D0805676

COPING
AND ADAPTATION

COPING
AND
ADAPTATION

EDITED BY

George V. Coelho

NATIONAL INSTITUTE OF MENTAL HEALTH

David A. Hamburg

STANFORD UNIVERSITY

John E. Adams

STANFORD UNIVERSITY

BASIC BOOKS, INC., *Publishers*   *New York*

Copyright © 1974 by Basic Books, Inc.
Library of Congress Catalog Card Number 73-88058
SBN 465-01427-5
Manufactured in the United States of America
10 9 8 7 6 5 4 3

We dedicate this volume to the memory of Dr. Alfred Weisz (1934–1970). He understood and exemplified more about coping than we can possibly convey here. Although he had just begun his contributions to the field, he showed great promise as a teacher, researcher, and clinician. His strong commitment to preventive psychiatry made issues of coping and adaptation particularly relevant for him, and all of behavioral science has suffered a loss as a result of his tragic illness and death. His many contributions to this project were invaluable, and it is with deep respect that we offer this tribute to him.

Contents

III

COPING WITH REAL-LIFE CRISES

IV

ASSESSMENT OF COPING FUNCTIONS

V

COPING AND ADAPTATION

Contributors

JOHN E. ADAMS, M.D. Assistant Professor of Psychiatry, Stanford University School of Medicine, Stanford, California.

JAMES R. AVERILL, Ph.D. Associate Professor of Psychology, University of Massachusetts, Amherst, Massachusetts.

NAOMI H. BISHOP, Ph.D. Assistant Professor of Anthropology, University of Massachusetts, Boston, Massachusetts.

SIDNEY COBB, M.D. Director, Psychiatric Epidemiology Research Unit, Butler Hospital, Brown University, Providence, Rhode Island.

GEORGE V. COELHO, Ph.D. Social Psychologist, National Institute of Mental Health, Rockville, Maryland.

JOHN R. P. FRENCH, JR., Ph.D. Professor of Psychology and Program Director, Research Center for Group Dynamics, Institute for Social Research, University of Michigan, Ann Arbor, Michigan.

ALEXANDER L. GEORGE, Ph.D. Professor of Political Science, Stanford University, Stanford, California.

WALTER GOLDSCHMIDT, Ph.D. Professor of Anthropology, University of California, Los Angeles, California.

ROY R. GRINKER, SR., M.D. Director, Institute for Psychosomatic Research and Training, Michael Reese Hospital and Medical Center, Chicago, Illinois, and Professor of Psychiatry, Pritzker School of Medicine, Chicago, Illinois.

BEATRIX A. HAMBURG, M.D. Director, Child Psychiatry Clinic and Assistant Professor of Psychiatry, Stanford University School of Medicine, Stanford, California.

DAVID A. HAMBURG, M.D. Reed-Hodgson Professor of Human Biology and Psychiatry, Stanford University School of Medicine, Stanford, California.

IRVING L. JANIS, Ph.D. Professor of Psychology, Yale University, New Haven, Connecticut.

RICHARD S. LAZARUS, Ph.D. Professor of Psychology, University of California, Berkeley, California.

ERICH LINDEMANN, Ph.D., M.D. Visiting Professor of Psychiatry, Stanford University School of Medicine, Stanford, California.

DAVID MECHANIC, Ph.D. John Bascom Professor of Sociology, University of Wisconsin, Madison, Wisconsin.

RUDOLF H. MOOS, Ph.D. Professor of Psychiatry, Stanford University School of Medicine, Stanford, California.

LOIS B. MURPHY, Ph.D. Clinical Professor Emeritus, Child Health and Development, George Washington School of Medicine, Washington, D.C.

EDWARD M. OPTON, JR., Ph.D. Senior Research Associate, Wright Institute, Berkeley, California.

WILLARD RODGERS, Ph.D. Study Director, Survey Research Center, Institute for Social Research, University of Michigan, Ann Arbor, Michigan.

SHERWOOD L. WASHBURN, Ph.D. Professor of Anthropology, University of California, Berkeley, California.

ROBERT W. WHITE, Ph.D. Professor Emeritus, Clinical Psychology, Harvard University, Cambridge, Massachusetts.

Foreword

This volume and the conference that preceded it approach the question "What do we typically do in the face of painful elements of experience?" The contributors to this book represent different scientific disciplines and their papers deal variously with theoretical and empirical data. As is often the case with interdisciplinary efforts, most people have an initial fascination with the empirical data from disciplines other than their own, and there is a risk in the tendency to over-estimate the ease of certain operational approaches. Attention must be paid to the risks of subtle homologies and analogies since, although systems or levels may be partially isomorphic, each has in addition its own methods of control and regulation.

The contributors represent traditionally demarcated disciplines and may subtly reflect degrees of reductionism or "extensionism." Although they may, in combination, fail adequately to present modern integrated or unitary thinking about the total biopsychosocial field, the very existence of this book offers testimony to the fact that the behavioral sciences have been moving closer to each other. Clinical psychology is concerned not only with psychopathology but also with the "healthy" or "normal" laws of mentation. The social sciences are becoming involved in actions oriented toward intervening in various sized social groups. Psychiatrists are moving toward the study of the normal phases of the life cycle, to develop base lines for longitudinal studies of development and the life history of disease. They are also trying to redefine what they strive to accomplish with therapy.

Concepts of "health" or "normality" have sometimes been used as the common ground for interdisciplinary discussions, but these terms have increasingly been seen as heavily charged with value judgments and as actually representing often fictional states. The present volume focuses instead on concepts of "stress" and "coping," where coping represents classes of transactions among components of a biopsychosocial system. While these concepts show promise of providing a specificity superior to generalities about normality or the health-disease axis, even they do not easily yield an acceptable common definition. To avoid direct confrontation with this definitional issue, there is a strong temptation to employ apparent synonyms such as adaptation, mastery, and defense. Use of these terms, however, may only add complexity, since each embodies its own frame of reference.

As with many terms used in the social and behavioral sciences, it is unfortunate that adaptation, defense, mastery, and coping are everyday words, since it makes more difficult our attempts to clarify conceptual differences. Thus, while adaptation may stand alone as a good biological term, we use the others to differentiate degrees of awareness or closeness to consciousness, differences in adaptation to a present real or past inner danger, and differences in success or failure. To make these distinctions is to fragment the totality into often invalid dichotomies, since all adaptations partially master, all have utility and cost, all require stimuli or releasing mechanisms, and all represent some form of conflict at some level but become unitary at a higher level. Mastery and even creativity are best viewed as adaptations derived from components of the integrated system of mentation-behavior. In all instances, internal and external environmental stimuli instigate an equilibrating process on the part of the organism. This process sometimes leads to avoidance or attack, to accelerated or compensatory internal changes, or to novel solutions.

Stimulus conditions that evoke these responses have been termed "stresses." Several authors here present at least tentative lists of classes of conditions or stimuli that may evoke coping processes. As sources of information they may contain too little or too much, or they may be ambiguous. The nature of the stress and the susceptibility of the organism give meaning to the stresser. This meaning occurs at some biopsychological level without respect to consciousness and may be "reevaluated" at any level over time. After many years of research we have tended to abandon the simple term "stress," except as expressed by "stress-stimuli" or "stress-response," and we have further come to realize that it is not the stimulus that is specific, but rather the response. This response specificity is clearly based on phenotypic patterns derived from combinations of genic and experiential factors.

Coping also has an ontogeny and may be considered as related to phases of the individual's life cycle, particularly an amplification of Erikson's epigenetic phases involving and including the social aspects of change. In general, it appears that each such phase has its own pattern of organization, its own vulnerabilities, and its own methods of coping. Strategies of coping thus depend on genetic constitution, experience, phase of life, and particular features of the environment. While such a system cannot by its very nature be fully understood by artificially dissecting it, the authors presented in this book provide a wide variety of useful perspectives on the total coping process.

In order to maintain a systems approach I would tend to classify adaptation according to the components of the biopsychosocial system. All adaptation at lower levels represents phases of conflict, perturbation, or change from idling to active states. These at a higher level are invisible but appear integrated. Biologically, we adapt to survive both as individuals and as members of the species. People also cope at the psychological level in order to develop and maintain self-esteem, self-identity, and object relations. The biological roots in primates and other infrahuman species extend by evolution to psychological methods based on new symbolic systems. At the social level we learn how to tolerate frustrations imposed by society and to accept delay of gratification. We incorporate by identification and develop the repertoire of social roles that our culture requires. In a changing and complex industrial society, the individual must deal with novel situations, temptations, and opportunities both at work and off the job. He must be able to cope with novelty, to control himself in the absence of ritual and social pressure, to postpone immediate gratification, to operate at a high level of symbolic thought, and to enjoy and be gratified by relatively abstract and intangible operations.

This volume provides the reader with a feast of information about a wide variety of topics from representatives of a number of disciplines. While a sense of full coherence and integration is sometimes lacking still, this appears to reflect the current state of our various fields and particularly results from the fact that our theoretical propositions are not yet broad enough to include the empirical referents. In reviewing the contributions contained here, I believe that we should above all become more cognizant of the complexities of human adaptation. Defense, mastery, or coping require a theoretical position extending beyond each discipline. They also require methodological approaches that combine and compliment data from experimental, field, and clinical settings. A unified field or systems theory seems to be required. The literature of all our disciplines is beginning to reflect this broadening, and a shift of thinking from dualistic to unitary thinking is evolving. I believe that this volume takes important steps in this direction.

Roy R. Grinker, Sr.

Acknowledgments

As with any edited volume, we must first express deep gratitude to our contributors. Their patience with the inevitable delays and their ready acceptance of editorial modifications have made our task both much easier and more pleasant.

The National Institute of Mental Health, which provided financial support for the Conference on Coping and Adaptation that preceded and contributed to this volume, has afforded an exciting working environment for each of us at various times and has funded a very significant proportion of the research work described herein. Stanley F. Yolles, former Director of the NIMH and Louis Wienckowski, Director of the Division of Extramural Research Programs at the NIMH consistently offered encouragement for the interdisciplinary research approach we espouse.

The Commonwealth Fund, through its president, Quigg Newton, and its former vice president, Robert J. Glaser, has provided vital core support to the Laboratory of Stress and Conflict at Stanford, California, where two of us now work. Their support has made possible not only the completion of this book but also new research programs to further our understanding of human coping and adaptation.

Finally, our sincere appreciation to Valarie Munden for assisting in the coordination of the Conference itself as well as her patience and persistence in working on the final technical details of the manuscript, and to Janet Robertson for reference research and typing of numerous drafts of the various chapters. We also extend our thanks to Jeanne Kennedy who skillfully prepared the index and to Ruth Rozman who was responsible for the final production phases of the volume.

George V. Coelho
David A. Hamburg
John E. Adams

Introduction

There are many ways in which common human experiences can be traumatic, and the mental health literature amply documents the variety of stressful situations which can result in failures of adaptation. Some stresses reflect the residua of man's evolutionary heritage, some are crises associated with normal developmental changes during the life cycle, and others reflect major features of new environmental demands that are related to social and technological change in rapidly industrializing cultures. With all of the stresses to which we are exposed, why is it that we are not usually shattered by them? If we can understand the processes and mechanisms of creative adaptation, how can we help individuals and groups to cope?

These are some of the questions that guided the planning of the literature survey (Coelho et al. 1970) and the Conference on Coping and Adaptation [1] held in Palo Alto, California, March 20–22, 1969, under the sponsorship of Stanford University's Department of Psychiatry and with the support of the National Institute of Mental Health.[2]

The framework of coping and adaptation provides a useful focus of attention for the biological and social sciences that are concerned with the behavior of individuals and groups exposed to the inevitable hazards of living.[3] Within this framework, we need to look at the human as an animal who is as fully subject to nature's laws and social requirements as any other animal and is no more capable of changing them; we also need to look at man not merely as an animal, but also as a symbolizing creature capable of imagination, foresight, and choice, and uniquely capable of using his culture to cope with the stresses of environmental change.

There is a wide range of individual difference in response to stress. How individuals appraise threatening elements in such situations depends on the personal significance of these situations. The extent to which a given element is relevant to motives or values of the person, which are often influenced by an individual's past experiences, and to conflict among these motives or values will tend to affect how the individual appraises threat in unfamiliar situations. This orientation is generally familiar in clinical psychiatry. However, both clinical observation and psychiatric research have neglected the study of the ways in which people cope with the threatening implications of difficult transitional experiences. Psychological research has also tended to neglect the interactive role of biosocial and cultural factors that shape the meaning of these situations for different population groups in different stages of the life cycle.

The following are examples of common stressful experiences that have been emphasized in recent behavioral research and clinical discussions: separation from parents in childhood; displacement by siblings; childhood experiences of rejection; illness and injuries in childhood; illness and death of parents; severe illness and injuries of the adult years; the initial transition from home to school; puberty; later school transitions, for example, from grade school to junior high school and from high school to college; competitive graduate education; marriage; pregnancy; menopause; necessity for periodic moves to a new environment; retirement; rapid technological and social change; wars and threats of wars; migration; acculturation; and social mobility.

What do we typically do in the face of painful elements of new experience? The literature of psychiatry and closely related fields overwhelmingly gives the impression that what we do is to avoid the painful elements at all costs and reject them as part of ourselves—even if this requires extensive self-deception. The classical mechanisms of defense are very largely in this category. They rely heavily upon avoidance and reduction of information. Is it possible that such mechanisms represent only one important class of responses to threatening elements of experience? Are there other major ways in which the human organism copes with stressful experience? In recent years, there has been increasing recognition of the need to explore the latter question. These are no doubt broad and complex concerns; they provoke questions that are not easily answered within the categories of any one disciplinary specialty in the behavioral and social sciences.

From a variety of vantage points, behavioral scientists have begun to be seriously concerned with coping, interpersonal problem solving, the development of competence, and adaptive behavior. The Conference on Coping and Adaptation provided an opportunity to bring the various points of view into sharper focus, and relevant bodies of data and theory into a meaningful interdisciplinary framework.

It provided impetus for the development of the present volume, which incorporates the conference proceedings, but represents a greatly enlarged and substantially new work. Additional contributions were especially invited to broaden the topical and methodological scope of the volume and to point out important directions for multidisciplinary work and promising guidelines for research and practice. These new materials make up over half of this volume. Moreover, all but one of the papers presented at the conference were revised for publication in the light of the conference discussions. An introduction has been added to provide an orientation and synoptic preview of the contents. The final chapter attempts to integrate the contributions from several disciplines and to formulate a working synthesis of biological, psychological, and sociocultural knowledge relevant to human coping.

The volume is organized into five major sections. The first section is concerned with basic concepts of adaptation viewed from a biological and cultural perspective. Cognitive organization of social reality is central to human adaptation, a process that all authors of this volume see to be facilitated by emotionally valued group support of an individual's positive self-image. The second section deals with developmental aspects of adaptive behavior in early childhood and adolescence and with different meanings and modes of competence in meeting the challenges of growing up. The third section reports on studies of coping behavior in complex, real-life decision-making situations. It discusses the implications of real-life stress research for theory as well as for practical interventions in clinical, educational, and organizational settings. The fourth section begins with two detailed reviews of technical issues in personality assessment viewed in the context of interactions between individuals and their environments; it concludes with a compendium of psychological methods and measures that have been central in research on coping behavior. In its totality the volume attempts to articulate the cumulative evidence of biological and social scientists who have worked effectively in strong multidisciplinary environments, scientists whose studies have been concerned with behavioral problems of practical significance for individual survival and innovation in stress.

For those readers who wish a somewhat more detailed preview of the volume, we have tried in the following pages to provide a conceptual road map to indicate the main features of this territory as viewed from the deliberate perspective of adaptation and coping. The map does not provide a summary nor an evaluative abstract of each chapter. It suggests the diversity and complementarity of approaches and highlights their distinctive contributions. Each of the main sections is introduced by a brief orientational statement and is followed by a précis of their respective chapters.

PART I. SOCIAL INTERACTION AND MOTIVATION IN ADAPTIVE BEHAVIOR

The first three chapters are concerned with the emotional and cognitive implications of social organization and group cooperation. The social system is emphasized as the vital basis for the development of the biological, symbolizing, and learning capacities of a species. The social system defines the species-specific tasks of survival, provides institutionalized support for human problem solving, and offers a means of anticipating commonly recurring developmental problems in the life cycle.

Chapter 1, "Social Adaptation in Nonhuman Primates," by Sherwood L. Washburn, David A. Hamburg, and Naomi H. Bishop, focuses on the role of social communication in the biological adaptation of nonhuman primates in their natural environments. The comparative method in field studies of animal behavior provides pertinent hypotheses about the nature of primate social organization and the interrelatedness of biology, social behavior, learning, and ecology. As an example, the locomotor biology of gibbons and patas monkeys is very different, and yet in both instances the social group maximizes the chances of survival by increasing the number of possible ways the animals meet the demands of their environment. The social group is seen as both permissive and restrictive, but clearly supportive of both individual and species survival.

While reminding us that the apes are *not* the ancestors of man, the authors conclude that studies of nonhuman primates, combining naturalistic field investigations and laboratory experiments, provide instructive models for the exploration of variables that are crucial in the interaction of biological and social processes in adaptive behavior. These variables are most often not amenable to direct experimental manipulation in human beings.

Chapter 2, "Ethology, Ecology, and Ethnological Realities," by Walter Goldschmidt, cites cross-cultural evidence to support the view that when social systems function adaptively they provide institutional supports to an individual's maintenance of a positive self-image—a minimally satisfactory self-image being necessary for coping with social stigma or failure. Using the comparative method, Goldschmidt points out that cultures operate in themselves as adaptive mechanisms for collective problem-solving behavior. For example, data from an interdisciplinary research project is used to contrast the behavioral consequences of a farming and pastoral way of life in East African communities whose natural resources and physical environment are very different. The data show that cultural adaptation involves the development of social institutions, in conjunction with the development of appropriate personality orientations, which fit with the ecological demands.

Chapter 3, "Social Structure and Personal Adaptation: Some Neglected Dimensions," by David Mechanic, brings into historical focus the adaptive issues in contemporary industrialized societies that are characterized by rapid technological and social change. For 99 percent of the time of man's existence as a distinct species, human biology evolved under conditions requiring adaptation to the social structure of hunting and gathering societies. With current vastly different patterns of social organization, adaptation requires that a high premium be placed on the individual's learning self-sufficiency and autonomy and related values of foresight and planning. Mechanic emphasizes, however, that major stresses on modern man are not amenable to individual solutions, but depend on institutionally organized efforts of group cooperation. Of particular importance is the role of the processes of social perception, which operate to maintain the individual's positive self-image under the most adverse social realities.

PART II. COPING TASKS AND STRATEGIES
IN THE DEVELOPMENT OF COMPETENCE

This section contains three chapters that identify the range of individual and group differences that must be taken into account in defining the coping issues relevant to each developmental phase in the life cycle. It examines the basic biosocial tasks of survival and growth in early childhood and adolescence, and their implications for child care, education, and mental health research and practice.

The adaptive tasks are seen to be different at each phase; and coping patterns vary depending upon biological factors, the learning opportunities, and environmental experiences that are associated with the individual's sex, ethnicity, and social class.

Chapter 4, "Strategies of Adaptation: An Attempt at Systematic Description," by Robert W. White, deals with the dynamic processes of adaptation as seen in competent children and adolescents. The dimension of time is emphasized: adaptation typically does not have to occur all at once, but with progressive changes and refinements of strategy over time. Both the normal stresses of the life cycle as well as the exceptional crises of injury and illness are considered. White points out that coping, mastery, and defense may, in the same individual, variously serve the purposes of adaptation in the long run, and the distinctions between these concepts are clarified. As examples, various clinical and field studies are cited, including the management of grief, the anticipatory activities of high-school students preparing to go away to college, and young children entering a psychologist's or doctor's office for the first time.

The author reminds us that individual adaptation is a compromise that involves the simultaneous management of three tasks—securing adequate information, maintaining satisfactory internal conditions, and keeping up some degree of autonomy or freedom of action. All of these balancing processes imply learning over time.

The chapter concludes with the suggestion that in psychotherapeutic settings it may be easier and more economical to suggest to the patient some of the promising pathways and potentialities for action on his part, rather than to concentrate exclusively on intrapsychic states of feeling.

Chapter 5, "Coping, Vulnerability, and Resilience in Childhood," by Lois B. Murphy, draws on rich case-study materials to document the biological, physiological, and interpersonal processes involved in the development of children's coping skills. Individual differences in adaptational styles are documented in a developmental scheme; and a range of variations is identified in the emergence of functions that contribute to the management of adaptive tasks. Especially noteworthy are the skill variations in sensory and motor responses to the particular external and internal stresses of the situation, the various reactions to pain and soothing, and perhaps most important the variability of the mother's responses to the infant's coping efforts. For example, the often shifting balance between autonomy and the ability to use help is crucial for the development of resilience—a key concept, according to the author, for observing the ups and downs of adaptation in vulnerable children. The need for further research is stressed, with particular attention to mother-child interactions in families with multiproblem children as compared with well-adapted parent-child pairs.

Chapter 6, "Early Adolescence: A Specific and Stressful Stage of the Life

Cycle," by Beatrix A. Hamburg, discusses the developmental aspects of the adaptive tasks relevant to early adolescence or puberty. This is a relatively neglected, yet critically important, developmental stage. The author describes the interrelationships between hormonal, cognitive, and cultural factors that influence the developing self-image and coping skills of the adolescent in this difficult phase. Emphasis is placed on the tasks, challenges, and coping possibilities facing the biologically changing individual at a time of culturally imposed social and psychological stress. A framework is provided for clarifying the interactive effects of biological changes in puberty and socioenvironmental changes on adaptive behavior during the stressful transition from elementary school to junior high school and the "teenage culture" in American society. The differential impacts of maturational rate on the early adolescent's self-image and self-esteem are discussed, as are the implications for sex and socioeconomic differences. As an example, it is shown that early-maturing adolescents, in comparison with late-maturing adolescents, tend to view themselves and to be viewed by significant others very differently. The psychosocial consequences are also likely to be very different for boys and for girls.

The author discusses a peer counseling project and a related training curriculum and concludes with practical recommendations that might be useful to pediatricians, school counselors and teachers, parents, and adolescents themselves.

PART III. COPING WITH REAL-LIFE CRISES

This section is concerned with the mastery of acute stressful situations that involve high risk and conflict for the individual. In all three chapters the authors examine the dynamic processes of decision making at each stage in the coping strategy. In each case the tasks involved in the critical situation are reviewed and the sources considered which provide the relevant information for rational problem solving.

Chapter 7, "Coping with Long-term Disability," by John E. Adams and Erich Lindemann, formulates coping principles that are derived from the study of catastrophic, disabling injuries. Selected case material from quadriplegic patients is used to illustrate the vastly different outcomes that are possible despite virtually identical anatomical lesions, physical disability, and physical rehabilitation programs. The difference is seen to lie in the psychological adaptation. Emphasis is placed on the need for the patient to focus on current and future reality and to anticipate and rehearse new behaviors and forms of social encounter. There is also a focus on conjoint adaptation on the part of the individual's family and network of significant others. They are required to readjust their expectations of the changed individual while maintaining full acceptance of him as a person. Coping principles that can equally apply to alcoholics, narcotic addicts, and chronically hospitalized psychiatric patients are set forth. All of these may require adaptive guidance in their social rehabilitation and relearning.

Chapter 8, "Vigilance and Decision Making in Personal Crises," by Irving L. Janis, examines in detail how individuals cope with fear-arousing communications in the face of impending disaster or potential deprivation. Drawing on empirical data from a broad program of studies of heavy smokers, draft resisters, and other classes of individuals facing complex decisions that seriously affect their health, career, or marriage, the author explores individual differences in response to warnings. The two sets of interacting factors selected for experimental study of real-life situations are the individual's personality predispositions and the intensities of threat-stimuli. He presents a sequential five-stage model of decision making that makes possible the identification of subgroups of individuals with varying predispositional characteristics. The model also identifies the interacting variables relevant to predicting the type of coping response to fear-arousing communications about impending personal crises.

Chapter 9, "Adaptation to Stress in Political Decision Making: The Individual, Small Group, and Organizational Contexts," by Alexander L. George, discusses three interrelated systems of resources for political decision making. These include the chief executive's individual system, his small informal face-to-face group of advisers, and the larger bureaucratic system of the chief executive and his official advising system. The author discusses the special processes that are relevant to the operation of each system and that may affect favorably or adversely efforts to cope with the task of rational decision making within the other two systems. As examples, presidential decision-making styles are reviewed with particular focus on recent crises in foreign policy. A pragmatic theory is proposed for bringing together the concepts of personality functioning in its adaptive aspects with special reference to small-group dynamics and organizational behavior.

PART IV. ASSESSMENT OF COPING FUNCTIONS

This section presents several research approaches that attempt to identify meaningful personality variables in adaptive functioning. The first two chapters provide psychological research models that illustrate the interaction between personality dispositions and situational requirements in experimental situations of problem solving. Perceptual and cognitive processes are particularly emphasized as important for mediating stressful outer demands on the individual's inner resources. The final chapter provides a comprehensive review of psychological techniques used for assessing those variables that are significantly related to adaptive behavior in personality development.

Chapter 10, "The Psychology of Coping: Issues of Research and Assessment," by Richard S. Lazarus, James R. Averill, and Edward M. Opton,

Jr., begins with the authors' review of their own and others' research concerning the specification of various coping processes. The authors spell out the formal requirements of any classification scheme that takes account of the dynamic interaction between organisms and environments. They define coping to emphasize problem-solving efforts of an individual faced with demands that are highly relevant to his welfare but tax his adaptive resources. It is pointed out that the demand characteristics of the situation cannot be understood without reference to the person exposed and responding to it.

The theoretical approach presented emphasizes cognitive processes of appraisal and reappraisal by which the individual obtains and evaluates information about the adaptive significance of an environmental event. Four basic strategies of empirical research on the cognitive mediators of emotion and coping are reviewed and a variance model is presented to attempt to account for individual coping responses in given situations.

The authors finally point out the limitations of isolated research on particular contexts of threat or challenge and conclude that their review dramatizes the need for a broad conception that brings such diverse though limited and particular research contexts within a comprehensive theoretical framework.

Chapter 11, "Adjustment as Person-Environment Fit," by John R. P. French, Jr., Willard Rodgers, and Sidney Cobb, is a report of work in progress in a major research program on psychological adjustment viewed as the goodness of fit between persons and their environments. Utilizing data from several longitudinal studies, a quantitative model is presented and the dynamics of adjusting are discussed. Hypotheses are generated about the techniques that the person uses over time in dealing with the discrepancies in the fit between his assessment of himself and of his environment.

The authors point out the different consequences of various techniques for adjusting. Also, there may be marked individual differences in the stability of defense preferences and coping styles that influence choices across all situations. The importance of longitudinal data is emphasized for the meaningful evaluation of these factors.

Chapter 12, "Psychological Techniques in the Assessment of Adaptive Behavior," by Rudolf H. Moos, provides a comprehensive inventory of psychological methods and techniques that have been devised to assess the adaptive behavior of individuals. Special emphasis is placed upon coping variables identified in current theories of motivation and personality dynamics and upon concepts related to ego-functions.

Research on coping behavior is viewed as a significant arena for the interplay of three distinct goals. First is the theoretical understanding of the various processes that enable individuals to handle problems that are stressful in the life cycle, as well as the unusually difficult circumstances involving injury or illness. The second goal is to develop a sound technology for behavioral assessment that is relevant to human problem solving in a variety of situations. The third goal is to manage effective therapeutic intervention in life crises.

This chapter focuses particularly on the second goal and reviews in detail a variety of assessment techniques which have been utilized in coping research. The importance of defining specific research goals is emphasized, because the goal of understanding and the goal of prediction may lead respectively to different kinds of methodologies.

PART V. COPING AND ADAPTATION

In the final chapter the editors provide a thematic overview of central topics in the area of coping and adaptation. An attempt is made to integrate the biological and social contributions to our understanding of coping behavior in critical phases of the life cycle. Beginning with biological and evolutionary concepts, the role of behavior in mediating individual development and species adaptation is explored. Social and cultural factors are seen as of major importance in supporting or defeating the attempts of an individual to cope with crisis in the short run, and also as contributing heavily to species survival and development. Methodological problems requiring further exploration are discussed, and promising research directions and practical guidance are suggested. A paradigmatic approach with considerable clinical relevance is presented with illustrative material from puberty and menopause—the various tasks and strategies involved in coping with developmental crises in these eras.

The contributors and editors of the volume are acutely aware, personally and professionally, of the turbulent events that seem to have progressively changed the social climate of the nation since the Conference on Coping and Adaptation was proposed in March 1968. American society witnessed its marvelous technological achievements in space exploration; it also experienced major cultural shocks and institutional crises that deeply disturbed many sectors of its population, but perhaps particularly its young people. Several national leaders were slain. Many cities exploded in epidemics of violence. A number of colleges and universities, which had been the humanistic witness to the values of reason and of learning, were for a time shut down and almost paralyzed by episodes of complex, powerful, but often seemingly irrational, disruption. On the other hand, at least some of the forces that aggravated the social disorders also served to expose long-festering wounds of poverty, hunger, cultural deprivation, and self-depreciation.

Conventional wisdom has not worked well in our attempts to define and deal with these crises. The range of destructive forms of aggressiveness that we have witnessed in our time challenge us to deepen and utilize our knowledge of human behavior and coping in development.

This volume indicates that our human genetic and cultural heritage provide us with the capacity to cope with stress in a very broad range of social and psychological habitats. Modern man is required to learn to adapt creatively to the challenges of rapid environmental and social change. Given this requirement and given our present knowledge of human adaptive capacities, what additional and perhaps unique stresses and conflicts will he have to face? What biological and emotional costs to our humanity are involved in the process? What are some of the nonhateful nonviolent ways of coping with stress? This volume has attempted to make these questions not only relevant but researchable.

In designing the format of the volume and the organization of its contents, we have attempted to help the informed citizen and student of behavior increase their appreciation of the nature and range of human resourcefulness that is often displayed in situations of stress and conflict. We have also attempted to define for practitioners in the fields of education, organizational development, and mental health some of the fundamental principles that can be useful in bringing conceptual unity to their helping efforts in their respective service settings. Above all, we have attempted to provide a framework and guidelines for interdisciplinary work among biological and social scientists who are concerned with sources and strategies of human adaptation in individual development. To the extent that these attempts have succeeded in some measure, this volume will have been of value.

George V. Coelho
John E. Adams

NOTES

1. The following participants at the conference presented invited papers, informal reports of work in progress, or commentary:

David A. Hamburg, M.D., Chairman	John R. P. French, Jr., Ph.D.
George V. Coelho, Ph.D., Co-Chairman	Sheppard Kellam, M.D.
	James W. Kelly, Ph.D.
Robert Bechtel, Ph.D.	Richard S. Lazarus, Ph.D.
Ernst Caspari, Ph.D.	David Mechanic, Ph.D.
Bruce Dohrenwend, Ph.D.	Rudolf H. Moos, Ph.D.
Barbara Dohrenwend, Ph.D.	Gardner Murphy, Ph.D.
Professor Erik H. Erikson	Lois B. Murphy, Ph.D.
Raphael Ezekiel, Ph.D.	John R. Newbrough, Ph.D.
Alexander L. George, Ph.D.	Melvin Sabshin, M.D.
Marvin Goldfried, Ph.D.	M. Brewster Smith, Ph.D.
Walter Goldschmidt, Ph.D.	Sherwood L. Washburn, Ph.D.
Roy R. Grinker, Sr., M.D.	Robert W. White, Ph.D.
Irving L. Janis, Ph.D.	John W. M. Whiting, Ph.D.

The following individuals attended the conference as observers, and several participated in the discussion:

<table>
<tr><td>From the National Institute
of Mental Health</td><td>From the Department of Psychiatry
Stanford University School
of Medicine</td></tr>
<tr><td>John E. Adams, M.D.</td><td></td></tr>
<tr><td>Berthold Brenner, Ph.D.</td><td>P. Herbert Leiderman, M.D.</td></tr>
<tr><td>James E. Lieberman, M.D.</td><td>Paxton Cady, Ph.D., M.D.</td></tr>
<tr><td>Benjamin Z. Locke, M.S.</td><td>David N. Daniels, M.D.</td></tr>
<tr><td>Robert E. Markush, M.D.</td><td>Peggy Golde, Ph.D.</td></tr>
<tr><td>Loren Mosher, M.D.</td><td>Beatrix A. Hamburg, M.D.</td></tr>
<tr><td>David Pearl, Ph.D.</td><td>Herant A. Katchadourian, M.D.</td></tr>
<tr><td>Louis A. Wienckowski, Ph.D.</td><td>Warren B. Miller, M.D.</td></tr>
<tr><td>Richard H. Williams, Ph.D.</td><td>Alfred E. Weisz, M.D.
(deceased)</td></tr>
</table>

Additional guests were:

James R. Averill, Ph.D. Edward M. Opton, Jr., Ph.D.
Carl N. Edward Pirkko Niemela

2. The Conference on Coping and Adaptation and the preparation of several chapters in this volume were supported under contract no. PH 43-68-1033 from the National Institute of Mental Health.
3. Coping and adaptation as a fundamental topic in psychiatric research is discussed in David A. Hamburg, ed., *Psychiatry as a behavioral science* (Englewood Cliffs, N.J.: Prentice-Hall, 1970), chap. 4.

REFERENCE

Coelho, G. V., Hamburg, D. A., Moos, R. H., Randolph, P., eds., *Coping and adaptation: A behavioral sciences bibliography*, Public Health Service Publication no. 2087, National Institute of Mental Health. Washington, D.C.: U.S. Government Printing Office, 1970.

I

SOCIAL INTERACTION AND MOTIVATION IN ADAPTIVE BEHAVIOR

1

Social Adaptation
in Nonhuman Primates

SHERWOOD L. WASHBURN,
DAVID A. HAMBURG,
AND NAOMI H. BISHOP

Our ancestors lived active and dangerous and short lives. As Vallois (1961) has shown, very few fossil men reached the age of forty. It was not only that life expectancy was short, but very few old individuals survived at all. Even after the advent of agriculture, life expectancy was still short because of high death rates of infants and children, but many individuals survived well beyond the age of sixty (Dublin, Lotka, and Spiegelman 1949). If we think of a human male becoming fully adult by about the age of twenty, few of our ancestors could have practiced those skills they had learned for a comparable period of time. In general, man's situation was not very different from the baboon's. Bramblett (1969) has shown that the male baboon is fully mature, both physically and socially, at about ten years, and in Africa few live beyond the age of twenty. In zoos, however, baboons sometimes live for more than forty years; and just as in the case of man, life under civilized conditions is twice as long as in the natural state. Only with modern medicine and technology has life expectancy radically increased. For more than 99 percent of the time that man has existed, he survived in small populations and lived by gathering and hunting (Lee and DeVore 1968).

Recently, all technical environmental conditions have changed—not only have they changed at an unprecedented rate, but never before has any single species attained this degree of power over the world. Yet the creatures who wield this power in a new world have a biology that evolved in an old one. The products of modern technology—the population explosion,

This paper is part of a program on primate behavior supported by the U. S. Public Health Service (grant MH 08623). We wish to thank Mrs. Alice Davis for editorial assistance.

pollution, space, and the bomb—are new, but interpersonal relationships are old. Such problems as sex, mother-infant relationship, play and independence, social position and dominance are not only common to all human cultures (Murdock 1945) but have their roots in a biology that man shares with other primates (Schultz 1969). For this reason, we may gain some insights into the nature of man by considering his evolution and the behavior of his nearest relatives.

We stress that we do not regard man as "only an ape" (and a "naked ape" at that!), but we think that comparison and evolution may help in the understanding of man. For example, some prosimians reach sexual maturity in approximately two years, some monkeys in four. Chimpanzees mature sexually at eight, and man at sixteen.[1] Comparison with other mammals suggests that this delayed maturity is a rare and remarkable adaptation. If we can understand *why* the delay of maturity has been advantageous in other primates, we are more likely to understand the background of the human situation. But comparison does not reduce the differences between man and ape. On the contrary, such comparisons emphasize man's uniqueness by placing it in context. Viewing man as a product of the evolutionary process, then, does not reduce the uniqueness of man (Simpson 1966), but an understanding of human evolution should help in interpreting human nature. On the one hand, this help is specific; it aids in the selection of laboratory animals that are most appropriate for particular comparative problems; and, on the other hand, it suggests the selective forces under which we evolved. Obviously, the comparative, evolutionary approach is only one of many avenues to the study of man. We think that it offers some insights that are unlikely to come from other approaches, and if our understanding of man increases only a bit, we regard it as worthwhile.

In this paper we shall be concerned with the social system of monkeys and apes [2] as an adaptive mechanism. At no stage in their lives can individual animals, living alone, cope with all the problems of their environment, and evolution has produced a variety of social systems through which the successful biology of one generation is transmitted to the next. The importance of the social system may be illustrated by the behavior of patas monkeys (Hall 1965). These monkeys are built for speed: their long trunk and limbs contrast markedly with the proportions of the genus *Cercopithecus*, their closest living arboreal relatives. By the use of speedy locomotion the patas monekys have adapted to life in the grasslands away from trees. When danger threatens, the single adult male of the troop jumps up and runs away as obviously as possible. His bright color, his motion of leaping up, and his tail-up attitude, all attract attention. The females and young freeze in the grass and "play possum." Without the decoy behavior of the adult male, the young, lacking the speed to escape, would be caught. Both possum and decoy behaviors are practiced by the young animals in play. Speed of running alone does not insure survival, but combined with a particular social system, it is highly successful.

The patas's system is based not only on the decoy and possum behavior, but also on a troop composed of one adult male and a number of females with young. The other adult males are driven away and form all-male groups. If this one adult male is killed, he will be replaced by a male from an all-male group. In patas country, the low trees offer little protection from predators at night, and the monkeys have adapted to this by sleeping separated from each other. This minimizes the number of animals likely to be caught when daytime escape behavior is not possible. Preparation for meeting predators, then, is helped along by biological structure, social structure, play behavior, and sleeping habits; but this whole pattern will not work if the grass is short, thus ecologically limiting the distribution of the species.

Adaptations of this sort are complex biosocial systems, and reproductive success of the species depends on the adaptation of the local groups. As Yerkes stated many years ago, a solitary chimpanzee is not a normal chimpanzee; and we can add that, with the exception of adult males, a solitary monkey will soon be a dead monkey. The bonds that hold the group together are as essential for survival as any other biological condition, and the genes that link generation to generation join nothing unless they are carried by members of a successful social group. Different species of monkeys and apes have widely divergent life styles; but in spite of the diversity, all are social, and survival is dependent on the success of a social pattern of living. The social system is the setting in which all other behavior makes sense. It provides the context for eating and drinking, for learning, predator defense, and reproduction. Hence, a monkey's most important adjustments are to other members of its group, rewards and pleasures being a product of group life.

The gibbon's way of life offers another example of biosocial adaptation. In this case, the group consists of a male-female pair and their offspring (Carpenter 1940; Ellefson 1966). Older juveniles are driven off by the adults, so that the maximum group size is approximately six individuals, though four is usual. This little group lives in a small, defended territory. Groups announce their locations by very loud calls in the early morning, and males engage in noisy, swinging displays when other gibbons, usually near the borders of the territory, are encountered. The gibbon group moves only over short distances, and individuals spend 85 to 90 percent of their time feeding while hanging by one hand, a habit unique to gibbons. This hanging-feeding adaptation is reflected in the anatomy of the arms, in the mode of locomotion (frequently by swinging under branches), and in the separations of thumb and of great toe that make it possible for a small animal to grasp a large trunk or branch.

The feeding adaptation dominates the whole of gibbon life. Sexual activity is infrequent, for the single female is rarely in estrus, and the male is probably the least potent of the Old World primates. In the gibbon's system, there is no play group, and many young gibbons have no playmates. The temperament of the young gibbon changes from the mild to the irascible. Starting around four years of age the juveniles become peripheral, both because of their own actions and the antagonism from the adult pair. The changes in temperament are clearly related to puberty and hormones, and by the time the canine teeth have erupted, the juvenile will tolerate only one adult animal opposite in sex to itself. In marked contrast to other monkeys and apes (*Cercopithecidae* and *Pongidae*), female gibbons have long canine teeth, are nearly as large as males, and are intolerant of other adult females.

In summary, the gibbon adaptation to hanging-feeding in a small area is correlated with territorial defense, male-female pairing, minimum sexual activity, minimum social play, and agonistic behavior by both sexes, including the peripheralization of the juveniles. The gibbon has adapted through the whole biosocial pattern, and in this way has been very successful. In some areas—where Carpenter observed gibbons in Thailand, for example—gibbons far outnumber monkeys. But the high cost of this way of life is revealed by their daily aggressive activities. According to Schultz (1939, 1969) fractures are frequent, and preponderantly all old gibbons have evidence of major injuries from falling, frequently attributable to display and territorial behavior.

Patas monkeys and gibbons represent opposite poles of primate adaptation. Patas live in open country in large undefended ranges. Gibbons live in forests in small, defended territories. Patas are quiet, while gibbons loudly proclaim their locations. A troop of patas monkeys numbers about twenty, with eight to ten adult females. The gibbon group is constituted of a pair and its young. In patas, juvenile males become peripheral and form all-male groups. In gibbons, juveniles of both sexes leave the group. The terrestrial patas retreat on the ground, while the arboreal gibbons escape by swinging a short distance away from the threat.

The contrasts between patas monkeys and gibbons illustrate several fundamental points on the nature of primate adaptation. The mode of locomotion, feeding, territory, social system, and temperament are all interrelated. The animals must be so constituted that they can *easily learn* the whole pattern (Hamburg 1963). The importance of learning, for example, is readily demonstrated by gibbon locomotion: it took two gibbons approximately three months to learn the optimum use of a large cage. The precise timing of the swings for speed and accuracy had to be learned, even in this relatively simple situation. In the natural habitat, particular arboreal pathways are repeatedly used; and the high-speed swinging displays are probably possible only in well-known trees. Obviously, the locomotor biology of gibbons and patas monkeys is very different; yet both must learn skill in a social group. Adaptation arises both from biology and from experience. Therefore, we use the concept "ease of learning" to stress this dual relationship.

As the animal grows, the pattern of learning changes. First, the infant is nursed, is groomed, and is constantly cared for and carried by its mother. As a juvenile, it is tolerated by troop members; but in the later juvenile period, gibbons of both sexes and male patas monkeys become peripheral.

In development, there is first a period of protected learning. Marked changes in temperament then occur which lead to adult behaviors normal for the species. This is accompanied by a changing *readiness to learn*. The deprivation studies (Mason, Davenport, and Menzel 1968) show that there is a large element of learning in social behaviors; but what is easily learned depends on the species, and the timing of the learning depends both on maturation and on the readiness to learn (Hamburg, personal communication).

Through evolution, each species is so constituted that it easily learns the behaviors that have been important in the history of the species. In other words, there is a feedback relationship between successful behaviors and the biological bases that make them possible. The result of behaviors in each generation determines the gene flow to the next generation and ultimately the course of evolution of the species. The notion of ease of learning is an attempt to view learning in a biological perspective. If the concept of instinct had become modern, as the concept of evolution has, then ease of learning would not be necessary. Unfortunately, to most people the word *instinct* means behaviors that are genetically, almost reflexively, determined.

Hinde and Tinbergen (1958) discuss this problem and use the expression "propensity to learn." Because the whole biology of the species (including its propensities to learn) is the product of evolution, species are adapted to the conditions of the past, and coping with the present may involve new elements for which the species is not adapted. In the vast record of evolution, the inability to cope has led to the extinction of most species, and the most important lesson from the study of evolution is that a successful species cannot be totally bound by the past. Because a structure or a behavior was adaptive long ago does not mean that it is still adaptive, or that it permits coping with the present in a way that will allow survival in the future. Man meets the problems of the atomic age with the biology of hunter-gatherers and many customs of times long past.

At the Conference on Coping and Adaptation, a motion picture on baboon behavior made by Professor Irven DeVore in the Amboseli Game Reserve in Kenya was shown. The film vividly presents the social life of these large, terrestrial monkeys. We think that such a visual aid is essential to understanding the life of nonhuman primates, which the written word alone is quite inadequate to convey. The conclusions that were drawn from the motion picture, from our previous discussion, and from our field experiences follow.

Monkeys and apes learn to be intensely social. The form of the group differs from species to species, but primates stay near one another, making great efforts to do so. The struggles of sick or injured animals to stay with the group indicate the intensity of this drive. It is, however, obvious that the attraction of the social group far surpasses its protective function, and the relationships within the group are themselves a cohesive force.

The social group is the seat for all of the learning and practice that a young primate requires. This learning can take many forms, one of which is play. The play situation has several features that make it a good arena of practice for young primates. It appears to be pleasurable, and here the judgment of pleasure is made on the basis of the animal actively seeking out other animals. Both social skills and motor skills are acquired through continuous repetition over the years (Dolhinow and Bishop 1970).

Play is the predominant activity during the juvenile stage of development, and it is also at this stage that adult behaviors are being noticed and practiced. The whole pattern of juvenile life is preparation for a clearly visible adult life. Juvenile female vervets, for example, play with infants long before they are old enough to have infants of their own. During the periods when juvenile males are playfighting, juvenile females are practicing carrying, holding, and grooming the newborn black infants of the adult females. After the infants are three months old, the juvenile females shift from mothering them to playing with them (Lancaster 1970).

Exploration, another form of learning, takes place when animals are well fed and secure. Monkeys and apes—if they are not prevented from doing so—investigate, explore, and manipulate a wide variety of things in their environments. Novelty, of a moderate degree, can lead to exploration, but exploration occurs only when tensions within the group are low; hence, the social group may both permit and prevent its occurrence. Exploratory behavior is most characteristic of young primates, because their lives are relatively more secure and freer from tension than the lives of older animals. In a crisis situation, animals revert to stereotyped behavior, and the practice of flight and escape behavior gained through play is one form of assurance that the animals will perform properly in crises.

This occurrence of stereotyped behavior in fearful situations is, in a sense, another form of learned behavior. Fears are easily learned and hard to extinguish; and while this is highly adaptive under natural circumstances, it also may lead to useless behaviors. A troop of protected baboons, for example, learned to fear shooting after two shots were fired from a car. In fact eight months later, the troop could not be approached by a car. By way of contrast, a troop in the park at Victoria Falls fled at the sound of a railroad train, even when well away from the tracks. Innovation cannot occur in stressful situations; this may be why infant and juvenile primates are at their most innovative and exploratory, because they are surrounded by relatively positive affect, first their mother's, later from their peers, and continuously from other troop members.

As a young primate matures, the surrounding emotional environment changes. In early infancy it is almost completely protected from the hostility of troop members. This is assured by its close association with its mother, the natal coat color, and probably its "infantile" behavior. As a juvenile, it is propelled into the center of the group, and the primary focus shifts from mother to peers. At this point, troop members are less tolerant of its behavior—although in the early juvenile period, it is often protected by its mother, and its involvement in play activities keeps it occupied and out of the way of the adults.

Late juvenile and subadult males are, however, the most active, exploratory, aggressive, and socially disruptive class of individuals. Building on the sexual differences in the play patterns of the infants and younger juveniles, older juvenile males play roughly, threaten adults, and are peripheralized to varying extents. This peripheralization, while always social, can also be seen spatially. In some species, the juvenile and subadult males spend most of their time on the periphery of the group; in others, they form all-male groups that may be spatially separate from the main group (which then has one male). A third alternative is to leave the troop temporarily, later returning to the troop of origin, or joining a new troop. Of eighteen male rhesus monkeys departing to solitary status from troops on Cayo Santiago, for example, sixteen were males between four and seven years of age (Koford 1966). And lastly, peripheralization may be the result of a gradual process, as in the case of the hamadryas baboon. The male juvenile hamadryas spends most of his time playing in the male play groups. At three years of age, he spends most of his time grooming on the periphery of the troop. As a subadult male, he is further peripheralized: only 18 percent of his resting time is spent in social interaction (Kummer 1968). Although females usually maintain the social bonds of childhood and stay in the group of origin, males go through some period of alienation. The degree of separation varies widely from species to species, but at least some peripheralization of males and some antagonism between old males and young ones seem to be universal in monkeys and apes.

Eventually the peripheral, or separated, males attempt to become dominant in the troop and gain access to estrus females. A satisfactory masculine position in the troop implies access to food, grooming, and social position as well as sex. A satisfactory position is judged by the animal's actions: the way it moves relative to others, the way it communicates and gestures, and the conditions of access to food, grooming, and sex. Dominance means that an animal achieves these goals without being harassed by other members of the group.

Individual motivation for sexual behavior is essentially distinct from reproduction of the species. Copulation must be pleasurable, so that an essential biological act will be accomplished; but a very wide variation in the amount of copulation among the various primate species leads to the same result—the female bearing as many infants as is biologically possible. Obviously, the effects of sexual behavior on the social group supersedes the reproductive aspects of sex. It is a potentially disruptive force; and in the mating season, wound and death rates among rhesus macaques are three times higher than usual (Wilson and Boelkins 1970).

In looking at primates, it becomes apparent that the social system cannot be fully described, let alone understood, without considering the emotions of the animals. All interactions are accompanied by external indications of emotion, and the personalities of the individuals vary by age, sex, and previous experience. And the emotions are not all positive—in the interpersonal relationships within the group, stress (as judged by the animal's actions) is common. The most noticeable example of this is the social position and life of the subadult male, but actually from infancy on, an animal's activity is restricted, first by its mother, and later by other adults and peers. Many species of primates do not have rigid dominance hierarchies, and even among the ones that do, this does not alleviate tension and aggression within the group. When a troop is excited, there may still be many threats and chases long after the danger has passed. DeVore's film, which showed excited behavior continuing for forty-five minutes after a lion had threatened baboons, illustrates this well. "Scapegoat" behavior, in which a frustrated animal turns on another subordinate animal, is common.

In examining the ways in which the nonhuman primates cope with their environment, the central role of the group immediately becomes apparent. The social group maximizes the chances for survival by increasing the number of possible ways the animals can interact and cope with their environment. As man's environment changes, so does that of the nonhuman primate, and the number of vanishing species of primates attests to their problems of coping. The social group is both permissive (in the sense that it can provide an environment conducive to exploration, close affectional ties, and increasing population) and restrictive (in that it limits individual possibilities). The number and kinds of coping strategies seen among the nonhuman primates are relatively limited when compared with those available to man. While both man and the nonhuman primates share common problems, the advantages conferred on humans by such features as language, or longer maturation with its concomitant increase in possibilities for learning, are obvious. But we must continually keep in mind that our biology is far behind our environment and that our methods for coping may be equally obsolete.

These remarks are intended to be expressions of a point of view, rather than final conclusions. Many more field studies are necessary before the whole range of primate social behaviors is even described. Uncontrolled field studies must be supplemented by experiments before we can be sure of how the observations can be interpreted. In the field, animals can be added or subtracted (Kummer 1968) or operated on (Kling, Lancaster, and Benitone 1970) or interaction rates can be changed by the use of drugs (Brown, personal communication). Controlled study of social groups in large compounds will add information essential for the interpretation of field studies. We do think, however, that there is enough information to state a point of view now and indicate some promising directions for further research.

SUMMARY

The primate field studies show the importance of understanding the biology of the individuals, the social system, and the ecology as these are interrelated in the adaptive system. As the environment changes, so (hopefully) does the social system and the biology. Through the primate field studies as examples, and through the potentials for experimental manipulation, we may come closer to an understanding of the costs and problems of biosocial development.

NOTES

1. Clearly, such figures can only be approximate. There are differences between species, between males and females, and other differences as well. The estimates in years are only to suggest the magnitude of the differences (Schultz 1969).

2. In this paper we use *monkey* to mean Old World monkey and *ape* to mean one of the African apes, unless the term is qualified.

REFERENCES

Bramblett, C. A. Non-metric skeletal changes in the Darajani baboon. *American Journal of Physical Anthropology*, 1969, *30*, 161–172.

Carpenter, C. R. A field study in Siam of the behavior and social relations of the gibbon, *Hylobates lar*. *Comparative Psychology Monograph*, 1940, *16*, 1–212.

Dolhinow, P. C., and Bishop, N. The development of motor skills and the social relationships among primates through play. In J. P. Hill, ed., *Minnesota Symposia on Child Psychology*, 1970, *4*, 141–198. Minneapolis: University of Minnesota Press.

Dublin, L. I., Lotka, A. J., and Spiegelman, M. *Length of life*. New York: Ronald Press, 1949.

Ellefson, J. O. A natural history of gibbons in the Malay Peninsula. Ph.D. diss., University of California, Berkeley, 1966.

Hall, K. R. L. Behaviour and ecology of the wild patas monkey, *Erythrocebus patas*, in Uganda. *Journal of Zoology*, 1965, *148*, 15–87.

Hamburg, D. A. Emotion in the perspective of human evolution. In P. Knapp, ed., *Expression of the emotions in man*. New York: International Universities Press, 1963.

Hinde, R. A., and Tinbergen, N. The comparative study of species-specific behavior. In A. Roe and G. G. Simpson, eds., *Behavior and evolution*. New Haven, Conn.: Yale University Press, 1958.

Kling, A., Lancaster, J. B., and Benitone, J. Amygdalectomy in the free-ranging vervet, *Cercopithecus aethiops*. *Journal of Psychiatric Research*, 1970, 7, 191–199.

Koford, C. B. Population changes in rhesus monkeys: Cayo Santiago, 1960–1964. *Tulane Studies in Zoology*, 1966, *13*, 1–7.

Kummer, H. *Social organization of hamadryas baboons*. Chicago and London: University of Chicago Press, 1968.

Lancaster, J. B. Maternal behavior directed towards infants by free-ranging juvenile female vervet monkeys. Paper presented to the American Anthropological Association, 1970.

Lee, R. B., and DeVore, I., eds. *Man the hunter*. Chicago: Aldine, 1968.

Mason, W. A., Davenport, R. K., Jr., and Menzel, E. W., Jr. Early experience and the social development of rhesus monkeys and chimpanzees. In G. Newton and S. Levine, eds., *Early experience and behavior*. Springfield, Ill.: Charles C. Thomas, 1968.

Murdock, G. P. The common denominator of cultures. In R. Linton, ed., *The science of man in the world crisis*. New York: Columbia University Press, 1945.

Schultz, A. H. Notes on diseases and healed fractures of wild apes. *Bulletin of the History of Medicine*, 1939, 7, 571–582.

———. *The life of primates*. London: Weidenfeld & Nicolson, 1969.

Simpson, G. G. Biological nature of man. *Science*, 1966, *152*, 472–478.

Vallois, H. V. The social life of early man: The evidence of skeletons. In S. L. Washburn, ed., *Social life of early man*. Chicago: Aldine, 1961.

Wilson, A. P., and Boelkins, C. Evidence for seasonal variation in aggressive behaviour by *Macaca Mulatta*. *Animal Behaviour*, 1970, *18*, 719–729.

2

Ethology, Ecology, and Ethnological Realities

WALTER GOLDSCHMIDT

INTRODUCTION

In this chapter I want first to present the theoretical case for an ethological basis for human behavior—which is an assertion of human consistency in the face of cultural diversity—and second to suggest that differential behavior between cultures relates fundamentally to the ecological circumstances under which the cultures are operative, illustrating this with data taken from my current research activities. Finally, I want to turn to the individual and discuss his adaptations to his own milieu, pointing up that cultures provide, or should provide, institutional means for individual adaptation.

TOWARD A HUMAN ETHOLOGY

I consider it necessary to assume that there is some significant, genetically based preprogramming in man; that there is something that may be called human ethology. Such preprogramming must be taken into account in understanding human behavior and human institutions, but, because man is a single species, it cannot account for the differences in such behavior from one community to another. Such differences are always differential cultural programming, responsive to situational factors. I believe that we must posit biologically based social characteristics, but that we must also be extremely cautious in positing such inborn traits. This doctrine of parsimony separates me from my more ethologically and biologically oriented colleagues, just as my willingness to accept inborn tendencies separates me from established ethnographic doctrine that treats man as essentially a *tabula rasa*—a behavioral lump of clay capable of being molded into any shape or form. I justify the former stand on two grounds: first, that it is always unwise to borrow more from one discipline when working in another than is absolutely necessary for explanation of the phenomena under discussion and, second, because evidence suggests that genetic behavioral preprogramming is volatile and, hence, that with increased cultural preprogramming it would tend to be lost in the processes of natural selection. (I might note that, for instance, species adapted to cave life usually retain the structures for seeing after they have lost the functional attribute of sight.) I justify the latter stand also for two reasons. First, I find that when I examine the writings by social theorists they always sneak in assumptions about man's innate behavior—usually without being aware of it—and I consider it to be better to make such assumptions explicit. Second, because the ethnographic record, despite my colleagues' love of the exotic and unusual, tends to be almost boringly consistent from place to place.

Let me exemplify what I mean by caution and parsimony. There has been building up over the past few years a kind of ethological philosophy, starting with careful and scientific observations on vertebrate behavior that show (among other things) certain forms of aggressive action under prescribed conditions and certain tendencies to spacing, nesting, and defense of the nest. This philosophy is being built into assumptions about man's aggressive tendencies and innate territoriality and ends up (at least in the hands of popularizers) as a kind of justification for institutions of private property and nationalism. It is obvious that the last elements in this syllogistic chain cannot be sustained by ethnographic fact, for man displays a widely variant degree of interest in property and institutions of nationhood, both between cultures and intraculturally. Aggression and territoriality as preprogrammed characteristics of the naked ape are therefore suspect—if not actually disproved. The ethnologist, therefore, has a tendency simply to discard these theories—either politely, by suggesting they are unwarranted extrapolations; hostilely, by attacking the motives of those who have put them forward; or foolishly, by asserting that man is a special kind of being and not subject to such genetic rules (presumably out of some atavistic belief in the human soul).

I believe there exists something that can be called a human ethology. But difficulties that do not bother those who watch sticklebacks and herring gulls face those who seek a human ethology, a human nature; for whatever is ethological is overlain by culture, and it is necessary somehow to peel away the culture to discover the naked ape underneath. Recent primate studies make one thing certain: we cannot build the human ethology simply from the least common denominator of our primate cousins.

My ethnological observations lead me to an ethological conclusion about *Homo sapiens* that is different from that made by those that assert preprogrammed aggression and territoriality. It is not that the individual is quintessentially aggressive and possessive, but rather that he is quintessentially concerned with the maintenance and furtherance of a positive self-image. I have elsewhere (Goldschmidt 1959) called this a need for positive affect.

There is no little evidence that such a need is preprogrammed, and I read both Spitz's and Harlow's work as supportive of this in humans and among infrahuman primates. It seems to me that one thing that has emerged from the studies by Washburn and his students is that such self-interested, status-oriented behavior has survival value for the individual primate. Whatever aggression and territoriality may be in infrahuman vertebrates, they are, in my view, merely two of several appropriate responses designed to satisfy this deeper preprogrammed need for ego-satisfaction.

I will return to this point in a moment, but I must here remind you that we are dealing with the *human* animal, and certainly what is quintessentially human is man's capacity to symbolize. The evolutionary value of this capacity, which so clearly underlies the cultural programming in man, is also quite clear. But we must not forget that every animal has the defects of his virtues and that man not only is able to manipulate symbols, but also that he is entrapped by them.

It is, as Hallowell (1967) has pointed out, the symbol of the self that lies at the very center of man's symbol system. That is, each normal individual in a normal community acts in such ways as to enhance the quality of that symbolic self. It is enhanced by the tokens that the community recognizes as significant and relevant to what makes a person good, substantial, powerful, prestigious. These may vary from the admiring glances of a pretty girl to the acquisition of a Nobel Prize. Significantly, however, they are meaningful to the purpose precisely because they are the perception of others. The idiom for an individual's evaluation of himself varies from culture to culture, for it is lesson one in anthropology that values differ from culture to culture. Hence, the actions requisite to self-aggrandizement (using that phrase in a nonpejorative sense) will vary from culture to culture. It may involve aggressive action; it may involve possessive orientations; but it may involve neither of these qualities.

There is one further point that must be made about man's symbolic actions relevant to this self-image, and one that is of primary importance to man's institutional behavior. This is the universal occurrence of a process of identification. That is, in every society, each individual identifies himself with one or more groups of individuals and finds not merely material advantage through such identification, but, more significantly, finds ego-gratification (or loss) in response to the fortunes of such groups. The similarity with ethological observations of flocking animals, and of many primate groups, needs merely be noted. However, the analogy should not lead us into the false premise of an identity. Whether or not the base mechanism is shared with these animals, what is quite clear is that the identification process is not limited by territoriality, proximity in kinship, nurturant person, age, or sex, but may be based on any of these criteria or on some entirely different one, such as occupation. These ethnological facts do not deny the reality of an ethological preprogramming, but it seems to me that they significantly change its locus.

Meanwhile, man is also preprogrammed for appetitive considerations as well: he seeks food, sex, survival, and creature comforts. In every society some or all of these desires may come in direct conflict with those virtues that enhance the symbolic self. Thus each individual must pick his way between those forms of behavior that satisfy his ego-needs and those that satisfy what can perhaps be called more primitive urges.

We cannot, on the basis of present ethnographic literature, prove that ego-aggrandizement or any other behavioral attribute is universal in man, though one can find little basis for doubting it. We cannot prove them through primate studies. I have elsewhere suggested that a new kind of ethnography is necessary if we are to demonstrate its existence. While among the Sebei, I made a practice of recording (by virtue of an unusually skilled interpreter) the verbal interactions of persons engaged in social encounters. The result of this study is a book (Goldschmidt 1969) whose substance is the verbatim record of two such events—one a matter of allocating a legacy among four sons of the deceased and the other an accusation of intent to engage in witchcraft brought by the mother of a newlywed junior wife against the senior wife. What impresses me most about this record is that, when we learn a few elements of law and belief, we are quite at home with the kinds of interactions that take place—interactions of the kind found in the novels of C. P. Snow and J. P. Marquand. My point, however, is to note that what we need is a sample of ethnographic reporting of this kind from societies the world over. Such reporting does not precode events in terms of the preconceptions either of the ethnographer or of the informant, and, therefore, it allows us to see interaction as it takes place. This is precisely the way ethologists work in the analysis of animal social behavior.

Such ethologically based individual self-aggrandizement means that social institutions must not merely cope with a recalcitrant external environment, but with man himself. The centrifugal force of individual self-aggrandizement, in my view, must be countered by established institutional mechanisms. If, as Ashley Montagu (1952) would have it, we are all Prince Kropotkin's mutual-aiders, there would be no need for institutional systems, reinforced by myth, ceremony, psychological apparatus, and frequently the use of force, to provide for that cooperation that is a requisite for human productivity. Instead, as Durkheimian social anthropology makes clear, human institutions provide the mechanisms for collaborative social action, and religious and ceremonial life reinforce through symbolic expression the imperative that the individual must be submerged in this community requirement.

FUNCTIONAL REQUISITES
AND INSTITUTIONAL SOLUTIONS

The ethnological literature dealing with adaptive processes is now beginning to take shape, and the theory of ethnology is being transformed by these interests: ecology is the magic word in today's theory, as Harris (1968) makes clear. It emerges as a confluence of two basic trends: (1) the evolutionary development in American anthropology of the past ten years, particularly as inspired by White (1949), but made viable by Steward's ecological studies stemming back over thirty years (1949, 1955); and (2) the functionalist approach that examined institutions in their setting as instrumentalities—but with ecology largely, if not wholly, absent. The marriage of the two approaches, as I pointed out in *Man's Way* (1959), is essential, for the evolutionists are deficient in social theory (which I think shows up very clearly in Steward's cultural-causality paper, 1949), while the Durkheimian functionalists never worked cross-culturally and, therefore, could merely assert the fitness of institutions, not their ecological relevance.

The ecological movement began with the early work of Steward (1938), who related the formation of primitive band organization, with its patrilineal bias and communal use of territory, to the exigencies of exploiting land under circumstances of dry-land economies utilizing primitive hunting and gathering technologies. It took a long time to make this viewpoint stick, largely because of a bias against economic thinking. This negative attitude was supported by an authoritative but fallacious ethnographic understanding of Algonquin hunting practices—a matter that had to be cleared up by further work. The consistency of this ecological adaptation has been shown by Service (1964). Meanwhile, Birdsell (1953) has demonstrated that Australian bands show a high level of size consistency, their territories being expanded or contracted in relation to the carrying capacity of the land, suggesting that there is an optimal size of social groups under conditions of a simple hunting economy. Lévi-Strauss (1969), though hardly an ecologist, has brought this theoretical orientation to Europe and England. Working cross-culturally, he was endeavoring to explain the closely related concepts of incest and exogamy, and he has suggested the functional relevance of marital rules in maintaining alliances—certainly an instance of the instrumental purpose of institutionalized behavior. And Leach, both in his Burma study (1968) and in his Ceylonese monograph (1961), uses ecology as a prime factor. Younger men, notably Barth (1956) and Gulliver (1955), have fully accepted ecological theories.

Yengoyan (1968, pp. 185–199), in his presentation to the "Man the Hunter" Conference, showed that the famous section system of the Australian tribes offered a mechanism for meeting two concomitant needs: (1) the need for a small integrated group to exploit a specific territory known intimately; and (2) a system of close alliances that made it relatively easy for such units, under local stress, to have access to the territory of neighboring sections. The point has a nice counterpart from another part of the world: Peters (1964) has shown that among some Arab peoples of North Africa the local group maintains close affinal alliances that are utilized from time to time when an individual, under conditions of local drought, seeks out his affinals who, through the vagaries of highly localized rainfall, are temporarily better situated.

I should acknowledge that there remains some recalcitrant data. Woodburn (1968), also in the "Man the Hunter" Conference, reporting on the Hadza, raises serious doubts of the functional necessity of institutional mechanisms. Turnbull's discussion (1968) of the Ik raises similar questions.

It may be that peoples like the Hadza and Ik were being gradually reduced by pressures of more advanced cultures and that their deficiency in coping against such outside forces may have been institutional rather than technological and that, therefore, the inadequacy of their social organization, as much as their impoverished productive technology, is responsible for the gradual decline of these groups. It is not self-evident that people will "invent" institutional apparatus to meet vicissitudes as they arise, any more than they will invent or take over technical apparatus. Yet I must confess that the specter of these amorphous, apparently non–value-oriented societies haunts me, and if institutions are instrumentalities, these people manage to cope with a most inadequate armamentum. At the very least, such data suggest that the institutional machinery of Australia is more elaborate than would appear to be absolutely necessary, unless some environmental parameter that we do not yet understand is operative.

To some extent, the Australian pattern may be an evolutionary product not unlike that classic analog, the Irish elk. What is quite clear in the Australian initiation system is that, whatever other functions it may perform, it is a powerful means of social control by senior men over the youth and the young men. And there is little reason to doubt that the exertion of this control relates to sexual practices, for the polygyny of Australia delays the marriage of the young (see, for instance, Hart and Pilling 1960), thus depriving them of their share of the one scarce resource of the community that is inequitably shared. This is an example of institutional means of coping with man himself—his greed and cupidity, as well as his sexuality. Those who know the current thinking on the evolutionary force that accounts for the elk's exaggerated antlers will recognize that the analog is a close one.

In biological development there can be more than one solution to a particular problem, such as, for instance, temperature maintenance. The situation is similar with respect to social problems. A recurrent functional requirement among marginal hunters is the establishment of food-sharing practices, particularly when large game has been killed. Failure to do so would be wasteful in a situation where the people simply cannot afford the loss. But food sharing may be built on particularistic kin obligations as among the Aranda, concepts of generosity as among the Andamanese, notions of perfect equity as among the Hadza, or free access when under duress to every cache as among the Arctic Eskimo. The secondary consequences of these divergences, as well as the factors determining which will be the solution of choice, are matters that deserve careful consideration. We will here only note that the Aranda, with their sadistic rituals and their strong control by the older men, do not rest on internalized notions of generosity, but on highly specific legal demands to share with particular kin; that is, the solution is consistent with other aspects of the culture.

Sharing the risks inherent in the vicissitudes of life is not a problem of hunting peoples only. Industrial society has developed a major industry in the form of insurance, which is the capitalistic means of handling this recurrent problem. The institution of insurance began in the seventeenth century in the form of "Tontine societies," which were mutual aid groups, largely to cover loss at death. It is no mere coincidence that organizations closely resembling these early European developments have sprung up in diverse parts of the world where tribal peoples have migrated to the cities in search of employment. The insurance provided them in their tribal communities, usually in the form of clans or other corporate groups with shared land, capital, or responsibilities, was no longer available in their new urban conditions. The best documented cases of such institutions have been provided by Little (1957) for West Africa, but Ardener (1964) has brought together numerous occurrences from diverse parts of the globe. It is a prime example of a felt need, and a recurrent institutional solution.

I have thus far suggested that in human societies there are recurrent problems requiring institutionalized solutions. These problems are the result of a combination of two generic circumstances: (1) the vicissitudes of the environment within which the society must maintain life; and (2) the preprogrammed self-seeking characteristics of the human animal that must be curbed or channelized. The former factor is a variant from one society to another; the latter is a constant, but one that takes on different involvements under different circumstances.

ECOLOGICAL ADAPTATION
OF SOCIAL INSTITUTIONS

With these theoretical considerations in mind, we can turn to the second phase of my discussion—namely, the manner in which a people's institutions and behavior are adapted to external circumstances. For if culture is an adaptive mechanism, a means of coping, then it follows that the specific forms that the adaptation will take depend upon the external circumstances to which they are subjected. I intend to illuminate this with data derived from an extensive research project in which my colleagues and I have investigated the adaptive process in culture. This research has been centered on four East African tribes, each of which is characterized by the fact that a part of its territory is arid, and there the people engage in cattle pastoralism, and part of it is better watered, and there they engage in hoe-farming. The essence of our research has been to examine in detail the community life and the population characteristics of each of these sectors of the four tribes in order to discover where certain consistent differences between them appear and whether such differences can be shown to relate to the economic circumstances in terms of the theoretically relevant consequences of these forms of economy.

It is not necessary here to go into detail regarding the methods and procedures we used, which have been delineated elsewhere (Goldschmidt 1965). Suffice it to say that we were concerned both with institutional behavior and with the attitudes, values, and personality traits of the population, that each of four ethnographers studied a pastoral and a farming community in one of the four tribes, that an anthropologist trained in psychology took a battery of questions and instruments from samples of each of the eight communities, and, because we were treating the environment as the ultimate independent variable, that a geographer studied land potentials and land use. Though numerous publications of an ancillary kind have emerged from this research, I am sorry to say that the full report on our work will be some time in coming. Hence, what I can here report is not only partial, but also preliminary.

It is important to point out that the demands of these two modes of economy are quite different—perhaps as different from one another as it is possible to find within the range of primitive economies. It is also necessary to point out that in dry, grassy, plains country the herding of cattle, sheep, and goats is the most advantageous use of land that can be made by a people lacking modern machine technology and market systems, but that where there is sufficient rainfall to render agricultural production reasonably certain, a much larger and more stable population can be supported by cultivating the soil, even when using primitive methods. Hence we argue, and the data in Africa substantiate, that people will rapidly take to the one or the other mode of economy in accordance with such circumstances (though there are of course intermediate conditions that permit considerable mixture of the two forms of production). That this is a reasonable assumption is attested to by the fact that in one of the four tribes we studied, five separate ecological adaptations were operative (Winans 1965), all of which have developed in the last hundred years. Our geographer generally found that dependence on agriculture related closely to the probability rates for rainfall adequate to grow crops (Porter 1963).

What is it that makes pastoralism so different a life form from farming? There are many factors, and we shall focus on but a few of the more important ones. The pastoralist must be mobile; he must be free to move with his cattle to meet their requirements for grass, water, and salt. By contrast, the farmer must remain in one place if he is to realize the investment of his labor on the land. Let us follow through some of the implications of this very simple and self-evident difference for what it means in terms of human adaptation.

First, there is the matter of control of land. The pastoralists cannot define locally owned plots of land, but must recognize free access to the grass and water for cattle if they are to maintain maximum use of their sparse resources. Throughout East Africa, and elsewhere when livestock are herded on natural grass (including our own pioneer West), there is a recognized territoriality, but no private land ownership. But the farmer must have established rights to the soil if he is going to invest in its maintenance; that is, some form of private landholdings. Thus among the Sebei, who originally were pastoralists, but took to farming on the well-watered slopes of Mount Elgon, legal sanctions for an institutional recognition of private land ownership became established, and by the time of our study all arable land was in such holdings. Nevertheless, when a group of these same farming Sebei returned to their plains territory (from which they had been driven by marauding tribes to the north) under the umbrella of British colonial protection about fifty years ago, they treated the land as public property. Only as a plot of land was brought under cultivation was it treated as a private right. Legal institutions, therefore, rapidly develop to meet the specific circumstances for which they are requisite.

Although a pastoral people are not free-roaming, but operate within a recognized territory in order to avoid direct confrontation with other tribes (except as they want to provoke such confrontation), they are nevertheless quite mobile. As no man is bound to one location, he is not bound to one set of neighbors. But the farmer does not have this mobility; he must remain in the community if he is to retain an interest in that capital which is the source of his sustenance and his well-being. He cannot escape his neighbors. Therefore, the farmer must adjust to a particular community of men, and among them there must be some internal control of a kind that is not requisite among pastoralists, who frequently operate under a legal system (known to us from the Bible) in which each clan or kin-group acts as an independent jural entity between which disputes are negotiated by vendetta or wergild.

A development that took place among the Sebei some time before Europeans entered their part of the world demonstrates the emergence of an appropriate institution (Goldschmidt 1967). The basic legal system of the Sebei was, and still remains, of the kind I just described. If a man murdered another, the victim's clansmen took vengeance by claiming a life from the clan of the offender or agreed on a payment of cattle. Failing either of these two methods, however, they would resort to magical oaths, which also worked against the clan rather than the individual who committed the murder. Whichever mode they utilized, it is clear that the matter was seen as one between the two clans, and the community or tribe had no part in the action—not even a mediating role There developed, apparently at the instigation of Matui, one of the leading prophets of the tribe, a new institution that the Sebei call *ntarastit* and which they gloss as "passing the law." In its ceremonial aspects, it was in almost all particulars the same as that used in the oathing ritual, with one important exception: in this instance it was taken not to avenge a crime, but as an affirmation of mutual community peace. The rite was a solemn statement involving sacred elements and was made by all adult men of the community as an affirmation that spiritual forces would destroy whoever should break the pledge. Moreover, by taking this oath, the community acquired the right to punish any person who broke the peace. *Ntarastit* thus established an institution of community law; it sanctioned the role of the community as judge and executioner. It was at least in two ways a very imperfect institution: (1) it was not adequately realized; and (2) it was crudely formed. Because the ritual was not held at regular intervals, but only when the prophet felt that lawlessness had reasserted itself, it obviously failed to perform its Durkheimian functions very effectively, suggesting the value of regular periodic reaffirmation in ritual form. Furthermore, the punishment that was meted out was very severe, even for minor thefts, so that it failed to make nice or consistent discriminations of the kind that are appropriate for legal redress. Nevertheless, we must credit the aboriginal Sebei leadership with having devised an institutional form to take care of a need that arose as a result of changed circumstances prior to the advent of Europeans in the area.

The ecological conditions of the two forms of economy also influence the nature of warfare, and this in turn has relevance for other aspects of institutional behavior. Among pastoralists the world over there is endemic raiding, a constant pattern of small-scale conflicts intended as a mode of gratification by the annexing of enemy property. Cattle are particularly susceptible to such a pattern: they are valuable, they are necessarily held in relative isolation, they graze in open country where natural protection is limited, and they can be moved great distances in a very short time and hidden away with relative ease—all of which I discovered when I accompanied a retaliatory raid to recapture some animals that were stolen by neighbors of the Sebei. Land cannot be thus stolen (though other valuables, including wives and children, can be). The ideal form of cattle raid is a small, highly mobile, and rapid foray against which the defense is eternal vigilance in equally small numbers and at the site where the cattle are at the moment; that is, by the herdsmen themselves. A second line of defense involves the existence of institutional machinery for rapidly mobilizing retaliatory raids. For such purposes it is necessary to have some means by which the otherwise independent individual herdsman can be articulated to a larger group. Two institutional devices for such action are found repeatedly in pastoral societies: (1) the so-called segmentary lineage system that articulates the agnatic kindred by using the ties of blood relationship; and (2) age-sets that cemented by ties of initiation into a common corporate group of warrior-aged men. Both types are found in East Africa, sometimes in conjunction.

Farmers, on the other hand, must protect their territory; they are involved in a defensive operation vis-à-vis a spatially defined community, whether or not they also engage in raiding. While patterns of raiding are also found among farmers, as is classically illustrated by the New Guinea Highland peoples, the economic motive for such action is certainly less insistent. For defensive action there must be the potential of mobilizing all able-bodied men who share a residence, without regard to age or affiliation. On the other hand, age-sets in a farming community merely create an organization of young men whose potential for disruption is great, particularly if they have no external target against which to express their aggression. Under such circumstances it is not surprising that the Sebei have reduced the age-sets, which they retain from pastoral times, to function less ceremonial entities, without either internal organization or recognized responsibilities. The Arusha, who are sedentarized Masai, have, according to Gulliver (1963), made a similar kind of adaptation.

These institutional and cultural changes indicate the manner in which a people, either by conscious acts of their leaders or by gradual alteration of their habitual activities, manage to change their patterned modes of life, usually by adapting some earlier pattern, sometimes by sloughing off old patterns, and perhaps occasionally by sheer invention.

ECOLOGICAL ADAPTATION
OF INDIVIDUAL BEHAVIOR

There is another level at which the adaptive process takes place, for man alters not merely his institutions, but also his characteristic form of behavior, his values and attitudes, and even his personality, to meet new exigencies of life. As indicated earlier, we had as part of our research team an anthropologist trained in psychology who took a battery of tests from thirty or more men and thirty or more women from each of eight communities—a total of 505 protocols. These tests were designed not merely to get expressed preferences, but also to obtain unexpressed values by diverse methods, including a picture value test (Goldschmidt and Edgerton 1961), and personality attributes, largely by means of the Rorschach. The responses have now been fully analyzed (Edgerton 1971), and although I cannot go into them in full detail, the conclusions are so relevant to the subject of adaptation and coping that I want to discuss them briefly.

Edgerton (1971) writes: "At the most general level of comparison, I believe that farmers and pastoralists are differentiated on two dimensions: (1) open versus closed emotionality, and (2) direct versus indirect action." Among the pastoralists, the first of these dimensions is built on such traits as ready expressions of affection, sexuality, depression, and, to a somewhat lesser extent, fear, bravery, and brutality; these stand in contrast to the farmers' emotional constraint and expressions of hatred. The second dimension contrasts the pastoralists' willingness to take direct aggressive action, expressions of independence, frequency of adultery, as against the farmers' tendency to conflict avoidance, to indirect forms of aggression, and, as might be expected, impulsivity. A third set of contrasts, which Edgerton does not raise to the "general level," but which I, with my more sociological orientation, find of equal saliency, is what one might call social commitment. Here the pastoralists express more concern with their social unit, showing more respect for authority, more sense of cooperation, of involvement with clan and kinsmen, a greater concern with wrongdoing, and a heightened sense of guilt and shame. By contrast, the farmers are less respectful of authority, express a greater degree of hatred, are more apt to seek out friends rather than kinsmen, and are more given to insults and litigiousness.

This last set of contrasts may seem to run counter to our earlier discussion of the fact that the farmer is more involved with a spatially based community than the herdsman. But the point is precisely the opposite: the farmer is forced into an involvement with a community from which he cannot escape by geographic mobility; furthermore, it is one in which it is more difficult, because of the greater fixity of wealth, to rise by vertical mobility. The situation is also more fraught with internal conflict, for if one man amasses more land than another this fact not only is clearly visible, but it means that he has acquired a greater sector of a finite store of resources. The pastoralist who has a larger herd is not similarly depriving others of fortune. Thus the closed community of the farmers is a breeding ground for hostility, and where hostility is rampant there also is a need to avoid open expression of emotion and acting out of feelings.

Whereas farming places constraints on emotional expression and directness of action, the pastoral economy supports the individual who is capable of direct action and is free to express himself. The pastoralist is faced with a constant and recurrent set of choices, and his ultimate success depends upon the cogency of his decisions. In this he is very much like our traditional capitalist, and indeed he may be viewed as, if not the original, at least the aboriginal capitalist.

This freedom of action and individuality in pastoral life are qualities that make it seem particularly attractive to Westerners. But one must not lose sight of the obverse of this coin. It is also a difficult life, one with a harshness, with many hardships and constant danger from enemies and animal predators. Such conditions require a ready-to-act, brutal personnel, strongly attached (through culturally reinforced supports) to its virtues. Perhaps nothing is more telling of the differences than that, while the farmer's greatest fear is of poverty, the pastoralist's greatest fear is of death.

It should be needless to point out that these are differences in tendencies and frequencies, not absolute differences, and some individuals "conform" more to the ecologically relevant patterns of behavior of their community than do others. But all the differences I have discussed are statistically significant at the .0005 level, despite the fact that our investigation dealt with very short-range changes, despite the fact that most of our communities were not purely farming or purely pastoral, but were ranged along a continuum from one to the other, and also despite the fact that they were not isolated from one another, but were in communication and even intermarried, thus "contaminating" the differences.

All of this suggests that man is an adaptive being, that he has learned to cope with an environment not merely in terms of technological apparatus and knowledge, but also by means of his institutions, values, attitudes, and even manifestations of personality. (It is perhaps relevant to point out that some wives in one of the pastoral communities had been born in farming communities; yet these women were in most particulars more like their husbands than they were like their fathers.) This does not mean that man is infinitely flexible, that there are no tendencies to continuity in behavior, even in the face of disfunction and disharmony, but it does mean that the human animal, in coping with his environment, is able to make adjustments of a significant and far-reaching kind, rapidly bringing institutional changes, attitude changes, and even measurable differences in personality attributes into conformity with the external circumstances of life.

THE INSTITUTIONALIZATION
OF INDIVIDUAL COPING BEHAVIOR

One of the central implications of the foregoing analysis is that, as indicated earlier, institutions must cope with the egoistic demands of the individual and that, conversely, the individual must cope with institutional situations. I should now like to give some consideration to the fact that in a well-functioning social system the individual's problems of adjustment are met by institutional means, whereas in other societies such needs are poorly met or not met at all. Let me exemplify what I mean by the institutionalization of individual behavior with an event that I observed among the Sebei.

Sebei women undergo an initiation in which the main and most difficult ordeal is a "circumcision," an excision of the labia minora, with a not very sharp iron knife. The cutting is usually done in groups of half a dozen girls in a ceremonial that begins one dawn and lasts until the sun breaks the horizon the next morning. During those twenty-four hours the girls are given medicines and instruction and visit the homes of their friends and relatives, dancing and singing. The day is the prelude to a long ceremonial cycle, lasting about six months, at the close of which the girls are ready for marriage. It is quite clearly the female counterpart to the male initiation rite, and nowadays sometimes the boys and girls go through the preliminary phase together, though never the actual cutting. A part of the activity involves the singing of bawdy and frightening songs, and relatives will emphasize the pain and hardship of the cutting and the initiate's inability to meet the ordeal. To "cry the knife" is a major disgrace, and to this day the Sebei sing songs of derision of those who have failed the ordeal in the distant past. It is more frequent for a girl to cry, perhaps because it is a more vital incision, but if a girl does she suffers a social disability throughout her life—she is forbidden to be a man's senior wife, is not permitted to the circumcisions of future generations, and is otherwise made to suffer minor indignities that will not let her forget her moment of shame. I might add that it is an ordeal to watch, and by the time I was witnessing my third instance of the ceremonial, I found myself hoping that one of the girls would fail the test in order that I might witness the reaction—a sentiment that still gives me a twinge of guilt. Indeed, the senior girl, one who was particularly popular and had the highest status in the group, refused to let the operation be completed. The consternation was dramatic; her old father was in a rage and literally had to be held, and finally it was made clear that my presence was no longer desirable, as they would have to catch the girl, hold her down, and complete the cutting.

A week or so later I called on the initiate, who was alone in seclusion. I expected to find this girl in a fit of remorse and self-recrimination for her failure. Nothing of the kind; her response to me was quite specific: "I know who caused me to cry." All initiates learn, during the course of their initiation, the magical means by which they can make novices cry, and this fact is the basic sanction that gives all adults authority over all youths. She told me how a particular man had accosted her, demanding sexual acquiescence, and that she had refused and insulted him; therefore she knew that he had done magic against her. What is relevant to us here is that the culture of the Sebei provides a ready-made external "cause" for the individual dereliction. Although she will still suffer the social disabilities of her failure, she is protected from loss of self-esteem by the culturally established and socially approved externalization of her act. This is what I mean by providing an institutional means for an individual to cope with a personal situation.

Cultures do not always provide such necessary elements. For a concrete example, I urge you to go back and read Fortune's analysis of Dobu (1932)—not, however, merely Benedict's *"Readers' Digest* version" in *Patterns of Culture* (1934). You will recall that in this society there is a pervasive and universal fear; that no relationships are pleasant, or easy, or even without explicit dangers. The hostility between the sexes is so great that the married couple, when they live together, alternate residence between the kinsmen of the husband and the wife, each remaining an outsider to the spouse's kinsmen. In my recent analysis of this situation, I suggest "that the quality of Dobuan interpersonal relationships derives from the failure to provide *any* kind of identity for the Dobuan child" (Goldschmidt 1966, p. 79). Indeed, it is my belief that the prevalence of brother-sister incest is to be accounted for by the fact that this is the only relationship that is not fraught with jealousy, hatred, and the threat of witchcraft. I continue as follows:

. . . the society inadequately provides the institutionalized means for the individual to internalize the constraints of society and the constraints upon his own ego-aggrandizing impulses. This is not merely an absence of controls. Controls, in fact, abound; they are in the magical practices of his fellows of which each man is fully aware, and every Dobuan makes at least a public front of controlled behavior and restraint of impulses. Not only are there strict rules of propriety, but also the Dobuan makes every effort to display a face of good behavior (with the result that the missionaries are deceived but the traders are not) and outward signs of conformity and friendliness. (The avoidance of witchcraft talk, of sexual reference, or uncovering one's sexual organs is explicit, while all persons secretly are involved in witchcraft or sorcery and in extramarital sexual activity. Only those too young or too old for sexual affairs are free to use terms of sexual reference.) No, it is neither absence of rules nor the absence of efforts to control others that accounts for the pervasive anarchy on Dobu. It is, I feel certain, the failure to provide internalized restraints on individual impulses through appropriate institutionalization, with the result that these impulses are constantly being enacted for the private purposes of the individual (whenever he can escape detection and direct punishment), who is then suffused with guilt and (by reason of feeling guilty) assumes that others are secretly endeavoring to punish him for these acts (Goldschmidt 1966, pp. 79–80).

I want now to turn to another instance where society has failed to provide institutional means for individual coping; one which leads us to some of the more pragmatic aspects of the problems we have been discussing. For this purpose I want briefly to summarize some of the findings regarding the post-hospitalization life of a group of mentally retarded persons as developed by Edgerton in *The Cloak of Competence* (1967). Edgerton made a follow-up investigation of a group of the higher-level mental retardates who had been released from Pacific State Hospital. He found these people beset with the problem not merely of self-maintenance, but of what can best be called ego-maintenance. To be found wanting in mental capacity is the most devastating of all possible stigmata, at least in our culture—indeed, mental competence is very close to what we might call the soul. The fact that these people had been certified as mentally incompetent by an agency of the state is so destructive of the ego that they simply could not accept their condition for what it was. As a result they had to develop mechanisms of defense—social mechanisms—by means of which to establish a cloak of competence, even if woven from the same thread as that of the emperor. To do this they were forced into two patterns of behavior, which Edgerton calls "passing" and "denial."

The first of these has to do with concealing the fact of their retardation from others; the second with concealing the implications of this fact from themselves. The latter they do by various devices: their "illness" was temporary or the result of alcoholism; it had to do with some particular deficiency such as "nerves" or physical illness; it was the result of a conspiracy by others. All of these are means by which the individual encapsulates the reality into a specific and explainable deficiency, or denies by projecting blame, so that he may keep his ego intact.

Passing, of course, relates to the social interrelationships of the post-hospitalized patient. One of the important elements of passing is that he must conceal the fact that he had been an inmate, particularly from a potential employer or a potential spouse, but also from casual acquaintances. The responses Edgerton received suggest that sterilization, which is practiced on most patients at the hospital, affects their ego-structure less by the denial of sexuality than by the affirmation—and the ineradicable evidence of such affirmation—of their stigma. Thus, for instance, one woman said:

I was all engaged to marry a man that I really loved. He loved me too, but one day we were sitting and talking with his mother and father and they were saying how happy they would be when we were married and had children. I couldn't do it, because his parents wanted us to have children. When I heard this, I said, "No, I don't never want to get married." I almost told her [the mother] why but I just couldn't bear to tell her (Edgerton 1967, pp. 155–156).

The ingenuity of efforts made by these people, to hide their stigma, despite their limited competence, is touching and impressive. They invent such devices as wearing a broken watch, so when they need to know the time (which they do not know how to tell) they can ask somebody what time it is, explaining that their watch has stopped.

A frequent and the most effective aid for passing is the acquisition of a sponsor—some person who knows the inadequacies of the ex-patient and is willing and able to help in the recurrent minor crises of everyday life: setting his alarm clock, helping with his marketing, filling out forms, and the like. Such sponsors may be relatives or a spouse, but often they are employers, landlords, or others who have chanced to take on the relationship. It frequently appears to be a kind of psychological symbiotic relationship in which the giver of aid receives satisfactions as much as the recipient.

The contrast between the situation of these mental retardates, who suffer such devastation of their self, and that of the Sebei initiate, whose actions brought her a similar loss of face, is most instructive. In one instance there stands ready an institutionalized ego-defense, however much the initiate must suffer a social stigma, while in the other there is not even an awareness on the part of those most concerned with the problem of mental retardation to provide anything that will help maintain an adequate sense of the self.

The lesson to be drawn from this contrast is relevant to the central subject of this book, namely, the coping behavior of individuals. Society creates situations with which each individual must cope; it does so by establishing barriers to the successful administration of the symbolic self. I do not see how it can be otherwise, though manifestly cultures differ greatly in the degree to which they erect such barriers, the demands they make on individuals, and the measures they provide for self-gratification. But however much they establish differences in status and well-being among the population, and however much they make demands upon the individual, cultures can also provide means by which the individual ego can be sustained, by which the individual may preserve at least a minimally satisfactory image of his self. The psychiatrists have long recognized the existence of ego-defense mechanisms as part of the individual repertoire of behavior; what we have not recognized is that there is also an institutionalization of such mechanisms, and that such institutionalization is important to the maintenance of a harmonious society and a healthy population.

Above all, what we forget is that new situations require new institutions and that ultimately these must be conceived in the minds of men if they are to come into existence. We must, therefore, take a lesson from the old Sebei prophet Matui and create appropriate institutions for individuals who must cope with new or unmet problems that derive from our own ever-changing social milieu.

One wonders that the responsible agencies have failed to work out standard means by which the mental retardates can meet their constant and recurrent problems. It would be easy to provide for such young people the necessary cover stories and techniques so that each would not have to invent them for himself. Could not there be, for instance, a means of explaining away the sterilization that would at least make possible the "passing" if not the "denial"? If we appreciate the relevance of ego-maintenance as a social problem, it is clear that these actions would be more important than the provision of ex-patient clubs, which serve merely to reiterate and reinforce the stigma itself.

This is not merely a matter of mental retardates. Elsewhere in this book there is consideration of problems of youth in modern schools, and nowhere are there greater difficulties for individuals endeavoring to preserve—and to create—a self. Consider what must be a constantly recurrent problem for young blacks in this age of dissent, those who are motivated to seek some culturally approved goal in the larger society, but must face the pressures of their peers to engage in the militant protest or face the accusation of Uncle Tomism. Is there some way in which we can help them to formulate their choices in terms of their personal aspirations without denying the relevance of the protest? Can we institutionalize compromise between the dominant culture of white America and the subculture of the black youth? Though the answer is not easy, it is a question worth asking.

SUMMARY

Culture is the adaptive mechanism in man for meeting the diverse conditions in which he lives. It has the dual task of providing the means for exploiting the environment and (because this is necessarily done by human collaboration) of providing the means by which individual pressures to personal self-aggrandizement are held in check and channelized. Essential to such a view of society is the recognition that each person lives in terms of a symbolic self whose fate he is motivated to control and whose public and private quality it is his chief concern to advance. With this thesis outlined, I showed how cultural institutions are adaptive to diverse circumstances, using as illustration the data we derived from our Culture and Ecology Project. A second kind of adaptation takes place on the individual level; for clearly the individual must learn to cope not only with diverse exterior circumstances, but also with the diverse institutional mechanisms that are relevant to these circumstances.

Next we saw that culture provides socially acceptable means for the individual to cope with the institutions themselves, in such a way that he can, despite personal inadequacy and social stigma, maintain his ego intact, though not all cultures in all circumstances provide such mechanisms, as the description of Dobu suggests. Nor do we provide such mechanisms in our own society, as we saw by examining the problems of mental retardates living in the outside world.

All this suggests that we must conscientiously seek ways of establishing institutionalized means for individuals to cope with an ever-changing society in order that they may preserve an adequate sense of self. The problem is pervasive in our society, as even the most cursory examination of youth subculture or ghetto subculture will demonstrate. For this purpose I recommend that the reader consult such a book as Claude Brown's *Manchild in the Promised Land* (1965).

REFERENCES

Ardener, S. The comparative study of rotating credit association. *Journal of the Royal Anthropological Institute*, 1964, *94*, 201–229.

Barth, F. Ecologic relationships of ethnic groups in Swat, North Pakistan. *American Anthropologist*, 1956, *58*, 1079–1089.

Benedict, R. *Patterns of culture*. Boston and New York: Houghton Mifflin, 1934.

Birdsell, J. B. Some environmental and cultural factors influencing the structuring of Australian aboriginal populations. *The American Naturalist*, 1953, *87*, 171–207.

Brown, C. *Manchild in the promised land*. New York: Macmillan, 1965.

Edgerton, R. B. *The cloak of competence: Stigma in the lives of the mentally retarded*. Berkeley and Los Angeles: University of California Press, 1967.

————. *The individual in cultural adaptation: A study of four East African peoples*. Berkeley and Los Angeles: University of California Press, 1971.

Fortune, R. F. *Sorcerers of Dobu: The social anthropology of the Dobu islanders of the Western Pacific*. New York: Dutton, 1932.

Goldschmidt, W. *Man's way, a preface to the understanding of human society*. New York: Holt, Rinehart & Winston, 1959.

————. Theory and strategy in the study of cultural adaptability. *American Anthropologist*, 1965, *67*, 402–408.

————. *Comparative functionalism: An essay in anthropological theory*. Berkeley and Los Angeles: University of California Press, 1966.

————. *Sebei law*. Berkeley and Los Angeles: University of California Press, 1967.

————. *Kambuya's cattle: The legacy of an African herdsman*. Berkeley and Los Angeles: University of California Press, 1969.

Goldschmidt, W., and Edgerton, R. B. Picture technique for the study of values. *American Anthropologist*, 1961, *63*, 26–47.

Gulliver, P. H. *The family herds: A study of two pastoral tribes in East Africa, the Jie and Turkana*. London: Routledge & Kegan Paul, 1955.

————. *Social control in an African tribe*. London: Routledge & Kegan Paul, 1963.

Hallowell, A. I. The self and its behavioral environment. In A. I. Hallowell, ed., *Culture and experience*. New York: Schocken, 1967.

Harris, M. *The rise of anthropological theory: A history of the theories of culture*. New York: Thomas Y. Crowell, 1968.

Hart, C. W. M., and Pilling, A. R. *The Tiwi of Northern Australia: Case studies in cultural anthropology*. New York: Holt, Rinehart & Winston, 1960.

Leach, E. *Pul Eliya, a village in Ceylon: A study of land tenure and kinship*. Cambridge: University Press, 1961.

————. *Political systems of Highland Burma*. Boston: Beacon Press, 1968.

Lévi-Strauss, C. *The elementary structures of kinship*. Translated by J. H. Bell and J. R. von Sturmer; edited by R. Needham. Boston: Beacon Press, 1969.

Little, K. The role of voluntary associations in West African urbanization. *American Anthropologist*, 1957, *59*, 579–596.

Montagu, M. F. A. *Darwin, competition and cooperation*. New York: Henry Schuman, 1952.

Peters, E. L. Camel herding pastoralism and lineage organization in Cyrenaica. Lithographed papers prepared for the Symposium on Pastoral Nomadism, Wenner-Gren Foundation, New York, 1964.

Porter, P. W. Suk views on Suk environment. *Annals of the Association of American Geographers*, 1963, *53*, 615–616.

Service, E. R. *Primitive social organization: An evolutionary perspective*. New York: Random House, 1964.

Steward, J. Basin-Plateau aboriginal sociopolitical groups. Bureau of American Ethnology, Bulletin 120, Washington, D.C., 1938.

———. Cultural causality and law: A trial formulation of the development of early civilization. *American Anthropologist*, 1949, *51*, 1–27.

———. *Theory of culture change*. Urbana: University of Illinois Press, 1955.

Turnbull, C. The importance of flux in two hunting societies. In R. B. Lee and I. DeVore, eds., *Man the hunter*. Chicago: Aldine, 1968.

White, L. *The science of culture: A study of man and civilization*. New York: Farrar, Straus, 1949.

Winans, E. V. The political context of economic adaptation in the southern highlands of Tanganyika. *American Anthropologist*, 1965, *67*, 435–441.

Woodburn, J. Introduction to Hadza ecology. In R. B. Lee and I. DeVore, eds., *Man the hunter*. Chicago: Aldine, 1968.

Yengoyan, A. A. Demographic and ecological influences on aboriginal Australian marriage sections. In R. B. Lee and I. DeVore, eds., *Man the hunter*. Chicago: Aldine, 1968.

3

Social Structure and Personal Adaptation: Some Neglected Dimensions

DAVID MECHANIC

The study of social adaptation is most typically pursued without seriously considering the pervasive influence of social structural variables on personal and social adaptation. Traditional approaches to adaptation have developed from psychodynamic studies and ego psychology, and there has been a continuing tendency to see mastery of the environment in terms of intrapsychic mechanisms that allow individuals to control psychologically the environmental stimuli impinging upon them and to maintain a state of personal comfort. More recently, with growing emphasis on environmental mastery and effective performance, some investigators have broadened their scope of study to include such concerns as the learning and use of skills and the direct manipulation of the environment, but this new development has not been very systematically developed. Almost all stress investigators, irrespective of their orientations, neglect consideration of the relationship between social structure and mastery.

From a social psychological point of view, it has increasingly become apparent to investigators of stress that adaptation must be considered in terms of the relationship between external physical and social demands on the person and his resources to deal with these (McGrath 1970). It has become commonplace to consider the potentialities for adaptation in terms of the fit between person and environment, and even therapeutic approaches are frequently based on achieving a more congruent fit. Because the approach to adaptation has been primarily a psychological one, the person-environ-

Supported in part by grant 5 R01 MH 14835 from the National Institute of Mental Health.

ment fit usually considered is an attitudinal fit, or one based on how the person perceives himself in relation to the environment. Only more recently has there been greater emphasis on the issue of whether the person's actual skills are capable of dealing with true external demands.

Successful personal adaptation has at least three components at the individual level. First, the person must have the capabilities and skills to deal with the social and environmental demands to which he is exposed; for the sake of simplicity I shall designate these skills as coping capabilities. Such capacities involve the ability not only to react to environmental demands, but also to influence and control the demands to which one will be exposed and at what pace. Second, individuals must be motivated to meet the demands that become evident in their environment. Individuals can escape anxiety and discomfort by lowering their motivation and aspirations, but as we will see later there are many social constraints against this mode of reducing stress. As motivation increases, the consequences of failing to achieve mastery also increase, and level of motivation is frequently an important prerequisite for experiencing psychological discomfort. Third, individuals must have the capabilities to maintain a state of psychological equilibrium so that they can direct their energies and skills to meeting external, in contrast to internal, needs. It should be apparent that much of the psychological literature on adaptation concerns itself with this third dimension—one which I refer to as defense. Although psychologists who have studied stress have viewed defense as an end in itself, it is more reasonable to see defense as a set of mechanisms that facilitates continuing performance and mastery. Defenses that may be very successful in diminishing pain and discomfort may be catastrophic for personal adaptation if they retard the enactment of behavior directed toward real threats in the environment. To put the matter bluntly, such defenses as denial—a persistent and powerful psychological response—will do a drowning man no good!

There is still another kind of person-environment fit that is rarely discussed in the literature on stress and adaptation, but it is probably the most important of all. This fit between the social structure and environmental demands is probably the major determinant of successful social adaptation. Man's abilities to cope with the environment depend on the efficacy of the solutions that his culture provides, and the skills he develops are dependent on the adequacy of the preparatory institutions to which he has been exposed. To the extent that schools and informal types of preparation are inadequate to the tasks men face, social disruption and personal failure will be inevitable no matter how strong the individual's psychological capacities. Similarly, the kinds of motivation that people have and the directions in which such motivation will be channeled will depend on the incentive systems in a society—the patterns of behavior and performance that are valued and those that are condemned. Finally, the ability of persons to maintain psychological comfort will depend not only on their intrapsychic resources, but also—and perhaps more importantly—on the social supports available or absent in the environment. Men depend on others for justification and admiration, and few men can survive without support from some segment of their fellows (Mechanic 1970).

The foregoing is so obvious that I state these points with some embarrassment. As every introductory student of sociology learns in the first few weeks of his first course, solutions to life tasks become institutionalized and tend to be cumulative through the generations. Men learn through the experience of others, and solutions to environmental demands and challenges are taught from one generation to another. The ability of men and societies to adapt to the conditions of their lives depends in large part on the adequacy of such institutionalized solutions.

The influence of social structure is, of course, more complicated than this discussion suggests. The community not only defines solutions to environmental challenges, but also imposes new challenges through the social values it perpetuates. On the most primitive levels, the community defines territoriality, mobility, the pattern of fertility, food acquisition and use, mating, and social responsibility. But complex social structures also involve a large and varied set of demands that impinges on almost every aspect of life from survival to the most trivial of interrelationships.

Institutionalized solutions to environmental problems must change as the problems themselves change. To the extent that preparatory and evaluative institutions in a society are fitted to the types of problems people in the society must face, then most persons are likely to acquire the skills and capacities to meet life demands and challenges. But with rapid technological and social change, institutionalized solutions to new problems are likely to lag behind, and the probability increases that a larger proportion of the population will have difficulties in accommodating to life problems. In large part, the literature on stress and coping has aided the myth that adaptation is dependent on the ability of individuals to develop personal mastery over their environment. Indeed, most psychological studies of adaptation are studies of individuals and not of groups. But even a superficial thrust into the anthropological literature will make clear how interdependent men are even in the most simple of societies and how dependent they are on group solutions in dealing with environmental problems. Increasingly, it is clear that major stresses on modern man are not amenable to individual solutions, but depend on highly organized cooperative efforts that transcend those of any individual man no matter how well developed his personal resources.

THE INFLUENCE OF SOCIAL NETWORKS ON ADAPTIVE BEHAVIOR

Although the stress literature often refers to group influences on adaptation to stress, such references are frequently diffuse and unenlightening. Men relate to groups in a great variety of ways, and they may relate to the same group in different ways. Many groups define values and goals and serve as a reference point from which individuals may evaluate themselves. Or they may serve to encourage persons and help allay anxiety. But most important from the perspective of this paper is that group organization and cooperation allow for the development of mastery through specialization of function, pooling of resources and information, developing reciprocal help-giving relationships, and the like. It is a truism, but nevertheless important, that men are highly interdependent, and only through complex organization are the more complicated jobs of the community fulfilled. The effectiveness of individuals in many spheres of action is dependent almost exclusively on the maintenance of viable forms of organization and cooperation that allow important tasks to be mastered.

Much of the confusion in the stress literature results because stress is frequently seen as a short-term single stimulus rather than as a complex set of changing conditions that have a history and a future. Man must respond to these conditions through time and must adapt his behavior to the changing character of the stimuli. Thus mastery of stress is not a simple repertoire, but an active process over time in relationship to demands that are themselves changing, and that are often symbolically created by the groups within which man lives and new technologies which such groups develop. Adaptation itself creates new demands on man that require still further adaptations in a continuing spiral (Dubos 1965).

Moreover, many demands are ambiguous and intangible; they are created out of the social fabric and social climate that exist at any time. Challenges, therefore, are a product of the transaction between man and his environment, and many of the demands to which man must adapt are those that he has himself created. People to some extent can determine what demands they will be exposed to and at what pace. They can select from alternative environments and reference groups in testing themselves against their environments. They not only respond themselves, but require others to respond to them. This complex interplay between men involves adaptive techniques that are infrequently referred to in the study of short-term single stressors. Men pace themselves; they selectively seek information in relation to their needs for developing solutions on the one hand and for protecting their "selves" on the other; they anticipate future situations and plan solutions that they test; they frequently select the grounds on which their adaptive struggles will take place and carefully choose appropriate spheres of action. In short, they are more than seeds carried by the winds, or at least they can act as if they are.

One of the most impressive tests of the limits and potentialities of man's adaptive capacities occurs in those situations where men must live in controlled environments that are contrary to their values and goals, and where they are victims of arbitrary power, such as in concentration camps and prisons. We know from such situations that men often lose hope and become apathetic, accepting their fate without a fight. But we also know that even under the most desperate and unencouraging circumstances men succeed in developing competing forms of social organization that allow them to resist their oppressors and may allow survival under the most unpropi-

tious of circumstances. Eugen Kogon (1958), a long-term resident of Bu-
chenwald, describes the underground organization of inmates under the
most hellish of conditions:

There were a number of effective means by which the prisoners could assert their
interests. They were all based on two essential prerequisites: power inside the
camp, and a well-organized intelligence service. . . . . Functional cohesion was in-
sured by the prisoner intelligence service. Such a system was built up in every camp
from the very outset. Reliable key members of the ruling group—or the group seeking power—were systematically wormed into all important posts, sometimes only
after bitter and complex maneuvering. There they were able to observe everything
that happened in the ranks of the SS and the prisoners, to obtain information on
every personnel shift and policy trend, to overhear every conversation. . . . Every
detail had its official "runners" ostensibly appointed in order to maintain liaison
with the numerous scattered SS offices. Actually three-fourths of their time was
taken up by work on behalf of the prisoners (pp. 254–255).

Kogon describes in detail how the underground organization was successful
in controlling work assignments and reassignment of inmates to other
camps and outside work details, and how they were successful in hiding
and protecting valuable members of the underground from the SS. Kogon
concedes that the prisoners were not strong enough to forestall general SS
directives involving mass liquidations and similar actions, but they had vast
influence on matters involving "the ordinary minutiae of camp life."

The type of organization which Kogon dramatically describes has been
similarly observed in prisons (Sykes 1958; Sykes and Messinger 1960), mental hospitals (Goffman 1961, pp. 173–320), military organizations (Cohen
1966), and a great variety of other organizational contexts. To the extent
that participants in organizations do not share the goals and values of its
managers and authorities, an informal organization emerges that often im-
pedes directives and programs that are seen as threatening to the welfare of
organizational participants. I have described the principles underlying the
power of such subordinate personnel elsewhere (Mechanic 1962a); let it suffice to note here that much of organizational power stems from small decisions made on daily tasks, or what Kogon refers to as "ordinary minutiae."
Because higher-status organizational participants wish to be relieved of such
burdensome "dirty work" or are dependent on others to perform it for other
reasons, the dependency relationship and access to the performance of daily
work give the subordinate considerable opportunity for effective vetoes on
organizational policies.

As solutions to important problems become more complex, these problems are less likely to be resolved by individual initiative and action. In contrast, they are likely to depend on the ability of men to work out organized
solutions involving group actions. It is within this context that it is necessary to note that individuals who may be adaptive and effective persons
from a psychological perspective may be unfitted because of their values
and individual orientations for the kinds of group cooperation that are nec-

essary in developing solutions to particular kinds of community problems. Thus many effective copers may become impotent in influencing their environment because of their resistance or inability to submerge themselves into cooperative organized relationships with others.

It is not difficult to cite examples in modern life where men's disdain for organized participation interferes with effective performance. In the sphere of medicine, for example, the development of technology and associated growing costs of medical care require new forms of medical practice better fitted to the needs of the population than the highly individualized practice of medicine. Even in the absence of economic disincentives, doctors who are highly individualistic in their orientations tend to be reluctant to work within more organized practice settings (Mechanic 1968). Similarly in science, because of the costs and expansion of technology and specialized knowledge, team research is becoming more of a necessity. Yet, there are strong resistances to working cooperatively among many scientists who are highly individualistic and competitive in their orientations (Hagstrom 1965). Or to take another example, it is clear that organization of various aspects of the work force into groups that can bargain collectively is more effective than each man bargaining for himself. Although collective action is developing among a variety of professionals, in the higher professions there are very strong values that mitigate against collective action. To move more directly into the political realm, the futility of individual action in contesting such actions as the Vietnam war or the ABM in contrast to collective opposition is evident. Group action is not necessarily effective, but it may provide at least a fighting chance.

In considering the conditions under which men will confront their environment, the symbolic aspects of threat and adaptation are extremely important. It is rarely the most oppressed who rise up to the challenges of their fate, but more usually those who have had a taste of the possibilities of improving their condition (Runciman 1966). Revolutions feed on faith and rarely occur when men see no way out. The unwillingness of many concentration camp victims to oppose their murderers may have, in part, resulted from the uncertainty of their individual fates, but more likely such efforts seemed futile and hopeless. In contrast, when men have hopes of success they are often willing to take on the most powerful of adversaries. This is, of course, all very speculative. Students of coping and adaptation would do well to invest greater attention to the question of how men see their environment and their own potency in meeting the challenges of that environment.

This brings me to consideration of a serious misconception that appears to run throughout the stress literature—the notion that successful adaptation requires an accurate perception of reality. There is perhaps no thought so stifling as to see ourselves in proper perspective. We all maintain our sense of self-respect and energy for action through perceptions that enhance our self-importance and self-esteem, and we maintain our sanity by suppressing the tremendous vulnerability we all experience in relation to the risks of the real world (Wolfenstein 1957). It is the beauty of symbolic environments that they allow men to enhance their sense of self-importance while permitting the community to persist at the same time. Most men tend to rate themselves and their qualities somewhat higher than their fellows would rate them, and the social contract among men allows each to control the definition of the situation to some extent on matters most close to his own self-interest. When the contract breaks down, one can usually locate groups that help sustain one's own self-definition, and social life is loosely enough organized so that most men can manage to sustain comforting self-perceptions.

The appropriate criterion for evaluating various defensive processes is the extent to which such defenses facilitate coping and mastery. Obviously, if defensive processes reach too far beyond what is acceptable to one's fellows, they create difficulty and interfere with successful adaptation. But many misperceptions of reality aid coping and mastery, energize involvement and participation in life endeavors, and alleviate pain and discomfort that would distract the person from successful efforts at mastery. Reality, of course, is a social construction, and to the extent that perspectives are shared and socially reinforced they may facilitate adaptation irrespective of their objective truth. It is well known that if men define situations as real, they are real in their consequences.

There are other concepts that have been taken up by psychologists who study stress that are probably more important to their own self-conceptions than they are for most people. A variable like "accessibility to self" may have some importance for introspective psychologists, but there is no good evidence that I know of that relates such variables to successful adaptation. In fact, there is some reason to believe that in many life endeavors too much self-awareness or introspection retards successful coping efforts. Many successful copers tend to be rather insensitive to their own intrapsychic experience and tend to orient themselves more to their outer environment than to their inner world (Korchin and Ruff 1964). Some very successful performers are truly public personalities in that they orient themselves outwardly and tend to have no very elaborate inner life. In contrast, there are persons who, by their abilities to see complexities in every issue, find it difficult to mobilize to attack any issue.

SOME PROBLEMS IN THE THEORY
AND METHODOLOGY OF STRESS STUDIES

If we take the position that adaptation is anticipatory as well as reactive and that men frequently approach their environment with plans, the study of such processes takes a somewhat different direction. Within such a view, man attempts to take on tasks he feels he can handle, he actively seeks information and feedback, he plans and anticipates problems, he insulates himself against defeat in a variety of ways, he keeps his options open, he distributes his commitments, he sets the stage for new efforts by practice and rehearsal, he tries various solutions, and so on. One cannot study such activities very effectively within an experimental mode that subjects man to specific stimuli and only measures limited reactions to these. But methodological models to successfully study such active processes of coping are very much undeveloped, and the lack of richness in the experimental stress literature reflects the lack of a successful experimental technology for studying adaptive attempts over time.

However much we may lament the fact, the development of fields of study follows the development of research technologies more than theoretical problems. In the stress field we have been the victim of many technologies that were useful and interesting in their own way, but that diverted researchers from basic issues. Perhaps most prominent have been the clinical interview and psychological assessment techniques popular among ego psychologists. The clinical interview depended too fully on retrospective reports, and the structure of such data in the absence of controls allowed each investigator to promote his favorite set of conceptions. Similarly, the use of personality assessment tools frequently allowed the investigator to explain, but not illuminate, performance differences. Thus we learned that men achieved because they had a need for achievement, that they were prejudiced because they were authoritarian, and that they did not participate in organizations because they were alienated. This form of absorption by naming took on the character of a popular sport, and although each of these conceptions involved an underlying theory of personality, the theory itself was either discredited or forgotten while the technologists continued to use the various measures that they could correlate with a host of other information. Because the study of stress has been to some extent limited by the fashionable methodologies of the past few decades, the picture of adaptation that emerges from the literature is one that depicts man as reactive and individualistic and his mode of coping as largely intrapsychic.

The major exception to this generalization has been the study of disasters and other real-life stresses under natural conditions. Approaches to natural stresses can follow a quasi-experimental design and, under some conditions, can utilize appropriate comparison groups. These studies for the most part present a much richer picture of the complexity of social adaptation and related factors. But given the complexity of such situations, it is often difficult to ferret out very precisely the variables most influential in modes of adaptation. The literature on social adaptation would benefit substantially from a richer interaction between field studies and more precise laboratory experiments, and more experimentation utilizing simulations of real situations. There are obvious ethical barriers in simulating stressful life circumstances, but there are many real circumstances that are amenable to study using experimental methodologies. Also, we have to develop more complex experimental models that do not restrict so closely the subject's opportunity to exercise his adaptive repertoire in dealing with laboratory situations. We must provide richer opportunities for subjects than the option of pushing one or another lever. Particularly impressive use of quasi-experimental models under natural circumstances are such investigations as the study by Epstein (1962) of paratrooper exercises and the Skipper and Leonard (1968) study of response to the stress of hospitalization and tonsillectomy.

It is likely that in the near future we have most to learn from field studies of adaptation to particular stress events over time. Such involvement requires greater emphasis on prospective and processual studies. Because this need has been expressed many times before, I will emphasize some more specific considerations rather than the more general points.

It is clear that we must go beyond people's subjective reports of how they feel and how they have responded to particular stressful circumstances. Such reports are particularly dubious when they describe events retrospectively, because we know that part of the process of adaptation involves the subtle restructuring of the individual's attitudinal set toward events that have taken place (Davis 1963; Robbins 1969). Successful adaptation requires changes in attitudes and perspectives that are sufficiently subtle so that the person hardly recognizes the changes himself. Large and sudden modifications of attitudes and perspectives are likely to produce new stresses, and, indeed, such large changes are themselves evidence of difficulties and disruptions in successful adaptation. We thus must be suspicious of reconstructions of the past as true representations of what really took place.

But even reports of events involving continuing activities and use of short recall periods may have dubious reliability. If we are not to throw the baby out with the bath water, we have to devote considerable effort to defining what kinds of reports are generally trustworthy and which ones are not. We can anticipate that persons will more reliably report their sex, age, family composition, and similar matters than they will their mental status, marital happiness, and like matters. Even when dealing with "harder" variables, persons frequently distort their responses, as women do, for example, in their tendency to underestimate their age, as very old people who tend to overestimate their age, and as many others who tend to report their age in round numbers. In contrast, reports on such variables as loneliness have very low test-retest reliability (Nefzger and Lilienfeld 1959). To some extent this is characteristic of all mood responses, which may widely vary from one day to another. Investigators, however, must be reasonably clear as to what degree of reliability of measures their studies require and the general range of reliability of varying measures they might utilize.

Take, for example, data dealing with people's reports of their use of medical services. Such data may or may not be worthy of collection, depending on the interests of the investigator and the research question he is asking. If the investigator wishes to know whether a person has been to a dentist, a doctor, or has been hospitalized during the preceding year, respondent reports will provide a reasonably reliable approximation. If, for some reason, small differences in utilization of medical services are important to the study, then it is reasonably clear that respondent reports will be too biased to be of any use (Mechanic and Newton 1965). Similarly, if an investigator wishes to note no more than crude differences between social categories on some measure of utilization, respondent reports will serve his purpose more than if he wishes to assign specific reliable scores to individual persons. Even in the case of more crude analyses of such data, respondent reports are likely to be unacceptable if there is reason to believe that there are systematic biases in reporting among different social groups.

Reports on such matters as having a heart condition, undergoing surgery, being hospitalized, and going to a doctor are reasonably "hard" in that these situations will have required specific actions on the part of the respondent that are not routine. But most studies of stress involve questions about very ordinary things that concern routine behavior and common attitudes, and such data are particularly suspect. For example, in family studies when identical questions are asked of husband and wife concerning routine activities in the family, husband-wife correlations are very small (Brown and Rutter 1966). Similarly, we know, for example, that what mothers tell you about themselves and what they tell you about the behavior of their children tend to be more highly correlated than data obtained independently from mother and child (Mechanic 1964). Too frequently investigators end up studying subjects' tendencies to respond and little else.

It is extraordinary that there are so few attempts to obtain independent data on behavior, because it is often accessible to research investigators willing to put in a little effort. It is possible, for example, to obtain medical and other records that allow some assessment of the value of what people tell you. These records, of course, have their own sources of unreliability, but investigators are on much firmer ground if they have both respondent and record data available to them. We need, in general, further development of behavior ratings that are likely to depict the variables we are really interested in more satisfactorily than do the measures more ordinarily used. This is no simple task, but it is one we will have to take on at some point. Those who deceive themselves that in the future we will develop some simple paper-and-pencil test to measure coping or adaptive potentialities are bound to be disillusioned; for the concern we face is so complex and multifaceted that it should be apparent that when we do develop some adequate measures, they are likely to be very complex ones. My own view is that such measures will have to be in the form of behavioral tests, and that the ordinary paper-and-pencil tests are incapable of the task.

At the theoretical level, one of the largest tasks that stress researchers face is the development of models that specify in a predictive sense under what conditions one set of adaptations will develop in contrast to some other set. If the study of adaptation is to develop as a theoretical area, then we must do more than describe the array of behaviors characteristic of persons' adaptive attempts; we must begin to specify the relative probabilities that, under given circumstances, one coping attempt will follow rather than another. This theoretical approach will depend on rich field studies that depict the scope of alternatives, followed by more controlled laboratory studies that attempt to determine the conditions under which one or another form of behavior follows. In short, theoretical needs require a range of methods, and if investigators do not choose to be eclectic themselves, at least some dialogue among approaches must be maintained.

One is beginning to see a more sophisticated theoretical approach emerging from this kind of interaction. It is promising, for example, that experimentalists who previously took the view that people avoided "discomforting information" are now more appreciative that sometimes they do and sometimes they do not and that the entire matter is more complicated than earlier views suggested (Freedman and Sears 1965). It may be too early to suggest convergences, but it may be that persons seek out information contrary to their views and perspectives when such information is important to their future coping efforts; discomforting information may primarily be avoided when it is believed to be of little utility. Or to take another example, early studies were concerned with the simplistic question as to whether or not high interactors were more or less successful at various tasks. There is a growing appreciation of not only the fact that there are different kinds of interaction (which I previously referred to as interaction for instrumental purposes and interaction for the purposes of support), but also that interaction may not only facilitate activity and support people, but also arouse competition and anxiety and lead to interference with effective performance (Hall 1969; Mechanic 1962b). Such variables as rate of interaction are too crude to be informative theoretically in understanding adaptation.

It is encouraging that social psychologists in general are moving away from using their concepts to absorb existing data and are giving increasing efforts to developing an understanding of the contingencies affecting behavior. For example, when dissonance theory (Festinger 1957) first became fashionable it was frequently used to explain the results of a variety of studies by citing a dissonance explanation. Recently, however, there have been more serious attempts to specify on the basis of various contingencies the likely route of dissonance reduction. Similar efforts are taking place in the study of social comparison processes. It has been very common for social scientists to explain data after the fact by arguing that a person's behavior was a result of choosing particular reference groups. The more interesting issue—and one now receiving more attention—concerns the conditions under which identification with various possible reference groups occurs. Ego psychology has similarly been handicapped by the failure to specify in any rigorous way the conditions under which one set of defenses will occur in opposition to another mode of adaptation, and under what conditions particular defenses will be selected. The literature abounds with discussions of particular defenses in isolation from others. Thus we find discussions dealing with compensation (that is, the tendency to do particularly well in some areas to overcome inadequacies in others) without awareness of a literature on status congruency (the psychological tendency to maintain one's various statuses at approximately the same level), which appears in opposition to it. The theory of compensation argues that people strive toward maintaining unequal levels of performance, while the theory of status congruency maintains that people strive toward maintaining equal levels of performance. Such contradictions lead to theoretical contributions in that they suggest that important intervening variables have been neglected. In the example cited it is likely that people tend to compensate when a particular dimension of their status or performance is blocked or unalterable. However, when there is opportunity to perform in any of several spheres, it may be that the need for congruency is dominant. I know of no specific data that clearly resolve the contradiction, but the recognition of a contradiction raises new issues.

In conclusion, I think that it would be advisable to pursue studies of adaptation with two particular models in mind. (1) On the one hand, we need more emphasis on field studies of adaptive struggles over time. Further attention must be given to collecting data at various points in time in contrast to using retrospective reports. Moreover, such studies should give greater emphasis to the development of behavioral measures. (2) At the same time, we should be pursuing a variety of cross-sectional studies that link particular adaptive strategies and coping devices to effective behavior on a variety of life tasks. Although there are many studies of a cross-sectional nature in the stress area, few are concerned with the relationship between what people do and how effective they are. In the past, more than a reasonable proportion of the total research effort has gone into attempts to link personality traits with effectiveness, and in many ways this has been a disappointing effort. My guess is that greater emphasis on coping strategies themselves will provide a greater payoff. Finally, I believe that a field has the greatest payoff when there is constant interplay between studies in natural settings and more precise experimental investigation. We should do all we can to nurture those bridges that make such collaboration possible and fruitful.

REFERENCES

Brown, G., and Rutter, M. The measurement of family activities and relationships. *Human relations*, 1966, *19*, 241–263.

Cohen, A. *Deviance and control.* Englewood Cliffs, N.J.: Prentice-Hall, 1966.

Davis, F. *Passage through crisis: Polio victims and their families.* Indianapolis: Bobbs-Merrill, 1963.

Dubos, R. *Man adapting.* New Haven, Conn.: Yale University Press, 1965.

Epstein, S. The measurement of drive and conflict in humans. In M. R. Jones, ed., *Nebraska symposium on motivation.* Lincoln, Neb.: University of Nebraska Press, 1962.

Festinger, L. *A theory of cognitive dissonance.* Evanston, Ill.: Row Peterson, 1957.

Freedman, J., and Sears, D. Selective exposure. In L. Berkowitz, ed., *Advances in experimental social psychology*, vol. 2. New York: Academic Press, 1965.

Goffman, E. *Asylums.* New York: Doubleday, 1961.

Hagstrom, W. *The scientific community.* New York: Basic Books, 1965.

Hall, D. The impact of peer interaction during an academic role transition. *Sociology of Education*, 1969, *42*(2), 118–140.

Kogon, E. *The theory and practice of hell*. New York: Berkeley Medallion Books, 1958.

Korchin, S., and Ruff, G. Personality characteristics of the Mercury astronauts. In G. H. Grosser, H. Wechsler, and M. Greenblatt, eds., *The threat of impending disaster: Contributions to the psychology of stress*. Cambridge, Mass.: M.I.T. Press, 1964.

McGrath, J., ed. *Social and psychological factors in stress*. New York: Holt, Rinehart & Winston, 1970.

Mechanic, D. Sources of power of lower participants in complex organizations. *Administrative Science Quarterly*, 1962a, 7, 349–364.

———. *Students under stress*. New York: Free Press, 1962b.

———. The influence of mothers on their children's health attitudes and behavior. *Pediatrics*, 1964, *33*, 444–453.

———. General medical practice in England and Wales. *New England Journal of Medicine*, 1968, *279*, 680–689.

———. Some problems in developing a social psychology of adaptation to stress. In J. McGrath, ed., *Social and psychological factors in stress*. New York: Holt, Rinehart & Winston, 1970.

Mechanic, D., and Newton, M. Some problems in the analysis of morbidity data. *Journal of Chronic Disease*, 1965, *18*, 569–580.

Nefzger, N., and Lilienfeld, A. Item reliability and related factors in a community survey of emotionality. *Sociometry*, 1959, *22*, 236–246.

Robbins, L. Follow-up studies of behavior disorders in children. Paper presented to the W.P.A.-R.M.P.A. Symposium on Psychiatric Epidemiology, University of Aberdeen, July 1969.

Runciman, W. G. *Relative deprivation and social justice*. Berkeley and Los Angeles: University of California Press, 1966.

Skipper, J. K., Jr., and Leonard, R. C. Children, stress and hospitalization: A field experiment. *Journal of Health and Social Behavior*, 1968, *9*, 275–287.

Sykes, G. *The society of captives*. Princeton, N.J.: Princeton University Press, 1958.

Sykes, G., and Messinger, S. The inmate social system. In R. Cloward et al., eds., *Theoretical studies in social organization of the prison*. New York: Social Science Research Council, 1960.

Wolfenstein, M. *Disaster: A psychological essay*. New York: Free Press, 1957.

II

COPING TASKS
AND STRATEGIES
IN THE DEVELOPMENT
OF COMPETENCE

4

Strategies of Adaptation: An Attempt at Systematic Description

ROBERT W. WHITE

At the outset of this inquiry we are confronted by four commonly used words with overlapping claims upon the territory to be discussed. The words are *adaptation, mastery, coping,* and *defense.* No attempt at systematic description is likely to prosper if these words are left in a state of free competition, jostling for the thinly scattered grains of truth that might nourish their meaning. Their peaceful coexistence requires, as in any well-regulated hen yard, the establishment of some sort of pecking order that everyone observes and fully understands. The first step in this direction is simple: clearly the boss hen is *adaptation.* This is the master concept, the superordinate category, under which the other three words must accept restricted meanings. Descriptions of mastery, of defense, or of coping alone cannot be systematic in any large sense, but they can become part of a system if they are ordered under the heading of *strategies of adaptation.*

PRELUDE ON TERMINOLOGY

The concept of *defense,* to take it first, is an obvious one, signifying response to danger or attack, but it comes to us with a somewhat swollen meaning because of the position it has been given in psychoanalytic theory. Freud's genius as an observer, so apparent in his unveiling of sexual and aggressive inclinations, never burned more brightly than in his perception of what came to be called the *mechanisms of defense:* repression, projection, undoing, and the other devices whereby danger was parried and peace restored in the frightened psyche. Psychoanalytic therapists, following this lead, became expert at scenting anxiety in the free associations of their patients; expert, moreover, at unraveling the ramified operations whereby security was achieved. Presently these operations were seen to have worked over long periods of time, producing such complex results as character armor and the protective organization of personality. Unwary theorists even jumped to the generalization that development was a simple counterpoint between instinctual craving and defense. It became necessary after Freud's death for those who called themselves "ego psychologists" to restore explicitly the concept of adaptation and to confine defense to those instances of adaptation in which present danger and anxiety were of central importance.

The concept of *mastery*, perhaps an equally obvious concept, has never enjoyed the same vogue among psychologists. When used at all, it has generally been applied to behavior in which frustrations have been surmounted and adaptive efforts have come to a successful conclusion. The alternatives suggested by the word are not, as with defense, danger and safety, but something more like defeat and victory. This might imply a limiting definition, but in fact the concept of mastery has been used with no sense of limits. The English language, loved by poets for its flexibility, offers only pitfalls to the systematic thinker. There is nothing wrong with saying that danger and anxiety have to be mastered, which allows us to classify defense mechanisms as a form of mastery. It is equally correct to say that efforts at mastery serve as a defense against anxiety, which permits us to consider counteractive struggle a mechanism of defense. If mastery is to be used in any limited technical sense it should probably be confined to problems having a certain cognitive or manipulative complexity, but which at the same time are not heavily freighted with anxiety.

Where does the concept of *coping* stand? We can find out what we mean by it by noticing the kinds of situation chosen for studies of coping behavior. Sometimes these situations represent an acute dislocation of a person's life: serious crippling sickness, the death of close relatives, financial disaster, the necessity to live in a radically new environment. Sometimes the situation is less drastic, but it is still unusual in the subject's life: going to school for the first time, going to visit the child psychologist, or making the transition from high school to college. Nobody has chosen going to school for the sixty-third time as an occasion for coping. The freshman year at college, with all its new experience, clearly qualifies as coping, as does the sophomore year now that we are alert to the possibility of "sophomore slump" and dropping out, but nobody has yet detected any large-scale common problems that would justify choosing the junior year for an investigation of coping behavior. For "when the sea was calm," said Shakespeare, "all boats alike show'd mastership in floating"; only in a storm were they obliged to cope. It is clear that we tend to speak of coping when we have in mind a fairly drastic change or problem that defies familiar ways of behaving, requires the production of new behavior, and very likely gives rise to uncomfortable affects like anxiety, despair, guilt, shame, or grief, the relief of which forms part of the needed adaptation. Coping refers to adaptation under relatively difficult conditions.

This discussion of terms demonstrates the necessity of making *adaptation* the central concept. It may well be that in stressful situations things happen that have no counterpart in easier circumstances, but some of what happens is likely to come straight from the repertoire that is common to all adaptive behavior. There is a sense in which all behavior can be considered an attempt at adaptation. Even in the smoothest and easiest of times behavior will not be adequate in a purely mechanical or habitual way. Every day raises its little problems: what clothes to put on, how to plan a timesaving and step-saving series of errands, how to schedule the hours to get through the day's work, how to manage the cranky child, appease the short-tempered tradesman, and bring the long-winded acquaintance to the end of his communication. It is not advisable to tell a group of college students that they have no problems, nothing to cope with, during the happy and uneventful junior year. They will quickly tell you what it takes to get through that golden year, and as you listen to the frustrations, bewilderments, and sorrows as well as the triumphs and joys you will have a hard time conceptualizing it all as well-adapted reflexes or smoothly running habits. Life is tough, they will tell you, in case you have forgotten; life is a never-ending challenge. Every step of the way demands the solution of problems and every step must therefore be novel and creative, even the putting together of words and sentences to make you understand what it is like to cope with being a college junior.

Adaptation, then, is the only firm platform on which to build a systematic description. What is needed is an ordered account of *strategies of adaptation*, ranging from the simplest ways of dealing with minor problems and frustrations to the most complex fabric of adaptive and defensive devices that has ever been observed from the chair at the head of the psychoanalytic couch. If this can be done, the uses to be made of defense, mastery, and coping can be much more readily decided.

ADAPTATION AS COMPROMISE

There is another preliminary issue that is likely to get in the way if we do not deal with it at the start. Perhaps we can put a little blame on Freud for having started something that often crops up today as an unwitting tendency to think of adaptive behavior in a dichotomy of good and bad. Uncensorious as he was toward the neurotic behavior that circumstance and a repressive society had forced upon the patient, Freud was a stern and moral man who would not call a patient well until all neurotic anxieties were understood, all defense mechanisms abandoned, and all behavior brought under control of the clear-eyed ego that perceives everything exactly as it is. But this heroic prescription was meant to apply only to neurotic anxieties, legacies of childhood that did not correspond to present dangers. The ideal patient, issuing from his analysis cleansed of all anxiety, was really cleansed only of defenses against dangers that no longer existed. So we must attach less blame to the fastidious Freud than to the careless popularizers of mental health wisdom who have communicated the thought, utterly bizarre in one of the most frightening periods of human history, that the mentally healthy person is free from all anxiety and meets life with radiant confidence. Of course we all know better than that when we stop to think, but in the psychological and psychiatric literature there lies a concealed assumption that dangers must be faced because they are not really there, that any delay, avoidance, retreat, or cognitive distortion of reality is in the end a reprehensible piece of cowardice. We must march forward, ever forward, facing our problems, overcoming all obstacles, masters of our fate, fit citizens of the brave new world. Foolish as it is, this unwitting assumption sufficiently pervades our professional literature so that we really do have to stop and think. What are the transactions that actually take place between a person and his environment?

In actuality, of course, there are many situations that can be met only by compromise or even resignation. Events may occur that require us to give in, relinquish things we would have liked, perhaps change direction or restrict the range of our activities. We may have no recourse but to accept a permanent impoverishment of our lives and try to make the best of it. Furthermore, when dangers are real and information incomplete it is in no sense adaptive to march boldly forward. History provides many examples, none better than General Braddock in our own colonial days, who marched his column of British regulars through the forests of Pennsylvania straight into a French and Indian ambush. Described not inappropriately in military metaphors, adaptation often calls for delay, strategic retreat, regrouping of forces, abandoning of untenable positions, seeking fresh intelligence, and deploying new weapons. And just as recuperation from serious illness is not the work of a day, even though in the end it may be completely accomplished, so recovery from a personal loss or disaster requires a long period of internal readjustment that may not be well served at the start by forceful action or total clarity of perception. Sometimes adaptation to a severely frustrating reality is possible only if full recognition of the bitter truth is for a long time postponed.

The element of compromise in adaptive behavior can be well illustrated from that rich storehouse of information provided by Lois Murphy (1962) in her study of young children in Topeka. She describes a number of three-year-olds brought for the first time from their homes to her study center, where the business of the day is to meet a psychologist and engage in some activities that constitute a test of intelligence. Her first two illustrations, boys named Brennie and Donald, present us at once with a striking contrast. Brennie appears to be confidence incarnate. He climbs happily into the car, alertly watches and comments upon the passing scene, charms everyone with his smile, walks into the testing room with perfect poise, accepts each proffered task with eager interest, makes conversation and asks for appropriate help from adults, and finally leaves the scene with a polite expression of thanks. Brennie might be judged a paragon of mental health, and any three-year-old so easy to deal with is certain to be a psychologist's delight. In contrast, the day of Donald's visit is a taxing one for the staff. The child comes accompanied by his mother, described as "warm and ample," and he utters not a word either during the ride, when entering the building, or for some time after he enters the psychologist's office. Invited to sit down, he stands resolutely beside his mother, his feet spread slightly apart. He will string beads only when his mother has done so first, and once embarked on this operation, he refuses to be diverted by the psychologist, who would like to get on with the test. Slowly he warms up enough to dispense with his mother's mediation and deal directly with the psychologist, but the testing still drags because Donald becomes involved in, for instance, building-block constructions of his own instead of those required for the test. The session ends with the assessment far from complete.

It is easy to imagine what Donald's session would look like in the records of a typical guidance agency. He has displayed two highly disquieting symptoms. He has a bad case of separation anxiety, clinging to his mother when he should be facing reality, and he also displays withdrawal and introversion by building with blocks according to his fantasy instead of responding properly to social stimulation. But before we hurry Donald into psychotherapy let us look at the situation from a child's point of view. As adults we know something that he does not know: we know that Mrs. Murphy and her staff are full of kindness and patience and that they will go to great lengths to keep discomfort and anxiety at a minimum. Donald can know only that he is being taken to a strange place for a purpose he cannot fathom. Many children by the age of three have been to the pediatrician's office, to the barber, and perhaps even to the dentist, and they may well have noticed a credibility gap between parental assurances and the discomforts actually experienced during these visits. Now they are being taken to play games with a nice lady—a likely story indeed! If such conditions existed for Donald, he exhibits commendable common sense in sticking close to his mother, the one familiar object, until he can figure out the nature of the racket. It is his good fortune that his principal observer, Mrs. Murphy, understands his position, perceives him not as anxiously dependent but as a "sturdy boy," and appreciates his strategy of adaptation. She says:

Over the years we have seen Donald, this pattern has continued: cautious, deliberate, watchful entrance into a new situation, keeping his distance at first, quietly, firmly maintaining his right to move at his own pace, to make his own choices, to set his own terms, to cooperate when he got ready. These tendencies persisted long after he became able to separate from his mother (1962, p. 32).

And what of the perfectly adjusted Brennie? In reviewing Mrs. Murphy's book, I likened Brennie to a genial cocker spaniel who welcomes friend and burglar with equal joy. He seems to trust everyone without discrimination. This is fine as long as he stays in a highly restricted circle consisting of family, nursery school teachers, and sympathetic psychological researchers, who support him lovingly and demand a minimum amount of compromise. But eventually Brennie is going to find out that life is not a rose garden. Before long he will be entering what Harry Stack Sullivan described as the "juvenile era," a time when crude competition and aggression among peers are only slowly brought under the control of ripening social understanding. He will find that there are adults who do not respect children and may even take advantage of them. In his teens some of his contemporaries will urge him not to trust anyone over thirty. It is easy to project his career line further into the still competitive adult world with the self-seeking, scandals, and rackets that fill the daily newspapers. By that time Brennie may have been badly burned for his innocent credulity and thus learned to be circumspect, but if we compare him with Donald at the age of three, we reach the painful conclusion that it is the cautious Donald who is better adapted to the average expectable human environment.

This is a long introduction to the main task of this paper, but it will not have been wasted if we now start that task with a clear realization of these points: (1) that the described phenomena of coping, mastery, and defense belong in the more general category of strategies of adaptation, as part of the whole tapestry of living; and (2) that adaptation does not mean either a total triumph over the environment or total surrender to it, but rather a striving toward acceptable compromise.

THE TREND TOWARD
INCREASED AUTONOMY

The point of departure for a systematic description of strategies of adaptation should be the broadest possible statement. Let us put it this way: adaptation is something that is done by living systems in interaction with their environments. It is important to emphasize both the noun *systems* and the adjective *living*. Our whole enterprise can founder at the very start if the basic image is allowed to be mechanical rather than organismic. It is characteristic of a system that there is interaction among its various parts, so that changes in one part are likely to have considerable consequences in at least several other parts. A system, furthermore, tends to maintain itself as intact as possible and thus displays more or less extensive rebalancing processes when injured or deformed. This much is true of inanimate systems as well as animate ones, which makes it necessary to qualify the systems under discussion here as *living*. For it is characteristic of living systems that they do something more than maintain themselves. Cannon's historic studies of homeostasis have familiarized us with the remarkable mechanisms whereby animal and human living systems maintain internal steady states, such as body temperature and fluid content, and restore such states when circumstances have forced a temporary departure. But Cannon was well aware that maintaining homeostasis was not the whole story; he saw it as a necessary basis from which living systems could get on with their more important business. This further business consists of growth and reproduction. Living systems do not stay the same size. They grow dramatically larger: the puppy that you once held in your hands becomes the big dog that you can no longer hold in your lap. This increase eventually reaches its limit in any one system, but not until arrangements have been made to start a whole fresh lot of tiny living systems on their way toward maximum growth.

The fundamental property of growth in living systems was well described in 1941 by Andras Angyal. Looking for "the general pattern which the organismic total process follows," Angyal pictured the living system as partially open to the environment and as constantly taking material from the environment to become a functioning part of itself:

It draws incessantly new material from the outside world, transforming alien objects into functional parts of its own. Thus the organism *expands* at the expense of its surroundings. The expansion may be a material one, as in the case of bodily growth, or a psychological one as in the case of the assimilation of experiences which result in mental growth, or a functional one as when one acquires skill, with a resulting increase of efficiency in dealing with the environment (1941, pp. 27–28).

Thus the life process necessarily entails expansion, but Angyal carried the matter further. Living systems, he pointed out, exhibit *autonomy.* They are in part governed from inside, and are thus to a degree resistant to forces that would govern them from the outside. If this were not true, the whole concept of adaptation would be impossible. Angyal then describes the direction of the organismic process as one toward an *increase of autonomy:*

Aggressiveness, combativeness, the urge for mastery, domination, or some equivalent urge or drive or trait is assumed probably by all students of personality. All these various concepts imply that the human being has a characteristic tendency toward self-determination, that is, a tendency to resist external influences and to subordinate the heteronomous forces of the physical and social environment to its own sphere of influence (1941, p. 49).

It was an evil day, we may imagine, for the inanimate world when living systems first broke loose upon it. Conservative boulders doubtless shook their heads and predicted gloomily that if this subversive trend gained strength the day might come when living systems would overrun the earth. And this is indeed exactly what has happened. Most of the land surface is completely buried by living systems, and even the oceans are full of them. When we consider this outrageous imperialism it is small wonder that the expansion of peoples and of nations has been a besetting problem throughout human history. And even when we concentrate on strategies of adaptation, we must keep it in mind that human beings are rarely content with maintaining a personal homeostasis. Unless they are very old they are almost certain to be moving in the direction of increased autonomy. It can be a threat of disastrous proportions to discover in the midst of life that all avenues are blocked to further personal development.

Living creatures, in short, will constantly strive for an adaptive compromise that not only preserves them as they are, but also permits them to grow, to increase both their size and their autonomy. Consider an animal as it steps forth in the morning from where it has been sleeping and moves into its daytime environment. If all goes well, it will ingest a portion of that environment, maintain its visceral integrity by homeostatic processes and by eliminating waste material, add a tiny increment to its size, explore a little and thus process some fresh information about its environment, gain a bit in muscular strength and coordination, bask in the warm sunshine, and return at night to its den a little bigger, a little wiser, a little stronger, and a little more contented than it was in the morning. If the season is right, it may also have found an opportunity to set those processes in motion whereby a number of offspring will come into existence. A day like this can be described as one of maximum animal self-actualization. If all does not go well, the animal may return to the den hungry, cold, perhaps battered and bruised, yet still essentially intact as a living system, capable of recuperating during the night and setting forth again in the morning. Of course, it may have failed to keep itself intact or even alive, but we can be sure disaster occurred only because the animal's adaptive repertoire, employed with the utmost vigor, has not been equal to the circumstances. Animals try to go up; if they go down, they go down fighting.

SOME VARIABLES
OF ADAPTIVE BEHAVIOR

The adaptive capacities of any species of animal are to some extent represented in bodily structure, the product of natural selection. Protective coloring, great weight and strength, or such features as the rabbit's powerful hind legs that enable it to make bewildering hairpin turns in the course of its flight are part of the inherited equipment that favor certain styles of adapting. When we speak of strategies of adaptation, however, we are referring more particularly to the realm of behavior, the realm that is directly controlled by the nervous system and that is in various degrees open to learning through experience. This realm is traditionally broken down into receptive processes, central storage and organizing processes, and motor processes that lead to further sensory input. In the case of animals, whose inner experience, whatever its nature, remains forever closed to us, strategies of adaptation have to be described in behavioral language. They have to be described in terms of what can go on in a behavioral system of receptors, central structures, and effectors, not overlooking, of course, the contributions of the autonomic nervous system and the input of information from inside the body. How can we best describe the possibilities of adaptive control and regulation in an animal's behavioral system?

We could start with a flourish of analytic logic by talking sequentially about regulation in the sensory, the central, and the motor spheres. But this is a dangerous piece of abstraction; in actuality the whole thing operates not as a sequence but as a system. What happens when we surprise a squirrel feeding on the ground? There is a whisk of tail and before we know it, the animal has darted up a tree and is sitting on a branch chattering angrily at us. You might judge from a carelessly written mental health tract that the squirrel's behavior was neurotic and deplorable, inasmuch as it retreated instead of facing reality. But the squirrel is facing reality all right; it has simply elected to face it from a position of strength rather than from one of weakness. When you are on the cluttered ground and a huge creature is approaching, fear and flight are adaptive. When the cognitive field has thus been changed so that you are above the huge creature and have at your disposal all the escape routes provided by the branches of a tree, it is adaptive to sit down, be angry, and try the power of scolding. The squirrel has regulated the cognitive field, but has done so in large part by motor activity, and this is surely typical of adaptive strategies in the animal world.

Because the living animal is a system, adaptive behavior entails managing several different things at once. The repertoire by which this management is carried out can be conceptualized at this point in terms of action. One possibility is simply orientation with a minimum of locomotion. When locomotion is employed, it can consist of approach, avoidance while still observing the object of interest, or flight, and a final option is the complete immobility of hiding. Those are the possibilities stated in the most general terms. In order to behave adaptively the animal must use this repertoire to produce what prove to be, even in simple instances, fairly complex results. It seems to me that there are at least three variables that are regularly involved in the process, three aspects of the total situation no one of which can be neglected without great risk. If the animal is to conduct a successful transaction with the environment, perhaps leading to enhancement and growth, but in any event not resulting in injury or destruction, it must (1) keep securing adequate information about the environment, (2) maintain satisfactory internal conditions both for action and for processing information, and (3) maintain its autonomy or freedom of movement, freedom to use its repertoire in a flexible fashion.

I shall enlarge upon these three variables in a moment, but let us first place them in concrete form in order to secure the point that they must all be managed as well as possible at the same time. When a cat hears a strange noise in a nearby thicket, locomotion stops, eyes and ears are pointed in the direction of sound, and the animal's whole being seems concentrated on obtaining cognitive clarity. But if this were the only consideration, the cat might now be expected to move straight into the thicket to see what is there; instead, it explores very slowly and with much circumspection, for it is combining the third variable with the first, maintaining a freedom of movement that would be lost in the thicket. If the noise turns out to have come from a strange cat intruding on the territory, and there ensues a battle of vocal and hair-raising threats leading to an exchange of blows, the second variable becomes decisive. We know from the work of the ecologists that animal battles rarely go on to the death. The animal that sustains injury, feels incompetent, or is slowed by fatigue, shifts its tactics from approach to flight, and wisely lives to fight another day. This result is more probable if the first and third variables have been sufficiently heeded so that the animal is not cornered and has kept escape routes open.

Information

Securing adequate information about the environment is an obvious necessity for adaptive behavior. Action can be carried on most successfully when the amount of information to be processed is neither too small nor too great. If the channels are underloaded, there will be no way to decide what to do, as we would express it in adult conscious experience. If the channels are overloaded, there will again be no way to decide what to do, this time because the number of possibilities creates confusion. Of course this is not just a quantitative matter; what really counts is the meaning of the information in terms of potential benefits and harms. With this modification, however, it is permissible to use a quantitative metaphor and say that there is a certain rate of information input that is conducive to unconfused, straightforward action, and that both higher rates and lower rates will tend, though for different reasons, to make action difficult. Adaptive behavior requires that the cognitive field have the right amount of information to serve as a guide to action. Depending on circumstances, then, adaptation may take the form either of seeking more information or of trying to cut down on the existing input. The cautiously exploring cat illustrates the former process, behaving as though it asked the question, "What is it?" But if the same cat is in the nursery and is exposed to the affection and curiosity of several children, it will try to get away from some of the overwhelming input and might be imagined to ask, "What is all this, anyway?"

Departure in either direction from the preferred level of information is illustrated in Murphy's descriptions of the Topeka three-year-olds. There is likely to be a shortage of information before the children arrive at the testing center, and this is not easily dispelled by adult explanations. Once they have arrived, however, the children are flooded by an input that, because of its newness, they cannot easily put in order. There is a new room, a psychologist, an observer, and a collection of more or less unfamiliar materials. We have already seen how the sturdy Donald dealt with this situation, standing close to his mother, surveying the scene with alert eyes, and consenting to take action only when he had structured the cognitive field sufficiently to isolate an activity he felt competent to undertake. Another of Murphy's procedures was to have groups of children come to her home for a party, a situation quite new, strange, and bewildering to them and possibly a little odd even to adult eyes, inasmuch as each child had an observer assigned to keep account of everything he did. Donald faced this situation with his characteristic determination to get the ˋcognitive field straight. After a long silent survey, he discriminated a zone of likely competence in the toys in the garage and went there to examine them. Later, he picked out a safe entry into the social scene and ended the afternoon in fairly active participation. In this he was more daring than another boy who found his first manageable zone to be building blocks in a corner of the garage and stayed with it the whole afternoon.

Internal Organization

Working on the cognitive field alone will not guarantee adaptive behavior if the internal organization of the system gets too far out of balance. This is crudely obvious if an animal is injured in a fight, weakened by loss of blood, or exhausted in a long struggle. It is clear also in the lowered alertness, curiosity, and effort of children who are feeling sick. Even in young children it is possible to detect another form of internal disorganization that can seriously hamper adaptive behavior: the disorganization produced by strong unpleasant affects such as anxiety, grief, or shame. Some of the Topeka children confronted their first session with the psychologist with a degree of emotion that made it difficult for them to make use of the available information. One little girl, for instance, became tearful and inert, as if drained of energy. When able to try the tasks at all, she could scarcely muster enough force to attend, handle objects, or speak above a whisper, and her most characteristic movement was to push the materials gently away. The inhibition vanished magically when she started for home. A normally active boy showed the paralyzing effect of anxiety first by keeping close to his mother, avoiding contact with examiner and test materials, and then by tentative work on the tasks with quick giving up in the face of difficulties. He was able by these tactics to control the anxiety and work up to an active part in the testing. As his internal organization came back to its usual balance, he spoke more loudly, moved more vigorously, explored the materials more boldly, initiated conversation, and became increasingly master of the situation.

Autonomy

Even if the internal organization is in good balance and the cognitive field is being dealt with competently, adaptive behavior may come to grief if freedom of action is not to some extent maintained. Animals, we may suppose, often enough get trapped in situations from which they cannot escape, but to a remarkable extent they seem to avoid this mishap, as if they were constantly monitored by a small built-in superego reminding them to keep their escape routes open. Once when I kept hens, I was worried to see a large hawk circling high above the yard, but my neighbor reassured me that a hawk would go without its dinner rather than drop down into a nar-

row, high-fenced pen that might hamper its return to the realms of safe
soaring; and, sure enough, no hens were taken. Preserving space in which
to maneuver is always an important consideration in strategy.

Among the Topeka children Donald again comes to mind as one who
kept initiative in his own hands by refusing to be drawn into situations until
he had given them a thorough scrutiny. Tactics of delay and refusals to participate, frustrating as they may be to the psychologist and thus all too
readily given a derogatory tag like "anxious avoidance" and "withdrawal,"
may actually be in the highest tradition of adaptive behavior, following the
adage to "look before you leap." Especially adept at maintaining autonomy
was a girl named Sheila, not quite three, who after looking at the test materials announced that she did not want to watch them and instead would
play with the toys on the floor. There was no sign of anxiety, and very
quickly she involved the examiner in her game with the toys. Momentarily
intrigued by a performance test set up before her, Sheila began to play with
it, but when gently pressed to follow the examiner's rules rather than her
own, she returned to the floor, announcing, "I want to do *this*. We don't
like the game we had." Murphy comments as follows:

Here we see a child who in the face of continuing and skillfully applied adult pressures maintained her own autonomy. And it was not merely a matter of refusing
and rejecting; it was a matter of doing this without allowing the pressures to depress
her mood or to restrict her freedom of movement. Instead, during most of the time,
the pressures served to stimulate her to her own best efforts in structuring the situation and obtaining enjoyment from it and from the relationship with the adult (1962,
p. 82).

In adult life, Sheila possibly will become one of those who regard psychological tests as an invasion of privacy, and we should hesitate to criticize her
for this because it may be part of a courageous career in the cause of civil
rights.

Adaptive behavior, in short, involves the simultaneous management of at
least three variables: securing adequate information, maintaining satisfactory internal conditions, and keeping up some degree of autonomy. Whatever the specific nature of the problem may be, those other considerations
can never be safely neglected. But if we think in these terms, it becomes
clear that strategies of adaptation typically have a considerable development
over time. The temporal dimension is of the utmost importance for our
problem.

THE TIME DIMENSION
IN ADAPTIVE BEHAVIOR

I doubt if any serious student of behavior has thought about the adaptive
process without considering it to be extended over time. Yet it seems to me
quite common in clinical assessments to look for samples of such behavior,

for instance the client's initial reaction to the examiner or the way inkblots are dealt with on first meeting, and then jump to the generalization that these are the client's characteristic ways of meeting his problems. Undoubtedly this is one of the reasons for the well-known fact that psychological assessments based on tests picture everyone, even the healthiest, as a clinical case needing some kind of improvement. The client's characteristic ways of meeting a problem the first time may not be how he meets them the second and third times, still less the twentieth time. On their first visits to the study center Donald and Sheila would not have been recorded as secure children; in neither case could the psychologist come anywhere near to completing the examination. Fortunately, they were studied over a long period of time, and we know that both are strong sturdy specimens of humanity with sense enough to take their own time and deal with things in their own way. Strategy is not created on the instant. It develops over time and is progressively modified in the course of time.

If illustration of this principle were needed, the Topeka children could again furnish us with vivid examples. There is the little girl at the party, physically slowed by a slight orthopedic defect, who at the outset cannot manage the jumping board even with help, and at the end jumps joyfully entirely by herself. There are the two sisters, age five and three, who have to accommodate themselves to the awesome prospect of moving to another city. Their strategies are traced through the months of anticipation and preparation, through the move itself, and through the first few weeks of finding security and satisfactions in the new environment (Murphy 1962, pp. 69–75, 168–170, 178–185). But if we think in terms of the three variables just discussed, the importance of the time dimension becomes self-evident. The values of the variables are not likely to stay long unchanged. Perhaps clearer cognition will reveal danger, increase fear, and precipitate flight, but a good many of the situations encountered by children are simply new. There is, of course, always a little risk in newness, so what is required is a cautious approach allowing time to assess both the risk and the possibility of benefits. The input of information may lead to sharper discrimination of the field, discovery of areas of likely competence and enjoyment, quieting of disturbing affects in favor of pleasurable excitement, and a lowering of the premium on maintaining strict autonomy. All such rebalancing of the variables implies processes of learning extended over time. A profitable familiarity with the cognitive field can be gained simply by protracted inspection with no motor involvement beyond moving the eyes and head. Closer familiarity requires the making of behavioral tests, discovering one's competence to deal with promising portions of the environment. There are great individual differences among children in the speed and apparent ease with which they deal with the newness of the world around them. Considering the many and varied adaptations that have to be made, we should not hastily conclude that the quickest strategies are necessarily the best.

HUMAN COMPLICATIONS
OF THE ADAPTIVE PROCESS

Up to this point we have described strategies of adaptation almost wholly in behavioral terms. Illustrations have been confined to the behavior of animals and quite young children. The purpose of this maneuver has been to lay down a descriptive framework—one might say, a sort of biological grid—upon which to place the vastly more extensive strategies available to human adults. The human brain makes possible a transcendence of the immediate present that we do not suppose to exist in even the most intelligent subhuman primates. This is partly a matter of language and communication. As Alfred Kroeber memorably expressed it:

A bird's chirp, a lion's roar, a horse's scream, a man's moan express subjective conditions; they do not convey objective information. By objective information, we mean what is communicated in such statements as: "There are trees over the hill," "There is a single tree," "There are only bushes," "There were trees but are no longer," "If there are trees, he may be hiding in them," "Trees can be burned," and millions of others. All postinfantile, nondefective human beings can make and constantly do make such statements, though they may make them with quite different sounds according to what speech custom they happen to follow. But no subhuman animal makes *any* such statements. All the indications are that no subhuman animal even has any impulse to utter or convey such information (1948, p. 41).

The result of this capacity to talk about and think about things that are not immediately present is in the end an immense extension of the human horizon. Asch describes this in the following words:

Men live in a field that extends into a distant past and into a far future; the past and the future are to them present realities to which they must constantly orient themselves; they think in terms of days, seasons, and epochs, of good and bad times. . . . Because they can look forward and backward and perceive causal relations, because they can anticipate the consequences of their actions in the future and view their relation to the past, their immediate needs exist in a field of other needs, present and future. Because they consciously relate the past with the future, they are capable of representing their goals to themselves, to aspire to fulfill them, to test them in imagination, and to plan their steps with a purpose.

An integral part of man's extended horizon is the kind of object he becomes to himself. In the same way that he apprehends differentiated objects and their properties he becomes aware of himself as an individual with a specific character and fate; he becomes *self*-conscious. . . . Because he is conscious of himself and capable of reflecting on his experiences, he also takes up an attitude to himself and takes measures to control his own actions and tendencies. The consequence of having a self is that he takes his stand in the world as a person (1952, pp. 120–122).

It is in this vastly expanded world of experience that human beings must devise their strategies of adaptation.

One's first thought may be that the ensuing complexities are certain to drown us. I believe, however, that we stand to gain by fitting human strategies as far as possible into the three behavioral variables deduced from animals and young children. Take first the second variable, the maintaining, and if possible the enhancing, of the system's internal organization. It is here that awareness of the remote, the past, and the future, and especially awareness of oneself as a person, most dramatically expand the meaning of the variable. Clearly there is much more to be maintained than bodily integrity and control over disruptive affects. One thing that must be enhanced if possible, and desperately maintained if necessary, is the level of self-esteem. In part this shows itself as a struggle to keep intact a satisfactory self-picture, in part as attempts to preserve a sense of competence, an inner assurance that one can do the things necessary for a satisfactory life. Wide are the ramifications of keeping up one's self-esteem. Almost any situation that is not completely familiar, even casual and superficial contacts with new people, even discussing the day's news, can touch off internal questions like, "What sort of impression am I making?" "How well am I dealing with this?" "What kind of a person am I showing myself to be?" When self-esteem is tender or when the situation is strongly challenging, such questions, even if only vaguely felt, can lead to anxiety, shame, or guilt with their threat of further disorganization. No adaptive strategy that is careless of the level of self-esteem is likely to be any good. We certainly regard it as rare, unusually mature, and uncommonly heroic when after an unfortunate happening that diminishes his importance or shows him to be wrong, a person quietly lowers his estimate of himself without making excuses or seeking to lodge the blame elsewhere.

Less dramatic but still important are the expanded meanings of the other two variables. Securing adequate information is no longer confined to the immediate cognitive field. Information about things absent assumes increasing significance, especially when it bears on courses of action that extend into the future. Resources for information are also much richer: other people can be asked, relevant reading matter can be sought, and in some cases it is possible to send friends, employees, or students out to increase the scope of one's informational net. The maintaining of autonomy similarly gains a future dimension and a wider meaning. Looking ahead into the future and frequently making plans of one kind or another, we soon learn to be at least somewhat careful about committing ourselves. We feel better if things can be left a little open, if there are options; if, for example, in taking a job we see room for varying its duties or believe that in any event it will be a good springboard toward other jobs. "If I take this job," so many have asked themselves, "with its demands for teaching or medical service, will I have time for my own research?" Preserving an acceptable level of freedom of movement continues to be an important consideration even when the present physical field of the exploring animal has expanded into the imagined future social field of the human adult.

ILLUSTRATIONS FROM RECENT RESEARCH

The understanding of strategies of adaptation can start from any one variable provided we bear in mind that the simultaneous management of all three variables is constantly involved. In one of the first psychiatric studies of severe life stress, Lindemann (1944) described the working-through of bereavement and grief in a way that includes all three. The need for information is important following bereavement because a great many established patterns of conduct both in the present and in the expected future have been fatally disrupted. As Lindemann put it, "the bereaved is surprised to find how large a part of his customary activity was done in some meaningful relationship to the deceased and has now lost its significance" (p. 142). New burdens will have to be assumed, new patterns of meaningful conduct discovered; how will all this be managed, and where will opportunities be found? Yet often enough the bereaved person is for some time unequal to contemplating the future, which would only emphasize the magnitude of the loss and increase painful and paralyzing grief. Internal organization cannot be maintained, thinking and action can hardly be carried forward at all, as long as this disruptive emotion remains strong. Self-esteem, too, is often put on trial, challenged by the intrusion of unexpected feelings of guilt. Lindemann noticed how often "the bereaved searches the time before the death for evidence of failure to do right by the lost one; he accuses himself of negligence and exaggerates minor omissions" (p. 142). Considerations of autonomy, of preserving or opening up some sense of free movement, present themselves as soon as the immediate crisis has passed. Sometimes a death may be experienced as increasing the survivor's freedom, but typically a widowed spouse, especially if there is a family to bring up, looks into a future gravely constricted.

A few years ago, Hamburg and Adams (1967) reviewed a number of studies of behavior during major life transitions, putting a strong emphasis on the seeking and utilizing of information. They perceive the cognitive quest, however, in relation to the other two variables. Thus in patients with severe injuries that are bound to restrict their future activity the search for information is seen as serving the following purposes: "keeping distress within manageable limits; maintaining a sense of personal worth; restoring relations with significant other people; enhancing prospects for recovery of bodily functions; and increasing the likelihood of working out a personally valued and socially acceptable situation after maximum physical recovery has been attained" (p. 278). The time dimension proves to be significant in these cases. For a while, the depressing impact of the event must be controlled, and this is often accomplished by extensive denial of the seriousness of the illness. As time goes on, there is an increase of cognitive clarity, but this is usually achieved at the cost of an increase of depression, which now is better tolerated. The dismal truth is perceived only as rapidly as one can stand it. Similar processes of balance are revealed in studies of the parents of children suffering from leukemia. Again one can see delays in taking in the full meaning of the diagnosis and slow progress toward appreciation of the inevitable outcome. Again one can see the outcropping of guilt and the need of the parents to be reassured that more attention on their part to the early manifestations of the disease would not have changed the prognosis. In this situation, grief can be experienced in advance, and it was noticed that the more this was done, the less the parents were overwhelmed when the child's death finally occurred.

The use of strategies of adaptation in advance, in anticipation of problems that still lie ahead, would appear to be a peculiarly human attribute. It is unusually well exemplified in a study by Silber and colleagues (1961) of high-school seniors getting ready to enter college in the fall. The subjects were chosen because of their high level of competence in the more important aspects of adolescent life; their previous success gave them confidence, but did not exempt them from misgivings over the important step soon to be taken. The interviewers became aware of a large repertoire of adaptive strategies serving to increase information about college life, dampen anxiety, sustain and improve a self-image of adequacy, and provide reassurance that the new life would offer a variety of pathways to self-satisfaction. The students sought information by writing to their college, visiting the campus, and talking with the college students and graduates of their acquaintance. They filtered the information by selectively perceiving those aspects of their college that put it in the light of a benign, friendly, supportive environment. They sustained internal organization by the thought that worrying was normal, was shared by other prospective students—"Everybody feels this, everybody has to be a freshman once"—and might even have a useful function in preparing for eventualities. They further reminded themselves of previous analogous situations successfully dealt with, such as the transition from junior to senior high school, identified themselves as part of a group well prepared for college, and lowered their levels of aspiration with respect to academic performance and social prominence during the freshman year. Particularly significant was the building of a sense of competence by a process of role rehearsal during the spring and summer. The students began to read books they thought would be required at college, to exert themselves in courses considered to be on a college level, and to take special pains with term papers, understood by them to be of great importance in college performance. Anticipating their increased independence, some of them began buying their own clothes and practiced more careful budgeting of their time. In their choice of summer jobs they veered away from those associated with adolescent status, like baby-sitting and mowing lawns, looking instead for work that would put them in competition with adults and would increase their experience in dealing with adults on an equal level. With respect to autonomy, they rehearsed in fantasy the different things they might do to secure help, win popularity, and find avenues for their individual skills and interests. And if worse came to the worst, as one of them expressed it, "If I want to go home, I'll be able to."

It is worth noticing that the strategies of adaptation pursued by these prospective college students accomplished more than could reasonably be implied by the words *defense* and *protection*. I wonder if they do not imply more than most people have in mind when they use the word *coping*, which according to my desk dictionary means contending, striving, opposing, or resisting "on equal terms." The limits of definition are at this point shadowy, but we must be sure not to overlook what these young people actually accomplished while dealing with the problems of transition. The men and women who walked on to their respective campuses in September were not quite the same people who received news of their admittance the previous spring. Whatever distortions and defensive operations may have crept into their college-oriented behavior, these were greatly overbalanced by substantial increases in realistic information, in realistic expectations, and in actual competence through role rehearsal and through summer jobs. They had grown, they had matured, they had exhibited Angyal's trend toward increased autonomy, and as human beings they stood taller than the high-school adolescents they had been six months before. One of the great advantages of research on coping is that it brings back into the psychological and psychiatric literature the persistence, the will to live, the courage, and indeed the heroism that are as much a part of human nature as the retreats, evasions, and petty impulse gratifications that bulk so large in our thinking about psychopathology. Let us be sure that the concept of coping does not shrink in its meaning so that we lose this great advance over our constricted past and forget that strategies of adaptation lead not just to equilibrium but to development.

A CLOSING NOTE ON DEFENSE MECHANISMS

I shall now bring defense mechanisms back into the discussion. You may have thought that I was angry with them, but I am angry only with the overweening part they have been accorded in the understanding of personality. The mechanisms of defense, the ten of them listed by Anna Freud (1937), or whatever the number may be, have a legitimate place among strategies of adaptation. They *are* strategies of adaptation, and we can assume that in the course of human history they have relieved untold millions of people of anxiety that would otherwise have been overwhelming. Possibly when it comes to actual process, the defense mechanisms are not even very different in kind from other adaptive processes. Theodore Kroeber (1963) has pointed out the impressive continuities between defense mechanisms and estimable adaptive devices. Repression has a counterpart in suppression, reaction formation in substitution, and rationalization in the most strenuous and disciplined logical analysis. According to this way of thinking, defense mechanisms can be seen as adaptive devices gone wrong, and the way in which they have gone wrong is in failing to maintain a balance among the three variables I have been discussing. Presumably because the threat to internal organization is acute—the anxiety unbearable—obtaining further information is sacrificed, and the cognitive field is either partially blacked out or subjected to a major interpretative distortion. As far as our knowledge of defense mechanisms goes, derived largely from psycho-analytic treatment, they work for the time being; in short range they are adaptive. They cause trouble in the long run because they contain no provision, so to speak, for learning anything new about sources of danger. Closing the cognitive field is a static solution, guaranteeing that dangers will not be reexamined and may, therefore, retain their original power to precipitate anxiety. Thus defense mechanisms can be considered poor devices, the work of which must sometimes be undone for the sake of psychological health, but they cannot be denied their place as a class of strategies of adaptation.

WHAT DIFFERENCE DOES IT MAKE?

The question "What difference does it make?" is often asked by laymen about our technical and theoretical discussions and is, I believe, one which we should always ask ourselves. What value can we anticipate from imposing a grid of three very general variables upon the seemingly endless phenomena of adaptive processes? What good is accomplished by distributing the phenomena into categories labeled (1) securing adequate information about the environment, (2) maintaining satisfactory internal conditions both for action and for processing information, and (3) maintaining autonomy or freedom of movement? What practical virtue is there in asserting that strategies of adaptation in order to be reasonably successful require the simultaneous management of these three considerations, the holding of some sort of balance among them?

I do not for a moment think that this descriptive maneuver illuminates all our difficulties or contains inherent advice for mental health practices. The variables may not be the best ones, and they may be too big. The second one, for example, which might be called maintaining and enhancing the inner structure and functional capacity of the system as a whole, contains in the human case aspects as disparate as controlling disruptive affects and maintaining a satisfying self-picture. For practical purposes a breakdown into separate subvariables would certainly be necessary. But whatever may be the shortcomings of the description offered in this essay, however small the step that has been taken, I am going to close with the claim that it is a step in the right direction.

As a profession—and here I mean to include psychiatrists, psychologists, social workers, and all others who work in the domain broadly called mental health—we have been for a long time heavily concerned with how people feel, not so much with what they do. It has been our faith that if people could be made to feel right inside, to experience trust, to feel loved and valued, to relinquish their jealousies and competitive aggression toward the members of the family circle, then only could we expect their behavior to change; then only could we confidently leave them to their own devices. So we have been tempted to concentrate on these inner states, trying to influence them directly through the power of insight and the efficacy of a relationship in which the most regularly described element is warmth. Yet increasingly we have been confronted by the painful fact that this method of getting at the roots of the difficulty is, after all, something short of a startling success, even though many have benefited greatly from it, and that in any event it is likely to take quite a long time. Now comes the movement for community mental health, with its ideal of making our services available to all segments of the population. Whatever reservations we may have about so vast an aspiration, it is inevitable that a democratic society should try it, just as in the last century it was inevitable that an education through high school should come to be considered the right of every child regardless of economic circumstances. Community mental health may not work, but there is no doubt in my mind that we are going to try it.

It would be good, therefore, if it *did* work, but its working will certainly require astonishing economies of professional time. We are forced to think about doing things faster. And I submit that one way to do this is to concentrate more carefully on what clients do, or on what they can be encouraged to do by advice or a suitable arrangement of circumstances. There has never been doubt that action is capable of changing feeling. The most telling example is the gain in confidence and the reduction of anxiety that follow the successful performance of some act that has been the object of misgivings. Giving instruction and advice, offering explanations and suggestions to parents, suggesting changes in the environment—these have always been part of the helping strategy. The medical profession, always quick to erect polysyllabic defenses, has lately reasserted its claim to stay on top of these activities by calling them "paramedical," while the psychologists, equally jealous, have attacked the whole disease model of behavior disorders and pinned on psychotherapy the new label of "behavior change." As a pacifist with respect to professional prestige quarrels, I argue only that we may find, if we try it modestly but persistently, using our best insight and taking care to evaluate our results, that fairly simple and direct methods of influencing behavior can produce a good deal better results than we have been taught to suppose. But our best insights will not be enough if they all have to do with inner states, defense mechanisms, and the precipitates of interpersonal relations. There must be a new sensitivity to potentialities for action, to what the client might just be capable of doing for himself with a little encouragement, and to what he might be able to do if he knew that it was important and would help him with his problems. Into this we can have insight only if we are thoroughly familiar with strategies of adaptation as they occur in everyday life.

To emphasize the point, let us suppose that in that high school where the competent adolescents were studied there is a less competent boy, admitted to college like the others, but facing the prospect with far less spirit. His parents notice that he seems preoccupied and worried, complains of not sleeping, looks thinner, and acts less inclined to seek the company of his friends. He announces that he feels tired and will spend the summer at home, mowing the lawn, rather than looking for a summer job. The parents, wanting their boy to have everything of the best, send him to an expensive psychiatrist. What will happen? My hope would be that the psychiatrist, aware of the wide range of strategies of adaptation shown by other boys in this situation, would use his influence chiefly to persuade his patient to try some of them. The boy may be afraid of the total experience, but he may not be afraid to visit the campus, obtain literature, talk to college students he knows, buy some clothes alone, write school essays as if they were college essays, and apply for a man-size summer job. And if these can be managed, even if only with encouragement and one at a time, he has already moved along the path toward college and will make the final transition with less difficulty. But one can imagine that the talks might settle on the boy's passive-dependent tendencies, which he certainly has, and perhaps on resentment against the parents who seem willing to let him leave home, which he may also have. He can be shown that he is a passive-dependent spiteful little brat, but he can also be shown, without mentioning this, how he can become a man. It seems to me the path of wisdom to try the latter first. If it works, there is a solid victory that will probably fortify the patient somewhat against future difficulties. We all know that it may not work without change in archaic anxieties and wishes that have become preemptive, and this would call for a second and different strategy of therapeutic intervention. In community mental health work, however, there will rarely be time and staff to provide this second chance. What is tried first will generally be all that is tried.

A paper written several years ago bears on this issue in a rather amusing way. It is probably tactless to speak of it because it deals with the delicate topic of giving up smoking. In their research the authors (Leventhal, Watts, and Pagano 1967) exposed their subjects, cigarette smokers all, to a variety of urgings to stop smoking, including a somewhat alarming film, and in some cases an extremely disquieting one, that showed in color the surgical removal of a blackened lung. In contrast to a control group, these measures produced marked effects in the form of fear, determination to stop smoking, and an actual reduction in number of cigarettes smoked during the following week. The subjects were also divided another way: part of them received instructions on how to stop smoking, and part of them did not. The instructions were taken from a booklet used in antismoking clinics and were highly detailed. They dealt with avoiding conditions conducive to smoking, with the preparation beforehand of excuses for declining cigarettes, with tricks like carrying gum, not carrying matches, and taking deep breaths when the urge to smoke became strong. They also advocated a heightening of awareness by writing down the reasons for smoking and for stopping. At the end of the first week, the instructed and the uninstructed groups had both smoked much less, there being little difference between them. But when questioned after a month, and again after three months, the instructed subjects were holding their gains nicely, while the curve for the uninstructed group was moving suspiciously back in the direction of the original level of cigarette consumption. Would we have expected this result? Should it not have been that the subjects who experienced the most fear would make the greatest change in their smoking behavior? Apparently not: in this situation the effects of fear could easily peter out, whereas lasting effects occurred in those who knew what to do, who were equipped with instrumental acts that gave them a strategy of adaptation to carry out their intention.

There are many influences today that make us reluctant to tell people what to do. Partly, no doubt, it is the effect of the contemporary culture that has become so extravagantly negative to anything that smacks of direction and authority. Partly it comes from our profound absorption of Freud's image of man, based on neurotic man in whom an enfeebled and compromised ego opposes in vain the vast powers of unconscious id and superego. But partly, I think, the trouble is that we do not know what to say. Knowing so much about the ways in which common sense, realism, inventiveness, and courage can be spoiled, we have dismissed them rather than studying how they still work. Herein lies the importance of the study of strategies of adaptation. We all need to become paramedical experts, widely familiar with behavior change, keenly aware of the whole range of strategies of adaptation. At this point, our democratic society needs community mental health. What we professionals need to do to make it work is to rediscover at a new level of sophistication the homely wisdom of the past.

REFERENCES

Angyal, A. *Foundations for a science of personality.* New York: The Commonwealth Fund, 1941.

Asch, S. E. *Social psychology.* Englewood Cliffs, N.J.: Prentice-Hall, 1952.

Freud, A. *The ego and the mechanisms of defence.* London: Hogarth Press, 1937.

Hamburg, D. A., and Adams, J. E. A perspective on coping behavior: Seeking and utilizing information in major transitions. *Archives of General Psychiatry,* 1967, *17,* 277–284.

Kroeber, A. *Anthropology.* Rev. ed. New York: Harcourt, Brace & World, 1948.

Kroeber, T. C. The coping functions of the ego mechanisms. In R. W. White, ed., *The study of lives.* New York: Atherton Press, 1963.

Leventhal, H., Watts, J. C., and Pagano, F. Effects of fear and instructions on how to cope with danger. *Journal of Personality and Social Psychology,* 1967, *6,* 313–321.

Lindemann, E. Symptomatology and management of acute grief. *American Journal of Psychiatry,* 1944, *101,* 141–148.

Murphy, L. B. *The widening world of childhood: Paths toward mastery.* New York: Basic Books, 1962.

Silber, E., Hamburg, D. A., Coelho, G. V., Murphey, E. B., Rosenberg, M., and Pearlin, L. D. Adaptive behavior in competent adolescents: Coping with the anticipation of college. *Archives of General Psychiatry,* 1961, *5,* 354–365.

5

Coping, Vulnerability, and Resilience in Childhood

LOIS B. MURPHY

INTRODUCTION

In the century that has passed since the publication of *The Origin of Species* (Darwin 1859) an increasingly balanced understanding of adaptational processes in human beings has gradually emerged. The concept of phylogenetic evolution, with its insight into the prerequisites for survival of a given organism in a specific environment, was followed by a series of steps in the understanding of ontogenetic development. It is not surprising that different streams of scientific work had to continue to be separate for half a century. Those initiated by Sigmund Freud's contributions to the understanding of epigenesis of drive (Freud 1905, 1953) aspects of mental functioning influenced by drives remained relatively remote from the successive discoveries of experimental and developmental psychology of the universities. This was true despite the interest of G. Stanley Hall (1883), founder of child psychology, in Freud's work and, later, the interest of Susan Isaacs (1930) as early as the 1920s in contributions from experimental work.

Only when Freud's own formulations regarding the ego were followed by Hartmann's monograph *Ego Psychology and the Problem of Adaptation* (1958) was the way opened for more spontaneous rapprochement of the broad streams of investigations comprising the psychoanalytic and the academic approaches. The later work of Piaget on the development of intelligence (1952) captured the interest of a large body of workers, some of whom have also been interested in analyzing parallels and differences between Piaget and Freud (Anthony 1957). But there is room for much more work toward

This paper is based upon studies supported by U. S. Public Health Service grants M680 and 5 R12 MH 9236-02, by the Gustavus and Louisa Pfeiffer Foundation, and by the Menninger Foundation; and also by U. S. Public Health Service grant MH 10421, Children's Hospital of the District of Columbia.

a comprehensive view of the adaptational process. This discussion of coping tasks is one step in the direction of further study of the adaptational process as seen in growing children.

BIOGRAPHICAL BACKGROUND OF OUR RESEARCH ON CHILDREN'S WAYS OF COPING

Long before the beginning of my first formal study of young children in 1932, I was interested in individual differences in temperament and equipment and their relation to the development of personality. This was reflected in *Social Behavior and Child Personality* (Murphy 1937), in my discussion of individual children in *Life and Ways of the Seven-to-Eight-Year-Old* (Biber et al. 1942), in the approach to individual students in *Emotional Factors in Learning* (Murphy and Ladd 1944), and especially in my outlines in *Methods for the Study of Personality in Young Children* (Lerner and Murphy 1941). This naturally led to a concern with the different ways in which different children dealt with new or difficult situations, adult demands, and pain; but also included was the question of the young child's struggle with apparent feelings of helplessness and anger resulting from illness or from adult aggression, as illustrated by the documentary *This is Robert*, by L. J. Stone, which used primarily Stone's photographic records of children in our Sarah Lawrence Nursery School, and by *Colin: A Normal Child* (Murphy 1956), based on longitudinal records from the same setting.

This emphasis on the *child's* solutions and efforts was evoked by my dissatisfaction with the research of the period which I had reviewed in the 1931 edition of *Experimental Social Psychology* (G. Murphy and L. B. Murphy 1937). It seemed that many people were preoccupied with such questions as negativism, aggression, and other undesirable behavior as seen by adults in terms of normative standards, and that hardly anyone was trying to understand how the child might be experiencing and facing his situation. My orientation was probably deeply influenced by Freud's *The Ego and the Id* (1923) and *Group Psychology and Analysis of the Ego* (1921), published in English during my undergraduate years. Susan Isaacs' *Social Development in Young Children* (1933) also seemed to me more understanding than the current American work. I wrote to her about Dan, one of the children she described in full detail, who seemed to be an intense, warm, sometimes violent, often loving, little boy who confronted life very directly—and she agreed with my impressions. The writings of Anna Freud and Dorothy Burlingham, especially their detailed observations of children removed from their families and cared for in the Hampstead Nursery, brought this interest into still sharper focus. These records (Freud and Burlingham 1943, 1944) were replete with examples of young children's coping efforts under stressful conditions. Anna Freud's (1951) comments on the potential contribution of *observations* of infants and young children supported my belief that our understanding of processes of adaptation could be strengthened by careful observation of the interactions between children and their environments.

Finally, as I observed active infants, I was impressed by the multiple serendipities—chance discoveries of successful devices for coping with infantile tasks, challenges, obstacles, and frustrations. All of this helped me to pull together and see in the context of basic human processes the coping efforts of a baby; of a severely handicapped person like our polio child (Murphy 1962) or Franklin Roosevelt; of blind or deaf children I had observed in numerous special schools, and Helen Keller; of people who were more frail or vulnerable than others or had been weakened by illness. The writings of Bernfeld (1929), Hartmann (1958), as well as those of Sigmund and Anna Freud, helped to strengthen my emphasis, along with biographies of vulnerable geniuses such as Michelangelo and Beethoven, and the ingenious and heroic coping strategies of my mother who was severely crippled by rheumatoid arthritis.

Becoming interested in the universal scope of coping, I was intrigued by observations of "lower species"—an ant faced by an obstacle as it carried home a burden of food, circumventing the barrier while still maintaining a sense of direction; a young robin teetering on the edge of its nest (with its chattering mother close by), vigilant, hesitant, then daring to take off and frantically beating its wings in the effort to fly; our little dog defying my command to come in the house (and stop barking at the postman), then looking me in the eye, dashing in through the house and out the unlatched back screen door as if he had formed a clear idea of how to cope with me.

Coping came to include all those efforts to deal with environmental pressures that could not be handled by reflexes or organized skills, but involved struggles, trials, persistent focused energy directed toward a goal. So responses to threats and dangers, frustrations and defeats, obstacles, loss, strangeness and the new or unknown, demands from the adults or others in the environment, all required study.

What I wanted to do then was just to call to the attention of American workers with children the child's way of getting along—with whatever equipment he had at his developmental stage—and his own individual makeup, as he faced the particular external and internal problems of his situation.

BEGINNING THE SYSTEMATIC STUDY
OF CHILDREN'S COPING

During World War II, and with various other demands, I could not focus on this until I went to the Menninger Foundation in 1952 with an open ticket from Dr. Will Menninger to do what I wanted to do. Sibylle Escalona and Mary Leitch, child psychiatrists, had collected very intensive, naturalistic observations on 128 babies, using three simultaneous observers in a laboratory situation, supplemented by home visits and movies; but the main thing is this incredible body of very delicate observations by very sensitive observers. When Escalona decided she wanted to get back East and persuaded Gardner and me to go to Topeka, the bait for me was her offer: "You can do anything you want to with the children and the infancy data, there's enough material there for lots of us to work at and we won't get in each other's way." It was a total bequest with absolute generosity and no strings at all tied to it. Their approach to the individual infant, with his idiosyncratic capacities, tastes, sensitivities, and ways of dealing with stimulation, was remarkably congruent with mine.

Along with the children, I inherited the gifted Grace Heider of Escalona's staff, and some other talented people from the Menninger and larger Topeka community, notably Povl Toussieng, M.D., a young child psychiatrist in training; [1] Walter Kass, Ph.D., clinical psychologist in the Children's Division; [2] Alice Moriarty, Ph.D., clinical psychologist from Yale University, recently arrived in Topeka; and Patricia Schloesser, M.D., a pediatrician, Director of Maternal and Child Health for the State of Kansas. The late Dr. Nelly Tibout, M.D., an experienced and creative child analyst, was consultant for the first two years.

With this experienced and able staff to begin our exploratory study, I felt that it was important to utilize their most perceptive observations fully rather than to impose a prestructured format on their observations that could limit the scope or depth of our exploration of children's individual coping methods in relation to their capacities, temperament, and so forth. We spent a year in weekly sensitizing discussions, sharing questions about possible factors in coping capacity, and the implications of the concept.

We then developed a plan for recording that included two observers in each situation, where we looked for the children's responses to a variety of familiar and novel situations involving mild challenge or threat. We were intrigued with the idea of making intensive studies with normal children that would focus on how the children get along, how they cope with the ordinary ups and downs of life's challenges and frustrations. We did not undertake to make a big deal out of the word *coping*. It was just that we wanted to see what was going on with children. The mood was very much like that of Robert Coles's *Children of Crisis* (1967), where he also does not deal with coping as a concept to push around theoretically, but rather as an entrance into an area.

My first research on sympathy (1937) included fifty-five children, and afterward I decided that was too many for the kind of close study I preferred. What I wanted to do was to follow intensively just a few, maybe ten or fifteen. Gardner Murphy and my other chief consultant, Nelly Tibout, said that we could not do anything at all statistically with such a tiny number, and urged me to take enough for at least some elementary statistical analysis; they suggested thirty. So we took thirty-one, just to allow a little for the inevitable loss that every such undertaking has to anticipate.

I was really mothering a group of investigations by different people, not dictating what they should do, but making it possible for them to use the pool of material as it accumulated. The children were three to five years old when we began.

But in addition to the intensive, multidisciplinary study at the preschool level, we offered hospitality to other investigators. The concept was that of a "pool of data" on a sample of children. Interested researchers were to have the use of the data pool on the condition that they contributed their own data to the pool. Dr. H. A. Witkin sent an assistant, Carol Johnson, to carry out perception tests on our group, and she added over thirty more children from the Escalona sample (Witkin et al. 1962). All of these children were studied later by Dr. Riley Gardner's staff (Gardner and Moriarty 1968), and Wayne Holtzman's inkblot test (1961) was administered to most of these children. Additional studies included Dr. Charles Stewart's work on the role of religion as a coping resource in this church-going culture (1967) while Drs. Bernardez and Davidson made studies of individual children based on the total data from infancy to puberty (Bernardez 1965; Davidson 1967). Dr. Tarlton Morrow (1965) followed C. J. Morgan's intensive study (1964) of three pubertal boys who were losing the level of integration they had reached. Mary Engel (1958) was at the Menninger Foundation in training and developed a Children's Insight Test, which I think is quite fruitful for coping, although this is not the way the analysis of it is ordinarily structured.

In addition to the study of individual children's ways of coping with standard examinations, we wanted to pick up the unexpected events, crises, and special problems or opportunities. Under the heading of "special problems" I had about a hundred hours in weekly sessions over about three years with a child who had been so ill from polio that she had not really been expected to survive. I was able to follow the steps she went through from the time when I first saw her at the age of five years, crawling along the floor, to graduation from high school, when she received academic honors, had a boyfriend, and was ready to go to college. Then, when a boy was in a car accident in which his mother was killed, his father terribly injured, and the boy himself had two broken legs, a younger member of our staff spent time with him in the hospital. He wrote this up in process records (Murphy and Moriarty, to be published). These records were dictated in full detail after each encounter with the child, whereas in most of the regular examinations we were using tape recordings or dictaphone belts and other devices to supplement our dictated observations. (Several different kinds of publications have come out of it, as different people wrote on different problems that appealed to them.)

I have been rather intrigued by the many kinds of observations you can make in an undertaking like this, and this has led me to reflect on studies in which the major research tool was empathy. This may be true for the observations of animals or humans, and I find myself wondering in such circumstances, "How did the researcher come to this conclusion?" In clinical terms, many statements in these studies would be considered an "interpretation" of why the subjects were doing what they were doing, and I come to the conclusion that the only way such questions could be answered would be by wondering (consciously or unconsciously) "Why would I have done this if I were the subject?" I am saying this because I think this approach has been important for some of the people working with our Topeka material; and this is one reason why we have kept our subjects so well, although a number of them have moved to another state. For instance, the last time I went to Topeka, Alice Moriarty said, "Lenny called me up last night and wanted to know how to get in touch with you because he is stationed seventeen miles from Washington and wants to come and see you." They have all been told that the research is finished, that our grant is ending soon, and that they have been seen for the last time, but they are not accepting that idea. They have been coming back to see us. Why? We haven't been doing anything for them; we haven't been giving them anything. We haven't been offering any advice. All we've been doing is listening, at successive phases. It hasn't been an ongoing contact, but every few years there is another "go-around," and they have been telling us that to be a part of this has meant a great deal to them. They say it has helped them to think about themselves and where they are going as they wouldn't have otherwise. Empathizing can be done only if we manage to throw off the shackles of the preconceptions that we bring to a group that is very different. (Actually, the kind of experience you have had and I have had working with a hard-core poverty day-care center is more different than, let's say, the experience of getting acquainted with healthy Nigerians at their university, Nigerians who are more like us than they are like some other Nigerians.) I think the physical science model that has shaped the superego of psychology has deprived psychology of some of the most important, productive, enlightening experiences that we might have been having over the years in our attempts to understand human beings and what they are all about.

DEVELOPING AN APPROACH

We approached our study thinking of coping in terms of struggling, trying, managing, dealing with a situation. We thought of it as a modest, unassuming word, a modifier to be used with other words; that is, coping devices, coping techniques, coping strategies, and we were using it because the concept of adjustment is so loaded with honorific implications, and maladjustment is so pejorative. In the early 1930s there were monographs on "resistance" in young children, and labels like "withdrawn" were put on children. But then I would look at the children and see the kinds of things that Robert White was quoting (1959). For instance, little Sheila, two years old, said, "I don't like your game, I don't want to do it any more." This is a very sensible remark; she was actually expressing quite clearly what Erikson (1963) has told us a two-year-old should be capable of being; that is, autonomous. She is stating her own point of view in a two-year-old way, whereas testers expect a child to cooperate with the authority. The concept of coping focuses on what the child is trying to do. In itself it does not imply success, but effort. Defensive maneuvers can be part of coping processes. Successful coping may contribute increments of competence as Robert White (1959) has discussed this.

At first we did not formulate tightly knit definitions that might also have interfered with the scope of our findings. Rather, we shared a common orientation to, and interest in, exploring the child's experience and understanding his struggles. To do this we used some of the tools already familiar and well sharpened by previous work, but now applied to a new task, along with other specially planned "situations," such as parties and a trip to the zoo.

Intelligence and projective tests, pediatric examinations, and social occasions were to be seen not just as methods of ascertaining the resources of the children so that they could be identified in normative terms and compared with others, although we did do this. But also, all of these would be viewed as demands made upon the child, in new situations, new places, by strange adults. We planned to scrutinize as carefully as possible the different ways in which individual children seemed to experience and deal with these demands. We ourselves picked up the children and returned them to their homes, dictating records of "to-and-fro" observations.

Through home interviews with mothers we obtained reports of the children's ways of coping with developmentally typical fears and stress in the family, such as the arrival of a new baby, loss of pets or of relatives, and moving. One mother made detailed records for us of her three children's ways of coping with daily experiences, while another mother outside the study group kept notes on stress experiences such as starting nursery school and coping with an accident and the hospital treatment it required. Unusual threats such as tornadoes, reactions to the kidnapping and death of a child in a nearby city, and the death of a child when his home burned down across the street from one of our families were reported in interviews or records by mothers. And in some instances, we attended funerals, visited hospitals, or saw a sick child at home.

At annual meetings of the American Psychological Association in 1954 and 1955 we presented symposia (Murphy 1954, 1955) in which the range of coping behavior in certain children was described by each of several members of the research team; and at the Fifteenth International Congress of Psychology in Brussels in 1957, I presented a brief summary—"A Longitudinal Study of Children's Coping Methods and Styles" (Murphy 1959). In this I illustrated the strategic and complementary use of active, overt coping efforts *and* defense mechanisms using the example of two-year-old Molly's way of coping with fear of thunder, and successive steps toward relative mastery of this fear by the age of five. A brief summary of the stages Molly went through in conquering her fear of thunder and the noise of a jet plane follows:

1. As a two-year-old, Molly cried many times and was completely terrified during thunderstorms or when a jet plane passed overhead.
2. A year later she was able to get into bed with her older sister during a thunderstorm and accept comfort from her.
3. At about the same time Molly began to reassure herself (and her baby brother), saying, "It's just noise and it really won't hurt you at bit."
4. A month after this storm Molly was again terrified as a jet plane flew unusually low overhead; she cried and clung to her sister for comfort. A few hours later she repeated several times to herself, "Thunder really doesn't hurt you; it just sounds noisy. I'm not scared of planes, only thunder."
5. The next month she opened the door into her parents' room during a thunderstorm, saying that her younger brother was afraid (although he was really fast asleep).
6. Nine months later, at four years and two months, she was awakened from a nap during a thunderstorm, but remained quietly in bed. Afterward she said to her sister, "There was lots of thunder, but I just snuggled in my bed and didn't cry a bit."
7. Four months later, at four and a half years, Molly showed no open fear herself during a storm, and comforted her frightened little brother, saying, "I remember when I was a little baby and I was scared of thunder and I used to cry and cry every time it thundered."

Here we see the two-steps-forward, one-step-backward process: (1) overt expression of fearful affect and helplessness; (2) actively seeking comfort from a supporting person; (3) internalizing the comfort and the image of the comforting person, acting as comforter to herself; (4) differentiating sources of fear while still reverting to the need for physical comfort from her sister; (5) projecting the fear to her baby brother (as a way of rationalizing getting the support she needed) and seeking a symbol of support (opening the door without demand for physical or other active comforting); (6) combining actively comforting herself with formulation of a self-image in terms of pride in control and mastery of her fear; (7) reaction formation, achievement of bravery and referral of the fear to her past.

Nothing in our records in the fifteen years of study has suggested that we should revise this basic point that defense mechanisms are normally and constructively used in the total process of coping, especially when the child is in danger of being overwhelmed or is confronted with threats that cannot be mastered at his current stage of development or in his current situation. Defense mechanisms become pathological or contribute to pathology only when they interfere with progress in coping.

Thus we see coping as a process, involving effort, on the way toward solution of a problem, as contrasted on the one hand with ready-made adaptational devices such as reflexes, or on the other hand, with complete and automatized mastery and resulting competence. The following may illustrate relationships of these concepts.

Adaptation involves:

   reflexes (built-in mechanisms) and *instincts* (broader built-in patterns);
   coping efforts (to deal with situations not adequately managed by reflexes);
   mastery resulting from effective and well-practiced coping efforts;
   competence as the congeries of skills resulting from cumulative mastery achievement.

In human beings, reflexes and instincts do not go far to cope with the complexities of demands, threats, opportunities, life offers. Therefore, constant invention, incessant trial-and-error stabs at managing, supplement the limited (if impressive) repertoire of reflex capacities.

Moreover, coping could be seen as in the following diagram.

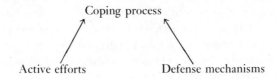

Implied in the above is the observation that coping efforts may be successful or unsuccessful, or unsuccessful at one time and successful at another time.

Of course I was glad to find Roy Grinker's study of coping capacities of young men (R. Grinker, Sr., R. Grinker, Jr., and Timberlake 1962) and David Hamburg's documentation of the poignant coping processes of people desperately ill from severe burns (D. Hamburg, B. Hamburg, and deGoza 1953) along with the evidence that those who could utilize useful denial managed to cope better than those who were overwhelmed by the lethal threat they faced, unable to modulate their perception by strategic denial.

In some situations, as with our polio child, early strategic denial gradually became unnecessary as the total process brought her to a state where she could realistically pass for normal and "not feel handicapped any more," to use her own words. The long struggle took over a dozen years.

Because, obviously, the challenges and threats and relevant ways of coping with them could be expected to vary in different environments and cultural settings, we did not attempt a definitive taxonomy of coping. Rather, we regarded our task as that of alerting or sensitizing workers with children to the child's experience. This use of our work was characteristic of, for instance, pediatricians dealing with hemophiliac children, clinicians dealing with retarded or handicapped children, some child psychiatrists dealing with disturbed children, some nurses dealing with children in hospitals, and research investigators making cross-cultural studies of children's coping.

We did, however, conceptualize coping devices and coping styles. We also distinguished between Coping I, or capacity to deal with the opportunities, frustrations, obstacles of the environment, and Coping II, or capacity to maintain internal equilibrium. And we formulated items describing characteristics of the child's equipment, temperament, and home life, which could be analyzed in relation to his capacity.

The variations in a given child's capacity to cope effectively with different situations, and between different children's capacities to cope with a given situation, led to a focus on differences in vulnerability. Our study of this took shape in a Vulnerability Inventory (Murphy and Moriarty, to be published), the items in which could be seen to contribute interactively and cumulatively to the intrinsic problems with which the child had to cope.

This now permitted an overall view of the interrelations of coping and vulnerability with development and the outcomes of coping efforts for the child's adaptational style (Murphy and Moriarty, to be published). As part of these studies we have formulated an outline of coping tasks in infancy illustrated in the following section. Our observations of the preschool children were uncontaminated by contact with the Escalona data on infants, and all the staff but Grace Heider remained "uncontaminated" until sequential data were analyzed at the puberty stage. Thus the important and statistically significant correlations between infancy and later data provided an impetus to take a closer look at the earliest coping efforts of the infants.

COPING EFFORTS IN INFANCY

The first and most basic task of human development, as well as the one that lasts the longest—in fact for the lifetime of the individual—is to survive. For the very young baby in the critical early weeks of postnatal life, this is a matter of achieving adequate integration in the basic vegetative functions, such as breathing, feeding and digesting, elimination, resting, and sleeping.

Achievement of smooth organic functioning is important not only in its own right, but also as a prerequisite for a stable positive mood-level. Without a dependable experience of feeling good within himself (narcissism), the infant has little basis for attributing goodness to the external world (trust). Moreover, when difficulties in oral and gastrointestinal functioning, lack of skin comfort, or other primitive gratification, contribute to overwhelming and persistent distress with autonomic flooding, the autonomous development of perceptual and other cognitive functions may be jeopardized.

The baby's persistent efforts to achieve efficient sucking and feeding can be seen most clearly in those infants who have to cope with difficult nipples—those small or poorly erected nipples that are hard to grasp. The efficiency of the sucking reflex varies in different infants; babies also vary in their ability to get a thumb into the mouth, and we can observe the varying persistence of effort to cope with this problem.

Mild discomforts that the young infant can handle through motor coping devices such as turning away, wiggling into a different posture or position in the crib can stimulate effective coping efforts from the age of a few weeks. Success in these efforts reinforces the tendency to make further spontaneous coping efforts, to devise new solutions to problems.

Along with motor solutions to discomfort, the baby may comfort himself when hungry, or alone without stimulation, through sucking on thumb, fingers, or fist; or such sucking may be continued after feeding when, as the mother says, "He didn't get enough sucking out of it." When the early balance of oral and motor solutions to discomfort problems is too heavily weighted on the oral zone, interference with development of motor coping efforts may result. Interactions of gratification and frustration in the oral and motor zones can lead to varying patterns of readiness for more mature use of each.

Broadly speaking, survival implies another basic task of the infant: to grow up at a pace consistent with optimal functioning and use of his own equipment and the development of his capacities, in cooperation with appropriate stimulus, support, and protection from the environment. Every organ of perception, motility, cognition, and so forth, requires nutriment and exercise for adequate development.

Thus stimulus management is another basic coping task in relation to the following: (1) evoking enough and sufficiently relevant stimulation for the development of specific aspects of perceptual-motor and other cognitive functioning as well as to meet social and affective needs; (2) protection against excessive or painful stimulation; (3) selecting the stimuli needed for gratification of individual interests and needs, for progressive familiarization with the environment, for exercise of currently emerging functions, and for extension of variety needed to maintain alertness.

In view of much recent research (Brackbill 1967), the baby needs not only some degree of pattern or complexity, but also enough newness to maintain the eagerness that we later ascribe to curiosity. By now we can think of the primitive searching and scanning efforts of the young baby as part of the active effort to find perceptual and cognitive nutriment. Curiosity is as important in the effort to support cognitive development as food finding and ingestion are important to support physical growth. The coping aspect of this can be seen in some babies of two to three months—or in our sample, even in a baby of four weeks—who struggle for a vertical posture that brings a more complex scene within visual range than is available when the baby is held in a supine position.

Emerging integrative functions of the ego include the organization of perceptual traces (cognitive map-building) (Tolman 1948); the mobilization of motor resources in goal-directed action evident in the early stretching to reach and bang a toy hanging from the crib; developing both the capacity to accept substitutes at times and to wait at times. Primitive precursors of imitation can be seen in some three-month-old babies' effortful approximations of the grown-up's waggling tongue. Along with the baby's efforts to adapt his posture comfortably to the mother's holding pattern, this can be seen as part of the baby's active coping with tasks involving ways of relating to the mother and other persons in the environment.

Active participation in the development of basic relationships to other persons as differentiated individuals (with or without exclusive attachment to the mother) is another major task of the first year. This involves the infant's ways of evoking satisfying action from the caretaker in times of need, mutually responsive communication, and affective exchange. These contribute to foundations for basic identification.

Closely related to the above are the complex efforts to cope with loss, separation, and unexpected or extreme change. Although we can almost literally watch the effort of some babies to master the environment with a protracted, intent, focused gaze, we feel less sure of the inner aspects of coping with loss and with separation. I have watched closely the reactions of babies in a hospital foundling ward when I had to leave after a period of play. In each case I had held the baby on my lap, feeding, fondling, talking to, and playing with the baby. In each case I put the baby down with a toy in his bassinet or crib. One baby reached out to hold and to stroke the sleeve of my bright, textured suit. A second turned to his toy, a balloon suspended from the foot of his bassinet, kicking, then reaching over to scratch, pat, and push it. A third focused his gaze on decorative plaques on the wall. A fourth turned away, apparently oblivious to the environment. It was as if he had totally lost interest in (decathected) the world—or as if, when I put him down, he felt that "Nothing exists for me anymore." His body went limp and flaccid, and he seemed to be coping by total renunciation, instead of by using one or another of the substitutes available in the environment as the other babies did.

These were all babies about four months old, and I have illustrated these coping devices to underscore how crucial the baby's response to the task of coping with separation may be for the development of his relation to the environment. With the first baby, some of the pleasure of the interaction with me was used in his stroking of, and playing with, substitutes as I had stroked and played with him. The baby who looked at the wall decorations might be more inclined to develop fantasy resources for coping. The last baby seemed unable to cope actively at all without sustained support. I felt that I was seeing a possible precursor of autistic development (and I strongly urged that he be placed as soon as possible with a responsive foster family).

I have tried so far to illustrate how each basic zone of adaptive equipment—oral, perceptual, motor—involves its own range of coping tasks and resources. These arise from the interrelation of the baby's equipment and what the environment provides. Thus a baby with poorly integrated sucking reflexes has to work at improving his sucking, and a baby who copes with a poor nipple has to struggle with that. In the latter case, the coping task is greater if along with a poor nipple his sucking pattern is poorly integrated.

COPING WITH DISCOMFORT AND FRUSTRATION

Now suppose we look at the general problem of discomfort in the young baby. What can he do if he is uncomfortable—from muscle fatigue, boredom, wet or soiled diapers, too bright lights, unpleasant noises, too long offering of the bottle or breast, or any of the myriad conditions that can make a baby uncomfortable? We scrutinized and rated the baby's coping efforts at whatever period within the first six months he was studied by Escalona's team. Interestingly enough, our ratings correlated with later behavior far beyond our expectations (Murphy and Moriarty, to be published). Capacity to protest or to terminate unwanted stimulation at this early age was significantly correlated with later active coping with the environment.

Now what does this mean for our cherished concept, frustration tolerance? I think we are learning the hard way that frustration tolerance may be a much overrated capacity. Certainly the people of India (and of some other developing countries) developed frustration tolerance (and resignation) to the nth degree, and we are spending millions of dollars and much human effort to help them give up some of this and cope more actively with their needs for food, sanitation, prevention of illness, and so forth. Similarly, the passivity developed in southern Negroes through generations of resigned tolerance has had tragic consequences. The capacity to do something to change frustration to progressive satisfaction, whether by slow, piecemeal steps or with revolutionary speed, may run less risk than static tolerance. And the capacity to cope actively with frustration begins in earliest infancy; it can be encouraged and directed or starved to atrophy. Probably the optimum is the development of enough frustration tolerance to support the delay involved in slow progress toward reaching a goal; in other words, to support a sustained coping effort.

THE CONTRIBUTION OF MOTHERS

Mothers differ widely in their response to the young baby's coping efforts. Some mothers regard the small baby as helpless and try to anticipate every need and protect him from every discomfort. When carried to an extreme this does not allow him to discover his own coping capacities. Other mothers support and encourage coping efforts as they are spotted—when the baby of two or three months stretches and wiggles to be held in a more vertical situation, they help him with pillows or a different slant to the babyseat, in response to his own active effort. Still other mothers instigate coping efforts by holding a toy just out of reach to stimulate the baby to "come and get it," or stretch for it. But some mothers determinedly defeat the baby's initiative or struggles by forcibly pushing him down with a threatening remark, "You lie down there," by ignoring signals for help or gratification of needs, and by suppressing his cries—one of his few ways of communicating before language matures.

CRITICAL PHASES

Special coping problems are involved at times of "sensitive phases" or "critical phases" (Scott 1962). These terms are sometimes differentially referred to as the period of emergence (but still incomplete integration) of new evolving functions, or the time period when stimulation is required specifically for consolidation of a new process or function, as in the critical phase for imprinting as discussed by ethologists (Lorenz 1953). With infants, as we saw, the first days after birth may be considered a critical phase for the integration of early feeding mechanisms; but the whole first year (during which the infant triples his weight) is a phase when oral needs are intense, although often no more important than the infant's need for contact, for adequate stimulation (nutriment), for all the basic sensory-motor functions, for the integration of basic motor skills, and for the establishment of the primary human relationships.

Thus a series of critical phases for coping may be seen in the first year of life as new functions are emerging, functions involved in handling the tasks outlined above. These may be roughly summarized as follows, with the proviso that wide individual differences in timing of the emergence of function have been documented in many investigations. Chapters in Brackbill's *Behavior in Infancy and Early Childhood* (1967) document the following:

1. The first weeks after birth are critical for organic integration and the related sense of well-being, as mentioned above.
2. At four to eight weeks the emergence of more coordinated, sustained, and selective looking and listening presents a sensitive phase for perception, with a danger of apathy in the case of understimulation. This does not mean that perception "begins" at this time; the "orienting reflex" may even interrupt feeding in the newborn (Sokolov 1958). Newborn visual fixation, scanning, preference for pattern and for movement are all evidence of the early steps in development of perceptual capacities (Stone, Smith, and Murphy 1973). Even very young infants apparently need stimuli of some degree of complexity as indicated by recent evidence for their preferential responses to patterns, to movement, and to change. The emergence of the "smile of recognition" (Erikson 1963) in response to the human face parallels the increased organization of visual and auditory perception.
3. At about four months or later, differing with different infants, the beginning emergence of differentiation between self and the external world (Jacobson 1954) is a sensitive phase for the consolidation of both objectivity and a delighted response to stimulation as opposed to a confused or suspicious, affectively loaded perception of the external world. Normally at this stage we see a peak of joyful, eager response to social stimulation, and beginnings of deliberate and vivid, if still vague, affecto-motor behavior to evoke interaction with other persons. The suspicious or hostile orientation may become patterned or fixed

when persistent acute distress (presumably accompanied by autonomic upheaval and flooding of the brain with chemical by-products) prevents adequately neutral or serene perceptual development. This can be seen most vividly in extreme cases of unreachable, frantic, disorganized children who are not merely "emotionally disturbed" at a later stage, but who do not have foundations for dependably satisfying perceptions.

The development of discrimination between self and the world is supported by the emergence of more active sensory-motor interactions with major objects in the environment. Now the infant has the task of extending his repertoire of resources for making something (pleasurable) happen.

Persistent experience of both strong pleasant and unpleasant reactions to the same stimulus before the maturation of capacity for differentiation of aspects of objects in relation to varying levels of gratification and frustration may contribute a predisposition to ambivalence that shapes responses to new objects. Conflicts arising from this ambivalence present another kind of coping problem, as seen in our subjects.

4. Parallel with the basic self-object differentiation is the discrimination between factors relevant and irrelevant to pain or pleasure. Memory of painful inoculations is global during the early months; anxiety regarding anticipated pain is aroused by perception of the doctor's office or the doctor in a white coat, in contrast to the only gradually differentiated association of anxiety specifically with the inoculating needles (Levy 1960). The task of learning exactly what to blame or to be anxious about thus involves increasing differentiation of threatening parts in an experience-whole, which generally develops only from six months on.

5. At six to eight months, differentiated recognition of mother in contrast to strangers has emerged or is emerging, although some infants show this much earlier. We find now a sensitive phase for separation-anxiety and for anxiety regarding the stranger. Some infants are able to cope with the task of mastering this anxiety within a few weeks, and Buhler included this capacity as an eight-months developmental test (1930). For other infants these sources of anxiety remain acute through the second year of life, or until autonomy in basic functions and pleasurable experiences with strangers have provided added security. A variety of coping devices may be developed to deal with anxiety regarding strangers, including strategic or self-protective withdrawal, and the elaboration of multiple ways of maximizing contact with the mother (turning toward, running to, climbing onto her lap, clutching at her skirt, and so forth).

6. Meantime, parallel with the increasing perceptual organization of the environment and discrimination between self and the environment is the increasing awareness of and cathexis of self (Jacobson 1954) that has to proceed to a point of clarity about what one can manage alone before separation from mother (as protector and buffer against the world) can be tolerated; this blossoms during the second year, intensified by the vivid consciousness of control of the body as toilet training is accomplished, and also control of the environment.

Fundamental for these basic tasks of achieving secure and gratifying differentiation between self and the world, and the sense of control of both, are the motor developments (rolling over, sitting, standing, creeping, beginning to walk) that present a multitude of challenges to the infant, new opportunities for information about the world, ways of using it, and both potential gratification and potential pain to be encountered in his explorations. The earliest motor activities do not come as automatically as examiners may think when they test babies on a monthly schedule. When we watch babies in home settings we see the daily struggle, the sometimes defeated, gradually more successful efforts to turn over, then to creep. Each new step in progress is the outcome of such repeated efforts. The baby also has to learn to cope with the dangers of collisions as soon as he learns to creep, as well as to avoid hot or sharp or other hurtful objects.

The major body achievement of a vertical position (standing, walking) often brings the first excited expressions of triumphant mastery, after endless struggles to pull up, to maintain balance, to hold on. Even when holding on to the railing of a playpen, some babies cannot maintain a standing position for long. They drop down to rest, then struggle up again.

Such achievements contribute to new dimensions of the sense of well-being that arises not only from sensations associated with good vegetative functioning, but also from striped muscle sensations involved in the successful practice of the new coordination. These experiences of delight in mastery, or triumph, are doubtless important in motivating the further efforts needed to move on to new stages of control, and of integration of basic skills with more complex interactions with the personal and the impersonal world.

The period of first emergence of *any* of these skills may be a sensitive phase: Shirley (1931) and others have noted instances of inhibition of walking after it had begun, following painful encounters or falls, doubtless at a time of sensitization increased by other factors. And we had records at Sarah Lawrence of infants whose motor efforts were defeated by being tied into the crib, or kept in a playpen too long. When such an infant copes by resignation, the ego increments of autonomy normally contributed by this phase of emerging motor skill as discussed by Erikson (1963) are lost, and active coping efforts are reduced.

The infant's capacity for expression and communication of wants, needs, frustrations, pleasure, and unhappiness actually begins after birth with crying. This is at first a reflex, but is soon used as an expression of discomfort or need of attention, and a device for evoking response from the adult. As the mother recognizes the infant's increasingly differentiated expressions of protest, demand, interest, hunger, or pain, as well as expressions of comfort and delight that develop during the first months, she is increasingly able to respond appropriately to her perception of "his hungry cry," or "his tired cry." The mutual responses of baby and mother lead not only to increased smiles and vocalization, but also to further differentiation of the baby's communication and his perception of expressions and communications from his mother.

By the age of eight months babies have been observed to differentiate between different emotional expressions from the mother (Buhler 1930), although even earlier some babies can be inhibited by controlling words expressed by the mother, such as "shh," or "no, no." This marks a new stage in the use of communication. Imitation of the differentiated actions and expressions of the mother is increased and further extends the coping resources of the baby.

Each child, including each baby, however young, has to get along in his culture, meet its demands, put up with the frustrations it imposes, and exploit its opportunities while at the same time accomplishing even more basic tasks, namely: (1) achieving sufficient equilibrium or balance to support all vegetative functions important for survival; (2) managing sufficient intake of nutrition and exercise to support all aspects of physical, including neurological, maturation; (3) activating and developing adaptive resources, including sensory, perceptual, and sensory-motor activity; (4) memory and recognition; (5) mastery of space, and development of a cognitive map to guide explorations of the environment; (6) developing selective investments in, and affective responses to, specifics in the environment that fit the idiosyncratic capacities for gratification of the individual child; and (7) evolving sustained relationships sufficiently profound to evoke identification with satisfying individuals who can serve as models of the society in which the child must come to feel he belongs.

All of these contribute to, and make possible, some modulation and guidance of drives in a way that integrates them with these adaptive resources.

A series of developmental *paradigms* will highlight the individuality of coping problems of the very young infant.

1. In the earliest feeding experiences:
    a. If sucking reflexes do not function smoothly, the baby has to work at improving his sucking technique. (Variations in pattern result, as with some babies sucking is a matter of lips alone, while with others there is more use of suction from the cheeks.)
    b. He has to deal with the problem of "enough." Some babies terminate decisively, ejecting the nipple, pulling away from the nipple, keeping the lips closed, turning the head away, and so on. Others do not do this, but just stop sucking.
    c. Food preferences: Infants differ in their response to different tastes and textures of food. As soon as variety and semisolids are introduced, the baby has to cope with those he doesn't like. He may clamp his mouth shut, refusing to take in distasteful food, or push it out of his mouth, or wriggle or get fussy, or even cry in protest.
    d. Fatigue: Some small or weak babies get tired before they have taken as much as they need or want. They may rest a bit, then return to sucking, in contrast to energetic infants who finish the bottle without stopping.
    e. Difficulties may arise with the mother's nipples when they are inverted or poorly erected; or with the flow of milk. Some babies pat or knead the breast or jab at the nipple with their mouths, as if to rectify these conditions.
2. Babies differ in their tactile needs and responses, and in their ways of coping with tactile contact:

a. Some babies seem to crave the sense of being surrounded, as when cuddled into a corner, and even four-week-old babies and younger have been observed to wriggle into a corner or to one end of the crib.

b. Babies differ in their need or craving to be held: some protest when put down, while others do not; some infants wriggle restlessly and distastefully when they are held, or held in unpreferred ways.

3. Sensory stimulation has different values for different infants:

a. Some as young as two months will protest being in a position where they cannot see anything.

b. Some cope with departure of the grown-up by turning to visual stimuli; others turn to tactual stimuli such as toys, or they rub the blanket, scratch the side of the crib, and so on, or induce sensory experience by banging, bouncing, rocking themselves.

4. The maturation of motor resources and development of motor skills is of greater interest to some babies than others, and those who are "motor-minded" will struggle persistently to perfect a nascent skill:

a. Some four-month-old babies have been observed to push repeatedly in the effort to turn over, "practicing" the necessary movements of coordinated pushing and turning until they succeed.

b. The Escalona-Leitch records (1949) contain an observation of a twenty-four-week-old baby struggling to get up on all fours. Over a period of thirty-five minutes the baby pushed up until he was exhausted, collapsed and rested, sucking his thumb, then pushed up again until he finally succeeded. Similar efforts are seen in many babies as they struggle to master creeping, pulling up to a standing position, and walking. After they have mastered walking, they have to develop techniques for managing falls, and recovery from falls.

5. Management of space—avoiding collisions, circumventing obstacles—presents new coping problems: these involve coordination of space perception and motility, memory, development of a cognitive map, and others, and also utilization of these functions in the use of opportunities provided by the environment. Control of motor impulses so as not to fall out of infant chair, high chair, or walker also involves a coordination of space perception with memory of consequences, and inhibition of sudden movement.

6. Infants differ in their perception of strangeness, their timing of this, their cognitive-affective reaction, and their ways of coping with stranger-anxiety if it is aroused. Records by Katherine Wolf and others note anxious reactions to strangers as early as twelve and sixteen weeks. Avoidance, withdrawing, protest, seeking comfort from the mother, are different ways of coping with such anxiety when it is aroused.

7. Loss of mother may arouse anxiety at any age from three to four months on, more usually from six months on—after a baby has become capable of differentiating mother from others (Murphy 1964).

8. Pain: Let us now use the paradigm of an infant who was received an immunization shot from a strange man in a white coat, in a strange room full of strange things, in a building he never went to before. Most babies scream. It hurts. And they remember. The differentiation of memory will affect what they have to cope with on the next trip.

a. One baby will begin to cry when mother brings him to that building.

b. Another will cry when they enter the office.

c.   Another will cry only when he sees the doctor in the white coat.

d.   Only *one* six-month-old baby in 2,000 was able to keep details sufficiently separate so that he did not cry until he saw the needle (Levy 1960). (Smart baby to know that the needle and *only* the needle was what hurt him.)

The baby's coping problem will be influenced also by (1) the individual pattern of his sensory responses, and (2) his reaction to the shot. Many factors are involved here. Babies differ in their skin sensitivity, pleasure or discomfort in being handled, sensitivity to temperature changes, and to pain; and they differ in their feelings about posture and lying supine. So the experience is quite different for different infants. One baby does not mind being laid down on the doctor's table, where another dislikes it and protests. One doesn't mind removal of his clothes, and another feels chilled all too easily. For one the shot itself is a passing twinge and for another an acute pain.

Their bodies react differently too. One gets a rise in temperature, another loses his appetite for a few days, another suffers continued discomfort from a large, red swelling at the site of the shot, and so on.

A shot is a routine assault by the environment, which all the babies have to put up with. But the exact experience differs widely from one baby to the next, and many babies experience one or another sort of threat to integration.

Depending upon the coping styles developed to that point, one may retreat into extra sleep, another withdraws or becomes moody and unresponsive, while another cries until comfort comes. If sleep is healing enough so that the pain is lessened by the morrow, integration may be gradually restored. If comfort is successfully soothing and the baby is consoled, not only is integration restored, but trust in the environment as well. I deliberately used the phrase "if the baby is consoled" because some babies seem inconsolable, and when this is the case, restoration of integration comes far more slowly, and the baby's threshold for experiencing threat may be lowered.

The Widening World of Childhood: Paths toward Mastery (Murphy 1962) was based on the preschool observations. Now, years later, the young children in that book have graduated from high school, are getting married, starting work, or going to college. We have seen them through the anxieties of shifting to junior high school, the shock of the assassination of President Kennedy, the fascination of America's worst tornado; and Drs. Moriarty and Toussieng have interviewed them on the threshold of adulthood. Over these years Dr. Heider has studied vulnerability in infants and young children (1966), Dr. Moriarty has studied continuity and changes in cognitive functioning (1966), Drs. Riley Gardner and Moriarty (1968) have reported on the relation between cognitive functioning and personality structure, and numerous other reports have been presented. Also, Dr. Irene H. Wiemers and I have made an intensive analysis of infants aged one month and four months to document the range of individual differences to be seen at this early age (Wiemers and Murphy, to be published).

Although our subjects represented a normal sample—and this was confirmed later by Wayne Holtzman's evaluation of the HIT scores obtained at the puberty stage—we early became aware of vulnerabilities in certain children and the relation of these vulnerabilities to their experience of stress

(Murphy and Moriarty, to be published) and their coping tasks. We also became aware of the sequences of stress that they experienced, and Alice Moriarty made a preliminary report on this to a staff conference in 1960. The circular relation between vulnerability and stress experience was highlighted by the children's responses to a questionnaire about their reactions to President Kennedy's assassination (Ginsparg and Moriarty 1969).

THE VULNERABILITY CONTINUUM

In comparison with a clinic group, it should be remembered that in our sample, infants with defects were excluded insofar as this could be determined in the pediatric examination at that time. Also, infants whose parents had marked illness or emotional disturbance or defect were excluded, along with illegitimate infants and those from the lowest socioeconomic group. None was living in slum conditions, or was extremely mobile, or alienated (most were church members). And the group included none from minority groups. Thus, both on the organic dimension and on the sociocultural dimension, "high risk" infants were excluded. Our group began as a "normal" sample with the possible exception of an instance where the father died during the mother's pregnancy.

But these children, as noted above, revealed patterns of vulnerability and ways of handling vulnerability that were not foreseen at the beginning of this study. If we consider that many, if not most, children regarded as disturbed have had to deal not only with environmental frustrations, deprivations, and other stress, but also their own frailties of many sorts, we can think in terms of a continuum of vulnerability. At one end we would place the most vulnerable infant, frail, perhaps defective, poorly integrated, so lacking in equipment for survival that his chances of growing up even with the best of care were slight. At the other end, the relatively invulnerable baby would be the one who is so robust, adaptable, and resilient that he can survive even severe deprivation, mishandling, and environmental stress.

Because the extremes of defect and likelihood of severe mishandling or deprivation were excluded from our group, we are confined to a relatively narrow range of vulnerability. Yet from this narrow range we have learned a great deal. The very exclusion of extremes has forced us to look more carefully and to consider the implications of the child's subjective situation from more different angles.

When we began to study the preschool children, we observed in some of them overt evidence of decreased smoothness or effectiveness of functioning under the stress of excitement, threat of failure, or conflicts and anxiety evoked by projective tests. We added the pediatrician's observations, mild defects such as flat feet, acquired hearing loss, allergies, autonomic lability, and low thresholds for tension-arousal; and observations by the team as a whole of extremes of activity or passivity, extreme sensitivity or reactivity to stimulation in any modality, variable positive and negative response to different degrees or qualities of stimulation in one modality, among other patterns in the individual children.

As we worked toward an understanding of the children's coping capacity we saw that specific patterns, and also interacting tendencies, interfered with the capacity of some children to cope with the environment and with the ability of others to maintain sufficient equilibrium to support optimal functioning. Heider (1966) undertook the intensive study of vulnerability in infancy and at the preschool stage.

Typical vulnerable children showed some combination of the following: they were firstborn; they had had pregnancy or birth difficulties; they were colicky babies and were hard to comfort; they showed a labile pattern of autonomic reactivity; they were accelerated in certain areas and average or behind their age level in other areas of development—thus finding it hard to integrate the range of basic functions; they had zones of high sensitivity (or reactivity to specific stimuli) or of highly ambivalent responsiveness (intensely pleased by one level or degree of stimulation, then displeased by a slightly more intense or different level).

STRESS

In this subculture, although many gross diseases have been eliminated, several children were still subject to frequent upper-respiratory infections and secondary illness related to these, as well as to other illnesses. Minor defects, such as flat feet and handicaps due to heredity, pregnancy, or birth difficulties, and consequences of severe illnesses such as polio, were present in certain children. Accidents injured some children, or members of their families; death came to some close relatives or to family pets during the children's early years. Unemployment of the father and moving caused insecurity directly and indirectly to some children. Marital strains, depressiveness in the mother, alcoholism in the father were disturbing to a few.

Marked shifts from freedom to restrictions are typically experienced as the infant grows from a relatively limited baby to an active exploring child and as he moves from the preschool stage to the rigidities of school where pressures for achievement also mount through the years. We have to think of the multidimensional "normal expectable stress" for any group (greater for low socioeconomic groups and some minority groups, with their greater economic, health, and familial difficulties—but these were not represented in our sample).

However, the impact of, or the stressfulness of, specific or combined pressures, frustrations, or pain differs with different children depending on constitutional and acquired thresholds (or sensitivities), affective and autonomic lability, consequences of previous traumata, conflicts, anxiety, or suspicion, the subjective or objective mitigating factors, and effectiveness of defenses. One family "feels poor," while another family, which is equally hard-pressed economically, finds itself low on money—but not on spirit. A wide range of factors in the child, both organic and psychological, affect the stressfulness to the individual of any particular experience.

RESILIENCE

We did not really bring resilience into focus until recently. In cases where a child showed disintegrative reactions under stress, we found that we wanted to talk about recovery and resilience as well as recovering from autonomic upsets as seen in the medical examination. For instance, a child functioning very smoothly when comfortable became jerky or disorganized under excitement or anxiety; or a child regressed and behaved in a more infantile way, thumbsucking or just acting like a baby, then recovered from this. When the recovery to smooth, appropriate functioning was quick and stable, we thought of the child as resilient. This is not exactly the same as coping, because although coping efforts may contribute to recovery, there is something underneath that gives the push and contributes to the flexibility or the possibility of being resilient—whether it is recovery from such relatively minor things as I have described or from depression or even from illness. Readiness to recognize, trust, and welcome progress was associated with Helen's progress. Helen was described by Heider (1966) as one of her vulnerable babies who was ill a great deal through infancy and the preschool stage; but she could still manage for herself. As an infant, when she got too tired she learned to signal to her mother that she would rather be left alone, and at the preschool level she would alternate between being very active and responsive and taking time out to be quiet. About the age of seven or eight she was found to have a combination of the upper-respiratory difficulty she had been having all along, with a very bad kidney infection as well. Finally, her tonsils were taken out, and she became quite a healthy child.

The intriguing thing was that she was so ready to be somebody different, that there was no persistence of the sick little girl who had had to have a lot of attention before. Now she could move into life in the way she had always wanted to. When she was about ten I asked her how she was able to change so much. Her answer was interesting. She said, "Well, I know that bad things can turn into good things"; and I asked, "How do you know?" She said, "After my operation my grandmother took me to visit her in California and out of her house I could see the lights of Hollywood and she took me to Disneyland." In other words, this linked the painful illnesses and operation with something very good. Some people would interpret this as an image selected to represent what she had internalized from early experiences of the alternation between being unwell and then getting better, between being exhausted and then getting rested. And here comes the mystery part of it. Why didn't she develop a pattern of "I no sooner get rested and feel good than I get tired again," a negative pattern instead of a positive pattern?

A clue that I was interested in was that one of the things she could do for herself when she was a little baby of six months old was to elaborate oral pleasure. She could bubble, mouth her toys, suck her thumb, and do ten or twelve different things with her tongue, lips, and mouth. She was very playful, and, for a little baby, creative. So it seemed to me that this capacity to do something for herself that was fun and satisfying was one clue. Incidentally, around the age of eleven she got four 4-H prizes in the county fair, and there were other instances of ways in which she elaborated or multiplied sources of gratification. Her mother had had postpartum depression, had been somewhat distant, and, all the observers thought, not completely satisfying or sensitive to the child. Perhaps what happened was that very early the autonomous discovery of ways of getting satisfaction for herself, which evidently chased away the discomforts, became formulated for her in this central orientation to life.

There are enormous individual differences in the reactions of babies, first, to pain stimuli, like shots, and second, to the soothing that you try to give them. This involves detailed study of many different aspects of the equipment: of the child's skin sensitivity and how much of the sensitivity produces satisfaction, so that being cuddled and patted induces a positive experience that is introjected at the expense of the pain experience, which then is displaced or fades out.

Another connection between infancy and later experience in relation to resilience is suggested in our positive correlations between an infant's capacity to protest, or to terminate something it didn't like, and later coping capacity. At the earliest level, an infant may push out food that it doesn't want. Sometimes babies will clamp their mouths shut if they don't want any more, or push out the food with their tongues, or just roll it around in their mouths and not swallow it, and in some way make it very clear that they are just not going to put up with it. In other words, at a very young age, at two or three months, the babies are coping very actively and in ways that can remove the unpleasant stimulus.

There's one other kind of thing. Our polio child, whom I'm calling Ann, tended to be fairly easily upset as an infant. She was colicky, and she had skin sensitivity that contributed to some discomfort. When she cried, her mother would pick her up, hold her, and laugh with her to induce laughter to displace the crying. The cuddling and gay playfulness were part of this mother's way of helping her. Ann became an extraordinarily resilient child. In the sessions I had with her when she was eight, she drew clowns. The clowns were colorful and jolly, but each one had a limping, distorted left leg like Ann had after polio.

When she had to go to the hospital at the age of ten to have nine vertebrae fused in a five-hour operation, she was completely immobilized. The services provided by the nurses on the surgical ward for children was totally inadequate in Ann's case; for instance, while she was lying in a cast from her chin to her hips, unable to turn or to reach anything, a nurse put a complex jigsaw puzzle on a litter next to hers. It was useless to her—she couldn't even get a good look at it. I asked her afterward what she would try to provide if she were running a hospital. She said, "Well, if you can't do anything at all, it would be nice if they could just send a clown around." In other words, the pattern of coping with pain by laughter and gaiety persisted from infancy.

Ann remained in a cast from her chin to her hips for a year, but she could get around two weeks after the operation. After she got out of the hospital, the question arose whether she could go to school. Her teacher thought it was nonsense to send a child in a cast like this back to school where she could not bend her back, her head, or her neck; she couldn't look down to see to read. Her father said, "No, she's going back to school, and I'll put up an easel at her desk. We'll put the books on the easel so that she can see them, and she'll be able to manage." So this was done. Ann then burlesqued her rigid posture; she moved around like a queen, in such an amusing way that all the boys came along to pick up her books and put them on the easel. She really made a very gay time out of it. Of course there was some denial in this, but what effective denial! How useful was her way of actively coping with the situation in the service of recovery, participation with other children, and making progress in school.

I went to the hospital to visit Ann after the operation, and I had picked her up and brought her over for the play sessions with me when she was first recovering from polio. I took Richard to the cemetery to see the grave of his mother when he hadn't been able to go to the funeral. Some of my staff went to another funeral when I wasn't able to go, and I went to graduations.

You would need to spend extensive time in a surgical ward of a hospital if you wanted to make a broad study of recovery patterns of children who had had severe operations. This is an important thing to do, and it ought to be done, but I was not able to add that on to the things that we were doing; we were busy just following our own subjects.

So we have been interested in processes contributing to recovery. Obviously, first of all is elimination of the stress by reducing infection with antibiotics, and so on; restitution by sleep, rest, or food in connection with fatigue or depletion of energy supplies after struggle. I mentioned above a baby who struggled for thirty-five minutes to turn over, and tried to get up on all fours. When exhausted, he would collapse and suck his thumb, then go at it again, until he finally succeeded. The restitutive value of his self-comfort and rest was important as a prerequisite to resumption of his efforts. Food and the gratification it provides also contribute to a child's valiant struggle. In Robert Coles's (1967) descriptions of black children facing the stress of integration, one of the grandmothers said, "Before she goes to school I give her grits and when she gets back from all that we have some ice cream." This very poor grandmother appreciated the support value of the oral treat as desperately important for this child struggling with the terrible tasks of getting along in the process of desegregation of a Mississippi school. The contribution of prosthetics is, of course, not just the action made possible, but the renewed hope for approximating normal functioning that is made possible. Fantasy can sustain an image of participation. When Ann was in a respirator for three months, she was lucky enough to have good nurses who caught on to her vivid imagination and kept entertaining her with stories about a little pink rabbit who was running down the hall. Ann was a child with enormous capacity for enjoying fantasy, even desperately sick as she was; the fantasy itself had a restitutive quality. Also under restitution, of course, we include substitute love-objects. Here the capacity to accept a substitute object is basic to making new friends when we move or in other ways lose old ones. Janice, moving from Topeka to Wichita at the age of twelve and missing all her Topeka friends, joined two churches and went to weekly Friday night dances at the Presbyterian church and monthly Saturday night dances at the Baptist church. This you might call the reaching for, exaggerating, and multiplying gratifications to compensate for the losses. Later, she got over that extreme kind of reaching out, but it helped her at that time. Certain children, including Lennie, who had had a severe loss experience at the critical age of nine months, had difficulty in making new friends when his family moved.

Changing the pain-pleasure balance, both through reduction of pain by soothing (there are great differences in children's capacities to be soothed) and the increase of pleasure through fun, love, work, narcissistic reward, is important here. When Richard lost his mother, his sister who was about seventeen years old took over very warmly and really mothered the younger children in a restorative way. This was a major factor in the children's resilience in that family.

Several chapters in this book discuss issues of cognitive mastery. I would like to emphasize one additional point: that is, the role of differentiation and cognitive mastery in limiting stress, in clarifying with oneself that it is this, but not this or this; or "I've lost this and this, but I still have this." The circumscribing of stress is important in holding on to the still positive resources and allowing them to contribute to resilience.

Strategic use of defenses was perhaps particularly clear with Teddy. After his parents were divorced, his mother's new husband got into terrible fights with the former husband. This was a very miserable time for Teddy. Finally the first father left town. Teddy is a wonderful boy, a musician, and doing extremely well in college. He said, "I've had two lives, my life with my first father and my life now; I've just got to forget the first." I call this strategic use of repression and forgetting. It helps Teddy, although he's paying a price for it because he's not letting himself remember and hold on to the very important good image his first father was in Teddy's first three years—an image that was internalized and made it possible for Teddy to become the kind of young man that he is now.

I also want to emphasize another point. We have talked so much about autonomy, and this is par for the course in discussions on maintenance of mental health; but the capacity to evoke help, to use help, to relate to new objects, and to accept support is equally important. In our children we see that a balance of autonomy and ability to use help is crucial for resilience.

Struggle for mastery depends upon available energy and also upon expectation and trust in future gratification; that is, the capacity to entertain fantasies of future gratification, believe them, and work toward them, to make your own wish come true.

The drive to grow, progress, and achieve, of course, is vivid in little children, as in Sally's comment at the age of four, "I'll eat lots of soup and I'll grow up and be big." Anna Freud has talked about this a great deal. The push to grow is a huge factor on the side of resilience in a child.

In addition to the efforts made by the child and his caretakers is the pressure from the environment and the "model of resilience." The cultural factors and the demand for resilience contribute to the emergence of it: for example, the resilient mother, father, grandmother, or whoever, who then expects you to be resilient and rewards your resilience. With a self-image as one who recovers, an image structured after there have been experiences of recovery, as with Sam and the accident described in *Widening World of Childhood* (Murphy 1962), the child comes to see himself as a person who is resilient and expects himself to recover.

The idea of a "propitious phase" for access of energy was suggested to me by observations of several children. One of them was Colin, one of the children from Sarah Lawrence Nursery School, written up as volume 2 of *Personality in Young Children* (Murphy 1956). He had a brief, but acute, illness at about the age of three and felt very helpless and confused. After that he went through a phase of being very aggressive, having to dominate and master everything and everybody. This surprised his teachers, because earlier he had been a cooperative, friendly, and not extremely aggressive little boy. The outburst of aggression at four seemed to utilize and to exaggerate the upsurging energies typically available in the phallic phase. He might not have been so successful in regaining his vitality and self-confidence at a critical phase.

I saw this same thing happening with another of our Topeka boys who had a mild case of polio at the age of three, followed by unexpected initiative and mobilization of energy in subsequent years.

This contrasts with the failure of development of autonomy and initiative in a child who was kept in a crib during infancy and until the age of two because of very severe infantile eczema. I saw the kind of thing that Erikson, Freud, and others have talked about—if a trauma, disturbance, or abnormal kind of experience happens during a phase in which an important function should be developing, then that function may not develop adequately. That was the picture with Rachel, who had been so restricted during the phase when autonomy is typically consolidated (Murphy and Moriarty, to be published). When we saw her at four, she was completely stymied in the play situation and every new situation. During all the years that we saw her, she was never able to move autonomously into any new situation. This contrasts with the children who had already developed autonomy, along with speech and motor skills, and who suffered the illness *after* basic ego functions had been consolidated, and when phallic phase energies were emerging. The propitious phase then provides energy that can be utilized for resilience.

Other favorable changes following recovery have been experienced either in ourselves or in watching our children. What I am calling the euphoric rebound, for instance, is illustrated by a child who has had braces on her teeth for two or three years, then is released from them with delight, excitement, and eagerness, the release of energy after recovery. We also see triumph of mastery and new sense of competence when a difficult skill is mastered, as with Darlene, reported in *Widening World of Childhood* (Murphy 1962). A tendency to accent the positive, as with Teddy, may involve constructive selective repression or forgetting. Similarly, a positive view of stress involves being able to appreciate the positive aspects that you were not aware of at first, that go along with some difficulties. This may be referred to as a "blessing in disguise," as with Helen's "Bad things can turn into good things," or, with several children, "I got stronger through it." Coles mentions this in some of his Mississippi children (1967).

Important sequelae of recovery may include the reinforced confidence in a therapy case, expressed in the child's statement, "I can put up with a lot"; or in the changed values after enormous threat, coming through it and surviving, then feeling, "It's good just to be alive." I mention this in relation to the tornado, but we also see this after recovering from dangerous operations or accidents. Reinforced hope, and expectations of the future, readiness to use support, new constructive defenses, are now part of the character and lower the threshold for recovery. And again—this last point is from therapy cases primarily—"I'm a new me," the child says when he feels the release from anxiety and the push to move into areas he didn't feel free to move into before. Most of these favorable outcomes, then, refer to the strength of ego and more positive self-image contributed by triumph over stress. In the records of Dr. Coles and in interviews with some of our Coping Project mothers, we see the reinforcement of *faith* that comes from positive outcomes of recovery efforts. The belief that "God was on our side" adds a deep support to the increased ego strength.

On prerequisites for resilience—and this bothers me most—I have listed energy reserves, one of the things that we watched in our early coping records—namely, the capacity to mobilize resources under stress, to be strained and yet still to be able to pull up extra energy, the "second wind" phenomenon, the positive physiological response to restitution when it is available. Then there is what Van der Waals calls "healthy narcissism," feeling good about oneself, wanting good for oneself, and feeling entitled to it. This is derived from very early infantile experience and is basic to the whole orientation toward what happens to you.

There is also the factor of flexibility. It seems to me that it is an extremely important variable in relation to recovery and resilience: flexibility in distribution of effort, and in affect; that is, to be able to feel differently in response to new perceptual structuring, to be able to see things differently, to modify defenses, to develop capacity for change.

Finally, there is yet another factor emerging from early infancy which also provides the capacity for responding to substitutes, new objects, and new opportunities: namely, the capacity for struggle and the constructive use of anxiety and of aggression. This facilitates fending off pressures, making it possible for the child to change the situation or his relation to it so as to release potential resilience. Imposing structures on the environment is included here. Integrative and creative drive has been emphasized in several of the chapters in this volume and I would include not just conscious creativity, but also, as Erikson (1963) has implied, unconscious creativity as it occurs in sleep and gives the child something to wake up with and go on with.

The biological model for resilience is self-healing, the capacity of many organisms to recover functions and even some body parts after damage. We must add to that (1) the infant's experience of recovery from pain as a result of shifted cathexis initiated by mothering or by autonomous efforts, (2) restoration of equilibrium after autonomic upheaval, (3) the child's experience of positive changes through growth, (4) the reinforcement of this sequence by repeated positive experiences, (5) the infant's and child's perception of such sequences, (6) the unconscious or conscious expectation that when pain occurs, recovery will follow, (7) the extended capacity to make relevant efforts to bring about or to help recovery.

Resilience can be conceived, then, as an active psychophysiological push to restore a satisfying state of being, evolving from a highly cathected psychic construct of experienced shifts from pain to pleasure, or disturbance to comfort, supported by the physiological capacities to resolve disruptions of smooth autonomic functioning by returning to optimal levels, and by the physiological capacity for self-healing. Coping efforts that institute steps to assist this process provide additional support, but do not in themselves constitute resilience; they are in part an expression of this active push from within.

SUMMARY

In this essay I have reviewed some of the major steps in the emergence of the coping concepts as we have developed them in our Topeka studies. I have not attempted to review the recent investigations that have focused on special problems of coping, nor the theoretical discussions that have sometimes attempted to divorce coping and defense mechanisms as opposite in their adaptive implications.

And I have not dealt with the important new potential of the coping concept both for individual therapy and for rehabilitation of the capacity for effort in the economically and culturally deprived and hopeless, or "copeless," sector of American life.

Rather, I have outlined in some detail steps in the development of coping capacity in childhood, and I have illustrated some of the processes and steps in coping that have contributed to resilience in children observed in our longitudinal study.

Further research is needed, and the most important questions require further longitudinal studies. Many investigators have reported on the lack of curiosity, differentiation capacities, problem solving, and integrative constructive play in seriously deprived preschool children. In view of the importance of mother-infant interaction for the development of the infants in our longitudinal series, it seems urgent to study the patterning of such interactions and their relation to the child's capacity for integrated functioning in all basic areas of response to the impersonal and personal environment. It has been customary to categorize the child's perceptual and perceptual-motor dealings with the impersonal environment as "cognitive," while his dealings with the human environment are classified as "social." It seems likely that underlying both are capacities for orientation, differentiation, organization, and integration of perception with action that are characteristic of the child's coping style. The seriously deprived children I have observed are equally inept in using mealtime tools, building with blocks, mobilizing a play group, and solving a new problem actively.

If we follow the Freud-Piaget paradigm that assumes that inner structures—organized and organizing—are formed through the infant's and child's active exchanges with the environment, we can infer that inadequate coping capacity as revealed in poor self-care, play, learning, organizing, and social functioning is a result of inadequate interaction in the first two years of life. Documentation for this hypothesis could be provided by careful observation of mother-infant interactions in families with multiproblem children as contrasted with those in families whose children play, learn, and get along well with peers and adults; that is, children who function adequately in both cognitive and social spheres. In such studies, elimination or control of organic factors differentially complicating the child's functioning would be necessary.

NOTES

1. Povl Toussieng is now Director of Child Psychiatry, University of Oklahoma Medical School.

2. Walter Kass is at the Albert Einstein College of Medicine, in the Department of Psychology.

REFERENCES

Anthony, E. J. The system makers: Piaget and Freud. *British Journal of Medical Psychology*, 1957, *30*, 255–269.

Bergman, P., and Escalona, S. Unusual sensitivities in very young children. *Psychoanalytic Study of the Child*, 1949, *3/4*, 333–352.

Bernardez, T. The feminine role. *Bulletin of the Menninger Clinic*, 1965, *29*, 198–205.

Bernfeld, S. *The psychology of the infant*. New York: Brentano, 1929.

Biber, B., Murphy, L. B., Woodcock, L. P., and Black, I. S. *Life and ways of the seven to eight-year-old*. New York: Basic Books, 1942.

Bowlby, J. *Maternal care and mental health*. 2nd ed. Geneva: World Health Organization, 1952.

Brackbill, Y., and Thompson, G. G., eds. *Behavior in infancy and early childhood*. New York: Free Press, 1967.

Buhler, C. *The first year of life*. Translated by P. Greenberg and R. Ripin. New York: John Day, 1930.

Chandler, C. A., Lourie, R. S., and Peters, A. D. *Early child care: new perspectives*. Edited by L. L. Dittmann. New York: Atherton, 1968.

Coelho, G. V., Hamburg, D. A., and Murphey, E. B. Coping strategies in a new learning environment. *Archives of General Psychiatry*, 1963, *9*, 433–443.

Coles, R. *Children of crisis: A study of courage and fear*. Boston: Atlantic Monthly Press, Little, Brown, 1967.

Darwin, C. *The origin of species by means of natural selection* (1859). With additions and corrections from the 6th and last English edition. New York and London: Appleton, 1912.

Davidson, J. Infantile depression in a "normal" child. *Journal of the American Academy of Child Psychiatry*, 1967, 7, 522–535.

Drillien, C. *Prematurely born infants*. Baltimore: Williams & Wilkins, 1964.

Engel, M. Children's insight test. *Journal of Projective Techniques*, 1958, *22*, 13–25.

Erikson, E. *Childhood and society*. 2nd ed. New York: Norton, 1963.

Escalona, S., and Leitch, M. The reactions of infants to stress. *Psychoanalytic Study of the Child*, 1949, *3*, 121–140.

Escalona, S., and Weider, G. *Prediction and outcome*. New York: Basic Books, 1959.

Frank, L. K. *On the importance of infancy*. New York: Random House, 1966.

Freud, A. Observations on child development. *Psychoanalytic Study of the Child*, 1951, *6*, 18–30.

———. *Normality and pathology in childhood*. New York: International Universities Press, 1965.

Freud, A., and Burlingham, D. *War and children*. New York: International Universities Press, 1943.

———. *Infants without families*. New York: International Universities Press, 1944.

Freud, S. *Three contributions to the theory of sex* (1905). Standard Edition, 1953, 7, 125–245.

———. *Group psychology and analysis of the ego* (1921). Standard Edition, 1955, *18*, 67–143.

———. *The ego and the id* (1923). Standard Edition, 1961, *19*, 3–66.

Gardner, R., and Moriarty, A. E. *Personality development at preadolescence: Explorations in structure formation*. Seattle: University of Washington Press, 1968.

Gesell, A., and Ilg, F. *Infant and child in the culture of today*. New York: Harper, 1943.

Ginsparg, S., and Moriarty, A. E. Reactions of young people to the Kennedy assassination. *Bulletin of the Menninger Clinic*, 1969, *33*, 295–309.

Ginsparg, S., Moriarty, A. E., and Murphy, L. B. Young teenagers' responses to the assassination of President Kennedy: Relation to previous life experiences. In M. Wolfenstein and G. Kliman, eds., *Children and the death of a president*. New York: Doubleday, 1965.

Grinker, R., Sr., Grinker, R., Jr., and Timberlake, J. "Mentally healthy" young males. *Archives of General Psychiatry*, 1962, *6*, 405–453.

Hall, G. S. The contents of children's minds. *Princeton Review*, 1883, *2*, 249–272.

Hamburg, D., Hamburg, B., and deGoza, S. Adaptive problems and mechanisms in severely burned patients. *Psychiatry*, 1953, *16*, 1–20.

Hartmann, H. The mutual influences in the development of ego and id. *Psychoanalytic Study of the Child*, 1952, *7*, 9–30.

———. *Ego psychology and the problem of adaptation*. New York: International Universities Press, 1958.

Hartmann, H., Kris, E., and Lowenstein, R. Comments on the formation of psychic structure. *Psychoanalytic Study of the Child*, 1946, *2*, 11–38.

Heider, G. Vulnerability in infants and young children. *Genetic Psychology Monographs*, 1966, *73*, 3–216.

Holtzman, W. *Inkblot perception and personality*. Austin: University of Texas Press, 1961.

Isaacs, S. *Intellectual growth in young children*. London: Routledge, 1930.

———. *Social development in young children*. New York: Harcourt, Brace, 1933.

Jacobson, E. The self and the object world. *Psychoanalytic Study of the Child*, 1954, *9*, 75–127.

Lerner, E., and Murphy, L. B. Methods for the study of personality in young children. *Monographs of the Society for Research in Child Development*, 1941, *6*(4).

Levy, D. The infant's earliest memory of inoculation: A contribution to public health procedures. *Journal of Genetic Psychology*, 1960, *96*, 3–46.

Lorenz, K. Z. *Discussions on child development*. New York: International Universities Press, 1953.

Luria, A. B. *The nature of human conflicts*. New York: Liveright, 1932.

Menninger, K. Psychological aspects of the organism under stress. *Journal of the American Psychoanalytic Association*, 1954, *2*, 67–106, 280–310.

Morgan, C. J. An individual action-research method for intensive exploration of adaptive difficulties in the prepuberty stage. *Journal of Psychology*, 1964, *58*, 439–458.

Moriarty, A. *Constancy and I.Q. change: A clinical view of relationships between tested intelligence and personality*. Springfield, Ill.: Charles C. Thomas, 1966.

Morrow, T. Providing growth experiences. *Bulletin of the Menninger Clinic*, 1965, *29*, 177–189.

Murphy, G., and Murphy, L. B. *Experimental social psychology*. New York: Harper, 1937.

Murphy, L. B. *Social behavior and child personality*. New York: Columbia University Press, 1937.

———. Symposia presented at the meetings of the American Psychological Association, 1954, 1955.

———. *Personality in young children*, vol. 2, *Colin: A normal child*. New York: Basic Books, 1956.

———. Learning how children cope with their problems. *Children*, 1957, *4*, 132–137.

———. A longitudinal study of children's coping methods and styles. In *Proceedings of the 15th International Congress of Psychology*. Amsterdam: North Holland Publishing Co., 1959.

———. Preventive implications of development in the preschool years. In G. Caplan, ed., *Prevention of mental disorders in children*. New York: Basic Books, 1961.

Murphy, L. B. *The widening world of childhood: Paths toward mastery.* New York: Basic Books, 1962.

————. Some aspects of the first relationship. *International Journal of Psychoanalysis,* 1964, *45,* 31–44.

Murphy, L. B., and Ladd, H. *Emotional factors in learning.* New York: Columbia University Press, 1944.

Murphy, L. B., and Moriarty, A. *Development, vulnerability and resilience.* To be published.

Piaget, J. *The origins of intelligence in children.* New York: International Universities Press, 1952.

Rheingold, H. The modification of social responsiveness in institutional babies. *Monographs of the Society for Research in Child Development,* 1956, *21*(2).

Rust, M. The effect of resistance on intelligence test scores of young children. *Child Development Monographs,* 1931, *6.*

Scott, J. P. Critical periods in behavioral development. *Science,* 1962, *138,* 949–958.

Shirley, M. *The first two years, a study of twenty-five babies.* Minneapolis: University of Minnesota Press, 1931.

Sokolov, E. N. *Perception and the conditioned reflex.* Moscow: Moscow University, 1958.

Stewart, C. *Adolescent religion.* New York and Nashville: Abingdon Press, 1967.

Stone, L. J. *This is Robert* (film). New York University Film Library.

Stone, L. J., Smith, H., and Murphy, L. B. *The competent infant.* New York: Basic Books. 1973.

Tolman, E. C. Cognitive maps in rats and men. *Psychological Review,* 1948, *55,* 189–208.

Toussieng, P., and Moriarty, A. *Responsive youth: A Midwest spectrum.* To be published.

White, R. Motivation reconsidered: The concept of competence. *Psychological Review,* 1959, *66,* 297–233.

Wiemers, I. H., and Murphy, L. B. Individuality in infants at four weeks and four months of age. To be published.

Witkin, H. A., Dyk, R. B., Faterson, H. F., Goodenough, D. R., and Karp, S. A. *Psychological differentiation: Studies of development.* New York: Wiley, 1962.

Wolf, K. Personal communication.

6

Early Adolescence: A Specific and Stressful Stage of the Life Cycle

BEATRIX A. HAMBURG

In the past two decades, there has been a steep upsurge of interest in, and concern about, adolescent behavior. At the present time, public opinion polls consistently reveal that for a majority of American people, problems of youth are viewed as a primary concern facing the nation. In some cases this concern has related to violent confrontations over social issues. For others there has been equal concern about the alienated, often drug-abusing, dropouts from society. There is general public awareness of the ever-increasing rises in youthful suicides and in rates of juvenile delinquency. It has been puzzling and alarming for us to realize that these severe problems are manifesting themselves in younger and younger age groups. Whereas concern had previously been focused on college-age students, it is painfully clear that some of the most flagrant examples of disturbing antisocial behavior are probably occurring in early adolescents in the junior high schools.

As a result of a long experience with school consultation, it has become clear to me that even for the modal individual, early adolescence is intrinsically a period of great stress, impoverished coping skills, and consequent high vulnerability. I have chosen to focus on this period (ages twelve to fifteen) because it would appear to be of crucial importance to understand the challenges of the biological and psychosocial variables that confront individuals at this time. In both of these arenas there is the sharpest possible discontinuity with the immediate past. In almost no sphere is it possible to draw on analogous past experience as a support or guide. Early adolescence is clearly a critical period of development that involves the negotiation of unique biological, psychological, and social demands. The adaptive challenge posed by *superimposed* tasks in this era has been underestimated. The nature of the discontinuities and challenges will be discussed at length.

The psychiatric literature on adolescence is vast and continues to proliferate. However, only recently has there begun to be an effort to look at the generic category of adolescence in a truly differentiated way. Early adolescence is an era that has suffered relative neglect in the literature. A review of the literature reveals that most current discussions deal predominantly with the cultural impacts on the late adolescent (college-age youth) as he is being socialized into adult roles. Until very recently, the literature was further skewed in that it tended to deal chiefly with males. There is need for reappraisal of this concept of a homogeneous "subculture" of adolescence, which has been fostered both in the popular press and in professional literature.

There is every reason to believe that at the present time the total adolescent period can and should be divided into three distinct eras that have their characteristic tasks, challenges, and coping possibilities. With the insidious lengthening of the adolescent period, we have now arrived at a situation in which there are two largely nonoverlapping critical developmental periods in the transition from childhood to adulthood. The contemporary length of the adolescent era has, in fact, led to a situation in which the middle period between early and late adolescence has become a third developmental stage of adolescence in its own right.

In Kestenberg's (1967) impressive studies there is a differentiated look at the category of adolescence. She discusses phases of adolescence in terms of psychic and hormonal correlations and also addresses herself to sex differences in the negotiation of these phases. Although she, too, sees adolescence as tripartite and would roughly make the same age divisions as I propose, her nomenclature is quite different. This perhaps points to the need for a standard set of reference terms. In any case, what I refer to as puberty or early adolescence is defined by her as prepuberty. According to her definition, "The onset of prepuberty is marked by an activation of inner genital organs and the appearance of secondary sex characteristics. Prepuberty diffusion coincides with a rapid increase in sex-specific hormones, and the subsequent reintegration parallels the regularization of sex-specific hormonal patterns." What I would refer to as middle adolescence is called puberty by Kestenberg. She states, "Puberty begins with the maturation of gonads (mature spermatazoa and ovulation)." Late adolescence in her nomenclature is the preadult phase of consolidation. Her discussion of all of these phases of adolescence is in terms of sex hormones, sex organs, and libidinal effects, with an emphasis on the reactivation and resolution of Oedipal conflicts (Kestenberg 1968).

As will be discussed, it is my impression that it may be misleading to view the changes of the gonadal hormones as preponderantly libidinal in their behavioral impacts. Nonetheless, it is certainly true that the dominant themes of early adolescence are related to the endocrine changes of puberty. However, these changes transcend the changes in secondary sex characteristics or libido. The other biological changes, such as changes in height, facial contours, fat distribution, muscular development, mood changes, and energy levels are of striking importance and function powerfully and independently in shaping the course of adolescent development. This chapter represents an effort to explore the tasks, challenges, and coping possibilities that face the biologically changing individual at a time of culturally imposed social and psychological stress.

The long period of adolescence that characterizes contemporary Western society is a product of influences that have acted to prolong adolescence at both ends. It has been prolonged at the inception of adolescence (puberty) due to biological effects that have lead to a secular trend toward the onset of puberty at an increasingly earlier age. Tanner (1962) has reported a trend for the lowering of the age of menarche by four months per decade. Thus, the average age of menarche in 1860 was sixteen and a half years. The average age today for comparable populations is twelve and a half years. This has generally been attributed to better nutrition, in particular, to more protein and calories in early infancy. The overall improvement of health and lessening of debilitating childhood disease probably has also contributed (Tanner 1971). Undoubtedly, there are other as yet unspecified factors that play a role in hastening the biological changes that mark the beginning of adolescence. In males, comparable events of puberty show a lag of roughly two years (Blizzard et al. 1970), but it is assumed that the same secular trend is reflected in males as well.

The termination of adolescence is characterized by a change in social status. The induction into adult social roles is taking place at an increasingly older age in Western industrial society. There are those who view the phenomenon of contemporary adolescence as a social invention chiefly designed to keep young people out of the labor force as long as possible (Eisenberg 1970). A common definition of the end point of adolescence is the achievement of an adult work role. Ideally, this includes the pursuit of a goal in which talents are used, interests are focused, and a sense of efficacy is established. This commitment to work generally occurs in a context of autonomy and renegotiation of the relationship to the nuclear family. The newly achieved independence should not mean estrangement, but rather a new level of adult-adult relationship that is based on more equality and mutual respect. This generally involves a more realistic appraisal of the family with an acceptance of shortcomings and an appreciation of assets. Finally, there is the challenge of intimacy and the establishment of a stable, mature heterosexual relationship. Mutuality and the ability to relate tenderly and with trust are issues of importance in this task. Clearly, the end point of adolescence is a complex matter with more than one adult role to be negotiated. In addition to the tasks just described above, there are adult responsibilities such as voting, conscription into the army, legal age for drinking of alcohol, and legal responsibility for making valid contracts. These varied adult rights and responsibilities have no regular pattern. This ambiguity about admission into adult roles, and consequent termination of adolescence, is often experienced as a stress in its own right. The entry into adolescence, or puberty, would appear to be simpler and more clear-cut. This assumption will be examined.

The earliest and, at one time definitive, description of adolescence was the encyclopedic two-volume work of G. Stanley Hall in 1904. Basically, he defined adolescence in biological terms as the period spanning the time from the changes of puberty to full adult physical growth. Hall also heavily emphasized the inevitability of storm and stress during adolescence and perceived this turbulence as a function of instinctive behaviors. These strongly biological notions were never appealing to his colleagues and, when coupled with his own version of social Darwinism, they soon fell into professional neglect. It is notable that even as early as 1928 in the preface to a standard textbook on the psychology of the adolescent, Hall's work was dismissed as being "of historic value primarily rather than of scientific or practical value today" (Hollingworth 1928).

The tendency for the pendulum to swing sharply toward a cultural, rather than a biological, explanation of adolescence was given impetus by Margaret Mead in 1930 when she published *Coming of Age in Samoa* and pointed out the overriding importance of cultural determinants in shaping the course of adolescent development. She described a simple culture in which there was a very early introduction of children (ages six and seven) to aspects of adult roles and she depicted their gradual, smooth movement toward assumption of full adult status without any of the turbulence previously described as biologically inevitable by Hall. This cultural relativism was reiterated and underscored by other anthropologists (Benedict 1938) and thus launched the cultural interpretation of adolescence that pervades much of current thinking.

The heavy emphasis on the male in late adolescence derives in part from the classic works of Erik Erikson. His work epitomizes the behavioral, rather than physical, definition for the end point of adolescence. In Erikson's schema of eight psychosocial crises in course of development, the adolescent crisis deals with the achievement of "identity" versus role diffusion. Erikson (1959) has written very persuasively about the vicissitudes of the "quest for identity," and this does not need to be discussed here. It is significant that Erikson is very widely read by adolescents themselves and, in part, has become a blueprint for them as well as parents, teachers, and mental health professionals. The inference tends to be made that the descriptions and prescriptions that derive from the model of the late adolescent male pertain to all ages and stages of adolescence and speak equally validly for the female as well as the male. It now seems likely that this assumption is questionable. Early adolescents have very little in common with late adolescents in terms of either developmental tasks or coping strategies.

Mention must be made of the social setting in which the biologically changing early adolescent finds himself. By and large, the institution of the junior high school will be his school experience. Theoretically, the junior high school was designed to ease the transition from the experience of self-contained classroom and single teacher throughout the day, the pattern of the elementary school, to the large population, large campus, rotating classes, and multiple teacher situation of the high school. In fact, junior high schools, as they now exist, duplicate in all particulars the conditions of the high school, so that the transition is not eased, but instead the radical shift in school experience is displaced downward by two years. As generally followed, the system involves elementary school for six years and then junior high school for two or three years, followed by high school for three or four years. As it works out, the entry into junior high school is timed with significant pubertal changes in most girls. There are, however, only a small number of early-maturing boys who have comparable pubertal changes at this time. The implications of this for the adolescent's development will be discussed later. The quality of academic performance expected shows a sharp increase. Achievement pressures are sharply escalated. There is, as mentioned, the new experience of a very large institution with a succession of six or seven different teachers each day whose personal relationship with the student cannot have the same meaning or intensity it had in elementary school. There are ultimate advantages as well as disadvantages to this sytem, but it is, nonetheless, a sharp discontinuity with the past.

Parents also view the junior-high-school student as entering a new world. They expect to treat their child differently and think of him now as an "adolescent." As mentioned previously, the stereotype thus evoked refers to late adolescents, and so parental attitudes and behaviors tend to derive from this model. The applicability of the late-adolescent model for providing useful prescriptions for dealing with early adolescents is dubious.

It is worth noting some of the continuities with the past that do exist. The early adolescent continues to live with his parents, and the issue of actual physical separation from them and living on his own (autonomy) is remotely viewed, if perceived at all. There is a sharp increment in the school demands, but he is a student and continues to think of himself as continuing to exist in the student role for considerable years ahead. There is no pressure for real commitment to an adult work responsibility. Although "going steady" may or may not be the custom in a particular community, there is rarely any question of a more than "playful" and exploratory relationship with the opposite sex in the twelve-to-fifteen-year age group. According to Offer (1972), the younger teenagers report very little involvement with sex in either thought or deed.

It was previously mentioned that there are three sets of new preemptive demands for the early adolescent. First, there are the challenges posed by the biological changes of puberty. The individual must cope with the flagrant and undeniable impact of change in body configuration. He perceives, at times erroneously, his emerging size and shape as the physique that will characterize him throughout his adult life. This concern over body image is pervasive, and there are deep concerns about physical attractiveness and vulnerability to real or imagined assaults on bodily integrity. There is, at the same time, relatively little information about the wide range of normality or the timetables for the appearance of the various physical manifestations that affect his total body image. There are baffling mood and temperament effects that are probably partially the result of direct effects of the gonadal hormones, but are experienced as interpersonal stress.

Second, there are the challenges that are posed by the entry into a new social system, junior high school. With this transition, the student relinquishes the former security of membership in one stable classroom and is faced with the task of negotiating six or seven changes of teachers and classes each day with no group support. This raises threats of failure in the face of vastly greater requirements for autonomy. There are greater academic demands and concerns, therefore, about achievement. Finally, there is uncertainty about the ability to make new friendships.

The third set of challenges derive from the sudden entry into a new role status. The admission into junior high school has become a convenient marker for the conferrring of adolescent status and the badge of entry into the "teen culture." In a dimly perceived way, the early adolescent urgently feels himself in need of a new set of "adolescent" behaviors, values, and reference persons.

Clearly, each of these sets of challenges is formidable in its own right. Additional stress is engendered by the fact that these challenges are superimposed. No child can escape the necessity for major reorganization and reorientation at this time. There would appear, however, to be sex, class, and cultural differences in the experiencing of the crisis, and these will be discussed.

BIOLOGICAL CHANGES OF PUBERTY

Much is now known about the details of endocrine changes associated with pubertal development. There have been major advances in recent years primarily due to the development of newer methods that permit accurate measurement of pituitary and gonadal hormones in the blood. The current information about puberty can be summarized as follows. The onset of puberty is determined by the interaction of gonadal hormones and the hypothalamus. In childhood, until eight or nine years of age, there are trace levels of circulating gonadal hormone. Evidence in mammals (Donovan 1959) indicates that prior to puberty the cells of the hypothalamus are sensitive to these minute amounts of circulating hormone. A resultant feedback system is set up, in which the anterior lobe of the pituitary, via the hypothalamus, is inhibited from secreting gonadotrophins that would otherwise evoke secretion of sex hormones in functional amounts. The significant change of puberty is the "maturation" of the cells of the hypothalamus and their escape from the restraining influence of minute quantities of gonadal hormone. The factors influencing this "maturation" of the brain in man are not yet elucidated.

The prepubertal pituitary gland is also functional. Trace amounts of the gonadotrophins FSH and LH have been measured in the urine as well as in the plasma of young children (Rifkind, Kulin, and Ross 1967). The LH excretion is reported to increase tenfold at the time of puberty. The elevated gonadotrophins, in turn, stimulate the gonad, which leads to increased secretion of androgen or estrogen. In early puberty there is still a tendency to heightened sensitivity to circulating gonadal hormone and thus a feedback equilibrium at a low level of hormone production. The gonadotrophin level does not reach the adult "set-point" until after mid-adolescence. In the female, there is a late development of the mid-cycle peak in LH production that is necessary for ovulation. Typically, this may not occur for a year or two after menarche. Maximum fertility and regular ovulation probably is not achieved until the early twenties (Tanner 1962).

It is of great interest to note the dramatic pubertal increase in testosterone in pubertal males. By the method of Gandy and Peterson (1968), this has been reported as a tenfold increase. The possible behavioral implications of these sharp increases in gonadal hormone levels at puberty must be considered.

Do such changes alter responsiveness to provocative stimulation or lower frustration thresholds? Curiously, not a single study has so far related the hormonal changes of puberty to specific, reliable measures of any aspect of aggressiveness in humans. Nonetheless, several recent reports suggest a role for sex hormones in relation to personality development in the adolescent and young adult human and draw attention to the promotion of aggressiveness in adolescents by androgen administration (in this case, the mildly potent androgen, dehydroepiandrosterone) (Wolstenholme and O'Connor, 1967). Moreover, recent biochemical studies implicating dehydrotestosterone as the "biologically active form" of testosterone accentuate the desirability of obtaining more detailed information about the various androgenic compounds present in the plasma of adolescents. Their possibly fluctuating concentrations during this period of development should also be examined in view of the cyclicity of levels of testosterone excretion in normal males reported by Corker and Exley (1968). The application of gas chromatographic methods can greatly clarify such problems on the endocrine side.

Unfortunately, the endocrine changes of puberty in man have largely been studied by one set of investigators, while the behavioral changes have been the object of an entirely different set of investigators. There is clearly a need for interdisciplinary research, so that the interplay of events in this critical period can be meaningfully understood. In the Laboratory of Stress and Conflict at Stanford University, preparations are underway to study these issues on a biobehavioral basis.

Some of the same questions must be asked about the specific relationship between female sex hormones and behavior. Do the changes in levels of gonadal hormones at the time of puberty have a significant effect on the emotionality of early adolescent girls? Again, no studies have attempted to relate the hormonal changes of puberty to specific, reliable measures of anxiety, hostility, or self-esteem. There have been a number of such studies (Coppen and Kessel 1963) for adult women in relation to the hormonal fluctuations of the menstrual cycle. The importance of such information is underscored by the findings (Dalton 1964; Mandell and Mandell 1967) that suicides, acts of violence, and psychiatric admissions are related to periods when levels of estrogen and progesterone are rapidly changing. At present, the moodiness and hostility of early adolescent males and females is generally cast in an interpersonal context. It would be helpful to all concerned if the hormonal contribution to these affective states could be realistically assessed.

If these sex hormone-mood correlations were established for puberty, it would offer an important new insight into one of the distressing aspects of early adolescent behavior of both sexes. Often, the adults dealing with early adolescents are hurt and baffled by their unpredictable, hostile, or moody behavior. Unfortunately, many adults tend to react automatically in a counterpunitive style, and thus a downward spiral of negative interaction may ensue, leading, at times, to explosive outbursts on both sides. Both parent and child would feel better if they knew that the mood had, in part at least, a biological base.

Tanner (1971) has stated: "For the majority of young persons, the years from twelve to sixteen are the most eventful ones of their lives so far as their growth and development is concerned. Admittedly during fetal life and the first year or two after birth developments occurred still faster . . . but the subject himself was not the fascinated, charmed or horrified spectator that watches the developments, or lack of developments, of adolescence" (p. 907).

Despite the secular trend toward earlier maturity, the pattern and sequence of adolescent growth and bodily change have shown surprising consistency since studies have been recorded. Indeed, there is some reason to believe that they have not changed appreciably since the time of early man. Hamburg (1962) has discussed the general issues involved in the genetically determined biological adaptations of early man to his ecological situation; he also discussed the implications of the slowness and lags of evolutionary change in terms of the psychological consequences and coping challenges for modern man in continuing to carry anachronistic genetic endowment in modern times when the environmental and cultural demands are so utterly different. In general terms, it can be stated that the bodily changes of early adolescence have the net effect of enhancing sexual dimorphism. Mature males, in general, notably excel in size, strength, and physical endurance. As was mentioned earlier, they probably also have a specific rise in aggressivity. These adaptations had a high salience for early man, but their utility is less clear in industrialized society.

In his classic studies of growth curves and patterns of development, Tanner (1964) has shown that the form of the human growth curve is shared by primates, but not by other mammals. Most mammals show a peak velocity just prior to birth and a slower but steady growth velocity from weaning until the completion of pubertal change. In the primates, on the other hand, there is a gradual *decrease* in velocity of growth between weaning and the pubertal growth spurt. This trend toward increasingly slower growth in childhood is carried successively further in the progression from monkeys and apes through man. The maturation of the hypothalamus and consequent initiation of pubertal change occurs *after* the association areas of the cortex are quite well developed. The net result is a long childhood learning period in which the young individuals are relatively small and docile. Thus, at a much earlier time, the cognitive, physical, and temperamental changes associated with adolescent change occurred at a time when the postpubertal individual was immediately inducted into needed adult roles for which the changes were well suited. The adolescent male is well adapted for hunting, fighting, and the other feats of endurance and strength that are important in a hunting-gathering society. Modern postindustrial society has a prolonged adolescent period that accentuates the discrepancy between the biological proclivities of the young person and the demands of the culture and its social institutions. It would, indeed, be convenient if individuals today remained small and docile until immediately prior to full induction into adult roles.

In discussing the pattern and sequence of pubertal change, *average* ages will be given. Later on, I will return to the issues raised by deviations from these averages in terms of early versus late maturing. The range of ages at which pubertal events occur is very great for both boys and girls.

The initial change in the pubertal male is testicular cell growth and secretion of male sex hormone by the cells of the testis. This typically occurs at eleven and a half years (Wohstenholme and O'Connor 1967) in response to the increase in gonadotrophin. There is a concomitant acceleration of growth of the testes and scrotum. As this progresses, there is reddening and wrinkling of the scrotal skin, and downlike pubic hair begins to appear about age twelve. The height spurt begins roughly a year after the first testicular acceleration (twelve and a half). The peak of the height spurt is about fourteen years of age, but mature height is not typically reached until about eighteen years of age. There is noticeable growth in the penis at the same time. Along with the growth of the penis and as a function of the same hormonal stimulus, there is growth of the seminal vesicles, the prostate and bulbo-urethral glands. The first ejaculation will typically occur about one year later (age thirteen and a half). Very commonly there is the development of subareolar nodes on the nipples at this time.

Roughly two years after the first appearance of pubic hair, the axillary hair appears (age fourteen). The facial hair, beginning with down on the upper lip, appears at the same time as the axillary hair. Facial hair progresses to include hair along the upper part of the cheeks, the mid-line below the lower lip, and finally along the lower border of the chin. The remainder of the body hair grows slowly and over a lengthy period. During this same period there is enlargement of the pores, and acne is very common, particularly in boys inasmuch as the characteristic skin changes are due to androgenic activity.

The changing of the voice is a somewhat late and rather gradual process. The change in pitch is due to enlargement of the larynx and lengthening of the vocal cords. This will typically begin about age fourteen and a half or fifteen, and the true adult pitch will not be reached for several years.

For girls, pubertal events occur about two years earlier than comparable events in the boys. As early as nine or ten, there is a significant increase in gonadotrophin. The ovarian follicles begin to develop, and uterine growth is initiated. The development of the breast is the earliest external manifestation of beginning sexual maturation. Budding of the breast is associated with increased estrogen secretion. Breast changes are usually well underway before pubic hair appears in noticeable quantity. In the following year (eleven years old) the uterus and vagina show accelerated growth. The labia and clitoris also enlarge. Pubic hair is well developed. Vaginal secretion commences. There is growth and remolding of the bony pelvis. Estrogen secretion is increased and tends to be cyclic. At age twelve, nipples show pigmentation, and the breasts show further development toward mature size and shape. At about twelve and a half years, menarche, the first menstruation, occurs. Axillary hair appears at roughly the same time. It is clear that menarche occurs relatively late in the sequence of events. Although it marks a definitive and relatively mature stage of development, it does not signify complete development. Full reproductive function may not be attained until a year or two after menarche. Early menstrual cycles are often irregular and may be anovulatory. Menarche always occurs after the peak height velocity is passed. An accurate overall height prediction can be made to the postmenarchal girl. This may be important for the early-maturing tall girl who towers above her classmates and has grave concerns about her eventual height.

Although typical or modal ages have been used for convenience in these brief summaries of pubertal change, the range of ages for all of these changes is very large. In other words, children mature at different rates. It has been established that the timing of puberty has significant and differential behavioral consequences for boys and girls. Reynolds and Wines (1951) studied onset and end point of pubertal change in fifty-nine adolescent boys longitudinally at the Fels Research Institute. The age range for the onset of puberty in boys was nine and a half to fifteen years. The age range for the end point was thirteen and a half to eighteen and a half years. In a companion study of girls at the Fels Research Institute, Reynolds and Wines (1948) found a range of ages from eight and a half to thirteen for the onset of pubertal change as defined by the appearance of the breast bud. It is clear, therefore, that there are instances in which some children have not yet begun any pubertal change at an age at which their peers have entirely completed all of the pubertal events. Therefore, in a mixed group of boys and girls between the ages of eleven and fifteen, there is enormous variability in the level of maturational development. It will be remembered that this coincides with the junior-high-school experience. Mary Cover Jones (1965) and associates have done long-term investigations of the different impacts and varying outcomes of early versus late maturity in boys and girls. Skeletal age was used as a stable and reliable index of physical maturity. On the average, the physically accelerated and physically retarded adolescents of the same chronological age are separated by two years in skeletal age. In girls, as early as eleven years of age, all of the late maturers are shorter than the mean for the early maturers. At the mean age of fourteen, the height distributions for early and late maturers show an extreme separation with no overlap. At the peak of growth, early-maturing girls are not only taller than their girl classmates, but also much taller than most of the boys in the class. From that age onward, the differences tend to decrease, and by eighteen or nineteen the mature heights of the early- and late-maturing girls are very similar.

Strength tests in boys show that late maturers are relatively weak and are low in tests of athletic ability. Early-maturing boys are more "masculine" (mesomorphic) in their builds and late-maturing boys more "childish" (slender and long legged) in their builds. Late maturers are likely to be perceived and treated as immature by both adults and peers.

These classic studies (Jones 1965) revealed that systematic comparisons between the behavior and personality characteristics of early- and late-maturing adolescents have indicated that acceleration in growth tends to carry distinct advantages for boys, but disadvantages for girls.

In early adolescence, early-maturing boys were given more leadership roles, were more popular, excelled in athletic ability, were perceived as more attractive by adults and peers, and enjoyed considerably enhanced heterosexual status. When studied (Mussen and Jones 1957) at seventeen years of age, the early-maturing boys showed more self-confidence, less dependency, and were more capable of playing an adult role in interpersonal relations.

The findings on the late-maturing boys showed more personal and social maladjustment at all stages of adolescence. When studied at seventeen years of age, the group showed negative self-concepts, prolonged dependency needs, rebellious attitudes toward parents, strong affiliation needs, and profound feelings of rejection by the group. Interestingly, the groups did not differ in needs for achievement and recognition.

The early reports of systematic comparisons among girls ages eleven to seventeen years (Jones and Mussen 1958) showed that early-maturing girls were seen as "submissive, listless, or indifferent in social situations and lacking in poise. Such girls have little influence upon the group and seldom attain a high degree of popularity, prestige, or leadership" (p. 492).

Late-maturing girls in early adolescent years were seen as relatively more outgoing and assured. They were described as being confident and having leadership ability.

In early adolescence, early-maturing boys, and, to a somewhat lesser extent, late-maturing girls, share a fortuitous adaptive advantage. Early-maturing girls stand in an intermediate position adaptively despite their extreme position developmentally. A possible explanation for this may be that while their body configuration and tallness is viewed by the girls themselves and others as discordant, it occurs while the girls are in the elementary school. Essentially this means that the task of coping with physical change occurs as the single major challenge confronting her. She does not have the superimposed academic and social pressures inherent in junior high school. Her status with her peer group is buffered by halo effects that can continue to operate inasmuch as she is remaining in a stable social setting and does not have to establish herself with new peers. Also, despite the fact that her appearance is different both to herself and others, the changes are recognized by all concerned as desirable steps toward maturity. Finally, within the continuity of the elementary-school period, parents are less likely to alter their expectations of her or drastically change their accustomed ways of relating to her. She is usually perceived by them as a "large child" rather than as an "adolescent." Again, needed stability may thus be achieved. In instances where the parents collaborate in permitting an early shift to "adolescent" behaviors at ages nine or ten, there is much more turmoil, as she strives to find a niche.

The late-maturing boy is at the most severe disadvantage. He is at least as highly discordant as the early-maturing girl, but under much less favorable circumstances. He continues to look like an elementary-school boy at a time when it is important to him to be as grown up as possible. He has a developmental lag of about four years as compared to the average girl of the same age and perhaps two years in relation to the age-matched boy. This degree of discordance is experienced as a severe stress. The distress is heightened by the fact that generally the afflicted individual is unaware that he will, in fact, catch up to his more fortunate early-maturing peers. At this critical time in development, however, his self-esteem is very low, and he develops maladaptive patterns of adaptation either in terms of appeasement and overcompliance or swaggering, pseudoadult behavior. In both instances anxiety level is likely to be high. There is some reason to believe that for some individuals the ultimate adult adaptive ability is enhanced if the boy succeeds in mastering this developmental challenge.

The widespread concern of the early adolescent with his body has been generally sensed and has been documented in nationwide surveys of thousands of adolescents in such studies as the Purdue Opinion Polls. Their figures show that 52 percent of adolescents report a dissatisfaction with their weight. Generally boys tend to want to gain weight, while girls want to lose it; 24 percent of girls want to "improve their figure." About 37 percent of boys would like to change their "body build"; 12 percent are deeply concerned about pimples; and 37 percent are dissatisfied about their posture. Frazier and Lisonbee (1950) studied 508 tenth-grade students and found that among tall girls, 49 percent were very concerned about their height and that 39 percent of short boys expressed equally great concern. In their sample, 82 percent of the students expressed concern about pimples or other skin problems. Nearly 67 percent of the entire group expressed a desire for some type of physical change. It has been found (Frazier and

Lisonbee 1950; Jersild 1952) that when junior-high-school students were asked what they did not like about themselves, physical characteristics were the most predominant response. There was a very much lower percentage of high-school students who responded in this way. In early adolescence, the individual must come to terms with his definitive body image through an integration of his self-perceptions and those reflected to him by significant others. The negotiation of this task has profound implications for his sense of identity as an adult. The psychological development of the individual is closely related to the course of his physical development.

PSYCHOSOCIAL CHANGES
OF EARLY ADOLESCENCE

The drastic change in school format from the self-contained classroom of elementary school to the rotating classes of junior high school has already been described. It has been clear for some time that the entry into junior high school probably represents the most abrupt and demanding transition of an individual's entire educational career. This is a crisis period that has important educational as well as personal consequences.

A major issue in early adolescence is the recognition of sharp escalation in academic demands both in terms of expected output and complexity of tasks. A great many students have deep-seated fears of inadequacy and failure. Some students are buffered by the support of older siblings who have served as models and sources of information for them in negotiating the transition. But for many others, siblings are negative and disturbing models or the student is himself the eldest or perhaps an only child. Evidence tends to confirm that their fears may be well founded. Studies have demonstrated (Finger and Silverman 1966) that a startling drop in school performance is associated with entry into junior high school. In a study by Armstrong (1964) in New York, 45 percent of the boys and girls with good elementary-school records performed at a fair or poor level in junior high school. The work of Finger and Silverman replicated this finding and furthermore has shown that students who experienced a drop in performance in junior high school were rarely able to improve at a later point in their careers. It is possible, therefore, to make rather accurate predictions of eventual academic performance in junior high school. The authors further note that whereas grades in elementary school are highly related to intelligence, intelligence was largely unrelated to the change in performance at the junior-high level. In junior high school, motivation seems to be the important factor. It is certainly our impression that similar findings characterize the academic careers of children in the Palo Alto, California, School District, and we are collecting data to check this point.

Kagan (1971) feels that "youths are finding it increasingly difficult to rationalize working for grades." He believes that in the current climate of public opinion the power of the incentive to utilize education as a passport to higher status and financial security has been eroded, and so academic achievement is meaningless to many. I am in accord with his hypothesis that motivation to deal with problems of body image, role change, and relation to peers preempts academic concerns. Kagan states it well: "The adolescent needs a firmer set of motivational supports that will allow him to work at school requirements while he is trying to fit the catechism of academic competence into the larger structure we call the self" (p. 1006).

Despite the fact that intelligence *per se* is not at issue in the school performance of early adolescents, it is worthwhile to reexamine their style of cognitive functioning. By and large, it has generally been assumed that these early adolescents have moved on from "formal operational thinking" to logical operations and abstract thinking (Inhelder and Piaget 1959). There are several lines of evidence that would suggest that this is not generally true. First, teachers who have previously taught high-school students invariably report that they are unable to be successful with the same approach in junior high school. Martin (1971) states: "when I moved I moved from high school to junior high school teaching I was an experienced teacher with a reputation for good performance. I went to my class of eighth graders with confidence. After forty-five minutes, I knew I had entered a different world and would have to begin learning about teaching again. . . . These were people who were different from the fifteen to eighteen year olds I had been teaching" (p. 1088). Teachers are frustrated unless they revise their presentations from the predominantly logical and abstract to a concrete approach. The junior-high-school student is deficient in his ability to generalize, to use symbols, and to process information with objectivity.

Elkind has described the egocentrism of adolescence (1967) as showing its peak in the ages that correspond to early adolescence (twelve to fifteen). Objectivity is, by definition, inversely proportional to egocentrism. In this same paper Elkind further states that in his experience, it is not until the age of fifteen or sixteen that formal operational thinking becomes firmly established. Clearly in any transition to a new stage, there are rate differences between individuals and fluctuations within a given individual until the newly emerging stage is consolidated. It can be said that abstract thinking generally appears earlier in areas of science and mathematics because children are given much more experience in learning these symbols and mediating terms and have more practice in manipulating these relationships and propositions (Peel 1960). Even in these areas, however, early adolescents will tend to revert to concrete operations if confronted with an unfamiliar or unusually difficult problem. The egocentrism that Elkind describes, although pervasive, is most obvious in the early adolescent's preoccupation with his bodily changes and his concerns with responses of others to his appearance.

Our experience with the Peer Counseling project (more fully described below) has also strikingly confirmed the cognitive difference between junior-high-school and high-school students. Our training groups uniformly consisted of a combination of both junior-high-school and high-school students. It was consistently reported across all training groups (a total of nineteen groups) that junior-high-school students were unable to profit from material unless it was presented in concrete terms. For example, high-school students can readily role play an interpersonal interaction from the basis of a hypothetical situation. Junior-high-school students usually cannot. They need first to construct a situation out of their own personal knowledge or experience before they can role play the interactions. In other ways as well, it was repeatedly observed that there is generalized difficulty in reasoning about things that are outside of the direct, personal experience of early adolescents. Although they do show remarkable gaps in their areas of knowledge, it was also clear to us that their intelligence, worldliness, and verbal sophistication had initially obscured the true nature of their cognitive limitations. Initially there was a tendency to equate them with the high-school students in ability for abstract thinking. It would appear that this is another example of coping burdens imposed on the early adolescent because of inappropriate expectations of him that are derived from late adolescence.

The entry into junior high school presents opportunity as well as stress. It is generally acknowledged that cognitive development is susceptible to environmental influence as well as maturation. This "learning to learn" potential has far-reaching implications for teaching methods and curriculum planning. It needs to be generally appreciated that there is a definite sequence in moving from concrete to abstract cognitive functioning (Ausubel and Ausubel 1966). The individual needs to acquire a working body of inclusive concepts, and a vocabulary of mediating terms, in order to understand meaningfully and to manipulate symbolically stated relationships and relational propositions. Without these tools, the same manipulation cannot be performed without the aid of the concrete props. We had the opportunity to see this kind of developmental cognitive change in the paced presentations of material to junior-high-school students in our Peer Counseling curriculum. More research is needed into the details of the cognitive processes of early adolescents. Since almost all cognitive studies of adolescents have been carried out on high-school populations, we have little evidence about modal functioning or the range of differences, and nothing about sex differences, in the timing or nature of cognitive functioning in early adolescents. It is likely that these are interpersonal as well as academic issues and many of the problems derive from our failure to appreciate the egocentric and concrete level of thinking that characterizes this period of early adolescence.

In addition to the drop in academic performance, other indicators of high distress can be noted in the junior high schools. Many students, particularly boys, who had been tractable and diligent in elementary school show rebellious, acting-out behaviors that make them intolerable to teachers. There is a high incidence of drug abuse and alcohol consumption. Significant numbers of students are captives of negatively oriented peer groups. Other students are isolated or alienated. In the educational field, it is generally acknowledged that junior high school is the period of highest turbulence.

When the schools have felt the impact of heightened emotional needs on the part of their students, all too often, the available counseling and guidance services have been inadequate both in terms of manpower effectiveness and also in terms of acceptability to a significant percentage of the students. In view of this, we felt that a comprehensive program of peer counselors would fill an important mental health need. It would also serve to act as a "window" on the inner world of the junior-high-school student and would enable us to study the coping tasks and challenges of these students in detail. Accordingly, a Peer Counseling project in the schools was initiated by my colleague, Barbara Varenhorst, a school research psychologist, and myself in the fall of 1970 (Hamburg, Varenhorst 1972).

The Peer Counseling project is an effort to utilize specially trained secondary-school students to help troubled students. There is also an emphasis on prevention through the assignment of peer counselors to target groups of children who show either personal or situational vulnerability. An important aspect of the program has been to assign peer counselors to help students with the stressful transition from elementary to junior high school. These counselees are initially seen in the sixth grade toward the end of the school year when their anxiety about the challenge of junior high school is starting to mount. In the pilot phase of the program, all of the sixth-grade students in the Palo Alto School District were contacted in this way. It was universally acknowledged by the sixth graders that they have strong apprehensions about the transition to junior high school. It was reassuring to them to be able to obtain specific information about what to expect and to know that the same Peer Counselor speaking with them would be on hand at the junior high school when they arrived in the fall. It was very clear that gaining information and knowledge of a reliable personal support were of crucial coping importance for them. It was also useful for them to realize the universality of their fears. They learned that their classmates felt as they did and also that the Peer Counselor had been concerned at a comparable stage.

The anxieties expressed were (1) fear of academic failure, (2) insecurity about their ability to cope with the interpersonal demand of having to relate to a different teacher and a different group of students on an hourly basis, (3) concern about the ability to make and hold friends, (4) ignorance about role expectations now that they would be treated as adolescents, and (5) a general sense of confusion about the bigness and complexity of the new school format. Many students worry about actually getting lost and failing to appear for classes.

In recruiting for the Peer Counseling program, the training curriculum was described to the students. In this description it was implicit that individuals taking the training could derive substantial personal benefit. It was clear that the course would give specific training and practice in skills for understanding and getting along with other adolescents. It would also offer a chance to gain peer and adult perspectives on topics of high saliency.

In brief, the training consists of a twelve-week course carried out in small groups under the supervision of mental health professionals with expertise in group work and adolescence. The curriculum follows an orderly sequence. Initially there is teaching of interpersonal and communication skills both on a one-to-one and group basis. This is followed by in-depth discussions of topics of student concern such as (1) academic motivation, climate and relevancy of school, (2) family relationships and problems, (3) peer relations and problems, (4) future goals, (5) special problems such as drug abuse, sexual concerns, ethnic or religious difference, physical handicap, or other bodily concerns. It has been gratifying to note that trainees enthusiastically report that personal help to themselves is an outstanding attribute of the program. The use of students as surrogates, models, bridging persons, and sources of useful information for one another has proven to be of great value.

As has been mentioned, most of these students are experiencing a developmental crisis in which the sharpness of the discontinuity with the past severely limits the individual in his ability to draw on past learning and information in trying to cope with the new tasks. As a result the student is quite dependent on environmental supports in attempting to anticipate and regulate responses to the challenges he faces. The school has the necessary ingredients for playing a major role in meeting many of the needs of early adolescents.

The use of the peer group as a reliably constructive reference group is very important and can be structured in a variety of ways. In addition to a project such as Peer Counseling, it is also possible to teach "affective education," communication, and interpersonal skills to these students who are eagerly seeking such information. There are possibilities for other types of prosocial groups. It seems clear that in the future schools will exert increasing influence in the socialization of the students through such programs of nonacademic education.

ROLE CHANGE OF EARLY ADOLESCENCE

Although it has never been formally defined as such, entry into junior high school has functioned as a rite of passage. It is the convenient marker for defining the crisis of social identity when the individual is no longer perceived as a child and is viewed by himself and others as entering the teen culture. For almost all early adolescents there is doubt and tension with the realization that a mostly comfortable, and in any case well-understood, phase of his life is over and that a challenging, as yet poorly defined, phase is about to begin. He feels himself in immediate need of a new set of behaviors, values, and reference persons. He is aware that significant adults relating to him often have a reciprocal expectation that they will, in turn, now have different standards and new ways of relating to him. The uninitiated person, when aspiring to a new status, often tends to respond to the most conspicuous and stereotyped features of the new role. The early adolescent will often tend to assume postures of exaggerated independence with accompanying derisive and rebellious attitudes toward his parents in particular, and perhaps all adults in general, in response to the stereotype of adolescent emancipation. He may also slavishly conform to styles of hair and clothing that he identifies as characteristic of the youth culture.

Unfortunately, as mentioned previously, most literature on adolescence derives from the late-adolescent phase. Parents seeking guidelines for their appropriate behavior in relation to their child's role transition find an emphasis on the adolescent's need for independent decision making and the development of autonomy. This can easily lead to a significant renunciation of parental prerogatives and support. This type of response can lead to heightened distress on the part of the child. The result is that in a time of major discontinuity, accustomed parental guidance is withdrawn, and the young person is thrust toward uncritical acceptance of the peer group as a model and a major coping resource. Although this uncritical allegiance to the peer group may be useful in allaying immediate anxieties, it has serious limitations. The peer group at this stage is usually too shallow and rigid to afford the necessary resources for growth and development. When the peer group is organized around drugs or acting-out behaviors, there is potential for considerable damage. There are significant class and cultural differences in the experiencing of the crisis of adolescent role change.

In reviewing the data on adolescent turmoil, it is noteworthy that there is a consistent finding in large survey studies of adolescents of far less turbulence than more theoretically oriented sources and case studies would lead one to expect. It now seems likely that the bulk of other types of professional literature may represent a sampling effect that has tended to exaggerate the disturbances. It should also be noted that the surveys have typically been studies of public senior-high-school populations. The relative calm of this high-school era as a general phenomenon deserves brief mention.

While in high school (ages fifteen to eighteen) there are no distinctive new challenges or changes in status. The format of school and the intellectual demands are by now a familiar extension of the junior high school. The bodily growth and developmental changes are merely refinements of the major pubertal changes that occurred earlier.

Likewise, interpersonal transactions are more constructive, but not radically different. There is a more highly critical use of the peer group. There are planned experimentations and role rehearsals. Instead of previous stereotypes, peers are used in a variety of roles, such as helpers, foils, critics, models, and so on. The previous concern with exploratory learning about the opposite sex, in general terms, is giving way to the nurture of specific relationships in which there is mutuality and the beginning of tenderness. The mid-adolescent is making many refinements in his self-image and sense of identity.

The adaptions are smoother in high school, not only because the tasks are less new and challenging, but also because the coping assets within the individuals are greater at that time due to maturational and learning effects. By the time of high school, full cognitive development has been achieved. This makes new dimensions possible in dealing with psychosocial, as well as intellectual, tasks. Mid-adolescents are capable of generalizations, abstract thinking, and useful introspections (Inhelder and Piaget 1959; Ausubel and Ausubel 1966; Elkind 1967). As a result, there is less response simply to the novel, exotic, or contradictory aspects of the environment, but a more differentiated approach to their milieu.

The survey data, while primarily directed to high-school students, do contain some direct data and retrospective materials that shed light on the responses of junior-high-school students. (Incidentally, paucity of material and the great need for research directly on junior-high-school students is again notable in this area as in so many others.) The survey material has, by design, tended to include all strata of the population in representative numbers. This means that the middle classes, contribute by far the largest total number of students. There is reason to believe, and this will be elaborated on further, that the youth of the lowest and highest social classes have disproportionately influenced the psychiatric literature on adolescence. In contrast, the bulk of students in the survey studies come from middle-class, white-collar and blue-collar families who are moderately affluent and traditional in their orientation. They and their children tend to expect a continuity of generations in terms of values and occupational niches. There is mutual expectation of conformity or very little early striving toward autonomy. By and large, these individuals live in stable communities, and the children respect and wish to emulate their parents. Religious values and affiliations tend to be stronger than in the surrounding classes.

Offer (1969) has extensively studied two large groups of adolescents in public high schools in Illinois. He calls them "modal adolescents," and he found that among them only very few were members of deviant groups where parental values would be seriously challenged. "The relationship between the subjects and their parents was stable, consistent, and emphatic" (p. 223). The same findings are reported by Douvan and Adelson (1966) in their survey of 3,500 adolescents in Michigan. They also concluded that the process of detachment from the parents seems less dramatic and full of conflict than tradition and theory hold.

The early adolescents in the traditional families are buffered in meeting the combination of crises of early adolescence. They continue to have, and want to utilize, the guidelines and resources of the parents in developing new strategies for dealing with the pubertal and school challenges. They are, therefore, less susceptible to peer pressure. The impact of the teen culture on them is less striking. It should be remembered that the early adolescent, the junior-high-school student, is typically between twelve and fourteen years of age. There is a four-to-six-year period before the issue of actual separation from the home and parents will become real. A strong posture of independence at this early stage is not, therefore, linked with a valid development transition.

When the child had continued into eighth grade in an elementary school, there was further stability in the parent-child relationship. The mutual perception of change in social status and role was postponed until ninth grade and occurred after some mastery of the self-image problems related to pubertal changes had taken place. However, the modal adolescents of today, with their multiple superimposed developmental crises of early adolescence, show effects of the stress. In discussing his modal students, Offer (1969) notes: "In our subjects rebellion manifested itself most clearly in early adolescence, at ages twelve and fourteen" (p. 70). Even at worst, however, this defensive behavior on the part of the traditionally oriented early adolescent is within bounds.

Undeniably, the extreme disturbance of behavior described in much of the literature on adolescence does actually exist. It occurs in families where there is expectation by both parent and child of sharp discontinuity between the child and adolescent role. It also occurs where there is repudiation of parental values. These families tend to cluster in two groups. One is the lower-class, "disadvantaged" population. The other is the upper-middle-class and intellectual group. The "enlightened," high-status parents in the second group have usually derived their prescriptions for dealing with their adolescents from professional sources. Unfortunately, as mentioned previously, virtually all the literature, although not explicitly stated, deals with the late-adolescent phase. These parents find, therefore, an emphasis on the need for independent decision making and the development of autonomy. There is a heightened need for parental stability and guidance at the time of major biological, school, and social discontinuity. The early adolescent cannot possess the competence and mastery needed for full independence. Instead, the early- and mid-adolescent phases are the training grounds and preparation for the achievement of autonomy by the time of late adolescence. The success with which these earliest phases are negotiated will, of course, affect the final outcome of adolescent development.

In the poverty group, the adolescent finds a heightening of an already preexisting tendency to find his guidance and support among peers rather than adults, that is, in the "street gang" (Short 1966). There have frequently been weak or missing fathers. In response to this, the adolescent males often tend to adopt styles of exaggerated masculinity including hyper-independence, high risk taking, and aggressive behaviors. Of course, father absence occurs sporadically in all social groups. Whenever absence is prolonged, the negative impact on the development of the adolescent male is significant (Lynn and Sawrey 1959; Hetherington 1965; Sears 1951). Grinker, Grinker, and Timberlake (1962) emphasized that the history of strong identification with father and father-figures was significant in the cluster of conditions found in their sample of emotionally healthy college freshman males.

Where there is a lack of firm parental guidance and where the parent does not serve as model and coping resource, there is a more urgent need for the individual to uncritically seek peer support and adopt the badges of conformity with the attendant risk of antisocial outcomes.

There are data on the relation between parental interest and involvement and the adolescent self-image (Rosenberg 1965). Data from the same source deal with the effects of level of self-esteem on behavior. Rosenberg has studied 5,977 juniors and seniors in public high schools throughout New York State. He studied parental interest as indicated by the parents' knowledge of, and relationship to, his child's friends, by parents' reactions to academic performance, and by parents' responsiveness to the child as judged by dinner-table interactions. There is retrospective information pertaining to the early-adolescent period. He concludes that low parental involvement and interest are highly correlated with low self-esteem in the child. He says it is "not the punitive responses which are most closely related to low self-esteem but the indifferent ones" (p. 138). He points out that low self-esteem leads to characteristic responses. The individual is more vulnerable in interpersonal relations (deeply hurt by criticism); he is relatively awkward with others (finds it hard to make talk, does not initiate contacts); he assumes that others think poorly of him or do not particularly like him; he tends to put up a "front" to people; he feels relatively isolated and lonely. There is low faith in people. In some, "This low faith in people takes the form of contempt for the great mass of humanity; among others, mistrust, and among still others, hostility" (p. 182). Low self-esteem makes him relatively submissive or unassertive in his dealings with others. It is thus apparent that the individual's self-conception is not only associated with attitudes toward other people, it is also associated with his actions in social life and the position he comes to occupy in his high-school peer groups.

In summary, available evidence supports the concept that parental interest, guidelines, and support, particularly of the parent of the same sex, offer the most effective help to the early adolescent in negotiating his tasks. There is a need for public understanding of a differentiated view of adolescence and specific information on early adolescence. Rather than accepting the notion of the generation gap as modal and even somehow growth promoting, parents need education about the underlying needs of early adolescents. They need to be supported in carrying out appropriate parental functions and in learning about effective communication with their children.

SUMMARY OF IMPLICATIONS FOR RESEARCH WITH EARLY ADOLESCENTS

In America there are good reasons to define the junior-high-school period as early adolescence and to recognize it as a time of major developmental stress. The superimposed challenge of sharp discontinuity with the immediate past in three major areas of development has been explored. Some of the hormonal, cognitive, and cultural reasons for impoverishment of coping skills in the early adolescent have also been described.

The relative neglect of the period of early adolescence as a distinct area of research continues to represent a striking gap in our knowledge of adolescence. Very little research has been directed primarily to this period in terms of its specific coping challenges. It might be fruitful to study the transition from elementary school to junior high school in a fashion similar to the study of the transition from high school to college carried out by Coelho, Hamburg, and Murphey (1963). Some educators are experimenting with alternatives to the traditional sequence of elementary, junior high, and high school. These deserve study in terms of the psychosocial and coping outcomes, in addition to curricular and learning considerations. We hope to do some of this in our continuing work in the Stanford-Palo Alto School project. The shift from thinking in terms of "concrete operations" to mature abstract thinking that occurs during the period of early adolescence has not been studied in detail. We need to learn more about the variability, rate of change, or other attributes of cognition peculiar to this period. There is increasing evidence that information processing in this period is significantly different from that in the middle- and late-adolescent periods. The implications for teaching methods and curriculum design need to be further explored for both academic and nonacademic subjects.

The desirability of further investigation into the relation of gonadal hormones to the moodiness of adolescence, particularly for the female, has already been mentioned. There is also a need to investigate the possible relation of gonadal hormones to aggressive behavior in males. It is, of course, important to study the problem of aggressive and antisocial behavior in the broader psychosocial aspects as well. Finally, there is a need to look at the ways in which the peer group can be more reliably used as a constructive coping adjunct. The Peer Counseling program (Hamburg and Varenhorst 1972) in which students learn interpersonal skills and exchange relevant information is but one of many models for utilizing the potential of the peer group. We need to explore as many as possible.

In general, there is a need for interdisciplinary research on early adolescence that links biological and psychosocial variables. This critical period of turbulence and potentiality clearly deserves far more study than it has so far received.

REFERENCES

Armstrong, C. Patterns of achievement in selected New York state schools. Mimeographed. Albany: New York State Educational Department, 1964.

Ausubel, D., and Ausubel, P. Cognition development in adolescence. *Review of Educational Research*, 1966, *36*, 403–413.

Benedict, R. Continuities and discontinuities in cultural conditioning. *Psychiatry*, 1938, *1*, 161–167.

Blizzard, R., Johanson, A., Guyda, H., Boghdassarian, A., Raiti, S., and Migeon, C. Recent developments in the study of gonadotrophin secretion in adolescence. In F. P. Heald and W. Hung, eds., *Adolescent endocrinology*. New York: Appleton-Century-Crofts, Educational Division of Meredith Corporation, 1970.

Coelho, G., Hamburg, D., and Murphey, E. Coping strategies in a new learning environment. *Archives of General Psychiatry*, 1963, *9*, 433–443.

Coppen, A., and Kessel, N. Menstruation and personality. *British Journal of Psychiatry*, 1963, *109*, 711–721.

Corker, C. S., and Exley, D. Daily changes in urinary testosterone secretion in the male. *Clinical Endocrinology*, 1968, *2*, 552–568.

Dalton, K. *The premenstrual syndrome*. Springfield, Ill.: Charles C Thomas, 1964.

Donovan, B. T., and Van der Werfften Bosch, J. The hypothalamus and sexual maturation in the rat. *Journal of Physiology*, 1959, *147*, 78–92.

Douvan E., and Adelson, J. *The adolescent experience*. New York: Wiley, 1966.

Eisenberg, L. Student unrest: Sources and consequences. *Science*, 1970, *167*, 1688–1692.

Elkind, D. Egocentrism in adolescence. *Child Development*, 1967, *4*, 1025–1034.

Erikson, E. Identity and the life cycle. In *Psychological Issues*. New York: International Universities Press, 1959.

———. *Identity: Youth and crisis*. New York: Norton, 1968.

Finger, J., and Silverman, M. Changes in academic performance in the junior high school. *Personnel and Guidance Journal*, 1966, *45*, 157–164.

Frazier, A., and Lisonbee, L. K. Adolescent concerns with physique. *School Review*, 1950, *58*, 397–405.

Gandy, H., and Peterson, R. Measurement of testosterone and 17-ketosteroids in plasma by the double isotope dilution derivative technique. *Journal of Clinical Endocrinology*, 1968, *28*, 949–977.

Grinker, R. R., Sr., Grinker, R. R., Jr., and Timberlake, J. A. A study of the "mentally healthy" young males (homoclites). *Archives of General Psychiatry*, 1962, *6*, 27–74.

Hall, G. S. *Adolescence: Its psychology and its relations to physiology, anthropology, sociology, sex, crime, religion and education*, vols. 1, 2. New York: Appleton, 1904.

Hamburg, B., and Varenhorst, B. Peer Counseling in the secondary schools: A community mental health project for youth. *American Journal of Orthopsychiatry*, 1972, *42*, 566–581.

Hamburg, D. The relevance of recent evolutionary changes to human stress biology. In S. Washburn, ed., *Social life of early man*, pp. 278–288, Chicago: Aldine, 1962.

Hetherington, M. E. A developmental study of the effects of sex of the dominant parent on sex role preference, identification, and imitation in children. *Journal of Personality and Social Psychology*, 1965, *2*, 188–194.

Hollingworth, L. S. *The psychology of the adolescent*. New York: Appleton, 1928.

Inhelder, B., and Piaget, J. *The growth of logical thinking from childhood to adolescence*. New York: Basic Books, 1959.

Jersild, A. T. *In search of self*. New York: Columbia University Press, 1952.

Jones, M. C. Psychological correlates of somatic development. *Child Development*, 1965, *36*, 899–911.

Jones, M. C., and Mussen, P. H. Self-conceptions, motivations, and interpersonal attitudes of early and late maturing girls. *Child Development*, 1958, *29*, 491–501.

Kagan, J. A conception of early adolescence. *Daedalus*, Fall 1971, pp. 997–1012.

Kestenberg, J. Phases of adolescence: With suggestions for a correlation of psychic and hormonal organizations. II. Prepuberty diffusion and reintegration. *Journal of American Academy of Child Psychiatry*, 1967, *6*, 577–614.

———. Phases of adolescence: With suggestions for correlations of psychic and hormonal organizations. III. Puberty, growth, differentiation and consolidation. *Journal of American Academy of Child Psychiatry*, 1968, 7, 108–151.

Lynn, D. B., and Sawrey, W. L. The effects of father absence on Norwegian boys and girls. *Journal of Abnormal Social Psychology*, 1959, *59*, 258–262.

Mandell, A., and Mandell, M. Suicide and the menstrual cycle. *Journal of the American Medical Association*, 1967, *200*, 792–793.

Marshall, W. A., and Tanner, J. M. Variations in the pattern of pubertal change in boys. *Archives of the Diseases of Childhood*, 1970, *45*, 13–23.

Martin, E. C. Reflections on the early adolescent in school. *Daedalus*, Fall 1971, pp. 1087–1103.

Mead, M. *Coming of age in Samoa.* New York: Morrow, 1928.

Mussen, P. H., and Jones, M. C. Self-conceptions, motivations, and interpersonal attitudes of late- and early-maturing boys. *Child Development*, 1957, *28*, 243–256.

Offer, D. The psychological world of the teen-ager: A study of normal adolescent boys. New York: Basic Books, 1969.

———. Attitudes toward sexuality in a group of 1500 middle-class teen-agers. *Journal of Youth and Adolescence*, 1972, *1*, 81–90.

Peel, E. A. *The pupil's thinking.* London: Oldbourne, 1960.

Reynolds, E. L., and Wines, J. V. Individual differences in physical changes associated with adolescence in girls. *American Journal of Diseases of Children*, 1948, *75*, 329–350.

———. Physical changes associated with adolescence in boys. *American Journal of Diseases of Children*, 1951, *82*, 529–547.

Rifkind, A. B., Kulin, H. E., and Ross, G. T. Follicle stimulating hormone (FSH) and luteinizing hormone (LH) in the urine of pre-pubertal children. *Journal of Clinical Investigation*, 1967, *12*, 1123–1128.

Rosenberg, M. *Society and the adolescent self-image.* Princeton, N. J.: Princeton University Press, 1965.

Sears, P. Doll play aggression in normal young children: Influence of sex, age, sibling status, father's absence. *Psychology Monographs*, 1951, *65* (6), 1–42 (whole issue).

Short, J. F., Jr. Juvenile delinquency: The sociocultural context. In L. W. Hoffman and M. L. Hoffman, eds., *Review of Child Development Research*, vol. 2. New York: Russell Sage Foundation, 1966.

Smith, L. M., and Kleine, P. E. The adolescent and his society. *Review of Educational Research*, 1966, *36*, 424–436.

Tanner, J. M. *Growth at adolescence.* 2nd ed. Oxford: Blackwell Scientific Publications, 1962.

———. The human growth curve. In G. A. Harrison, J. S. Weiner, J. M. Tanner, and N. A. Barnicott, eds., *Human biology.* Oxford: Oxford University Press, 1964.

———. Sequence, tempo and individual variation in the growth and development of boys and girls aged twelve to sixteen. *Daedalus*, Fall 1971, pp. 907–930.

Wolstenhome, G. E. W., and O'Connor, M. *Endocrinology of the testis.* Boston: Little, Brown, 1967.

III

COPING WITH
REAL-LIFE CRISES

7

Coping with Long-term Disability

JOHN E. ADAMS
AND ERICH LINDEMANN

As medicine has progressively learned to conquer or at least control acute illness, its concern has increasingly become chronic disease and long-lasting incapacity. In many fields of medicine the major therapeutic task has become rehabilitation. Although great strides have also been made in the development of techniques to restore or at least minimize the effects of lost physical or psychological function, the final psychosocial outcome of rehabilitative efforts often remains uncertain. Despite prompt and skillful intervention, the "recovered" patient may continue to function at far less than his full psychobiological capacity. We shall review here several conceptual approaches to the understanding of disability and shall consider ways in which new information, formulations, and experimental evidence can aid professional work in this field. Earlier discussions of the social and psychological aspects of disability developed from several disciplinary approaches and utilized a variety of theoretical frameworks (Finesinger and Lindemann 1945; Goodman et al. 1963; Wing 1966). Because the final outcome of rehabilitation must depend heavily on the patient's capacity to deal successfully, often over a relatively long time course, with disease and handicap, we shall focus particularly on the growing body of observation and theory relating to the mechanism of human coping and adaptation.

Over the last twenty-five years there has been increasing interest on the part of behavioral scientists in situations requiring relatively rapid psychosocial adaptation. The study of responses to stressful circumstances in clini-

Some of the material in this chapter was originally presented at a Clinical Symposium in the Department of Psychiatry at Stanford University. Daniel J. Feldman, M.D., participated with the authors in this symposium. We wish to express our appreciation to Dr. Feldman for provision of the case materials presented here and for his theoretical contributions to the discussion of biological coping.

cal settings has led to the development of the concept of "crisis." This refers to a situation in which one or several individuals are confronted with adaptive tasks that demand the mobilization of new resources in psychological competence and social skills. It has been elaborated with respect to "developmental crisis" by Erikson (1963) in connection with the various stages of personality development and as "situational crisis" by Caplan (1964) and Lindemann (1965). The concept of crisis may be used to view the need for adaptation both in terms of the situational requirements and the various phases over time of the mobilization of resources. The perception and definition of the tasks facing the individual, as well as the strategy selected for attempted management of these tasks, become important parts of the process of resolving the crisis. The critical issues arise over the choice of these patterns of adaptation. These patterns may be predominantly regressive and defensive, functioning primarily for the protection of the self from disintegration, or may represent efforts to master the environment, restructure the task ahead, and solve the problems of dealing with a novel situation. In most crisis situations the adaptive process is a complex and changing mixture of these regressive and progressive components, and it is to this dynamic process of search for individual styles and strategies of mastery that the term *coping* has been applied (Hamburg and Adams 1967).

A number of acute crisis situations have been studied from this general perspective. Lindemann's research on grief and mourning has emphasized the psychological consequences of bereavement and loss, including loss of body parts (Cobb and Lindemann 1943; Lindemann 1944). Studies have been made of patients with severe burns (D. Hamburg, B. Hamburg, and deGoza 1953), of those in the acute stages of paralytic polio (Visotsky and Hamburg 1961), and of parents of children fatally ill with leukemia (Chodoff, Friedman, and Hamburg 1964). Janis (1958, 1962) has described responses to major surgery and the behavior of populations exposed to natural catastrophies. All of these have focused primarily on those aspects of the acute situation that make it a crisis for the individual and have delineated the psychological means by which the crisis is at least managed, even if not mastered.

In this essay, we are concerned with the coping strategies of individuals suffering from long-term illness or disability. In these situations major and permanent adjustment is most often obligatory. The emphasis must be not only on the management of an acute psychosocial threat, but also on the development of new patterns of behavior and the design of new interpersonal roles.

In an effort to make quite vivid some of the issues involved, we will now present two brief clinical vignettes drawn from a physical rehabilitation setting. These are not intended to be full case histories, but are rather meant to highlight the psychosocial problems of permanent disability.

The first case is that of an eighteen-year-old white, single, male, a high-school senior who was in excellent health until February 3, 1962. In the early hours of that morning, the truck in which he was riding with two friends entered sudden fog, the driver lost control, and the truck overturned. The patient did not lose consciousness and realized almost immediately that he could not move his legs. He was admitted to a local hospital, where X rays revealed a fracture-dislocation of the sixth cervical vertebra, and examination showed him to be totally paralyzed below the waist. He had only minimal gross function of his arms and sensory loss below the mid-sternum. A laminectomy was performed and traction applied, but over the following six weeks there was no significant return of function. The records do not indicate what he may have been told regarding his prognosis, but he was described as reasonably cheerful and cooperative. He was transferred to a university medical center and was admitted to its rehabilitation service on March 20, 1962.

The patient was raised on a ranch in rural California, on which his father was a foreman. He was always physically active and spent much time working around the ranch. He had no particular fondness for this type of life, however, and had joined the Naval Reserve and planned to enter active duty following graduation from high school. He had considered making a career of the service. He had been a mediocre student academically, but was socially popular and a star in athletics. Although he had had a girlfriend throughout high school, there were no plans for marriage, and his goals within the Navy were apparently not well-defined. He was the youngest of three boys in the family, and his two older brothers had joined the Navy shortly before his accident.

During the early part of his rehabilitation hospitalization, the patient expressed the firm conviction that he would again walk and cooperated fully with the physical therapy program. Recurrent pain in his neck and arms soon forced reduction in his program, and several neurosurgical procedures caused further delay. Each operation apparently produced expectations of a magical cure, and there was disappointment when this did not occur. These feelings were reinforced by the patient's parents, and especially his father. The father was repeatedly described by the ward staff as silent and apparently uncomprehending of his son's condition. He became involved only when he mirrored his son's disappointment and criticism of the staff for not doing more. The mother was talkative and superficially involved, but she too held rather magical expectations and was unable to carry her expressed concern into concrete action. For example, there were long delays by the family in initiating application for financial assistance through the local Aid to the Totally Disabled Program. In this setting the patient's first visit home, frequently a milestone in rehabilitation, was a disappointment to all concerned. For the patient, it apparently confirmed his worst fears of the extent of his incapacity, and the friends whom he had expected to involve him in all of their activities failed to do so. His mother had grave doubts of her ability to care for him at home, and ultimately she spent much of the weekend in bed herself.

Early in his hospitalization, the patient was visited by the vocational rehabilitation counselor to plan for his completion of high school and later vocational training. Arrangements were made for a teacher to work with him at the hospital, but his episodic pain and "other appointments" prevented his making any progress. Attempts at completing high school were finally suspended. In terms of long-range vocational planning, the patient repeatedly spoke of unrealistic physical activity. At one point, when the counselor stressed the necessity of a more realistic view, the patient became very upset and accused the counselor of telling him that he would never walk again. The ensuing uproar ultimately involved the parents and the entire staff and ended only with the patient's and his parents' denial being reestablished.

With the coming of fall and the departure for college of the friends who had visited him during the summer, the patient became more overtly depressed and un-cooperative. Pain, without clear organic basis, became almost constant, and the patient spent much time in bed with the curtains drawn and frequently with the sheet over his head. At this point, psychiatric consultation was requested, and psychotherapy was continued on a fairly regular basis for the next eighteen months. In therapy, the patient was alternately severely depressed and suicidal, or angry, hostile, and demanding. The psychotherapist felt that he viewed the rehabilitation program as a "package," and that to cooperate with this was to also accept his ultimate disability. Many attempts were made to find a middle ground and establish other sources of self-esteem, but none of these proved helpful.

The patient was discharged after ten months' hospitalization, to return home with his parents. Physical rehabilitation had gone well, but no real progress had been made on the psychological front. Over the next two years, the patient did complete high school, but only after many social agencies had been involved and their various plans had been either rejected or severely criticized as inadequate. Several additional hospitalizations were required for attempted control of his pain. Plans for the patient to attend a local junior college were rejected because "it's a place for people who can't make it anywhere else." Arrangements were finally made, again by social agencies, for the patient to live in a nearby city with his brother and attend the city college. This lasted for less than a semester, and ended with the patient's readmission to the hospital in semicoma, apparently from medication overdose, although the details were never clear.

The patient now lives at home, but is reportedly very unhappy. His vague plans have shifted slightly to more sedentary activities, but again nothing has been done and he apparently still clings to the hope that he may again walk.

In the second case, a seventeen-year-old white, single, male, high-school junior suffered a sixth cervical vertebra fracture in a diving accident in September 1960, while on vacation with his basketball coach and a group of friends. He was also rendered immediately quadriplegic, with only minimal gross hand function. Local hospitalization again brought little improvement, and he was admitted to university rehabilitation service in April 1961, with chronic urinary tract infection and rapidly developing decubitus ulcers.

This patient was born and raised in the San Francisco Bay area and lived there with his parents at the time of his accident. He was an only son, with an older married sister living next door to the family. He had attended local parochial schools, was popular with teachers and other students, an average student, and an athletic star. At the time of his accident he had vaguely planned a high-school teaching career in physical education.

On admission to the rehabilitation service, this patient also expressed the hope that he would again walk. His parents shared this hope, and on initial contacts with the staff they showed minimal distress and indicated that "everything will be fine." Despite this verbalized denial, however, they behaviorally began adjusting to their son's condition by placing ramps in their home and widening doorways to accommodate a wheelchair. The family is repeatedly described by the staff as very close-knit, and his friends and teachers also provided much support.

This patient's rehabilitation was also complicated by medical problems, and evaluation for severe anemia and recurrent fevers delayed his program for more than two months. His first visit home was very successful, and many friends gathered to welcome him. The patient attended the graduation of his high-school class in the spring following admission, and by fall he had completed his junior year courses with a teacher visiting the hospital. With the beginning of planning for vocational training, the patient became periodically depressed, but was able to discuss his feelings with the rehabilitation staff. He initially had little interest in academic teaching as a career and thought of pursuing his former hobby of radio and television repair. His physical limitations prevented the mechanical aspects of this work, and after a brief exposure to electronic theory he decided that this did not interest him. In further discussion with the counselor, the patient developed an interest in history, and at the time of discharge after ten months' hospitalization he was considering college with a history major. He was discharged home and adjusted well. Although attendant care was offered, the patient chose not to accept this, but to depend instead upon passersby if he needed assistance. Over the next year he completed high school and began college at a local Catholic institution. He continued to live at home, with his mother or a friend driving him to and from school, but operated independently during the day. He ultimately graduated from college, and is now teaching history at the high-school level. He recently considered marriage, but after discussing his sexual limitations with physicians decided against this for the time being. His interest in sports has not been totally lost, for during a recent hospitalization for urinary tract infection he arranged to coach a local boy's club basketball team from his wheelchair.

The two young men described above had apparently quite similar pre-accident resources and interests and neither history suggests serious personality defects. They had virtually identical anatomical lesions and physical disabilities and parallel courses of physical rehabilitation. Both used psychological "defenses" during the early part of their hospitalization, and indeed those who have studied crises have pointed out that such behavior may be highly adaptive in "buying time" during the acute phase (Cobb and Lindemann 1943; Chodoff, Friedman, and Hamburg 1964; Hamburg and Adams 1967). Yet their final outcomes could hardly have been more disparate, with one carving out a new and apparently quite satisfactory life for himself, while the other has made little progress during the almost ten years since the accident. On the basis of the data presented, we cannot hope to explain the difference in outcome of the two patients described. We will aim instead to point to what appear to be highly significant variables in the adaptational process involved in rehabilitation. It is useful first, however, to review briefly the three conceptual frameworks in which rehabilitation has traditionally been considered. These frameworks focus respectively on the biological, psychological, and social aspects of the adaptive process.

If the human being is viewed as an organism coping with a physical environment, certain biological mechanisms will be required in order to deal with this environment adequately. There are perhaps four fundamental mechanisms necessary for successful biological coping, and these are present in all higher animals. The first of these is *movement*. An adequate moving mechanism capable of providing purposeful and effective movement, and for sufficiently long periods of time, is clearly necessary. Vir-

tually all response to environmental challenge involves purposeful movement, either of the total organism or its appropriate parts. *Sensing* may be
considered as a second biological mechanism. Through this mechanism all
environmental inputs are received and appropriate responses evoked. This
input-output relationship is a fundamental biological rule of behavior, and if
either of these systems is disturbed, the biological capacity to cope is severely impaired. As a third essential component of function, the organism
must have an *energy-producing* mechanism. In this sense, all of an organism's
vegetative functions may be seen as providing for the conversion of ingested
fuel into energy for sensing and movement. Thus cardiac or pulmonary disability, within this framework, is an impairment of the energy-producing
mechanism. A fourth component might be called the *cerebral-integrating*
mechanism. This is a biological process that makes learning possible, stores
information, and appropriately integrates sensory input and motor output.
It can be seen as the control mechanism of a sensitive feedback system. Any
disease must in some way impair one of these four mechanisms, and disability results. Disability can thus be seen as a diminished capacity to "cope"
physically with the environment. We have mentioned so far only the "coping" organism, and yet from a biological viewpoint the environment must
also be considered. We must ask the important question, "coping with
what?" There are many features of the physical environment, so taken
for granted by the intact organism, that pose great problems for an individual who has lost the ability to walk, talk, hear, see, or perform fine hand
movements. To a considerable extent, failure in adaptation may be seen as a
product of insurmountable obstacles in the environment. Disturbances in
the four mechanisms described and their expression as physical disability
are the areas of primary concern of rehabilitation medicine. The goal is to
restore physical function insofar as it can be restored by the techniques
available, and thus to minimize remaining disturbances and permit the individual to cope maximally with the environment. Alteration of the physical
environment likewise plays a major role in rehabilitative efforts.

What has been disturbing is the fact that there is often too little correlation between the degree of physical disability, the success of physical restoration or environmental modification, and the ultimate social function of the
patient. The cases presented amply demonstrate this discrepancy, and
many further examples could easily be cited. Obviously, factors beyond the
biological must be considered, and the focus is most often on the individual's psychological state.

Psychological approaches to the understanding or assistance of patients
with long-term disability have most often been based in the concepts and
techniques of psychoanalytic psychotherapy. Although oversimplified, the
following summarizes the underlying focus of this approach. In this system,
emphasis is placed primarily on the preexisting personality of the disabled
individual, and an understanding of his failure to adapt to disability is
sought in unresolved conflicts from his past life. Much time may be spent in

reviewing developmental history in an effort to formulate the dynamic structure of the individual's personality at the time of the crisis. Current difficulties in adaptation are viewed in terms of the continuity of past personality and behavior, and there may well be less emphasis on current and future reality. As an example, difficulties in working effectively with rehabilitation personnel may be seen only as a carry-over from strained parental relationships. Psychiatric "symptoms" of depression and anxiety, and various manifestations of psychological "defense," seen almost universally in the acute phases of disability, may be understood in terms quite appropriate for dealing with psychoneurotic patients, but they have little relevance for an individual with gross physical limitations. Psychotherapy utilizing such an approach may produce considerable "insight" on the part of the patient, but there is all too often a failure to translate this understanding into effective coping behavior.

As a matter of fact, even in cases of severe psychoneurosis, the removal of pathological defenses only opens the way for a second phase of the therapy, in which habituated behavior patterns belonging to the neurosis are gradually replaced by more realistic ones. New forms of behavior and new social encounters have to be anticipated and rehearsed. The attending anxiety must be tolerated, and the new behavior must actually be tried and evaluated. The support of the therapist and his continued interest in successive levels of accomplishment is a crucial aspect of this "rehabilitation" phase of the program. The mastery of the emotions involved is intimately related to the appropriate rehearsal of the next steps to be taken. Indeed, the concept of emotion, both in anxiety and in depression, has been much enriched by observations carried out on primates in the context of programming and rehearsing future activities (Pribram and Melges 1969).

The success or failure of the planned behavior is always determined by the social context in which it is executed, and the environmental variable most often centrally considered in psychological approaches to rehabilitation is the patient's family. There is concern with their psychological response to the crisis they share with the patient, and emphasis may be placed on their instrumental value in caring for him physically. Therapeutic intervention with the family is often aimed at assisting them in managing their distress and in effectively assuming the caretaker role without fostering undue "regression." Even broader physical and social environments may likewise be viewed as contributors to overall personality structure, and these environments may be searched primarily for supporting or regressive elements with respect to the patient's pattern of functioning.

Both of the patients discussed here were, at the time of their accidents, in the process of emancipation from their families and were about to enter the peer groups of adult life. Their successful participation in these peer groups required mastery of the necessary dependency and need for care that were inevitably a part of their paralysis. The temptation for the parents to overly satisfy these dependent needs—and the patient's conflict between participating in the family in a childlike, dependent role versus striving for a rewarding set of activities outside the family—can severely complicate rehabilitation.

This highlights the importance of a recurring question that complicates the patient's efforts. For whom is he getting rehabilitated? If the paralysis is experienced as a deformity, producing an ugly cripple, then the fear of never being able to count on a loving and accepting response from the family or peer group may lead to hopelessness and resignation. That these fears are plausible and must be specifically disproved has been shown repeatedly by studies of the great differences in acceptance and aversion with respect to more or less disfiguring types of impairment (Goodman et al. 1963).

While the general psychological condition brought to the crisis of physical disability, like the mechanical aspects of the disability itself, clearly has major relevance to outcome, it appears that focus on the adaptive tasks is required for full understanding and effective intervention.

Clinical observation, over long periods of time, of fairly large numbers of patients whose problem is ongoing disability suggests that this is a peculiar kind of social predicament in which the issue is not "get well or die," but rather becoming "permanently different." Stated bluntly, the individuals we are talking about no longer possess the range of capacities that are taken for granted in human conduct, namely, the ability to walk, grasp and release, and perform an almost infinite range of other sensory-motor functions. These universal human attributes are not simply temporarily suspended, but are rather permanently lost.

This issue of "differentness" often seems central to the resolution of the kind of crisis we are considering. The important distinction is between being "sick" and being "different." As long as the disabled individual sees himself and is seen by the environment as sick, he continues to demonstrate appropriate illness behavior and to have appropriate expectations of getting well. Such behavior patterns are well demonstrated by the first patient described above. Basic to adequate coping with permanent disability is the awareness and acceptance by the individual and his environment that he is no longer sick, but different. If this transition is successfully made, he may then function as a different kind of human animal, with distinctive needs, problems, and ways of adapting. It thus becomes evident that a most important prerequisite to effective assistance in rehabilitation is a clear picture of the individual's self-image. The important contribution of the psychiatrist in such a setting is often the elucidation of a dynamic psychological understanding of the origins, development, and current environmental supports for the individual's view of himself.

Because the old basis for self-respect and the confidence that one will be liked by family and peers have been shattered, or at least severely strained, by the illness, the patient needs a great deal of testing and reaffirmation on the part of a readily accessible network, consisting of both handicapped and healthy persons, so that he has positive expectations about his future performance and participation.

Previous studies have repeatedly stressed the maintenance of self-esteem as a primary task in a variety of crisis situations (Chodoff et al. 1964; Coelho, Hamburg, and Murphey 1963; Hamburg and Adams 1967; D. Hamburg, B. Hamburg, and deGoza 1953; Silber et al. 1961; Visotsky and Hamburg 1961). Without this stabilizing force, the risks involved in behavioral change become overwhelming. We must next ask what psychological factors contribute to the maintenance of self-esteem, and we would submit that of major importance is the individual's sense of movement toward an image of himself in the future, or an ego ideal. It is precisely this sense of continuity and progress that may be totally disrupted by physical catastrophy. A second prerequisite to rehabilitation is thus an understanding of the sources and supports of the ego ideal. The opportunity to observe and identify with others who can serve as models for successful and rewarding new patterns of role behavior must be considered as indispensable for a successful program (Bandura and Mischel 1965).

A recent preliminary study by Suinn and Feldman (unpublished data) strongly supports the central importance of self-image in the outcome of physical rehabilitation. This study utilized a relatively simple and brief self-description scale that required the patient to agree or disagree with statements describing himself either as permanently sick and disabled or as capable of altering his goals for the future. Response patterns to this scale, collected early in the course of rehabilitation of patients suffering severe physical trauma, were correlated with ultimate functional outcome following maximum feasible physical rehabilitation. The results indicated a high correlation between flexibility of future goals and optimal functioning. It is important to note that the more global factor of "motivation," often invoked in explaining the results of rehabilitation, but seldom reviewed in detail, was not considered in making the outcome predictions in this study.

In further illustration, we turn again to the first case presented earlier. The young man described clearly clung tenaciously to the image of himself as sick and disabled. It is also quite evident that this view was shared by his family and other significant members of his environment. With regard to future goals, there is again little ambiguity. For this patient, physical activity and roles requiring it seem the only route to personal achievement. Athletics had provided important past experiences with success, and family tradition for the "manly" Navy life was clearly very strong. The mere suggestion of more realistic roles, for example those of student and perhaps eventually teacher, proved to be an overwhelming threat to self-esteem. Such responses were again reinforced by the patient's family, and this total system proved resistant to the various efforts of the rehabilitation staff.

Although the distinct perspectives described above have perhaps been somewhat overdrawn, they do in fact exist. More importantly from a therapeutic standpoint, these tasks are often delegated to different members of the rehabilitation team. Thus, physical restoration is the responsibility of physicians and physical therapists, psychological skills are often requested only when evidence of gross distress appears, while planning for future social and occupational roles is delegated to social workers and occupational therapists. In contrast to this fractionation, it seems clear that for maximum effectiveness rehabilitation must be viewed in terms of the dynamic and complex relationships among these interacting systems. They must be regarded as interpenetrating and interdependent systems that affect the patient's sense of unity of self in doing, feeling, and becoming. Changes within each system have repercussions on each of the others, and they must be articulated in a feedback communication network. As an example, the patient's experience of his changed body functions has a bearing not only on his body image, but also on his feelings about himself and the world. This self-image is in turn affected by his actual behavior in coping with the changed environmental situation, and the tasks that he can perform depend in part on how his social environment supports his self-image and induces new role expectations that may legitimately be fulfilled in the task environment. It seems obvious, then, that the first step must be an exploration by members of the rehabilitation team among themselves and the search for congruence of their values with those of the patient and his family. Some such congruence will have to be achieved in order to facilitate effectively the patient's efforts and to avoid exposing him to overwhelming conflict.

To review now, from the viewpoint of coping behavior, successful rehabilitation can be seen to involve effective engagement with several broad bio-psycho-social tasks. These tasks include maintaining a sense of personal worth, keeping distress within manageable limits, maintaining or restoring relations with significant other people, enhancing the prospects for recovering bodily functions, and increasing the likelihood of working out a personally valued and socially acceptable life style after maximum physical recovery has been attained. As applied to the process of rehabilitation for those with long-term disability, these various tasks appear to be vital component parts of the ultimate goal of altering the patient's view of himself in the future and establishing a modified ego ideal. Such redirection may be an option in many of the crisis situations that have been studied, but would appear obligatory in the adaptation to gross physical limitation. To accomplish this complex task of social learning, skills beyond those of the psychiatrist or expert in physical medicine alone may be required. The great importance of maintaining self-esteem during the period of uncertainty and exploration of new goals require the coordinated support of all members of the rehabilitation team. In addition to their supportive function, rehabilitation staff can be significant sanctioners of new goals and behaviors. The patient's family and broader social contacts must obviously be made an integral part of the adaptive process, for they are often required to make considerable value adjustment themselves in support of the "changed" individual. The importance of the early and continuous involvement of significant others cannot be overstressed, for they are all too often seen merely as agents to take over the patient's care once physical rehabilitation has been completed.

Institutions well beyond the hospital walls must be involved in effective rehabilitation. Schools can play a major part in the redirection of life style and values of the handicapped; and industry could well develop a wide range of productive and self-esteem-fostering roles. The British rehabilitation model, involving the establishment of communities for the handicapped, perhaps produces excessive isolation from the rest of society, but may well point to important social variables (Wing 1966). To understand the operation of these larger social systems and to assist them in change, the medical specialists must use the skills of the social psychologist and sociologist, while the anthropologist may add an understanding of cultural values and their evolution. Rehabilitation truly becomes a broad task for all of the behavioral sciences.

In summary, it appears that the process of rehabilitation after severe physical injury presents a series of complex and often unanswered questions to the clinician. Studies of crisis behavior following a variety of loss situations provide the basis for inferences concerning the phases and stages of the restorative process. A significant point is reached after the initial period of denial, when experiences and behavior analogous to mourning are observed. The accustomed life style and its range of functions and rewards are not abandoned without pain, and the attending depression must be accepted before new functions and roles can be learned. There must be detailed review of the major tasks faced by the individual and his environment. These include defense against recurring negative emotions, the maintenance of self-esteem in the face of impaired functioning, the search for models for the successful creation of a new life style, and the development of access to reference groups whose values and goals support a new set of roles. Specific coping strategies must be collaboratively developed to approach each of these major challenges.

We have concentrated here on the effective adaptation to physical disability, but the principles outlined have applicability in many other areas. The alcoholic, the narcotic addict, the chronically hospitalized psychiatric patient, and even the neurotic, while often not demonstrating the kind of acute crisis that we have described, share with the victim of physical trauma a need for rehabilitation and social relearning. The study of coping behavior in a wide range of settings may provide important clues to the understanding and facilitation of individual and social change.

REFERENCES

Bandura, A., and Mischel, W. The influence of models in modifying delay of gratification patterns. *Journal of Personality and Social Psychology*, 1965, *2*, 698–705.

Caplan, G. *Principles of preventive psychiatry*. New York: Basic Books, 1964.

Chodoff, P., Friedman, S., and Hamburg, D. Stress, defenses, and coping behavior: Observations in parents of children with malignant disease. *American Journal of Psychiatry*, 1964, *120*, 743–749.

Cobb, S., and Lindemann, E. Coconut Grove burns: Neuropsychiatric observations. *Annals of Surgery*, 1943, *117*, 814–824.

Coelho, G., Hamburg, D., and Murphey, E. B. Coping strategies in a new learning environment. *Archives of General Psychiatry*, 1963, *9*, 433–443.

Erikson, E. *Childhood and society*. New York: Norton, 1963.

Finesinger, J., and Lindemann, E. A discussion of the psychiatric aspects of rehabilitation. *Diseases of the Nervous System*, 1945, *6*, 1–8.

Goodman, N., Richardson, S. A., Dornbusch, S. M., and Hastorf, A. H. Variant reactions to physical disabilities. *American Sociological Review*, 1963, *28*, 429–435.

Hamburg, D., and Adams J. E. A perspective on coping behavior. *Archives of General Psychiatry*, 1967, *17*, 277–284.

Hamburg, D., Hamburg, B., and deGoza, S. Adaptive problems and mechanisms in severely burned patients. *Psychiatry*, 1953, *16*, 1–20.

Janis, I. *Psychological stress*. New York: Wiley, 1958.

———. Psychological effects of warnings. In G. W. Baker and D. W. Chapman, eds., *Man and society in disaster*. New York: Basic Books, 1962.

Lindemann, E. Symptomatology and management of acute grief. *American Journal of Psychiatry*, 1944, *101*, 141–148.

———. The timing of psychotherapy. In 6th International Congress of Psychotherapy, London 1964, Selected Lectures. New York: S. Karger, Basel, 1965, 75–90.

Pribram, K. H., and Melges, F. T. Psychophysiological basis of emotion. In P. J. Vinken and G. W. Bruyn, eds., *Handbook of clinical neurology*, vol. 3. Amsterdam: North-Holland Publishing Company, 1969.

Silber, E., Hamburg, D., Coelho, G., Murphey, E. B., Rosenberg, M., and Pearlin, L. Adaptive behavior in competent adolescents: Coping with the anticipation of college. *Archives of General Psychiatry*, 1961, *5*, 354–365.

Suinn, R., and Feldman, D. Unpublished data.

Visotsky, H., and Hamburg, D. Coping behavior under extreme stress: Observation of patients with severe poliomyelitis. *Archives of General Psychiatry*, 1961, *5*, 423–448.

Wing, J. K. Social and psychological changes on a rehabilitation unit. *Social Psychiatry*, 1966, *1*, 21–28.

8

Vigilance and Decision Making in Personal Crises

IRVING L. JANIS

In contemporary society, national and local authorities frequently alert the public to emerging threats so as to encourage precautionary actions. Public health officials regularly warn people about cancer and heart disease by giving vivid descriptions of the threatening aspects of disease in an attempt to induce them to adopt preventive measures. The press, radio, and television constantly transmit warnings and precautionary recommendations about how to prevent automobile accidents and various large-scale disasters. The mass media also present communications that recommend precautionary social actions to prevent future economic dangers and social disorganization. The ostensible purpose of all these various types of warnings and admonitions is to help people cope more effectively with potential dangers and deprivations in the future. But the success of any such communication depends initially on the emotional reactions of members of the audience, as they are being exposed to it, and, subsequently, on the way in which they think about and assimilate the message.

RESPONSIVENESS TO WARNINGS AND EMOTIONAL INOCULATION

A number of social psychological investigations have begun to explore systematically the conditions under which warnings succeed in inducing acceptance of whatever course of preventive action is recommended by the com-

This chapter is based on material from several chapters in a forthcoming book by I. L. Janis and L. Mann, Decision Making: A Social Psychological Approach. The research studies reported in this chapter were facilitated by grant MH-08564 from the National Institute of Health, U. S. Public Health Service. Preparation of this chapter was facilitated by grant GS-30514X from the National Science Foundation.

139

municator. Most of these studies use authentic warning messages presented by sources who are authoritative public health experts or organizations. The findings, therefore, are most relevant for public health campaigns intended to induce people to take such precautionary measures as cutting down on smoking, coming to medical clinics for diagnostic checkups, and obtaining inoculations against infectious diseases.

Some of the results also have implications for a different type of warning communication, one that is designed to have an emotionally inoculating effect on persons who are about to be exposed to severe life stress. Studies of people facing major surgical operations, debilitating illness, and community disasters point to the need for emotional inoculation (Caplan 1961; Egbert et al. 1964; Janis 1958; Janis and Leventhal 1965). These studies indicate that if a normal person is given accurate prior warning of impending pain and discomfort, together with sufficient reassurances so that fear does not mount to a very high level, he will be less likely to develop acute emotional disturbances than a person who is not warned. We know that there are exceptions, of course, such as neurotic personalities who are hypersensitive to any threat cues. There are also some unmitigated types of personal disasters, as in the case of terminal cancer victims and severely burned persons, who are only "withered remnants of their former selves," for whom blanket denial may be the only effective means of avoiding overwhelming anxiety and depression (D. Hamburg, B. Hamburg, and deGoza 1953). But these considerations do not preclude the following hypothesis for a wide range of anticipated sources of stress: moderately fear-arousing messages about impending dangers and deprivations will function as a kind of emotional inoculation, enabling normal persons to increase their tolerance for stress by developing effective coping mechanisms and defenses (Janis 1958, 1971). I call this process emotional inoculation because it may be analogous to what happens when antibodies are induced by injections of mildly virulent viruses.

To produce successful emotional inoculation it is necessary to interfere with the person's spontaneous efforts to ward off his awareness of the signs of impending danger. Unwelcome information has to be given in order to convey a realistic picture of the disturbing events each person is likely to experience. How can this be done without running the risk of provoking either panic or adverse avoidance reactions, such as defensive indifference and denial? Tentative answers are suggested by some of the same communication experiments mentioned earlier, which assess the effects of different dosages of fear-producing material—for example, in warning messages about lung cancer that urge people to cut down on smoking.

Systematic field studies and controlled experiments show that persuasive messages containing fear-arousing warnings or other motivating appeals generally mobilize powerful resistances (Janis 1967). But communications research also indicates that there are certain conditions under which audience resistance to distressing warnings and unwelcome admonitions can be overcome sufficiently to induce a vigilant attitude concerning realistic threats and to instigate decisions that lead to adaptive coping actions. A number of communication variables have been found to affect the success of any communication that attempts to influence a person's outlook about the future, to change his attitudes, or to induce him to adopt a new course of action. Here I am referring to such well-known factors as conveying the expert credentials of the communicator, referring to opposing arguments in a way that avoids apparent bias, and presenting recommendations that explicitly convey the implications of the arguments and emotional appeals presented in the persuasive message (Cohen 1964; Hovland, Janis, and Kelley 1953; Janis and Smith 1965).

In addition to a variety of stimulus variables, individual differences among people exposed to the same communications have also been investigated. We are beginning to accumulate some data concerning the types of persons who are likely to be most resistant and least resistant to various types of messages. In other words, we know that the success of an authoritative message depends not only on *who* says it and *what* he says but also on the predispositional characteristics of the persons to *whom* it is said.

In this chapter, I focus on the findings concerning predispositional factors that help to account for individual differences in responsiveness to warnings that present fear-arousing information. Because these individual differences are usually investigated in studies that consider the effects of different intensities of threat material, we are able to take account of interactions between predispositional attributes and variations in threat stimuli.

Many of the studies that furnish us with relevant data have been focused on one main question, namely, whether high emotional arousal elicited by a warning generally facilitates, or interferes with, acceptance of the communicator's recommendations. But the accumulated evidence indicates that emotional arousal gives rise to both facilitating and interfering effects, sometimes with one being dominant and sometimes the other (Janis 1967). Consequently, we cannot expect to find any broad generalization that will tell us whether a high-threat or low-threat version will be more effective. Rather, we must expect the optimal level of fear arousal to vary for different types of warning communications and for different types of personalities. By the optimal level of fear, I mean the point on the fear continuum where the facilitating effects of fear arousal are most powerful and outweigh the interfering effects. Once the level of fear arousal exceeds the optimal level, interference gets the upper hand, and acceptance of the communicator's recommendations will decrease.

In an earlier paper (1967) I tried to show how a new theoretical model, which postulates a family of inverted U-shaped curves to account for the relation between intensity of fear arousal and adaptive coping responses, might enable us to bring some order out of the seemingly contradicting findings from research on the effects of fear-arousing communications. Later in this chapter I shall indicate the implications of this model for our understanding of individual differences. For the present, I merely want to point out that instead of expecting the optimal level of arousal always to be

at one end or the other of the fear-arousal continuum, we should reformu-
late our questions in terms of factors that determine whether the optimal
level will be relatively high or low whenever a given type of warning is
presented to a given type of person. For example, we should try to find the
answers to such questions as these: When a warning communication deals
with such a grave and imminent danger that it arouses an extraordinarily
high degree of fear, as when a physician recommends emergency surgery to
remove a cancerous growth, what factors can be introduced into the situation that will help to promote an optimal level close to the maximum possible level of stress tolerance, in order to reduce the chances that the upset-
ting recommendation will be misunderstood, rejected, or defensively
avoided? In general, under what conditions will stress tolerance be maximal, so that any warning message that arouses strong fear will be interpreted correctly, without inducing panic or other maladaptive responses?
What types of personalities generally have low tolerance for the stresses
generated by warning messages and what types generally have high tolerance? In what ways and to what extent can predispositions be modified so
that someone who initially overreacts to a given type of warning can be
helped to cope more effectively? The implications of these questions will
perhaps become more apparent after we examine a number of relevant findings from studies that suggest, at least indirectly, the kind of answers to be
expected.

The sources of individual differences in stress tolerance within a given
population are difficult to determine, because many of the most relevant
variables, such as chronic level of anxiety, cannot be experimentally manipulated. Moreover, most personality tests available for investigating correlations between personality attributes and acceptance of a communicator's
recommendations are of low or unknown validity. The most frequently
used of these tests are personality inventories that subjects fill out themselves. These self-reports are notoriously affected by the subjects' conscious strivings to represent themselves as socially acceptable persons.

The assessment of responsiveness to fear-arousing communications is
especially complicated, because defensive personality tendencies incline
many individuals to deny potential danger or to repress their negative feelings. Some indications of these distorting response patterns are provided in
studies by Lazarus and his co-workers on fear reactions to distressing sights
of genital mutilations in documentary movies. In one study, Lazarus and
Alfert (1964) compared the emotional reactions of subjects scoring high and
low on various self-rating scales from the Minnesota Multiphasic Personality Inventory. When asked to report their affective states, the subjects who
scored high on scales that were presumed to measure denial, repression, or
repression-sensitization were less likely than others to say that they were
disturbed by the vivid scenes of genital damage. Nevertheless, on various
physiological measures of arousal taken during exposure to the stressful film,
the deniers obtained higher scores than the nondeniers.

Because assessment of arousal varies with response mode, research on individual reactions to stress may be more productive if assessments are made on a variety of indicators in order to determine preferred mode of emotional expression. In other words, we may need to extend to the verbal sphere the well-known suggestion by Lacey (1959) to investigate each individual's "channel" for expression of affect among the various physiological changes that are likely to be induced by stressful stimuli.

Most of the pertinent evidence on predispositional factors comes from a small number of studies in which the reactions of persons who are high and low on a given personality attribute are compared shortly after all of them have been exposed to the same warning communication. Although the data are fragmentary, we can extract a number of hypotheses about predispositional factors that determine the intensity and quality of stress reactions.

In general, two types of predispositional factors have been investigated. One type has to do with *ego-involvement*, or the degree to which the individual perceives the threat as relevant to his personal goals, decisions, and social commitments. The second general category includes chronic level of anxiety and other *basic personality characteristics* that presumably determine an individual's sensitivity to a much wider range of threat or stress stimuli.

EGO-INVOLVEMENT IN THE THREAT

Before examining chronic personality attributes, let us look first into some of the less well known predispositional factors making for individual differences in ego-involvement, which are amenable to environmental influence. Some relevant evidence comes from studies that compare the reactions of smokers and nonsmokers to fear-arousing communications on smoking and lung cancer. Several such studies indicate that smokers tend to be more resistant than nonsmokers to communications that play up lung cancer or other dangers of smoking (Cannell and MacDonald 1956; Feather 1962, 1963; Janis 1959; Leventhal and Watts 1966). Leventhal and Watts, for example, give evidence to suggest that heavy smokers, after being exposed to a fear-arousing movie on smoking and lung cancer, tended to express "blanket reassurance" attitudes involving denial of personal vulnerability, which function as a defense against the arousal of fear. Many more heavy smokers than light smokers said they would *not* be vulnerable to lung cancer. Because they felt they had little to worry about, it is not surprising that the heavy smokers were less likely to accept the public health recommendations to stop smoking. Similar results were reported from a study on the effects of a warning concerning automobile accidents. Drivers minimized the potential dangers more than nondrivers and were less likely to accept the recommendation to use seat belts (Berkowitz and Cottingham 1960).

Additional studies bearing on the role of ego-involvement as a determinant of stress reactions have been reviewed by Iverson and Reuder (1956) and in subsequent discussions by Vogel, Raymond, and Lazarus (1959), and Lazarus (1966). Lazarus (1966) cites evidence showing the expected relationship between the degree of emotional arousal induced by a threat of deprivation and the strength of the individual's need to avoid the deprivation.

From these and other studies of ego-involvement it appears that there are two main ways in which the members of an audience for whom the threat is most applicable tend to differ from those who are less ego-involved: (1) the highly ego-involved persons become more *vigilant* and more *interested* than others in obtaining information about the threat; but (2) they are more *reluctant* than others to conclude that the danger is sufficiently great to warrant protective action. From verbal comments recorded during exposure to a fear-arousing communication, we have found (Janis and Terwilliger 1962) that some highly ego-involved smokers start off by feeling personally vulnerable to the potential dangers depicted in an antismoking communication and become momentarily fearful, but then they promptly think of some way to minimize the threat or to discredit the communicator. Once they are able to restore their feelings of invulnerability, their temporary fear reactions subside and they no longer regard the threat of lung cancer as a challenge to their long-standing complacency. No one is likely to go through the painful process of considering changing his long-standing policy unless he becomes convinced that certain dangerous events might arise in the foreseeable future that could be escaped or mitigated by some alternative course of action. Withey (1962, p. 106) points out that when a person is induced to take a threat seriously he may make a series of thoughtful appraisals, trying to estimate: (1) the nature of the impending danger and its expected unfavorable consequences; (2) the probability that the dangerous event will occur; (3) the severity of the loss to himself if the event does materialize; (4) the means available to him for coping with the potential danger; (5) the probability of success of alternative means; (6) the probable cost of using each of the alternative effective means; and (7) the course of action that is most likely to succeed at minimal cost. These cognitive appraisals, along with appraisals of the imminence of the danger, lead to coping plans that can function in the long run as effective reassurances, which differ from the cruder forms of blanket reassurance in that they are more oriented toward reality, enabling the person to anticipate a limited, tolerable degree of personal vulnerability and to take account of his own coping resources.

Even when we restrict our observations to heavy smokers, we find marked individual differences in readiness to be exposed to challenging information about the health hazards associated with smoking. There are some who regularly adhere to the policy of smoking more than a pack each day, but feel quite perturbed about what they are doing and wish they could change. Such smokers are actually in a state of postdecisional conflict, usually induced by one or more impressive communications that have successfully challenged their former complacent attitude of personal invulnerability. Other heavy smokers are only partially challenged and do not manifest very much postdecisional conflict. They acknowledge being personally vulnerable to the danger, but they set aside any challenging message about lung cancer, emphysema, or heart disease by assuming that there is no need to worry about these hazards at present: "I can wait until there are signs of the danger materializing; maybe it never will." Thus, even though partially challenged, the smoker may maintain a type of resistance that interferes with his acceptance of the recommended precautionary measures; he is able to retain his emotional equanimity by sincerely denying that at present anything needs to be done about the potential threat. But even though they are only partially challenged, these smokers, like those in a state of acute conflict about continuing to smoke, are disposed to be more vigilant and impressed by new fear-arousing information than those smokers who have not yet been challenged at all.

These latent differences among smokers who manifestly are displaying the same smoking behavior have their counterpart among persons who are pursuing any other course of action that is labeled as risky or dangerous by some influential sector of our society. That is to say, the same differentials in latent responsiveness to new warnings probably hold for persons who are pursuing any course of action, whenever authoritative warnings are issued that call attention to its potential risks.

PREDISPOSITIONAL DIFFERENCES IN EGO-INVOLVEMENT CORRESPONDING TO STAGES IN THE DECISION-MAKING PROCESS

The foregoing statements about latent predispositional differences are in line with recent conflict-theory analysis of changes in attitudes and decisions (Janis 1959, 1968; Janis and Mann 1968). We view the decision-making process as a sequence of stages that starts off with challenging information that motivates the person to reconsider whatever course of action (or lack of action) constitutes his current policy. We view successful challenges as having the effect of arousing interest in new information and persuasive messages concerning the desirability of alternative courses of action, because the person has become motivated to find an adequate solution to the problem posed by the challenge. This theoretical approach also gives considerable emphasis to the decision maker's capacity to resist impressive persuasive communications and signs of social disapproval after he has committed himself to a course of action.

Most discussions of personal decision making distinguish between two major phases in the decision process—the predecision and postdecision phases (Festinger 1964). Similarly, many studies of attitudes merely differentiate between those people who are in favor of adopting a given course of action and those who are opposed. However, a finer classification from the standpoint of a conflict-theory analysis of the decision process differentiates among the sequential stages through which a person goes in arriving

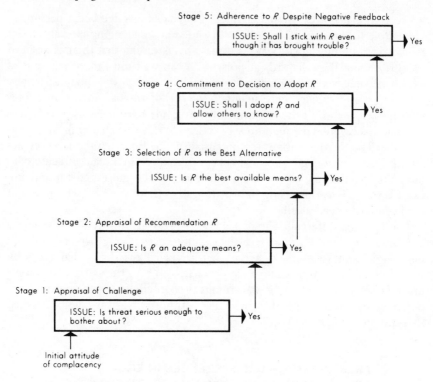

Stage 5: Adherence to *R* Despite Negative Feedback

> ISSUE: Shall I stick with *R* even though it has brought trouble?   ▶ Yes

Stage 4: Commitment to Decision to Adopt *R*

> ISSUE: Shall I adopt *R* and allow others to know?   ▶ Yes

Stage 3: Selection of *R* as the Best Alternative

> ISSUE: Is *R* the best available means?   ▶ Yes

Stage 2: Appraisal of Recommendation *R*

> ISSUE: Is *R* an adequate means?   ▶ Yes

Stage 1: Appraisal of Challenge

> ISSUE: Is threat serious enough to bother about?   ▶ Yes

Initial attitude
of complacency

FIGURE 8-1   Stages in making a decision to adhere to a new policy recommended as a means for coping with a serious threat. From: Irving L. Janis, Stages in the decision-making process, in Robert P. Abelson et al., eds., *Theories of Cognitive Consistency: A Sourcebook*, © 1968 by Rand McNally and Company, Chicago, p. 579. Reprinted by permission of Rand McNally College Publishing Company.

at a stable decision, such as giving up smoking, going on a diet, or undergoing a prescribed course of medical treatment (Janis 1968). The five main stages shown in Figure 8-1 have been differentiated on the basis of observations of the changes people undergo when they commit themselves to a new policy and successfully adhere to it.

1. APPRAISAL OF A CHALLENGE.   Until his present course of action (or inaction) is challenged by some form of negative feedback that calls attention to real or anticipated losses, the person remains complacent about the policy to which he has been adhering. Once a communication or event challenges the old policy by making the person realize that it has some undesirable consequences that should be avoided, he will begin to have doubts about continuing it and will consider the possibility of selecting an alternative course of action.

2. APPRAISAL OF RECOMMENDED ALTERNATIVES FOR MEETING THE CHALLENGE.   After the person has become doubtful about the desirability

of his old policy as a result of an effective challenge, he will seek information about the available alternatives and will begin to appraise them from the standpoint of averting the negative consequences that have come to the focus of his attention. During this phase, the decision maker discards any alternative that appears to be too unsafe or too costly and ends up selecting for further consideration those alternatives that he judges as feasible candidates for averting the losses made salient by the challenge.

3. MAKING A TENTATIVE DECISION ABOUT THE BEST AVAILABLE POLICY. During this phase, the decision maker continues to seek information and to think over the pros and cons of each of the potential alternatives. He ends up by selecting the one that he decides will work best for him. Whereas stage two may be likened to nominating the candidates, stage three corresponds to selecting the best candidate. By scanning and weighing each alternative in terms of its advantages and disadvantages, the decision maker attempts to select the one that will best meet his personal criteria for maximal gains and minimal losses. There are four major types of considerations that enter into the balance sheet for any predecisional conflict during stage three: (1) anticipated utilitarian gains or losses for oneself; (2) anticipated utilitarian gains or losses for significant others; (3) anticipated approval or disapproval from significant others; and (4) anticipated self-approval or self-disapproval. (An illustrative example of a balance sheet during stage three is presented in Table 8-1, which is based on interview data from a heavy smoker who participated in one of our preliminary experiments on changing smoking attitudes and habits.)

4. COMMITTING ONESELF TO THE NEW POLICY. After having covertly decided to adopt a new plan of action, the decision maker sooner or later reveals his decision to others. This may involve a series of substages as the person commits himself more and more, starting off by telling only a few close friends or members of the family, and then gradually allowing more and more persons in his community to know about it. As soon as he takes the first step of informing someone, the person anticipates some degree of social disapproval and a corresponding loss of self-esteem if he fails to carry out the new policy. Each fresh commitment to another person or group becomes an added incentive for bolstering and sticking with the decision.

5. ADHERENCE TO THE NEW POLICY DESPITE CHALLENGES. Starting with the very first act of commitment, the person may encounter negative social feedback in the form of overt or covert disapproval of his new decision. In addition, negative feedback arises whenever any of the calculated risks materialize and whenever any expected gain fails to materialize. Each of these setbacks—and any impressive communication that predicts ultimate failure—is a potential challenge that could create postdecisional re-

TABLE 8-1 HYPOTHETICAL BALANCE SHEET AT THE STAGE WHEN Examples of Conflicting Cognitions Verbalized by an Average Smoker the Surgeon General's Report on Smoking and Lung Cancer

ANTICIPATED UTILITARIAN CONSEQUENCES

Alternative courses of action (policies)	*+ or − incentive values*	*For self*	*For significant others (spouse, friends, family, reference group)*
1. Original policy (Continue smoking about one pack per day)	+	Provides daily pleasure; sometimes relieves emotional tension.	By relieving tension, it helps me get along better with my family and fellow workers.
	−	Possibility of my developing a lung cancer; it will make ordinary respiratory illness more serious; costs money.	Family would also suffer if I were to become a cancer victim.
2. New recommended policy (Stop smoking)	+	Chances of lung cancer will be greatly reduced; respiratory illness will be less troublesome; money could be put to good use.	Family will be more secure if I reduce chances of lung diseases; my abstinence might exert a good influence on our children.
	−	Unsatisfied craving will be unpleasant; I'll be more irritable and angry; might develop severe anxiety symptoms; might become overweight.	I already cause enough trouble to my spouse without becoming even more irritable and tense; this could be the last straw that breaks up our home.
3. Alternative compromise policy (Smoke only one-half pack per day)	+	Same as No. 2 to a milder degree, with risk of cancer greatly reduced.	Same as No. 2 to a milder degree.
	−	Same as No. 2 to a milder degree, with no problem of becoming overweight; a slight risk of lung cancer.	Same as No. 2 to a milder degree.
4. Alternative non-recommended policy (Switch to filtered cigarettes, one pack per day)	+	Same as No. 2 to a milder degree, but no money saved and not sure of lung cancer risk.	Same as No. 2 to a milder degree.
	−	Same as No. 1 and No. 2 to a milder degree.	Same as No. 2 to a milder degree.

From: I. L. Janis and L. Mann, A conflict-theory approach to attitude change and decision-making. In A. G. Greenwald et al., eds., *Psychological foundations of attitudes*. New York: Academic Press, 1968. Pp. 338–339.

ANTICIPATED APPROVAL OR DISAPPROVAL

From self	From significant others	Final judgment
I pride myself on not scaring easily.	My statistician friend will be pleased that I do not accept correlation as proving causation.	Unsatisfactory—Wants to change if a satisfactory alternative is available to provide a net gain (or less net loss).
If I don't live up to my commitment, I shall feel like an untrustworthy, weak character; if I ever develop a serious respiratory illness, I'll feel guilty.	Several friends will lose respect for me, since I committed myself to change my smoking habits; my family doctor will continue to disapprove.	
I shall feel satisfied with myself for living up to my commitment; also, taking action on the basis of new evidence shows that one is mature, realistic, and intelligent.	My friends will see that I am living up to my commitment; my family doctor and a few antismoking friends will strongly approve.	
I might lose my temper more often, which would make me feel like a heel.	My statistician friend will think I am stupid.	Mixed attitude—Prefers a less conflictful alternative if available.
Same as No. 2 to a milder degree.	Same as No. 2 to a milder degree.	
Going only part way may show a lack of self control.	My family doctor and several friends will not approve of this compromise.	Most satisfactory—Ready to adopt this policy since no available alternative is more attractive.
Same as No. 2 to a milder degree.	Same as No. 2 to a milder degree.	-
Same as No. 3 to a stronger degree.	Same as No. 3 to a stronger degree.	Satisfactory—But less attractive than an available alternative.

gret and conflict. All such challenges tend to be ignored, refuted, or somehow counteracted when the decision maker remains unshaken in his resolve to adopt the new policy. This stage persists indefinitely until an effective challenge occurs that is powerful enough to provoke another stage one type of crisis, following which the decision maker may again go through the four successive stages to arrive at a firm new decision. Thus, for assessing a person's initial position on a given decisional issue, such as whether to stop smoking, a sixth category must be added: unchallenged adherence to the *original* policy. This category can be regarded as prestage one for any new policy; it is equivalent to stage five for the original policy.

Sometimes, of course, the five stages cannot be sharply differentiated, especially when relatively minor decisions are made: the person may approach the task quite casually or simply make a final choice impulsively, so that some of the stages are coalesced or omitted. However, the five-stage model may provide a useful framework for analyzing predispositional differences in ego-involvement and other determinants of responsiveness to new information concerning precautionary measures that could avert a predicted source of danger.

One of the main types of problems to which the sequential model is intended to apply has to do with the receptivity of any audience exposed to warnings and persuasive messages that oppose his current course of action. A few years ago we had an opportunity to investigate this relationship in a field study of participants in the draft resistance movement (Janis and Rausch 1970). During the spring of 1968, there was a growing movement among students throughout the United States to oppose being drafted to fight the war in Vietnam. At Yale University, an antidraft petition—known as the "We-Won't-Go" pledge—had been circulating for many months and was signed by hundreds of students. Our study involved presenting persuasive messages on both sides of the draft resistance issue to men who had already signed the pledge and comparing their reactions with those of nonsigners who held varying positions with respect to the desirability of signing the pledge.

During the month when the interviews were being conducted, the local press, radio, and television newscasts gave daily reports about Senator Eugene McCarthy's campaign, which was devoted mainly to attacking the Johnson Administration on moral grounds for its failure to end the war in Vietnam and was receiving strong student support. Moreover, just before our study began, another antiwar campaign was also receiving considerable publicity. The Yale chaplain, Rev. William Coffin, had been indicted, along with Dr. Benjamin Spock and other leaders of a draft resistance movement. Coffin and the others were repeatedly appealing to Yale students to examine their own consciences on the morality of refusing to participate in an immoral war. Thus the draft resistance movement was constantly in the focus of attention of the Yale community.

The antidraft pledge, which was circulated in all the residential colleges, declared:

We are men of draft age who believe that the United States is waging an unjust war in Vietnam. We cannot, in conscience, participate in this war. We therefore declare our determination to refuse induction as long as the United States is fighting in Vietnam.

The signers realized that they were making a very strong personal commitment to resist being drafted, especially because all their names, along with the text of the pledge, were regularly published in local newspapers.

Although there was a great deal of controversy about the legal and moral status of the pledge and about its probable effectiveness as a political tactic, there was general agreement that adhering to it could have serious personal consequences. The students knew that the legal penalty for refusing induction was five years in prison and a $10,000 fine. Moreover, many draft resisters expected their careers to be seriously disrupted, particularly if they were planning to obtain a U.S. government fellowship, to enter the legal profession, or to work on any project or in any agency financed by government funds.

Our main purpose in comparing men who took varying stands on the antidraft pledge was to investigate theoretical issues bearing on responsiveness to persuasive messages in relation to stages in the decision-making process, particularly with regard to the problem of selective exposure.

There is fairly general agreement among social psychologists that after people become committed to a given course of action they show an increase in resistance to any persuasive communication that opposes their position (Festinger 1964; Janis and Mann 1968; Jones and Gerard 1967; Kiesler 1968; McGuire 1968a). But there is considerable controversy about how commitment affects interest in opposing communications. Until a few years ago, it was taken for granted by social scientists that people have little interest in exposing themselves to any message that challenges their existing beliefs and attitudes, particularly if they have already committed themselves on the issue (Klapper 1960). But the early opinion surveys on which this conclusion was based provide at best highly equivocal evidence, and the results of subsequent experiments leave us with a mixed picture (Freedman and Sears 1965). Several years ago, McGuire (1968b) pointed out that although a few experiments provide supporting evidence, a larger number of others fail to confirm the selective-exposure hypothesis, even though some of the authors had expected a positive outcome on the basis of one or another theory of cognitive consistency.

During the late 1960s, social psychologists began to realize that a number of additional factors may enter into exposure, including expected utility of the information and expected social rewards for acquiring information about what one's opponents are saying (Freedman and Sears 1965; Katz 1968; McGuire 1968b; Mills 1968; Sears 1968). The view that is beginning to emerge is that no single generalization can be expected because people have strong tendencies to satisfy curiosity and to obtain information about potential setbacks, as well as strong tendencies to avoid the tension generated by information that is inconsistent with existing expectations and preferences (Katz 1968; McGuire 1968*b;* Sears 1968). The problem then becomes that of determining the conditions under which one or another tendency will become the dominant one. This view fits in well with a conflict-theory approach: the choice of whether or not to expose oneself to a given communication can be conceptualized as a decision, albeit a minor one. Like all other decisions, any exposure decision would be partly influenced by prior commitments, but also by other important factors in the decisional "balance sheet"—utilitarian gains for oneself and for significant others, anticipated social approval from significant others, and anticipated self-approval for living up to one's own standards of conduct (Janis 1959).

This theoretical orientation inclined us to direct our inquiry beyond the question of whether increased commitment has the effect of increasing or decreasing a man's interest in opposing communications; we wanted to learn something about how and why such interest in opposing communications varies as a function of the stage the person has reached in the decision-making process.

Because the vast majority of Yale students had not, in fact, signed the "We-Won't-Go" pledge, we took special steps in order to have a sizable subgroup of men who had overtly committed themselves by signing it. We started off working from the published lists of signers of the "We-Won't-Go" pledge; as was mentioned earlier their names had appeared in the local newspapers as part of the signers' act of overt commitment. After selecting a sample of the names on a random basis, we sought out the men in their residential colleges. A total of twenty-three signers were interviewed. A sample of forty nonsigners was obtained in the same residential colleges by knocking at doors, in the same way the signers were approached. On the basis of a standardized interview, the sixty-three Yale undergraduates were sorted into those favoring and those opposing the "We-Won't-Go" pledge, by classifying them into four groups: (1) signers of the pledge, whose names had been published in local newspapers; (2) potential signers who were still undecided; (3) formerly conflicted refusers; and (4) prompt (unconflicted) refusers. These four categories were found to be highly predictive of expressed intentions to engage in alternative forms of antiwar protest, such as participating in demonstrations and sit-ins.

After the interviewer asked the men to read persuasive articles, significant differences were found indicating the expected relation between initial position and acceptance: the farther the men had gone in the direction of committing themselves to refuse to be drafted, the more likely they were (1) to accept communications favoring the draft resistance movement, and (2) to reject opposing communications. But just before being asked to read the articles, they showed the reverse outcome when they were asked to indicate how interested they would be in reading propledge and antipledge articles. (The type of material to be expected in each article was conveyed by the title and a fifty-word summary.)

For the four propledge articles, there were no significant group differences. For the four antipledge articles, however, there were large and significant differences in interest scores [1] (see Table 8-2). It will be noted, however, that the linear trend is the reverse of what would be expected on the basis of an inconsistency-avoidance hypothesis.

Thus, those who opposed signing the "We-Won't-Go" pledge were less interested in reading antipledge articles (which would support their own initial position) than were men who favored signing the pledge. When we examine the pertinent data in Table 8-2, it looks like this outcome is mainly

TABLE 8-2 COMPARISON OF MEN WHO OPPOSE
THE "WE-WON'T-GO" PLEDGE WITH
MEN WHO FAVOR THE PLEDGE
Mean Scores on Interest in Being Exposed
to Pro and Anti Articles

	OPPOSED TO PLEDGE		IN FAVOR OF PLEDGE		
	Promptly refused to sign (N = 12)	*Refused after deliberation* (N = 16)	*Might sign* (N = 11)	*Have already signed* (N = 23)	OVERALL MEAN
Propledge articles	9.83	11.81	11.09	10.83	10.94
		10.96		10.91	
Antipledge articles	7.50	9.38	10.09	11.31	9.84
		8.64		10.82	

Analysis of Variance: Interest Ratings by *S*s's Initial
Position (Dichotomized) and Type of Article Rated
(Pro versus Anti Draft Resistance)

Between Ss	*df* 62	*Mean square*	*F*
Initial position (A)	1	35.02	2.59
*S*s within groups	60	13.52	
Within Ss	62		
Pro versus anti articles (B)	1	44.55	7.35 [a]
A × B	1	38.10	6.28 [b]
B × *S*s within groups	60	6.06	

From: I. L. Janis and C. N. Rausch, Selective interest in communications that could arouse decisional conflict: A field study of participants in the draft-resistance movement. *Journal of Personality and Social Psychology*, 1970, *14*, 46–54.
[a] $p < .01$
[b] $p < .05$

attributable to the low mean score (8.64) for the men opposed to signing the pledge. In view of their low interest ratings, one might surmise that these men may have been uninterested in reading anything more on their own side of the issue because they were already overfamiliar with the supporting arguments.

Other plausible factors that might account for the observed outcome are suggested when we take note of the obvious fact that the men who favor signing the pledge deviate as much above the overall mean score of 9.84 for the antipledge articles as the men who oppose signing differ in the opposite direction. Perhaps there were some special reasons why those in favor of signing were more strongly interested than the others in being exposed to statements by their opponents concerning the allegedly bad consequences that might be in store for them if they were to live up to the "We-Won't-Go" pledge. Some clues along these lines were obtained from a separate series of intensive interviews of twenty-eight Yale men, which focused on attitudes and plans concerning resistance to the draft and was carried out as a pilot study to supplement the data from the present study. Almost all of the men described themselves as strongly opposed to continuing the war in Vietnam and hoped that they would not be drafted, although only twelve of the twenty-eight expected to refuse induction if drafted, in accordance with the "We-Won't-Go" pledge. Every one of the twelve resisters acknowledged that his refusal to be inducted would be a legally punishable offense and stated that if necessary he would leave the country or go to jail. When queried about the considerations that entered into their decision, the twelve resisters admitted feeling considerable conflict, anxiety, and uncertainty about their decision. Their comments suggest two specific sources of vigilance that would incline them to pay attention to counter arguments: (1) vigilant interest in information about the type of objections to the draft resistance movement that they were likely to encounter, so as to deal effectively with their parents or others in their personal social network who do not share their views; and (2) vigilant interest in information about the probable unfavorable consequences of adopting one or another specific course of action as a means for implementing the general policy stated in the pledge (for example, to apply for conscientious objector status, Project Vista, the Peace Corps, or a draft-deferred teaching job, or to escape the draft by leaving the United States).

The important point is that no matter how deeply committed a man might be to support the draft resistance cause, he still faced the question of what he would do personally to circumvent being drafted. One reason why each man's decisional conflict was so intense was his realization that every one of the alternatives open to him was very risky. Even those inclined to apply for the Peace Corps or some other means of obtaining a draft exemption or deferment knew that the attempt might fail and therefore that they might be required to resort to a more drastic means of avoiding the draft, which would result in a jail sentence and possibly permanent damage to their careers. Assuming that the signers and would-be signers in our field study were facing this type of predecisional conflict, we would expect them to be especially vigilant concerning any of the risks entailed by evading or opposing the draft laws.

Obviously, there are other motivations that might also enter into the decision to read a communication that goes counter to one's own stand. For example, a desire to be regarded as a fair and judicious person might incline a man to express a strong interest in being exposed to the opposing communications. These and related tendencies, which have been repeatedly mentioned in publications on selective exposure, could be operating among the college students in our field study. Furthermore, because our data are correlational, we must also consider the possibility that some important predispositional attribute—such as a personality or ideological variable that makes for marked differences in open-mindedness—might be the underlying determinant both of attitudes toward the "We-Won't-Go" pledge and of readiness to expose oneself to the pro or anti communications.

Although we have no basis for selecting among the alternative mediating factors that could account for the differences in interest ratings shown in Table 8-2, the data, nevertheless, bear directly on the status of the selective-exposure hypothesis, which predicts the opposite outcome from what we found. Our data on recall of pro and anti arguments also indicate that the reality-testing orientation of the college students in our study remained unaffected by whatever motivation they may have had to avoid decisional conflict. The findings show that the men's initial position had no relation to the number of pro or anti arguments they were able to recall after reading two persuasive communications.

Our findings are consistent with Sears's (1968) conclusions in his critique of the selective-exposure hypothesis. He points out that although several communication experiments show a selective-exposure tendency, at least twice as many studies fail to yield any significant differences that would show the predicted preference for supportive communications or avoidance of nonsupportive communications. He also cites findings from experiments by Waly and Cook (1966) and Greenwald and Sakumura (1967) showing that nonsupportive arguments are learned as readily as supportive ones. Sears concludes that the available evidence calls into question the earlier reports of selective exposure and selective learning, because it implies that in everyday life people do *not* generally resort to information-avoidance techniques to soften the impact of unpleasant information, even though such avoidance may be displayed in extreme situations of psychological stress involving the threat of bodily injury, death, or the loss of a loved person.

The results from our field study not only fail to support the selective-exposure hypothesis, but also indicate that at least under certain conditions we should expect the reverse tendency to be dominant. We have suggested several factors that might prove to be the determining conditions—such as overfamiliarity with supporting arguments and vigilant concern about unfavorable consequences to be averted when one is facing the dilemma of selecting the most appropriate means for implementing a policy to which one has already committed himself (or is about to do so). Such factors will require systematic investigation as potentially interacting variables in subsequent studies of selective exposure.

Certain of the explanatory concepts put forth to account for the results of this field study have important implications for the way a person will respond to opportunities for obtaining potentially distressing information about anticipated threats. Among the pertinent hypotheses are the following: when people commit themselves to a general course of action that they know is difficult to implement without sustaining serious losses, such as imprisonment or career disruption, they will retain a vigilant interest in opposing communications. More specifically, the decision maker's general level of vigilance concerning anticipated social or physical punishment for an obviously illegal or counternorm action will increase when he reaches the stage where he feels almost ready to commit himself, and it will continue to remain high, or possibly increase to an even higher level, after he actually does commit himself, even though he may prefer to avoid information that will induce decisional conflict or cognitive dissonance. During and after the commitment stage, the decision maker will display a relatively high degree of interest in two types of conflict-inducing information: (1) objections and arguments that he is likely to encounter from his family, friends, or other significant persons who may express strong disapproval; and (2) information about specific punitive consequences that he might be able to avert when he decides on the most appropriate means for implementing his risky decision.

SOME IMPLICATIONS
OF THE FIVE-STAGE MODEL
OF THE DECISION-MAKING PROCESS

The study of draft resisters suggests that the five-stage model of the decision-making process might provide a useful classification scheme for sorting people into predispositional subgroups representing qualitative and quantitative differences in ego-involvement that influence the way people will respond to fear-arousing information. In our recent group studies conducted in a clinic at Yale University for persons who want to change their smoking habits, we have encountered subjects who are at each of the various stages (Janis 1968). Some of the volunteers who come to the clinic merely feel a bit concerned about the unhealthy consequences of smoking and wonder what they ought to do about it (stage one). There are other volunteers, however, who have reached the later stages. Some feel convinced that they should quit smoking and have repeatedly committed themselves to do so, but they simply cannot tolerate the withdrawal symptoms (stage four). Subjects at each of the various stages seem to be able to benefit and move on to the next stage as a result of the added commitment and social support that comes from joining a "common-problem" group conducted by a psychologist or from being paired up with a partner with whom they maintain daily contact by telephone. Nevertheless, the types of information that appear to be especially effective for people at an early stage in the decision-making process do not appear to be very effective for persons at a later state, and vice versa. For example, when a member of a discussion group vividly describes his concerns about the threat of cancer, his statements meet with strong resistance from those members who have not yet gone through stage one. The latter are inclined to question their personal vulnerability to the dangers of lung cancer. The members at stages two, three, and four, however, seem to be progressively less resistant and become more strongly motivated by the same bit of warning information.

Having observed this type of differential response on many different occasions in working with these common-problem groups, I have been led to surmise that once a person has gone through the earliest stages of the decision-making process with respect to cutting down on smoking, he becomes much less resistant to subsequent fear-arousing information about the nature of the threat. Although the observations could be interpreted in a number of different ways, the following hypothesis is suggested: the higher the stage of the decision-making process at which the individual is located with respect to arriving at a new policy, the less his resistance will be to warnings that call his attention to the potential threats or risks pertaining to his initial policy. This hypothesis embodies the concept of latent dispositions mentioned earlier. Thus, for example, among a group of people who currently smoke a pack of cigarettes each day (initial policy) less resistance to a communication that plays up the danger of lung cancer would be expected among those who have already reached stage three in moving toward a decision to cut down on smoking than among those who are at stage two or stage one, even though none of them have as yet changed their smoking habits in any way. A special case of this hypothesis is the proposition stated earlier that those who have already been challenged (that is, reached stage one) will be less resistant than those who have been partially or not at all challenged (prestage one).

Although only indirect evidence is available so far, there is some reason to expect that the postulated inverse relation between stages and resistance to warnings about the initial policy will have a high degree of generality. In contrast, the postulated relation between stages and vigilance concerning warnings about the implementation of the new policy (discussed in connection with the study of draft resisters who showed strong interest in communications dealing with the risks of opposing the draft laws) would be much more restricted in scope, because it applies to certain types of decisions and not to others. Whenever a given policy can be easily put into practice, with little or no risks involved in implementing it, we would not expect to find the type of vigilant interest in opposing communications that we find among the draft resisters. Thus, for example, we would expect that if a middle-class American college student is moving toward a decision to become a cigarette smoker, he will not show this type of increase in vigilance; whereas, if he is moving toward a decision to become a marijuana smoker (or to use LSD or any other illegal drug), he will show it. The difference, of course, is that tobacco products are readily available and cost very little; whereas marijuana, like other illegal drugs, is more difficult to obtain, and the act of procuring it could lead to serious trouble with the police or other authorities. If antimarijuana laws were to change in the United States, observable differences in vigilance would be expected to disappear. For the present, however, we predict that most would-be marijuana smokers at stage three or four in the decision-making process will show relatively strong interest in antimarijuana communications, especially if they play up the dangers of trafficking in this drug, but most would-be cigarette smokers at the corresponding stages will show relatively little interest in antitobacco communications. Similarly, middle-aged men and women who are habitual marijuana users (stage five) would continue to take a strong interest in all antimarijuana communications in the mass media that promise to present new threatening information; those who are habitual tobacco users would not ordinarily show this type of vigilance concerning antitobacco communications in the mass media. These considerations have some obvious implications for the problem faced by those public health officials who are trying to induce the American public to avoid cigarette smoking.

The same problem would exist for all warnings that are intended to induce people to take account of the long-run dangers of any current practices that are *easy* and *unrisky* to carry out. This category might include, for example, a warning about the risks of heart disease from going without exercise, from overeating, or from not restricting the amount of polysaturated fats in one's diet. I do not mean to imply that all such warnings are forever doomed to go unnoticed and unheeded (see Hamburg and Adams 1967). Many a man will start to pay close attention to these warnings after he has had his first heart attack. But this type of reaction points up the problems of the mass media gaining the attention of large numbers of people before their usual expectations of personal invulnerability have been rudely shaken by a personal disaster or near-miss experience.

EMOTIONAL ROLE PLAYING AS A
DEVICE FOR CHALLENGING COMPLACENCY

One question that arises from the preceding discussion is whether predispositions to become vigilant can be changed in some way by introducing some form of effective challenge whereby people can be shifted from their chronic unchallenged status to stage one (or beyond), in the decision-making process. Is there some way to be challenged without being exposed to the actual danger itself? An affirmative answer is strongly suggested by several recent experiments that show the effectiveness of a psychodramatic role-playing device in inducing unchallenged smokers to change their smoking habits.

In the first in a series of experiments, Leon Mann and I used twenty-six young women as subjects (Janis and Mann 1965). All of them were cigarette smokers who had not expressed any intention of cutting down on their tobacco consumption. Half were assigned at random to the experimental group, and half to the control group. None were aware of the purpose of the study.

We set up a psychodrama situation for the experimental group, in which each subject was asked to play the part of a patient suffering from the

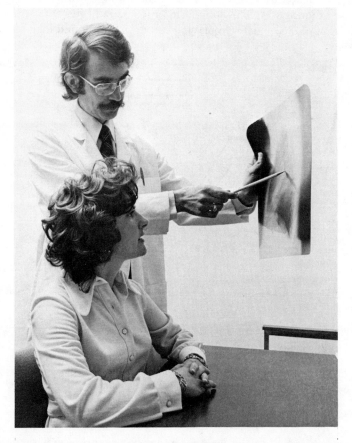

FIGURE 8-2   The subject ("patient") and experimenter ("doctor") in an emotional role-playing experiment dealing with smoking and lung cancer.

consequences of smoking. The investigator played the role of physician. Five scenes were acted out. In one, the "physician" pointed out the X-ray indications of a malignant mass in the patient's lung as he gave her the bad news that diagnostic tests indicated the presence of lung cancer (see Figure 8-2). The women in the control group were exposed to the same information, but they did not participate in the role playing. Instead, they listened to a tape recording of a session with one of the experimental subjects.

The role playing proved to be an extraordinarily disquieting experience, but the subjects apparently were able to tolerate a high level of fear without mobilizing resistances. Although the role playing generated a great deal of emotional tension, it had a markedly greater effect in changing smoking habits than did the tape recording. In a follow-up study conducted eighteen months after the role-playing episode (Mann and Janis 1968), the experimental subjects continued to report a significantly greater decrease in the number of cigarettes smoked than did the young women in the control group (see Figure 8-3). This long-term outcome indicates that a single one-hour session of emotional role playing can have a profound long-term effect

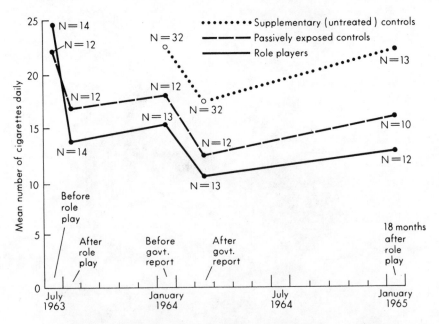

FIGURE 8-3   Long-term effects of emotional role playing on cigarette smoking. From: L. Mann and I. L. Janis, A follow-up study on the long-term effects of emotional role playing, *Journal of Personality and Social Psychology*, 1968, *8*, 339–342.

upon smokers who initially have no intention of cutting down on cigarette consumption. The results suggest that significant changes in smoking habits may persist for years. This technique of emotional role playing seems to provide unusual empathic experiences similar to those that occasionally lead to spectacular "conversions" among physicians, relatives, and friends of cancer victims. There are numerous indications that the high level of fear and vigilance aroused by the realistic quality of the experimental procedures may be a major factor in the increased antismoking attitudes and the changes reported in smoking habits.

A study by Leon Mann (1967) indicates that this type of emotional role playing is more effective with both male and female smokers than cognitive role playing (enacting the role of a debater arguing against smoking). Mann also found that the amount of attitude change produced by this fear-arousing procedure increases when subjects are given the opportunity to verbalize their own ideas while acting. Other recent studies also support the general conclusion that emotional role playing induces the person to "repackage" already available information in a way that changes his feelings of personal vulnerability to health hazards.

Thus, under appropriate conditions, a person's initial attitude of denial or unwarranted complacency may be transformed by a strong fear-arousing experience via psychodramatic role playing into a more adaptive attitude—an attitude that combines vigilance with high receptivity to precautionary recommendations. So far as our present evidence goes, it seems plausible to assume that the emotional role-playing procedure induces a mild, benign form of near-miss experience. But in exploring such devices, we are mindful of the possibility that more extreme near-miss experiences can induce a maladaptive state of hypervigilance together with other symptoms of a transient traumatic neurosis.

CHANGES IN PREDISPOSITION INDUCED BY NEAR-MISS EXPERIENCES

The effects of near-miss experiences have been described in studies of acute war neurosis. Grinker and Spiegel (1945), for example, present a series of case studies showing that the overreactions of traumatized soldiers and flyers to relatively mild signs of threat result from a basic change in self-confidence involving a loss of feelings of personal invulnerability. They were able to trace the onset of these attitude changes to near-miss experiences that preceded marked decreases in efficiency of performance among combat flyers. Practically all of these men had begun their series of missions with high morale, as volunteers who were confident about being able to survive the hazards of combat flying. Most of the flyers had originally felt that "others may die but nothing will happen to me." But they began to lose this sense of security after a few difficult missions, especially if they had a narrow escape or saw friends in their formation being shot down. Their fear of enemy attack markedly increased on the first occasions when they encountered a convincing demonstration of damage from antiaircraft fire or enemy fighter planes. After a dramatic, unnerving experience of helplessness in the face of danger, some flyers became so apprehensive that they could no longer perform their flying tasks dependably, and had to be grounded at least temporarily. In these men, there was a morbid change in basic attitude, from "nothing terrible will happen to me" to "something terrible is bound to happen to me."

Grinker, in collaboration with several psychologists, obtained some systematic data on this relationship from a questionnaire study of 544 flying officers who had recently completed their tour of combat duty (Grinker et al. 1946). Feelings of personal invulnerability were investigated by including a question concerning whether they had felt that "while others might be hurt or killed, it couldn't happen to you?" Affirmative answers were given by only a small percentage of the 284 flying officers who had developed acute neurotic symptoms during their combat duty or immediately after; whereas such answers were given by a relatively high percentage of the 260 flying officers who had undergone similar combat experiences without developing symptoms. Although the findings do not establish the causal sequence, the statistically significant difference between these two groups is consistent with the general hypothesis under discussion, which predicts that if a man develops the characteristic pattern of hypervigilance and other anxiety symptoms following exposure to danger, he will also show a change in attitude concerning his personal vulnerability.

A similar conclusion is supported by observations of civilians exposed to the destructive impact of air raids or peacetime disasters (Janis 1951; Schmideberg 1942; Wolfenstein 1957). The critical disaster experiences that give rise to acute anxiety reactions appear to be those capable of evoking a feeling of being powerless to avert actual danger. Narrowly escaping from danger, losing close friends or relatives, and witnessing maimed bodies appear to have the effect of shattering the entire set of psychological defenses involved in maintaining expectations of personal invulnerability.

In general, it is expected that hypervigilant behavior will be produced by information or danger episodes that interfere so drastically with anticipations of personal invulnerability that the person is no longer able to ward off strong fear whenever he encounters new danger signs. Not all near-miss experiences necessarily have this effect, however, even though there is evidence indicating that maladaptive reactions are more likely to be produced by near-miss experiences than by remote-miss experiences. There appears to be a benign type of near-miss experience that merely breaks down blanket immunity reassurances and induces the person to become aware of his potential vulnerability, without rendering him incapable of evolving effective reassurances. For example, after the San Angelo tornado, many survivors described themselves in interviews as having "learned a lesson" and reported that they now planned to build dependable storm shelters before there were any more tornado warnings (Moore 1958). Similar indications of new fear-reducing decisions have been noted after other disasters and danger episodes (Janis 1971).

Taking account of a theoretical analysis of "reality-oriented" or "reflective" fear, presented in an earlier publication (Janis 1962), we can view the learning effects of a benign near-miss experience as resulting in the acquisition of a set of discriminatory attitudes, which has a twofold benign outcome: (1) in the normal course of events, when no warning signal is present the person's level of fear remains very low, with blanket reassurance as the dominant reaction; and (2) when clear-cut warnings are perceived, the person's fear mounts to a moderate level, well above the threshold for discriminatory vigilance, but below the threshold for hypervigilance.

In contrast, when a person has been emotionally shocked by a severe near-miss experience, the level of fear evoked by subsequent threat stimuli will frequently exceed the threshold for hypervigilance, and he will display inappropriately intense fear, including excited overreactions to mild warnings and other remote threat cues.

Using "near miss" and "remote miss" as purely descriptive terms to designate, respectively, a high versus low degree of proximity to actual danger stimuli in a stressful situation, we can say that the former is more likely to produce hypervigilance, whereas the latter is more likely to produce an attitude of blanket reassurance. Despite these differential tendencies, however, the effects of near-miss and remote-miss experiences can overlap to a considerable degree, and both types are capable of giving rise to adaptive compromise defenses. In short, the sustained effects of any given stressful episode, whether near miss or remote miss in character, can range over the entire continuum, motivating the development of blanket reassurances, adaptive coping responses, or hypervigilance. Which type of outcome will ensue depends upon two main factors, according to the postulates presented in the analysis of reflective fear: (1) the type of information conveyed by the stress experience; and (2) the person's original level of fear in response to the threat stimuli (prior to the onset of the danger stimuli). When the information conveyed by the episode is of the type that breaks down expectations of personal invulnerability, the predicted poststress reaction to any recurrence of the threat will be the following: (1) maladaptive hypervigilance if the person's fear level initially was moderate or high; and (2) adaptive vigilance if the person's fear level initially was low. On the other hand, if the information conveyed by the episode is of the type that fosters expectations of personal invulnerability, the predicted poststress outcome will be the following: (1) blanket reassurance if the person's fear level initially was low; and (2) adaptive vigilance if the person's fear level initially was high.

The above-stated propositions serve to link the psychological impact of stress experiences with the antecedent predispositional status (average level of fear evoked whenever the person has been exposed to the given type of threat in the past) and the temporary (and sometimes persisting) changes in his predispositional status (increase in level of fear evoked by the same type of threat). These propositions also point to the continuity between the impact of direct confrontation with environmental stress and the impact of purely verbal warnings. We would expect that the effects of any pertinent informational input bearing on personal vulnerability to danger will depend upon the person's original level of fear, whether the information is conveyed by direct exposure to danger stimuli or by purely verbal warnings.

CHRONIC PERSONALITY PREDISPOSITIONS

So far we have been dealing mainly with readily modifiable types of predispositions, such as changes in ego-involvement from exposure to challenging psychodramatic or real-life experiences that increase vigilance and decrease resistance to warnings about a specific type of threat. Now we turn to the more persisting types of personality predispositions, such as chronic level of anxiety, which are not likely to change except when a person undergoes successful therapy.

Regardless of whether a person is highly ego-involved with a specific threat, he will overreact to any sign of danger if his predispositional tendencies include a low threshold for anxiety arousal to a broad class of threat stimuli. Even with relatively crude diagnostic techniques, we may be able to select persons who display very high anxiety in the presence of any sign of oncoming physical danger, whether it involves potential pain, body damage, or severe deprivation. An assessment of chronically high anxiety in response to external threats of physical danger should allow better-than-chance predictions as to who will display high, medium, or low emotional arousal in response to warnings as well as danger stimuli. Among surgical patients, for example, there are some hyperanxious personalities who characteristically react with high anxiety to any sign of potential pain, restraint, or body damage (Janis 1958). Such persons show disproportionately high fear when a nurse or physician enters the room, both before the operation and afterward. Long after the main ordeals of surgery are over, they continue to react as though facing an enormous danger when told about such minor threats as taking penicillin injections. Studies by Leventhal (1965) and Leventhal and Sharpe (1965) also indicate that chronically anxious patients can be identified on the surgical and maternity wards as those persons who become excessively disturbed when confronted with any minor threat before and after the crisis of surgery or delivery. These patients remain hypervigilant and never develop the kind of self-delivered reassurances that would allow them to cope adequately with the stresses they encounter in the hospital. Surgical patients who display more moderate levels of fear before the operation are likely to develop more effective reassurances.

Some indications of the ways in which predispositional characteristics are likely to interact with communication stimuli in producing adaptive behavior are provided by studies in which differentially frightening communications are exposed to equivalent groups of subjects whose personality attributes are assessed by personality tests. In the first study on personality differences in relation to acceptance or rejection of fear-arousing communications, Janis and Feshbach (1953, 1954) divided their subjects into high and low anxiety subgroups. This was done on the basis of the subjects' answers to a personality inventory that dealt with somatic anxiety symptoms (for example, questions about how often they suffered from pounding of the heart, trembling hands, cold sweats, clammy hands, and so forth). Acceptance of the recommendations given in a standard dental hygiene communication was found to be dependent upon the interaction of two variables: (1) the amount of fear-arousing material concerning the damaging consequences of neglecting one's teeth presented in the communication; and (2) personality predispositions, as assessed by the somatic anxiety scale. Within the audience exposed to the strong threat-appeal version, those students with high anxiety predispositions (that is, those manifesting many chronic anxiety symptoms) were less influenced than those with low anxiety predispositions. But, within the equivalent audience exposed to the minimal threat version, the opposite outcome was found. That is, the students with high anxiety predispositions were more influenced by the mild fear-arousing version than those with low anxiety predispositions (see Figure 8-4).

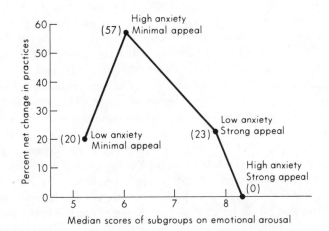

FIGURE 8-4 Observed relationship between level of fear arousal and acceptance of the communicator's recommendations, based on data from Janis and Feshbach 1954. From: I. L. Janis, Effects of fear arousal on attitude change, in L. Berkowitz, ed., *Advances in Experimental Social Psychology*. New York: Academic Press, 1967, vol. 3, p. 194.

This interaction indicates that a person's threshold for fear or anxiety arousal will determine the degree to which he will be resistant to a communication containing precautionary recommendations that are bolstered by statements that depict severe threats. The highly anxious students became more subjectively apprehensive while exposed to the fear-arousing statements in the strong-appeal version of the communication, but they were more likely to develop defensive reactions of the type that interfere with long-run acceptance. Thus, the strong-threat version appears to have exceeded the optimal level of fear arousal for the high-anxiety subjects, but not for the low-anxiety subjects. On the other hand, the mild appeal was found to have a comparatively favorable effect on the highly anxious students. These findings suggest that when a mild-threat appeal is presented (for example, one that refers to potential danger without "spelling out" any of the threatening details), the chronically anxious persons, by virtue of their low threshold for anxiety arousal, will be more likely than others to display a slight increase in fear. As long as the emotional state does not become too intense, they will be more likely than their unruffled neighbors to develop attitudes that conform with the communicator's recommendations. When their emotional state does become too intense, as with severe-threat communications, the chronically anxious person will become emotionally disorganized or will resort to habitual defenses. Interfering responses then predominate and prevent acceptance of the recommendations.

Several other experiments on fear-arousing communications provide comparative personality data similar to that obtained in the Janis and Feshbach experiment (Berkowitz and Cottingham 1960; Goldstein 1959; Haefner 1956, 1964; Leventhal and Singer 1966; Niles 1964; Singer 1965). (For a review of these findings see Janis and Leventhal 1968.) Some of the findings are confirmatory, but other findings are inconsistent with the Janis and Feshbach data, and are also inconsistent with each other. Perhaps the unreliability of the paper-and-pencil personality measures and the attitude-change measures used in these studies gives rise to so much error variance as to obscure whatever relationships might be present. The negative findings, however, serve to introduce a note of caution about the interaction hypotheses just discussed. Obviously, some of the inconsistencies may arise from unspecified variables that may prove to be limiting conditions for any general propositions about the relationship between anxiety proneness and acceptance of mild versus strong fear-arousing communications. The best that can be said for the interaction hypothesis at present is that it is supported by some, but not by all, of the relevant evidence, and, consequently, it is worthwhile to continue to investigate the individual differences in reactions to stress stimuli predicted by the hypothesis.

The continued search for this type of interaction effect is in line with an analysis of stress behavior by Lazarus and Baker (1956), who point out that the effects of stress sometimes remain undetected if the investigator fails to examine individual differences in response to the stressful situation. Illustrative examples are provided by the findings from experiments by Lazarus and Eriksen (1952) and Hardison and Purcell (1959). In both experiments, no main effects were found in comparing the laboratory stress and the nonstress conditions, but there was, nevertheless, an increase in variability of response attributable to the stress condition. In the Hardison and Purcell experiment, improvements in performance under stress occurred in subjects rated as independent and flexible, while deficits appeared in a contrasting group rated as dependent and constricted. Similar interaction effects are also reported in a stress experiment with grade-school children by Penny and McCann (1962), and the results closely parallel those found in the Janis and Feshbach (1954) study.

I suspect that one reason why the data from other pertinent studies are not consistent is that the formulation of the interaction hypothesis is a bit too simpleminded. A more adequate formulation, it now seems to me, would be in the following terms: the optimal level of fear arousal is generally lower for highly anxious and defensive personalities than for those who are less anxious and less defensive. The formulation of the interaction hypothesis presented earlier (p. 165) would be a special case of this more general reformulation, which is based on a somewhat more complex theoretical model than has been used in our thinking in the past. In the remainder of this paper, I shall briefly sketch out the main features of the theoretical model, and I shall try to show some of its implications for research on predispositional variables that account for individual differences in responsiveness to warnings.

A THEORETICAL MODEL
FOR ANALYZING CONTENT VARIABLES
AND INDIVIDUAL DIFFERENCES

In the search for differential responses among different personalities to the same warning communications, it may be useful to take account of the implications of a theoretical analysis of the determinants of the optimal level of fear arousal (Janis 1967). This analysis takes as its point of departure the basic assumption that adaptive attitude changes depend upon the relative weight of facilitating and interfering responses, which are evoked whenever a warning arouses fear. Consequently, it is inappropriate to expect to find any broad generalization about either a high- or low-threat type of warning being generally more effective in inducing people to take protective actions, because the optimal level of fear arousal will vary for different types of conditions and audiences. For example, some of the experiments mentioned earlier point to the perceived protective value or efficacy of the recommended course of action as a critical factor in determining the optimal level of fear arousal.

A hypothetical model has been constructed (Figure 8-5) in order to illustrate the notion that the optimal level of fear arousal for inducing acceptance will vary for different types of warning communications and for different types of persons. In the diagram of the three-dimensional model, the X-axis represents level of emotional arousal elicited by a warning communication, which can vary from zero at the left end to extreme panic at the right end. The Y-axis represents the probability of acceptance of an authoritative recommendation that will help the person to cope effectively with the threat. The third dimension, labeled "Determinant of optimal level," represents any situational or dispositional factor that influences the relative balance of interfering and facilitating effects at any given point on the fear continuum.

This diagram consists of a family of inverted U-shaped curves that relate fear arousal to acceptance. Each curve has a different peak (A, B, C, D, and

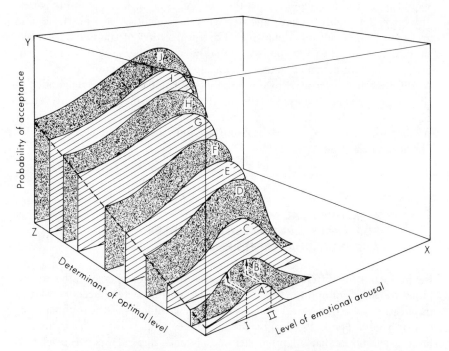

FIGURE 8-5 A three-dimensional model for analyzing the effects of fear-arousing communications. From: I. L. Janis, Effects of fear arousal on attitude change, in L. Berkowitz, ed., *Advances in Experimental Social Psychology.* New York: Academic Press, 1967, vol. 3, p. 207.

so on), which represents a different optimal level of arousal. A central task of research on the psychological effects of warnings and other stress stimuli, it seems to me, is to discover the interacting variables (represented by the third dimension) that determine whether the optimal level of fear will be relatively high or relatively low on the arousal continuum.

In an earlier paper (Janis 1967), I have shown how this model led us to the work on emotional role playing, in searching for psychological techniques that will reduce a person's resistances so as to enable him to reach a higher optimal level. In the same paper, I indicated how this model might help to reconcile some of the seemingly contradictory findings from past experiments on the effects of content variables. I think that the model may have similar implications for research on predispositional variables.

Lazarus (1966) has described four broad classes of personality attributes that can influence the process of coping with threat: (1) motivational patterns that determine which stimuli pose important threats and which ones are nonthreatening; (2) ego resources that reduce vulnerability to threat and facilitate adaptive forms of coping; (3) defensive dispositions that determine whether the person will characteristically respond with vigilance, avoidance, or some other form of defense when he is threatened; and (4) general beliefs about the threatening environment and one's own resources for coping with the source of danger. In combination, these various factors make for marked individual differences in the intensity of fear evoked by any communication that refers to a source of potential danger or loss.

The family-of-curves model inclines us to regard all such predispositional attributes as variables that determine whether an emotionally aroused person will be located on the ascending or descending sector of the inverted U-shaped curve. A general assumption about anticipatory fear is that the more vulnerable a person perceives himself to be, the higher his level of emotional arousal will be when he receives threatening information. Chronic anxiety has been treated as one of the variables that influence anticipated vulnerability to a wide variety of threats. Other variables that can influence anticipated vulnerability to any given threat, such as the threat of lung cancer from smoking, include ego-involvement (smoker versus nonsmoker), prior warnings about the extent of the danger (familiarity versus ignorance about the painful and incapacitating aspects of lung cancer), and prior information about the chances of coping with the danger should it materialize (awareness of the adequacies and inadequacies of available medical and surgical treatments of lung cancer).

Interactions like those we found in the Janis and Feshbach (1954) study incline us to ask these questions for any given warning: which type of personality is most likely to be aroused at or near the optimal level, where the facilitating effects of fear exceed the interfering effects? Which type is likely to be far above the optimal level, where the facilitating effects are no longer dominant?

One way to account for the interaction findings is suggested by the family-of-curves diagram in Figure 8-5. Suppose that we have available the results of a personality test that enables us to assess the chronic anxiety predispositions of a large number of people, so that we could sort them roughly into two groups—those who are highly sensitive to threats of pain or body damage and those who are not. (The scores on any test used to assess this personality variable may approximate a normal distribution curve, but it will be more convenient for purposes of theoretical exposition to oversimplify a bit and talk in terms of a simple dichotomy: persons who obtain relatively high scores will be referred to as "the anxious type" and those who obtain relatively low scores will be referred to as the "unanxious type" of personality.) When exposed to a very mild fear-arousing communication—let us say an antismoking movie that merely alludes to the threat of lung cancer, without elaborating on it—the unanxious persons will be aroused only slightly, if at all. The anxious persons, however, being acutely sensitive to any such allusions, will have thoughts and fantasies about their personal vulnerability that result in their becoming much more aroused. Now, if their fear is *not* so intense as to exceed their optimal level (as when a communication presents very mild threat cues along with some reassuring recommendations), we would expect more of the anxious personalities than the unanxious to adopt the recommended protective action. This is illustrated by the ascending portion of the curve up to point I on the first curve (A) in Figure 8-5. Point I might correspond to the level of arousal evoked in the anxious subjects, and a lower point on the X-axis would correspond to the level of arousal evoked in the unanxious personalities by the same mild fear-arousing communication. But a difference in the opposite direction would be expected whenever a stronger fear-arousing communication is presented that (1) does not exceed the optimal level of arousal for the unanxious (below the peak of A in the diagram), and (2) does exceed the optimal level for anxious personalities (for example, at point II). The latter persons would then become much more defensive and constricted, with the result that they would be less likely to accept the message, as indicated by the descending portion of the curve between the peak at A and point II.

These examples illustrate one way that the optimal-level concept could be used to explain the interaction findings described earlier. The main hypothesis suggested by the above discussion is that *the chronically anxious type of personality will generally have a lower threshold than the unanxious type with respect to feeling vulnerable and becoming emotionally aroused when subjected to either mild- or strong-threat stimulation.*

In addition to having a lower threshold, the anxious type of personality might differ from the unanxious type in other important ways, which could affect their capacity to cope effectively with stress. When the anxious and the unanxious personalities are equally aroused (say at point II in Figure 8-5), the anxious might be much more disposed than the unanxious to become either hypervigilant or defensively avoidant (Coelho, Silber, and Hamburg 1962; Lazarus 1966). If so, the anxious type would be less likely to develop an adaptive type of attitude that combines discriminative vigilance with reassurance and that leads to effective coping actions.

Thus, a second hypothesis to consider is that *the chronically anxious type of personality tends to have a lower optimal level of emotional arousal for acceptance of any recommended protective action, on the average, than the unanxious type.* In terms of Figure 8-5, the average optimal level for the unanxious type, for a given type of warning, might be at optimal-level B (on the second curve); whereas, the average optimal level for the anxious type would generally be lower, at optimal-level A (on the first curve). If this were the case, even when a moderate fear-arousing message evokes approximately the same degree of arousal in everyone (say, at point II), the anxious type would still show less acceptance than the unanxious type. We can see in the figure that point II intersects the curve for optimal-level A in a region where it is descending, whereas it intersects the curve for optimal-level B near the peak. But this large difference in degree of acceptance of the warning message would not be expected when a very mild version of the message is presented. If the level of arousal for both types of personalities is low (for example, at point I), both acceptance curves are intersected below the optimal level, before they begin to diverge.

The point is that the observed interaction effects could occur partly because of the relatively low chronic level of stress tolerance of the chronically anxious type of personality, as specified by the second hypothesis. Insofar as personality factors affect coping capabilities, they would be determinants of the optimal level, and the resulting individual differences would correspond to different curves on the third dimension in Figure 8-5.

It remains an open question, of course, whether either of the two hypotheses just suggested will provide an adequate explanation for observed interaction effects. In order to obtain definitive answers, it will probably be necessary to develop more precise methods of assessing emotionality than are currently used. We shall have to develop better techniques to classify people validly with respect to chronic anxiety predispositions and to detect differences in their momentary levels of emotional arousal in response to warnings. It seems to me that if research investigators expend the time and energy necessary to develop such techniques and to test theoretically oriented hypotheses, such as those suggested by the three-dimensional theoretical model, new vistas might start opening up for personality research. We might then begin to achieve some long-sought advances in our understanding of how personality predispositions influence the decisions people make in response to communications about impending crises and disasters.

NOTE

1. For the pro articles, the absence of any significant differences among the four groups was shown by a one-way analysis of variance: $F = 1.08$; $df = 3.58$; $p < .25$. For the anti articles, the same type of analysis of variance revealed significant differences in interest scores among the four groups: $F = 3.18$; $df = 3.58$; $p < .05$. The same outcome was obtained when we compared the combined mean for the two groups who were opposed to signing the pledge with the combined mean for the two groups who were in favor of signing it. The results of a 2 x 2 analysis of variance (bottom of Table 8-2) show: (1) a significant main effect for type of article, indicating that for all subjects the mean interest ratings were significantly higher for the propledge articles (10.94) than for the antipledge articles (9.84); and (2) a significant interaction effect, indicating that the outcome was not the same for the two types of articles—that is, when asked about the antipledge articles, the men opposed to signing the pledge expressed less interest than did the men who favored signing the pledge; whereas when asked about the propledge articles, the two groups did not differ in their interest ratings.

REFERENCES

Berkowitz, L., and Cottingham, D. R. The interest value and relevance of fear-arousing communications. *Journal of Abnormal and Social Psychology*, 1960, *60*, 37–43.

Cannell, C., and MacDonald, J. The impact of health news on attitudes and behavior. *Journalism Quarterly*, 1956, *33*, 315–323.

Caplan, G. *An approach to community mental health*. London: Tavistock Publications, 1961.

Coelho, G. V., Silber, E., and Hamburg, D. A. The use of the student TAT to assess coping behavior in hospitalized, normal and exceptionally competent college freshmen. *Perceptual and Motor Skills*, 1962, *14*, 355–365.

Cohen, A. R. *Attitude change and social influence*. New York: Basic Books, 1964.

Egbert, L. D., Battit, G. E., Welch, C. E., and Bartlett, M. K. Reduction of postoperative pain by encouragement and instruction of patients. *New England Journal of Medicine*, 1964, *270*, 825–827.

Feather, N. T. Cigarette smoking and lung cancer: A study of cognitive dissonance. *Australian Journal of Psychology*, 1962, *14*, 55–64.

———. Cognitive dissonance, sensitivity, and evaluation. *Journal of Abnormal Psychology*, 1963, *66*, 157–163.

Festinger, L. *Conflict, decision and dissonance*. Stanford, Calif.: Stanford University Press, 1964.

Freedman, J. L., and Sears, D. O. Selective exposure. In L. Berkowitz, ed., *Advances in experimental social psychology*, vol. 2. New York: Academic Press, 1965.

Goldstein, M. Relationship between coping and avoiding behavior and response to fear-arousing propaganda. *Journal of Abnormal and Social Psychology*, 1959, *58*, 247–252.

Greenwald, A. G., and Sakumura, J. S. Attitude and selective learning: Where are the phenomena of yesteryear? *Journal of Personality and Social Psychology*, 1967, *7*, 387–397.

Grinker, R. R., and Spiegel, J. P. *Men under stress*. Philadelphia: Blakiston, 1945.

Grinker, R. R., Willerman, B., Bradley, A., and Fastovsky, A. A study of psychological predisposition to the development of operational fatigue, sections 1 and 2. *American Journal of Orthopsychiatry*, 1946, *16*, 191–214.

Haefner, D. Some effects of guilt-arousing and fear-arousing persuasive communications on opinion change. Unpublished technical report, Office of Naval Reserve, contract N 6 ONR 241, August 1956. Mimeographed abridgment of Ph.D. dissertation, University of Rochester.

———. The use of fear-arousal in dental health education. Paper presented to the 92nd Annual Meeting of the American Public Health Association, Dental Health Section, October 1964.

Hamburg, D. A., and Adams, J. E. A perspective on coping behavior: Seeking and utilizing information in major transitions. *Archives of General Psychiatry*, 1967, *17*, 277–284.

Hamburg, D. A., Hamburg, B., and deGoza, S. Adaptive problems and mechanisms in severely burned patients. *Psychiatry*, 1953, *16*, 1–20.

Hardison, J., and Purcell, K. The effects of psychological stress as a function of need and cognitive control. *Journal of Personality*, 1959, *27*, 250–258.

Hovland, C. I., Janis, I. L., and Kelley, H. H. *Communication and persuasion:*

Psychological studies of opinion change. New Haven, Conn.: Yale University Press, 1953.

Iverson, M. A., and Reuder, M. E. Ego involvement as an experimental variable. *Psychology Report,* 1956, *2,* 147–181.

Janis, I. L. *Air war and emotional stress.* New York: McGraw-Hill, 1951.

———. *Psychological stress.* New York: Wiley, 1958.

———. Motivational factors in the resolution of decisional conflicts. In M. R. Jones, ed., *Nebraska symposium on motivation.* Lincoln: University of Nebraska Press, 1959.

———. Psychological effects of warnings. In G. W. Baker and D. W. Chapman, eds., *Man and society in disaster.* New York: Basic Books, 1962.

———. Group identification under conditions of external danger. *British Journal of Medical Psychology,* 1963, *36,* 227–238.

———. Effects of fear-arousal on attitude change: Recent developments in theory and experimental research. In L. Berkowitz, ed., *Advances in experimental social psychology.* New York: Academic Press, 1967.

———. Stages in the decision-making process. In R. P. Abelson et al., eds., *Theories of cognitive consistency: A sourcebook.* New York: Rand McNally, 1968.

———. *Stress and frustration.* New York: Harcourt Brace Jovanovich, 1971.

Janis, I. L., and Feshbach, S. Effects of fear-arousing communications. *Journal of Abnormal and Social Psychology,* 1953, *48,* 79–92.

———. Personality differences associated with responsiveness to fear-arousing communications. *Journal of Personality,* 1954, *23,* 154–166.

Janis, I. L., and Leventhal, H. Psychological aspects of physical illness and hospital care. In B. Wolman, ed., *Handbook of clinical psychology.* New York: McGraw-Hill, 1965.

———. Human reactions to stress. In E. Borgatta and W. Lambert, eds., *Handbook of personality theory and research.* New York: Rand McNally, 1968.

Janis, I. L., and Mann, L. Effectiveness of emotional role playing in modifying smoking habits and attitudes. *Journal of Experimental Research in Personality,* 1965, *1,* 84–90.

———. A conflict-theory approach to attitude change and decision-making. In A. G. Greenwald et al., eds., *Psychological foundations of attitudes.* New York: Academic Press, 1968.

Janis, I. L., and Rausch, C. N. Selective interest in communications that could arouse decisional conflict: A field study of participants in the draft-resistance movement. *Journal of Personality and Social Psychology,* 1970, *14,* 46–54.

Janis, I. L., and Smith, M. B. Effects of education and persuasion on national and international images. In H. Kelman, ed., *International behavior.* New York: Holt, 1965.

Janis, I. L., and Terwilliger, R. An experimental study of psychological resistances to fear-arousing communications. *Journal of Abnormal and Social Psychology,* 1962, *65,* 403–410.

Jones, E. E., and Gerard, H. B. *Foundations of social psychology.* New York: Wiley, 1967.

Katz, E. On reopening the question of selectivity in exposure to mass communications. In R. P. Abelson et al., eds., *Theories of cognitive consistency: A sourcebook.* New York: Rand McNally, 1968.

Kiesler, C. A. Commitment. In R. P. Abelson et al., eds., *Theories of cognitive consistency: A sourcebook.* New York: Rand McNally, 1968.

Klapper, J. T. *The effects of mass communication.* Glencoe, Ill.: Free Press, 1960.

Lacey, J. I. Psychophysiological approaches to the evaluation of psychotherapeutic process and outcome. In E. A. Rubinstein and M. B. Parloff, eds., *Research in psychotherapy.* Washington, D. C.: American Psychological Association, 1959.

Lazarus, R. S. *Psychological stress and the coping process.* New York: McGraw-Hill, 1966.

Lazarus, R. S., and Alfert, E. The short circuiting of threat by experimentally altering cognitive appraisal. *Journal of Abnormal and Social Psychology,* 1964, *69,* 195–205.

Lazarus, R. S., and Baker, R. W. Psychology. In E. Spiegel, ed., *Progress in neurology and psychiatry,* vol. 2. New York: Grune & Stratton, 1956.

Lazarus, R. S., and Eriksen, C. W. Psychological stress and personality correlates: Effects of failure stress upon performance. *Journal of Experimental Psychology,* 1952, *43,* 100–105.

Leventhal, H. Fear communications in the acceptance of preventive health practices. *Bulletin of the New York Academy of Medicine,* 1965, *41,* 1144–1168.

Leventhal, H., and Sharpe, E. Facial expressions as indicators of stress. In C. Izard and S. Tompkins, eds., *Studies of emotion.* New York: Springer, 1965.

Leventhal, H., and Singer, R. P. Affect arousal and positioning of recommendations in persuasive communications. *Journal of Personality and Social Psychology,* 1966, *4,* 137–146.

Leventhal, H., and Watts, J. Sources of resistance in fear-arousing communications on smoking and lung cancer. *Journal of Personality,* 1966, *34,* 155–175.

Mann, L. The effects of emotional role playing on desire to modify smoking habits. *Journal of Experimental Social Psychology,* 1967, *3,* 334–348.

Mann, L., and Janis, I. L. A follow-up study on the long-term effects of emotional role playing. *Journal of Personality and Social Psychology,* 1968, *8,* 339–342.

McGuire, W. J. The nature of attitudes and attitude change. In G. Lindzey and E. Aronson, eds., *Handbook of social psychology.* Reading, Mass.: Addison-Wesley, 1968*a.*

———. Selective exposure: A summing up. In R. P. Abelson et al., eds., *Theories of cognitive consistency: A sourcebook.* New York: Rand McNally, 1968*b.*

Mills, J. Interest in supporting discrepant information. In R. P. Abelson et al., eds., *Theories of cognitive consistency: A sourcebook.* New York: Rand McNally, 1968.

Moore, H. E. *Tornadoes over Texas.* Austin: University of Texas Press, 1958.

Niles, P. The relationship of susceptibility and anxiety to acceptance of fear-arousing communications. Ph.D. dissertation, Yale University, 1964.

Penny, R. K., and McCann, B. The instrumental escape conditioning of anxious and nonanxious children. *Journal of Abnormal and Social Psychology,* 1962, *65,* 351–354.

Schmideberg, M. Some observations on individual reaction to air raids. *International Journal of Psychoanalysis,* 1942, *23,* 146–176.

Sears, D. O. The paradox of *de facto* selective exposure without preferences for supportive information. In R. P. Abelson et al., eds., *Theories of cognitive consistency: A sourcebook.* New York: Rand McNally, 1968.

Singer, R. P. The effects of fear-arousing communications on attitude change and behavior. Ph.D. dissertation, University of Connecticut, 1965.

Vogel, W., Raymond, S., and Lazarus, R. S. Intrinsic motivation and psychological stress. *Journal of Abnormal and Social Psychology,* 1959, *58,* 225–233.

Waly, P., and Cook, S. W. Attitude as a determinant of learning and memory: A failure to confirm. *Journal of Personality and Social Psychology*, 1966, *4*, 280–288.

Withey, S. Reaction to uncertain threat. In G. W. Baker and D. W. Chapman, eds., *Man and society in disaster*. New York: Basic Books, 1962.

Wolfenstein, M. *Disaster*. Glencoe, Ill.: Free Press, 1957.

9

Adaptation to Stress in Political Decision Making: The Individual, Small Group, and Organizational Contexts

ALEXANDER L. GEORGE

In a report on severe adjustment problems experienced in a variety of settings, Hamburg and Adams (1967) begin with the question "Why doesn't everyone break down?" The question may well be asked about political leaders who must somehow deal with one complex, difficult situation after another in never-ending array. Yet, as we know, few political leaders actually break down under the stress of decision making or under the even greater stress of having to cope with the consequences of decisions already made.

Certainly we would like to know more about the psychological coping mechanisms that help keep political leaders intact and functioning. But, so construed, the "mental health" of the political executive is too narrow a focus for studies of ways to improve his policies and decisions. Obviously, the quality of his decisions is affected by many other factors, including the adequacy of the information, analysis, and advice available to him, the extent to which he profits from it, and the exigencies of politics he experiences. Obviously, too, someone in good mental health does not necessarily

For helpful comments on earlier drafts of this paper, the author expresses his appreciation to Irving L. Janis, George V. Coelho, Ole R. Holsti, J. Victor Baldridge, Brian R. Fry, Juliette L. George, James David Barber, Paula Gordon, Thomas E. Cronin, Scott C. Flanagan, Robert Jervis, Seyom Brown, Thomas Ehrlich, Paul Y. Hammond, and Lawrence E. Lynn. The research on which this paper is based was made possible by grants from the Foundations Fund for Research in Psychiatry and the Committee on International Studies, Stanford University. Copyright © 1974 by Alexander L. George.

make good policies and decisions. A relatively well-adjusted man, after all, may be lazy or stupid. Such a person may be disastrously ineffectual as a political leader even if he is well-meaning and manages not to break down under the stress of decision making.

Nor can we confine our concern solely to the consequences of a leader's decisions for his own emotional well-being. We must be at least equally concerned with the *consequences for others*, for the psychological coping devices a decision maker employs to maintain personality equilibrium may be dysfunctional for the group or polity on whose behalf he has acted.

When political scientists, some years ago, were exposed to early developments in ego psychology, they were struck particularly by the fact that arousal of a leader's anxieties and ego defenses could severely impair his ability to deal rationally with a situation. As a result, they tended (as did some psychiatrists and psychologists) to regard any display or ego defenses by a political leader in a stressful situation—such as denial, projection, rationalization—as a telltale sign that his ability to cope rationally and effectively had been impaired. Decisions made under such conditions were regarded with suspicion, and any inadequacy perceived in their substantive content was "explained" as an unfortunate by-product of the leader's resort to ego defenses.

More recent refinements in ego psychology and in studies of coping processes afford political scientists better tools for the evaluation of political decision making. We understand now—thanks to the work of Murphy, Hamburg, White, Janis, and others—that many of the classical ego-defense mechanisms can be used *constructively* by an individual in the total process of coping. Defensive operations such as withdrawal, denial, and projection need not preclude eventual adaptation to a difficult situation; rather, they may give the individual time to regroup ego resources and provide him with the short-run, tactical ego-support that facilitates a longer-term process of coping. In due course he may be able to rely upon more constructive ego capacities, such as information seeking, role rehearsal, or advance planning. Coping, then, includes not merely processes for maintaining emotional well-being, but also some that facilitate realistic problem solving.

What is noteworthy here is that coping is no longer seen exclusively in terms of a simple stimulus-response sequence, but as a process that may extend over time and utilize not just one, but several coping mechanisms. Moreover, coping may take on some of the characteristics of an improvised or patterned "strategy" for problem solving, a process in which emotion and reason may interact and coexist without mutual violence. Finally, coping is no longer viewed solely in terms of an individual's intrapsychic behavior; it may include important elements of a social and organizational process. For all these reasons, the broader conceptualization of coping behavior that has emerged in modern psychology is now more relevant for the study of stressful political decision making. Of course, experimental studies of coping responses do not all face subjects with the need to make a rational choice among alternative actions, and the results are of limited value for the study and management of political decision making. Some psychologists, how-ever, particularly Irving Janis, have gone further and have attempted to adapt stress and coping concepts and hypotheses directly to decision mak-ing. In his studies of the difficulties subjects encounter in making decisions in fear-arousal situations—for example, the danger of cancer from cigarette smoking—Janis has developed a reasonably comprehensive decision-making model that encompasses a variety of the sources of predecisional stress and postdecisional conflict. This approach to stress and coping lends itself to identifying strategies of "preventive intervention" of the kind I shall iden-tify in this paper.

Having noted the relevance of psychological theory for the study of polit-ical decision making, I must emphasize the need for supplementing it with social psychological and sociological theory. For in the context of such orga-nizations as the U.S. government there are only limited opportunities for employing conventional methods of psychiatric "intervention" to assist deci-sion makers in coping with stresses. And in any case, psychiatric knowl-edge is not sufficiently relevant and adequate for this purpose. Accordingly, theoretical perspectives and inquiries must be broadened to encompass the behavior of units larger than the individual—that is, the dynamics of small-group behavior and the dynamics of complex, bureaucratized organiza-tions—in which multiple actors, each with a special viewpoint and inter-ests, join in the struggle to influence the executive's decision. A similar conclusion has been reached by social psychologists: "the psychological approach to the study of problems in the social world has been impeded by an inability to deal with the facts of social structure and social organization. . . . Behaviorism, Freudianism, and field theory have been too individual in orientation and hence of very limited usefulness . . ." (Katz and Kahn 1966, pp. 1–2).

It must be noted, however, that role theory has had a minimal impact on the study of decision-making processes within organizations. This limita-tion is due fundamentally to the sociologist's traditional overemphasis on role as an integrating mechanism, which leads, in turn, to a neglect of the diversity of goals pursued within an organization and a neglect of conflict among the actors involved. The study of organizations indicates that extra-role forms of influence—bargaining, negotiation, compromise, coalition making, and so on—are often at the heart of decision-making process. Role theory in fact stands in danger of "not leaving any room for rationality in behavior" (Simon 1958, pp. xxx–xxxiii). Hence, a broader theory of influ-ence than that linked with the sociological concept of role is needed.

This chapter, then, will focus selectively on problems of stress and cop-ing in the pursuit of rational policy making within the government. It will not be possible or necessary to deal with all substantive policy questions. Rather, reflecting on the research interests I have pursued for many years, I shall focus on decision making in the sphere of foreign policy and will arbi-trarily limit the inquiry to the activities of the top layers of policy making—

the president and his leading advisers on national security affairs. Much of the conceptualization and many of the hypotheses advanced may be found to have relevance for the problem of improving rational decision making at lower levels of government and, more generally, for the politicized aspects of policy making in any complex organization; but I shall not comment explicitly on these broader implications.

A major task of this chapter is to develop a broad framework within which to locate and to interrelate different sets of variables that can affect efforts at rational choice among policy alternatives. I have chosen to do this by examining three contexts, or "subsystems," in which the task of achieving rational determination of complex policy matters may be, and frequently is, pursued in the executive branch of the government: *the individual context* (the chief executive); *the small-group context* (the informal, essentially spontaneous face-to-face relationships the president engages in with a relatively small number of advisers); and *the organizational context* (the more formal and structured role relations between superiors and subordinates in the executive branch as a whole). I shall not attempt to deal with still other contexts affecting the foreign policy-making process and its policy outputs—for example, the executive-congressional linkage, the context of domestic public opinion, and the context of allied and neutral opinion.

The analysis proceeds on the premise, which can be empirically justified, that each of these three subsystems generates its own adaptive and maladaptive ways of coping with the task of rational decision making. Part of the research task, then, is to identify the important dynamic processes of this kind associated with each context. But, of course, the three subsystems are also interrelated. Another aspect of the research task, therefore, is to identify ways in which dynamic processes associated with each context are capable of affecting adversely or favorably the efforts to cope within the other two subsystems. In examining available theory and empirical materials, we are particularly interested to show that each of the three contexts offers distinct leverage points and opportunities for preventive and interventive measures that might be exploited to reduce the likelihood that rational decision making will be impeded.

A satisfactory way of conceptualizing and interrelating these three subsystems, with the aim of producing a prescriptive theory of rational policy making, can be expected to emerge only after many successive approximations. The task is indeed a formidable one (for earlier attempts and discussion see Horwitz 1953, pp. 309–328, and Singer and Ray 1966). Despite advances in relevant portions of theories of individual psychology, small-group dynamics, and organizational behavior, the linkage and synthesis of these theories is still primitive and, certainly, inadequate for the research objective stated here. We need a more substantial integration of ego psychology with group dynamics, small-group dynamics with organizational behavior, and executive leadership with organizational behavior.

THE INDIVIDUAL CONTEXT

Cognitive Constraints on Rational Decision Making

It is customary to regard "stress" as something the individual experiences when he perceives and tries to cope with a severe threat to one or more strongly held values. The study of "decisional stress," however, requires a broader conceptualization of both sources and types of stress. Our concern is with decision making in which an effort is made to calculate the utility of alternative courses of action. The anticipated utility of a contemplated course of action, however, is often difficult to judge—there are *cognitive limits* on rational choice. In contrast to the models of "pure" rationality formulated in statistical decision theory and elaborated by economists, efforts at rational calculation in political life usually run aground on one or another of the following intellectual difficulties:

1. The political decision maker often must operate with incomplete, possibly erroneous, *information* about the situation at hand.
2. His *knowledge* of ends-means relationships is generally inadequate to enable him to predict with confidence the consequences of choosing one or another course of action.
3. It is often difficult for him to formulate a single criterion or *value* by virtue of which to choose the "best" of alternative options.

We shall be dealing with these three cognitive constraints throughout and will be particularly interested to note how they are coped with in the three contexts of political decision making. This section will focus on the individual context in which these constraints arise. Our first need is to find a framework for this purpose that is sufficiently broad to deal not merely with the individual *qua* individual, but with the individual executive who enters into small-group relationships with advisers and associates within a complex organization.

In another respect as well we shall have to broaden our framework. Much of the work on stress by psychologists and psychiatrists (definitions and conceptualizations are given in Lazarus 1966 and in Janis and Leventhal 1968) has focused somewhat narrowly on a single class of important situations, which pose strong and rather well-defined threats and dangers to the individual. When we turn to political decision making, we must consider a broader variety of situations, situations that activate motivational structures of greater diversity and complexity. Thus, for example, the stakes in politics and government pose not merely dangers, but also opportunities for the executive-leader to obtain gratification and rewards of various kinds.

The conceptualization and framework that will best fit immediate needs, without our becoming mired in the complexity and detail inherent in the subject, is the kind of simple "balance-sheet" model that Janis uses in his approach to the study of decisional stress (see Fig. 9-1). Janis distinguishes between "anticipated utility" and "anticipated approval or disapproval." He distinguishes further between anticipated utilitarian gains "for self" and "for significant others." Similarly, approval or disapproval can come "from self" or from "significant others." Although relatively simple, Janis's model has considerable heuristic value. It can be adapted and elaborated, as appropriate, for many kinds of research problems.

It is difficult, of course, to convert the kind of complexity embedded in the balance-sheet model into adequate explanatory and predictive models. The possibilities for resolving motivational conflicts are numerous. In one situation, for example, the decision maker may act to enhance utilitarian benefits for some significant others at the expense of other significant others. His decision may also be shaped by an expectation of utilitarian gain

	Anticipated utility		Anticipated approval or disapproval	
	For self	For significant others	From self	From significant others
Current policy				
Proposed new policies				

FIGURE 9-1   Irving Janis's "Balance-Sheet" model.

for himself—he may expect increased popularity or votes at the next election or increased political credit with the interest groups or other political actors who have gained by his decision. In another situation, he may be influenced largely by a strong need to prevent damage to his self-esteem or, on an unconscious level, to gain satisfaction of aggressive impulses or to prevent "domination" by others. Maintaining self-esteem may be so important to such a person that he will be led to secure it at the expense of utilitarian benefits for significant others—or even for himself. (See, for example, the case study of Woodrow Wilson's "self-defeating" behavior in George and George 1964; also George 1968, 1971a.) We recognize the role that unconscious motives and needs may play in decision making without, however, singling them out for major attention. The position taken is that insufficient attention has been given to stress occasioned not primarily, or even in the first instance, by conscious factors in personality, but rather by various congitive constraints on the individual's efforts to exercise his rational capacities for problem solving.

In the following discussion I shall deal with the strains occasioned by the three cognitive constraints on rational calculation given above. The third constraint, having to do with the difficulty of forming a single criterion or value for choosing among alternatives, will be dealt with first in a discussion of "multiple stakes." The other two constraints, emerging from limits on information and knowledge, will be dealt with together in a discussion of "cognitive complexity." This separation is somewhat artificial, because the three kinds of constraints on rational calculation often interact with one another and can be justified only as a means of facilitating analysis.

Coping with Motivational Conflict: The Problem of Multiple Stakes

Many of the political situations to which the decision maker must respond typically arouse or engage several different components of his motivation. Stress is experienced insofar as some of these motives and values compete with others in influencing his evaluation and choice of action. (The words *motivation* and *conflict* are, of course, taken more broadly here than in the customary psychiatric sense.) We may assume that the executive has internalized and shares with others some of the social norms and values that exist within the organization and in the larger social system of which he is a part. In addition, however, there are likely to be other values and interests held by other members of the organization and the social system that he has not internalized, though he is aware of them. These, too, he may feel it prudent to take into account. We expect him to be more readily responsive to social values he has internalized, whereas those not internalized enter into his decisional choices in a more fortuitous and calculated manner.

When multiple stakes are present, the decision maker may experience conflict and stress because he finds it difficult to satisfy all the competing considerations or to choose among them. Viewed from this standpoint, the simplicity of the balance-sheet model is deceptive, for "anticipated utility for self" in Janis's model can refer to a variety of the decision maker's personal (conscious and unconscious) or political values, interests, and needs; and "anticipated approval and disapproval from self" encompasses a similar variety of personal and political consequences.

Some of the value criteria that enter into and affect the executive's cost-benefit calculations will be distinctive and of a somewhat different order from value criteria that enter into the corresponding cost-benefit analyses of the small group or the organization. Not only does the balance-sheet model allow consideration of the decision maker's idiosyncratic personality, but it also reminds us that he often assesses his choices from the standpoint of political survival and advancement, whether for himself or for his party or both. To the executive, a decision on a given policy issue may pose a special set of cost-benefit consequences for his political prestige and reputation, for his accumulation of political resources, for the formation or maintenance of a political coalition on which he is dependent for reelection, or for ratification and implementation of other elements of his political program. Failure to take account of the distinctive value criteria that affect the decision maker's cost-benefit calculus has led advocates of systems-analysis techniques in government to underestimate the difficulties of applying their narrower *efficiency* criteria of cost effectiveness to issues that in fact activate a broader range of political values. Even restricted efficiency criteria are often difficult to reduce to a single measurable criterion of value.

Precisely because it is so difficult to employ objective analysis to deal with this particular cognitive constraint, an executive is often expected by others in the policy-making group to reconcile competing values and interests by going through an "internal debate." Their hope is that a subjective ordering and aggregation of competing considerations by the executive will enable him to offer a satisfactory solution to what would otherwise be left to be settled entirely via conflict and bargaining among the actors within the policy-making system—that is, in the third context, which we shall consider later. To the extent that he accepts and discharges adequately this unique task of leadership, the executive may be able to make a decisive contribution to lessening the social-political tensions and costs associated with making corporate decisions. His own intrapersonal tensions are "more easily resolved, since [he] can better subordinate one value to another" (Pruitt 1965, p. 62; see also McDonald 1970, p. 121). Of course, he may be unwilling to accept the task; or, if he does, he may not encompass all the social values that are vying for satisfaction in the political arena, or may not give some of them the weight in his own calculus they clearly deserve. Even when he is reasonably successful, it may require considerable skill at communication on his part to be credited by those concerned with having made the best decision in the overall public interest.

Internal debate and subjective aggregation of competing values and interests does not always work. The executive may forego this mode or supplement it with other modes. I find it useful to distinguish three ways in which an individual may attempt to cope with stress that is aroused when diverse motives and values are competing for satisfaction in the decision he has to make: (1) conflict avoidance or reduction; (2) conflict resolution; and (3) conflict acceptance.

CONFLICT AVOIDANCE OR REDUCTION.   This reaction seems to have received the most attention in psychiatrically oriented studies of stress and coping. A variety of specific psychological mechanisms have been identified which have in common that they enable the individual to banish or sharply reduce the motivational conflict he experiences in making a decision, or, when exposed to pressures, to reexamine a decision he has already made. These mechanisms are well known (Janis 1959*a* and 1959*b* offer a useful inventory of them); I shall mention only a few:

1. Various devices for *cognitive restructuring* that help the individual to avoid or minimize the cognitive dissonance occasioned by new information that is relevant to the decision he is making, or has already made, but that challenges its wisdom or its presuppositions (see Holsti 1967, pp. 25–96; Smith, Bruner, and White 1956, p. 251).
2. The tactic of *devaluating* a value held by the self or significant others when that value loses out in the competition with other motives.

3. The tactic of *reducing or abandoning one's identification with the significant others* who suffer utilitarian loss as a result of the decision.
4. Acts of *expiation and ascetism* when a difficult decision results in self-disapproval and guilt.

Conflict-reduction devices of this kind may indeed be functional for the leader in the sense of enabling him to keep going, but, as noted earlier, the consequences of coping with decisional stress in this way may sometimes be highly dysfunctional for the group or polity on whose behalf he is acting. We are interested in the quality of the decisions the leader makes, not merely with whether he finds a way of reducing or avoiding unpleasant decisional stress for himself. The consequences for the group are likely to be less harmful, for example, when he searches for appropriate compensation; when he attempts to convince significant others damaged by his action that his decision was the right or necessary one; when he attempts to demonstrate to, or persuade, significant others that he is still a worthwhile person and still identified with them, in hopes of ensuring that their disapproval will be temperate and temporary.

CONFLICT RESOLUTION. The second way in which motivational conflict is sometimes handled by political decision makers is less likely to have socially dysfunctional consequences unless it is pursued rigidly and inflexibly. Conflict resolution, as its name implies, consists essentially in an effort by the leader to satisfy somehow, to some extent at least, all or most of the competing considerations that are salient for him in a problematic situation. Often, of course, this is a formidable, if not impossible, task; but we must immediately add that the rewards of success are great, not only with respect to the inner psychological satisfaction a leader thereby achieves, but also in terms of the political rewards to be gained. Particularly in a democracy, in which there are many competing interests and a pluralistic distribution of power, and when, as noted earlier, the executive is expected to internalize or at least aggregate in his decision making the various interests and values striving for satisfaction, some facility at conflict resolution of one's intrapsychic decisional stresses is a requirement for success and survival as a political leader.

Two modes of seeking conflict resolution at the intrapsychic level may be distinguished. In the first, the individual tries to invent a single policy or option that will yield some satisfaction for all or most of the salient stakes and motivations involved. We may call this the strategy of *seeking multiple payoffs*. Some political leaders are unusually inventive and ingenious in this respect. If we examine their behavior more closely, we find that they are committed to an "optimizing" rather than a "satisficing" approach to decision making (the distinction is taken from Simon 1955). They like to extract every ounce of value and credit from every decision and action they take, and to minimize all of its possible costs and risks. As a result, the optimizer is often extremely reluctant to act or to reveal his intentions until he is ready. He attaches unusual importance to careful preparation and planning. And he does not take a passive stance toward the environment on which he is dependent for the multiple payoffs he seeks; rather, while deferring his decision, he takes soundings, prepares the ground, interacts with other political actors whose interests are involved or who can be helpful to him, and manipulates and orchestrates the political process as part of his search for a decision that will secure for him as much as possible of the multiple stakes he seeks.

We do not know enough about the kind of person or personality who develops such a facility. Certainly many kinds of persons can be drawn in this direction by the obvious political rewards for coping so successfully with the demands and complexities of politics. But in looking more closely at some political leaders who have mastered the style, one senses that they are, to some extent, driven by personal needs. Like any good thing, the optimizing of multiple payoffs can be pushed too far, or be relied upon too rigidly.

The second approach to achieving conflict resolution arises when the individual realizes he can satisfy only some of the multiple motives involved by the decision he must make. He may then try to satisfy the remaining ones sequentially over a period of time by a series of additional actions. We may call this the tactic of *sequencing* or *scheduling* competing motives.

It should be noted that the executive may achieve conflict resolution "prematurely"; that is, before the latent conflict among multiple values and interests has been brought fully into his awareness and adequately explicated. To avoid indulging in easy and premature solutions, he may depend upon those around him (the small-group context) and upon a process of decision making (the organizational context) to alert him to the full dimensions of the conflicting values and interests before exercising his facility at optimizing.

CONFLICT ACCEPTANCE.   In some situations, a political leader accepts and acts upon the fact that he cannot gain for himself all of the multiple stakes involved. Instead, he selects some of the multiple values as constituting the objective he will strive for. He accepts the fact that he will have to neglect the other salient considerations and attempts to live with the consequences of his choice stoically, without engaging in a desperate and perhaps wasteful search for multiple payoffs, and without resorting to possibly dysfunctional ways of reducing or avoiding the decisional conflict. Some leaders are evidently better able than others to deal with decisional conflicts in this manner. Personality variables are no doubt relevant, as are the learning experiences that have gone into the individual's political socialization. Some political leaders are more at ease with conflict and the processes of "politics" than others—but politics and conflict are inextricably intertwined.

In any case, among the major role tasks of the political leader is the task of making difficult decisions. It was with reference to this that Harry Truman used to say, with evident self-satisfaction, "the buck stops here," pointing to his desk; or "If you can't stand the heat, stay out of the kitchen." Truman's remarks in fact suggest one of the ways in which a political leader can deal more effectively with decisional stress. He can do so, as Truman did, by identifying with the role, understanding that one cannot be a decision maker without facing up to the fact that there will be many occasions on which one simply cannot make a good decision without some sacrifice to one's own interests or those of some significant others. We may recall that it was Truman who made the difficult decision—which cost him a great deal politically—to withdraw U.S. backing from Chiang Kai-shek in 1949, and who later resisted strong domestic pressure—again at high political cost—to expand the Korean War against the Chinese mainland.

By identifying with the role and accepting oneself as being a role player, the individual may find it possible to make difficult decisions with somewhat greater detachment and with greater sensitivity to priorities among competing considerations. Being a good role player may also enable him to experience less psychological stress and less personal damage when he is obliged to make a decision that sacrifices some interests, whether his own or those of significant others. Finally, as was surely true in the case of Truman, the individual who knows he is fulfilling difficult role requirements may in fact thereby derive compensatory gratification that bolsters as well as protects his self-esteem. (Particularly useful among the many discussions of relationships between role and personality variables in the study of stress are Levinson 1959; Hodgson, Levinson, and Zaleznik 1965; Thomas 1968, pp. 691–727; Kahn, Wolfe, Quinn, and Snoek 1964; Lasswell 1948, pp. 64–88; and Seligman and Baer 1969, pp. 18–35.)

Coping with Limits on Information and Knowledge: The Problem of Cognitive Complexity

It has long been recognized that cognitive limits on information and knowledge needed for rational decision making can be the source of acute stress for the executive. Thus, in a pioneering essay, Snyder, Bruck, and Sapin (1962, p. 167) called attention to the need to look for "devices whereby the decision makers minimize the psychological tensions which accompany decision making under circumstances of uncertainty and lack of complete information." Continuing, they asked: "How does [the decision maker] learn to live with unacceptable error? If devices to compensate for uncertainty are used, what effect do these have on deliberations?" (See also Gawthrop 1969, pp. 98–103.) It is understandable that in the face of stress-generating cognitive complexity some executives find it difficult to act. Indeed, some go so far as to conclude that the best strategy of leadership is to do as little as possible, hoping that the problems will go away or that they will find some other solution. Of the many executives who have adopted this coping strategy, it will suffice to take note of Calvin Coolidge's "calculated inactivity." As Fenno (1959, pp. 40–41) has observed, Coolidge's strategy "was to 'sit down and keep still' in the face of problems rather than to confront them, to 'remain silent until an issue is reduced to its lowest terms, until it boils down to something like a moral issue.' 'If you see ten troubles coming down the road, you can be sure than nine will run into the ditch before they reach you and you have to battle with only one.' "

But how *does* a leader overcome inhibitions to act that are generated by the difficulties of making a good cognitive appraisal of the situation? Even if we assume that his effort at rational decision making is unencumbered by unconscious needs and anxieties, he can still experience considerable stress merely trying to cope with the cognitive limits on his problem-solving ability. This we may refer to as "cognitive stress"; in a particularly vivid example, President Harding unburdened himself to a friend on one occasion thus:

John, I can't make a damn thing out of this tax problem. I listen to one side and they seem right, and then God! I talk to the other side and they seem just as right, and there I am where I started. I know somewhere there is a book that would give me the truth, but hell, I couldn't read the book. I know somewhere there is an economist who knows the truth, but I don't know where to find him and haven't the sense to know him and trust him when I did find him. God, what a job (Fenno 1959, p. 36).

There are many familiar strategies for avoiding or coping with predecisional stress that is occasioned at least in part by cognitive complexity. An incomplete listing would include:

1. A satisficing rather than an optimizing decision strategy (see Simon 1955; see also March and Simon 1958, pp. 140–141; Cyert and March 1964).
2. The strategy of "incrementalism," or "muddling through," as identified by Lindblom (1959, pp. 79–88; 1963 [with Braybrooke]; 1968, chap. 4).
3. Deciding what to do on the basis of "consensus politics," that is, what enough people want and will support, rather than attempting to master the cognitive complexity of the problem by means of analysis.
4. Using historical models to diagnose and prescribe for present situations (see Bobrow 1966, p. 931; Jervis 1970).
5. Reliance on ideology and general principles as a guide to action (see Hull 1948, p. 173; Schlesinger 1948).
6. Beliefs about the nature of politics and history, and about correct political strategy and tactics, that is, employment of an "operational code."

The executive's premature resort to (or overreliance on) any of these coping strategies can be dysfunctional insofar as it interferes with the search and analysis activities that should precede choice of policy.

The last of these strategies for coping with cognitive complexity is the most comprehensive and, therefore, of particular interest. Following the lead of Brim, Glass, Lavin, and Goodman (1962), psychologists who have studied the role of epistemological and instrumental beliefs in an individual's decision making, I have attempted to develop a systematic approach for research on the operational-code belief systems of political leaders (George

1969). Operational code, a term originally employed by Leites (1953), is a misnomer insofar as it implies that a leader has a set of recipes or rules for action that he applies mechanically in his decision making. Rather, the term should be understood as referring to a set of general beliefs about fundamental issues of history and central questions of politics as they bear, in turn, on the problem of knowledge and action. These beliefs serve as a cognitive map, or prism, that influences an actor's perceptions and diagnoses of political situations and provides decisional norms and standards to guide his choice of strategy and tactics. The beliefs are relatively few in number and large in scope, and each is capable of being differentiated and elaborated. Moreover, we expect them to be relatively stable over time and to exhibit some mutual consistency or connectedness.

Eleven philosophical and instrumental questions have been explicated as a first approach to formulating a given political actor's operational-code belief system. The "answers" he gives to these general questions define his fundamental orientation to the problem of leadership and action. The philosophical questions, phrased briefly here, include the following: What is the fundamental nature of political conflict and the image of the opponent? What are the prospects for eventual realization of one's political values and aspirations? Is the political future predictable; in what sense and to what extent? How much control or mastery can one have over historical development? What is one's role in moving and shaping history? What is the role of chance and accident in historical development? The instrumental questions are the following: What is the best approach for selecting goals and objectives for political action? How are the goals of action pursued most effectively? How are the risks of political action calculated, controlled, and accepted? What is the best approach to timing action? What is the utility and role of different means for advancing one's interests? A number of scholars are currently employing these questions as a basis for formulating the operational-code belief systems of various leaders. A standardized approach is being followed in order to facilitate comparisons. Ole Holsti (1970) has studied John Foster Dulles; David McLellan, Dean Acheson; Gordon White, Mao Tse-tung and Liu Shao-chi; Dennis Kavanagh, Ramsey Mac-Donald; and Ned Ashby, Kurt Schumacher and Willy Brandt. (These studies will be published together with evaluative essays in a forthcoming volume that I am editing.)

A leader's operational-code beliefs are not always well formed or easily deduced by the investigator on the basis of the kinds of data, observational opportunities, and methods generally available to social scientists. However, the methodological problems are no different in principle from those encountered in other forms of systematic research on beliefs and attitudes. At the same time, it is one of the attractive features of the operational-code construct for behaviorally inclined political scientists that it can serve as a useful bridge or link to psychodynamic interpretations of possibly unconscious dimensions of political belief systems and their role in behavior under different conditions (George 1969, pp. 195–196, 219).

An executive brings to his office an operational-belief system and coping style shaped by his whole life experience. It is the student's task to identify that style, to discern his characteristic ways of functioning in decision-making relationships. His functioning in political and executive roles is part and parcel of his personality—there is no such thing as "political personality," but rather the expression of a man's personality in political and executive roles and situations. A coping style that is highly adaptive in one political role may have severe maladaptive consequences in another political role.

The simplest part of the student's task is to construct a profile of the subject's patterns of coping with his decision-making tasks. The factors that governed the leader's adoption of the coping devices he brings to office, or that emerge in response to the special demands and pressures of an executive position, are embedded in his life experience. Some of these coping strategies will reflect an accurate appraisal of reality and will constitute constructive, flexible responses leading to creative problem solving. Others may reflect distortions of perception and impairment in some degree of the capacity to respond freely and flexibly to the demands of reality.

In pursuing these matters further we can begin with the useful general proposition that the more complex the task of determining utilitarian gains and losses, the greater the chance that nonutilitarian factors will play a determining role in decision making. One possibility, of course, is that certain types of cognitive complexity experienced by the individual arouse his unconscious motives or open the door for their expression in his decision making. Another possibility is that the criterion of what significant others will approve of may easily fill the vacuum left for the decision maker who finds it difficult to make a good cognitive appraisal of the policy issue. This highlights the importance of small-group dynamics, to which we now turn.

THE SMALL-GROUP CONTEXT

Political scientists have long agreed, as Sidney Verba (1961) has noted, that "it is to the face-to-face group that one must look if one is to find the locus of decision-making in political systems." Action-taking groups tend to be small in membership. One investigator found that groups in business and governmental organizations in which actual decisions were made tended to number between two and seven members (James 1951). In any case, the size of the decision-making group is often reduced in crisis situations. Moreover, "when crucial choices are forced on an organization from the environment," the decisional subsystem will be characterized not only by a smaller core unit, but also by "a simpler role structure" (Snyder and Paige 1958). The consequences of the latter for the quality of decision making, however, do not lend themselves to easy generalization.

It may be true, as Snyder and Paige suggest, that fewer alternatives are likely to be considered by a smaller decisional unit with a simpler role structure. Nonetheless, in other respects the model of means-ends rationality may be more closely approximated in the smaller group insofar as decision making is then concentrated among top-level officials who operate with a broader view of the values at stake and are less inclined to engage in bargaining and protection of narrow bureaucratic interests (Verba 1961; Holsti 1972). Though this may serve to improve the quality of decisions in one respect, it may also introduce new constraints on effective problem solving. For when decision devolves to the top of an organization there is some risk that harassed top-level officials will lack relevant expertise and will lose contact with experts at lower levels of the hierarchy. Related to this problem is the danger of "uncertainty absorption," whereby the critical uncertainties identified in an analysis of the policy problem by experts at lower levels of the organization are left out or deemphasized in the transmission of the results of analysis to top-level policy makers through hierarchical channels (March and Simon 1958, p. 165).

Though much has been written about the impact of particular small groups on political decisions, few attempts have been made to study systematically the ways in which primary relationships within small decision-making groups affect political outcomes and, more generally, the political process (see Verba 1961; Collins and Guetzkow 1964; DeRivera 1968). Field studies are particularly important for this purpose, given the difficulty of extrapolating laboratory results to the prediction and explanation of phenomena in the political arena. At the same time, access to real-life, decision-making political groups is not easily arranged (two important exceptions are Barber 1966 and Eulau and Prewitt 1973).

As noted earlier, coping takes place not only via intrapsychic ego-functions of the individual, but also by means of interpersonal processes within the small group to which he belongs. Thus, for example, information about a threatening situation that is likely to create stress for the executive may be distorted or repressed not only by the executive's ego defenses, but also by the efforts of those around him to shield him. But, of course, the control exerted by other members of the small group can operate in quite a different way to compensate for tendencies on his part to distort or repress bad news. Thus, small-group processes are capable of forcing and assisting an executive to face up to the dimensions of a policy problem. Members of the group may also monitor his anxiety and try to strengthen his self-esteem while he is performing the tasks required by the situation. Obviously, then, the structuring and performance of role tasks within the small group deserve the closest attention.

Not all of the possible functions of the small group that affect decisional stress and coping by the executive will be taken up here. Rather, the discussion will focus on small-group dynamics that can affect rational decision making. Some of these processes will also provide a bridge between the individual context already discussed and the larger organizational context to which we shall turn later. It should be clear, finally, that our concern is with the small group in which—however informal its face-to-face rela-

tions—an individual, the executive, has formal authority and final responsibility for decisions (see DeRivera 1968, p. 222).

Decision-Making Norms and Culture
of the Small Group

We are particularly interested in the role the executive can play in structuring and regulating the problem-solving activities of the small group of
policy advisers around him. It is obvious that political leaders vary quite a
bit in the way they relate to their advisers. Some attempt to anchor their
decision making in the special culture and deliberations of a small group of
colleagues or associates. The problem-solving culture of the group, however, is a variable that takes many different forms, some of which may not
be conducive to rational decision making.

An executive may attempt to stabilize beliefs, knowledge, and judgments
that affect decisions in order to keep himself—and his colleagues—immune
to the day-to-day fluctuations of moods, emotions, and sentiments to which
he and they, as individuals, are subject. Noteworthy in this coping style is
the leader's effort to create a group suited to reinforcing his own constructive, adaptive ego-functions; and, conversely, his reliance upon members of
this group and the group's decision-making culture to ward off, control, or
compensate for any of his or their ego-defensive involvements in policy
making that might impair his judgment. Some leaders, by contrast, will try
to minimize their dependence on close associates, and to control the impact
they are allowed on decision making. In an effort to do so, an executive
may distinguish sharply between receiving factual information from others,
which he is willing or even eager to do, and entertaining specific advice on
what to do, of which he is distrustful. This is often true of leaders who
have a marked compulsive bent to their behavioral styles. Such a person
(for example, Woodrow Wilson) may attempt to cope with the strains and
stresses of decision making, not by anchoring himself in the culture and deliberations of a congenial group, but rather by pursuing a terribly conscientious and, in the last analysis, largely private search for "truth" and the
correct course of action (George and George 1964; George 1968; see also
Fenno 1959; Seligman 1956, pp. 410–426; Barber 1971; Anderson 1968; and
DeRivera 1968).

As this brief discussion indicates, the norms governing the deliberations
of the small policy-making group are of considerable importance. These
norms or expectations, more or less shared by members of the group, "regulate" the way in which they will go about dealing with the various tasks
involved in policy analysis. These tasks embrace not only (1) the way in
which the intellectual side of problem solving (for example, search, evaluation, and choice, which we shall discuss in the next section) is to be handled
within the group, but also (2) the processes of forming and maintaining consensus within the group on behalf of policies finally chosen, and (3) the

"rules" governing the expression of disagreement, bargaining, and compromise during different phases of policy making.

Norms of this kind may or may not be well-defined, comprehensive, or fully shared. A critical task of the executive is the shaping and enforcing of a set of norms; he will need to cover questions of the following kind: how will policy alternatives be identified, discussed, and evaluated within the group? How will participants satisfy their need for information and analysis? Will the same or different kinds of contributions to the problem-solving and consensus-building tasks be expected from the several participants? What "rules" will regulate the competition among participants for influencing the leader's choice? How will the task of intellectual synthesis of the various elements of a complex policy problem be handled? In making a decision, what relative weight will be given to arriving at the "technically best" option as against one that commands the desired kind and magnitude of consensus within the group? What degree of "support" will be expected of the participants once a decision is made by the executive? What "rules" will govern reconsideration of a past decision?

A review of the literature on small groups from the standpoint articulated here highlights the need for differentiating more precisely in small-group research the various subtasks of policy analysis and policy making. The familiar distinction in small-group leadership theory between "instrumental" and "affective" tasks does not offer a sufficiently refined basis for studying the effect of several different variables on the quality of the group's decisions. Status differences among members of the group are important in this respect, but they should be related not merely to differences in their communication and interaction patterns (for example, who speaks when, about what, and more often to whom, and so on), but also to participation in, and performance of, the various subtasks of problem solving. (One familiar and useful multiactivity model of problem solving is based on the distinction between "search," "evaluation," and "choice.") Relating status differentials more intimately to the quality of performance of these interrelated problem-solving tasks will result in a more refined analysis of the "instrumental" task that should be more useful both from the standpoint of theory and of practice. It will also permit a more incisive analysis of the leader's role in facilitating the instrumental task. (On this point see the important work of Maier 1963, 1970; Hoffman 1961; Vroom and Yetton 1971; Bower 1965.)

These questions concerning the norms of the problem-solving groups admit of different answers. One leader may convey to the group that he attaches higher priority to arriving at a policy choice that achieves consensus within the group than to seeking a better policy that fails to achieve consensus. Another leader, however, may signal the opposite. It is obvious, moreover, that leaders vary in the degree to which they will use their authority to block or hamper consideration of certain policy alternatives and to achieve consensus within the group for their own preferred course of action. But, as is well known, this can occur even when it is not the executive's intention. Other members of the group develop a sensitivity to what the leader is thinking, and some may wish to please him by channeling their advice in the same direction (Sorensen 1963, pp. 57–77). Or they may feel under pressure not to pursue a line of thought the leader is obviously opposed to. The executive may have to take special precautions to prevent this authority from hampering discussion of policy alternatives.

The various conformity-inducing dynamics of behavior in small groups are well known (see DeRivera 1968, pp. 207–244). They have been identified in laboratory studies and in field situations, and need not be recapitulated here. At the same time, it seems to me useful to distinguish two different dynamic patterns that produce conformity, but that have not been clearly differentiated in the literature. There is, first, the familiar pattern of group pressure on individual members that leads them to varying degrees of conformity. In the other, less frequently studied pattern, conformity flows from strong group cohesion brought about, or accentuated by, a threatening, stressful environment. We shall consider both.

Conformity through Group Pressure on the Individual

Of particular interest is the danger that advisers holding unpopular views will be inarticulate or ineffectual when subjected to group pressure for conformity. Group rejection of a "deviant" member was produced experimentally in Schachter's well-known study (1960). Pressure on dissident members of a policy-making group often occurs in natural settings as well, which may lead to their rejection by, or expulsion from, the group (Kennan 1967, pp. 474, 480, 491–496, 499; R. F. Kennedy 1969, p. 117). Rejection of a dissident, however, is an extreme outcome; dissidents may be controlled, and even used, in more subtle ways.

Indeed, social psychologists have for some time emphasized that the internal dynamics of a group can take different forms and can affect performance of the group's instrumental tasks in different ways. Nearly two decades ago, Cartwright and Lippitt (1957) warned against the tendency to conclude from the results of existing laboratory studies that cohesive groups must always produce unanimity on matters of importance. Urging that a distinction be made between "conformity" and "uniformity," they emphasized that the critical variable was the *content* of the prevailing group standards or norms: "A group might have a value that everyone should be as different from everyone else as possible. Conformity to this value, then, would result not in uniformity of behavior but in nonuniformity." Continuing, they conceded that "the pressure to uniformity which arises from the need for 'social reality' " and the necessity for the group to act cannot "simply be obliterated by invoking a group standard of tolerance. . . ." We would agree that the introduction by a permissive leader of a simple group norm of "tolerance," while helpful (see Maier and Solem 1952), will generally not suffice to create an optimal problem-solving culture. But although some useful work along these lines emerged thereafter, Cartwright felt himself obliged ten years later (Cartwright and Zander 1968) to note that the group's tolerance of dissident members and, more generally, its encouragement of creativity had still not received the study it deserved.

The critical importance of group norms emerges with sharper clarity when we review the disappointing results of studies that have attempted to account for conformity and uniformity of views within a group on the basis of individual personality characteristics. In the past twenty-five years, much attention has been given in laboratory studies and in related theoretical speculation to the possibility that persons with certain personality characteristics are particularly vulnerable to group pressures for conformity. The findings that have accumulated in this heavily researched field (as noted by McGuire 1968; Marlowe and Gergen 1969), however, have turned out to be increasingly complex and inconsistent. McGuire was led to conclude that no simple generalizations about the personality-influenceability relationship are likely to be valid; rather, the relationship appears to be complex and situationally interacting, or else of very narrow generalizability.

For similar reasons, political scientists specializing in the study of personality correlates of political attitudes have recently concluded that not all conformity springs from the same motivations, and that it may be best henceforth to regard conformity and deviation as *descriptive* terms that merely denote an individual's response to norms. "Indeed, conformity may be a behavior category so broad as to be almost equivalent with the concept of learning itself, rather than an identifiable, specific propensity or personality trait that some people possess in significantly greater measure than others" (DiPalma and McClosky 1970, p. 1059).

Although a more discriminating look at group norms is strongly indicated, the bulk of the systematic research to date has dealt with laboratory groups that possess a relatively simple *modus operandi* and problem-solving culture. One must go outside the laboratory for a picture of the range and complexity of motivations within small groups respecting the encouragement, control, and use of dissident members. In the first instance, executives and other members of small policy-making groups often do recognize that performance is likely to be degraded if pressures for conformity within the group are permitted to discourage informational inputs and a balanced evaluation of options. Accordingly, steps are often taken to structure the processes of the group, particularly by developing special norms and a group culture that will encourage members to offer all relevant information, however worrisome, to advocate unpopular views, and thus to secure a many-sided evaluation of policies under consideration. In recent years much attention has been given to the usefulness of the "devil's advocate" role from this standpoint, and various proposals have been made for institutionalizing this role in policy-making groups (see DeRivera 1968, pp. 61–64, 209–211; Jervis 1970; R. F. Kennedy 1969, p. 112; Holsti 1972). Policy makers themselves, under fire for their controversial decisions, have taken pains to give assurance that dissident views were encouraged and that someone in the policy-making group has played devil's advocate (see, for example, Graff 1970, pp. 46, 50–51, 69–73, 87, 125, 136–137).

Indeed, even a cursory examination of historical materials on the making of U.S. foreign policy in recent years makes it amply clear that, in contrast with laboratory groups, countervailing considerations often make it unnecessary or undesirable to squelch or reject a dissident member of the small policy-making group. Rather, the likelihood that dissidents will increase anxiety within the rest of the group is often accepted and legitimized as an emotional inoculation serving to strengthen the coping abilities of the group.

But this by no means suggests that the mere provision of a devil's advocate role in small decision-making groups guarantees improved policy performance or, indeed, that the role itself can be easily performed with the integrity required to yield the desired impact. Indeed, available evidence on this score is of a mixed character and on the whole sobering. Thus, a perceptive account of Vietnam policy making in the upper levels of the government by a participant-observer casts considerable doubt upon the feasibility of the much vaunted devil's advocate role. James C. Thomson (1968, p. 49) reports that doubters and dissenters did appear and persisted in the policy-making circle; but rather than being rejected, he notes, they were subtly "domesticated"—that is, dissent was institutionalized and the impact of the devil's advocate role was effectively neutralized. Thomson accounts for this domestication process as a manifestation of the "clubbish need" felt by virtually all members of the upper level of policy making: "On the one hand, the dissenter's desire to stay aboard; and on the other hand, the nondissenter's conscience." Once Undersecretary of State George Ball began to express doubts, "he was warmly institutionalized: he was encouraged to become the in-house devil's advocate on Vietnam. The upshot was inevitable: the process of escalation allowed for periodic requests to Mr. Ball to speak his piece; Ball felt good, I assume (he had fought for righteousness); the others felt good (they had given a full hearing to the dovish opposition); and there was minimal unpleasantness. The club remained intact. . . ." Thomson adds: "I must confess my own considerable sense of dignity and acceptance (both vital) when my senior White House employer would refer to me as his 'favorite dove.' " George E. Reedy, a former press secretary to President Johnson, puts it more directly (1970, p. 11): "It is well understood that [the devil's advocate] is not going to press his points harshly or stridently. Therefore, his objections and cautions are discounted before they are delivered."

Moreover, the dissident may so moderate his dissent or his style of expressing it as to fall into what Thomson calls the "effectiveness" trap—the trap that keeps men from resigning in protest and airing their discontent outside the government. Though an uncharitable judgment may be fully justified in some cases, the reality of the dilemma cannot be ignored. As Thomson puts it: "To preserve your effectiveness, you must decide where and when to fight the mainstream of policy . . . one may be able to prevent a few bad things from happening." But as for George Ball, who presumably acquiesced in his "domestication," Thomson is quick to concede that matters might have got worse faster if Mr. Ball had kept silent or had left before his final departure in the fall of 1966.

There are additional incentives, not mentioned by Thomson, that may encourage an executive to hold on to dissident policy advisers, however weakened or illusory the multiple advocacy may be. First, hearing negative opinions expressed *and* rebutted may provide top-level officials with the psychologically comforting feeling that they have considered all sides of the issue and that the policy chosen has weathered challenges from within the decision-making circle. Paradoxically, then, having some dissenters within the group may help the others, in particular the leader, to cope with some of the stresses of decision making.

Second, there is rehearsal value in listening to, and debating with, dissenters within the policy-making group. Those who support the policy are then better equipped to reply when they encounter similar challenges in the public arena.

Third, the formal modalities of multiple advocacy can help hold the group together. The feeling that consultation and debate took place before the chief executive made his decision may assuage some of the disappointment of those whose advice was not followed. It may be easier for them to close ranks, at least temporarily, behind the policy chosen. This is consistent with research findings in other settings that suggest that as long as the individual is satisfied that proper deference has been granted his point of view by organizational superiors, his hostility reaction will, in all probability, be minimal if his superiors do not accept his judgment (Horwitz 1964, pp. 79–82).

Fourth, if the dissenter can then be pressed into the role of defending the policy in public forums, he may well do a better job than would firm, enthusiastic advocates of the policy. To the extent that his original doubts are shared by outsiders, the defense of the policy he manages to develop is likely to focus on considerations that will be especially salient for them. Philip Geyelin (1966, p. 210) notes that "It was a familiar Johnson stratagem to send known dissenters to argue on behalf of his policies."

Finally, there may be important public-relations values for the executive who follows the practice of hearing multiple advocates and, more generally, who structures the policy-forming process to ensure orderly consideration of alternative options. As George Reedy puts it (1970, p. 11), the objections and cautions of the official devil's advocate "are actually welcomed because they prove for the record that decision was preceded by controversy." In an earlier era a leader could leave the question whether he had acted wisely to the judgment of history some generations hence. This possibility has been increasingly denied leaders of democratic governments in our era of rapid communications; important elements of the public are no longer satisfied to wait for that judgment. Thus, faced with the public's demand for "instant history," presidents and their advisers increasingly cooperate in enabling journalists to write inside accounts of how and why a recent decision was made. The impact of these public expectations may, of course, be shallow. The administration may respond to them by routinizing its procedures for policy making, ritualizing the conduct of multiple advocacy, and "domesticating" devil's advocates in order to secure public-relations advantages. As a result, top-level officials may learn to enact their policy making in such a way as to meet the informed public's expectation of how important decisions should be made and to project a favorable image into the "instant histories" that will be written shortly thereafter. But one can be too cynical about this; we can hope that shadow and substance cannot exist wholly apart from each other, and that the striving for a good image may serve to reinforce the hand of those in government who also strive for an effective system of policy making.

Conformity as a Function of Strong Group Cohesion in a Stressful Environment

The second of the dynamic patterns producing and maintaining conformity within small decision-making groups has been less well articulated and studied, because the group processes associated with it are more subtle. Without detracting from the importance of the first pattern, we may agree with Marlowe and Gergen (1969, p. 610) that it is unsatisfactory and "unduly restrictive" to view conformity solely within "the narrow context of a group exerting pressure on individuals, some of whom are susceptible (or suggestible) and consequently conforming." A broader perspective can be gained by observing that small decision-making groups sometimes take on the characteristics of a "primary group." Sociologists and psychologists who have studied the remarkable cohesion that develops at times in small combat groups in military organizations have noted the special kinds of mutual identifications and emotional ties that bind members of the primary group together—and sustain individual members in coping with the stresses of combat (see, for example, Shils and Janowitz 1948, pp. 280–315; and Janis 1963, pp. 227–238). (The writing of this section has been made possible by the stimulating thesis articulated by Irving Janis in his book on *Groupthink*, and summarized in his "Groupthink among Policy Makers," 1971a, pp. 71–89. Janis employs available theories of group dynamics as a diagnostic tool for illuminating flaws in policy making and decision making that preceded certain fiascoes, such as the Bay of Pigs and Pearl Harbor. He also postulates, as I have here, two patterns of group dynamics in developing his theory of "groupthink.")

Though it may seem far-fetched to apply the analogy of a combat group to the small political decision-making group, it is well known that executives often rely upon primary-group ties with one or more close associates or friends as a means of coping with the stresses of decision making. From membership in the small intimate group, the individual may secure some of the psychological support—esteem, respect, protection, affection—needed to sustain him in his efforts to cope with the cognitive complexity, the uncertainty and risks, and the criticism from outsiders that are inevitably a part of political decision making. The executive himself may become dependent for emotional support upon policy advisers, as against friends outside the policy circle, though some executives are evidently aware of the risks here. Woodrow Wilson could accept Colonel House as both a friend and policy adviser only because House occupied no official position (George and George 1956, 1964). Calvin Coolidge "found it necessary to keep his friend Frank Stearns around him as a kind of buffer-companion-confessor, yet he would not work through him or consult him in any way" (Fenno 1959, p. 42). Adlai Stevenson noted that Lyndon B. Johnson was very uncomfortable if none of his policy advisers wholly approved of a decision he had just taken (Geyelin 1966, p. 234). A number of participant observers, including Bill Moyers and George Reedy, have commented on the tendency of Johnson's top-level policy-making group on the Vietnam war to take on some of the characteristics of an embattled group in order to protect itself from critical views.

Janis (1971*b*) hypothesizes that "concurrence seeking" in small decision-making groups is "a form of striving for mutual support based on a powerful motivation in all group members to cope with the stresses of decision making." This striving for mutual support, Janis postulates, "has functional value for the members insofar as it alleviates distressing emotional states . . . feelings of insecurity or anxiety about risks and possible errors . . . conflicts between different standards of conduct, between ethical ideas and humanitarian values on the one hand and the utilitarian demands of national or organizational goals. . . ."

We noted earlier that one of the major cognitive constraints on rational decision making arises from the fact that it is often difficult to formulate a single criterion of value to apply in choosing the best course of action. Janis suggests that under these circumstances, and particularly in highly cohesive groups, *group concurrence* tends to replace reality testing of the morality and efficacy of the policy being chosen or pursued. Thus, Schachter (1960) postulated, on the strength of Festinger's theory (1950, 1954), that "on any issue for which there is no empirical referent, the reality of one's own opinion is established by the fact that other people hold similar opinions."

In Janis's theory, strong cohesion facilitates the emergence of what he calls "groupthink," a way of coping with stress that is likely to be highly maladaptive for rational decision making. Groupthink is characterized by a "shared illusion of invulnerability," an exaggerated belief in the competence of the group, a "shared illusion of unanimity" within the group, and a number of other symptoms. It would appear that under conditions of stress the existence of strong primary-group ties within a small decision-making group can encourage *regressive forms of thinking* (as well as regressive emotional states), such as the following: (1) global or undifferentiated thinking, that is, a simplistic cognitive view of the external world and of other political actors; (2) dichotomized modes of thought; (3) oversimplified notions of causation; (4) loss of sense of proportion; and (5) confusion of means with ends. Regressive forms of thinking are recognizable from time to time in small cliques of "fanaticized" policy advocates who fight for a certain highly valued policy option in the face of great and persistent difficulties.

Janis, then, deliberately challenges the conventional wisdom that a highly cohesive group is a high-performance group. Though recognizing the usefulness of strong group cohesion, he warns that it can have an adverse impact on the group's performance and assigns it the status of a necessary, but insufficient, condition: "The more amiability and esprit de corps among members of an executive group, the greater the danger that independent critical thinking will be replaced by groupthink." The very fact that the decision makers enjoy strong group cohesion may lead to an erosion of critical intellectual capacities when they resort to concurrence seeking in a stressful decisional environment. This is a far more subtle and insidious thing than is social pressure to conform exerted against a member of the group who entertains dissident policy views.

A number of coping mechanisms related to small-group dynamics have been noted; some of these facilitate rational decision making, while others disrupt it. We face next the difficult task of showing how small-group processes are linked or can be linked with the additional set of processes peculiar to the broader and more complex organizational context. Though a great deal of research attention has been given to each of these contexts, relatively little has been given to studying the two relationally—this despite the fact that leading theorists of personality have traditionally looked to organization as a means of controlling and minimizing disruptive effects of certain types of group dynamics on individual rationality and group performance. Thus Bion (1952, pp. 235–247) holds that "organization and structure" are the means by which a work group prevents obstruction of its tasks by one or another of the emotional drives that characterize the underlying motivation of a group.

Organizations can indeed provide opportunities for reinforcing the individual's constructive, adaptive, ego-functions. They employ institutionalized procedures for assisting executives to face up to the need for seeking and utilizing relevant information and advice, conducting rehearsals of plans, and identifying and evaluating alternative courses of action. Organizational structure can also strengthen the role and impact of a dissident member of the small advisory group around the executive. The isolated policy adviser who, as we have seen, may be ineffective as the devil's advocate in the small group can become a powerful advocate if he possesses a power base within the organizational structure.

We noted earlier various ways in which an executive may try to cope with the difficult task of formulating a single criterion aggregating all relevant values and interests in the political arena. If an executive cannot cope with this problem via an internal debate of his own, or is prevented from settling the problem in this way by other political actors, he may attempt to orient himself to an *external* play of these values and interests on the part of other members of the policy system. We have seen that the small group may be a poor arena in which to secure an adequate airing; for in that context, pressures for conformity, group cohesion, and concurrence seeking as a vehicle for reality testing may get in the way. These processes are absent or at least weaker in the organizational context; and it may be easier, therefore, for the executive to secure within the organization the external play of conflicting values he needs. The clash over policy on the part of officials identified with different subunits of the complex organization and reflecting different social values and interests provides this possibility. But it is only a possibility and, as we shall note, a new set of dynamic processes that are peculiar to the internal workings of complex organizations must be contended with as the arena of political decision making expands to include the organization.

THE ORGANIZATIONAL CONTEXT

Policy performance in a complex organization, such as the executive branch of government, is sensitive to many factors. In trying to outline a policy-making system that will facilitate adaptive choices of policy and help avoid certain types of costly malfunctions, we do not ignore or underestimate the simultaneous importance of ideological, cognitive, and other variables. Moreover, even a good policy-making process cannot guarantee adaptive decisions; rather, it must be judged in terms of probabilities.

Political scientists and students of administration have long been intrigued by the possibility that though an organization should not be regarded as a unitary rational actor it might still achieve rationality in policy making by breaking down its problems and assigning the subproblems to different parts of the bureaucracy. But although organizations do in fact pursue such a course, it has been found that few decision-making problems of any scope can be so neatly subdivided and dealt with successfully in isolation.

This limitation certainly applies to the making of foreign policy, many of whose issues cut across jurisdictional lines of special competence and responsibility. Some writers have emphasized this point by defining a "policy question" as one for which there are no experts, only advocates and referees. Effective problem solving in such cases cannot be achieved by decomposition and decentralization of policy analysis; rather, it requires a holistic framework within which provision is made for iterative interaction among various specialized competencies. Interaction of this kind is often difficult to arrange and manage properly, because the relevant competencies are typically institutionalized in different subunits of the organization.

The task is further complicated by the fact that there is often no clear or dominant overall organizational goal to guide subunits in their efforts to identify the best policy option. Rather, the subunits tend to perceive goals and interests of their own that compete for satisfaction in the choice of policy for the entire organization. To engage in effective policy making under these circumstances, therefore, requires coordination, standard operating procedures, rules for decision making, and a monitoring or custodianship of the whole.

The Centralized Control and Bargaining Models of Policy Making

Classical writers on the administration of large organizations have traditionally placed great reliance upon centralized, hierarchical systems for achieving coordination and control over internal processes. And through the 1930s, as one political scientist recently noted, American students of public administration were almost totally preoccupied with formal structural arrangements. Since then, however, their "principles" (mainly mechanistic) of administrative management have been devastatingly attacked, if not replaced, by an alternative set of "principles" (Altschuler 1968, pp. 212–213). Nonetheless, critics did effectively challenge one of the fundamental assumptions of the highly centralized, hierarchical model—the assumption that the top-level executive could be expected to determine and apply the broad public interest better than lesser officials identified with subunits at intermediate and lower levels. Thus Lindblom (1955), being concerned that the pendulum of organization theory had swung too far toward favoring a system of centralized, hierarchical policy making, advanced an alternative model of policy making via "bargaining" (or, as he renamed it in 1965, "partisan mutual adjustment") among the interested parties and actors. Lindblom was not as sanguine as other theorists concerning the chief executive's ability to internalize, subjectively aggregate, and reconcile the competing values and interests engaged by a policy issue. That task, in his judgment, would be best left to the free play of bargaining processes among the different interested parties within the system.

Two quite different prescriptive models of policy making emerged, therefore; and because theoretical formulations of both the centralized, hierarchical, and the bargaining models were initially cast in oversimplified terms, they seemed to offer stark, polarized alternatives. In contrast, organizational practice in formulating policy-making systems within the government has experimented with various "mixed systems." And in the past decade or so, organizational theorists, too, have begun to look more closely for ways of combining elements of both models to improve policy performance. It is increasingly recognized, moreover, that a given mixed system cannot be expected to be optimal for policy areas as diverse as defense planning, foreign policy, and domestic welfare.

Trends in Organizing Foreign Policy Making

Since the forming of the National Security Council (NSC) in 1947 there has been a steady, if inconsistent, trend toward an increasingly centralized system of foreign policy making. This has meant increased presidential-level involvement in, and control of, the processes of policy formation and implementation. The staff of the NSC has been called upon, particularly in the past decade, to reach deeper into the relevant departments and bureaus in order to gain control over a wider range of issues at earlier stages. Several variants of a mixed system have been employed, with the pendulum swinging during the Nixon Administration to the most structured and centrally directed variant of this entire period.

Under Truman, the functions and role of the newly created NSC were limited in various ways. Though Truman often used a type of "adversary proceeding" in discussions with foreign policy advisers from the various departments to enable all viewpoints to be heard, he had serious reservations about the new NSC and generally did not rely on it for this purpose. Moreover, the hierarchical level at which foreign policy making was to be coordinated under Truman was not the NSC but rather the State Department. Truman turned aside early efforts to have the secretary of defense preside over NSC meetings in his absence. Instead, he designated his secretary of state as the second-ranking NSC member, who then presided over council meetings during the first two and a half years of the NSC's existence, after which Truman began to attend and preside himself. The workings of Truman's foreign policy-making system clearly rested on the relationship of confidence and trust between the president and his secretary of state.

For Eisenhower, the NSC offered an opportunity to put into effect his preferred style of decision making. He immediately upgraded the role of the NSC and strengthened its functions; at the same time he introduced into the system a new official, the Special Assistant for National Security Affairs (previously the NSC staff was headed by an executive secretary), to administer the NSC staff and oversee its communications with the departmental officials most concerned with foreign affairs. These changes toward more orderly and increased staff work were not allowed to undermine the secretary of state's position as chief foreign policy adviser to the president, though they shifted upward to the NSC level the burden of central coordination. The NSC meetings also became the setting for formal adversary proceedings in the debate of foreign policy.

With the Kennedy Administration, the formal NSC machinery was deliberately weakened, and it was hoped that the State Department would lead and coordinate the making of foreign policy. This hope was not realized, and for this and other reasons the Office of the Special Assistant began to exercise important informal and formal presidential-level leadership tasks that went beyond the carefully defined and delimited functions of the NSC staff under Eisenhower.

President Johnson's approach was, if anything, even more informal than Kennedy's. Johnson relied on his regular Tuesday lunches with his top-level advisers to achieve coordination of high-level policy; otherwise, coordination took place at lower levels. In 1966 Johnson attempted to restructure the central coordinating functions of the foreign policy system and to locate them, not at the NSC level, but rather so as to enable the State Department to serve as the formal kingpin of various interdepartmental committees. The new system was slow in getting underway and did not really "take" before the change of administrations in 1968.

Under President Nixon, the coordinating apparatus that Johnson introduced has been further strengthened, but is now drawn back to the presidential level. He has revived the trend begun by Kennedy toward converting the Special Assistant into a semiautonomous actor in the policy system. As a result, centralized direction and coordination of foreign policy making from above is now stronger than ever before. Henry Kissinger plays an active role in influencing and shaping the processes of policy analysis throughout the executive branch in order to formulate well-developed options for the president's consideration. The enhanced role of the Special Assistant indeed incorporates features of the management model developed earlier by Secretary of Defense McNamara in the sphere of defense planning. (For a detailed description and analysis of these developments see Davis 1970, pp. 4–23; R. H. Johnson 1969; Falk 1964; Hammond 1961; Kolodziej 1969; and Destler 1972).

This brief review can usefully end with two seemingly contradictory observations. As one long-term staff member and student of the NSC has noted, "The factor that dominates everything else is the president's style of decision making" (R. H. Johnson 1969, p. 720). Indeed, the variation in personal styles of presidents helps account for the zigzags we have noted in degree of institutionalization and use of the NSC. At the same time, however, the tend toward an increasingly centralized system of foreign policy making is unmistakable. What we have seen since the NSC was introduced in 1947, therefore, is a continuing process of experimentation with different kinds of mixed systems.

"Bureaucratic Politics" and Its Persistence in Centralized Policy-Making Systems

In the sphere of foreign policy the case for centralized direction of the policy-making process is, of course, a strong one. The specialized competences relevant to foreign policy, however, are widely distributed within the government. Moreover, foreign policy issues are typically complex and often ambiguous; they generate a diversity of views among policy makers, and the search for a rational calculation of policy often encounters sharp disagreements among system participants. The strongly centralized system that has emerged under the Nixon Administration has weakened, but not altogether displaced, the bargaining model alluded to earlier. Rather, as its predecessors, the present arrangement for foreign policy making turns out to be, on closer inspection, a mixed system.

Anyone who has worked in government or observed it closely knows that policy formation can be neatly organized or very untidy or, paradoxically, both. Thus, policy formulation often proceeds on two tracks simultaneously: the official track consists of the prescribed routines and standard operating procedures for policy formulation and coordination that are visible to authorized participants. A second track operates with some of the same participants and others as well, but on a more subterranean level; its activities are more spontaneous and less visible and are influenced by what is occurring or is expected to occur on the official track, and, of course, its purpose is to influence and control the official track.

As in any complex organization, policy making within the executive branch of the government characteristically takes place, at least in part, through informal political processes. Although not fully perceived by outsiders, there is within the executive branch an erratic, if not continuous, collision of viewpoints and interests; incumbents in the various subunits are not just bureaucratic officials carrying out chain-of-command orders from above. Rather, they are advocates of different interests and viewpoints, and at times reflect or represent the views of interest groups outside the organization itself. As Allison (1969, pp. 699–707) puts it: " 'government' consists of a conglomerate of semi-feudal, loosely allied organizations, each with a substantial life of its own. Government leaders do sit formally, and to some extent in fact, on top of this conglomerate . . . [but they] are not a monolithic group. Rather, each is, in his own right, a player in a central, competitive game" (see also Halperin 1970).

The competitive, politicized aspect of the policy-forming process, which has been variously called "bureaucratic politics" or "administrative politics," operates on the second, more informal track. Bureaucratic politics is characterized by competition and conflict, by bargaining, negotiation, and compromises, and by strategies of coalition formation and consensus building (see Feldman and Kanter 1965, pp. 638–641). On large issues of policy there is often disagreement not only between departments, but within individual departments and agencies. As a result, rival policy coalitions that cut across departments and agencies may come into being. Membership in these ad hoc coalitions often draws persons and groups outside the executive branch—congressmen, newspapermen, interest groups, and even scientists and scholars—into the competitive struggle to influence the president's decisions.

How these struggles over policy are resolved within the government depends in part upon the relative power and bargaining advantages of the participants and in part on the manifold processes of persuasion, bargaining, negotiation, compromise, and coalition building. To be sure, there are also efforts at intellectual persuasion based on analysis of the issues; analysis can usefully moderate bargaining processes and clarify for each advocate the relative utility of different compromises. But policy analysis often remains intertwined with advocacy. And in fact, because bargaining has potentially disruptive consequences, it "will frequently be concealed within an analytic framework" (March and Simon 1958, p. 131).

Though most observers agree that the process of policy formation within the executive branch is often highly politicized, they disagree substantially in their evaluation of its impact on the quality of the decisions that emerge. Additional disagreement arises over the question of what, if anything, can be done to improve the structure and workings of the policy-making system. Some specialists take a dim view of bureaucratic politics; they deplore the fact that important policy decisions are influenced by bargaining and compromise within the policy-making circle rather than through detached intellectual analysis of the problem. Other students of government, myself included, see possible merit, as well as necessity, in this system. For us, conflict is normal, expected, and potentially healthy, if it is properly managed and resolved.

Indeed, it is well established that social conflict can have positive functions for adaptation. But the social theorists of conflict have not extended their analysis to decision-making systems. A multiactivity model of decision making with the group is needed. Thus, a distinction is made between the following: (1) *search*—finding alternatives, obtaining and sharing relevant information; (2) *analysis*—examining the relationships among available information, establishing the appropriateness of defined alternatives; and (3) *choice*—choosing from among the alternatives. In his study of experimental groups, Bower (1965) found that conflict was an important factor motivating constructive thought and analysis. The effect of conflict on search and analysis was particularly noteworthy. "The personal commitment of a subject to an initial position," Bower noted, "motivates him to defend his choice by presenting all the information which supports his position. . . . group search is stimulated in both extent and quality." Moreover, Bower's study contradicts a major premise of other normative theories of social choice; thus, his groups were not successful problem solvers when they were concerned solely with "what is best for the group."

These findings, and the multiactivity model of search, analysis, and choice on which they are based, are relevant for our evaluation of bureaucratic politics. Direct observation of the impact of bureaucratic politics on the quality of policy making indicates that it sometimes works poorly, on other occasions surprisingly well. Accordingly, there is a need for systematic, comparative case studies addressing the following questions: Under what conditions do the workings of bureaucratic politics help produce "good" decisions? Under what conditions do they tend to produce "poor" decisions? What, in other words, are the prerequisites for effective functioning of the bureaucratic politics process? Only provisional answers to these questions are possible at this time. Halperin's recent study (1971) concludes that a president and his senior assistants should know how the game of bureaucratic politics is played so that they can learn to master it and perhaps put it to constructive use (see also Allison and Halperin 1972).

Converting Bureaucratic Politics into Effective Multiple Advocacy

What is needed is a pragmatic theory indicating how the game of bureaucratic politics can be converted into an effective system of multiple advocacy. I shall argue here that instead of exorcising bureaucratic politics, as the present NSC system attempts to do, the policy-making system should be structured so that the bargaining game itself works to improve the quality of search and evaluation. At the same time, multiple advocacy must be not only retained and strengthened, but made an integral part of a mixed system that includes centralized coordination and policy initiative from the top. Thus our theory of multiple advocacy is not a simple plea for dispersing power more widely to subunits and actors within the bureaucratic-politics model.

Under the present highly centralized NSC system, the modalities of involvement are such that cabinet officials and other senior players are seriously weakened in their role as advocates. Development of policy options through the government via the intricate network of formal NSC machinery "co-opts" departmental specialists and analytical resources. As a result, when senior players finally do have an opportunity, at top-level NSC meetings, to express their views on alternative options—as the system indeed permits—they may not be in a position to offer well-considered departmental points of view backed by independent analysis (this is implied in several accounts of the Cambodian decision; see Smith 1970; Maxey 1970).

To reintroduce the prescriptive approach into the study of bureaucratic politics, as pioneered by Richard Neustadt in his *Presidential Power* (1960), we must return to leads provided by earlier scholars. Curiously, a prominent advocate of the bargaining model, Charles Lindblom, while recognizing that it can and does perform badly on occasion, has displayed little interest in articulating the conditions necessary for effective bargaining and bureaucratic politics in policy making. Critics of the extreme bargaining model have been more helpful in this respect, but they have been content to argue the case for centralized management tools and have stopped well short of developing a theory for putting the bargaining model on a sounder basis (see, for example, Rowen 1966; Capron 1970).

In 1959, Roger Hilsman suggested some of the conditions under which the bureaucratic-politics process might be rather efficient in identifying and assessing major foreign policy alternatives. "The chances should be good," he suggested, "that the resulting policy will be a wise one . . . if the subject under debate is one on which the different groups of advocates are knowledgeable, . . . and if the top levels of government participate fully in the process or are sensitive to the verdict. . . ." Hilsman's observation was offered parenthetically and linked casually with a few illustrative cases. A fuller statement is possible, however. Because conflict over policy and advocacy is inevitable within a complex organization, one solution lies in the direction of ensuring that multiple advocates within the system will cover the range of interesting policy options on any given issue. A system of multiple advocacy is likely to be at its best and to produce its best decisions when three conditions are satisfied:

1. When the following resources are evenly distributed among the various actors:
    a. Power, weight, influence (including influence beyond the executive branch).
    b. Competence relevant to the policy issues.
    c. Information relevant to the policy problem.
    d. Analytical resources.
    e. Bargaining and persuasion skills.
2. When the executive monitors and variously participates in the interactions among the advocates.
3. When there is adequate time for debate and give-and-take.

The importance of the third condition is largely self-evident and will not occupy us here.

Concerning the first condition, it is clear that the mere existence within the policy-making system of actors holding different points of view will not guarantee adequate multisided examination of a policy issue. Competence, information, and analytical resources bearing on the policy issue in question may be quite unequally distributed among these advocates. As a result, one policy option may be argued much more persuasively than another, and the policy that is objectively best may be defeated by an inferior policy that happens to be more fortunate in its sponsorship. Moreover, policy issues are often not decided solely on the basis of the intellectual merits of the competing positions. Thus the distribution among the actors of the other two resources identified in our theory—power and bargaining skills—may be critical in shifting the decision toward one or another of the options. An option put forward by an advocate with superior competence, adequate information, and good analytical resources will not necessarily prevail over options advanced by advocates with superior power and bargaining skills. But it is not our purpose to develop predictive theories on the combinations of these five resources that are most likely to enable a player or coalition to prevail in the clash over choice of policy.

"Multiple advocacy" is a more apt description of this kind of competitive, but balanced, policy-making process than "bargaining model" or "partisan mutual adjustment." Multiple advocacy is not a pure, or "free market," bargaining game, but a "mixed system" that enables management to make use of internal competitive processes. Effective multiple advocacy does not just happen. Centralized management must structure and interrelate several contrasting roles within the policy-making system. Nor are all actors cast into the role of advocate. Two other top-level roles are also required: the *custodian* of the policy-making process and the *magistrate*, who presides at the apex. We shall discuss these roles later—for assistance in their formulation, I am indebted to Flanagan (1971).

Before proceeding, it will be useful to identify more sharply the fundamental respects in which the multiple-advocacy model differs from Lindblom's (1965) "partisan mutual adjustment." At risk of oversimplification, we note that he sees various factors as operating naturally to induce effective coordination in the absence of centralized control or intervention. The logic of partisan mutual adjustment implies not merely automaticity and inevitability of coordination, but also the emergence of a policy decision that is about as good as can be obtained. In contrast, the multiple-advocacy model makes explicit the assumption that effective competition is usually necessary if the processes of bureaucratic politics are to produce the functional equivalent of rational consideration and choice. Specialists in organizational behavior have noted a tendency on the part of subunits of complex organizations to engage in "quasi-resolution of conflict" and to avoid uncertainty in relations with each other by "negotiating" the internal environment (see Cyert and March 1963, pp. 116–120). Left to their own devices, subunits of the organization may adapt by restricting their competitive role. Thus, for example, one of the familiar criticisms of the State Department is that it adapted to the emergence of the United States as a world power after World War II by avoiding the opportunity for an enlarged role in national security affairs in favor of the safety of the more familiar and smaller role to which it was accustomed by tradition.

Decentralized, unregulated bargaining systems may also degrade organizational decision making insofar as each subunit of the organization attempts to restrict its contribution to organization-wide search and evaluation in order to enhance its influence on top-level choice. Thus a subunit (for example, the State Department or the Joint Chiefs of Staff) may provide the chief executive with a single preferred option that reflects its own internal bargaining politics and obscures or conceals information and analysis supporting other options. Hence top-level management must find ways of stimulating multiple advocacy, not merely among the major subunits, but also within each of them, or at least utilize devices for releasing upward and outward the contributions of specialized personnel in each subunit.

In contrast with partisan mutual adjustment, therefore, the theory of multiple advocacy warns that the presumed beneficial effect of internal competition and conflict on organizational policies is something else again if the competitors are unevenly matched, divide up the market, engage in unfair competition, squeeze out or buy off weaker competitors, and so forth. Accordingly, multiple advocacy assigns to top-level authority the task of maintaining and supervising the competitive nature of policy making within the organization. This task belongs to the custodian, whom we have already mentioned and to whom we shall give considerable attention in the remainder of this paper. The custodian's role, it should be noted, can be introduced and maintained only by the chief executive. Moreover, the creation of the custodian's role by the chief executive implies that he wishes at times to regard himself as a magistrate who evaluates and chooses among the various policy options. The central importance of the magistrate should not be overlooked or taken for granted—it is only because there is a magistrate at the apex of the system that multiple advocacy can be maintained and regulated. The introduction of the magistrate role means that advocates are no longer competing against one another, but rather for the magistrate's attention. The custodian can influence the competition even where the resources of the advocates are unbalanced; and in fact, it is particularly important that he do so when there is a marked disparity in bargaining advantages among advocates. As this implies, in his role as magistrate the chief executive does not simply decide in favor of the strongest coalition of advocates. Rather, his central position and ultimate responsibility give him the obligation to evaluate the relative merits of competing positions and the power to decide against the majority.

The policy-making responsibilities of the chief executive are not necessarily confined to the role of magistrate, which he exercises himself, or to the role of custodian, which he would be wise to delegate to a senior assistant. From time to time the chief executive may also exercise the role of advocate, particularly when other actors do not advocate policy options that deserve serious consideration, either because they do not attach high enough priority to such options or because they perceive disadvantages in them for departmental interests. In such instances, the executive may play the advocate's role himself or encourage policy advisers on his staff to exercise the prerogatives of advocates. In the latter event, we shall argue, the chief executive should not ask his custodian to take the role of adviser-advocate.

In sum, multiple advocacy is, in contrast to partisan mutual adjustment, a management oriented theory. It requires that we give considerable attention to the role of the chief executive and his immediate staff.

Role of the Chief Executive

As the preceding discussion implies, the chief executive's orientation to bureaucratic politics in policy making is likely to be crucial to an effective multiple advocacy. We shall now show in some detail how the executive's personal style can influence the organization's norm structure.

In past decades, American presidents have had quite different orientations to the phenomenon of bureaucratic politics. In one of the most incisive studies of the subject, *Presidential Power*, Neustadt (1960) emphasized that the president must be an ever wary, active, and skillful participant if he is to protect his own interests. And presidential power, perhaps the president's primary interest, is not an ample and stable commodity that the incumbent receives upon entering office and that is ever available thereafter to be exercised when needed. The fierce competition for power and influence waged in the arena of bureaucratic politics inevitably affects the president's power position even when other actors are not deliberately attempting to profit at his expense. When the game really heats up, it is not unlike a jungle in which something like the Darwinian struggle for survival takes place. (Dean Acheson once remarked that what the secretary of state needed most was an instinct for the jugular.)

Neustadt saw little hope that these features of bureaucratic politics can be eliminated or tamed by organizational structuring, and on this particular point he is persuasive. But the advice he offers the president by no means exhausts the possibilities available to him. Nor does he attempt to develop the kind of broader theory for strengthening multiple advocacy that we are discussing here. Neustadt focuses his advice to presidents somewhat too narrowly on the problem of protecting their personal power position and their prestige. (This has inevitably made some political scientists uneasy and has led to the view that *Presidential Power* is too Machiavellian. Schlesinger [1965] reports that President Kennedy himself became uneasy at suggestions that he was modeling his presidency along the lines of Neustadt's prescriptions.) He does not address the broader question of what the president can do to ensure that better public policy decisions will emerge from the inevitable play of bureaucratic politics. There is indeed an underlying assumption in parts of Neustadt's book that if the president succeeds in protecting his personal power stakes in controversial policy matters he will thereby also ensure better policy decisions for the country at large. This is sometimes true, but the exceptions can be extremely important. By concentrating on the protection of his personal power, the president may become gradually locked into a disastrous policy.

Every new chief executive faces the task of deciding how to orient himself to the phenomenon of bureaucratic politics within the government and to the larger and often interlinked game of politics rounding the executive branch. An individual's preferred mode of adapting to the "politics" of policy making is influenced both by the "operational-code" beliefs mentioned earlier and by personality factors. The executive's general attitude toward political conflict—the first of the philosophical beliefs in his operational code—is of particular importance. Thus, some chief executives have viewed politics as a necessary, useful, and perhaps even pleasant game; others have regarded it as a dirty business that must be discouraged or ignored. A president, moreover, has a personal political style that is influenced by several of his operational-code beliefs and by experiences that have shaped his view of his own political efficacy. His behavior is thus influenced by the kinds of roles, skills, and tasks he *feels* particularly adept at and those he does not (Barber 1968*a*, 1968*b*, 1971). From this has developed the concept of leadership "style." Style differences among presidents (see Barber 1968*b*; Hargrove 1966) appear to be related to the stance presidents take toward bureaucratic politics.

Herbert Hoover, who had been a successful engineer and who had a strong distaste for "politics," tried to take the politics out of policy making within the executive branch and, indeed, within the government as a whole (see Fenno 1959; Hargrove 1966, chap. 5). He tried to do so by substituting centralized one-man control over the free play of bureaucratic politics and by relying upon a rationalized, technocratic approach to decision making in lieu of a system of multiple advocacy. In common with many other leaders who have attained high office, Hoover believed that the policy-making arena should be one in which reason and goodwill, rather than power and conflict, prevailed. According to Fenno (1959, pp. 37–38):

Herbert Hoover's decision-making procedure was characterized by the extent to which he dominated it through a personal involvement at all low levels. His secretary writes that "he had to originate every last recovery program put forward by his Administration. . . ." In all of his prior executive experience he had stressed the necessity of tight one-man control over an organization. It was, for instance, almost a conditioned reflex to the onset of a new problem for Hoover to call a conference of specially qualified experts. But he did not call it until after he had first formulated a set of proposals, laying out the line of approach he desired. . . . The group discussion was designed not to initiate, but to explore ramifications and consequences, to bring about a meeting of minds, and to enlist voluntary cooperation—all based on Hoover's original propositions. The tempo of decision making as well as the substance of policy was controlled by him. . . .

Franklin D. Roosevelt took the opposite course in search of a strategy of control over the vagaries of bureaucratic politics. Instead of trying to take the "politics" out of the policy-making process, Roosevelt deliberately exacerbated the competitive and conflictive aspects of bureaucratic politics. He sought to increase both structural and functional ambiguities within the executive branch in order to better preside over it. For Roosevelt, conflict among significant others around him was not a source of anxiety or of depression or pessimism; nor did he perceive it as threatening in a personal or political sense. Not only did he live with the political conflict and at times near chaos around him; but he enjoyed the game and manipulated bureaucratic politics in order to control and profit from it.

In Arthur Schlesinger's (1959) judgment, Roosevelt's stratagems and tactics for this purpose comprised an implicit "theory of competitive administration." (Roosevelt had a profound impact on American political scientists, for example, Neustadt.) Fenno (1959, pp. 44–46) noted:

He [Roosevelt] sought always to preserve his discretionary "freedom of action." He accompanied this by delegating responsibility and authority in small, vague, and sometimes conflicting fragments, to a point where only he could contribute consistency and direction. . . . The result was an essentially unpatterned technique of administration. It resulted in fuzzy lines of responsibility, no clear chains of command, overlapping jurisdictions, a great deal of personal squabbling, and a lack of precision and regularity. . . . The method of delegation left jurisdictional boundaries to be mapped out by conquest or agreement. It promoted much "stimulating" inter-departmental conflict which could and did eventually land in his own lap.

This is, indeed, an extreme strategy for converting bureaucratic politics into a system of multiple advocacy. It is one way of preventing domination of the policy choice by one powerful or misguided advocate; one way of ensuring identification and consideration of a variety of alternatives; one way of preventing several advocates from bargaining and compromising their way into a policy-controlling coalition and thus protecting their own bureaucratic interests at the expense of others, including those of the president and the public at large. And these are indeed some of the "malfunctions" that the system of bureaucratic politics is prone to.

What is noteworthy is that Roosevelt did not attempt to substitute a new centralized, hierarchical model of policy-making processes (as advocated, for example, in the later Hoover Commission proposals for reorganization of government agencies); rather, he introduced a strong degree of structural ambiguity and procedural confusion into the administrative politics system. As Fenno (1959, pp. 39–40) noted:

His personal involvement was regular only in its irregularity, and predictable only in its unpredictability. . . . All of these decision-making methods tended toward one result—keeping his advisers off-balance, unable to forecast or rationalize their own advisory role, and uncertain as to whether he was or was not taking their advice.

Harry Truman adopted a different strategy for coping with the complex morass that governmental structure had become as a result of Roosevelt's style and the wartime expansion of agencies. Initially, he tried to tidy up the mess by clarifying and dividing up the jurisdictions. He tried to weaken the game of bureaucratic politics by strengthening each department head's control over his particular domain and by delegating presidential responsibility to him. Truman attached special importance to his ability to delegate responsibility and to back up those he trusted. He learned through experience, however, that to delegate too much was to jeopardize his own job. As for the larger policy issues that overlapped several departments, Truman played the role of chairman of the board, hearing sundry expert opinions and then making the decisions himself. He not only accepted the responsibility of making decisions, he liked it. A modest man in many ways, he adjusted to the awesome responsibility of the presidency suddenly thrust upon him by respecting the office and determining to become a good role player. By honoring the office and doing credit to it, he would do credit to himself.

Dwight Eisenhower to some extent shared Hoover's distaste for "dirty politics." But he appears to have recognized the need for it and to have allowed others to play the game on his behalf, without paying much attention. He did not attempt to depoliticize and rationalize the policy process completely, but seems to have operated on the assumption or expectation that the necessary multiple advocacy at lower levels of the policy-formation process would lead to a depoliticized formulation of choices, if not an agreed-upon recommendation, before the matter reached him and his top advisers for decision. His awkward fumbling when confronted by unresolved policy disagreements among top-level advisers and advocates is noted by Neustadt (1960, chaps. 4, 6). Eisenhower seems to have defined his sense of personal political efficacy in terms of the important contribution he could make by remaining above politics and by emphasizing the shared values and virtues that should guide governmental affairs.

John Kennedy felt much more at ease with the conflict aspects of politics. Moreover, he "simply did not find the formal processes, large meetings and relative presidential passivity that had characterized the Eisenhower system compatible with his personal and activist approach to the presidency" (R. H. Johnson 1969, pp. 717–718). He recognized the value of competition among multiple advocates within the governmental process and deliberately encouraged it ("I can't afford to confine myself to one set of advisers. If I did that *I* would be on *their* leading strings.") But Kennedy stopped well short of the extreme measures Roosevelt had employed. Rather than introduce calculated chaos into the policy system of multiple actors, as Roosevelt had, Kennedy increasingly utilized other strategies for avoiding the many possible malfunctions that bureaucratic politics could generate, the painful consequences of which had been so glaringly illustrated in the Bay of Pigs fiasco in the third month of his administration. He made increasing use of the White House staff as an instrument for controlling the bureaucracy and bending it, if possible, to his will.

In addition, Kennedy employed a variety of organizational devices to counteract the narrowness of perspective of members of individual departments and agencies. New types of planning procedures attempted to encourage critical, broad-gauged consideration of all of the competing factors (political, economic, diplomatic, military) embedded in a particular policy problem. Ad hoc interagency task forces, which were staffed from different departments, were established to conduct policy planning on specific issues or on trouble spots in the world. And personnel with different policy and professional backgrounds were introduced into the staffing of each of the regular agencies and departments. (Materials on Kennedy's orientation to bureaucratic politics appear in the memoir literature produced by members of his administration; but see also Neustadt 1963; Anderson 1968, pp. 195–298; Clark and Legere 1969.)

What is noteworthy in Kennedy's strategy for coping with the narrowness of bureaucratic politics is his multisided effort to restructure the roles of top-level advocates from different agencies and to resocialize them with a new set of decision-making norms. This strategy reached a peak in the Cuban missile crisis, which we shall analyze shortly. Kennedy's method of coping with bureaucratic politics stands in contrast to the approaches of his predecessors: Hoover's effort to take the "politics" out of the policy system and convert it into a centrally directed rational problem-solving mechanism; Roosevelt's attempts to increase competition and conflict within the policy system by undermining its structure and norms; Truman's desire to divide up the jurisdictions and strengthen each functional specialist's control over his own domain; and Eisenhower's efforts to stay above politics and let the machinery run.

The effect of crisis situations on the rationality of organizational decision making has been the subject of considerable research. Holsti (1972) concludes his review of laboratory and field studies on this subject with the observation that "policy making under circumstances of crisis-induced stress is likely to differ in a number of respects from decision-making processes in other situations. . . . [and] such differences are likely to inhibit rather than facilitate the effectiveness of those engaged in the complex tasks of making foreign policy choices" (p. 23). He concludes soberly that the reactions of statesmen to crisis-induced stress are often, though not always, disturbingly similar to those of subjects in experimental settings. For this reason, if for no other, it is instructive to note the novel ways in which Kennedy sought to control the possibly disruptive influences of bureaucratic politics during the Cuban missile crisis.

"Collegial" versus "Bureaucratic" Styles of Decision Making

Organizations are periodically faced with novel situations in which important values are at stake, but that cannot, or should not, be dealt with by selecting one of the standard responses from the organization's repertoire. To cope adequately with such situations it is often necessary to rearrange the milieu and norms of policy-making personnel so that they are able to ask questions at variance with the ideology and policy doctrines of the organization as a whole or those of its subunits. This is difficult to achieve when the quest for an effective decision proceeds within the context of a narrow, formalized bureaucratic process of policy making. For various reasons a more loosely structured and informal milieu—that is, the "collegial" style of decision making—makes it easier for most participants to free themselves and others from the inhibitions of organizational doctrines and from the tendency to overprotect the special interests of their subunit and constituency. Particularly because these inhibitions tend to be implicit and deeply ingrained, they can easily stifle creative imagination and novel ways of looking at the new policy problems that have arisen.

The possibility for fruitful restructuring of roles and norms for this purpose was demonstrated by President Kennedy in the Cuban missile crisis. The lessons he and his close advisers had drawn from their inept policy making in the Bay of Pigs case were now quickly put to use in improvising a quite different approach to crisis decision making when they were suddenly confronted in October 1962 by Khrushchev's deployment of missiles in Cuba.

Following the discovery that a substantial number of surface-to-surface missiles of medium range were being emplaced in Cuba, many questions arose for U.S. policy that required integrated evaluation from political, diplomatic, and military standpoints. The president immediately created a special ad hoc group of advisers from different branches of the government to consider the implications for U.S. security interests and to identify, develop, and evaluate alternative courses of action for his consideration. This group came to be called the Executive Committee (ExCom) of the National Security Council.

As has been emphasized in all available accounts, Kennedy quickly established a *modus operandi* and ground rules for the deliberations of the ExCom that greatly facilitated performance of its critical tasks. The ExCom was given the character of an informal problem-solving group that was to concern itself with all relevant aspects of the problem. Each member of the group was encouraged to concern himself with the policy problem as a whole, not to confine himself to that element of it on which he was expert or for which he or his department was officially responsible.

This mode of policy deliberation enhances the role of the generalist and gives him more scope for interacting with specialists and challenging their expert opinions. Though the importance of the generalist has often been emphasized by experienced policy makers, the role does not appear to be well defined or to have received much formal attention in studies of group problem solving. We need not see the ideal generalist as one who is broad gauged without being, or having been, an expert of some kind. Even the expert can take the role of generalist on matters not within his expertise. But for an expert to do so he must be willing to violate the tacit agreement, often entered into by experts, not to challenge another's expertise. The essence of the generalist's role is to ask the questions his very ignorance, naïveté, and different perspective allow him to ask of experts, questions that might never occur to the experts or whose relevance would not be evident to them until pointed out. It appears to me questionable whether the role of generalist in problem-solving groups can be played adequately by the political leader or chief decision maker.

As the detailed accounts, particularly by Sorensen (1965, pp. 679–680, 684–686) and Abel (1966, pp. 47, 52, 69–73, 79, 86–88), indicate (see also George 1971*b*), the meetings of the ExCom were marked by considerable give-and-take. Protocol was suspended. Second-level officials were encouraged to give their views even when they were at variance with those of superiors who were present. The president was encouraged by some of his close associates to absent himself from meetings when it was found that the process of mutual exploration of views was freer and more productive without him. Most participants are reported to have changed their positions at least once during the course of the six days prior to the president's final decision on a course of action.

The fact that time was available before the president would have to act and that secrecy was preserved proved to be highly useful. Time permitted the ExCom to pursue an iterative approach to its problem-solving task, which facilitated mutual education and made it possible for the group to close in on the critical factors on which the final choice of action depended.

The ExCom drew upon specialized inputs from functional and technical experts on political, military, and diplomatic questions, acting as an informal steering group for bringing to bear the best knowledge and analytical capabilities available in the more specialized branches of the government. Indeed, the iterative process permitted an increasingly sharper edge to be put upon requirements for specialized inputs. But perhaps the major contribution the collegial mode made to effective policy making was to maintain a broad perspective in which all relevant considerations could be identified, and the relationships among them kept in mind in devising and assessing alternative courses of action.

A collegial model of policy making in matters of this kind has important advantages over models in which participants reflect more closely the characteristic organizational features of hierarchy, specialization, and centralization. In the ExCom case, though the collegial model probably operated at something approaching optimal performance, it did so for reasons that may not always be present. Nonetheless, it deserves study so that we might understand what these special factors were and judge whether and how they might be replicated on future occasions.

To sharpen appreciation of these features let us compare the collegial style with an extremely bad variant of the formal bureaucratic model. Planning and decision making in this deliberate caricature are highly structured, expertise is compartmentalized along narrow functional lines, and system operation is highly formalized. Information and judgment on each of the relevant elements of the policy problem up for decision are provided the chief executive solely by the recognized functional expert on that element. Role playing is narrow and inflexible, and there is no devil's advocate. Further, the chief executive makes no provision for having the functional experts engage in a genuine dialogue in order to explore the problem as a whole and to examine the interrelationships among its elements. A formal procedure is followed for obtaining each expert's judgment on his portion of the problem—a judgment, it is presumed, that others are not competent to question. Each actor may also be asked for his overall judgment, but he gives it without having understood or studied the problem as a whole; and because he is aware that he has not understood, he tempers his conclusions and holds to a conservative, even sterile, view to avoid risking strong measures in the wrong context.

Because there is little or no use of an iterative approach to problem solving in this process, the experts have no opportunity to revise their judgments. Further, the highly structured, compartmentalized approach casts each adviser in the role of spokesman for his group. This forces the participants to resort to bargaining and superficial compromises rather than to utilize analytic procedures as a means of dealing with disagreements over policy. A heavy if indeed not impossible intellectual burden is ultimately placed upon the chief executive and his immediate personal staff in attempting a blend or synthesis of the many elements of the problem. This variant of the bureaucratic model, therefore, fails to meet the critical challenge in problem solving, namely, analysis of the relationship of the various parts of the problem to one another, and of the relationship of the parts to the whole.

In sum, the collegial approach to problem solving strengthens the analytic component and reduces the influence of the bargaining component. It does so by restructuring the roles of special advocates, enhancing the role of the generalist vis-à-vis the functional experts, providing for interactive policy analysis, and introducing new norms for the process of deliberation.

The Concept of "Preventive Intervention": A Pragmatic Theory for Managing the Policy-Making Process

Though structural and procedural reorganization in foreign policy making has on occasion yielded more rational decisions, overall improvements have been marginal and uneven; there appears to be no single structural formula by means of which the chief executive and his staff can convert the functional expertise and diverse viewpoints of many offices and individuals into consistently wise policies and decisions. Not surprisingly, this sober observation is entirely consistent with the evaluation by organizational theorists of a far wider range of experience. The optimism of an earlier day, which saw principles of modern organization and administration, and indeed bureaucracy itself, providing a vehicle for greater rationality in social and governmental affairs, has long since faded. As one specialist has put it: "The pyramidal, centralized, functionally specialized, impersonal mechanism known as bureaucracy . . . was out of joint with contemporary realities. . . . Adaptive, problem-solving, temporary systems of diverse specialists, linked together by coordinating executives in an organic flux—this is the organizational form that will gradually replace bureaucracy" (Bennis 1969, pp. 44–61). See also Toffler 1970, chap. 7, "Organizations: The Coming Ad-hocracy." Though the outlines remain dim, the theorists of administration and organization are breaking new ground once again.

But Bennis asks (1969, p. 45), "How would these new organizations be managed?" Our examination of the foreign policy-making machinery faces a similar problem. We have indicated briefly how a collegial system of decision making within a small advisory group can be created and managed. How, then, can a system of multiple advocacy be managed within the larger organization? Experience indicates that any system for policy making, however well designed, is subject to periodic failures and gross malfunctions. As Wilensky (1967) has emphasized, all large-scale organizations have structural characteristics of hierarchy, specialization, and centralization that encourage chronic pathologies of information and advice. Organizational theorists have accordingly turned their attention increasingly toward the types of human failures, individual and group dynamics, organizational pathologies, and malfunctions that can occur in large policy-making systems.

Thus, provision must be made for monitoring the day-to-day workings of the policy system, for identifying and correcting possible malfunctions, for avoiding distortion in hierarchical communication by various means such as redundancy, counter-biases, elimination of middlemen, and distortion-proof messages (Downs 1967), and for strategies for "preventive intervention." Clearly the chief executive has unique opportunities as well as responsibilities in this array, but he cannot be expected to discharge them on an intuitive, improvised, and personal basis. What is needed is a pragmatic theory that will identify the conditions or prerequisites for strengthening the system of multiple advocacy and for avoiding the detrimental vagaries of bureaucratic politics.

Preventive intervention is not a novel concept. In trying to adapt and incorporate it into decision-making theory and organizational practice, it would be well to draw upon experience gained in other fields, such as medicine and public health, and upon the stimulating analogies from biological and cybernetic models of "self-organizing systems." In von Neumann's words (1956, pp. 2085–2086), such systems "contain the necessary arrangements to diagnose errors as they occur, to readjust the organism so as to minimize the effects of errors, and finally to correct or block permanently the faulty component." Thus, duplication and overlap in administrative agencies are not necessarily a sign of waste and inefficiency, though the task remains to distinguish between inefficient redundancies and those that are constructive and reinforcing.

The strategy we have chosen for developing this kind of pragmatic theory consists in diagnosing past policy making within the government with the object of inductively codifying the lessons of experience. Such an inductive approach gives our prescriptive model a strong empirical base. In reviewing historical cases we have tried to identify what it was about the workings of the policy-making process itself that may have contributed importantly in each case in shaping the final policy or decision adopted by the president. We have been looking, in other words, for "breakdowns" or flaws in the presidential advisory system. But we have also been attentive to components that enhance the president's ability to make good policy choices. It should be clear that our concern is with major policy decisions at critical-choice points, such as decisions for intervention, escalation, or termination of a conflict.

Admittedly, the effort to evaluate major policy decisions gets us into the difficulties of normative analysis. At the most fundamental level lies the question of the values that guided the decision makers. Thus the investigator may regard a particular policy decision as "good" or "bad," depending upon whether he agrees with the ideology and political values the policy maker was pursuing. In another normative judgment the investigator confines himself to considering whether the best decision was made under the circumstances that prevailed at the time; this proviso is necessary lest the quality of the decision be scored unfairly on the basis of hindsight. A third normative criterion concerns whether the decision makers judged correctly the feasibility of the option they chose. Did a "good" decision on paper lead to a poor policy outcome because of inept, lethargic, or uncooperative implimentation by the responsible department? And did the option chosen reduce the flexibility the policy makers would need later were they to encounter unexpected and threatening developments? There are, then, some explicit criteria for making the more circumscribed type of normative evaluation, including (1) the attainability of the policy goals chosen; (2) the suitability of the means employed; (3) the timeliness and flexibility of the response; (4) the accuracy of calculated support for the policy chosen; (5) the accuracy of relative estimates of one's own capabilities vis-à-vis the opponent's capabilities and intentions; (6) the accuracy of predicted long-term consequences. This is by no means to suggest that the difficult methodological problems of normative analysis have been resolved, but the question must be confronted if studies of foreign policy making are to have greater relevance.

Malfunctions in the System
of Multiple Advocacy

Diagnostic analysis of a number of critical incidents in foreign policy making has enabled us to identify nine general types of malfunctions that can easily occur and that are likely to have adverse effects on policy outputs when they do occur. That a malfunction of process actually occurred is easier to establish than its precise importance in determining the decision that was finally made. Other variables also affected the decision in each case and these, too, are considered. It should be noted in this connection that the objective of developing a pragmatic theory for operating the policy-making system does not require high-confidence explanations of the kind sought by the historian; for our purpose causal imputations that are at least plausible, if not compelling, will do. (I have omitted most of the historical documentation of the case studies from this chapter; it is available in George 1972.) Though the malfunctions often occur as interrelated phenomena, we take them up separately here.

WHEN THE PRESIDENT AND HIS ADVISERS AGREE TOO READILY ON THE NATURE OF THE PROBLEM FACING THEM AND ON A RESPONSE TO IT. An experienced, shrewd executive is likely to regard premature consensus within the policy-making group as a reason for postponing, rather than taking, action. Alfred P. Sloan, former chairman of General Motors, is reported to have said at a meeting of one of his top policy committees:

Gentlemen, I take it we are all in complete agreement on the decision here. . . . Then I propose we postpone further discussion of this matter until our next meeting to give ourselves time to develop disagreement and perhaps gain some understanding of what the decision is all about (Drucker 1967, p. 148).

The problem of deferring action is more complicated, of course, when the situation seems to demand a quick response, and when the chief executive himself is disposed to take action. In certain types of foreign policy crises, a kind of generalized, unfocused consensus for action may quickly emerge, in the name of preventing any damage to U.S. interests. But the fact that the president and his advisers spontaneously or readily achieve such consensus may serve (and typically does serve) to prevent adequate consideration of the attendant costs and risks.

For various reasons it appears to be particularly difficult for decision-making groups in these circumstances to soberly pursue a rigorous cost-benefit analysis of alternative options. Indeed, as is the case in psychological experiments on decision making in crisis situations (see, for example, Robinson, Hermann, and Hermann 1969), fewer alternatives are likely to be identified and evaluated. (But, as in the Cuban missile crisis, when decision makers are alert to the possibility that a crisis atmosphere may disrupt rational decision making they may be able to design or introduce ad hoc procedures to safeguard against these tendencies. This, in fact, is the focus of the present essay.)

This type of malfunction is vividly apparent in the events leading to President Johnson's decision to send U.S. military forces into the Dominican Republic in the spring of 1965. As Geyelin puts it: "If Lyndon Johnson had acted much differently than he did in the early, decisive days of the Dominican crisis, he would have had to invent his own alternatives and ignore the counsel of his principal advisers . . . " (1966, pp. 244–245). There is nothing in the available record to indicate that the Special Assistant for National Security Affairs, McGeorge Bundy, attempted to protect the president's options in this case.

Indeed, all available accounts indicate that consensus on the need for U.S. military intervention developed quickly, easily, and without challenge within the decision-making group. The reasons are suggested by Geyelin: "Not the least of the lessons of Santo Domingo is that President Johnson was remarkably at the mercy of the advice and activities of his subordinates on the scene . . ." (pp. 244–245). And they speedily concluded that a rebel victory carried with it the risk of an eventual Communist regime. This assessment emerged as quickly and firmly as it did because perception of the developing crisis was shaped by a strong policy predisposition antedating the crisis—the belief that the Dominican Republic should not be allowed to become another Cuba. A distorted, exaggerated perception of the threat emerged when available information on the rebels was viewed through the prism of the "Cuban syndrome." No attempt was made until well after the United States was committed to intervention to check its embassy's definition of the situation and of the policies most appropriate for meeting it.

But decisional premises of the kind we have seen at work in the Dominican crisis do not always blunt the ability of decision makers to make a reasoned calculation of the utility of intervention. Vigorous multiple advocacy within the Eisenhower administration in the Indochina crisis helped to control the effect of an ideologically reinforced decisional premise. In the spring of 1954, the Eisenhower Administration was suddenly faced with having to decide whether to intervene in Indochina. Intervention on behalf of the beleaguered French forces at Dien Bien Phu was strongly favored by chairman of the Joint Chiefs of Staff Admiral Radford and apparently also by Secretary of State John Foster Dulles, and was supported by other members of the administration. The psychological momentum for intervention took hold quickly. Administration advocates attempted to build wider consensus for intervention by emphasizing the expected damage to U.S. interests if Indochina were lost. These efforts were crowned by Eisenhower's invocation of the "row-of-dominoes" analogy.

But the president was ambivalent and had second thoughts about the costs and risks of intervention; and in any case he was unwilling to act without consultation with congressional leaders. Some observers feel that the president deliberately slowed up the momentum for intervention within his administration, and indirectly strengthened the hand of advisers who were opposed to it, by directing Dulles and Radford to take their case to congressional leaders. There it became readily apparent that the air strike advocated by Radford to relieve pressure on French forces at Dien Bien Phu did not have the backing of all members of the Joint Chiefs. Moreover, it was obvious that the air strike probably would not achieve its purpose; rather, it would quickly become the first step on an exceedingly slippery slope that could engulf the United States in another major ground war in Asia. As a result, a wholesome sobriety was introduced into policy calculations. The momentum for intervention was delayed and eventually reversed despite the fact that the cold war image of Communism and a perception of threatened damage to U.S. interests were widely shared by policy makers and congressional leaders. Intervention was avoided only because the process of policy making forced decision makers to face up to the sobering question of costs and risks.

General Matthew Ridgway, then Chief of Staff of the Army, led the opposition. At the first suggestion that air and naval forces be committed in Indochina, Ridgway labeled the proposed action "ominous"; he warned that such a commitment would inevitably lead to use of ground forces. It was "incredible" to him that Washington should forget the bitter lesson of Korea so soon. Ridgway quickly dispatched a group of army specialists under General Gavin to Indochina to determine firsthand the difficulties and requirements of a U.S. intervention. On the basis of this study Ridgway reported to Eisenhower that the cost in men and money would be greater than in Korea. Though it is difficult to assess the impact of Ridgway's advice on Eisenhower's decision, Ridgway himself believed that his report, brought before the National Security Council, played a considerable, perhaps decisive role in counseling the administration against intervention (Ridgway 1956).

WHEN ADVISERS AND ADVOCATES TAKE DIFFERENT POSITIONS AND DEBATE THEM BEFORE THE PRESIDENT, BUT DO NOT COVER THE FULL

RANGE OF RELEVANT HYPOTHESES AND ALTERNATIVE OPTIONS. There is no assurance that on any given policy problem the actors within the decision-making system will divide up all of the relevant options. Some options may fail to get serious consideration because it is felt that the president has excluded them or would reject them. Thus, the option of not giving direct military assistance to South Korea when it was attacked by North Korea in June 1950 was never really considered by Truman's advisers, in part because the president made it clear at the outset that the United States would not allow the attack to succeed.

Other options may fail to get adequate consideration or presentation to the executive because policy-making officials serving under him are themselves disinterested in them. There are various ways of reducing the executive's freedom of action even while seemingly providing him with multiple options. As Robert H. Johnson notes: "One of the chief problems with attempts to lay out major policy alternatives is the strong temptation to load the dice. A typical procedure is to set up a straw-man alternative on either side of a middle course of action which quickly becomes the logical choice over the more 'extremist' options" (1969, p. 723).

Whether this type of malfunction occurred during the planning of the Vietnam escalation in 1964–1965 and what weight to attribute to it are somewhat uncertain. Some of Johnson's advisers may have felt that, although the president did request all the options (Thomson 1968, p. 52), he had already excluded the withdrawal option; in any case, many of them were themselves against withdrawal and not motivated, therefore, to provide a well-considered, persuasive version of this option. The Pentagon papers (1971) give the impression that most of the principals in the policy-making system had for some time come to feel that the United States should not withdraw and, if necessary, should engage in some degree of military escalation. During 1964 Johnson was largely preoccupied with the forthcoming presidential election and with domestic policy; he did not participate actively in the extensive Vietnam planning. After his election in early November, his advisers succeeded in drawing him into serious discussion of the situation in Vietnam and consideration of additional U.S. assistance. The internal political situation in Vietnam was now so unstable, however, that in the policy review of late November it was agreed that no increase in assistance was to be contemplated until a more stable government and political climate emerged in Saigon. What policy the United States should follow in the event these improvements failed to take place was evidently not considered.

Ever since the Chinese civil war, U.S. policy toward Asian countries threatened by Communism had been constrained by the sound proposition that the United States should not become inextricably committed via economic and military aid to regimes lacking the will to help themselves, the capacity to govern, and popular support. In late 1964 the logical implication of this decisional premise was that further involvement should be avoided and indeed that preparations should be made for a face-saving exit from South Vietnam.

But although Johnson had stated that he wanted all options considered, there is no indication in the public record that the option of U.S. withdrawal became the subject of major study. Neither the president nor his Special Assistant for National Security Affairs, McGeorge Bundy, requested that the withdrawal option be given careful consideration. To be sure, elements of this point of view were articulated by Undersecretary of State George Ball, who served as the focal point of a weak dovish coalition. But Ball was regarded as a "Europe man," and never entered the mainstream of policy planning. And Vice-President Humphrey is reported to have made a last-ditch attempt to prevent the bombing of North Vietnam (Hoopes 1969, p. 31).

Thus the Vietnam policy review of late 1964 afforded, as it turned out, the last opportunity for calm, unhurried deliberation on the situation. What had happened was that a new decisional premise, that Southeast Asia had become strategically important to the United States, had supplanted the old. Though the origins of the new premise cannot be easily traced, the Pentagon papers (1971) suggest that it had emerged gradually and tacitly during the preceding years, evidently without the conflict between the two premises being clearly identified and subjected to a major policy debate.

WHEN THERE IS NO ADVOCATE FOR AN UNPOPULAR POLICY OP-TION. During the first week of the Korean War, President Truman assembled a policy-making group on the need for action to prevent damage to U.S. interests. The group's decisions leading to the commitment of American ground troops were reached in a piecemeal, incremental fashion, and the initial consensus was never subjected to serious challenge. That no such challenge emerged was not because agreed-upon contingency plans existed for such an event, which had only to be put into operation. Indeed, no such plans existed—the North Korean attack had come as a shock. The president immediately defined the situation as one in which too much was at stake to permit the United States to acquiesce. The ingredients for bureaucratic politics and multiple advocacy were present in the long-standing policy and personal conflicts between Secretary of State Dean Acheson and Secretary of Defense Louis Johnson, but the president's attitude and the atmosphere of crisis muted their expression. As a result, the military pressures of the quickly deteriorating situation in Korea determined the choices made. The participants in these decisions believed they had few alternatives to the actions they took. Indeed, in one sense of the word no "decision" was made; that is, the president and his advisers did not at any point sit down to weigh the political and military factors for and against direct U.S. military intervention. There was no search for alternative ways of limiting the expected damage to national interests. The decisional premises that defined the situation—such as, that the aggression in Korea was like Nazi aggression in the 1930s and, if unopposed, would encourage Communists to undertake new aggressions—were not singled out for any kind of critical examination.

During the first few days of the conflict, at a time when U.S. assistance was still limited to air and naval support, several of Truman's advisers, and indeed the president himself, expressed reluctance to see U.S. ground troops committed. Once the deteriorating battlefield situation made it imperative, however, no adviser spoke against the introduction of American combat forces except George Kennan, who hesitated on the grounds that it would increase the likelihood of Soviet intervention. Even so, Kennan did feel that the United States would have to react with all necessary force (1967, p. 486); he also favored prompt steps to protect Formosa from falling into Communist hands on the ground that "two such reverses coming one on the heel of the other could easily prove disastrous to our prestige and to our entire position in the Far East." But neither Kennan nor military advisers who were unenthusiastic about an Asian land war were encouraged to play a vigorous devil's advocate role in the policy discussions. Nor was any effort made to calculate soberly the cost or level of military effort that would be required to defend South Korea. General MacArthur's quickly improvised (and grossly optimistic) estimate that two divisions under his command from Japan would enable "early offensive action" to save South Korea was accepted without question.

Later on in the Korean War, when the decision was being made to send U.S. and U.N. forces across the 38th parallel to pursue the defeated North Korean army and to unite the two parts of the country, the threat of Chinese Communist intervention arose. Important officials in Truman's circle of policy advisers (Secretary of the Air Force Thomas Finletter, Chief of Naval Operations Admiral Sherman, and Kennan) were disturbed by the risks of Chinese intervention. Once again, however, Truman's structuring and management of the policy-making process discouraged those with reservations from playing articulate devil's advocates. Indeed, such a role was not generally congenial to President Truman. He preferred to structure the policy-forming process in terms of functional expertise. Each of the agency heads was expected to provide his considered view of that aspect of the problem for which he was responsible. Within each department, second- and third-level officials contributed their advice to their department head, and deviations from this hierarchically organized flow of advice were not encouraged.

Kennan's advice on this and other occasions when it differed from Acheson's was thus overshadowed and controlled by the secretary of state. In a laudatory account of the way in which Truman organized and managed the process of foreign policy making, Acheson credits him with infusing an "adversary process" into National Security Council meetings similar to that of the law court (1969, pp. 733–737). It is clear that what Acheson endorses in this respect is the formal, orderly variant of the adversary process—one that worked to Acheson's advantage because Truman acknowledged and leaned on his special competence in foreign affairs—and not the unstructured and unpredictable variants of multiple advocacy associated with the game of bureaucratic politics. Acheson's distaste for the informal variants of multiple advocacy—in which he enjoyed less influence—emerges clearly from his critical account of the workings of the ad hoc ExCom at the time of the Cuban missile crisis, in which Acheson participated at President Kennedy's invitation.

WHEN ADVISERS TO THE PRESIDENT THRASH OUT THEIR OWN DISAGREEMENTS OVER POLICY WITHOUT THE PRESIDENT'S KNOWLEDGE AND CONFRONT HIM WITH A UNANIMOUS RECOMMENDATION. In this variant of the workings of bureaucratic politics the other actors in effect "gang up" on the chief executive. Clark Clifford gives a succinct, authoritative account of this practice in an interview describing his role as assistant to President Truman on domestic affairs:

The idea was that the six or eight of us would try to come to an understanding among ourselves on what directions we would like the President to take on any given issue. And then, quietly and unobtrusively, each in his own way, we would try to steer the President in that direction. . . . Well, it was two forces fighting for the mind of the President, that's really what it was. It was completely unpublicized, and I don't think Mr. Truman ever realized it was going on . . . (Anderson 1968, p. 116).

In this case, as Clifford's account makes clear, two coalitions of advisers were competing for influence over policy. A more dangerous situation arises when all major advisers on a policy issue reach agreement among themselves before approaching the executive. This type of malfunction almost occurred in the late autumn of 1964 when President Johnson was confronted with a solid lineup of advisers recommending that he proceed with the Multilateral Force (MLF) for NATO. The MLF was to be a strategic force composed of surface ships manned by mixed crews drawn from a number of NATO countries; for several years a small but strong group within the administration had pushed this idea as a way of knitting the alliance together. An opportunity for final U.S. approval of the plan and its implementation arose in connection with Prime Minister Harold Wilson's visit to Washington for discussions with the president. The MLF advocates within the administration succeeded in coordinating a position paper with all of the president's chief advisers that would have firmly committed the United States. Hence, on the eve of his critical meeting with the prime minister, Johnson "was confronted with a spirited, consecrated, nearly united bureaucracy . . ." (Geyelin 1966, p. 162).

Now it is extremely difficult for a president to act contrary to the unanimous advice of his national security advisers. He is deprived of an adequate evaluation of available options when the actors thrash out or compromise their differences privately and confront him with a unified recommendation. It is for this reason that we stressed earlier the need for presidential-level participation in, or at least sensitivity to, the day-to-day workings of the bureaucratic-politics system. Because the chief executive cannot be expected to participate directly in this process or even to monitor it closely, the task becomes a critical function for his personal assistants; it is only through alter egos who clearly understand his responsibilities and needs that the chief executive can monitor the workings of the policy-forming system and intervene as necessary.

In fact, this critical task was performed ably by one of the president's alter egos in the MLF case. Geyelin (1966, p. 170) states that the position of McGeorge Bundy as "guardian of options and protector of the president" was perhaps never more effectively displayed than in this episode. Bundy had sensed trouble building up earlier in the year. "With the MLF partisans in full cry, the President's position was uncertain. . . ."

Sensing malfunction, Bundy quietly called upon Richard Neustadt, a part-time consultant to the White House, to make an independent appraisal of the MLF issue in Europe as well as in Washington. Armed with this and other information that Bundy had assembled, the president entered the final briefing conferences with his foreign policy advisers prepared to challenge their decisional premises, information, and recommendation. "In the course of the protracted conferences in preparation for the Wilson visit," Geyelin reports (1969, p. 162), "Johnson assailed the men around him, questioning their competence as well as their counsel. . . ."

Within NATO there had by no means been a clear consensus on behalf of the MLF, let alone enthusiasm; and senior members of Congress as well as many officials in the executive branch were not enthusiastic. What Bundy's timely intervention accomplished was to bring these factors into greater prominence for the president's benefit. He had initiated a strategy of preventive intervention to restore some semblance of multiple advocacy.

WHEN ADVISERS AGREE PRIVATELY AMONG THEMSELVES THAT THE PRESIDENT SHOULD FACE UP TO A DIFFICULT DECISION, BUT NO ONE IS WILLING TO ALERT HIM TO THE NEED FOR DOING SO. By early November 1950, large numbers of Chinese Communist forces had already intervened in the Korean War and had subjected U.S. and South Korean forces to sharp tactical combat; but they had not yet launched an all-out offensive against U.S. and U.N. forces. Nonetheless, Truman's chief civilian and military advisers in Washington were acutely concerned over the maldeployment of MacArthur's forces in North Korea in the presence of large numbers of Chinese Communist forces. The president's advisers seemingly agreed among themselves that MacArthur's directives should be changed to reduce the vulnerability of his forces, but this consensus was not translated into action. According to Neustadt's (1960) account, each adviser interpreted his official role quite narrowly in order to relieve himself of the obligation to take the initiative. "No one went to Truman," Neustadt (1960) writes, "because everyone thought someone else should go." Each had reasons of his own for not doing so.

The military chiefs deferred to State; let Acheson, as guardian of "policy," ask Truman to reverse MacArthur. But Acheson, already under fire from the Capitol, was treading warily between the Pentagon and that inveterate idealist about generals, Harry Truman. In immediate terms the risk was "military"; if it justified reversing the commander in the field, then the Joint Chiefs must make the judgment and tell Truman. So Acheson is said to have insisted, understandably enough, and there the matter rested (p. 145).

As for Secretary of Defense George Marshall, who had preceded Acheson as secretary of state and had himself been Army Chief of Staff when Bradley (now chairman of the Joint Chiefs of Staff) was subordinate commander, he had "leaned over backwards" since returning to the government as secretary of defense shortly before these events took place "not to meddle with the work of his successors in *their* jobs. He had also leaned over backwards not to revive the old Army feud between him and MacArthur. What Acheson and Bradley were not ready to initiate, Marshall evidently felt he could not take upon himself. . . . The President, meanwhile, had little thought of overriding, on his own, the tactical decisions of a qualified commander" (Neustadt 1960, p. 145).

This was a sorry example, indeed, of narrow bureaucratic role playing at the highest advisory level. One can only speculate what Truman's response would have been had his advisers shared their concern with him. If Truman had acted promptly, there would have been time to pull back MacArthur's forces before the Chinese launched their major offensive on November 28. The catastrophe that followed might have been avoided altogether or greatly reduced.

WHEN THE PRESIDENT, FACED WITH AN IMPORTANT DECISION, IS DEPENDENT UPON A SINGLE CHANNEL OF INFORMATION. It has seldom been noted that during the Cuban missile crisis, Khrushchev quickly established multiple channels for securing information on Kennedy's intentions. Too much was at stake for the Soviet government to wait passively for deliberate or inadvertent signals from Washington. Several channels were opened—at the U.N., through the Soviet ambassador's conversations with Robert Kennedy and others in the administration, and through the special contacts that Alexander Fomin, the top intelligence specialist in the Soviet embassy in Washington, established with John Scali, an American journalist known to have high-level contacts in the State Department. Faced with the imminent need to make important decisions, the Soviet premier grasped the value of redundancy in information coverage of his opponent's behavior.

In striking contrast, U.S. leaders have allowed themselves in several crises to remain dependent on a single channel of information for critical intelligence. Among the many malfunctions of the policy-making process evident in planning the Bay of Pigs fiasco in 1961 was the fact that Kennedy and his advisers, including the Joint Chiefs, depended on the Central Intelligence Agency's (CIA) estimates of Castro's military and political strength. Both were underestimated by the CIA. A substantial anti-Castro underground was to have spearheaded an uprising when the invasion by Cuban exiles took place. Castro's air force was reportedly weak and vulnerable, incapable of dealing with the invading force. The CIA argued that the invasion should not be delayed, because Cuba would soon receive modern air power from the Soviets. In fact, Castro had already received these aircraft (see Sorenson 1963, p. 302; Schlesinger 1965, chap. 10).

Although the single channel of information on these and other inputs to policy planning was controlled by the CIA, where the chief advocates and planners of the invasion resided, Kennedy's suspicions were not aroused. There was ample time to set up independent channels of information and intelligence evaluation, but the president and his alter egos made no such move. Rather, they allowed the CIA to maintain unchallenged its position as dominant advocate.

The Bay of Pigs disaster left the White House reluctant to depend on established procedures in other departments and agencies for the selection and analysis of information. Shortly thereafter a "situation room" was set up in the White House basement adjoining the offices of the NSC staff. Teletype machines were installed that received all important messages from military, diplomatic, and intelligence centers around the world simultaneously with their arrival at the State Department, the Defense Department, and the CIA. Though the purpose of the situation room was ostensibly to improve the president's ability to manage crises and to stay on top of fast-breaking events, by equalizing the White House's access to critical information it also improved its ability to deal with other actors in the system. The position of the Special Assistant for National Security Affairs was especially strengthened.

Timely access to available information, however, does not in itself assure that multiple channels will exist when they are most needed. The type of malfunction we have been discussing occurred again in the Dominican intervention of April 1965. Washington was dependent for its picture of the complex internal political situation in the Dominican Republic on a single channel of information—this time the U.S. embassy in Santo Domingo. Had Johnson (or any of his advisers) wished to act differently in this crisis, as Geyelin (1966, pp. 244–245) puts it, "he would have had to discount the overwhelming weight of intelligence he received from the scene. . . ."

The government's dependence on a single channel of intelligence cannot be explained on the ground that the crisis developed too swiftly. Washington had been warned that the internal political conflict in the Dominican Republic might get out of hand. But neither the president nor the Special Assistant for National Security Affairs, "the guardian of presidential options," took heed of the warning. A conscious attempt to develop an alternative source was undertaken only on April 29, *after* the U.S. decision to intervene had been made and was being implemented (this was the presidential mission of John Bartlow Martin).

WHEN THE KEY ASSUMPTIONS AND PREMISES OF A PLAN HAVE BEEN EVALUATED ONLY BY THE ADVOCATES OF THAT OPTION. A striking example of this type of malfunction occurred in the Bay of Pigs case. Considering that Kennedy persistently entertained grave doubts about the CIA invasion plan and, moreover, did *not* regard Castro as a direct threat to the United States, it is puzzling that the key premises of the CIA plan were not subjected to thoroughgoing scrutiny. But CIA Director Allen Dulles and Deputy Director Richard Bissell, both carry-overs from the Eisenhower Administration, in fact enjoyed considerable respect and prestige in the new administration, and Kennedy hoped to have them join his team.

Kennedy's reservations about the invasion plan were never translated into an effective search for an alternative. Instead, a number of partial constraints were imposed on the plan to make it more acceptable to the president (Sorensen 1963, pp. 304, 306; Schlesinger 1965, chap. 10). What was sorely needed was an independent, informed, and competent assessment of the critical premises on which the CIA plan rested. But the questions the president and other policy makers raised from time to time were answered only by those who were preparing the plan and supporting it, and the meetings degenerated into question-and-answer periods. When an occasional skeptic, like Senator Fulbright, who was invited by the president to attend one of the policy meetings, raised questions about the plan, Kennedy limited his own role to allowing the CIA representatives to answer.

In providing consistently reassuring answers the CIA representatives were not necessarily engaging in conscious deception, though wishful thinking may have been at work in their assessment of uncertainties. Nor is this surprising, for the CIA leaders firmly believed that action against Castro was necessary. They had created and trained a Cuban exile force to carry out the invasion; and the preparations had already achieved a certain bureaucratic momentum by the time the new president established himself in office and turned some of his attention to reviewing the plan. In the last analysis, the key premises of the invasion plan went unquestioned because the president allowed the CIA to dominate and weaken the multiple-advocacy system.

WHEN THE PRESIDENT ASKS ADVISERS FOR THEIR OPINIONS ON A PREFERRED COURSE OF ACTION, BUT DOES NOT REQUEST A QUALIFIED GROUP TO EXAMINE MORE CAREFULLY THOSE JUDGMENTS THAT RUN COUNTER TO HIS PREDISPOSITIONS. We have noted the danger that may arise when no actor in the system is willing to speak up for an unpopular option or to oppose the group's preferred course of action. A different kind of malfunction occurs when advisers who give negative counsel suffer from inadequate resources for advocacy or are discouraged by the president or his surrogates from using them fully. As a result, the president may "hear" the negative opinion of an adviser, but not really want to "listen" to a fuller, more thorough presentation of it.

There are indications of this type of malfunction of the advisory system in late 1961 during the events leading to President Kennedy's decision to commit additional U.S. military advisers to South Vietnam. All reports during the year had indicated an increasingly grave state of affairs; Diem's government was not expected to last without substantial additional help from the United States. But doubts and hesitations over this course of action were shared by important policy advisers as well as President Kennedy himself. The Pentagon papers (p. 102) disclose that at one point Secretary of State Rusk himself expressed reluctance to see American prestige committed too deeply for the sake of "a losing horse." On another occasion Undersecretary of State George Ball argued against more military assistance to Saigon because he feared it might eventually lead to a deployment of as many as 300,000 troops.

Though Kennedy was aware that the real problem in South Vietnam was Diem's lack of political strength, he felt compelled by global cold-war pressures to bolster the Saigon regime. Preferring to temporize and buy time, the president gave no encouragement to advisers who expressed doubts about the wisdom of sending more military advisers and warned him that this would harden the U.S. commitment. As a result of the president's attitude, the option of U.S. withdrawal did not attract the kind of vigorous advocacy for which sentiment existed within the advisory group. The possibility of working toward a neutral South Vietnam, advanced by Chester Bowles, was put aside rather quickly without serious study. The president evidently preferred to believe, contrary to advisers' warnings, that he would not be seriously reducing his freedom of action to withdraw later if he increased the number of U.S. military advisers. As in the Bay of Pigs case, the nature of the president's involvement in policy planning served to hamper rather than encourage full development of options and full-fledged multiple advocacy of them.

The same type of malfunction had been evident in more acute form earlier in 1961 during deliberations leading up to the Bay of Pigs incident. On various occasions the CIA plan to invade Cuba was strongly opposed by individual advisers—Chester Bowles, Arthur Schlesinger, William Fulbright. All accounts of Kennedy's management of the policy-making process in this case make clear that, far from seeking opportunities to encourage vigorous multiple advocacy, he was reluctant to see it develop and hoped to satisfy his own doubts about the plan by procedures that did not so directly challenge its advocates and supporters.

Following the president's cue, neither McGeorge Bundy, his Special Assistant for National Security Affairs in the White House, nor Robert Kennedy, nor Rusk attempted to initiate or encourage an independent evaluation. When Hilsman suggested that his office do so, Rusk refused on the grounds of secrecy. And at one point, Schlesinger, who had written two memos opposing the plan, was taken aside by Robert Kennedy and told to "lay off." Those who opposed the invasion were "heard," but were given no encouragement to develop the case against it. The Joint Chiefs, it is true, were asked to evaluate the CIA plan, but there was no disposition on the part of Kennedy or his leading advisers to ensure that the Joint Chiefs were sufficiently motivated to give it a properly critical scrutiny, or to look too closely at the qualified endorsement the Joint Chiefs came up with.

Thus the advice of policy dissidents that remains the mere opinion of the individuals concerned will not suffice to check the momentum of a dominant policy faction. In the Bay of Pigs case the futility of the dissidents' efforts cannot be explained on the grounds that the president enthusiastically supported the policy option in question. In fact, he disagreed with the major premise on which the CIA plan was based—namely, that Castro constituted a threat to vital U.S. interests—and had reservations about the plan itself. Rather the explanation must be sought in part, as Kennedy recognized later, in his failure to manage the policy-shaping process more effectively.

WHEN THE PRESIDENT IS IMPRESSED BY THE CONSENSUS AMONG HIS AD-VISERS BUT FAILS TO ASCERTAIN HOW FIRM THE CONSENSUS IS, HOW IT WAS ACHIEVED, AND WHETHER IT IS JUSTIFIED.   In malfunction number 4, which is similar to this one in some respects, the other actors thrash out their disagreements on a policy issue without the president's knowledge, and then confront him with a unanimous recommendation. But the chief executive may also be the victim of what Janis (1971a, 1971b) calls an illusory consensus among his advisers that reflects a rather different working of the system. Thus, at the important April 4, 1961, meeting it appeared to President Kennedy that there was no longer any opposition to the Bay of Pigs plan. Evidently he did not realize that the management of the policy-forming process had finally succeeded in discouraging the further expression of opposition. As Schlesinger (1965) recalled it, "Our meetings were taking place in a curious atmosphere of assumed consensus." And, as Sorensen (1963) put it, the advice offered Kennedy "was not so unanimous or so well considered as it seemed."

The chief executive, then, and his alter egos must not take the consensus among policy advisers at face value. Particularly when the consensus is agreeable to him, the president must nonetheless force himself to test it. Is it complete, or does it obscure important differences and unresolved issues? What is it based on and how was it achieved? Is it a well-considered consensus toward which all actors have done their homework and interacted with one another in a joint problem-solving exercise? Or is it a manufactured or synthetic consensus obtained through the dominance of one policy clique, or through bargaining among the actors that papers over difficult problems and shirks the task of identifying and evaluating relevant options?

Implications for Strengthening Multiple Advocacy and the Policy-Making System

This inventory of possibly dangerous malfunctions leads to the identification of a critical task for monitoring and managing the day-to-day workings of the policy-making process. General knowledge of these typical malfunctions should increase the likelihood that a custodian of the process will identify their emergence early on and undertake corrective action. The kinds of intervention strategies needed to correct or compensate for malfunctions are mostly self-evident and have been suggested in the preceding review of historical cases.

It seems both obvious and appropriate that responsibility for discharging this critical task at the highest level of policy making in the executive branch should be assigned to the Special Assistant for National Security Affairs. (Staff assistants to senior officials in departments can be assigned the corresponding task in their own agencies.) From the very inception of the office, the Special Assistant has been designated custodian and manager of the process.

It should be emphasized, however, that the Special Assistant will be able to perform the critical tasks associated with the custodian's role only if he scrupulously refrains from taking the role of advocate himself. Both roles are necessary at the presidential level, but effective operation of the policy-making system requires that the two remain separate. To combine them in one official would set up a severe role conflict: when important policy issues are being decided it would be extraordinary if an individual who is himself an advocate of a particular option could also discharge the critical tasks of custodian of the process.

The role of custodian-manager is critical. Performance of the role can be eroded and eventually robbed of its integrity only if its incumbent is encouraged by the chief executive to become a policy adviser, or otherwise succumbs to the temptation of becoming an advocate. Other persons with special competence on foreign policy matters can be appointed by the chief executive as his advisers on substantive issues, leaving the Special Assistant free to focus exclusively on the procedural aspects of policy making.

Both Truman and Eisenhower attempted to prevent leading staff personnel of the National Security Council from acting as policy advocates. Under Truman the NSC staff was headed by an executive secretary whose duties were carefully circumscribed. When Eisenhower created the Office of the Special Assistant he excluded from its duties the role of policy adviser. Robert Cutler, the first incumbent, reports that his role was defined by Eisenhower as that of a nonadvocate and a non-freewheeler. Only rarely, Cutler has written, did he undertake to suggest an independent position of his own inside or outside the NSC. Such forays "would sometimes bring down on my head an adverse storm." Interestingly, however, he adds (1966, pp. 315–316): "But if debate was intensified on a germane issue, it was worth a knock on the head."

Under Kennedy, however, a basic duality emerged in the role. In the looser organization of the NSC that Kennedy introduced, the Special Assistant emerged as an ad hoc policy adviser to the president; he was no longer restricted to being the neutral manager of well-defined NSC procedures. No careful, informed analysis has been made of Bundy's effort, and those of his successors (Walt Rostow and Henry Kissinger), to combine the task of custodian with that of advocacy, but there are indications that these two roles cannot easily be combined in one post.

The same kind of role conflict is likely to emerge if the Special Assistant acts as a spokesman on behalf of existing policy. Whether he speaks openly to explain and support decisions taken by the administration or does so in an ostensibly off-the-record manner, he may be constraining his performance as neutral custodian. The definition of Robert Cutler's role in this respect restricted him to the classical anonymity expected of a presidential assistant. He was not to issue public statements, provide the press with rationales for policy decisions, or even discuss or write about the way in which the NSC was organized and operated except as specifically authorized by the president (Cutler 1966, pp. 315–316).

In the past decade there has been a gradual and cumulative change in this spokesman component of the role. Since Bundy in 1961, the man serving as Special Assistant has increasingly acted as a major, though not the sole, spokesman for the president's foreign policy decisions. The explanation for this development is not difficult to grasp. The men selected for the job, beginning with Bundy, have been specialists on national security affairs to a degree that their predecessors under Truman and Eisenhower clearly were not. It is understandable that such an official, so close to the president's thinking and so well informed about the basis and rationale of foreign policy decisions, should be considered an ideal choice to serve as an important communication link and public-relations channel to the more alert and informed elements of the public. But serving as a spokesman-apologist for existing policies may in fact inhibit the Special Assistant in performing his more important responsibility for securing an adequate revaluation and reconsideration of current policy.

Another potential role conflict can be identified with respect to two different ways in which the custodian or "watchdog" function is defined. The Special Assistant, it may be argued, should be concerned with protecting the chief executive's broad responsibility for the quality of the policy-forming process rather than, more narrowly, protecting the president's personal power stakes. But these two tasks cannot be comfortably combined in one role. The attempt to do so may lead, as some critics have charged, to an erosion of the Special Assistant's performance of his primary responsibility. When he attempts to combine both watchdog functions, the Special Assistant risks losing the capacity for serving as the "honest broker" of ideas and analyses. Rather than keeping the president's options open, the guardian of the president's personal power stakes can help the president to keep them closed. This is a criticism leveled at Rostow's performance of the role (see, for example, Hoopes 1969, pp. 59–61, 116, 123). The question has also been raised whether serving as personal adviser to the president has required Kissinger to subordinate his institutional role as kingpin of the NSC system (Destler 1972).

Finally, at the risk of hopelessly complicating the problem, we must recognize still another role conflict that may degrade the Special Assistant's ability to discharge the custodian's task. If, as has been the case in the past, he is also expected to monitor and ensure the implementation of policy decisions once they are taken, can he preserve intact his chief role? After all, White House aides who might be able to fashion a fairly objective role in the process of policy formation often become advocates and unrelenting lieutenants for fixed views in the implementation stage. The importance of implementation notwithstanding, I would propose that the Special Assistant's personal involvement in it is likely to create serious constraints on his ability to perform as custodian of the policy-making process, especially where reevaluation of existing policies is concerned. The question is posed, therefore, whether the two tasks of custodian and implementer, both of which the executive requires, need to be combined in the same person and whether they can be kept sufficiently separate to avoid a dysfunctional role conflict.

I have argued that the Special Assistant, or someone like him elsewhere in the foreign policy advisory system, should be the custodian of the policy-making process, and that this critical task should not be combined with becoming a policy adviser-advocate, a public spokesman on behalf of existing policy, a watchdog of the president's personal power stakes in policy issues, or an implementer of policy decisions already taken. The attempt to do so will undermine the integrity of the incumbent's performance of his central role, which is to improve the workings of the multiple-advocacy system on behalf of the executive by balancing actor resources when necessary, by strengthening weaker advocates, by bringing in new advisers to argue for unpopular options, by setting up alternate channels of information, by arranging for independent evaluation of decisional premises and options that are not receiving objective, competent evaluation, and generally by monitoring the policy-making process for possibly dangerous malfunctions and instituting appropriate corrective action.

This "job description" is indeed a composite of some of the most useful tasks performed on occasion by the incumbent of the office. But these critical tasks have by no means been consistently undertaken, as we have seen, on all the occasions when there was a need for them. It is suggested, therefore, that the best performances of the job in the past now be codified and institutionalized into the Special Assistant's role.

The availability of this kind of pragmatic theory should help to institutionalize and regularize self-correcting mechanisms within the policy-making system. As a result, the kind of timely intervention McGeorge Bundy made in the MLF case would hopefully become the rule rather than the exception. As we have seen, what this Special Assistant did so well for John-son in this case, no one did for Truman in November 1950, when the pres-ident should have been alerted that his advisers had agreed something should be done about the maldeployment of MacArthur's forces. Perhaps one of Truman's assistants would have done so had essential features of the multiple-advocacy model been institutionalized in the norms of the system at that time.

Similarly, some of the glaring inconsistencies we have seen in Bundy's performance might have been smoothed out for the better had he incorpo-rated into his role a better understanding of his critical tasks. The insight and ingenuity he demonstrated so well in the MLF case in safeguarding the president's options were conspicuously absent from his performance in other cases we have examined—the Bay of Pigs, the 1961 decision to in-crease U.S. military advisers in South Vietnam, the decision in 1965 to bomb North Vietnam, the Dominican intervention. In none of these cases does it appear that Bundy either identified the ongoing malfunction or ini-tiated appropriate emergency action to correct or compensate for it. The explanation for his apparent failure to do so is no doubt complicated, but we do know that the role itself has not been clearly and consistently defined.

We have presented our theory of multiple advocacy in undiluted form and without caveats. It remains to acknowledge that, as with all other prescriptive theories, this one too has its practical limits and costs.

Multiple advocacy is not offered as a comprehensive theory covering all aspects of policy making. We have noted that the values of policy makers and their cognitive beliefs (that is, decisional premises) may be so firmly and uniformly held on occasion as to severely constrain the choice of policy. In such cases, the way in which policy-making procedures are organized and managed may have little independent effect on the quality of decisions taken. More often, however, there are competing values and a variety of decisional premises that, moreover, are not firmly held; in such instances, the nature of the policy-making process may indeed exercise a critical influ-ence on the evaluation and choice of policy.

It would be naïve, then, to argue that multiple advocacy can guarantee good decisions in every instance. Rather, the case for it must rest on the more modest, but not unreasonable, expectation that even an imperfect sys-tem of multiple advocacy will help forestall some very bad decisions. This is not to say that malfunctions of the kind we have identified always result in major policy errors. But they can.

The prerequisites for an effective system of multiple advocacy are not easily met in practice. It is not easy to recruit able persons for all the senior positions in the policy-making system and to provide them with the re-sources and staffs they need to become effective advocates—for example, competence, analytical capabilities, and bargaining and persuasion skills. Nonetheless, knowledge of the theory of multiple advocacy is useful even if its requirements cannot be fully achieved. Thus the chief executive and his staff can be made aware that the decision-making process on an important issue may be inadequate in certain respects that need to be corrected or taken into account.

Multiple advocacy may entail costs that one would rather avoid incurring. The time required for effective advocacy and for give-and-take among the advocates may on occasion impose undue delays on decision making at the executive level. In a full-blown system of multiple advocacy, competition and conflict may get out of hand, strain cohesion, impose heavy human costs, or create political difficulties for the chief executive in his relations with Congress and the public. Cast in the role of advocates, officials may be quicker to go outside the executive branch in search of allies in policy disputes. The chief executive may feel that his diminished control over final decisions outweighs the benefits of multiple advocacy. There is no denying that multiple advocacy entails costs that may be onerous and difficult to live with from time to time. On the other hand, other systems of policy making also entail costs and risks, though perhaps they are less conspicuous and of a somewhat different kind. The absence of effective multiple advocacy, as we have seen, can also have very serious costs in terms of the maladaptive policies it leads to.

Multiple advocacy, or some functionally equivalent system of organizational decision making, recommends itself by way of forestalling the severe risks of choosing a policy hastily, without proper information and analysis, or without adequate challenge to decisional premises. This is particularly so in the case of foreign policy decisions that, once made, are not easily reversible or correctable on the basis of feedback.

Finally, the chief executive's attitude toward multiple advocacy is, of course, critical. This model of organizational policy making is likely to suit the style and temperament of some presidents more than others. One can hope that the formulation of the theory here, together with the historical documentation provided of its importance, will at least call attention to some of the fundamental problems, lacunae, and defects in other policy-making models.

The executive obviously has the power and means to shape the roles of his advisory staff. Role analysis of the kind we have undertaken here, especially with respect to the Special Assistant for National Security Affairs, is needed for the presidential staff as a whole in order to identify critical role tasks and to clarify the conditions on which their effective performance depends (see Cronin 1969, 1971). Role analysis can lead to useful redistribution of role tasks among staff assistants and to redefinition and clarification of individual positions. Finally, role analysis associated with the theory of multiple advocacy can be helpful in selectively recruiting personnel for staff positions, in socializing incumbents into their roles, and in maintaining a milieu and incentive structure that foster effective performance.

SUMMARY AND CONCLUSIONS

A broad framework has been developed for the study of adaptive and mal-adaptive decision making within the policy-making system of a complex organization. Three subsystem contexts have been identified: the *individual* (that is, the executive); the *small group* (the president's informal, face-to-face relationships with his advisers); and the *organization*. We examined the interrelationship of these three subsystems in order to note how distinctive dynamic processes associated with each context may affect adversely or favorably the quality of rational calculation of policy in the other two contexts.

The analysis was structured by focusing on ways in which cognitive stress may be coped with in each of the three subsystems. Cognitive stress (and the deeper anxieties it may activate, about which less is said in this paper) arises from attempts to deal with three difficult constraints on rational decision making: (1) inadequate information about the situation; (2) inadequate knowledge by means of which to assess the consequences of alternative courses of action; and (3) the difficulty of reconciling the competing, conflicting values engaged by the situation.

Each of the three subsystems is capable of generating maladaptive ways of coping with each of these three cognitive constraints. At the same time, opportunities exist or may be created in each subsystem for (1) opening up and maintaining channels of information about policy problems that may require decision, (2) improving the identification and evaluation of alternative courses of action, and (3) dealing with the competing values and interests at stake in a given situation.

The fact that different actors within the system perceive the stakes differently complicates the already difficult task of reconciling competing, conflicting values. The executive may resort to one of three modes of dealing with competing values and interests. He may employ one of several psychological mechanisms to banish or sharply reduce the motivational conflict; we have called this mode of coping "conflict avoidance." Or he may attempt to satisfy, to some extent at least, all or most of the competing values and interests aroused by the policy issues; this mode of coping, "conflict resolution," is pursued by inventing a single policy that is expected to indulge all of the competing values simultaneously, or by the tactic of sequencing or scheduling separate efforts to meet different competing values at different times. The third mode, "conflict acceptance," finds the executive accepting the fact that not all of the competing values can be indulged and selecting some at the expense of others.

As for decisional stresses occasioned for the executive by the other two cognitive constraints (inadequate information and knowledge), a variety of coping strategies were identified but not discussed at length. We emphasized, rather, that the difficulty an executive experiences in coping with this kind of cognitive complexity may well make him more vulnerable to certain small-group dynamics. The criterion of what significant others will approve of may easily fill the vacuum created for him by the difficulty of making a good cognitive appraisal of the policy issue.

In considering the relationship between the individual and small-group subsystems, we emphasized first the need for more differentiated theorizing and empirical analysis of the ways in which the executive's reality testing and problem solving might be reinforced by favorable small-group processes and protected against disruptive small-group dynamics. A critical variable here is the set of norms comprising the problem-solving culture of the small group of policy advisers; these norms can be seen as regulating the performance of the many critical subtasks involved in the small-group policy-making activities. These subtasks, we feel, need to be differentiated much more precisely than they have been. Moreover, the problem-solving norms and culture of small policy-making groups are subject to considerable variation. We need to identify variants that reinforce the executive's own constructive, adaptive ego-functions, and contribute to warding off, controlling, or compensating for any of his or other group members' ego-defensive involvements in policy making.

Turning to the often noted fact that conformity-inducing dynamics in small-group behavior may seriously degrade the capacity for rational policy making, we noted first that we must go beyond the available simplified laboratory studies of this phenomenon to perceive the remarkable range and complexity of motivations affecting the treatment of real-life dissidents. Field observations in natural settings and, indeed, even the preliminary observations in this essay should stimulate the design of more complex laboratory studies of group-induced uniformity of opinion. The more insidious disruptive pattern occurs when small decision-making groups that enjoy strong cohesion attempt to cope with severe, persistent cognitive stress by substituting group concurrence for reality testing. The very fact that the policy makers enjoy group cohesion may lead to an erosion of critical ego-functions.

In any case, both types of conformity-inducing dynamics associated with the small group are absent or weaker in the organizational context. One looks, therefore, for ways in which organizational procedures and dynamics might discourage or compensate for these maladaptive small-group coping mechanisms.

We noted that policy dissidents who attempt with indifferent success to play the devil's advocate role within the small group, or who are easily co-opted into serving other functions for the group, may become more effective devil's advocates if they are given a power base within some subunit of the organization.

We noted that the executive who cannot deal with the difficult cognitive task of formulating a single criterion aggregating all relevant values and interests engaged by a policy issue, via an internalized subjective debate, has the alternative of benefiting from an external play of the conflicting values

within the organization. The clash over policy on the part of subunit officials reflecting different social values and political interests provides this
possibility. Ideally, the small group (organized to function in the "collegial"
mode) moderates the sectarian rivalries that develop within the bureaucratic
structure, while at the same time the diverse subunit loyalties within the organization prevent the development of excessive intimacy and cohesion
within the small policy-making group.

The organizational context has been closely examined because it is somewhat more accessible for interventive or preventive measures aimed at improving the quality of the decision-making process. Efforts to incorporate
such measures encounter the dilemma that although stress and conflict can
lead to maladaptive responses, they may also be necessary for creative
problem solving. How to deal with this dilemma challenges us to seek a better understanding of the conditions associated with each reaction. To this
end, we have outlined a theory of effective multiple advocacy. Whereas
other theories have stressed the necessity and advantages of highly centralized, hierarchical policy-making systems, I suggest that intraorganizational
conflict over policy cannot, and perhaps should not, be completely suppressed and controlled from above. Because policy advocacy is inevitable,
the solution lies in ensuring that there will be multiple advocates within the
organization who will cover the range of interesting policy options on any
given issue.

Effective competition is necessary for optimum multiple advocacy, but
because it cannot be taken for granted, the executive and his staff are
confronted with several critical tasks. First, the executive may have to take
steps to equalize (or at least to avoid gross disparities of) the resources that
policy-making officials need for effective advocacy, or to compensate in
some manner for inequalities among them. Second, the executive and his
staff assistants must be alert to the danger that in a given situation the preferences of the available advocates may not encompass a sufficient number of
policy alternatives. Third, the executive may have to develop and enforce
certain rules of the game to maintain fair competition and avoid "restraint of
trade" among advocates.

Our theory of effective multiple advocacy also emphasizes the need for
timely identification and correction of possible malfunctions in the policy-
making process. Provision must be made for monitoring the day-to-day
workings of the process, and strategies for preventive intervention must be
available. Clearly, the executive has unique opportunities as well as responsibilities in this respect. From an examination of historical cases of actual or
near malfunctions in U.S. foreign policy making we have identified nine
general types of malfunctions against which safeguards are necessary. Responsibility must be fixed within the system for identifying an incipient
malfunction and taking corrective action. Within the executive branch of
the government, the Office of the Special Assistant for National Security
Affairs seems to be a particularly appropriate focus for custodianship of
these critical tasks. The evidence suggests, however, that the Special Assis-

tant can discharge this responsibility only if he refrains from becoming a policy advocate himself. The possibility of role conflicts that could undermine his performance of critical tasks arises also where the Special Assistant attempts to combine custodianship with the role of watchdog for the executive's personal power stakes, the role of public spokesman for existing policies, or the task of implementing policy decisions.

A more satisfactory conceptualization and interrelation of the three subsystems discussed can be expected to emerge only after many successive approximations. I hope that the results of this initial effort will be found sufficiently promising to warrant further, more substantial efforts to develop its implications for theory development, empirical research, and pragmatic efforts to increase the coping capacity and rationality of policy-making systems. To this end, as I noted in stating my research purposes, we must seek a much more satisfactory integration of the relevant theories of individual psychology, small-group dynamics, executive leadership, and organizational behavior.

REFERENCES

Abel, E. *The Cuban missile crisis*. Philadelphia and New York: Lippincott, 1966.

Acheson, D. *Present at the creation*. New York: Norton, 1969.

Allison, G. T. Conceptual models and the Cuban missile crisis. *American Political Science Review*, 1969, *63*, 689–781.

Allison, G. T., and Halperin, M. H. Bureaucratic politics: A paradigm and some policy implications. *World Politics*, 1972, *24* (Supplement—entire issue).

Altschuler, A., ed. *The politics of the federal bureaucracy*. New York: Dodd, Mead, 1968.

Anderson, P. *The president's men*. Garden City, N.Y.: Doubleday, 1968.

Barber, J. D. *Power in committees*. Chicago: Rand McNally, 1966.

———. Adult identity and presidential style: The rhetorical emphasis. *Daedalus*, 1968a, *97*(3), 938–968.

———. Classifying and predicting presidential styles: Two weak presidents. *Journal of Social Issues*, 1968b, *24*(3), 51–80.

———. The president and his friends. In F. I. Greenstein and M. Lerner, eds., *A sourcebook for the study of personality and politics*. Chicago: Markham, 1971.

Bennis, W. G. Post-bureaucratic leadership. *Trans-Action*, 1969, *6*(9), 44–61.

Bion, W. R. Group dynamics: A review. *International Journal of Psychoanalysis*, 1952, *33*, 235–247.

Bobrow, D. International indicators. Paper presented to annual meeting of the American Political Science Association, September 1969.

———. The Chinese Communist conflict system. *Orbis*. 1966, *9*(4), 931.

Bower, J. L. The role of conflict in economic decision-making groups: Some empirical results. *Quarterly Journal of Economics*, 1965, *79*, 263–277.

Brim, O. G., Jr., Glass, D. C., Lavin, D. E., and Goodman, N. *Personality and decision processes*. Stanford, Calif.: Stanford University Press, 1962.

Capron, W. M. The impact of analysis on bargaining in government. In Louis C. Gawthrop, ed., *The administrative process and democratic theory*. Boston: Houghton Mifflin, 1970.

Cartwright, D. C., and Lippitt, R. Group dynamics and the individual. *International Journal of Psychotherapy*, 1957, 7(1), 86–102.

Cartwright, D. C., and Zander, A. Pressures to uniformity in groups. In D. C. Cartwright and A. Zander, eds., *Group dynamics*. 3rd ed. New York: Harper & Row, 1968.

Clark, K. C., and Legere, L. J. *The president and the management of national security*. New York: Praeger, 1969.

Collins, B. E., and Guetzkow, H. *A social psychology of group processes for decision-making*. New York: Wiley, 1964.

Cronin, T. E. Political science and executive advisory systems. In T. E. Cronin and S. D. Greenberg, eds., *The presidential advisory system*, pp. 321–335. New York: Harper & Row, 1969.

———. "Everybody believes in democracy until he gets to the White House": An examination of White House-departmental relations. *Law and Contemporary Problems*, 1970, 35(3), 573–625.

Cutler, R. *No time for rest*. Boston: Little, Brown, 1966.

Cyert, R. M., and March, J. G. *A behavioral theory of the firm*. Englewood Cliffs, N.J.: Prentice-Hall, 1963.

Davis, V. American military policy: Decision-making in the executive branch. *Naval War College Review*, 1970, 22(9), 4–23.

DeRivera, J. H. *The psychological dimension of foreign policy*. Columbus, Ohio: Merrill, 1968.

Destler, I. M. Making organization count. Unpublished manuscript. New York: Council on Foreign Relations, 1970.

———. *Presidents and bureaucrats: Organizing the government for foreign policy*. Princeton, N.J.: Princeton University Press, 1972.

DiPalma, G., and McClosky, H. Personality and conformity: The learning of political attitudes. *American Political Science Review*, 1970, 64, 1054–1073.

Downs, A. *Inside bureaucracy*. Boston: Little, Brown, 1967.

Drucker, P. F. *The effective executive*. New York: Harper & Row, 1967.

Eulau, H., and Prewitt, K., eds. *Labyrinths of democracy: Adaptations, linkages, representations, and policies in urban politics*. New York: Bobbs-Merrill, 1973.

Falk, S. National Security Council under Truman, Eisenhower, and Kennedy. *Political Science Quarterly*, 1964, 79(1), 403–434.

Feldman, J., and Kanter, H. E. Organizational decision-making. In J. G. March, ed., *Handbook of organizations*. Chicago: Rand McNally, 1965.

Fenno, R. F. *The president's cabinet*. Cambridge, Mass.: Harvard University Press, 1959.

Festinger, L. Informal social communication. *Psychological Review*, 1950, 57, 271–282.

———. A theory of social comparison processes. *Human Relations*, 1954, 7, 117–140.

Flanagan, S. C. Aborted democratization: The inter-war crisis in Japan. Ph.D. dissertation, Stanford University, 1971.

Gawthrop, L. C. *Bureaucratic behavior in the executive branch*. New York: Free Press, 1969.

George, A. L. Power as a compensatory value for political leaders. *Journal of Social Issues*, 1968, 24(3), 29–49.

———. The case for multiple advocacy in making foreign policy. *American Political Science Review*, 1972, 66(3), 751–785.

———. The "operational code": A neglected approach to the study of political leaders and decision-making. *International Studies Quarterly*, 1969, *13*(2), 190–222.

George, A. L. Some uses of dynamic psychology in political biography. In F. I. Greenstein and M. Lerner, eds., *A sourcebook for the study of personality and politics*. Chicago: Markham, 1971*a*.

———. The Cuban missile crisis, 1962. In A. L. George, D. K. Hall, and W. E. Simons, eds., *The limits of coercive democracy: Laos, Cuba, Vietnam*. Boston: Little, Brown, 1971*b*.

George, A. L., and George, J. L. *Woodrow Wilson and Colonel House: A personality study*. New York: Day, 1956.

Geyelin, P. *Lyndon B. Johnson and the world*. New York: Praeger, 1966.

Graff, H. F. *The Tuesday cabinet: Deliberation and decision on peace and war under Lyndon B. Johnson*. Englewood Cliffs, N.J.: Prentice-Hall, 1970.

Halperin, M. H. *Bureaucratic politics and foreign policy*. Washington, D. C.: Brookings Institution, 1970.

———. Why bureaucrats play games. *Foreign Policy*, 1971, (2), 70–90.

Hamburg, D. A., and Adams, J. E. A perspective on coping behavior: Seeking and utilizing information in major transitions. *Archives of General Psychiatry*, 1967, *17*, 277–284.

Hammond, P. Y. *Organizing for defense*. Princeton, N.J.: Princeton University Press, 1961.

Hargrove, E. C. *Presidential leadership: Personality and political style*. New York: Macmillan, 1966.

Hilsman, R. The foreign policy consensus: An interim research report. *Journal of Conflict Resolution*, 1959, *3*(4), 361–382.

Hodgson, R. C., Levinson, D. J., and Zaleznik, A. *The executive role constellation: An analysis of personality and role relations in management*. Boston: Harvard Business School, 1965.

Hoffman, R. L. Conditions for creative problem solving. *Journal of Psychology*, 1961, *52*, 429–444.

Holsti, O. R. Cognitive dynamics and images of the enemy: Dulles and Russia. In D. J. Finlay, O. R. Holsti, and R. R. Fagen, eds., *Enemies in politics*. Chicago: Rand McNally, 1967.

———. The "operational code" approach to the study of political leaders: John Foster Dulles' philosophical and instrumental beliefs. *The Canadian Journal of Political Science*, 1970, *3*(1), 123–157.

———. *Crisis, escalation and war*. Montreal: McGill-Queen's University Press, 1972.

Hoopes, T. *The limits of intervention*. New York: McKay, 1969.

Horwitz, M. The conceptual status of group dynamics. *Review of Educational Research*, 1953, *23*, 309–328.

———. Managing hostility in the laboratory and the refinery. In R. L. Kahn and E. Boulding, eds., *Power and conflict in organizations*. New York: Basic Books, 1964.

Hull, C. *Memoirs*. New York: Macmillan, 1948.

James, J. A preliminary study of the size determinant in small group interaction. *American Sociological Review*, 1951, *16*, 474–477.

Janis, I. L. Decisional conflicts: A theoretical analysis. *Journal of Conflict Resolution*, 1959*a*, *1*(4), 331–335.

———. Motivational factors in the resolution of decisional conflicts. In M. R. Jones, ed., *Nebraska symposium on motivation*. Lincoln: University of Nebraska Press, 1959*b*.

————. Group identification under conditions of external danger. *British Journal of Medical Psychology*, 1963, *36*, 227–238.

————. Groupthink among policy makers. In N. Sanford and C. Comstock, eds., *Sanctions for evil*. San Francisco: Jossey-Bass, 1971a.

————. *Victims of groupthink*. Unpublished. Yale University, 1971b.

Janis, I. L., and Leventhal, H. Human reaction to stress. In E. F. Borgatta and W. M. Lambert, eds., *Handbook of personality theory and research*. Chicago: Rand McNally, 1968.

Jervis, R. *How decision-makers learn from history*. Unpublished. Harvard University, 1970.

Johnson, R. H. The National Security Council: The relevance of its past to its future. *Orbis*, 1969, *13*, 709–735.

Kahn, R. L., Wolfe, D. M., Quinn, R. P., and Snoek, J. D. *Organizational stress: Studies in role conflict and ambiguity*. New York: Wiley, 1964.

Katz, D., and Kahn, R. L. *The social psychology of organizations*. New York: Wiley, 1966.

Kennan, G. F. *Memoirs, 1925–1950*. Boston: Little, Brown, 1967.

Kennedy, R. F. *Thirteen days*. New York: Norton, 1969.

Kolodziej, E. A. The National Security Council: Innovations and implications. *Public Administration Review*, 1969, *29*(6), 573–585.

Lasswell, H. D. *Power and personality*. New York: Norton, 1948.

Lazarus, R. *Psychological stress and the coping process*. New York: McGraw-Hill, 1966.

Leites, N. *A study of Bolshevism*. Glencoe, Ill.: Free Press, 1953.

Levinson, D. J. Role, personality, and social structure in the organizational setting. *Journal of Abnormal and Social Psychology*, 1959, *58*, 170–180.

Lindblom, C. E. Bargaining: The hidden hand in government. The RAND Corporation, RM-1436-RC, 1955.

————. The science of "muddling through." *Public Administration Review*, 1959, *29*(2), 79–88.

————. *The intelligence of democracy: Decision-making through mutual adjustment*. New York: Free Press, 1965.

————. *The policy-making process*. Englewood Cliffs, N.J.: Prentice-Hall, 1968.

Lindblom, C. E., and Braybrooke, D. *A strategy of decision*. New York: Free Press, 1963.

Maier, N. R. F. *Problem-solving discussions and conferences: Leadership methods and skills*. New York: McGraw-Hill, 1963.

————. *Problem-solving and creativity in individuals and groups*. Belmont, Calif.: Brooks/Coles, 1970.

Maier, N. R. F., and Solem, A. R. The contribution of a discussion leader to the quality of group thinking: The effective use of minority opinions. *Human Relations*, 1952, 277–288.

March, J. G., and Simon, H. A. *Organizations*. New York: Wiley, 1958.

Marlowe, D., and Gergen, K. J. Personality and social interaction. In G. Lindzey and E. Aronson, eds., *Handbook of social psychology*. 2nd ed. Reading, Mass.: Addison-Wesley, 1969.

Maxey, D. How Nixon decided to invade Cambodia. *Look*, 1970, *34*(16), 22–25.

McDonald, J. How the man at the top avoids crises. *Fortune*, 1970, *81*(1), 121–122, 152–155.

McGuire, W. J. Personality and susceptibility to social influence. In E. F. Borgatta and W. M. Lambert, eds., *Handbook of personality theory and research*. Chicago: Rand McNally, 1968.

Neustadt, R. E. *Presidential power*. New York: Wiley, 1960.

———. Approaches to staffing the presidency: Notes on FDR and JFK. *American Political Science Review*, 1963, *57*, 855–863.

The Pentagon papers. New York: Bantam Books, 1971.

Pruitt, D. G. Problem solving in the Department of State. Monograph series in world affairs, no. 2. University of Denver, 1965.

Reedy, G. E. *The twilight of the presidency*. New York: World, 1970.

Ridgway, M. B. *Soldier*. New York: Harper & Row, 1956.

Robinson, J. A., Hermann, C. F. and Hermann, M. G. Search under crisis in political gaming and simulation. In D. G. Pruitt and R. C. Snyder, eds., *Theory and Research on the Causes of War*. Englewood Cliffs, N.J.: Prentice-Hall, 1969.

Rowen, H. S. Bargaining and analysis in government. In L. C. Gawthrop, ed., *The administrative process and democratic theory*. Boston: Houghton Mifflin, 1970.

Schachter, S. Deviation, rejection, and communication. In D. C. Cartwright and A. Zander, eds., *Group dynamics*. 3rd ed. New York: Harper & Row, 1968.

Schlesinger, A., Jr. The Roosevelt era: Stimson and Hull. *The Nation*, June 5, 1948.

———. *The age of Roosevelt*, vol. 2. *The coming of the New Deal*. Boston: Houghton Mifflin, 1959.

———. *A thousand days*. Boston: Houghton Mifflin, 1965.

Seligman, L. G. Presidential leadership: The inner circle and institutionalization. *Journal of Politics*, 1956, *18*, 410–426.

Seligman, L. G., and Baer, M. A. Expectations of presidential leadership in decision-making. In A. Wildavsky, ed., *The presidency*. Boston: Little, Brown, 1969.

Shils, E. A., and Janowitz, M. Cohesion and disintegration in the Wehrmacht. *Public Opinion Quarterly*, 1948, *12*, 280–315.

Simon, H. A. A behavioral model of rational choice. *Quarterly Journal of Economics*, 1955, *69*, 99–118.

———. *Administrative behavior*. New York: Macmillan, 1958.

Singer, J. D., and Ray, P. Decision-making in conflict: From interpersonal to international relations. *Bulletin of the Menninger Clinic*, 1966, *30*, 300–312.

Smith, H. Cambodian decision: Why president acted. *New York Times*, June 30, 1970.

Smith, M. B., Bruner, J. S., and White, R. W. *Opinions and personality*. New York: Wiley, 1956.

Snyder, R. C., Bruck, H. W., and Sapin, B. *Foreign policy decision-making*. New York: Free Press, 1962.

Snyder, R. C., and Paige, G. D. The United States decision to resist aggression in Korea. *Administrative Science Quarterly*, 1958, *3*, 362.

Sorensen, T. C. *Decision-making in the White House*. New York: Columbia University Press, 1963.

———. *Kennedy*. New York: Harper & Row, 1965.

Thomas, E. J. Role theory, personality, and the individual. In E. F. Borgatta and W. Lambert, eds., *Handbook of personality theory and research*. Chicago: Rand McNally, 1968.

Thomson, J. C., Jr. How could Vietnam happen? An autopsy. *Atlantic Monthly*, 1968, *221*(4), 47–53.

Toffler, A. *Future shock*. New York: Random House, 1970.

Verba, S. *Small groups and political behavior: A study of leadership.* Princeton, N.J.: Princeton University Press, 1961.

von Neumann, J. The general and logical theory of automata. In J. R. Newman, ed., *The world of mathematics.* New York: Simon & Schuster, 1956.

Vroom, V. H. and Yetton, P. W. Normative and Descriptive Models of Participation in Decision Making. Paper prepared for the joint U.S.-Soviet Seminar on Organization Design. Kiev, U.S.S.R., June 1971. Unpublished.

Webb, E. J. *Individual and organizational forces influencing the interpretation of indicators.* Unpublished. April 1969.

Wilensky, A. *Organizational intelligence.* New York: Basic Books, 1967.

IV
ASSESSMENT OF COPING FUNCTIONS

10

The Psychology of Coping: Issues of Research and Assessment

RICHARD S. LAZARUS,
JAMES R. AVERILL,
AND EDWARD M. OPTON, JR.

Although the concept of coping has long been used informally in those fields of psychology in which adaptation or adjustment is emphasized, little systematic attention has been directed to it. A general analysis of the ways in which the psychological aspects of coping may be viewed and which can guide research and assessment seems urgently needed. The purpose of this chapter is to attempt such an analysis. Because ours is a preliminary effort to systematize a vast and ill-defined area, we will deal primarily with broad conceptual and methodological issues. The specific goals and substance of the paper include, in an initial section, the definition of coping, delineation of issues related to the description and classification of coping, and a review of our own theoretical frame of reference and research; the remaining sections are devoted to a detailed examination of three main sources of variance in coping, namely, the response variables from which coping processes are inferred, situational variables, and personal (dispositional) variables. In attempting to actualize such an ambitious set of objectives, we are conscious of the fact that we have written a broad, widely ranging, and very long essay whose structure may at times be difficult for the reader to keep in mind. One solution might be for the reader to move directly from this introductory statement to the summary, which reviews the main contents, and only then to proceed to the body of the text.

This paper and the research reported within it were made possible partly by a research grant (MH-2136) from the National Institute of Mental Health and by research training grant (RH-4) from the Rehabilitation Services Administration.

SOME PRELIMINARY ISSUES

The Definition of Coping

Most writers have used the term *coping* in an intuitive, everyday sense, relying on the context to make the meaning clear. As a consequence coping has accrued a variety of meanings. For example, Lois Murphy (1962) defines it as any attempt to master a new situation that can be potentially threatening, frustrating, challenging, or gratifying, a definition with which we basically agree. One of the present writers (Lazarus 1966) had earlier proposed a more restricted definition, applying the concept only to situations involving threat. Such a definition now seems too narrow in scope. Even more restrictive in some respects is the approach of Haan (1969) who differentiated coping from defense mechanisms on the basis of certain valuative properties (for example, coping is more flexible and reality oriented). Thus, the idea of coping has been used to cover the broadest possible forms of adaptive behavior, in which case it becomes nearly coextensive with the concept of adaptation, as well as to identify more specific and narrowly conceived adaptive processes.

The concept of coping includes the most casual and realistic forms of problem-solving activities as well as the most highly motivated or pathological efforts to be extricated from real or imagined dangers. Under conditions of relatively low stakes to the organism, the focus tends to be on deliberate, flexible, reality-oriented, or rational efforts at mastery; in effect, on what is usually called problem solving. When the context is that of strong drive, frustration, stress, or emotion, that is, when the stakes are high, the focus is likely to shift to more rigid, primitive, less adequate, and less realistic efforts at mastery. Instead of *problem solving*, *coping* and *defense* are frequently used terms to describe the efforts at mastery in the latter context.

There is no reason why the student of problem solving should not also concern himself with the context of high drive, emotion, and psychopathology. Actually, theory and research on problem solving have also been extended to conditions of frustration and conflict, as in the work on experimental neurosis of Masserman (1943), Maier (1949), Miller (1959, pp. 196–292), and others. Similarly, those interested in coping in the context of threat, frustration, emotion, and psychopathology also direct attention to the conditions under which adaptive efforts are maximally effective as well as ineffective. And although coping tends to be examined in the context of threat, frustration, and negatively toned emotions, the more positive contexts of challenge and potential gratification (and the positively toned emotions connected with them) are also relevant, as noted in Lois Murphy's definition of coping. Rational and irrational efforts at mastery, that is, realistic problem solving and primitive defenses, are two sides of the same coin, and both must somehow be examined in the same conceptual context.

We regard coping as problem-solving efforts made by an individual when the demands he faces are highly relevant to his welfare (that is, a situation of considerable jeopardy or promise), and when these demands tax his adaptive resources. Such a definition does several things; first, it emphasizes the importance of the emotional context in coping; second, it allows inclusion of both the negative or stress side of emotion, as well as the positive side of potential fulfillment or gratification; third, it recognizes the overlap between problem solving and coping; and fourth, it emphasizes adaptive tasks that are not routine or automatized, that is, those in which the adaptive outcome is uncertain and in which the limits of the individual's adaptive skill are approached.

Description and Classification of Coping-Defensive Polarities

As we have defined coping, the concept is exceedingly broad, just as it is in everyday use by researchers and clinicians concerned with adaptive functioning. As such, the concept remains a general rubric and does not refer to a specific kind of process. Varieties of coping must still be specified and classified so as to provide a basis for their assessment and for the study of their determinants and consequences. Such a descriptive and classificatory system needs ultimately to be exhaustive in encompassing the main varieties of coping activity, as well as detailed enough to include the individual forms of coping that fall within each main category. It must also have theoretical coherence and must be linked to observable antecedent conditions and measurable responses whose adaptive value to the individual can be determined over the short and long run.

At the present time, no adequate classificatory system exists, although there are some limited schemes that deal with segments of the total problem, such as descriptions and analyses of defense mechanisms (A. Freud 1946), descriptions of coping devices of the ego arranged from least to most pathological (Menninger 1954), a tripartite model of coping (Haan 1969), and other versions (for example, Lazarus 1966; Miller and Swanson 1960), each of which is seriously incomplete in meeting many of the requirements of a good classificatory scheme. Although we cannot undertake the task of reviewing these limited efforts, many of the problems of classification can be nicely illustrated by considering one particular instance in which defenses are divided into two opposing types or defensive polarities, for example, repression and sensitization (or isolation). Our discussion is not designed to review the research on repression-sensitization, but rather to highlight some of the more important conceptual and methodological problems that any classificatory scheme must face.

The differentiation between repression on the one hand and an opposing defensive process variously called sensitization, isolation, vigilance, and so forth, has long been of interest to psychologists engaged in research on personality dynamics. These postulated processes have their conceptual origins in the Freudian tradition of ego-defense mechanisms, although the original meanings have often been eroded. A peak of interest in this limited typology of defense occurred during the recent era of research on "perceptual defense," the substance of which has been reviewed by a number of writers (see Allport 1955; Brown 1961; Jenkin 1957). Comparable research today is less faddish with respect to method and instrument and is not specifically devoted to perceptual processes.

Research on defensive polarities may be divided into three main approaches, which differ in the conceptual emphasis, terminology, and type of assessment instruments employed. All three share a common bias in emphasizing the dispositional or personality attributes that lead to a defensive response, rather than the defensive response *per se*. That is, it is assumed that individuals differ in the disposition to employ one or another defensive reaction when exposed to conditions of threat. We shall first briefly characterize the three approaches, so that later we can use them to illustrate fundamental issues in the description and classification of coping processes. Because there are three discrete approaches, each employing overlapping terminology, we have had to find a language with which to identify the general area of concern that all three share in common. One approach uses the polarity of repression-sensitization, another refers to repression-isolation, and the third uses the terms *avoider* and *coper*. Therefore, in our subsequent discussion, these three specific approaches will be collectively referred to under the general rubric of *defensive polarities*.

The *repression-sensitization* dimension of coping is one of the most heavily researched in the current personality literature. On one pole (repression) is the hypothetical tendency to deal with threat by not admitting (that is, by denying) evidence of poor functioning, emotional disturbance, and socially undesirable traits or impulses; at the other end (sensitization) is the tendency to concede such traits readily, and to be oriented toward (sensitized to) the disphoric or threatening aspects of living. The exact definition and labeling of these tendencies varies among different investigators, along with the specific measures employed to assess them (although all use questionnaires). For example, Byrne (1964, pp. 170–220) constructed a scale from the MMPI (Minnesota Multiphasic Personality Inventory) item pool, employing the terms *repression* and *sensitization* to characterize the opposite poles of the dimension. Welsh (1956) factor analyzed the MMPI and identified two dimensions which he labeled R (repression) and A (anxiety). Of course, these scales overlap partly with that of Byrne. Welsh thinks of high R subjects as being characterized by repression and denial and low R subjects as being characterized by externalizing and "acting out" behavior. Others have interpreted similarly constructed questionnaires in quite different ways, for example, as introversion-extroversion (see Eysenck 1967, chap. 3; Kassebaum, Couch and Slater 1959), Yeasaying-Naysaying (Couch and Keniston 1960), overcontrol-undercontrol (Block 1965), or high versus low need for social approval (Crowne and Marlowe 1964). There is thus displayed a great variety of different concepts about the coping dispositions and processes that are assessed by the same or similar questionnaire tools.

Although employing overlapping terminology with that of repression-sensitization, a very different approach has been employed by a psychoanalytically oriented group following in the Rapaport (1967) ego psychology tradition of diagnostic psychological testing. The classification scheme consists of a dichotomy (as opposed to a dimension) between two presumably antithetical modes of defense, *repression* on the one hand, and *isolation* on the other. It is exemplified by the clinical diagnostic approach of Schafer (1954), and by the cognitive style research of Gardner, Holzman, Klein, Linton, and Spence (1959), Levine and Spivack (1964), and Luborsky, Blinder, and Schimek (1965). Assessment of these defensive dispositions is made on the basis of styles of thinking and perceiving as observed in the clinical setting or in protocols derived from Rorschach projective test data.

Two sets of criteria differentiating repression and isolation have been devised for research purposes. Gardner and colleagues (1959) have looked for evidence of repressive tendencies on the Rorschach inkblot test; constriction of ideation, naïveté, relatively unmodulated affect, unreflectiveness, and the absence of intellectualizing tendencies (analysis, qualifications, giving alternatives, and so forth) were considered indicative of this defensive disposition. The opposite pattern was used as evidence of isolation, along with such additional response characteristics as rumination about symmetry, intellectualization, and a high form quality (high $F + \%$). Adopting the same theoretical point of view, Levine and Spivack (1964) employed a somewhat different (though overlapping) assessment approach, emphasizing the degree to which the Rorschach response is specific, elaborated, incorporates movement, and contains impulse-content or self-references. In a study of the perceptual scanning behavior of repressors and isolators, Luborsky, Blinder, and Schimek (1965) simultaneously employed both types of assessment approaches with the same individuals and reported a high degree of agreement between them.

In a third type of approach, Goldstein (1959) has utilized a sentence-completion assessment technique, emerging with a trichotomous classification consisting of *avoiders, copers,* and *nonspecific defenders.* Avoiders are said to avoid threatening content, while copers are like sensitizers in being hyperalert to the threatening aspects of their environment, neutralizing threat by intellectualized means; nonspecific defenders are persons who emphasize neither type of defense to the exclusion of the other, presumably being capable of using whichever is appropriate at the moment. In Goldstein's approach to the assessment of these defensive dispositions, subjects have the task of completing sentence stems containing aggressive and sexual connotations. Avoidance involves refusal to acknowledge the threatening content of the stem by evasion, blocking, or by somehow neutralizing it. For example, an avoidant response to the stem "I hate . . ." might be, "I hate to be caught out in the rain without my umbrella"; copers, on the other hand, might respond, "I hate self-righteous people"; in the latter case the hostile connotation has been acknowledged and even embellished. Nonspecific defenders fall between the two extremes, sometimes elaborating the threatening content, sometimes avoiding it.

The above defensive polarities pose certain theoretical and methodological issues of particular importance for the classification and assessment of coping processes. The key issue concerns the nature of the coping process assessed by the various questionnaires and projective tests. A second major issue concerns the completeness of the system, that is, the extent to which the classification leaves out other important coping processes. A third important issue concerns whether or not the classification dimensions or dichotomies identify important forms of adaptive response to threat. Let us examine each of these issues more closely.

The Nature of the Coping Process.   The general question posed here is one of "construct validity," as it has been discussed by such writers as Cronbach and Meehl (1955), Campbell (1960), and others. This refers to the theoretical or interpretive meaning given to any assessment test. Such meaning must be based ultimately on the conditions that elicit the reaction, as well as on the response correlates of that reaction. What interpretive meaning should be given to such "coping traits" as repression, avoidance, sensitization, isolation, and coping as used in the above defensive polarities?

We can approach this question by asking first whether the defenses assessed by these various schemes deal with the same or different coping processes. The personality research literature reflects a very casual attitude toward the use of terms such as repression, denial, avoidance, and so on. For example, researchers using the Byrne scale, or other similar scales such as that of Crowne and Marlowe, commonly associate the disposition to repress with the processes of denial or avoidance; and similarly, sensitization is loosely associated with vigilance, approach, intellectualization, and isolation, without careful specification of the acts presumably involved in such processes, and their interrelationships. Research workers appear to assume that these scales assess Freudian defensive processes as implied in repression-isolation (see Gardner et al. 1959; Schafer 1954). Thus, Byrne uses the term repression as in repression-sensitization, as does Gardner and co-workers (1959), in referring to repression-isolation. Although Goldstein employs the language of avoiders and copers, the coping acts implied by avoidance appear to overlap with those in repression and denial, and the author himself readily slips into the older jargon of sensitization when speaking of people who are copers, or in scoring his test for coping. In fact, during the era of perceptual defense research, the terms sensitization, isolation, and intellectualization tended to be used interchangeably as stemming from the common theoretical root of the Freudian conceptions of defense.

There are grounds for serious doubt that the personality assessment tests used in the above approaches to coping are indeed measuring the same type of defensive disposition. The only direct evidence at present is Levine and Spivack's (1964) failure (with 150 subjects) to find a relationship between their Rorschach cognitive style measure of repression-isolation and a number of MMPI derived scales. It would appear most probable, therefore, that the coping processes tapped by questionnaire measures are different from those revealed by the Rorschach cognitive style measures. Furthermore, Lefcourt (1966) has obtained evidence suggesting that repression and sensitization as measured by the Byrne scale reflect attitudes of individuals toward the expression of emotion; moreover, if these attitudes are changed, the test score differentiation is eliminated. The research of Parsons, Fulgenzi, and Edelberg (1969) also suggests that repressors and sensitizers, as identified by Byrne's scale, say things about their affective life that do not correspond to their actual emotional behavior in social contexts. The questionnaire scales could thus be interpreted as reflecting values about emotion, or ways the person sees himself and wishes to present himself to others, rather than a form of unconscious, intrapsychic mastery over psychological threats as is implied in the Freudian concept of defense.

Further doubt about the meaning of the questionnaire measures of coping disposition has been contributed by the research of Golin, Herron, Lakota, and Reineck (1967), who obtained a correlation of .87 between the Byrne scale and the Taylor (1953) Manifest Anxiety Scale, high anxiety being associated with sensitization. Others have reported comparable findings in the past (for example, Deese, Lazarus, and Keenan 1953). This could mean merely that sensitization is a coping process that is also associated with considerable anxiety; on the other hand, it has been argued that the scale does not measure a coping process (sensitization) at all, but should be considered as a measure of dispositional anxiety or emotionality. But if sensitization is to be regarded as a defense against anxiety, as repression is also presumed to be, why should sensitizers show such high anxiety scores? How logically can the defense be at the same time a measure of the very affect that it is presumed to be a defense against? Presumably, only if it were an unsuccessful defense. Thus it is paradoxical that certain questionnaire measures appear to reflect equally well emotionality and defensiveness, rather than defensiveness alone (see Adelson 1969, pp. 217–252, for a similar analysis).

In spite of the above negative findings, studies that suggest indirectly that there may be some overlap between the coping processes assessed by different methods occasionally appear. For example, using a questionnaire (the Welsh R scale), Mendelsohn and Griswold (1967) have provided excellent evidence that repressors are less likely to use incidental cues in problem solving than nonrepressors; that is, they appeared unresponsive to what seemed irrelevant to the task at hand. Moreover, using the Rorschach cognitive style index of repression-isolation, Luborsky, Blinder, and Schimek (1965) also demonstrated that repressors exhibited perceptual constriction in their scanning of pictures (as measured by an eye movement camera), while isolators visually examined the pictures in more detail. This difference was found even when the picture did not contain emotionally loaded or threatening content, so that the difference between repressors and isolators seems to be a matter of functionally autonomous styles of looking, rather than a "defense" against specific threat. In any case, the same patterns of perceptual behavior seem applicable to repressors as defined by a questionnaire measure in the Mendelsohn and Griswold research and repressors as defined by the Rorschach cognitive style measure in the Luborsky research, as distinguished from the pattern displayed by both sensitizers and isolators.

One is left with the clear impression that a great deal of thinking and research must still be done before the coping dispositions and processes implied in the above defensive polarities are understood, and the construct validity of their assessment measures established. This applies not only to the specific systems that have been discussed, but to any other present scheme. Measures must be developed for coping processes so that the underlying theory can be verified and changed by empirical research.

THE COMPLETENESS OF A CLASSIFICATION SCHEME.   Because coping processes take a wide variety of forms, any classificatory scheme can be judged as to its completeness, that is, the extent to which it encompasses all or most of the diverse forms of coping. On the basis of the definition of coping given earlier, these forms would comprise all of the diverse acts people (and infrahuman animals too) engage in to meet an actual or anticipated challenge. These acts may be primarily behavioral—for example, avoiding and escaping danger; threatening, attacking, or mollifying an adversary; seeking allies or binding oneself to a group to increase one's power over danger; and taking substitute paths to an unachievable goal. These are only a few instances where the response may be largely overt. In other forms of coping, such as seeking knowledge or searching for cues, cognitive activity may be especially evident. In still other instances, the coping response may be largely intrapsychic, as when threat is neutralized by defensive thought processes (for example, by the Freudian defense mechanisms), or when goals are achieved in wish-fulfilling fantasies. This list simply emphasizes the great diversity of coping activities. As has been pointed out by Professor Mechanic in Chapter 3, our formal descriptive language about coping seems singularly limited in the light of all the things we can do to deal with threat, and this makes the task of successfully classifying coping all the more difficult.

In view of the richness and variety of coping processes, the three defensive polarities discussed previously seem each to be extremely limited in scope, being restricted to intrapsychic processes or defenses, and totally ignoring the many forms of overt action that people engage in under threatening conditions. Even with respect to intrapsychic defenses, the defensive polarities are woefully incomplete against the rich panorama of mechanisms identified by Freudian theory. Thus the defensive polarities are often assumed to apply to a whole family of associated defenses, including on the one hand repression, denial, and avoidance, and on the other hand, isolation, intellectualization, and undoing. It is not clear, however, what is to be done with other types of intrapsychic devices for neutralizing threat, such as sublimation, defensive identification, rationalization, reaction formation, compensation, displacement, projection, and so on. What relation, if any, do these other defenses have to repression-isolation? At present we do not really know. There is little empirical evidence to support even the concept of families of defenses, although Freud originally conceived of each defense as arising from a particular impulse characteristic of a particular stage of psychosexual development. Even the linking of repression, denial, and avoidance as is typically done is itself without much empirical support, although their association with given situations or in given persons makes intuitive sense. In sum, there is as yet little dependable evidence about the interrelationships, even among the various intrapsychic defensive processes.

The Importance of the Categories of Classification.   Although a classificatory scheme may be limited or incomplete, it may still deal with very important forms of coping. This is clearly the case in the defensive polarities we have reviewed. Such an assertion is warranted for two main reasons. First, and perhaps most important, the concepts of repression and its polar opposites play very important roles in the most influential theories of personality dynamics, especially Freudian psychoanalysis, but in many neoanalytic theories as well. Such defenses also are widely represented in clinical practice. Second, the concepts underlying these defensive polarities have stimulated a great volume of research that has been providing evidence about antecedent conditions (personality and situational) and response correlates. Thus these descriptive and classificatory schemes cannot be accused of dealing with trivial or inconsequential psychological processes in spite of the shortcoming that they encompass a limited range of coping processes. Ultimately the findings of such research will have to be incorporated within larger, more comprehensive schemes for describing and classifying coping processes.

Concluding Comments.   We have used the defensive polarities of repression-sensitization (isolation, and so on) to illustrate some of the problems involved in current approaches to the description and classification of coping. Schemes describing other forms of coping, for example, emotional reactions and "rational" problem solving, could have served the purpose as well; it is likely that whatever scheme were chosen, similar conclusions would be reached.

First, there is a general tendency to confuse dispositional variables with response variables, or at least not to distinguish between them. Thus most of the research reviewed above has not involved actual episodes of repression or sensitization; rather, it has been concerned with general tendencies to engage in one or another of these defenses. Because the dispositions we have been discussing are oriented about specific responses (for example, repression), it may be assumed that many of the statements that apply to one type of variable also apply to the other. This is not necessarily the case, however, either in theory or in concrete matters of research and assessment. Moreover, not all dispositions relevant to coping are so response oriented;

they may also refer to stimulus characteristics and underlying psychological dynamics. In a later section, we shall have much more to say about the distinction between dispositional and response variables, as well as various types of dispositions.

Secondly, while the defensive polarities emphasized personal or dispositional determinants of coping, they all but ignored another equally important class of determinants—the situation. That is, while much was said about repression and sensitization as personality characteristics, no analysis was made of the type of situations that would lead a person to engage in repression as opposed to sensitization. A central theme of this chapter is that coping represents a *transaction* between an individual and his environment. The actions or intrapsychic processes that take place in an emotional context certainly depend on the nature of the threat, frustration, challenge, or potential for gratification. If this were not so, then coping would rarely be adaptive in the sense of preserving the individual in a real world or making possible the carrying out of his plans. Thus, coping can never be assessed or evaluated without regard to the environmental demands that create the need for it in the first place. It is essential that we discover how each type of situation initiates, shapes, and constrains the forms of coping. Although this point may seem banal on reflection, it is repeatedly overlooked in discussions of the coping processes.

Thirdly, the discussion of defensive polarities also illustrates a certain parochialism that is characteristic of much research on coping. Thus, research and theory surrounding intrapsychic defense mechanisms comes largely from investigators with a clinical orientation and is heavily influenced by psychoanalytic concepts. Relatively little attention has been paid to the vast literature on emotional reactions in man and animals, which has grown up largely within a biological and physiological context. And neither group of theorists, those interested in defenses and those in emotion, have given due consideration to normal problem-solving behavior, which has been a traditional concern of "academic" psychology. One of the major advantages of the concept of coping is that it brings together under a single heading research interests that have much in common, but that have remained relatively distinct for historical and other reasons.

The parochialism of coping research is evident within, as well as between, traditions. It was noted, for example, that little cross reference is made between research on repression-sensitization as measured by questionnaires and research on repression-isolation inferred from the style of Rorschach responses. The few instances where direct comparisons were made indicated that these schemes had little in common in spite of the overlapping terminology and historical roots. Instead of speaking of "repression-sensitization" and "repression-isolation," it might have been more accurate to have distinguished between "defenses-as-measured-by-self-report-inventories" and "defenses-as-inferred-from-Rorschach-responses." It is an unfortunate but true observation that much psychological research and conceptualization is directed not so much by the nature of the problem, as by the availability of measurement devices. It goes without saying that if the unifying potential of the coping construct is to be realized, multiple research strategies will have to be employed and inferences will have to be based on a variety of response measures.

Finally, although present approaches to the description and classification of coping are parochial and limited in approach and lack adequate empirical support for their theoretical underpinnings, they do deal with behaviors that are generally regarded as important in human adaptation. However, the confusion over forms of coping behavior, lack of knowledge about their interrelationships and the conditions that bring them about, and the inadequacy with which our formal language of coping describes how humans and animals cope remain central handicaps for a behavioral science of coping. Progress in the development of an adequate psychology of coping is unlikely to be rapid until a theoretically based system of classification for coping acts has been evolved, linked to more general psychological theory, and tied to observable antecedents and consequences. At present this is more of a need and a wish than a reality.

Some Theoretical Distinctions and Relevant Research

Having gained a limited but not unrepresentative perspective on the state of the art, we shall now review briefly our own theoretical position with respect to coping and emotion, and then summarize some empirical research based on it. In contrast to the previous discussion of defensive polarities, our primary concern will be with the description and classification of coping episodes, not dispositions.

THEORY.   In our theoretical treatments of coping (Lazarus 1966, 1968; Averill, Opton, and Lazarus 1969; Lazarus, Averill, and Opton 1970), we have emphasized the mediating cognitive process of *appraisal*, which is a perception distinguishing the potentially harmful from the potentially beneficial or irrelevant. Coping processes are not viewed as primarily a response designed to reduce an emotional mediator, as is traditionally argued, but rather as a response to the perception of some threatening condition and of potential avenues of solution or mastery. In short, they are designed to actualize some promise or to take the organism out of some jeopardy, as judged or cognitively appraised by the individuals.

In suggesting this, we are not excluding the possibility that the object of coping may sometimes be to reduce an unpleasant emotion. An emotional response is also a stimulus that one appraises like any other, and its occurrence may itself be judged as threatening or satisfying, thus leading to some further efforts at coping. However, such feedback is only one aspect in the elicitation of coping processes. For example, effort to prevent failure on an examination is a form of coping involving the impulse of avoidance (and its associated fear), and including usually the necessary coping effort preparatory to taking the exam; however, at the same time, the "excitement" of fear and thoughts about it may interfere with the instrumental preparatory activity, and so must itself be coped with. One implication of the above distinction between coping with a threat and coping with an emotion that is itself a threat is that we can either attempt to examine the adaptiveness of a coping process in the sense that it preserves the organism against a potential harm, or evaluate its successfulness in the sense that it reduces a negative emotional state or produces a positive one. In one the focus is on *emotion and its reduction*, while in the other it is on the *plight of the individual* in his environment. The values underlying these two modes of evaluation can be quite different.

Three aspects of appraisal may be distinguished. *Primary appraisal* concerns the judgment that some situational outcome will be either harmful, beneficial, or irrelevant. *Secondary appraisal* refers to the perception of the range of coping alternatives through which harm can be mastered, or beneficial results achieved. Primary and secondary appraisal interpenetrate each other, and the distinction is mainly designed to point to the sorts of cues or information on which the subsequent coping activity and the type of emotion depend. *Reappraisal*, the third aspect, refers to a change in the original perception, say, from benign to threatening, or vice versa. Such reappraisal is a response to changing external or internal conditions; that is, it can arise from new cues, reflection about the original evidence, or feedback from the effect of the individual's own reactions. All coping and emotion flow from these mediating appraisals, and it has been our position that we must understand the appraisal processes and the conditions that influence it in order to understand coping and emotion.

It is important to recognize too that a coping episode is never a static affair, but changes in quality and intensity as a function of new information and of the outcomes of previous responses whose implications are appraised. The individual is continually searching, sifting through, and evaluating the cues that any situation presents. Some appraisals are rejected and others accepted on the basis of both the steady inflow of information and the presence of psychological dispositions that influence the individual's transactions with the environment.

In our initial discussion of the definition of coping, we pointed out that emphasis could be placed on the rational, problem-solving features or on the emotion-centered, irrational features of coping. Appraisal is the process by means of which the stakes or potential outcome of a situation, and of the coping efforts adopted by the person to deal with it, are judged or evaluated. These appraisal processes are partly a function of the situation, as well as of the belief systems, cognitive styles, and other personal dispositions (sometimes interpreted as unconscious "forces") that have developed over the person's lifetime. Both rational and irrational coping are products of this mediating cognitive activity. When the stakes are judged to be high, and the outcome difficult to manage effectively, strong emotions typically follow, and there is a greater likelihood of ineffective, rigid, and primitive forms of coping, such as reality-distorting defenses. The person takes desperate steps if he must, or draws upon unrealistic beliefs and expectations about the situation in an effort to find a solution. Moreover, there is more interference with problem-solving efforts from the strong emotions that are generated in such situations, and from the thoughts stemming from the situation that is judged to be critical to the person's welfare. The nature and adequacy of all three appraisal processes mentioned above determine the extent to which coping is flexible, rational, and effective, or rigid, irrational, and ineffective in meeting the threat or challenge. The conditions that shape appraisal and reappraisal must be known before the coping process and the emotional response can be understood or predicted.

In our approach to coping itself, two main modes of expression should be distinguished—those that fundamentally entail direct action on the self or the environment, and those that function primarily through intrapsychic processes. Examples of direct action modes include active preparation against harm, as in building physical defenses or arranging for escape routes, attack, and avoidance, to name some of the most obvious. As we have said, impulses toward any specific direct action on a particular appraisal, for example, the identification of a threatening agent, perceiving the presence (or absence) of avenues of escape from that agent, or of opportunities to demolish it. Intrapsychic coping modes work by creating an impression of safety or gratification, which may be realistic, but which often is the product of defensive distortion. It seems useful to distinguish three main subtypes of intrapsychic coping—attention deployment, reappraisal, and wish-fulfilling fantasy. In attention deployment, for example, the individual may attempt to tune out whatever is harmful by not thinking about it, or by occupying his mind with positive things. In defensive reappraisal, a benign or positive interpretation of the individual's plight is forged by a cognitive "tour de force" in the absence of confirmation from environmental or internal cues. Thus, the individual may cope with threat by misinterpreting the situation in a way leading to benign appraisal. In effect, the threat is "short-circuited" by the defensive reappraisal process. Included here would be most of the defense mechanisms that are usually acknowledged, although we are somewhat uncertain about whether to place processes such as suppression and repression in the category of defensive reappraisal or of attention deployment. Depending on how they are defined, they could have elements of both. Finally, challenge and promise can be promoted intrapsychically by positive, wish-fulfilling fantasies that may have little or no connection with reality, but nonetheless create positive emotional states such as relief, security, euphoria, joy, or love.

It should be noted that by dividing coping into two main modes of expression—direct actions and intrapsychic processes—we are not suggesting that actions and thoughts are mutually exclusive. Certainly, cognitive processes go along with particular direct actions, and vice versa. The individual continuously explores the situation for cues about his well-being, even as he is engaging in attack or flight, and as an integral aspect of such actions or impulses to action. Similarly, intrapsychic processes, such as defensive reappraisals, may also involve actions that validate the unrealistic interpretation of the situation that has been forged. For example, the intrapsychic defense of reaction formation or reversal usually includes extravagant verbal or motoric manifestations of the benign feeling that is being claimed: the individual who in this way defends against his angry feelings by affirming loving impulses acts out these impulses as part of the defense. Nevertheless, what is important in such a defense is that a particular reappraisal of the realities is cultivated, and this is primarily an intrapsychic process with the action secondary. The important thing is that the person believe he loves rather than hates. Similarly, in paranoia as seen by Freudian theory (see Freud 1911), the person first must disguise the original homosexual impulse by treating it as an urge to attack, and then project that urge onto another individual. Only after this distorted (defensive) reappraisal is achieved does the paranoid act out the interpretation with evidence of anger and the desire to attack. The stated goal of such actions is to eliminate the harmful condition by instrumental acts, in order to achieve safety against the imagined danger, rather than to achieve the fiction of safety sought in the process of defensive reappraisal.

One reason the distinctions between direct action and intrapsychic modes might be important is that the conditions determining the choice of coping should vary not only among the individual forms of coping within the major modes, but also between the modes themselves. Certain conditions of threat leave little or no opportunity for direct action on the environment and thus favor either some form of direct action on the self or an intrapsychic process. Examples include terminal illness or other conditions where the individual is relatively helpless to cope directly with the harm, for example, severe injury or the death of a loved one. In these instances and many more, direct actions on the environment have little or no value. The possibility of direct action on the self may still remain, however, as when the inevitable harm can somehow be mitigated by learning a new skill to counteract a disability (that is, rehabilitation), finding a new love object to replace that lost, and so forth. Moreover, the society may provide institutionalized forms of direct action for coping with situations that are beyond the competence of the single individual, for example, mourning rites that channel grief into direct action, even though they are ineffective in regaining the lost love object.

In any event, it is highly probable that the conditions that leave room for, or encourage, direct actions differ from those that encourage intrapsychic modes of coping, although relatively little is known about this at the present time. When avenues leading to direct action on the self and the environment are closed, the only thing left for the individual to do is to fall back on intrapsychic processes for coping, even though these do not succeed in changing the objective circumstances. Perhaps one reason why clinicians working with neurotics emphasize defense mechanisms so much is that neuroses are viewed as based on intrapsychic conflict. Because the neurotic aspects of the dangers that the individual faces are entirely internal and unknown to him, there may be no action he can take against the environment or in respect to the self that will help him master the problem, and he is forced into some kind of intrapsychic coping process.

Sachar's work (Sachar et al. 1968) with depressed patients illustrates an interesting functional relationship that might exist between intrapsychic modes of coping and direct actions. Using biochemical assays of level of stress reaction, it was shown that these are sometimes elevated in depressed patients, while at other times such patients show normal hormone levels. Sachar and his colleagues provided evidence that elevated hormonal stress levels occur when the patient is in a period of active struggle, stimulated either by being confronted with the loss, or by the momentary failure to sustain a consolidated defense. When, in contrast, the intrapsychic defense is well entrenched, stress hormone levels are normal, and the patient seems clinically to be reasonably comfortable and well adjusted. Such difference in the adequacy of coping activity characteristic of different periods of psychiatric illness explain, according to Sachar, the contradictory findings among hormone studies of depression in which some report elevated hormonal stress levels, while others report no differences from normal levels. In any case, when successful, intrapsychic forms of coping might be expected to eliminate or limit active efforts at mastery of the environment, and would thus be associated with minimal biochemical and behavioral evidences of stress (Wolff et al. 1964). This reasoning suggests that the conditions favoring one may be antithetical to the other.

The gross distinction between direct action and intrapsychic modes of coping is, in a sense, a rudimentary classificatory scheme. It goes beyond mere reference to intrapsychic modes, such as the defensive polarities, and takes cognizance of the fact that much of coping includes manipulations of the environment as well as of one's cognitions about that environment. However, the distinction fails to meet two requirements of a good classificatory scheme; first, to provide a detailed itemization of the various coping subtypes that make up the major classificatory categories and, second, to provide a full analysis of the processes, antecedent conditions, and consequences of each type.

Table 10-1 provides a summary of the theoretical distinctions we have made above with respect to coping processes. It is as yet far too incomplete in the details of coping responses, and in the analysis of the specific antecedent conditions, psychological mediators, and consequences of each type of coping process, to be more than a rudimentary classification system and analysis, although we think it does point the way in which some of the issues might ultimately be resolved.

RESEARCH.   We have attempted to investigate the cognitive processes of appraisal and reappraisal by employing four basic strategies, direct manipulation, indirect manipulation, inferences from self-report data, and manipulation by the selection of dispositional variables.

TABLE 10-1 SOME THEORETICAL DISTINCTIONS
RELEVANT TO THE ANALYSIS OF COPING

	Situational variables	*Dispositional variables*
Antecedent conditions	Ecological and stimulus conditions	Personality traits, beliefs, cognitive styles
	Cognitive appraisal	
Psychological mediators	Primary appraisal of threat; secondary appraisal of coping alternatives; reappraisal based on the flow of events and reflection	
	Direct actions	*Intrapsychic processes*
Modes of expression in coping	Largely motoric modes of eliminating danger or achieving gratification	Largely cognitive modes of conflict resolution
Specific coping responses	Avoidance, attack, depressive reactions, active striving toward goal	Attention deployment (vigilance or psychic avoidance), reappraisal (realistic or defensive), wish-fulfilling fantasies

The strategy of *direct manipulation of appraisal and reappraisal* involves in-tervening directly to alter the manner in which subjects interpret (appraise) events portrayed in stressful movies or other emotional situations. In an early study (Speisman et al. 1964), subjects viewed a disturbing film, called *Subincision*, portraying a primitive ritual of cutting (with a stone knife) the penis and scrotum of adolescents entering manhood. The manipulation of appraisal was accomplished by means of three experimental sound tracks: the "trauma" sound track emphasized the emotionally disturbing elements of the ritual; "denial" asserted that neither significant pain, harm, or distress resulted; and "intellectualization" encouraged a detached and intellec-tualized view of the film events. The trauma sound track enhanced both au-tonomic and self-report evidence of emotional disturbance, while the denial and intellectualization sound tracks reduced it. Subsequent experiments demonstrated that the defense-based sound tracks were even more effective in reducing stress reactions when they were presented as orientation pas-sages before the film was started (Lazarus and Alfert 1964). In such cases, the threat was said to be "short-circuited" by the orientation, which pre-sumably altered appraisal in such a manner that the film events seemed less threatening. Later studies also extended the principle of short-circuiting of threat to other stressful films (Lazarus et al. 1965). This research paradigm for the study of the cognitive mediators also has been used to evaluate the capacity of two components of desensitization therapy—relaxation and cog-nitive rehearsal—to lower stress reactions (Folkins et al. 1968).

Studies utilizing direct manipulation of appraisal and reappraisal have, in sum, demonstrated that the same potentially disturbing movie produces dif-ferent levels of stress reaction depending on how it is interpreted. They support the concept that cognitive processes determine the level of the emotional response and illustrate an experimental paradigm for the study of these processes and their emotional consequences. They also provide illustrations of intrapsychic forms of coping (for example, denial and intellectualization), provided ready-made for the subject by the experimenter in the form of movie sound tracks or orientation passages.

In the research strategy of *indirect manipulation of appraisal and reappraisal*, the role of mediating cognitions in coping and emotion is studied by varying the environmental parameters of which such cognitions presumably are a function. Thus, for example, the imminence of a harm, its ambiguity, and the activities in which the person is engaged while he awaits it should influence the nature of appraisal and reappraisal processes and, in turn, coping responses. One such parameter, anticipation time, has been of particular interest to us. In an experiment by Nomikos, Opton, Averill, and Lazarus (1968) it was shown that, as compared to very brief anticipatory periods, say from a few seconds to half a minute, longer periods of waiting resulted in greater stress reactions, measured autonomically. Presumably, very brief periods of anticipation do not give the subject time to assimilate the disturbing implications of what is about to happen, while longer periods permit mental elaboration of the negative appraisal and lead to a larger emotional response. Moreover, most of the disturbance is produced during the anticipatory period before the subject sees a disturbing event (in this case an accident) on film.

The above research dealt with very brief anticipatory intervals, and it is quite possible that longer time periods (minutes, hours, days) might provide sufficient time for the evolution of coping devices with which the individual can master the threat. Precisely this possibility was investigated in our laboratory by Folkins (1970), who made different subjects await an electric shock for varying periods of time, five seconds, thirty seconds, one minute, three minutes, five minutes, or twenty minutes. (Control groups, used for comparison, waited for an electric light to be turned on.) It was found that although the objective harm (electric shock) was a constant, there were marked differences in the autonomic and subjective levels of disturbance associated with the varying anticipatory intervals. As might be expected from the previously cited study by Nomikos and colleagues (1968), the level of stress reaction rose from a brief five-second wait to a thirty-second wait, reaching a maximum in the group that waited one minute for the shock; however, it fell sharply in groups waiting three and five minutes. Other evidence strongly supports the interpretation that the drop in emotional disturbance associated with the three- and five-minute waiting periods was the result of the opportunity provided by these relatively long time periods for the subject to think through the situation and to reassure himself about the prospects of being harmed. Thus, by varying anticipatory intervals, the cognitive mechanisms of appraisal were also indirectly manipulated.

The "other evidence" alluded to above came from systematic interviews about what subjects were thinking and doing during the various anticipatory intervals. These interviews illustrate the use of the third strategy of *using self-report data to develop inferences about appraisals and reappraisals.* For example, during the three- and five-minute intervals, subjects commonly reported thinking that as a responsible representative of the university community the experimenter would certainly not expose them to serious harm, or that an electric shock realistically represented a mild rather than severe source of pain. Evidently, insufficient time for such thoughts was available during the brief anticipatory intervals of a minute or less.

Another illustration of the use of self-report measures to assess coping comes from a study by Lazarus, Speisman, Mordkoff, and Davison (1962). In this study, the first in our laboratory in which stressful movies were employed, subjects had watched two films, one benign, the other portraying the stressful subincision ritual. At the end of the latter film, subjects were interviewed to determine their reactions and styles of coping. Three basic patterns were observed. In one type of reaction there appeared to be "emotional flooding," illustrated by subjects' statements to the effect that the film "was disgusting; it made me sick to my stomach," and so forth. A second type of reaction, interpreted as intellectualized detachment, may be illustrated by statements such as, "It was an interesting anthropological study." A third type suggesting "denial" was typified by the statement, "It didn't bother me a bit." It was this interview material that in the first place led us to develop the denial and intellectualizing sound tracks employed in the later experiment (Speisman et al. 1964), which resulted in the significant lowering of emotional reactions while viewing the film.

Paradoxically, however, in this earlier study no relationship had been found between the assessed style of thinking (that is, denial, intellectualization, or emotional flooding) and autonomic evidence of degree of stress reaction during the film. This seems contradictory to the findings of the study using sound tracks (Speisman et al. 1964; and all the experiments using prophylactic orientation passages), where such styles of thinking were imposed by the experimenter and succeeded in lowering stress reactions. Our resolution of this has been to assume that subjects require time or repeated experiences with a threat to develop adequate modes of coping. That is, in the initial study without sound tracks (Lazarus et al. 1962), subjects who exhibited denial or an intellectualized way of thinking about the film events may not have actually employed these as active defenses while watching the film—they did not have a chance to do so. In the interview, we were seeing merely a style of thinking characteristic of the subject, or perhaps an effort to assimilate the events of the film after the fact, rather than a successful mode of coping with those events as they were happening before the subject's eyes. The anticipation studies described above to illustrate the indirect manipulation of appraisal also indicate that the evolution of successful defenses requires a certain amount of time. Perhaps, in the film context, subjects would have to view the same movie a second or third time, or otherwise have some opportunity to work the material over before intrapsychic modes of coping become effective. We know very little about the processes by which disturbing events are worked through, or the correlates of the ways of doing this.

In any case, the main point is that our two studies (Lazarus et al. 1962; Speisman et al. 1964) provide an instance of apparently contradictory results derived from two of the alternative strategies of research into appraisal and reappraisal, direct manipulation, and assessment by self-report. In effect, in the experiments involving direct manipulation, sound tracks and orientation passages representing denial and intellectualization successfully reduced stress reactions produced by movies, while in the study using only self-report data to infer such modes of thinking, the styles of denial and intellectualization showed no association with level of stress reaction. Although the contradiction can be easily resolved by making additional assumptions about successful or unsuccessful defensive processes and the conditions that create them (for example, time or repeated exposure), the methodological message of importance should be that different strategies of research sometimes lead to different conclusions. The alternative strategies should not be employed singly, but, rather, one should be used to supplement the other.

In the final strategy of *manipulating appraisal and reappraisal by the selection of dispositional variables on which they depend,* subjects are selected on the basis of differences in personality or species-based predispositions to cope in particular ways, emotionally or otherwise. In our own research with personality-based dispositional variables, tendencies to use one or another defensive style comprised the usual basis of the selection. Thus, for example, in the study by Speisman and co-workers (1964) that used stress-reducing prophylactic sound tracks, two kinds of subjects were also contrasted— those who were disposed to employ repressive-denial forms of defense, and those likely to use intellectualizing defenses. It was found that deniers showed more stress reduction as a result of the denial sound track than they did in response to the intellectualization sound track, while intellectualizers achieved more stress reductions as a result of hearing the intellectualization sound track than as a result of the denial sound track. In other words, there was an interaction between the effects of the prophylactic treatment and the personality disposition to employ one or the other defense. This same principle has recently been extended by Andrew (1967) to patients undergoing minor surgery. In her field experiment, the effects of detailed information about the patient's illness and the strategy of surgery depended on the defensive dispositions of the patients, with recovery from surgery being more rapid or impaired depending on such personality variables.

GENERAL CONCLUSIONS.   We began the theoretical portion of this section by suggesting the importance of the cognitive processes of appraisal and reappraisal for understanding coping and emotion. One criticism of such a theoretical stance has often been that it is phenomenological in character, that it is circular, and that the intrapsychic processes are refractory to empirical study. This is simply not true as has been pointed up, we believe, by the research from our own laboratory as summarized very briefly above. Much more detailed reviews of it are available elsewhere (for example, Lazarus and Opton 1966, pp. 225–262; Lazarus 1968; Lazarus et al. 1970; and Averill et al. 1969). The four alternative strategies of research on these processes—direct manipulation, indirect manipulation, inferences from self-report data, and manipulation by selection of dispositional variables—make possible empirical evaluation of the appraisal processes, especially when all four strategies are used in a mutually supplementary fashion so that the limitations and defects of one can be overcome by reference to the others. Research and theory that go beyond the mere demonstration of the role of cognitive mediators in coping and emotional processes has really just begun, but we think that it will increasingly support the scientific fruitfulness of a cognitively oriented theory of coping and emotion. We need not shy away from theorizing about coping and emotion in terms of mediating cognitive processes, because its concepts are inferential. By limiting the above review to our own research, we do not mean to suggest that we alone have used such an approach, although systematic programmatic research along these lines is relatively scarce.

We turn now to some of the more concrete issues of coping research and assessment. This does not mean, however, that we shall leave theoretical matters behind. On the contrary, a primary goal of the following discussion, and indeed the remainder of this chapter, is to fill in some of the lacunae in our theoretical formulations. To do this, we have adopted a frame of reference in which attention is directed toward those features of the response, the situation, and the person that contribute to variability in coping behavior.

A Sources-of-Variance Model

The concept of coping refers to certain classes of response. As emphasized in our definition, these responses and the processes underlying them are viewed from the functional perspective of demands (needs, opportunities, threats, pressures, urgencies) that tax the person's, or animal's, resources. The variability of any set of responses can be analyzed according to its *sources;* that is, we can examine that total variation in the matrix of responses we call coping and ask what the factors are that might account for this variation. Statistically, such an approach has been widely employed in experimental research, and also can be profitably applied to problems of assessment (Cronbach 1960; Endler 1966; Endler and Hunt 1966, 1968; Fiske 1963). It has also been used to evaluate the relative amount of variance in psychiatric patient behavior in a therapeutic community milieu contributed by the social setting, persons, and modes of response (Moos 1968), and by the therapist's contribution to the patient's response (Moos and Clemes 1967). We are not concerned here with "analysis of variance" as a mathematical-statistical technique; rather, our concern is with a logical, conceptual analysis of the factors that contribute to variability in coping behavior. This sources-of-variance model provides a convenient way of organizing the research and assessment issues basic to coping. After we have described this style of thinking, the remainder of this chapter will be centered around three main sources of variance and their interactions. These are (1) varieties of coping responses, (2) stimulus or situational demands, and (3) personality dispositions to react in particular ways to these demands.

These three sources of variance are depicted in Figure 10-1 on two levels of analysis. The cube at the upper left represents the more abstract level, in which response, situational, and dispositional variables are qualitatively different. That is, R_1 may represent aggression, R_2 avoidance, R_3 repression, R_k a vigilant search for information, and so forth. In a narrowly defined situation it is theoretically possible that all subjects would make the same response, in which case there would be no variation from this source within that situation. Even in the most carefully controlled laboratory settings, however, one usually discovers many different acts of coping performed by the subjects, although usually only one or at most a few of the wide range of possible responses are actually assessed. One problem, then, for a sources-of-variance model is to define the response universe to be studied and to find ways to measure the different types of responses.

The other two sources of variance with which we will be concerned are situational and dispositional variables. On the abstract level, situational variables (S_1, S_2, S_3, . . . , S_j) refer to such things as the content of the threat (for example, pain versus embarrassment), its objective ambiguity, the response options open to the individual, or any other environmental or ecological factor which might affect the coping response. The dispositional variables (P_1, P_2, P_3, . . . , P_i) refer to different types of personal characteristics, for example, personality traits, abilities, attitudes, belief systems, and so forth. As in the case of response variables, a major task for any analysis of coping is to provide a means by which the multifaceted situational and dispositional variables can be conceptualized.

The cube at the bottom right in Figure 10–1 represents a more concrete level of analysis, the expansion of one cell formed by the variables described above. That is, instead of being concerned with different *types* of coping behavior, the response variables (r_1, r_2, r_3, . . . , r_n) on this level of analysis refer to different ways in which a particular coping response might be expressed and hence measured (self-reports, physiological reactions, expressive and instrumental acts). The situational dimension (s_1, s_2, s_3, . . . , s_m) refers to varying degrees or aspects of a given environmental context (for example, varying intensities of electric shock in a laboratory experiment). Correspondingly, on this concrete level, the dispositional dimension (p_1, p_2, p_3, . . . , p_l) might refer to the relative strength of some response tendency, such as repression-sensitization.

It is important to keep in mind the two levels of analysis—abstract and concrete—for they obviously affect the types of generalizations which can be made. Most laboratory research is conducted on the concrete level; that is, the investigator concentrates on a particular coping response as a func-

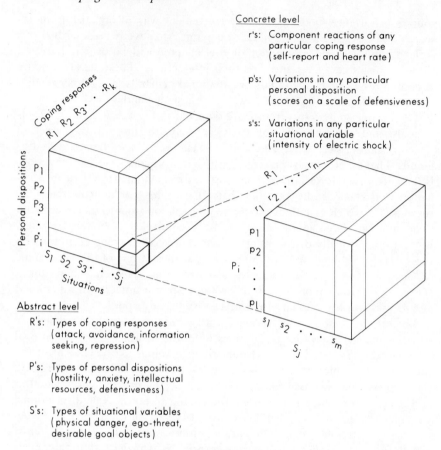

Concrete level

r's: Component reactions of any
      particular coping response
      (self-report and heart rate)

p's: Variations in any particular
      personal disposition
      (scores on a scale of defensiveness)

s's: Variations in any particular
      situational variable
      (intensity of electric shock)

Abstract level

R's: Types of coping responses
      (attack, avoidance, information
      seeking, repression)

P's: Types of personal dispositions
      (hostility, anxiety, intellectual
      resources, defensiveness)

S's: Types of situational variables
      (physical danger, ego-threat,
      desirable goal objects)

Figure 10-1   Three-way sources of variance model on abstract (left)
and concrete (right) levels of analysis.

tion of a single situational or dispositional variable. Such specificity is often
a necessity in quantitative, parametric studies where only a few parameters
can be varied at a time. In personality assessment, where use can be made
of an individual's symbolic capabilities, the levels of analysis may be mixed.
Thus, many self-report inventories are designed to measure one type of
coping disposition by asking the subject to imagine how he would behave in
a variety of situations. Other combinations of mixed-level analysis are also
frequent, especially in field research.

Ideally, one would like to see the simultaneous empirical employment of
both levels of analysis for all three sources of variance. That is, different
types of coping responses would be assessed, each by a variety of measures.
Similarly, different classes of situational and dispositional variables would
be sampled, each class being represented by a number of instances varying
along some relevant dimension. Such an ideal is, of course, practically impossible. Nevertheless, it is often *implicit* in the theoretical conclusions

drawn from more restricted designs. For example, when we say that an individual is high on disposition to repress as measured by a certain test questionnaire, it is implied that his high score relative to the group norm also reflects a tendency within that individual to favor repression over other modes of coping. Such an assumption may not be warranted unless a variety of coping behaviors have been sampled under different circumstances. A high normative score (between-subject comparison) may reflect hyperactivity of all coping behaviors, not just the one assessed, or, what is even more common in the case of self-report inventories, a general response bias with regard to the particular measure employed. The point we wish to emphasize is that the sources of variance outlined above, on both levels of analysis, contribute to the variability of coping behavior. When they are not measured, there is no way independently to assess their influence.

A concluding word might be added to indicate where the description and classification of coping into defensive polarities fits into the above sources-of-variance model. As we noted earlier, repression-sensitization and related constructs (repression-isolation; avoiders-copers) stand for personal dispositions, at least as they are typically assessed from self-report inventories, Rorschach responses, and the like. Moreover, these dispositions are oriented around particular responses; they say little about why a person tends to engage in repression, for example, or under what circumstances. As we shall see later, such response-oriented dispositions presuppose other tendencies stemming from one's beliefs about the nature of the environment and one's capacity to master it, from interpretations of interpersonal relations in terms of certain psychosexual conflicts, from expectations based on the previous history of success or failure in mastering threat by one or the other methods, and so on. Moreover, the analysis of a defensive polarity such as repression-sensitization ignores the many different ways or response modes with which the disposition may be expressed, such as concrete acts of repression, denial, avoidance, attention deployment, selective memory, perceptual or verbal suppression, and so forth. Nor does such analysis take into account the situational influences that might shape or modify the coping response, because its focus is on generalized dispositions that transcend situations. In short, these defensive classificatory schemes, and the research associated with them, deal on a very limited scale with only one of the three main sources of variance in coping, that of persons, whereas a complete attack on the problem would require explicit consideration of the other two main sources of variance, that is, situations and response modes.

The complexity of the problem addressed here is sharply pointed up by the relative absence of research and theory giving due weight to response and situational variables as sources of variance in coping behavior. Also relatively neglected is the great variety of personal dispositions that help determine coping, but that are not narrowly oriented toward specific types of response. The remainder of this chapter will be devoted to a more detailed discussion of these three sources of variance, with a separate section being devoted to responses, situations, and persons, respectively.

THE RESPONSE DIMENSION

In the presentation of our own theoretical viewpoint, we drew some distinctions between various types of coping behavior, primarily between direct actions and intrapsychic responses. Implicitly, then, we have already discussed the response dimension, but on a very abstract level. Moreover, in our discussion of appraisal we illustrated how inferences can be made about the cognitive processes that mediate coping. The present discussion will be concerned with a more concrete level of analysis as depicted in Figure 10-1. That is, we shall examine the various part-reactions, namely, verbal reports, physiological changes, expressive reactions, and behavioral acts, that are the raw material for inferences about coping and appraisal. In any given coping episode, measures based on these different reactions often stand in seeming contradiction. For example, a person may say that he is unperturbed and yet show high physiological arousal, or he may report considerable upset and yet not act accordingly. Therefore, we shall deal first with each type of reaction separately, and then consider the task of making inferences from the total pattern.

Verbal Reports

Verbalization may be used to infer coping, as when the person is encouraged to say how he is approaching a problem—whether he is angry, afraid, curious, concentrating, and so forth. Sometimes what is important is not so much the specific content of what a person says, but how he says it. In the discussion of defensive polarities, we have already indicated how the general style of a person's response, say, to a Rorschach card, may be used to assess coping dispositions. Stylistic changes may also be used to infer moment-to-moment changes in coping strategies, as has been indicated by the work of Mehrabian (1966) and others. Working with induced speech disturbances, Mahl (1963, pp. 77–105) found that effects on speech such as changes in form or content of a sentence, repetition, stuttering, omissions, and slips of the tongue were correlated with a speaker's immediate anxiety level during a psychotherapy session. Other aspects of speech were indicative of defensive maneuvers to cope with the source of threat. Such nonlexical analyses of speech are becoming an increasingly active area of research, and results are quite promising. It will undoubtedly remain a time-consuming and complex procedure, however, and its uses as a practical tool for assessment must therefore remain limited.

In the most common use of verbal reports, the literal meaning of a person's statement is taken more or less at face value. That is, if he says he is angry, he is assumed to be so, unless there is evidence to the contrary. Even in cases where it is believed that the response is feigned or the product of defensive distortion, the literal content of the expression is an important consideration. There are a variety of standardized tools for the direct assessment of verbal reports, of which adjective checklists are among the most widely used. The subject is presented with a list of adjectives having an affective connotation (angry, anxious, tense, sad), and he must indicate their appropriateness to his present state. The major differences between the various check lists center around the format of the rating scales and the method for deriving criterion scores.

The checklists developed by Nowlis (1965, pp. 352–389) and Clyde (1963) employ monopolar scales; that is, each scale is defined by only one adjective, and different scales are combined into affective dimensions on the basis of factor analytic studies. Nowlis (1965, pp. 352–389) has described twelve such dimensions, most defined by only three or four adjectives. A major difficulty with checklists based on factor analysis is that the specific adjectives defining a dimension may change from one study to another, and entire dimensions may disappear or coalesce depending upon the context. Strictly speaking, therefore, these checklists should be considered as approaches to assessment, rather than as well-standardized techniques. In any particular study, adjectives should be selected ideally on the basis of a careful analysis of that situation, and not blindly adopted from someone else's results.

A different approach to the construction of an adjective list has been taken by Zuckerman and his colleagues (Zuckerman 1960; Zuckerman and Lubin 1965). Here the subject indicates by a simple yes-no choice whether or not an adjective is descriptive of how he feels. Results are scored for three dimensions—anxiety, hostility, and depression. The adjectives for each scale were selected rationally and validated on criterion groups. The dimensions are, therefore, not factorially pure, but then neither are most affective states. Moreover, since a large number of adjectives define each dimension (twenty-one for anxiety, twenty-eight for hostility, and forty for depression), greater reliability across studies may be possible.

No discussion of adjective checklists would be complete without mention of the Semantic Differential developed by Osgood (Osgood, Suci, and Tannenbaum 1957). The Semantic Differential consists of seven-point scales anchored at each extreme by adjectival antonyms as good-bad, weak-strong, active-passive. The subject is asked to evaluate a concept or event by indicating its position on each scale. Factor analysis has revealed that most of the variance in the scales can be accounted for by three broad dimensions: evaluation, potency, and activity. These define what Osgood (1962) refers to as connotative meaning. Such meaning is presumably mediated by an affective system that is biologically determined and pancultural. In fact, the dimensions of the Semantic Differential are remarkably similar to those proposed by numerous authors (for example, Schlosberg 1954; Wundt 1902) to describe emotional reactions. It therefore is not surprising that the Semantic Differential also has been employed in the assessment and evaluation of coping behavior (for a thorough review of the Semantic Differential, see Snider 1969).

Another approach to the construction of self-report measures is the Personal Feeling Scales of Wessman and Ricks (1966). These scales assess twelve dimensions, including tranquility versus anxiety, elation versus depression, harmony versus anger, energy versus fatigue, among others. Each dimension is defined by a brief descriptive phrase, as are each of the points along the scale. The advantage of this approach is that the scales are described by a variety of words and phrases, thus lessening the chance of misinterpretation. It is for this reason that we have used this type of scale in our own cross-cultural research (Averill, Opton, and Lazarus 1969), where the precise translation of individual adjectives is practically impossible.

The creation of scales to assess the kind and intensity of affective states is relatively undeveloped, perhaps because of widespread distrust of self-report approaches. Existing techniques are rather insensitive to small changes in the intensity and quality of affects. One of the most important unresolved methodological problems is ambiguity about the standard against which a subject must evaluate his immediate feeling state. Thus, a subject is asked to say how anxious, angry, or depressed he is, but he is not told whether to use as a standard of reference his usual level of anxiety (to take one affect as an example), the level of anxiety immediately preceding the point of inquiry, or the strongest or weakest level of anxiety he has ever experienced. This poses no great problem when the experienced differences are gross, as, for example, when the subject has been exposed to a benign control condition to be compared with a strongly disturbing condition. But when the differences are subtle, most of the affect scales available probably do not pick them up. They tend to be gross, ordinal scales at best, where the subject can express only a judgment of "greater than" or "less than." Another problem is that the reports of subjects may be based on an intellectual assessment of the situation as one normally associated with fear, anger, or some other feeling, and it is not always clear whether a response is reflecting this cognitive judgment about the stimulus or an actual affective state. Thus, it would come as no surprise that the subject watching a stressful movie reports some form of distress, because the stimulus clearly implies such a response. Finally, most scales require the subject to report on his affective state retrospectively and often over a substantial period of time during which he may have experienced changing levels and qualities of affective reaction. Such a summary report is likely to obscure the variety of changing states a person normally experiences in any complex situation extended over time.

In addition to the above methodological problems, two important issues are·raised by the use of self-report to assess coping. The first involves the relationship between affect and coping. In the present context, which is oriented mainly to coping processes, the scales described above deal with only part of the total problem, the measurement of affective states. From our theoretical point of view, the type of affect displayed by the subject should be related to the coping impulse that arises from his appraisal of the situation and of the possibilities for mastering it. However, evidence relating coping processes to the degree or quality of emotional responses is as yet too meager to permit the use of the latter to infer the former. Still, it is worth remembering that most self-report measures oriented toward coping have a heavy component of items dealing with the presence or absence of disturbed affect. A good example is the Zuckerman scales of anxiety, hostility, and depression, the presence or absence of which is apt to form the basis for an inference about successful or unsuccessful coping. This is because successful defense is usually conceived in terms of the reduction of anxiety, suggesting that high anxiety is tantamount to a failure of coping (see, for example, Rosenwald 1961 for an explicit statement of this). The main danger of inferring coping from the presence or absence of disturbed affect is that the absence of negative affect may simply mean the absence of threat rather than the failure of coping. For this reason, affect scales alone are insufficient to infer coping, and some independent measure of the degree of threat must also be included.

A second issue concerns the forms of coping that can be assessed by means of self-report data. In the case of the problem-solving components of coping, that is, the way an individual thinks about the problem he faces, the sorts of information he seeks, the inferences he makes about the probable outcome, and so on, the subject can certainly be asked directly about his thought processes, with the prospect of learning much. An example is the already cited effort by Folkins (1970) in our laboratory; direct efforts were made through self-report methods to discover what subjects anticipating an electric shock thought and did while they waited. Moreover, self-report can also be used indirectly in evaluating the adequacy of such anticipatory coping efforts. For example, Haan's (1969) tripartite analysis of coping permits the judging of thoughts reported by subjects as realistic and flexible or inadequate and disrupted (she uses the term ego-failure for this). One of the problems with respect to Haan's category of ego-failure is that it is inferred partly from the affectivity reported by the subject, thus making the inference vulnerable to the possibility raised above that lack of disturbed affect may mean only the lack of threat, rather than successful coping.

Defensive forms of coping, on the other hand, cannot be assessed directly from self-report, because by definition, what the subject says is a distortion of the actual state of affairs. He cannot be expected to report defensive maneuvers if these are unknown to him. In such a case, the inference of defense must be made indirectly, by obtaining behavioral or physiological evidence that contradicts the contents of the self-report. We shall have more to say about this a bit later in the discussion of inferences from the total pattern of response.

Little systematic attention has been directed toward the assessment of coping by self-report methods. Mechanic's (1962) study of the coping of graduate students anticipating critical examinations was based essentially on clinical interviews and is an example of assessment efforts directed toward actual episodes of coping. Recently, Sidle, Moos, Adams, and Cady (1969) have designed a scale to measure coping. In Part I of this scale, for example, three problem situations are presented to the subject with instructions to list all of the coping strategies he might use to handle each problem; in Part II, the problems are repeated with a list of ten coping strategies, and subjects are instructed to check on a seven-point scale the likelihood that they would use each strategy. Gleser and Ihilevich (1969) have also developed a self-report device from which defenses are presumably inferred. Notice, however, that these two efforts are not directed at coping or defensive *episodes*, that is, of the manner in which persons handled a threatening experience, but are measures of coping *dispositions*, that is, tendencies to use one or another coping strategy in the event that actual exposure to threat occurred. In this they are similar to the previously examined defensive polarities, which also were assessed from verbal reports—(for example, Byrne's [1964, pp. 170–220] scale of repression-sensitization). Later we shall have occasion to spell out in full the distinction between a coping act or episode and a coping disposition. Most personality-centered efforts to assess coping represent attempts to measure coping dispositions rather than coping acts.

Physiological Changes

Activity of the autonomic nervous and endocrine systems is a frequently used channel of information for the assessment of coping. Until recently, there were few general references on this subject, and the prospective investigator had to consult many specialized journals in order to become acquainted with relevant techniques. Fortunately, the situation has now changed, and we can limit ourselves here to a few general observations. For short, general reviews of psychophysiological assessment, the reader may consult Averill and Opton (1968, pp. 265–288), Lykken (1967), and Shapiro and Crider (1969); three recent manuals (Brown 1967; Greenfield and Sternbach 1969; and Venables and Martin 1967) contain chapters describing the technical details involved in the measurement of individual autonomic variables.

Physiological variables have been used primarily to indicate the presence, absence, or degree of stress reaction, rather than to distinguish the quality or type of coping. This is not to say that all emotions are characterized by the same pattern of physiological activity. On the contrary, we believe that the evidence indicates that they are not. At the present state of the art, however, the existence of physiological patterns is of greater theoretical than practical importance. The most commonly used psychophysiological measures, such as skin resistance and heart rate, are too general to be used alone for differential diagnosis. On the other hand, as additional measures are recorded, the problems of data reduction increase geometrically. Even were this not an obstacle, individual differences in physiological reactivity are so great that it would be difficult to identify patterns characteristic of different emotions on the individual level, as opposed to general group trends. This situation may change with rapid advances in technology; but in the near future it seems that psychophysiological assessment will be limited to two broad classes of inferences regarding coping. On the one hand, psychophysiological measures may be used to reinforce or modify conclusions concerning the presence of emotionally arousing coping responses such as anger, fear, and so forth, when verbal reports and behavioral acts are somehow suspect. On the other hand, physiological changes may be used to indicate the success or failure of other coping modes, especially ego defenses, to achieve what Sachar and his colleagues (1968) have called psychological equilibrium (see also Fenz and Epstein 1962; Price, Thaler, and Mason 1957; and Wolff et al. 1964; all of whom have shown that defenses can lower physiological stress responses).

Expressive Reactions

The expression of emotion through facial and body displays has been a traditional concern of the psychology of emotion since the time of Darwin (1873). Unfortunately, early research on the judgment of affect from expressive cues was characterized by much contradiction, which raised doubt as to whether this was a useful channel of information. Recently, however, there has been a revival of interest in expressive reactions—their evolution (Andrew 1963; Hooff 1967, pp. 7–68), affective meaning (Frijda 1969; Osgood 1966), and use in psychotherapy research (Ekman and Friesen 1968, pp. 179–216). Conceptually, the use of expressive reactions in assessment of coping is similar to the use of physiological changes, although the technical problems of recording and evaluation are naturally quite different (see Ekman and Friesen 1969, pp. 49–98, for an excellent discussion of the classification and analysis of expressive reactions). Like physiological changes, expressive reactions are largely involuntary and may be quite unconscious, especially the micromomentary responses described by Haggard and Isaacs (1966, pp. 154–165). And although they are seldom sufficient by themselves to allow qualitative distinctions among different coping responses, they may reinforce or modify information provided via other channels. Moreover, through their close link with affect, expressive reactions may be used to indicate the failure of cognitive and other forms of coping to achieve conflict resolution. Ekman and Friesen (1968, pp. 179–216) have referred to this as the "leakage" of information.

Behavioral Acts

Coping involves an alteration, through intrapsychic cognitive responses or direct action, of the relationship between a person and his environment. As we have seen, intrapsychic cognitive responses can be inferred only through their effects on verbal, physiological, expressive, and behavioral variables. Direct actions (aggression, avoidance, information seeking, gaining new skills, and so on), on the other hand, may be more straightforwardly assessed. Direct action coping behavior has been observed and studied in a great many natural and semistructured situations. The problem for assessment, of course, is to select for analysis those aspects of behavior that can be easily and reliably coded and that are validly related to coping. Some behaviors, such as attack and avoidance, are quite obviously relevant. But a great variety of other behavioral responses are possible and of potential relevance. Proper selection of behavioral variables can proceed only after careful evaluation of the functional requirements of the situation (its demands and rewards) and the response options open to the individual.

These issues have been examined by Radloff and Helmreich (1968) in a study of the coping behavior of crewmen in Sealab II, a Navy experiment in underwater living. One of their findings can be used to illustrate some of the points we have been discussing. One of the most sensitive measures of an aquanaut's adjustment and work-effectiveness was the number of phone calls he made to the outside. Such calls were negatively correlated with diving time and other performance variables, but positively correlated with self-reported happiness. If one focused primarily on the self-report measure, it might be concluded that better adjustment resulted in feelings of happiness and a desire to communicate with others. On the other hand, the performance variables would indicate that the self-reported happiness was actually a defensive distortion and that outside phone calls were an indication of poor adjustment. In a later section we shall illustrate how, under certain circumstances, an increase in affiliative behavior is a common coping response to stress. At present, it is sufficient to note that inferences about coping can seldom be made from isolated reactions, regardless of type, but must take into consideration the entire patterning of responses, as well as the situation in which they occur.

Inferences about Coping from the Total Patterning of Responses

Responses, even verbal responses, do not come labeled as particular forms of coping. Whether the coping episode is one of repression, attack, or something else, must be inferred from characteristics of the response and the eliciting conditions.

A basic premise of our approach is that the various part-reactions comprising a coping episode, while often linked together functionally in a syndrome, may also occur independently of one another. Each element has its own particular adaptive functions (Lazarus 1968), and a comprehensive analysis of coping must be able to specify the individual and situational factors governing component reactions, as well as their integration into a behavioral whole. This means that any assessment program must encompass a variety of response elements. When these elements agree, that is, when there is redundancy among channels of information, then assessment is relatively straightforward and simple. But redundancy also implies a lack of information and hence is the least interesting case. The pattern of agreement and disagreement between the components of the total reaction contains within it information about the psychological, and even cultural, dynamics of coping—if only we are able to recognize and interpret the pattern.

The combination of response indicators is likely to be far superior in permitting accurate inferences about emotional states, because such a combination makes possible the uncovering of coping transactions that might serve to disguise the actual inner state. In their clinical studies of airmen in combat, for example, Grinker and Spiegel (1945) noted that psychosomatic symptoms might suggest a man overwhelmed by fear, yet who was unwilling to admit to himself or his buddies that this was so. And such disguise is possible not only in self-report measures and overt behavioral acts, where it has long been obvious to research workers, but also in so-called expressive acts as well, because these are often fastidiously controlled by the individual to create an impression. Thus, for example, Rosenfeld (1966) has shown that the conscious intention to seek approval from another person will lead in social interaction to evident smiles and gesticulations, demonstrating that so-called expressive acts may also have clearly instrumental functions. Clinicians make regular use of this principle.

Seemingly contradictory response patterns may take many forms. They may involve behavioral actions that lead to the inference of interest and concern, but that are contradicted by other actions simultaneously or on other occasions. Perhaps the most common example of such a discrepancy between response indicators is when a person says that he experiences no stress and yet gives contrary evidence through physiological arousal, or vice versa. Our research group (Weinstein, et al. 1968) has demonstrated that this discrepancy can be mediated by personality dispositions commonly interpreted as representing defensiveness, which lead the individual to deny psychological disturbance even when it is occurring. We did a reanalysis of six previously conducted experiments, dividing the subject populations into "repressors" and "sensitizers" on the basis of several MMPI-derived scales such as L, K, Hy-Dn, and Byrne's (1964, pp. 170–220) repression-sensitization scale, which we have discussed earlier. It was found that so-called "repressors" exhibited relatively greater autonomic and less self-report stress reaction to the film *Subincision*, the stimulus employed in all six of the reanalyzed studies. "Sensitizers," on the other hand, showed the opposite pattern in the two response modalities.

Two things are pointed up by this study. First, discrepancies between the component reactions of an emotional response are sometimes indicative of efforts to cope with different aspects of the situation and one's relation to it. We have already described Lefcourt's (1966) finding that repression-sensitization as measured by inventory scales reflects the attitude of a person toward the expression of emotion. In a threatening situation, therefore, "repressors" in this sense should withhold (not necessarily consciously) the display of emotion as in self-reports, while "sensitizers" should show a particular preference for this mode of expression. On the other hand, autonomic arousal should not—and did not—distinguish between these groups. In effect, although they overlap in some degree for the general population, self-reports and autonomic reactions also serve partially different functions, and hence should be expected to show meaningful discrepancies in certain kinds of persons and situations.

The second point raised by the study by Weinstein and co-workers (1968) has to do more strictly with assessment. If certain types of response discrepancies are related to reliable differences in personality, then questionnaires that help correct for these discrepancies may be constructed. By taking into account dispositions to respond in one manner or another, differences observed in response modalities can be explained and corrected for, achieving in this way a more accurate inference about intrapsychic processes. Moreover, many measures of coping dispositions are subject to the kinds of response bias that enter into the assessment of coping episodes. For instance, a person who will not report feelings of anxiety when threatened is not likely to answer items on a personality questionnaire that are indicative of anxiety. This is probably one reason for the very high correlation found between inventory measures of repression-sensitization and anxiety (for example, Golin et at. 1967). If a relative pure measure of this response bias could be constructed, it could be used to adjust inventory scores of coping dispositions, thus permitting better prediction of nonverbal responses in a threatening situation (see, for example, Bergan 1968).

Obviously, the permutations and combinations that different response variables may assume are many, and some may be normatively more common and psychologically more interesting than others. The rules for deciphering most discrepancies between response variables are not yet well established, and the conditions determining them remain largely unknown. Because adaptive situations, especially in humans, are highly complex and usually involve the type of reactions we have briefly reviewed above, that is, verbal reports, physiological changes, expressive reactions, and behavioral acts, those of us who wish to study coping and emotional processes inevitably depend on the discovery of the conditions influencing each of these indicators of such intrapsychic process.

THE SITUATIONAL DIMENSION

Viewed from our theoretical model (Table 10-1), situational and personality variables are the antecedent conditions or predeterminants of coping responses. Viewed from the standpoint of a sources-of-variance model (Figure 10-1), they comprise two of the three main dimensions that contribute to variability in coping. Our discussion of the situational dimension will remain primarily on the abstract rather than the concrete level of analysis. In an area so vast, we can only sample some important, general issues and indicate how they bear on the understanding, assessment, and prediction of coping.

To begin discussion of situational variables, we should repeat a fundamental point made earlier that coping (and emotional reactions too) represents a *transaction* between an individual and his environment. Let us take a research problem that is very well known in social psychology as a concrete example of this principle. Some time ago, Schachter (1959) attempted to test experimentally the notion that human affiliation had its origins, at least in part, in anxiety (or threat as we would be inclined to say). That is, he postulated that to prefer to be with other people rather than alone is a way of coping with threat. He created a basically simple but ingenious experimental situation with two treatment conditions. In the experimental condition, subjects were placed in an imposing laboratory setting and told to expect a severe and painful electric shock. The painful nature of the impending shocks was strongly emphasized to create a maximum of threat and anxiety. In the contrasting control condition, every effort was made to minimize the threat, with assurances given that the subject would barely feel the shock. Following this, subjects were permitted to select a comfortably furnished room during the ten minute delay while the equipment was being prepared. Some of the rooms supposedly contained other waiting subjects, while other rooms were empty. The subject was asked to indicate whether he preferred to wait alone or not. There was a marked tendency for the highly threatened subjects to choose to wait with others, in contrast with those exposed to low threat (the controls). Evidently, the company of others seemed to offer potential help in coping with the impending harm.

One might wonder whether the desire for affiliation would occur in all threat situations or, depend alternatively on such things as the nature of the threat or the quality of the social interaction that might be expected. A number of experiments were performed with the latter possibilities in mind. Of particular interest here is one by Sarnoff and Zimbardo (1961) who followed essentially the same procedure employed by Schachter, but varied the nature of the threat. As in Schachter's experiment, Sarnoff and Zimbardo told some subjects they would be given strong electric shocks; others (a control for degree of threat of shock) were told the shocks would be mild. A third group anticipated performing an action that was highly conflict laden—these subjects were told that they would shortly be required to suck on metal breast shields and other objects that were likely to arouse anxieties over oral impulses and to make them feel foolish (an altered type of threat). A fourth group (a control for degree of oral threat) was told they would suck on innocuous and acceptable objects, such as pieces of candy. Replicating Schachter's results, strong shock compared with weak shock led to a greater tendency to choose the company of others while waiting. However, the strong threat involving oral impulses produced a significant tendency in subjects to prefer waiting alone, compared with the low oral threat control condition.

The differences in affiliative behavior resulting from threat of shock as opposed to libidinal oral impulses may be interpreted in either of two ways. First, both types of stimuli may have aroused a *common state of threat*, and yet the different situational constraints created, of necessity, divergent forms of coping sensitive to such constraints. Second, the two stimuli may have aroused *different threat states*, say, "anxiety" in the case of shock and "embarrassment" in the case of sucking, each of which was manifested in different coping behaviors. We need not be concerned here about which interpretation is the better, for that is largely a matter of theoretical preference. Situational influences are involved in each interpretation, either in the production of different types of internal threat states or in requiring different coping processes. The net result is the same, that is, creation of different coping behaviors.

Situational variables operated somewhat differently to determine coping in an experiment by Taylor, Wheeler, and Altman (1968) on affiliative behavior under stress. This study explored the reactions of pairs of men subjected to eight days of isolation in small, twelve-foot square chambers. Three variables were manipulated: (1) degree of privacy—both members were confined either to one chamber or to separate chambers with free access between them; (2) amount of outside contact—such as voice communication, short music broadcasts, and the like; and (3) expected (not actual) length of confinement—four or twenty days. The authors had anticipated that the dual chamber arrangement, by allowing privacy when desired, would reduce stress in the twenty-day expected confinement condition. Just the opposite occurred. Individual quarters and expectancy of long confinement proved to be the most stressful conditions, especially when contact with the outside was minimum. On the other hand, when both members occupied the same quarters, stress levels were low and about the same in the twenty-day as in the four-day expectancy conditions. Moreover, privacy did not have a significant effect on stress reactions when a short confinement period was expected. There are many possible explanations for this seemingly paradoxical finding. One concerns the disruption of coordinated coping activities by the separate chamber condition. It was observed, for example, that the pairs that stood up best under the stress of confinement were comprised of individuals who coordinated their activities. Perhaps with the opportunity for privacy, such coordination was made more difficult.

The experiments by Sarnoff and Zimbardo (1961) and Taylor, Wheeler, and Altman (1968) both illustrate an important general principle, that is, to the extent that situational variables shape coping, inconsistency in individuals can be expected from situation to situation. This lack of consistency limits our ability to assert that one individual is, say, a repressor and another an isolator, except under carefully specified circumstances. To make reasonably accurate prediction of coping possible, it becomes necessary for us to classify situations on the basis of their "functional equivalence" for coping processes. That is, we must be able to specify the situations that have the common property of encouraging projection, repression, vigilance, attack, preparatory activity, or any other form of coping.

The above experiments also can be used to illustrate an important distinction between two broad classes of situational variables. In the Sarnoff and

Zimbardo (1961) experiment, the focal threat *stimulus* (for example, experiencing shock as opposed to sucking breast shields) was manipulated while other aspects of the environment were held constant. In the experiment by Taylor, Wheeler, and Altman (1968), the threat stimulus (confinement) was held constant while the entire ecology was manipulated, that is, different living spaces or "ecological niches" were created. The study of stimulus response or perceptual relationships has been a traditional concern of psychology, while the study of the total organism-environment interaction or ecological relationships has developed as a branch of biology. This separate development has created a considerable conceptual gap between perceptual and ecological explanations of behavior; only recently has the gap begun to be bridged (Barker 1968; Gibson 1966; Sells 1966). In the following discussion, we shall attempt to relate perceptual and ecological variables to each other and to coping via their influence on the process of appraisal, which is the cornerstone of our own theoretical position. We shall start with a consideration of ecological variables because they are the more general.

Ecological Variables

American psychology traditionally has been "environmentalist," in that differences between individuals have been attributed primarily to environmental and not constitutional factors. In spite of this, the environment has been the object of very little theoretical or empirical research by psychologists. This is due, in part, to the experimental emphasis in psychology, which necessarily limits the kinds of variables that can be manipulated. What is not so often recognized is the restriction that this limitation places on the generality of experimental findings. For example, frustration and its consequences (such as aggression and regression) have been for many years popular subjects for laboratory research. Using experimental methods, Barker, Dembo, and Lewin (1941) observed wide-ranging effects of frustration on children. In the field setting, on the other hand, Fawl (1963, pp. 99–126), a student of Barker, found fewer incidents of frustration than expected. Moreover, when frustration did occur, the consequences were different from those observed in the laboratory. In effect, the same relationship between frustration and its consequences that was observed in laboratory-based research was not duplicated in the field setting. Professor Washburn, in his chapter for this volume and elsewhere, has also noted this kind of discrepancy between generalizations based on laboratory experiments and those derived from field settings. The subject matter in this case dealt with the effect of brain lesions on the social behavior of monkeys. Uncinectomy in free-ranging rhesus monkeys resulted in social indifference and a lack of appropriate aggressive and submissive displays. The animals were expelled from the group and soon died or were killed (Dicks, Myers, and Kling 1969). Such behavior is not what would be expected on the basis of certain laboratory observations on temporal lobe lesions (compare with the Klüver-Bucy syndrome).

Psychologists have recently become increasingly aware of the need to consider the entire social and physical environment in the analysis of behavior. With reference to the former, Peters (1960) goes so far as to assert that "anthropology and sociology must be the basic sciences of human action in that they exhibit the systematic framework of norms and goals which are necessary to classify actions as being of a certain sort" (p. 7). In effect, merely by classifying behavior we place it within a sociological frame of reference. In a similar vein, social psychologist Muzafer Sherif has recently proposed what might be called a "psychosociology," in analogy to traditional psychophysics:

Study of the patterned properties of many social stimuli is beyond the level of *psychological* research, which is properly concerned with the behavior of individuals and deals in concepts appropriate to its analysis. In the past, psychologists borrowed freely from the work of physicists and chemists in specifying properties of stimuli like light, sound, and odor. The social sciences (sociology, anthropology, linguistics, economics, political science) study the patterned properties of social stimulus situations at a meaningful level. It is to them that we should properly turn for help in specifying the properties of the particular social situations we are studying and in defining the conditions bounding these particular situations (M. Sherif and C. Sherif 1963, p. 88).

While psychology is bounded on one side by the social sciences, it is bounded on the other side by the biological and physical sciences. Developments within biology, especially ethological analyses of animal behavior, have focused attention on complex features of the physical as well as social environment. This trend has been greatly reinforced by neurological observations that nerve fibers carry information about specific features of the environment that are of adaptive value to the organism. Thus, in a now classic paper, Lettvin, Maturana, McCulloch, and Pitts (1959) demonstrated how the optic nerve of the frog carries information regarding certain shapes, movements, contrasts, and the like, which are of ecological significance to the frog. This information is transmitted to the organism by means of physical energies, for example, by electromagnetic waves, in the case of visual information. The medium of transmission is, however, of relatively minor importance from an adaptive standpoint. To paraphrase a currently popular saying, the traditional concern of psychologists with the detection of physical energy *per se*, as in psychophysics, has too often confused the medium with the message.

The relevance of ecological analyses, whether biological or sociological, to the study of coping has been amply demonstrated by other contributors to this book (for example, by Washburn, Goldschmidt, and Mechanic). It is not our intention, nor is it within our competence, to expand upon their excellent discussions. However, we should indicate how ecological variables fit into our own theoretical model of coping. Our central theoretical construct is *appraisal*, that is, the evaluation of information regarding the relevance of an event to the individual's welfare. An ecological variable is, then, any environmental factor that influences appraisal. It may be the source of information, that is, a stimulus in the narrow sense, or it may be some other variable that influences the processing of stimulus information. For example, an infection or a state of fatigue is not a stimulus event; nevertheless, through its action on physiological and psychological functioning it may influence an individual's ability to process information. Hence, the same situation is liable to be appraised differently during illness and health, with a resulting difference in coping behaviors. Factors producing illness and fatigue are thus ecological variables from our point of view. This distinction is similar in many respects to that made by Kurt Lewin (1935) in the concepts of the "life space" and its "foreign hull."

Ecological variables may be related to (1) the physical environment (climatic conditions, terrain, natural and man-made resources), (2) the social environment (institutions, roles, customs, mores), (3) population characteristics (density and homogeneity as well as other demographic variables), and (4) the particular adaptive problem at hand (its difficulty, importance, and so forth). We cannot spare space to illustrate the influence of each of these classes of variables on appraisal, or to discuss their measurement. One example of the influence of the social environment on coping will suffice to illustrate the general point. Attack on, or flight from, a threatening agent is strongly constrained by socially shared values about, and sanctions against, such forms of coping under given circumstances, or by social groups or systems where such coping behaviors represent syntonic values. The individual faced with threat, for example, takes note of these circumstances and social values in choosing a coping response, because his response may have important consequences for his welfare, over and above the original threat. Moreover, some of these values and codes of conduct have also been internalized by him, and thus shape his appraisals as aspects of his personality. Much of the recent experimental research on aggression in social psychology deals with variables of this sort, although these have not been examined from an ecological perspective. Actually, very little psychological work meriting discussion has been done on the human level with ecological variables, although many authors have recognized the importance of ecological analyses and have contributed isolated studies. The work of Barker (1968) and his associates at the Midwest Psychological Field Station is an important exception to this generalization.

A few final points need to be made regarding the nature of the environment and its interaction with the individual, especially in the laboratory setting. Environmental events do not happen in isolation, and they cannot be analyzed as if they did. With few exceptions, for example, sudden disasters, most events have a past, a present, and a potential future course. This entire programmed sequence governs the organism-environment interaction, and not simply the point of contact at any particular moment. This is one reason for the frequent failure to replicate experimental findings in field settings; to attribute such failure solely to the existence of confounding variables is to miss an important point. The experiment is typically ahistorical. A subject is brought into the laboratory and presented with a situation that is relatively isolated from the normal stream of events. The same situation may mean very different things to the subject (will be appraised differently) depending upon whether it is encountered in the laboratory or in a natural ecological setting. This is not said to disparage experimentation—our own work is largely experimental—rather, it is said to point up an important gap between experimentation on situational variables and the broader concerns with the ecology of man as this gap applies to the study of coping.

The organism and environment are like two intermeshing gears. This means that there are three aspects of any organism-environment interaction that must be analyzed—the organismic gear, environmental gear, and the point of contact. Most psychological experiments are designed to investigate the point of contact. If the investigator happens to be interested in personality, he will probably also attempt to assess the influence of relevant dispositional variables. Rarely, however, does he attempt a similar analysis of relevant environmental variables. But the environment as well as the individual is possessed of consistencies; both are self-governing systems, which also happen to interact. The point of contact does not adequately define the environmental system any more than it does the individual. If psychologists are going to understand coping behavior, there is little doubt that they will have to expend as much energy in assessing the "personality" of the environment as they currently do with reference to the individual. We shall return to some of these points in a later section after we have considered the nature of personal dispositions. First, however, we must complete this discussion of the situational dimension with a brief consideration of stimulus variables.

Stimulus Variables

As noted above, stimulus variables are a subset of the entire ecological environment. They are the immediate source of information or raw material upon which appraisal operates. Stated another way, they represent one point of contact between the organism and his environment. Psychological analyses of stimulus variables abound, and we have no intention of reviewing this vast and readily available literature. Rather, we shall simply draw distinctions between three types of stimulus information that have aided our own experimental research, on the assumption that they may also prove of value to others. The three types of stimulus information include (1) that which is intrinsic or specific to a particular stimulus, (2) that which is extrinsic or common to a wide variety of stimuli, and (3) that which is determined by the individual's own response.

INTRINSIC STIMULUS PROPERTIES.   These convey information specific to a particular stimulus source. Information regarding height, for example, may be conveyed by a variety of visual cues. Most organisms, as soon as they are mobile, and evidently without prior learning, are able to use these cues to avoid approaching so close to a cliff's edge that they are in danger of falling over (E. Gibson and Walk 1960). In the present scheme, we would say that under natural conditions there are stimulus properties intrinsic to high places that convey information of functional significance to the organism. The *appraisal* of this information leads to an appropriate coping response, that is, avoidance.

In addition to the inanimate environment, the appearance and expressive reactions of other organisms are a rich source of intrinsic stimulus properties. Many examples could be taken from the ethological literature (Marler and Hamilton 1967), where intrinsic properties have been labeled "releasers" because of their ability to elicit or release a particular response pattern. Thus, the red belly of a stickleback is a potent stimulus for aggression; a red patch on the bill of a gull helps elicit begging in chicks; and so on for a wide variety of stimuli related to appropriate prey, predator, and sex objects. There is considerable debate concerning exactly how specific such releasers are to a particular response, and exactly what cues carry the information. Nevertheless, we can say that for lower animals, at least, some degree of specificity is the rule. In humans, the evidence is meager for the existence of intrinsic stimulus properties with a high degree of specificity due to biological factors. This does not mean, however, that evolution has not played an important role in determining which stimuli come to elicit particular coping responses in man. For example, it is easy to come to fear such things as height, darkness, mutilated or dismembered bodies, and other objects that may have played a role in primate evolution, but it is relatively difficult to learn to fear certain products of cultural evolution, for example, cigarette smoking and driving an automobile at high speeds. This differential ease of emotional learning has been emphasized by various investigators, most notably by Hebb (1946). It is obviously a fact of considerable significance for the study of coping, but one that has been relatively ignored by psychologists due to a lack of appreciation of intrinsic stimulus properties as a special class of stimulus variables.

Field investigators generally have shown greater cognizance of the importance of intrinsic stimulus properties than have experimental psychologists. The buzzers, lights, and other stimuli typically used in laboratory research do not have much intrinsic meaning; indeed, that is why they are selected. Associations to such stimuli can be built up within the laboratory, and greater experimental control can be ostensibly achieved. When dealing with more complex stimuli, however, even the experimental investigator must be concerned with intrinsic stimulus properties. We shall illustrate this with a problem from our own laboratory. This deals with differential emotional habituation, which might be considered the obverse of the differential learning problems considered above.

As previously described, much of our research has involved the use of motion pictures. One of our concerns has been with adaptation or habituation following repeated exposure to the same stressful film. This would seem to be a straightforward experimental problem; after all, habituation to simple stimuli has been a much researched topic and the relevant experimental procedures are pretty well understood. In a doctoral dissertation, however, Davison (1963) had shown the subincision film to subjects once a week for three consecutive weeks. The purpose was to study the psychological processes mediating adaptation to the film, defined in terms of progressively diminishing indices of reactivity from the first to third viewings. Specific hypotheses were made concerning the personality and coping dispositions underlying differential rates of adaptation. For the most part, these hypotheses could not be tested because the impact of the film was almost completely dissipated by one viewing. In another doctoral dissertation, Riess (1964) attempted to study the effects of different kinds of "therapeutic" techniques interposed between two showings of the subincision film. As in the Davison (1963) study, almost complete adaptation had occurred by the second showing so that differences between treatment groups were minor.

In contrast to the above findings, Alfert (1964) found little adaptation to a woodshop accident film (where fingers are lacerated and a board is driven through the abdomen of a workman) when the film was shown twice in the same session. Similarly, in a recent study on emotional involvement and detachment, Koriat and Melkman (unpublished data) found relatively little adaptation to the accident scenes of this film even after four exposures.

Thus, several experiments using the subincision film have seemingly resulted in considerable adaptation following one viewing, but several experiments using the woodshop accident film have suggested relatively little adaptation. Is it possible that adaptation to the type of events portrayed in the subincision film (that is, content) takes place readily, but adaptation to the portrayal of personal accidents occurs slowly? Such a suggestion goes counter to the psychoanalytically oriented assumption (Aas 1958) that the subincision film evokes a universal castration anxiety. However, the suggestion has also been made (Lazarus 1968) that the subincision film is extremely esoteric, and this makes the initial experience particularly difficult to assimilate. But once it has been seen and some way of thinking about it cultivated, there may no longer be any reason to react emotionally. In contrast to the woodshop accident film, the subincision operations have very little to do with everyday life in contemporary society, and hence may not maintain their emotional impact. In short, the above explanation of possible differences in rates of adaptation to both films emphasizes intrinsic factors, that is, the differential signal value inherent in the contents of the two films.

To test this speculative idea requires experiments that rule out factors other than intrinsic ones on which the films vary. Some of these fall within the rubric of "extrinsic stimulus properties," which will be discussed shortly. For the sake of continuity, however, it might be mentioned here that the two films, just discussed, differ in respect to their formats. For example, the accident film has three relatively discrete stressful moments, while six stressful operations are shown in the subincision film, and these are not so clearly demarcated from the surrounding neutral scenes. Thus the films differ in ways not specific to their basic subject matter, that is, in *extrinsic stimulus properties*, such as the discreteness of the emotion-producing episodes, and their frequency of occurrence. To investigate the role of intrinsic stimulus properties, such as the signal value of the stimulus content for day-to-day adaptation, it is necessary to hold the extrinsic properties constant. Ongoing research has been designed to do this by modifying the format of the subincision film to make it more similar to the woodshop accident film. It is hoped that the experiment will tell us (1) whether or not there is, indeed, differential adaptation to the contents of the two films, and (2) the nature of the cognitive mediators which are involved.

EXTRINSIC STIMULUS PROPERTIES. These refer to general dimensions common to a wide variety of stimuli, such as novelty, intensity or degree, inevitability, imminence, and ambiguity. Included also would be the variables of format mentioned at the end of the previous discussion. In that discussion of differential habituation, extrinsic stimulus properties were considered as confounding variables to be eliminated or held constant. Such is not always the case, however. In combination with intrinsic stimulus variables, extrinsic stimulus properties can be important determinants of coping, and hence are often the subject of investigation in their own right. A few examples will illustrate this point. *Novelty* is not a unique property of, nor is it intrinsic to, any particular kind of stimulus. Rather, it often enhances whatever coping response might normally be induced by intrinsic stimulus properties, including sexual arousal (Beach and Ransom 1967), aggression (Scott 1958), and fear (Hebb 1946), as well as curiosity and problem-solving behavior in general (Berlyne 1960).

Intensity is another extrinsic dimension along which any stimulus can vary and which has been the subject of much investigation and speculation. For example, Menninger (1954) has proposed that as degree of threat increases, coping mechanisms become more primitive, more costly to the psychic economy, and less integrated. The problem here, of course, is to obtain some measure of intensity independent of an individual's response. This is not as simple as it might sound, because a response is a function of both degree of threat and coping resources. Thus, if a person does not respond to a potentially stressful stimulus, it is sometimes difficult to determine whether he was really threatened but adequately defended or whether he simply was not threatened. A poorly integrated and primitive coping response, therefore, might reflect a high degree of threat, as Menninger suggests, or it might result from inadequate defenses against mild threat.

In addition to enhancing intrinsic cues (as in the example of novelty) and affecting the quality of response (as in the example of intensity), extrinsic stimulus properties may also "pull" for one mode of coping as opposed to another. Thus, as we have said earlier, an *inevitable* harm should result in forms of coping that are different from those present when harm can be prevented. For example, denial defenses seem to be extremely common in terminal illness where nothing can be done to prevent death.

Some of our own laboratory research has concerned the role of extrinsic stimulus properties in coping. We have already discussed the studies of Nomikos and colleagues (1968) and Folkins (1970) where *imminence,* or time to confrontation, was of primary interest. We have also recently undertaken a number of studies investigating the role of *ambiguity.* In one study just completed by Alan Monat (unpublished data), subjects had to await a painful electric shock. Under one condition, they knew that shock was certain and when it would occur (at the end of three minutes as indicated by a clock). Under another condition, subjects also knew when, but not whether, shock would occur, that is, they were told that there was only 50 percent probability of shock (actually it was 100 percent). A third group of subjects knew that shock would occur, but not when it would (the clock was removed). Thus, two types of ambiguity (in terms of probability and time of occurrence) were compared under a condition of minimally ambiguous threat. The results were not completely expected. Variations in the probability of shock produced the same amount of stress reaction, assessed by both self-report and physiological measures, as did shock that was certain, while temporal ambiguity was apparently less stressful than the other conditions. When the time of the shock was uncertain, subjects seemed to just "give up" and await their fate, showing lower levels of disturbance. There was also some evidence that subjects in the condition of temporal uncertainty tended to avoid thinking about the impending shock, in comparison with the other two groups, where the time of shock was known.

We need not dwell on possible interpretations of these findings. The important point is that much has been said about ambiguity in relation to coping, but very little research has been conducted on the topic. It is obvious from this experiment that "ambiguity" is itself an ambiguous concept, and the same could be said for the other extrinsic stimulus properties that we have mentioned. Unlike response variables, which have been subjected to many factor analytic schemes and other types of analyses to isolate underlying dimensions (for example, activation, pleasantness, potency, among others—Osgood 1966), stimulus variables have been relatively neglected in this regard. It is a trite, but nevertheless true, statement that a great deal of empirical research needs to be done in this area, and what evidence there is makes it clear that extrinsic stimulus properties of situations are powerful determinants of coping and emotional behavior.

RESPONSE-DETERMINED STIMULUS PROPERTIES.   These are the most difficult to define because they have received the least attention in research and theory. Yet it must be recognized that the dichotomy between sensory and motor, stimulus and response, does violence to the natural sequence of events. As Dewey (1896) pointed out many years ago, the stimulus is as much determined by the response as the response is by the stimulus. Recent experimental research leaves little doubt about the essential validity of this position, even with regard to simple sensory systems (Festinger et al. 1967; Gibson 1966; Werner and Wapner 1952). We have argued elsewhere (Lazarus 1966; Averill et al. 1969) that the perception of complex stimuli is a function, in part, of available coping options, in effect, that potential and actual responses influence the evaluation of the stimulus. This is what we mean by *secondary appraisal* (see the previous section, on "Some Theoretical Distinctions and Relevant Research").

For example, even in animals such as rats and dogs, the same potentially harmful stimulus, a painful electric shock, may induce active escape (Solomon and Wynne 1953), helplessness or passivity (Maier, Seligman, and Solomon 1968), aggression (Azrin, Hutchinson, and Hake 1967), or mating behavior (Barfield and Sachs 1968), depending upon situational constraints. Presumably, the secondary appraisal of the shock is different in each situation because the animal can—and did—do something different in each case (due to the presence or absence of an escape route, a target for aggression, or a receptive female, respectively). Such an interpretation of the animal's actions is not unwarranted anthropomorphism, as is indicated by a study by Bandler, Madaras, and Bem (1968). These investigators found that subjects rated an electric shock as more painful if they believed that a response, which was actually irrelevant to the stimulus, permitted escape. Subjects who believed that the same response had no influence on the shock reported less pain. Also of relevance is a study by Berkowitz (1967, pp. 243–254) indicating that subjects will become more angry if they believe that subsequently, after provocation, they will be able to retaliate.

To summarize the foregoing discussion of the situational source of variance, we have been concerned with pointing up the importance of environmental factors as a determinant of coping and have made an effort to relate the stimulus as seen by the experimental psychologist to the situation as seen by the ecologist. For us the common link is the theoretical construct of *appraisal* through which the person or infrahuman animal processes information, judges the relevance of events, and selects from his repertoire of coping acts that which is most nearly suited to the complex geometry of costs and gains with which his advanced or limited brain can put him in touch. Because the study of situations as determinants of coping requires ultimately the systematic classification of situational variables on the basis of their fundamental properties and their effects on the coping response, we have tried to suggest a few types of stimulus variables that could be important, some intrinsic to the specific stimulus, some cutting across given stimuli and applying to all stimuli, and some that must be defined by the response or potential response itself.

In the next section we turn to the third major source of variance in coping, that concerned with personality dispositions.

THE PERSONAL DIMENSION

Much research on the assessment of coping is concerned with personality structures, such as attitudes, beliefs, motives, and capacities, which in interaction with situational variables shape each coping effort. This research usually involves predicting how a person will respond in the future on the evidence of present and past characteristics, as measured by behavior in the laboratory, responses to a questionnaire, interpretation of a projective test, a life history, and so forth. In order to treat the theoretical and methodological implications surrounding the use of measures of personal dispositions in the study of coping, it is essential first that we have a clear conception of what is meant by a *disposition*, and how it differs logically from an actual response *episode*.

Dispositional versus Episodic Variables

The distinction between dispositional and episodic variables is common to all branches of science and is the topic of much debate among philosophers of science (Carnap 1956, pp. 38–76; Feigl 1951, pp. 178–213; Hampshire 1953; Pap 1962). Episodic variables are events, for example, specific instances of coping behavior as were discussed in the section on response variables. Dispositional variables, on the other hand, are not events, although they may be manifested in events. They may be defined by conditional statements of the "If . . . , then. . . ." variety (Hempel 1960, pp. 101–120). For example, the disposition of "hostility" might be defined: "If X is subjected to mild provocation, then X is hostile if and only if X attacks."

The difference between dispositional and episodic variables can be exemplified by an everyday physical example. To be combustible is a disposition; to burst into flame is an episode. If conditions are appropriate, then combustible material will burn, and the intensity of the reaction may be measured with a proper sensing device. When appropriate conditions are absent, however, the material will not burn, even though it is still combustible, and no thermometer can measure the heat of its nonexistent flame.

The distinction between combustibility and burning is obvious, but the parallel distinction between psychological dispositions and response variables has often been confused. It is important to avoid such confusion because the problems involved in the assessment of each are different. Moreover, theoretical as well as practical difficulties may arise when the distinction is blurred. We will illustrate this with reference to anxiety.

Anxiety, like many words that name affects, can refer either to dispositions or to responses. "Tom is anxious" may mean that he is anxiety-prone, that is, that he has a disposition to become anxious if even mildly threatened. "Tom is anxious" may also mean that Tom is experiencing an anxiety attack right now. In everyday conversation, context conveys the precise meaning. In psychological discussion, however, "anxiety" frequently is used as an abstract concept with the context unspecified. It is then only an easy, false step to reify dispositional anxiety as a chronic or continuous episode. It may be assumed, for example, that a person high on dispositional anxiety (usually called by another name, for example, "trait," "basal," "chronic," "tonic") is always in a state of anxiety, and that when such a person is not visibly anxious, the anxiety response is nevertheless present and could be detected if only more subtle and powerful measuring instruments were available. This conception is compatible with psychoanalytic and behavioristic theories that picture anxiety as a chronic drive state, sometimes conscious, sometimes not, but ever present as a source of energy for diverse behaviors.

The consequences of not distinguishing the dispositional and episodic meanings of anxiety are evident in the results of much research. For instance, frequent attempts have been made to relate dispositional anxiety as presumably measured by such tests as the Taylor (1953) Manifest Anxiety Scale (MAS) to physiological arousal. Not surprisingly, these attempts have been uniformly unsuccessful, except when the testing situation itself was threatening to the subject or when some specific threat stimulus was introduced (for reviews, see Averill and Opton 1968, pp. 265–288; McReynolds 1967; Speilberger 1966, pp. 3–20). The reasons for this failure can be readily seen if we compare anxiety and sexual arousal. A relatively well described physiological reaction accompanies sexual arousal (Masters and Johnson 1966; Wenger, Averill, and Smith 1968), including tumescence, increased heart and respiration rates, increased blood pressure, and so forth. These physiological changes are the sexual analogue of the physiological reactions accompanying episodic anxiety. But what is the sexual analogue of dispositional anxiety? Using the physiological studies of dispositional anxiety as a model, we might assume that the individual with high dispositional sexuality—the nymphomaniac or "Don Juan"—should have greater resting activity in those variables that show the greatest changes during sexual arousal. This would be ridiculous. The highly sexual individual is not in a continuous state of mild tumescence, with a slightly pounding heart and somewhat heavy breath. Rather, the full reaction can be induced more readily and by a larger range of stimuli in the person with a high sex "drive," and more of his everyday activity is devoted to bringing himself into contact with such stimuli. Similarly, the dispositionally anxious individual is not in a state of continuous anxiety, but becomes anxious more readily than do others.

It might be granted that dispositional anxiety does not imply a state of physiological arousal in the same sense as does episodic anxiety, but that there are nevertheless continuous phenomenal or experiential correlates (McReynolds 1968, pp. 244–264). The reification of dispositional variables as mental events is extremely common and is a part of our philosophical and scientific heritage (Ryle 1949; Sarbin 1968). The substitution of mental events for physiological ones, however, does not affect the logic of the situation. Indeed, it may be even more insidious, for when introspection does not reveal the requisite experiences, it is then a small step to say that the affect is still there, but is unconscious.

Dispositions such as anxiety and hostility traditionally have been conceptualized in terms of a drive or energy model (Freud 1926, 1936; Spence 1958). Because we reject the concept of drive as useful for the understanding of coping in general, and emotion in particular (Averill 1968; Lazarus 1968), we must formulate the operation of dispositions in some other fashion. The alternative best supported by current research and theory in motivation is in terms of differing thresholds of activation for specific coping episodes (Cofer and Appley 1964). These threshold differences may arise from biological, cultural, and psychological factors, and usually from a combination of all three.

Biological (phylogenetic) and cultural factors in the development of coping dispositions have been discussed by other contributors to this book (e.g., Washburn, Hamburg, and Goldschmidt); we shall, therefore, limit ourselves to a few observations concerning their psychological development.

One aspect of the theoretical task of the psychologist concerned with coping dispositions is to ascertain whether there is a regular developmental sequence for the appearance of certain modes of coping. For example, one might ask whether denial or repression as defensive modes precede the appearance of isolation or intellectualization, in very much the same way as Piaget (1952) did in proposing that a sensor-motor stage of adaptive thought preceded the conceptual stage, or as Freud did in proposing that paranoid projection and isolation arose in the anal stage of psychosexual development preceding the appearance of the mechanism of repression that arose in the later phallic or Oedipal stage. It seems highly likely from a logical point of view that the child must be capable of appropriate forms of thought before he can utilize certain processes of coping. The question has been stated quite clearly by Gardner and colleagues (1959), who have spelled out several kinds of possible developmental relationships between cognitive styles and defenses.

The answers to such developmental questions require systematic research on coping processes with children of varying ages, but such research is currently out of fashion. Developmental psychology is having a love affair with the intellectual functions and has tended for some time to ignore the motivational and emotional stages of development in which coping is a relevant consideration. It would be of great value to the understanding of coping processes to examine how the various classes of coping activity emerge in the infant and young child. Although some research along these lines in field settings has been reported by Escalona and Heider (1959), Murphy (1962 and in chapter 5 of this volume), and Heider (1966), this work is limited by a mainly descriptive, atheoretical orientation, by attention to some aspects of coping and not others, by a focus on a limited age and time span in the individuals studied, and by the absence of systematic concern with the role of situational factors as determinants of coping. Such a critique does not fault the fine work that is being done, but rather reflects the small numbers of people working and the limited range of approaches being utilized in tackling the developmental problem of coping. In the search for better understanding of the coping process, the developmental aspects are too important to be neglected indefinitely.

To conclude these general observations on coping dispositions, a few comments need to be made regarding the strength of an affective disposition and its relationship to nonemotional forms of coping. The intensity of an emotional episode can be measured by the intensity of verbal reports, physiological changes, expressive reactions, or behavioral acts, as previously described. Similarly, the strength of an affective disposition can be measured by the intensity or probability of an emotional episode upon stimulation. But the strength of the disposition may also be judged by its influence on behavior not normally classified as emotional. The power of an affective disposition depends on how much behavior can be explained by it (Kenny 1963). In fact, it is logically possible that the disposition might never be manifested in a strictly emotional sense. Like the combustible material that never bursts into flames because proper precautions are taken, so the dispositionally anxious person might never experience an anxiety attack because he has secluded himself in an environment protected from all threat (a form of coping). The protection may be behavioral, as when the phobic person avoids high places, or it may be intrapsychic, involving attention deployment or defensive reappraisal. In either case, if the avoidance response is well practiced and successful, episodes of disturbed affect will not be manifested; they are not thereby rendered unconscious, they are simply absent. In fact, defensive behaviors are among the more important signs of dispositional vulnerability to those affects, just as fire extinguishers and other defenses against fire usually indicate the presence of combustible materials.

A Classification of Coping Dispositions

Just as we attempted to do in the case of stimulus variables, we offer also a classification of dispositional variables that might be important in coping. There are, of course, many ways of proceeding with such a classification, for example, in traditional terms such as moods, motives, abilities, sentiments, and personality traits. We shall be concerned here with three types: those organized around coping responses, which we call *response-oriented* dispositions; those organized around particular stimulus objects, referred to here as *stimulus-oriented* dispositions; and those dictated by theoretical propositions about the underlying psychodynamics, termed *theoretically oriented* dispositions.

RESPONSE-ORIENTED DISPOSITIONS. Of the three categories of dispositional variables, response-oriented dispositions appear to be overwhelmingly the most frequently employed in personality research. Examples include dispositions to respond with anxiety, hostility, depression, and repression-sensitization, to name a few. Because we have already examined this type of variable in considerable detail in the discussion of defensive polarities, we shall devote little additional space to it here. It suffices to point out that as currently used, most response-oriented dispositional measures are largely descriptive and atheoretical; that is, they offer little understanding of the dispositions that they assess. This does not mean, however, that they cannot be of considerable practical value in the control and prediction of behavior. Unfortunately, that value is often not realized because of a failure to consider the great varieties of ways in which a coping response may be expressed (see the discussion of response variables as a source of variance). To take a simple example, dispositional hostility may be expressed in overt aggression, subtle verbal innuendoes, or the withdrawal of affection, depending upon the person and the situation. Thus, the general tendency to respond with hostility may subsume a number of more specific tendencies to engage in particular forms of aggression. Such individual differences in preferred modes of response may be considered an extension of the principle of *individual response specificity*, a concept derived from psychophysiological research (J. Lacey and B. Lacey 1958; see also Engel and Moos 1967). The existence of individual response specificity means that lower-order, as well as general response, tendencies must be assessed or a variety of responses measured. It also means that different measures of the same general response will show little relationship to one another if correlations are calculated across individuals. These points are illustrated in a recent study by Leibowitz (1968) in which the assaultive subscale of the Buss-Durkee Hostility Inventory correlated with direct physical aggression, while the verbal subscale was most highly correlated with role-playing aggression. Physical and role-playing aggression were unrelated.

STIMULUS-ORIENTED DISPOSITIONS.   While response-oriented dispositions emphasize the consistency of coping responses over various situations, stimulus-oriented dispositions refer to the tendency for diverse responses to be organized about some stimulus object or goal. For example, the individual who hates may not only strive to injure his enemy, but he will be sad and angry at his enemy's successes, happy at his defeats, skeptical of his accomplishments, and so on. In other words, the coping responses will vary as a function of the changing status of the stimulus object. Concepts that refer to stimulus-oriented dispositions include: "attitude," "belief," "motive," "sentiment," "complex," "value," and many more. There are important differences between these concepts (see Allport 1935, pp. 798–844; Katz and Stotland 1959, pp. 423–475; McDougall 1936; Rokeach 1968; Smith 1963), but we cannot go into the nuances here.

Stimulus-oriented dispositions include cognitive and behavioral components. The cognitive component is a system of knowledge and belief regarding what is true or false, good or bad, potent or benign, and so on, about the stimulus object. The behavioral component consists of one or more response-oriented dispositions, for example, toward fear, anger, and so forth. In the simplest case, one response tendency would be associated with a single stimulus object—for example, fear (response) of a domineering parent (stimulus object). The disposition may become more complex through the elaboration and differentiation of the cognitive component, so that what was simply fear of a parent may become fear of authority in general. Complexity can also increase as the stimulus object becomes associated, perhaps under different circumstances, with a variety of response tendencies. Thus, if the feared stimulus object became associated with wonder and affection, we might speak of awe and reverence; or hate and prejudice might arise if fear and anger became associated with the same stimulus object.

Numerous authors have emphasized how a person's myriad of beliefs, attitudes, and sentiments become organized into a stable and coherent structure, with attitudes toward the self forming the cornerstone. The forces that mold the structure and hold it together have been investigated under the headings of cognitive balance (Heider 1958), dissonance (Festinger 1957), and congruity (Osgood, Suci, and Tannenbaum 1957). The general line of thought developed in all three models has its origin in the work of Heider, who described cognitive balance as a state "in which the entities comprising the situation and feelings about them fit together without stress" (1958, p. 180). Bramel (1962) has applied this type of analysis to the study of trait attribution, one form of projection. Bramel noted that some traits, such as homosexuality, are anxiety producing because they are dissonant with the self-concept or superego. One way to reduce this anxiety would be to attribute the undesired trait to another person. However, if the individual is consciously aware of the undesired trait, the projection will be an effective coping device only if it is directed toward respected persons. That is, if a respected person possesses the same trait, then perhaps it is not so bad after all, and cognitive imbalance is reduced. Experimental tests (Bramel 1962, 1963) in which subjects were led to believe that they possessed homosexual tendencies confirmed this prediction. Other theorists who have emphasized the ego-defensive functions of attitudes and other stimulus-oriented dispositions are Freud (1930), Fromm (1941), Maslow (1943), Smith, Bruner, and White (1956), and Rokeach (1968).

Instruments have been constructed to assess broad, stimulus-oriented dispositions that may be shared by large numbers of people. The best known of these is perhaps the study of values by Allport, Vernon, and Lindzey (1960). These authors present scales for the assessment of theoretical, economic, aesthetic, political, social, and religious values, the theoretical rationale for which comes from Spranger's (1928) typology. Another ambitious attempt to classify and measure stimulus-oriented dispositions is by Cattell (1959, 1965) and his associates. Cattell's system is very similar to McDougall's (1936) theory of sentiment. His major innovation is the application of factor analytic techniques, with the development of tests to measure sentiments related to career, religion, spouse, parental home, superego, patriotism, and the self, among others (Sweney 1967). Guilford (1959), also using factor analysis, has identified what he calls hormic or motivational traits that appear to be closely related to Cattell's sentiments. Finally, mention should be made of the work of McClelland and his colleagues (Atkinson 1964; McClelland 1955) on the assessment of motives (*n* achievement, *n* power, *n* affiliation, and so forth) using projective techniques.

The above lists of theorists and assessment instruments might give the impression that stimulus-oriented dispositions have been the subject of much research. Such is not the case; the citations offered represent the exception rather than the rule. Actually, most of the research that has centered around stimulus-oriented dispositions has had a distinctly practical flavor—for example, the testing of interests for vocational counseling and attitude measurement in public opinion surveys. We shall, therefore, conclude this discussion with a brief illustration of how stimulus-oriented dispositions may influence the outcome of experimental research, even when they are not the primary focus of interest. Many studies have attempted to relate dispositional anxiety to physiological reactivity during stress. More often than not, no relationship has been found. An experiment by Hodges and Spielberger (1966) indicates one of the reasons why. They found that a subject's score on the Taylor Manifest Anxiety Scale did not predict his cardiac response to the threat of electric shock; however, the magnitude of heart-rate change was related to the subject's specific attitude toward shock. Thus, the lower-order, stimulus-oriented disposition (attitude toward electric shock) had an overriding effect as compared with the more general, response-oriented disposition (anxiety).

THEORETICALLY ORIENTED DISPOSITIONS.   The classification of dispositions as response- and stimulus-oriented is phenotypical, describing either a particular type of response or the organization of different responses about some stimulus object. Recently there has been a significant shift in emphasis from such empirical classifications to the analysis and assessment of underlying mechanisms. This trend is best exemplified by research on cognitive styles, which are characteristic modes of organization in perceptual and intellectual activities. For example, Witkin (1965) and his associates (Witkin et al. 1954) have investigated a dimension called "field–dependence-in-dependence," or "psychological differentiation" (Witkin et al. 1962). Perceptually, the field-dependent person is dominated by the overall organization of the field and has difficulty separating figure from ground. A field-independent person is more apt to see separate parts of the field as individual units. The embedded-figures and rod-and-frame tests used in this research allow easy assessment of these perceptual modes. Cognitively, the field-dependent person does less well at problems that require the use of essential elements in a variety of contexts, has a less articulated body concept, has a less well developed sense of separate identity, and tends to use "global" defenses such as repression and denial. Field-dependence is also characterized by behavioral dependency, is common among obese and alcoholic individuals, ulcer patients, and psychotics who have hallucinations rather than delusions. Field-independent persons, in contrast, tend to show an opposite pattern of response, including preference for intellectualization as a mode of defense (Schimek 1968). It has also been shown that field-independent subjects display sharp cardiovascular changes to insulin injection compared with field-dependent subjects (Silverman, McGough, and Bogdonoff 1967).

Many other types of cognitive styles have been suggested and investigated, including leveling-sharpening (Gardner et al. 1959; Holzman and Gardner 1959; Vick and Jackson 1967), tolerance for unrealistic experiences (Gardner et al. 1959), scanning (Gardner and Long 1962*a*; Holzman 1966), attention and inhibition (Gardner and Long 1962*b*), augmentation-reduction (Petrie 1967), physionomic perception (Rosett, Robbins, and Watson 1968), among others (see Shapiro 1965). At the present time it is difficult to say with any certainty which of these dimensions are valid and independent of the others. We will, therefore, limit ourselves to a few general observations.

Most speculation regarding cognitive styles and controls takes perception as its starting point, and most techniques of assessment are perceptual in nature. Cognitive styles are not restricted to perceptual functioning, however, but include other cognitive and behavioral activities as well. Cognitive styles are thus related to a broad range of coping responses, and their analysis must be in terms of the adaptive requirements of the situation. Gardner and co-workers have stated this point as follows:

Since coordination with reality looms large in our understanding of cognitive controls, their empirical definition must specify situational contexts. . . . The antecedents of cognitive controls must be sought in the task-sets, expectations, and options provided for response; these define the conditions for isolating and defining cognitive controls experimentally. The tendency to ignore the adaptive context of a task is perhaps one of the reasons it has been so difficult to establish the predictive generality of response in different test conditions (1959, pp. 14–15).

We have made similar arguments throughout this chapter with regard to coping in general.

In referring to cognitive styles as "theoretically oriented" we do not mean to imply that they are well understood in terms of underlying dynamics, or that they are founded on some well-established theory. Most investigators of cognitive styles have been strongly influenced by psychoanalytic theory, but the cognitive functions described are not conceived within any narrow theoretical scheme. Indeed, in most psychoanalytic practice, individual differences in characterized traits are still conceptualized primarily in terms of preferred modes of defense; that is, the emphasis is on response-oriented dispositions. Essentially, then, cognitive styles are theoretically oriented dispositions primarily in the sense that they are conceived to be somehow more fundamental or genotypic than are dispositions relating only to a person's preferred mode of response or his attitudes toward particular stimulus objects.

The genotypic nature of theoretically oriented dispositions means that they should exert their influence in a wide variety of situations and behaviors, as was illustrated in the case of field-dependency. Thus, cognitive styles are manifest in situations not necessarily involving threat or challenge, and dispositions for coping with threat as related to a particular style may, therefore, be assessed in nonstressful situations. An example of such nonstressful assessment may be found in the work of Holzman and Gardner (1959), who related the cognitive style of "leveling" to the tendency to use repression as a defense. Using a perceptual, "schematizing test," as they called it, Holzman and Gardner first divided their subjects into levelers and their opposites, sharpeners. Levelers tended to ignore small differences in the sizes of a series of circles, while sharpeners were strongly attuned to such differences, noticing them readily when they occurred. Using the Rorschach Test as the basis of assessing defenses, they found a striking tendency for the previously identified levelers to give Rorschach evidence of repression. The problem here is whether such Rorschach evidence depended on the actual elicitation of an active repressive process (a coping episode) or was merely a characteristic sample of a thinking style that might correlate with the defense mechanism of repression.

An even more striking example of the use of cognitive styles for the assessment of coping dispositions is in the work of Voth, Cancro and Kissen (1968). These investigators tested the hypothesis that certain ego-defense mechanisms are related to autokinesis, the apparent motion of a pinpoint of light in a dark surrounding. The theoretical link between defense and autokinesis is the postulated dimension of ego-closeness–ego-distance. Ego-closeness is characterized by an openness to, and even a dependency upon, environmental stimulation. People on this end of the dimension should experience little autokinesis, because their attention is directed outward and can be focused on the physical stimulus, which in reality does not move. These people presumably should prefer such defenses as repression, externalization, projection, and acting out. This is because the outward deployment of attention reduces awareness of one's inner life and allows discharge of libidinal and aggressive tendencies on external objects. Ego-distance, on the other hand, is characterized by a capacity to withdraw cathexis and to become absorbed in subjective experience. Ego-distant people should, therefore, experience greater autokinesis and a preference for such defenses as withdrawal, intellectualization, and isolation. In an experimental test of these hypothetical relationships, Voth and Cancro report statistically significant correlations in the predicted directions between autokinesis, on the one hand, and defenses (as judged from descriptive accounts of therapeutic interviews), clinical histories, and test results, on the other.

The usefulness of cognitive styles for the assessment of coping dispositions depends, of course, upon the theoretical and empirical relationships between the variable measured directly (for example, autokinesis) and the coping disposition (for example, defensiveness). Some of the correlations reported by Voth and Cancro (1968) were quite respectable in this regard, exceeding the validity coefficients of many psychological tests. For example, correlations ranging from .40 to .76 were found between autokinesis and a scale of defensiveness, depending upon the rater and type of information used to judge defenses. The low end of the scale was characterized by externalization, projection, flight, acting out, and denial through action, while withdrawal, isolation, and intellectualization were characteristic of the other extreme. If such a result proved reliable, then the autokinetic phenomenon would offer a convenient and objective means to assess general trends in defensive style. Unfortunately, although it has been under investigation for nearly a century, little is known about the physiological and psychological mechanisms mediating autokinesis (Royce et al. 1966).

By emphasizing the work on cognitive styles, we do not wish to imply that these are the only theoretically oriented dispositions of relevance to coping. Nevertheless, they do serve to illustrate many of the problems involved in this type of research. Moreover, most tests of cognitive style have one feature that may prove of considerable advantage for assessment—that is, they do not depend upon self-report, which is subject to the same kind of response bias discussed earlier in connection with verbal response variables.

Actually, all three types of dispositional variables discussed in this section are of *potential* theoretical relevance. The distinction between response-oriented, stimulus-oriented, and theoretically oriented dispositions has been made primarily for descriptive purposes, to make easier the discussion of a complex and poorly organized area. The distinction, therefore, refers only to the typical uses of the variables described, not to their potential use. For example, the typical use of the Taylor Manifest Anxiety Scale has been response oriented, that is, as a measure of the tendency to respond with anxiety, regardless of underlying dynamics. However, the test was originally constructed as a measure of Hullian drive, a theoretical construct (Spence 1958). Similarly, although the typical use of stimulus-oriented variables has been pragmatic and atheoretical, this type of disposition formed the theoretical foundation for McDougall's (1936) social psychology. One of the major issues of research and assessment in coping is undoubtedly the provision of a theoretical structure in which all types of dispositional variables may be embedded.

In our discussion of cognitive mediators of coping, three types of *appraisal* processes were distinguished—primary and secondary appraisal, and reappraisal. This three-way distinction was based on theoretical considerations and is independent of the descriptive trichotomy we have been discussing with regard to dispositional variables. Nevertheless, there is a rough correspondence between the two. Stimulus-oriented dispositions, for example, should exert their greatest influence on *primary appraisal*, which is an evaluation based largely on stimulus characteristics. Response-oriented dispositions, on the other hand, are of greater relevance to *secondary appraisal*, which takes into consideration the response options perceived as viable. Finally, what we have referred to as theoretically oriented dispositions are related in certain respects to *reappraisal,* as in the case of cognitive styles and defensive processes. The correspondences are not exact, but they do perhaps form a starting point for analysis and future investigation.

The Interaction of Dispositional and Stimulus Variables

In speaking as we did earlier of coping as a transaction between the person and the environment, it must also be recognized that one cannot properly be separated from the other, except for convenience and for assessment of isolable variables. The language of psychology tends to view the situation or stimulus as separate from the person's dispositions; yet in phenomenological personality analysis it is the latter that gives the former its psychological significance. Using our conceptual language of *appraisal,* whether or not a situation is threatening or gratifying to the person depends on how it is interpreted, and this interpretation derives in part from the cognitive structures that the person has acquired over his lifetime. That is, on the basis of his motives and beliefs, one person will respond to a situation as threatening, while another will respond to the same situation as benign or irrelevant. Thus, both the situation and the person together form, in a sense, a new conceptual unit of analysis that together is different from either variable separately. Said differently, the significance of the situation for coping cannot be considered without reference to the person who is responding to it, and vice versa.

The above point implies that research designs to study coping must utilize simultaneously both kinds of factors or sources of variance, situational and personal (in the case of infrahuman organisms, the most useful person variable might be species differences). This can be illustrated with a study by Lipsitt and Strodtbeck (1967) that highlights the interplay of situational and personal variables in determining the behavioral outcome. The experiment involved assessment of certain personality characteristics of the subjects and the presentation to them of four versions of a court transcript of a jury trial. Three hundred eighty male naval enlisted personnel between the ages of eighteen and twenty-nine were employed. Sex-role identities of these men were assessed first for "unconscious" sexuality by means of a projective test. The test required the subject to complete in any way he chose a series of drawings consisting of a few simple lines. The projective drawing test was scored by experienced judges on the basis of a variety of criteria of male and female symbolic expressions. For example, expanded drawings were scored male, while drawings left open were judged female. Active objects such as motorboats or steamboats were scored male, while passive objects like sailboats and containers were scored female. The criteria were clear enough to make it possible for the judges to achieve a high degree of agreement in judging. The overall score for this test was conceived by the authors as a measure of covert or unconscious masculinity or femininity, the assumption being that subjects would not be aware of the trends in themselves communicated in their drawings.

A second method of assessment was also used, consisting of a questionnaire to which the subjects responded with true or false answers, and which presumably revealed the subjects' conscious sex-role identification, because the implications to the subjects of a large proportion of the questions were considered obvious by the experimenters (this could be a disputed point). Some examples include: "I want to be an important person in the community"; "I prefer a shower to a bath"; and "I would like to work as a dress designer." On the basis of both test results, subjects could fall into one of four types, conscious masculine/unconscious masculine, conscious masculine/unconscious feminine, conscious feminine/unconscious masculine, and conscious feminine/unconscious feminine.

The experimental task consisted of listening to the transcript of the trial in order to make a decision about whether the accused was innocent or guilty. The accused was a former American soldier being tried for treason as a result of alleged activities while he was a Japanese prisoner of war after the fall of Corregidor in 1942. During the actual trial the judge had allowed the introduction of testimony about the defendant's alleged homosexuality on the grounds that it related to the character of the defendant. (On appeal, it was held that this testimony was irrelevant and prejudicial.) The judge had also made a controversial "charge" to the jury containing the assertion that it was appropriate for the jury to consider the defendant's character in arriving at a verdict of guilty or not guilty. This original transcript was edited by the experimenters so as to create four experimental conditions. These conditions involved variations around two basic themes based on the emotionally arousing testimony about homosexuality and the judge's controversial charge to the jury.

The four experimental conditions were as follows: The (ah) transcript serving as the basic case contained *neither* of the two types of touchy material. The (AH) transcript contained *both* the testimony about homosexuality (H) and the judge's charge to the jury (A). The (aH) transcript contained the basic case plus *only* the testimony about homosexuality. And the (Ah) transcript contained the basic case plus only the judge's charge to the jury. The stage was thus set to determine the extent to which the decision about innocence and guilt as given by the subjects is influenced by the two types of emotionally loaded material acting on the various personality types. This was done by exposing subjects from each personality subgroup (persons) to each of the various experimental treatments (situations).

Lipsitt and Strodtbeck reported three particularly interesting findings. First, the (Ah) transcript, which contained only the judge's charge to the jury to the effect that the defendant's character was relevant to the judgment of guilt or innocence, produced an increase in the tendency of *all personality types* to find the defendant guilty. Evidently the judge's point about moral character being relevant to the verdict resulted in a more punitive stance among all types of persons.

Second, in the (aH) treatment, where homosexuality alone was introduced, the personality group that was presumably *unconsciously feminine and consciously masculine* gave a greater number of guilty verdicts than would be expected by chance. Eighty-seven percent of that group voted guilty, compared with a little over 50 percent in the other groups. In effect, for this personality type the introduction of homosexuality into the trial produced a distortion of the basic judicial issue. The authors suggested that this type of person with "suppressed feminine impulses" has learned to inhibit, and feel punitively toward, his own feminine tendencies, and hence does not hesitate to be punitive toward the defendant for his own overtly expressed homosexuality.

Third, in the (AH) treatment condition, in which both the judge's charge and the homosexual testimony were included, the personality group identified as both *consciously and unconsciously feminine* showed a marked tendency to give not-guilty verdicts (65 percent), compared with the other groups which tended to vote guilty (82 percent). The authors suggested interpretively that in these persons, their own conscious as well as unconscious homosexual inclinations led them to be especially sensitive to the accusation of homosexuality brought against another and used as evidence against his character; they overreacted to a sense of injustice that they felt was reflected by the impugnment of the defendant's character by an irrelevant consideration.

Naturally, we must be cautious in accepting the assumption of Lipsitt and Strodtbeck that the projective test scores measured unconscious sexual identification, while the questionnaire measured its conscious counterpart, although this assumption does well in accounting for the results and is at least as reasonable as any other. But even if the assumption is rejected, the experiment illustrates very well the key point we made above, that *a situation affects people in different ways depending on the kind of person who is responding to it.* The study of the determinants of coping should be designed to include simultaneously situational variables and those relevant to personality with which such situational variables communicate. When the two factors are combined, as they are in the above experiment, the coping response outcome is not dependent on either alone, but on a new unit of analysis, for which we have no adequate vocabulary. For want of a better term we might call this unit "the *appraised* significance of the situation," which, as we have pointed out, will be the result of both situational and person variables, measurable beforehand so as to eliminate any circularity. Although we can study potent situational determinants of coping separately from personality determinants, especially those that tend to have similar effects on most persons, and although we can study potent personality variables separately also, in the long run we will have to consider the interplay of both. Although such a conclusion should be rather obvious, the principle underlying it is all too commonly overlooked in psychological research.

SUMMARY

In this chapter we have tried to provide a sweeping overview of the area of coping from a psychological perspective, enunciating a number of theoretical and methodological issues that must be tackled if a general psychology of coping is to be developed. In so doing we necessarily have given minimal attention to our own specific research and theorizing and have illustrated with, rather than reviewed, the huge volume of research that could be regarded as falling under the rubric of coping.

At the outset, we examined a number of preliminary issues. The one with which we began concerned the definition of coping, and the distinction between the healthy, positively adaptive problem-solving efforts characteristic of low-stakes situations, and the primitive and maladaptive forms of coping typically associated with conditions of high stakes (that is, severe threat, frustration, conflict, and great challenge). Next in line was a statement of the unfulfilled need for a *description and classification system* within which to view coping processes and their observed antecedents and consequences. We examined some of the issues involved in classification as illustrated by a group of approaches to defining defensive polarities, such as repression-sensitization, repression-isolation, and avoiding-coping. The key issue in such a rudimentary classification is theoretical and concerns the nature of coping processes implied in use of such terms. This discussion of defensive polarities offered a limited perspective on the current state of affairs in coping research. The following four points emerged and formed the rationale for much of the subsequent discussion. First, there is a general tendency to overlook the distinction between dispositional (personality) and episodic (response) variables. Second, the role of situational variables in shaping coping is seldom given more than token acknowledgment. Third, much current research in coping is parochial and limited in scope and does not encompass many varieties of coping responses. Finally, rapid progress in the development of an adequate psychology of coping is unlikely until a theoretically based system of classification for coping responses has been evolved.

At this point we provided a brief review of our own theoretical position concerning coping and emotions. This position emphasizes the mediating cognitive processes of *appraisal and reappraisal* by which the individual obtains and evaluates information about the adaptive significance of an environmental event. From such information a choice of coping alternatives is made. Four basic strategies of empirical research on the cognitive mediators of emotion and coping were reviewed—namely, direct manipulation of appraisal and reappraisal, indirect manipulation, making inferences from self-reports, and selection of subjects on the basis of relevant personality dispositions. Our empirical work using each of these research strategies was briefly examined.

A *sources-of-variance* model was then developed, around which the subject matter of coping was organized. Within this model, three main types of variables were distinguished: responses, situations, and persons. The last three sections of the paper have been devoted to separate discussions of each of these sources of variance.

Four classes of observable *response data* were considered, from which coping processes are inferred: verbal reports, physiological changes, expressive reactions, and behavioral acts. Perhaps the most difficult theoretical and methodological issue in making such inferences is the common situation where disagreement occurs between one or another of these classes of response. Although such disagreement could arise from artifacts of measurement, they also reflect the somewhat independent function of each response class in the organism's adaptation to physical and social demands. The point needs to be stressed that when individual responses seem to diverge, the resulting pattern often contains within it important information about eliciting conditions and the nature of the coping process. Rules for translating such patterns into theoretically meaningful concepts are still very primitive and without adequate empirical support.

Situations, the second source of variance considered, shape coping processes via the organism's appraisal of the event with which he must cope. Principles by which situations determine the coping process are badly needed, particularly rules about the different situations that are *functionally equivalent* in producing the same coping process. Certain situations, for example, may pull for sensitizing or vigilant forms of defense in threatening contexts, while others may tend to elicit repressive-avoidant ones.

To begin with, a distinction was made between the total ecology of the person or animal in the natural setting and the specific controlled stimulus to which he might be exposed in the laboratory. An ecological variable, within our theoretical framework, is any factor that influences the mechanisms underlying appraisal. It was also pointed out that the laboratory stimulus event is apt to be isolated from the stream of the organism's life events, and thus might have a different significance for him than a similar stimulus event might have in ordinary living. We then presented a preliminary classification of types of stimuli relevant to coping, which we divided into *intrinsic stimulus properties* (information related to the specific stimulus), *extrinsic stimulus properties* (general to a wide variety of stimuli, for example, imminence, ambiguity), and *response-determined stimulus properties* (those determined by the available response to that stimulus).

With respect to the dimension of *persons*, we first gave a brief overview of the logic of dispositional variables, also touching on the development of psychological dispositions and the fallacy of their reification in terms of drive or energy. There are many types of personality dispositions, and we offered a classification into three types. Two of these, *response-oriented* and *stimulus-oriented* dispositions, are essentially atheoretical; that is, they involve no necessarily postulated mechanism underlying the existence of the disposition to cope in one way or another. A third type, *theoretically oriented* dispositions, comprises those in which some mechanism is assumed, as in the case of the cognitive dispositions of field-dependence and field-independence.

Finally, it was argued that situations have no meaning for coping without regard to persons. Because situational variables interact with personality variables, a new integrative unit of analysis is needed to supplant reference to the two separate classes of variables, which for want of a better term we have called the *appraised significance of the situation*. Because appraisal is a function of both situational and personality variables, this unit expresses the transaction between the person and the environment in terms of the cognitive processes by means of which a given type of person processes and evaluates information about the environment.

An effective general science of coping depends on the ultimate resolution of all of the issues that we have posed here, those pertaining to the nature of the responses that define coping and from which the coping process is to be inferred, those concerning the situational and personality determinants of these processes, and those relevant to the evaluated coping outcome in the form of "healthy," adaptive mastery or maladaptation. Most research on coping at the present time very naturally chooses some particular context of threat or challenge, some given population, and some specific coping response to study, usually without regard to the connection of these to other contexts, types of persons, and responses. Our own research is no exception, being mainly limited to the experimental context of vicarious (motion picture) threats, college students, and situations in which intrapsychic coping processes are all that a subject can realistically bring to bear against the threat. Researchers usually attempt to generalize from these limited situations to broader contexts of coping responses, coping situations, and types of persons. A broad conception of coping requires bringing together such diverse though limited research contexts within a comprehensive theoretical framework. This chapter is intended to set the stage for progress toward this presently unattainable goal.

REFERENCES

Aas, A. *Mutilation fantasies and autonomic response*. Oslo, Norway: Oslo University Press, 1958.

Adelson, J. Personality. In P. Mussen and M. Rosenzweig, eds.. *Annual review of psychology*, vol. 20. Palo Alto, Calif.: Annual Reviews, 1969.

Alfert, E. Reactions to a vicariously experienced and a direct threat. Ph.D. dissertation, University of California, Berkeley, 1964.

Allport, F. *Theories of perception and the concept of structure*. New York: Wiley, 1955.

Allport, G. W. Attitudes. In C. Murchison, ed., *A handbook of social psychology*. Worcester, Mass.: Clark University Press, 1935.

Allport, G. W., Vernon, P. E., and Lindzey, G. *Study of values*. 3rd ed. Boston: Houghton Mifflin, 1960.

Andrew, J. M. Coping styles, stress-relevant learning, and recovery from surgery. Ph.D. dissertation, University of California, Los Angeles, 1967.

Andrew, R. J. Evolution of facial expression. *Science*, 1963, *142*, 1034–1041.

Atkinson, J. W. *An introduction to motivation*. Princeton, N. J.: Van Nostrand, 1964.

Averill, J. R. Grief: Its nature and significance. *Psychological Bulletin*, 1968, *70*, 721–748.

Averill, J. R., and Opton, E. M., Jr. Psychophysiological assessment: Rationale and problems. In P. McReynolds, ed., *Advances in psychological assessment*, vol. 1. Palo Alto, Calif.: Science and Behavior Books, 1968.

Averill, J. R., Opton, E. J., Jr., and Lazarus, R. S. Cross-cultural studies of psychophysiological responses during stress and emotion. *International Journal of Psychology*, 1969, *4*, 83–102.

Azrin, N. H., Hutchinson, R. R., and Hake, D. F. Attack, avoidance, and escape reactions to aversive shock. *Journal of the Experimental Analysis of Behavior*, 1967, *10*, 131–148.

Bandler, R. J., Jr., Madaras, G. R., and Bem, D. J. Self-observation as a source of pain perception. *Journal of Personality and Social Psychology*, 1968, *9*, 205–209.

Barfield, R. J., and Sachs, B. D. Sexual behavior: Stimulation by painful electrical shock to skin in male rats. *Science*, 1968, *161*, 392–395.

Barker, R. G. *Ecological psychology*. Stanford, Calif.: Stanford University Press, 1968.

Barker, R. G., Dembo, T., and Lewin, K. Frustration and regression: A study of young children. *University of Iowa Studies in Child Welfare*, 1941, *18*(1).

Beach, F. A., and Ransom, T. W. Effects of environmental variation on ejaculatory frequency in male rats. *Journal of Comparative and Physiological Psychology*, 1967, *64*, 384–387.

Bergan, J. R. A special scoring procedure for minimizing response bias on the School Anxiety Questionnaire. *Psychology in the Schools*, 1968, *5*, 210–216.

Berkowitz, L. Experiments on automatism and intent in human aggression. In C. D. Clemente and D. B. Lindsley, eds., *Aggression and defense*. Berkeley and Los Angeles: University of California Press, 1967.

Berlyne, D. *Conflict, arousal and curiosity*. New York: McGraw-Hill, 1960.

Block, J. *The challenge of response sets*. New York: Appleton-Century-Crofts, 1965.

Bramel, D. A dissonance theory approach to defensive projection. *Journal of Abnormal and Social Psychology*, 1962, *64*, 121–129.

———. Selection of a target for defensive projection. *Journal of Abnormal and Social Psychology*, 1963, *66*, 318–324.

Brown, C. C., ed. *Methods in psychophysiology*. Baltimore: Williams Wilkins, 1967.

Brown, J. S. *The motivation of behavior*. New York: McGraw-Hill, 1961.

Byrne, D. Repression-sensitization as a dimension of personality. In B. A. Maher, ed., *Progress in experimental personality research*, vol. 1. New York: Academic Press, 1964.

Campbell, D. T. Recommendations for APA test standards regarding construct, trait, or discriminant validity. *American Psychologist*, 1960, *15*, 546–553.

Cattell, R. B. The dynamic calculus: Concepts and crucial experiments. In M. R. Jones, ed., *Nebraska symposium on motivation*, vol. 7. Lincoln: University of Nebraska Press, 1959.

———. The scientific analysis of personality. Baltimore: Penguin Books, 1965.

Carnap, R. The methodological character of theoretical concepts. In H. Feigl and M. Scriven, eds., *Minnesota studies in the philosophy of science*, vol. 1. *The foundations of science and the concepts of psychology and psychoanalysis*. Minneapolis: University of Minnesota Press, 1956.

Clyde, D. J. *Manual for the Clyde Mood Scale*. Coral Gables, Fla.: University of Miami Biometric Laboratory, 1963.

Cofer, C. N., and Appley, M. H. *Motivation: Theory and research*. New York: Wiley, 1964.

Couch, A., and Keniston, K. Yeasayers and naysayers: Agreeing response set as a personality variable. *Journal of Abnormal and Social Psychology*, 1960, *60*, 151–174.

Cronbach, L. J. *Essentials of psychological testing*. New York: Harper & Brothers, 1960.

Cronbach, L. J., and Meehl, P. E. Construct validity in psychological tests. *Psychological Bulletin*, 1955, *52*, 281–302.

Crowne, P., and Marlowe, D. *The approval motive*. New York: Wiley, 1964.

Darwin, C. *The expression of emotions in man and animals* (1873). Chicago: University of Chicago Press, 1965.

Davison, L. A. Adaptation to a threatening stimulus. Ph.D. dissertation, University of California, Berkeley, 1963.

Deese, J., Lazarus, R. S., and Keenan, J. Anxiety, anxiety reduction, and stress in learning. *Journal of Experimental Psychology*, 1953, *46*, 55–60.

Dewey, J. The reflex arc concept in psychology. *Psychological Review*, 1896, *3*, 357–370.

Dicks, D., Myers, R. E., and Kling, A. Uncus and amygdala lesions: Effects on social behavior in the free-ranging rhesus monkey. *Science*, 1969, *165*, 69–71.

Ekman, P., and Friesen, W. V. Nonverbal behavior in psychotherapy research. In J. Shlien, ed., *Research in psychotherapy*, vol. 3. Washington, D. C.: American Psychological Association, 1968.

———. The repertoire of nonverbal behavior-categories, origins, usage and coding. *Semiotica*, 1969, *1*, 49–98.

Endler, N. S. Estimating variance components from mean squares for random and mixed-effects analysis of variance models. *Perceptual and Motor Skills*, 1966, *22*, 559–570.

Endler, N. S., and Hunt, J. McV. Sources of behavioral variance as measured by the S-R Inventory of Anxiousness. *Psychological Bulletin*, 1966, *65*, 336–346.

———. S-R inventories of hostility and comparisons of the proportions of variance from persons, responses, and situations for hostility and anxiousness. *Journal of Personality and Social Psychology*, 1968, *9*, 309–315.

Engel, B. T., and Moos, R. H. The generality of specificity. *Archives of General Psychiatry*, 1967, *16*, 573–581.

Escalona, S., and Heider, G. *Prediction and outcome*. New York: Basic Books, 1959.

Eysenck, H. J. *The biological basis of personality*. Springfield, Ill.: Charles C. Thomas, 1967.

Fawl, C. L. Disturbances experienced by children in their natural habitats. In R. G. Barker, ed., *The stream of behavior*. New York: Appleton-Century-Crofts, 1963.

Feigl, H. Principles and problems of theory construction in psychology. In *Current trends in psychological theory*. Pittsburgh: University of Pittsburgh Press, 1951.

Fenz, W. D., and Epstein, S. Measurement of approach-avoidance conflict along a stimulus-dimension by a thematic apperception test. *Journal of Personality*, 1962, *30*, 613–632.

Festinger, L. *A theory of cognitive dissonance*. New York: Row, Peterson, 1957.

Festinger, L., Burnham, C. A., Ono, H., and Bamber, D. Efference and the conscious experience. *Journal of Experimental Psychology*, 1967, *74*, (whole no. 637).

Fiske, D. W. Homogeneity and variation in measuring personality. *American Psychologist*, 1963, *18*, 643–652.

Folkins, C. H. Temporal factors and the cognitive mediators of stress reaction. *Journal of Personality and Social Psychology*, 1970, *14*(2), 178–184.

Folkins, C. H., Lawson, K. D., Opton, E. M., Jr., and Lazarus, R. S. Desensitization and the experimental reduction of threat. *Journal of Abnormal Psychology*, 1968, *73*, 100–113.

Freud, A. *The ego and the mechanisms of defense.* New York: International Universities Press, 1946.

Freud, S. Psychoanalytic notes upon an autobiographical account of a case of paranoia (dementia paranoides). In *Collected Papers*, vol. 3 (1911). London: Hogarth Press, 1933.

――――. *Inhibitions, symptoms and anxiety* (1926). Translated by A. Strachey. London: Hogarth Press, 1936.

――――. *Civilization and its discontents* (1930). Translated by J. Riviere. London: Hogarth Press, 1957.

Frijda, N. H. Recognition of emotion. In L. Berkowitz, ed., *Advances in experimental social psychology*, vol. 4. New York: Academic Press, 1969.

Fromm, E. *Escape from freedom.* New York: Rinehart, 1941.

Gardner, R. W., Holzman, P. S., Klein, G. S., Linton, H. B., and Spence, D. P. Cognitive control, a study of individual consistencies in cognitive behavior. *Psychological Issues*, 1959, *1* (4).

Gardner, R. W., and Long, R. Control, defense, and centration effect: A study of scanning behavior. *British Journal of Psychology*, 1962a, *53*, 129–140.

――――. Cognitive controls of attention and inhibition: A study of individual consistencies. *British Journal of Psychology*, 1962b, *53*, 381–388.

Gibson, E., and Walk, R. The "visual cliff." *Scientific American*, 1960, *202*, 64–71.

Gibson, J. J. *The senses considered as perceptual systems.* New York: Houghton Mifflin, 1966.

Gleser, G. C., and Ihilevich, D. An objective instrument for measuring defense mechanisms. *Journal of Consulting and Clinical Psychology*, 1969, *33*, 51–60.

Goldstein, M. J. The relationship between coping and avoiding behavior and response to fear-arousing propaganda. *Journal of Abnormal and Social Psychology*, 1959, *58*, 247–252.

Golin, S., Herron, E. W., Lakota, R., and Reineck, L. Factor analytic study of the manifest anxiety, extraversion, and repression-sensitization scales. *Journal of Consulting Psychology*, 1967, *31*, 564–569.

Greenfield, N. S., and Sternbach, R. A., eds. *Handbook of psychophysiology.* New York: Holt, Rinehart & Winston, 1969.

Grinker, R. R., and Spiegel, J. P. *Men under stress.* Philadelphia: Blakiston, 1945.

Guilford, J. P. *Personality.* New York: McGraw-Hill, 1959.

Haan, N. A tripartite model of ego functioning: Values and clinical and research applications. *Journal of Nervous and Mental Disease*, 1969, *148*, 14–30.

Haggard, E. A., and Isaacs, K. S. Micromomentary facial expressions as indicators of ego mechanisms in psychotherapy. In L. A. Gottschalk and A. H. Auerbach, eds., *Methods of research in psychotherapy.* New York: Appleton-Century-Crofts, 1966.

Hampshire, S. Dispositions. *Analysis*, 1953, *14*, 5–11.

Hebb, D. O. On the nature of fear. *Psychological Review*, 1946, *53*, 259–276.

Heider, F. *The psychology of interpersonal relations.* New York: Wiley, 1958.

Heider, G. M. Vulnerability in infants and young children: A pilot study. *Genetic Psychology Monographs*, 1966, *73*, 1–216.

Hempel, C. G. Operationism, observation, and scientific terms. In A. Danto and S. Morgenbesser, eds., *Philosophy of science*. Cleveland: World Publishing, 1960.

Hodges, W. F., and Spielberger, C. D. The effects of threat of shock on heart rate for subjects who differ in manifest anxiety and fear of shock. *Psychophysiology*, 1966, *2*, 287–294.

Holzman, P. S. Scanning: A principle of reality contact. *Perceptual and Motor Skills*, 1966, *23*, 835–844.

Holzman, P. S., and Gardner, R. W. Leveling and repression. *Journal of Abnormal and Social Psychology*, 1959, *59*, 151–155.

Hooff, J. A. R. A. M. van. The facial displays of the catarrhine monkeys and apes. In D. Morris, ed., *Primate ethology*. Chicago: Aldine, 1967.

Jenkin, N. Affective processes in perception. *Psychological Bulletin*, 1957, *54*, 100–127.

Kassebaum, G. G., Couch, A. S., and Slater, P. E. The factorial dimensions of the MMPI. *Journal of Consulting Psychology*, 1959, *23*, 226–236.

Katz, D., and Stotland, E. A preliminary statement to a theory of attitude structure and change. In S. Koch, ed., *Psychology: A study of a science*, vol. 3. New York: McGraw-Hill, 1959.

Kenny, A. *Action, emotion and will*. London: Routledge & Kegan Paul, 1963.

Lacey, J. I., and Lacey, B. C. Verification and extension of the principle of autonomic response stereotypy. *American Journal of Psychology*, 1958, *71*, 50.

Lazarus, R. S. *Psychological stress and the coping process*. New York: McGraw-Hill, 1966.

————. Emotions and adaptation: Conceptual and empirical relations. In W. Arnold, ed., *Nebraska symposium on motivation*, vol. 16. Lincoln: University of Nebraska Press, 1968.

Lazarus, R. S., and Alfert, E. The short-circuiting of threat. *Journal of Abnormal and Social Psychology*, 1964, *69*, 195–205.

Lazarus, R. S., Averill, J. R., and Opton, E. M., Jr. Toward a cognitive theory of emotion. In M. B. Arnold, ed., *Feelings and emotions*. New York: Academic Press, 1970.

Lazarus, R. S., and Opton, E. M., Jr. The study of psychological stress: A summary of theoretical formulations and experimental findings. In C. D. Spielberger, ed., *Anxiety and behavior*. New York: Academic Press, 1966.

Lazarus, R. S., Opton, E. M., Jr., Nomikos, M. S., and Rankin, N. O. The principle of short-circuiting of threat: Further evidence. *Journal of Personality*, 1965, *33*, 622–635.

Lazarus, R. S., Speisman, J. C., Mordkoff, A. M., and Davison, L. A. A laboratory study of psychological stress produced by a motion picture film. *Psychological Monographs*, 1962, *76* (34, whole no. 553).

Lefcourt, H. M. Repression-sensitization: A measure of the evaluation of emotional expression. *Journal of Consulting Psychology*, 1966, *30*, 444–449.

Leibowitz, G. Comparison of self-report and behavioral techniques of assessing aggression. *Journal of Consulting and Clinical Psychology*, 1968, *32*, 21–25.

Lettvin, J. Y., Maturana, H. R., McCulloch, W. S., and Pitts, W. H. What the frog's eye tells the frog's brain. *Proceedings of the Institute of Radio Engineers*, 1959, *47*, 1940–1951.

Levine, M., and Spivack, G. *The Rorschach index of repressive style*. Springfield, Ill.: Charles C. Thomas, 1964.

Lewin, K. *A dynamic theory of personality*. Translated by K. E. Zener and D. K. Adams. New York: McGraw-Hill, 1935.

Lipsitt, P. D., and Strodtbeck, F. L. Defensiveness in decision making as a function of sex-role identification. *Journal of Personality and Social Psychology*, 1967, *6*, 10–15.

Luborsky, L., Blinder, B., and Schimek, J. Looking, recalling and GSR as a function of defense. *Journal of Abnormal Psychology*, 1965, *70*, 270–280.

Lykken, D. T. Neuropsychology and psychophysiology in personality research. In E. F. Borgatta and W. W. Lambert, eds., *Handbook of personality theory and research*. Chicago: Rand McNally, 1967.

Mahl, G. F. The lexical and linguistic levels in the expression of the emotions. In P. H. Knapp, ed., *Expression of the emotions in man*. New York: International Universities Press, 1963.

Maier, N. R. F. *Frustration*. New York: McGraw-Hill, 1949.

Maier, S. F., Seligman, M. E. P., and Solomon, R. L. Pavlovian fear conditioning and learned helplessness: Effects on escape and avoidance behavior of (a) the CS-US contingency and (b) the independence of the US and voluntary responding. In B. A. Campbell and R. M. Church, eds., *Punishment*. New York: Appleton-Century-Crofts, 1968.

Marler, P., and Hamilton, W. J. *Mechanisms of animal behavior*. New York: Wiley, 1967.

Maslow, A. H. The authoritarian character structure. *Journal of Social Psychology*, 1943, *18*, 401–411.

Masserman, J. H. *Behavior and neurosis*. Chicago: University of Chicago Press, 1943.

Masters, W. H., and Johnson, V. E. *Human sexual response*. Boston: Little, Brown, 1966.

McClelland, D. C., ed. *Studies in motivation*. New York: Appleton-Century-Crofts, 1955.

McDougall, W. *An introduction to social psychology*. 23rd ed. London: Methuen, 1936.

McReynolds, P. Relations between psychological and physiological indices of anxiety. Paper presented to the convention of the Western Psychological Association, San Francisco, May 1967.

———. The assessment of anxiety: A survey of available techniques. In P. McReynolds, ed., *Advances in psychological assessment*, vol. 1. Palo Alto, Calif.: Science and Behavior Books, 1968.

Mechanic, D. *Students under stress*. New York: Free Press, 1962.

Mehrabian, A. Attitudes in relation to the forms of communicator-object relationship in spoken communications. *Journal of Personality*, 1966, *34*, 80–93.

Mendelsohn, G. A., and Griswold, B. Anxiety and repression as predictors of the use of incidental cues in problem solving. *Journal of Personality and Social Psychology*, 1967, *6*, 353–359.

Menninger, K. A. Regulatory devices of the ego under major stress. *International Journal of Psycho Analysis*, 1954, *35*, 412–420.

Miller, D. R., and Swanson, G. E. *Inner conflict and defense*. New York: Holt, Rinehart & Winston, 1960.

Miller, N. E. Liberalization of basic S-R concepts: Extensions to conflict behavior, motivation and social learning. In S. Koch, ed., *Psychology: A study of a science*, vol. 2. New York: McGraw-Hill, 1959.

Monat, A., Averill, J. R., and Lazarus, R. S. Psychophysiological response during the anticipation of shock under different conditions of uncertainty. Paper presented to the convention of the Western Psychological Association, Los Angeles, April 1970.

Moos, R. H. Situational analysis of a therapeutic community milieu. *Journal of Abnormal Psychology*, 1968, *73*, 49–61.

Moos, R. H., and Clemes, S. R. Multivariate study of the patient-therapist system. *Journal of Consulting Psychology*, 1967, *31*, 119–130.

Murphy, L. B. *The widening world of childhood: Paths toward mastery.* New York: Basic Books, 1962.

Nomikos, M. S., Opton, E. M., Jr., Averill, J. R., and Lazarus, R. S. Surprise versus suspense in the production of stress reaction. *Journal of Personality and Social Psychology*, 1968, *8*, 204–208.

Nowlis, V. Research with the mood adjective check list. In S. S. Tompkins and C. Izard, eds., *Affect, cognition and personality.* New York: Springer, 1965.

Osgood, C. E. Studies of the generality of affective meaning systems. *American Psychologist*, 1962, *17*, 10–28.

———. Dimensionality of the semantic space for communication via facial expressions. *Scandinavian Journal of Psychology*, 1966, 7, 1–30.

Osgood, C. E., Suci, G. J., and Tannenbaum, P. H. *The measurement of meaning.* Urbana: University of Illinois Press, 1957.

Pap, A. *An introduction to the philosophy of science.* New York: Free Press, 1962.

Parsons, O. A., Fulgenzi, L. B., and Edelberg, R. Aggressiveness and psychophysiological responsivity in groups of repressors and sensitizers. *Journal of Personality and Social Psychology*, 1969, *12*, 235–244.

Peters, R. S. The concept of motivation. 2nd ed. London: Routledge & Kegan Paul, 1960.

Petrie, A. *Individuality in pain and suffering.* Chicago: University of Chicago Press, 1967.

Piaget, J. *The origins of intelligence in children.* New York: International Universities Press, 1952.

Price, D. B., Thaler, M., and Mason, J. W. Preoperative emotional states and adrenal cortical activity. *AMA Archives of Neurology and Psychiatry*, 1957, 77, 646–656.

Radloff, R., and Helmreich, R. *Groups under stress: Psychological research in Sealab II.* New York: Appleton-Century-Crofts, 1968.

Rapaport, D. *Collected papers.* Edited by M. M. Gill. New York: Basic Books, 1967.

Riess, W. F. The effect of psychotherapy-like interviews upon adaptation to psychological stress. Ph.D. dissertation, University of California, Berkeley, 1964.

Rokeach, M. *Beliefs, attitudes, and values.* San Francisco: Jossey-Bass, 1968.

Rosenfeld, H. M. Instrumental affiliative functions of facial and gestural expressions. *Journal of Personality and Social Psychology*, 1966, *4*, 65–72.

Rosenwald, G. C. The assessment of anxiety in psychological experimentation: A theoretical reformulation and test. *Journal of Abnormal and Social Psychology*, 1961, *62*, 666–673.

Rosett, H. L., Robbins, H., and Watson, W. S. Physiognomic perception as a cognitive control principle. *Perceptual and Motor Skills*, 1968, *26*, 707–719.

Royce, J. R., Carron, A. B., Aftanas, M., Lehman, R. S., and Blumenthal, A. The autokinetic phenomenon: A critical review. *Psychological Review*, 1966, *65*, 243–260.

Ryle, G. *The concept of mind.* London: Hutchinson, 1949.

Sachar, E. J., MacKenzie, J. M., Binstock, W. A., and Mack, J. E. Corticosteroid responses to the psychotherapy of reactive depressions: II. Further clinical and physiological implications. *Psychosomatic Medicine*, 1968, *30*, 23–44.

Sarbin, T. R. Ontology recapitulates philology: The mythic nature of anxiety. *American Psychologist*, 1968, *23*, 411–418.

Sarnoff, I., and Zimbardo, P. G. Anxiety, fear and social affiliation. *Journal of Abnormal and Social Psychology*, 1961, *62*, 356–363.

Schachter, S. *The psychology of affiliation.* Stanford, Calif.: Stanford University Press, 1959.

Schafer, R. *Psychoanalytic interpretation in Rorschach testing.* New York: Grune and Stratton, 1954.

Schimek, J. G. Cognitive style and defenses: A longitudinal study of intellectualization and field independence. *Journal of Abnormal Psychology*, 1968, *73*, 575–580.

Schlosberg, H. Three dimensions of emotion. *Psychological Review*, 1954, *61*, 81–88.

Scott, J. P. *Aggression.* Chicago: University of Chicago Press, 1958.

Sells, S. B. Ecology and the science of psychology. *Multivariate Behavioral Research*, 1966, *1*, 131–144.

Shapiro, D. *Neurotic styles.* New York: Basic Books, 1965.

Shapiro, D., and Crider, A. Psychophysiological approaches in social psychology. In G. Lindzey and E. Aronson, eds., *Handbook of social psychology*, vol. 3. *Research methods.* Reading, Mass.: Addison-Wesley, 1969.

Sherif, M., and Sherif, C. W. Varieties of social stimulus situations. In S. B. Sells, ed., *Stimulus determinants of behavior.* New York: Ronald Press, 1963.

Sidle, A., Moos, R. H., Adams, J., and Cady, P. Development of a coping scale. *Archives of General Psychiatry*, 1969, *20*, 225–232.

Silverman, A. J., McGough, W. E., and Bogdonoff, M. D. Perceptual correlates of the physiological response to insulin. *Psychosomatic Medicine*, 1967, *30*, 252–264.

Smith, M. B. Personal values in the study of lives. In R. W. White, ed., *The study of lives.* New York: Atherton, 1963.

Smith, M. B., Bruner, J. S., and White, R. W. *Opinions and personality.* New York: Wiley, 1956.

Snider, J. C., ed. *Semantic differential technique: A source book.* Chicago: Aldine, 1969.

Solomon, R. L., and Wynne, L. C. Traumatic avoidance learning: Acquisition in normal dogs. *Psychological Monographs*, 1953, *67* (4, Whole No. 354).

Speisman, J. C., Lazarus, R. S., Mordkoff, A., and Davison, L. Experimental reduction of stress based on ego-defense theory. *Journal of Abnormal and Social Psychology*, 1964, *68*, 367–380.

Spence, K. W. A theory of emotionally based drive (D) and its relation to performance in simple learning situations. *American Psychologist*, 1958, *13*, 131–141.

Spielberger, C. D. Theory and research on anxiety. In C. D. Spielberger, ed., *Anxiety and behavior.* New York: Academic Press, 1966.

Spranger, E. *Types of men: The psychology and ethics of personality.* 5th ed. Halle: M. Niemeyer, 1928.

Sweney, A. B. Objective measurement of strength of dynamic structure factors. In R. B. Cattell and F. W. Warburton, eds., *Objective personality and motivation tests.* Urbana: University of Illinois Press, 1967.

Taylor, D. A., Wheeler, L., and Altman, I. Stress relations in socially isolated groups. *Journal of Personality and Social Psychology*, 1968, *9*, 369–376.

Taylor, J. A. A personality scale for manifest anxiety. *Journal of Abnormal and Social Psychology*, 1953, *48*, 285–290.

Venables, P., and Martin, I., eds. *A manual of psychophysiological methods.* New York: Wiley, 1967.

Vick, O. C., and Jackson, D. N. Cognitive styles in the schematizing process: A critical evaluation. *Educational and Psychological Measurement,* 1967, *27,* 267–286.

Voth, H. M., Cancro, R., and Kissen, M. Choice of defense. *Archives of General Psychiatry,* 1968, *18,* 36–41.

Weinstein, J., Averill, J. R., Opton, E. M., Jr., and Lazarus, R. S. Defensive style and discrepancy between self-report and physiological indices of stress. *Journal of Personality and Social Psychology,* 1968, *10,* 406–413.

Welsh, G. S. Factor dimensions A and R. In G. S. Welsh and W. G. Dahlstrom, eds., *Basic Readings on the MMPI in psychology and medicine.* Minneapolis: University of Minnesota Press, 1956.

Wenger, M. A., Averill, J. R., and Smith, B. D. B. Autonomic activity during sexual arousal. *Psychophysiology,* 1968, *4,* 468–478.

Werner, H., and Wapner, S. Toward a general theory of perception. *Psychological Review,* 1952, *59,* 324–338.

Wessman, A. E., and Ricks, D. F. *Mood and personality.* New York: Holt, 1966.

Witkin, H. A. Psychological differentiation and forms of pathology. *Journal of Abnormal Psychology,* 1965, *70,* 317–336.

Witkin, H. A., Dyk, R. B., Faterson, H. F., Goodenough, D. R., and Karp, S. A. *Psychological differentiation.* New York: Wiley, 1962.

Witkin, H. A., Lewis, H. B., Machover, K., Meissner, P. B., and Wapner, S. *Personality through perception.* New York: Harper & Row, 1954.

Wolff, C. T., Friedman, S. B., Hofer, M. A., and Mason, J. W. Relationship between psychological defenses and mean urinary 17-hydroxycorticosteroid excretion rates: I. A predictive study of parents of fatally ill children. *Psychosomatic Medicine,* 1964, *26,* 576–591.

Wundt, W. *Grundzüge der physiologishchen Psychologie,* vol. 2. 5th ed. Leipzig: Wilhelm Engelman, 1902.

Zuckerman, M. The development of an affect adjective check list for the measurement of anxiety. *Journal of Consulting Psychology,* 1960, *24,* 457–462.

Zuckerman, M., and Lubin, B. *Manual for the Multiple Affect Adjective Check List.* San Diego, Calif.: Educational and Industrial Testing Service, 1965.

11

Adjustment as Person-Environment Fit

JOHN R. P. FRENCH, JR.,
WILLARD RODGERS, AND SIDNEY COBB

The psychological literature contains a wide variety of conceptions and criteria of mental health that typically are descriptive, nonquantitative, and sufficiently vague so that one cannot be sure how one concept relates to another. This chapter presents a *quantitative* approach to adjustment and coping. By dealing with a limited segment of this area, we will attempt a more precise conceptualization that leads to quantitative measures. We will present a set of defined concepts, a notation, and a simple model that shows the relationships among the following conceptions of mental health: adjustment, adaptation, environmental mastery, contact with reality, accuracy of self-assessment, coping, and defense. The measures for elements in this model will be illustrated, and some preliminary data will be presented.

BASIC CONCEPTS AND NOTATION

Our basic notion conceives of *adjustment* as the goodness of fit between the characteristics of the person and the properties of his environment. Two meanings of "environment" must be distinguished as it pertains to our model: (1) the *objective environment* that exists independently of the person's perception of it; and (2) the *subjective environment* as it is perceived and reported by the person. A parallel distinction can be made between the *objective person* as he really is and the *subjective person*, or self-concept. Because self-perception is not always veridical, the person's self-concept (or self-identity) does not always correspond exactly with the objective person. These distinctions imply that there are at least two conceptions of adjustment: the objective fit between the objective person and the objective environment, and the subjective fit between the subjective person and the subjective environment.

In discussing person-environment (P-E) fit, we will distinguish between two kinds of *demands* and two kinds of corresponding *supplies* to meet these demands. First, we may think of the motives of the person as demands that must be met by environmental supplies. The hunger need, for example, can make all sorts of food supplies attractive to the person. Similarly, the achievement value can make attractive an opportunity to achieve or a chance to compete and win.

Another type of demand is located in the environment rather than in the person. It consists of role requirements and requests emanating from other people. One's job, for example, may demand that he perform certain activities. The supplies to meet these demands consist of abilities in the person.

In order to quantify P-E fit, conceived as discrepancies between demands and supplies, we would like to be able to conceptualize the demand and the corresponding supply on *commensurate dimensions*, that is, we must be able to measure them on the same scale. For motives, this means we must ask, "How much of the environmental supply does the person need to completely satisfy the motive?" and "How much of this supply is available in his environment?" The answer to both questions can be located on the same scale, and thus an exact quantitative measure of P-E fit can be derived by subtracting the demand from the supply. Similarly, the excessive environmental demand for typing speed compared to the secretary's typing ability can be quantified in terms of words per minute.

It is appropriate at this point to make explicit a basic assumption of our theory. We assume that the *derived* concept of P-E fit is a useful conception of adjustment because the basic concepts of demands and supplies have interdependent effects. Thus, the concept of fit, as measured by the discrepancy between demand and supply, should predict to various consequences of adjustment, even after the predictive power of its two compounds taken separately has been accounted for (that is, partialled out of the dependent variables). In principle, we would make an even stronger assumption; namely, that the basic concepts of demands and supplies (or demands and abilities) have *no* independent effects; each is important *only* in relation to the other. However, the existing means of measuring each concept are far from perfected, so that pure measures of supplies, uncontaminated by demands, or vice versa, are unlikely to be available for some time. For this reason, only the weaker assumption is made at this time.

Now we are ready to introduce a notation for our basic concepts. We will take the case of the person's needs and the relevant environmental supplies first and keep in mind that the other cases are parallel. Our aim is to formulate the concept of "fit" (F) of the person (P) to his environment (E) in quantitative terms. We will consider first the relation of person and environment at a point in time; later we will deal with changes over time.

The notation used is:

E_o = Objectively measured environmental supply available to the person.

similarly

P_o = Objectively measured amount of supply necessary to satisfy this person's need.

The difference between these last two variables provides a measure of P-E fit.

(1) $F_o = E_o - P_o$ = Objective P-E fit, that is, the difference between the environmental supply and the person's need for it.

A person may incorrectly report his need or the environmental supply because he has incorrect information, because his perception is distorted, or because he has personal characteristics that lead him to present something other than his true picture of himself and his environment. Therefore, we need notation for the subjective reports:

E_s = Subjectively reported amount of supply from the environment available to this person.

P_s = Subjectively reported amount of supply necessary to satisfy the person's subjective need.

In the same way that equation (1) describes objective P-E fit, equation (2) describes subjective P-E fit:

(2) $F_s = E_s - P_s$ = Subjective P-E fit.

With this notation we are able to write two further equations describing the agreement between the objective and the subjective evaluations of this person's need and the environmental supply:

(3) $R = E_o - E_s$ = Reality of the subjective report of the environmental supply. This is sometimes called *contact with reality*.

(4) $A = P_o - P_s$ = *Accuracy of self-assessment;* that is, of the subjective report of the amount of supply necessary to satisfy this person. This is sometimes called accessibility of the self.

In the parallel case of an environmental demand and a person's ability to meet that demand, we will use comparable notation. Note, however, that in this case, to retain consistency, we define P-E fit as:

(1a) $F_o = P_o - E_o$

and

(1b) $F_s = P_s - E_s$

Positive values again indicate excessive ability, while negative values indicate deficiencies.

THE MODEL

At this point it is useful to take an overall look at what we have done. Table 11-1 shows the relationships between the four variables we have defined and the four equations we have written.

It should be clear that each of the four equations describes a mental health parameter of some importance. In earlier work (French and Kahn 1962), we have discussed three of these variables: namely, P-E fit, or adjustment, reality contact, and accuracy of self-assessment. The contribution of this model is to point out that one can get both objective and subjective estimates of P-E fit and that these are related to reality contact and accuracy of self-assessment.

The basic assumption of the model is that a negative value of F_s is an indication of lack of adjustment and will be associated with psychological strain and with the probability of various coping or defensive behaviors.

TABLE 11-1 THE DESCRIPTION OF THE PERSON AND HIS ENVIRONMENT

	Objective report	*Subjective report*	*Reality or accuracy of report*
Environment	E_o	E_s	$R = E_o - E_s$
Person	P_o	P_s	$A = P_o - P_s$
P-E fit	$F_o = E_o - P_o$	$F_s = E_s - P_s$	

More specifically, it is assumed that, other things being equal, there will tend to be a monotonic and probably curvilinear relationship between the size of a perceived deficiency for a particular supply or ability and various dependent variables, including measures of psychological strain and of the probability of certain coping and defensive behaviors. Excesses of supplies (either too much environmental supply to meet a need or too much ability to meet an environmental demand) are not expected to have any direct effects on such variables. Thus the curve of strain plotted against F_s should decrease as the deficiency decreases reaching an asymptote at perfect fit ($F_s = 0$) and showing no further changes with increasing excesses of supplies (see the solid line in Figure 11-1).

Two qualifying comments need to be made about this assumption. First, the model assumes that the measures of the person and of his environment are commensurate, that both deal with a single dimension. Second, it must be recognized that the dependent variables (psychological strain, coping and defensive behaviors, and so on) are related to P-E fit on a large number of supplies; therefore, the relationship between such a variable and P-E fit on a

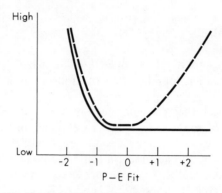

FIGURE 11-1   The hypothesized relationship between P-E fit (F_s) and psychological strain, where F_s = supplies minus demands (or abilities). Thus perfect fit = 0, deficiencies are indicated by negative values of F_s, and excesses are indicated by positive values of F_s.

particular supply will often be slight, and perhaps the direct relationship will be obscured if there are interrelationships between fit on different supplies.

For example, consider the supply of the "opportunity to affiliate" available to a population of persons. It is very possible that the supply of this commodity available in the environment of this population is inversely related to the supply of a second commodity, such as opportunity for privacy. Therefore, when a person reports that there is *more* opportunity for him to affiliate than he needs, this may often imply that there is *less* opportunity for privacy than he needs. The net result of this negative correlation between the pair of supplies might be a U-shaped relationship between the measure of perceived fit on opportunity to affiliate and, for example, psychological strain: too little opportunity to affiliate frustrates the need for affiliation, whereas too much opportunity to affiliate frustrates the need for privacy (see the broken line in Figure 11-1).

Another example of a U-shaped relation of strain to fit is the case of an environmental demand for an ability; here, a deficiency is often referred to as overload, whereas an excess is referred to as underload. The basic assumption of the model implies that overload is directly stressful; however, underload with respect to any ability often indicates a deficiency on another dimension—a lack of opportunity to utilize a valued ability—and this frustration of the need for self-utilization can be stressful. Again, the result of such interrelationships would be a U-shaped curve with strain being minimal where the demand equals the ability and with strain increasing with both increasing overload and increasing underload (underutilization).

In order to illustrate the model presented in Table 11-1, let us assume that we can discriminate affiliative behavior and need for affiliation commensurately on a scale from +1 to +4. A man with maximal needs for affiliation might find himself in the situation depicted in Table 11-2 with his objective needs, as assessed by his wife, really very poorly met because of her strong need to be alone. His objective P-E fit, $F_o{}^{aff}$, is minimal, that is -3. Or, we could say that he has a maximal deprivation of affiliation. His subjective report shows what might be called reduction of dissonance by distortion both of the environment and of the self resulting in a subjective fit, $F_s{}^{aff}$, of -1.

Of course, in the real world of measurement, things are not as simple as this; we must recognize that the "objective" assessment of the man's need by his wife may not agree very well with say a projective assessment of the same need. Similarly, if this wife with a strong need to be alone distorts her report of their collective affiliative behavior in order to reduce the discrepancy between her need and their actual social environment, we will be getting an untrue estimate of E_o.

Table 11-2 could just as well illustrate demands stemming from the husband's values. For example, he might strongly value equality of husband

TABLE 11-2 THE DESCRIPTION OF A MAN AND HIS ENVIRONMENT ON THE DIMENSION OF AFFILIATION

	Objective report (from wife)	Subjective report	Reality or accuracy of report
Environment	$+1$	$+2$	$R^{aff} = -1$
Person	$+4$	$+3$	$A^{aff} = +1$
P-E fit	$F_o{}^{aff} = -3$	$F_s{}^{aff} = -1$	

and wife, but he might find that his wife always behaved as an inferior and treated him as a superior. Such an objective discrepancy might well lead him to distort his perception of his wife's behavior and of his own value.

Turning now to the second type of P-E fit—the environmental demands on the person and the abilities available to meet these demands—it is immediately obvious that a table similar to Table 11-1 could be constructed. Table 11-3 deals with environmental demands and the relevant abilities. It illustrates the case of a job that requires a typing speed of fifty words per minute to keep up with the work load, $E_o = 50$, and a person holding the job who is able to type only thirty words per minute, $P_o = 30$. Let us further assume defensive distortion on the part of this person so that the subjective report is that the job requires forty words per minute and that ability is equal to that. Here, though the subjective P-E fit is good, the objective fit is poor. The good subjective fit is due both to unrealistic reporting of the real environment and to inaccurate reporting of the self. We are then describing this typist as having a poor objective P-E fit, which might be called an overload. Such an overload usually predicts poor mental health, either in terms of negative affect and physiological arousal or in terms of perceptual distortion. In this case, she has either defended against

TABLE 11-3 THE DESCRIPTION OF A TYPIST
WHO HAS INADEQUATE SKILL AND WHO IS
DEFENSIVELY DISTORTING BOTH THE
ENVIRONMENT AND HER SKILL
(THE NUMBERS ARE TYPING SPEED
IN WORDS PER MINUTE)

	Objective report	*Subjective report*	*Reality or accuracy of report*
Environment	$E_o = 50$	$E_s = 40$	$R = 50 - 40 = 10$
Person	$P_o = 30$	$P_s = 40$	$A = 30 - 40 = -10$
P-E fit [a]	$F_o = 30 - 50 = -20$	$F_s = 40 - 40 = 0$	

[a] In order to obtain a measure of P-E fit we again subtract the demands made from the supplies available to meet these demands, so equation (1) now becomes $F_o = P_o - E_o$ and equation (2) becomes $F_s = P_s - E_s$. Again a negative number indicates a deficiency, but this time the deficiency is in the person, rather than in the environment.

the anxiety that might otherwise be aroused by distorting her perceptions of the situation or is presenting herself in a socially desirable way and is hiding her true perception of herself.

Clearly some dimensions are more important to a given person than are others. Whereas ability in abstract thinking may have survival value for a mathematician, it may be of no importance at all to a house painter. Consideration of the relative importance of various dimensions is necessary in this model, for we can presumably sum over several related dimensions if they are weighted by their importance. Furthermore, one of the responses to a poor fit on a single dimension may be to reduce the importance of this dimension (Sherwood 1965).

Before proceeding to a theoretical discussion of the dynamics of adjusting, let us examine concretely some of the problems of measuring P-E fit.

THE MEASUREMENT OF ADJUSTMENT

The development of adequate measures of adjustment, conceived as P-E fit, is surely a task for the future; but a useful start has been made (Pervin 1967). To make our model more concrete, we present here selected measures from a current study of a national sample of about 2,000 high-school boys (Bachman et al. 1967). Because the measures were developed prior to the present model, the correspondence is crude, but hopefully illustrative. In this study, we obtained measures of fit along ten dimensions thought to be important to high-school boys. However, for purposes of illustration we present only two: one dealing with demands and abilities and the other dealing with needs and supplies. In accordance with the model, we present measures of both objective fit and subjective fit, and we add measures of perceived fit as a possible criterion of validity for the first two.

In order to measure objective fit with respect to intelligence, we operationalized the formula $F_o = P_o - E_o$ by using the Quick Test of Intelligence (R. B. Ammons and C. H. Ammons 1962) and by subtracting from it the intelligence required in that school as rated by a sample of teachers in the particular school. For the corresponding measure of subjective fit, we asked the following questions of the boys:

1. How intelligent do you think you are, compared with other boys your age?
   ( ) a. FAR ABOVE AVERAGE (TOP 10%)
   ( ) b. ABOVE AVERAGE (NEXT 15%)
   ( ) c. SLIGHTLY ABOVE AVERAGE (25%)
   ( ) d. SLIGHTLY BELOW AVERAGE (25%)
   ( ) e. BELOW AVERAGE (NEXT LOWEST 15%)
   ( ) f. FAR BELOW AVERAGE (BOTTOM 10%)

2. How much does your school give you a chance for using a lot of intelligence?
   ( ) a. VERY MUCH
   ( ) b. QUITE A BIT
   ( ) c. SOME
   ( ) d. A LITTLE
   ( ) e. NOT AT ALL

3. How much does your school actually *require* you to use a lot of intelligence?
   ( ) a. VERY MUCH
   ( ) b. QUITE A BIT
   ( ) c. SOME
   ( ) d. A LITTLE
   ( ) e. NOT AT ALL

4. How does this (the opportunity or requirement for using a lot of intelligence in school) fit in with what you want?
   ( ) a. TOO MUCH, COMPARED WITH WHAT I WANT
   ( ) b. A LITTLE TOO MUCH
   ( ) c. JUST ABOUT RIGHT
   ( ) d. NOT QUITE ENOUGH
   ( ) e. NOT ENOUGH, COMPARED WITH WHAT I WANT

F_s was then calculated by subtracting from the response to question 1 a score based on the responses to questions 2 and 3. These two questions on the environmental opportunities and requirements for using intelligence were combined by assuming that a boy could perceive too *much* (but not too little) *requirement* to use his intelligence; or too *little* (but not too much) *chance* to use his intelligence. This assumption was not fully consistent with the data, because a substantial number of boys gave contradictory responses (such as very much requirement and very little chance); this is an initial reminder that we are working with very imperfect measures of the concepts. Given the *post facto* nature of the analysis in the present case, we had little choice but to try to use an admittedly arbitrarily combined measure. Question 4 was used as the measure of perceived fit with respect to intelligence. This double-barrelled question with its cross references to two previous questions may have been too complicated for the less-intelligent and less-motivated boys in our sample.

With regard to affiliation with peers we asked:

1. Compared with other boys your age, how important is it for you to spend time with friends?
   ( ) a. MUCH MORE IMPORTANT THAN AVERAGE
   ( ) b. A LITTLE MORE IMPORTANT THAN AVERAGE
   ( ) c. ABOUT AVERAGE IMPORTANCE
   ( ) d. A LITTLE LESS IMPORTANT THAN AVERAGE
   ( ) e. MUCH LESS IMPORTANT THAN AVERAGE

2. How much does your school give you a chance to spend time with friends?
   ( ) a. VERY MUCH
   ( ) b. QUITE A BIT
   ( ) c. SOME
   ( ) d. A LITTLE
   ( ) e. NOT AT ALL

3. How does this (the chance for spending time with friends) fit in with what you want?
   ( ) a. TOO MUCH, COMPARED WITH WHAT I WANT
   ( ) b. A LITTLE TOO MUCH
   ( ) c. JUST ABOUT RIGHT
   ( ) d. NOT QUITE ENOUGH
   ( ) e. NOT ENOUGH, COMPARED WITH WHAT I WANT

Subjective fit with respect to affiliation was measured by the response to question 2 minus the response to question 1. Again, the inadequacy of the measures should be emphasized. Question 1, used as a measure of P, asks about the *importance* of affiliating, not *how much* affiliation is required. Question 3 was used to measure perceived fit.

For these measures of both intelligence and affiliation, we predicted that both deficiencies and excesses would be indicative of poor adjustment, so that as compared to boys reporting good P-E fit, boys reporting either type of poor fit would tend to have lower scores on measures of mental health; and they would be less satisfied with the school environment and so be more likely to consider dropping out of school. The reasoning behind this prediction is that an excess on the measured dimension will often indicate a deficiency on an unmeasured dimension. Boys reporting that the school gives them more opportunity to affiliate than they need probably often feel that they have too little chance to be alone or independent.

As a first step in evaluating the P-E fit measures, let us look at the concurrent validity of objective fit and of subjective fit as indicated by their correlations with perceived fit. Table 11-4 gives the relevant data. With

TABLE 11-4 THE CORRELATION RATIOS [a] (ETAS [b])
AMONG MEASURES OF P-E FIT

With respect to intelligence:

Objective fit vs. Subjective fit _____ .192

Objective fit vs. Perceived fit _____ .102

Subjective fit vs. Perceived fit _____ .356

With respect to affiliation:

Subjective fit vs. Perceived fit_____ .427

---

[a] All correlations are significant at the 1 percent level.

[b] The correlation ratio, Eta, is used in all tables in preference to the product-moment correlation (Pearson's r); the Eta statistic reflects non-linear as well as linear relationships, and, therefore, is preferable when non-linear relationships are expected. In this first table, the predicted and actual relationships both tend to be linear, and either statistic would be suitable, but for consistency, Eta is used throughout.

respect to both intelligence and affiliation the measures of subjective fit are substantially correlated with the criterion measure of perceived fit. Because objective fit with regard to intelligence is only weakly related to subjective fit, we would expect that objective fit should be less strongly related to perceived fit; the actual correlation is only .102 (which is, however, significant at the 1 percent level). Thus, there is mild preliminary support for the validity of our measure of subjective fit, but very little support for the measure of objective fit.

More important data for evaluating our measures of adjustment are presented in Table 11-5. We would predict that all three measures of fit should be related to the dependent variables of self-esteem, negative affective states (a cluster including depression, anxiety, resentment, and so on), and the subjective probability of dropping out of school (thereby changing the environment).[1] However, P-E fit along any single dimension could not be expected to be strongly related to these dependent variables. According to our theory each dependent variable is jointly determined by all ten dimensions and any one dimension should account for only a small percentage of the variance.

Objective P-E fit with regard to intelligence is significantly related to self-esteem, but not to the other two dependent variables. However, objective intelligence alone is more strongly related to each of the three dependent variables, while the objective demands for intelligence are not related to any of them. Thus, the P-E fit measure stands midway between its two component parts in predictive power.

Subjective P-E fit with regard to intelligence is significantly and a little more strongly correlated with each of the three dependent variables. Again, however, most or all of this relation seems to be produced by the even higher correlations of one of its components, subjective intelligence, with

TABLE 11-5 CORRELATIONS[a] (N'S) OF THREE MEASURES
OF P-E FIT (AND THEIR COMPONENTS) WITH THREE DEPENDENT
VARIABLES (SELF-ESTEEM, NEGATIVE AFFECTIVE STATES, AND THE
SUBJECTIVE PROBABILITY OF DROPPING OUT OF SCHOOL)

P-E fit and its components	*Self-esteem*	*Negative affective states*	*P of dropping out of school*
Objective P-E fit re intelligence			
Quick Test—demands for I.Q.	.114	.080	.066
Objective P = Quick Test	.143	.110	.145
Objective E = Demands for I.Q.	.050	.060	.052
Subjective P-E fit re intelligence	.198	.150	.131
Subjective P = Subjective intelligence	.329	.161	.180
Subjective E = Subjective demands	.065	.040	.035
Perceived fit re intelligence	.099	.121	.104
Subjective P-E fit re affiliation	.086	.126	.040
Subjective need to affiliate	.024	.027	.048
Subjective chance to affiliate	.124	.141	.074
Perceived fit re affiliation	.059	.154	.062

[a] All correlations above .08 are significant at the 5 percent level.

the three dependent variables. The environmental component is not related to any of the dependent variables.

Perceived P-E fit with regard to intelligence is significantly, but weakly, related to all three of the outcome variables.

Turning now to the measures of subjective P-E fit with respect to affiliation (there were no objective measures on this dimension), we see in the bottom part of Table 11-5 that fit tends to be related to the dependent variables, but less strongly than is the subjective chance to affiliate. The other component, subjective need to affiliate, is unrelated to any of the dependent variables. So most of the relation between P-E fit and the outcome variables could be attributed to one component; but for this dimension of affiliation it is the environmental component that produces the effects, whereas for intelligence it was the dimension of the person that did so. This difference may well be due to a methodological artifact: the correlations are higher wherever the measure of P or E appears to be more reliable. Finally, we see in the last line of Table 11-5 that perceived fit is significantly related to one of the dependent variables.

The eta statistics presented in Table 11-5 do not, in themselves, indicate whether the predicted curvilinearity of the relation of P-E fit to the dependent variables actually occurred. An examination of the actual cross-tabulations showed that there were slight curvilinear relations, more or less in the predicted direction, in about half the tables. In the other half, the relations were linear, just as they were for the dominant component that seemed to be producing most of the effect. Given the crudeness of the measures, this rather weak support for the curvilinear predictions of the model are about as good as could be expected.

On the basis of this preliminary analysis of only part of our data we conclude that: (1) our two theoretically derived measures of objective P-E fit and subjective P-E fit have modest concurrent validity as measured against perceived fit; (2) all three of these measures of fit have significant predictive validity, although as expected they account for only a very small percentage of the variance; (3) however, the predictive validity seems to have been achieved primarily on the basis of one of the component variables—the crudeness of the measures permitted only very weak support for the curvilinear relations and interaction effects predicted by the model; and (4) the data are sufficiently unreliable (often based on only one item and that one sometimes excessively complicated), so that they provide only a weak test of the model and do not permit any final conclusions on its usefulness.

Another problem that should be mentioned is the question of the proper analysis strategy for data such as these. When use is made of difference scores $(P-E$, or $E-P)$, several assumptions are made about the data that are probably unwarranted at this stage: it assumes that the two measures (of P and of E in this case) are both interval scales with the same zero point and with equal units. That is, it is assumed that the respondent who is at the same relative position on both scales has a good fit, and that a one-unit discrepancy on one scale is equivalent, in terms of lack of fit, to a one-unit discrepancy on the other scale. Other analysis strategies can and should be used that do not make such unwarranted assumptions.

Because the measures in the above study of high-school boys were only crudely appropriate for testing the model, we also will present some data from a study of adjustment to job stresses that used somewhat improved measures. This study by Robert Caplan (1971) examined the effects of a wide variety of job stresses on various risk factors in coronary heart disease. We shall examine here the relation of P-E fit to two psychological variables—satisfaction and perceived job-related threat—and to one physiological variable—cholesterol level, a completely objective variable (that is, there is no possibility that the measured cholesterol level is contaminated by response sets and other biases involved in subjective responses to questions). The measures of P-E fit are also better because they use more commensurate dimensions of the person and the environment, and because they are simple and more straightforward. Furthermore, because the 198 male subjects were NASA employees with a much higher educational level than the high-school boys, we expected that their responses to the questionnaire would be more valid and reliable.

For each of sixty-seven dimensions we asked two questions: one about the person's job environment and another parallel question about the kind of job environment they would like to have. (The latter is taken as a report of the person about himself.) One item, for example, asked the subject to respond on a five-point scale to each of the following commensurate dimensions:

1. The responsibility you have for the work of others.
2. The responsibility you would like to have for the work of others.

Clusters of P-E fit items were formed on the basis of intercorrelations among answers to the individual items. Ten clusters were formed of environmental items, and ten comparable clusters were formed using the analogous set of person items; then P-E fit scores were calculated by subtracting the score on each person cluster from the score on the analogous environmental cluster. These clusters were composed of from two to five items, and each could be labeled by the content of the items; for example, items in one cluster refer to responsibility for other people, items in another cluster deal with role ambiguity, and so on.

These P-E fit scores were then related to two psychological variables using one-way analyses of variance. One psychological variable is a measure of overall job satisfaction and is based on twenty-three items in which the respondent is asked to compare (on a four-point scale) his present job to alternative jobs open to him on various dimensions. The other psychological variable, a measure labeled "job-related threat," is based on seventeen items in which the respondent is asked to rate (on a five-point scale) his prospects for meeting his "own needs, for good health, for feelings of self worth," and so on, if each of various stressful aspects of his job continue to exist as they are now.

To summarize the results of the twenty analyses of variance (ten P-E fit measures versus two dependent variables), thirteen of the F-values were significant at the .05 level, and of these, eight were significant at the .001 level. Although no explicit hypotheses were made about which of these relationships would be U-shaped and which asymptotic, it is worth mentioning that six of the thirteen cases with significant F-values did show a U-shaped relationship, and three of the remaining seven cases seemed to level off at an asymptotic value. In the remaining four cases, there is neither a leveling off nor a reversal apparent in the curves. However, there is a general absence of respondents reporting poor fit in one direction or the other (either few people report excesses, or few people report deficiencies, depending on the particular dimension); this fact may well cut off the portion of the curves in which discontinuities in slope would occur.

Further analysis is continuing, but this preliminary analysis of the relationships between various P-E fit measures and two psychological variables seems to be generally quite consistent with the model.

Turning now to the physiological variable, serum cholesterol level, we will present a single illustrative analysis and comment on others. Again, we did one-way analyses of variance, using P-E fit as measured by each of the sixty-seven pairs of items as the control variable and cholesterol as the dependent variable. Most of the F-values were nonsignificant, but the exceptions are worth mentioning, although we are aware of the danger of capitalizing on chance in this case.

We predicted that both too much and too little responsibility would raise the level of cholesterol, so there should be a curvilinear relationship. In general, these predictions were supported. Figure 11-2 presents the results for an item on responsibility for the work of others. The relation of cholesterol to P-E fit shows the predicted U-shaped curve, with good fit being associated with significantly lower cholesterol levels than is lack of fit. The correlation ratio, eta, is significant; and it is higher than the correlations of cholesterol with the components (actual responsibility and desired responsibility).[2]

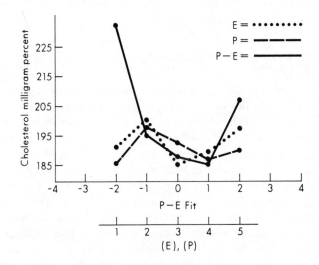

FIGURE 11-2   The relation of cholesterol level to P-E fit, to P, and to E related to the responsibility you have for the work of others. The correlation ratios (etas) are .23, .11, and .18, respectively. The relation of P-E fit to cholesterol is significant (F = 2.62, p < .05).

There were five additional dimensions for which P-E fit was significantly correlated with cholesterol and where the correlation with P-E fit was higher than the correlation with either of its components. In four of the five cases, the curves had the predicted U-shape. For the six dimensions where P-E fit was significantly related to cholesterol, two were dimensions of job responsibility, two described aspects of work overload and time pressure, and two were concerned with interpersonal relations.

Among the sixty-one dimensions that were not significantly related to cholesterol, there is further support for the above findings. Twenty of the sixty-one curves show the predicted U-shape, a number which seems to be somewhat greater than one would expect by chance. In thirty-one cases the eta for cholesterol is greater against P-E fit than it is against P alone or E alone (X^2 = 13.25, p < .005). The content of the dimensions also supports the significant findings; for example, there are four additional dimensions describing various job responsibilities, and all four of them show the predicted U-shaped relation to cholesterol.

Taken as a whole, these data provide strong, though preliminary, support for the P-E fit model. The data also serve to emphasize the great need for progress in the development of commensurate measures of the person and of his environment. Adequate tests of the usefulness of the P-E fit model will depend on our ability to measure both the demands of the person and of environmental supplies to meet those demands on a common dimension, so that difference scores become meaningful. Similarly, commensurate measures of the demands of the environment and of the abilities of persons to meet those demands must be developed.

THE DYNAMICS OF ADJUSTING

So far we have presented the concepts and notation for describing four criteria for the mental health of a person at a given point in time: his objective P-E fit, his subjective P-E fit, his contact with reality, and his accuracy of self-assessment. Now we turn to some hypotheses about the processes that the person uses over time in coping with, and adapting to, the discrepancies in fit and the inaccuracies in perceiving himself and his environment.

What are the forces toward change in the situation? The fundamental source of these forces is the deprivation of a need or a value (French and Kahn 1962, pp. 10 ff.). Such a deprivation induces motivational forces on the person in the direction of satisfying the motive. The strength of these forces will depend on the magnitude of the deprivation (how poor the P-E fit), the importance of the dimension on which the deprivation occurs, and the person's expectations for the future. If he expects a future deprivation, then the strength of the forces to change the situation will increase with the immediacy and the duration of this future threat. Finally, the strength of the forces will depend on *relative* deprivation; the person will evaluate the magnitude, importance, immediacy, and duration of his deprivations against those suffered by his reference group. In the case of value deprivations (for example, failure to achieve) the person will suffer both guilt and shame. His own forces will be powerfully reinforced by induced forces that stem from the expectations of his reference group.

When poor P-E fit involves an environmental demand greater than the person's ability, the strength of the forces to change will depend on the strength of the demands and the power of the role senders.

Inaccuracies in perceiving the environment or the self are assumed to involve forces toward a more accurate perception. The person will generally receive information, both from his own experience and from other people in his environment, that is dissonant with his perception; and there will be forces to reduce this dissonance.

The *techniques for adjusting* to these forces are complex and interdependent, but all of them are based on four elements: the person can change E_o or P_o or E_s or P_s. Changes in these elements provide the definitions and notation for the following techniques for adjusting:

$\Delta F_o = $ A change in objective P-E fit that defines *coping*.

Coping includes changing the supplies or demands of the objective environment or the motives or abilities of the objective person.

ΔE_o = A change in the objective environment that defines *environmental mastery* as one form of coping.

For example, our typist might persuade the boss to reduce her work load.
Or the husband in Table 11-2 might find another source to satisfy his need
for affiliation.

ΔP_o = A change in the objective person that defines *adaptation* to
the environment as another form of coping.

Our typist, for example, might take instruction to increase her typing
speed, or the husband described in Table 11-2 might reduce his need for
affiliation supplies.

ΔF_s = A change in subjective P-E fit that defines *defense*, if these
defensive distortions are brought about by ΔE_s and ΔP_s
without any corresponding objective changes.

Because changes in any of the four elements can be either an increase or a
decrease, there are eight basic adjustive behaviors. Moreover, any one of
these may vary in the motivation that induces the change, that is, in the extent to which it stems from an effort to improve P-E fit or an attempt to
improve accuracy of perception. And of course, the effect of any such adjustive behavior on fit and on accuracy will depend on the initial constellation of values of the four elements. Finally, we note that several basic adjustive behaviors may be combined in various sequences. Accordingly, many
adjustive behaviors, each with various consequences for mental health, are
encompassed by this simple model. We shall illustrate below only certain
consequences of the eight basic ones.

The success of these techniques for adjusting can be measured partly by
the degree to which they improve objective and subjective P-E fit. This can
be quantified by comparing the degree of fit before an adjustive behavior
with the same measure taken after the behavior. But this measure alone is
not sufficient, because these same techniques will also produce changes in
the accuracy of perception, other things being equal. These changes in the
other criteria of mental health can be deduced directly from the model. In
the following simple examples we assume that all other things are equal,
and thus we neglect, for the time being, certain expected empirical inter-
dependencies. We expect, for example, that any change in the objective environment will normally be perceived more or less veridically and will thus
produce corresponding changes in the subjective environment. We do not
consider such effects here.

Referring back to Table 11–1, we can see the following deductions:

1. Improvements in subjective fit that are brought about by defensive distortion
    of E_s will also change R, the person's contact with reality.

a. If $E_o > E_s$, then a defensive decrease in E_s will decrease the contact with reality. For example, the secretary who improves her subjective fit by defensively minimizing the demands of her boss will at the same time decrease her contact with reality, perhaps at the risk of being fired by the boss.

b. If $E_o < E_s$, then a defensive decrease in E_s will improve the contact with reality. The secretary who had been magnifying the job demands is now perceiving them more accurately.

c. If $E_o > E_s$, then a defensive increase in E_s will improve contact with reality. For example, the secretary who perceives the job demands as less than they really are and also as less than her own ability might increase her subjective fit by an increase in the perceived demand that would at the same time improve her contact with reality.

d. If $E_o < E_s$, then a defensive increase in E_s will increase the discrepancy from reality. Thus the secretary who perceives the job demands as more than they really are but less than her ability might increase her subjective fit by an increase in E_s that would simultaneously worsen her contact with reality.

2. Improvements in subjective fit that are brought about by defensive distortion of P_s will change A, the accuracy of the person's self-assessment. As in (1a) through (1d), the accuracy may be decreased or increased depending on the initial relation of P_o to P_s.

3. and 4. Parallel to (1) and (2), we can make similar deductions about the effects on accuracy of changes in objective fit that are brought about by environmental mastery, ΔE_o, and by adaptation, ΔP_o.

Just as various techniques for improving fit will have effects on accuracy, so these same techniques, when used for improving accuracy, will have specifiable effects on objective or subjective fit; and these effects can be deduced from the model.

These different consequences of the various techniques for adjusting may influence the person's choice of techniques. However, other factors may also be important. Individuals may have stable defense preferences and coping styles that influence their choices in all situations. Even more powerful influences on the choice may stem from the environment. It may be impossible, for example, to increase the environmental supplies for some need, so the person must choose some alternative technique for adjusting.

In order to test the dynamic aspects of our model, longitudinal data are required. We are now in the process of analyzing two such sets of data.

NOTES

1. These three variables were measured by ten items, forty items, and one item, respectively.

2. To check the possibility that age could somehow explain this relationship, cholesterol levels were corrected for age; this did not change the shape of the relationship between cholesterol and the P-E fit measure.

REFERENCES

Ammons, R. B., and Ammons, C. H. The quick test (QT): Provisional manual. *Psychological Reports*, 1962, *11*(7), pt. 7.

Bachman, J. G., Kahn, R. L., Mednick, M. T., Davidson, T. N., and Johnston, L. D. *Youth in transition*, vol. 1. Ann Arbor: University of Michigan, 1967.

Caplan, R. Organizational stress and individual strain: A social psychological study of risk factors in coronary heart disease among administrators, engineers, and scientists. Ph.D. dissertation, University of Michigan, 1971.

French, J. R. P., Jr., and Kahn, R. L. A programmatic approach to studying the industrial environment and mental health. *Journal of Social Issues*, 1962, *18*, 1–48.

Pervin, L. A. A twenty-college study of student × college interaction using TAPE (Transactional Analysis of Personality and Environment): Rationale, reliability, and validity. *Journal of Educational Psychology*, 1967, *58*, 290–302.

Sherwood, J. J. Self-identity and referent others. *Sociometry*, 1965, *28*(1), 66–81.

12

Psychological Techniques in the Assessment of Adaptive Behavior

RUDOLF H. MOOS

Important developments have taken place in personality theory during the last few years. These developments can in large part be traced back to the contributions of a small group of investigators—Angyal's (1941) concepts of autonomy and the organism's striving toward active mastery of the environment; Hartmann (1950) and Hartmann, Kris, and Loewenstein's (1949) emphasis on adaptive ego processes; Erikson's (1950) formulation of ego identity; Werner's (1957) ideas regarding the progressive differentiation of development; Maslow's (1954) and Rogers' (1961) writings on self-actualization and positive personality growth; White's (1959) conceptualization of effectance motivation and competence; and Kelly's (1955) notions regarding the importance of the active exploratory propensities of man as scientist. Research developments, which have emerged directly or indirectly from these theories, have contributed to the mushrooming increase of emphasis on the positive adaptive qualities of animal and human behavior. These include the study of the exploratory drive (Harlow 1953) and of curiosity (Berlyne 1960; Fowler 1965); experiments on the effects of stimulus deprivation and sensory isolation and, more recently, on various aspects of stimulus and variety-seeking motivation (Shapiro, Leiderman, and Morningstar 1964; Zuckerman, Persky, Link, and Basu 1968); the importance of cognition and plans (Miller, Galanter, and Pribram 1960); and the work on various styles of information seeking (Schroder, Driver, and Streufert 1967), cognitive complexity (Crockett 1965), and the motivating qualities of information present in the environment (Hunt 1961). This theory and re-

This work was supported in part by the National Institute of Mental Health, grants MH 10976 and MH 16026.

search has all-important consequences for our whole philosophy of human behavior, and also for the methodology and techniques that are used to assess that behavior. The purpose of this chapter is to focus on those psychological assessment techniques that appear to be most relevant to the conceptualization and measurement of adaptive behavior.

The extensive proliferation of new assessment techniques gives the unmistaken impression of a rapidly expanding area of inquiry that is currently still in its developmental infancy. The exponential growth of the area over the last several years makes it a relatively safe prediction that it will skip the latency stage and will soon blossom into a full-blown adolescent identity crisis. The work to date gives immediate and irrefutable testimony to the effects of exploration, curiosity, novelty, and stimulus seeking on the part of investigators concerned with assessing exactly those qualities. One of the healthiest aspects of the area is that there has been relatively good articulation between new theoretical developments and the creation of new assessment methods. This is true both in the sense that many of the techniques are an indirect outgrowth of the advances in theory development, and in the sense that specific techniques have been developed to measure specific relevant constructs such as self-esteem, self-actualization, ego identity, exploratory behavior, stimulus-seeking motivation, and feelings of efficacy and competence.

There are many reasons underlying the importance of focusing on adaptive behavior and coping processes that are relevant to the differential utilization of different types of assessment methods. A primary reason for assessment is to attempt to understand more completely the processes by which man handles everyday life stresses and major life crises and transitions. Full understanding can come only with detailed intensive study, either through interviews or through naturalistic observations of the actual day-to-day processes by which adaptation occurs. Understanding is essential because it tends to generalize to understanding of other individuals in similar crises and thus is relevant to empathy and helping behavior, because it helps to communicate the essential "flavor" of adaptive processes to inquiring students, because it helps the investigator to design better studies that include more relevant variables, because it may enhance the prediction of behavior in individual clinical situations, and because it tends to give the investigator-clinician a much needed feeling of competence.

A second, closely related reason involves the prediction of future behavior; for example, rapidity of recovery from surgery, relative success in Peace Corps training and field work, efficacy of adaptation to major life transitions such as migration and acculturation. It is often felt that a full intuitive understanding of adaptive processes is necessary before adequate prediction can occur. However, the past history of assessment attests to the conclusion that investigators' feelings of understanding are neither a necessary nor a sufficient condition for accurate prediction.

The goals of understanding and of prediction often lead to the choice of quite different assessment methods. Investigators interested primarily in understanding have tended to utilize more complex, intuitive, clinical, and global assessment methods; investigators interested primarily in accurate prediction have tended to utilize simple, objective, specific, and actuarial methods. Whether this is necessary, because different ends require different means, or whether the development of methods of intermediate complexity can effectively combine these goals is still unclear. For the present at least, understanding and prediction must be dealt with as somewhat separate goals, even though in the deepest and most relevant sense all of us fervently wish we could do both.

A third reason for assessment has to do with the public health aim of the prevention of maladaptation. For example, if it were possible to accurately identify children not coping adequately with the intellectual or emotional tasks of first grade, preventive counseling measures could be instituted. Specification of the reasons for maladaptation might even suggest the orientation and type of counseling measures that would prove most beneficial. A related, but essentially different, reason is the identification of superior adaptation, or, more properly, the search for talent. Importantly, this latter goal tends to arouse interest in new and different types of variables, for example, intellectual style, cognitive complexity; it also very closely articulates with an acutely felt societal need.

The goals of identifying adaptation and preventing maladaptation both imply still another reason for assessment—that is, to effect changes in adaptive behavior and in coping processes. Attempts to decrease maladaptive behavior are legion, and corresponding attempts to increase the probability of adaptive behavior, though not quite as frequent, are rapidly becoming more popular. On the other hand, direct attempts to alter individual coping processes experimentally are relatively rare thus far. The implications of the development of successful techniques to change individual coping styles could be enormous, especially if these styles actually do underlie extensive behavioral domains.

Another reason has to do with the changing of environments rather than of individuals. The assessment of coping can provide information about the general maladaptive consequences of certain institutional arrangements and thus may lead to institutional change. Langford (1961) has provided an excellent discussion of how the reactions of children and their parents to various aspects of hospital policies have resulted in important changes in these policies. Implied in all the preceding purposes is the overriding goal of understanding the fit between people and their institutions. Different individual coping predispositions should have differential costs and benefits in different institutions. Thus far there is relatively little hard information in this area, although there are encouraging signs of future progress.

An attempt is made to enumerate a large variety of relevant techniques and thus by induction to map the general contours of what is an immense and rather poorly defined research area. Decisions for inclusion were made on the criteria of clear relevance to the area, direct relationship to theory, authors' self-perceptions that they were dealing with adaptation variables, possible relevance to person-environment interaction, and "positive" labeling of assessed variables. Brief summaries of work on certain overarching variables, such as self-conceptions and cognitive styles, that may affect an individual's style of adaptation across a large variety of life settings, and variables that either measure actual attained skills or that may be relevant to attained skills (for example, marital status) have also been included.

Examples of various types of techniques are presented: techniques based on interview data, on tape recordings and films, on essays and written materials, on short-story and problem situations, and on objective assessment methods. These divisions are largely related to the following dimensions: (1) How complex and how true to life is the stimulus situation confronting the subject? (2) What type of response must the subject make; how complex and "real" is it? (3) How complex and difficult is the analysis of the data required by the investigator? The clarity and explicitness with which the response-analysis scheme is presented is important, as is the fact that increased complexity of analysis reflects on the time and money cost of the technique and may well be related to the ease of reproducibility of the results. Emphasis will be placed on what is one of the central problems in this area, that is, to preserve the complexity and richness of the subject's responses while at the same time reducing the complexity of the necessary data analysis and handling techniques.

The vast amount and range of relevant research makes it impossible to do justice to all the exciting work in progress, and thus only limited coverage is attempted. The primary purpose of the review is to call attention to the great variety of available assessment techniques that have heretofore been discussed in widely scattered literature. The field of inquiry is very new, and there are few established methods; it is thus too early to attempt a highly critical review. The major focus will, therefore, be on the descriptive comparison of different types of techniques. Selected methodological issues are discussed in the last section.

INTERVIEW AND OBSERVATIONAL TECHNIQUES

The attainment of systematic information in this area began with detailed in-depth interviews and observations of individuals in crisis situations. The major purpose of these studies was to understand the processes involved in coping. The long series of interview studies constitute a remarkable descriptive account of the actual processes that occur. They include accounts of adaptation to college (Coelho, Hamburg, and Murphey 1963; Silber et al. 1961a, 1961b), marriage (R. Rapoport and R. N. Rapoport 1964; Raush, Goodrich, and Campbell 1963), doctoral examinations (Mechanic 1962), severe burns (D. Hamburg, B. Hamburg, and deGoza 1953), poliomyelitis (Visotsky et al. 1961), the death of a leukemic child (Chodoff, Friedman, and Hamburg 1964; Friedman et al. 1963), major surgery (Abram 1965; Janis 1958), children's reactions to the death of a parent (Becker and Margolin 1967), adaptation to concentration camps (Cohen 1953), to natural disasters such as tornadoes and floods (Clifford 1956; Perry, Silber, and Bloch 1956), and to man-made disasters such as atomic bombs and prisoner-of-war camps (Janis 1951; Strassman, Thaler, and Schein 1956). These studies represent an unusually rich source of data and they must be carefully read by any serious investigator in the field.

There have been many attempts to reduce the complexity of information obtained from observations and interviews to reasonable quantitative proportions, and this section will briefly summarize two examples of rating methods, three utilizing Q-sorts, and two further studies, one of which developed a semistructured interview and the other an objective test to cover the same domain as the interview. Two studies focusing on classroom behavior and two others highlighting the utilization of the interview for assessing change in coping processes will also be mentioned. Insofar as practical, examples have been drawn from different content domains in order to illustrate the wide range of utility of the general types of variables assessed.

Wolff and co-workers (Wolff et al. 1964; Wolff, Hofer, and Mason 1964) tape recorded interviews ranging in length from two to four hours in a predictive study of thirty-one parents of fatally ill children. Effectiveness of defense referred to the immediate success of tension reduction, not to the defense's adaptive value. A parent was considered to be effectively defended if (1) he demonstrated little or no overt distress (affect criterion), (2) he showed little or no impairment of his functioning (function criterion), and (3) he demonstrated the ability to mobilize his defenses further in superimposed, acutely stressful experiences (defensive reserve criterion). These rating criteria were applied to the interviews, and the results showed significant correlations with mean 17-hydroxycorticosteroid excretion rates.

Hurwitz, Kaplan, and Kaiser (1965) devised a technique to assess parents' coping mechanisms relevant to the control of delinquency in their children. Parents were observed during an interview lasting an hour and a half and were then rated on each of five areas of parental coping—for example, parent-to-child communication, parent-to-parent communication, parental remedial action plan. Overall paternal and maternal coping scores were derived by summing the five area assessments. The items successfully differentiated between families who coped constructively and those who coped destructively with the court crises. These two are excellent examples of studies in which complex information obtained in long, detailed interviews was condensed by a quantitative rating scheme into a specific assessment of the effectiveness of coping and defense in a concrete stress situation.

Many studies have utilized the Q-sort as a means of quantifying complex interview and observational data. For example, Livson and Peskin (1967) attempted to predict the psychological health of young adults from personality evaluations through development in a longitudinal sample of thirty-one men and thirty-three women. They defined adult health by the correlations of a composite Q-sort description of each subject based on a lengthy and complex adult assessment, with a standard Q-sort based on experts' conceptions of a hypothetical psychologically healthy adult. Four developmental periods were used and only one (ages eleven, twelve, and thirteen) had significant correlations with adult health; adult health was essentially not predictable from personality measures taken at two phases of childhood and at late adolescence. Potentially healthy boys were, in early adolescence, relatively extroverted, expressive, and immune to irritability and temper tantrums, whereas potentially healthy girls were relatively independent and had a confident and inquiring orientation and a hearty attitude toward food. Baumrind and Black (1967) used a ninety-five-item Q-sort to relate children's behavior to socialization practices associated with dimensions of competence and found, for example, that paternal consistent discipline was associated with independence and assertiveness in boys and affiliation in girls and that demands for maturity correlated with independence and assertiveness for boys.

In a quite different area, Smith (1966) transcribed several hours of semistructured field interviews conducted with each of over forty Peace Corps teachers in Ghana and constructed two decks of Q-sort items that judges could use to quantify the interviews. The procedure was to hold "clinical" conferences in an attempt to formulate the interview information and then to translate it into Q-sort items. One deck of sixty-five items dealt with the volunteer's role perceptions, personal agenda, and role performance, whereas the second deck of sixty-four items permitted judges to characterize the volunteer's personality structure and processes. Factor analyses yielded global factors labeled "competent teaching in Africa" and "self-confident maturity." When varimax rotation was performed on the role-performance Q-sort deck, several quite different patterns of competent performance emerged; for example, one pattern emphasized constructive involvement with Africa, whereas a second emphasized exclusive teaching commitment. These results indicate the importance of a multidimensional conceptualization of competence. All three Q-sort studies illustrate how complex rich observational and interview data may be effectively quantified and the resulting data utilized in elaborate statistical analyses. Block (1961) has recently presented an excellent review of the details of the Q-technique.

Another method of reducing interview complexity is to attempt to develop either a more focused semistructured interview or to devise a self-report instrument that covers the same ground, at least for predictive purposes, as does the original interview. Neugarten and his colleagues (1961) reported having lengthy and repeated interviews covering many aspects of each respondent's life pattern, attitudes, and values in order to develop a life-satisfaction index. Interview ratings were made on several variables—for example, zest versus apathy, congruence between desired and achieved goals, and positive self-concept—and were summed to obtain an overall rating or index of satisfaction. Because this index necessitated at least one long interview and would have been cumbersome to use on a large scale, the investigators attempted to devise a self-report instrument that would take only a few minutes to administer. High and low scorers on the life-satisfaction indices were used as criterion groups, and items differentiating between these groups were selected for two preliminary instruments that correlated .52 and .59 with the initial life-satisfaction index. Thus, direct self-reports agreed substantially, but only partially, with evaluations of life satisfaction made by an outside observer.

In another example, Argyris (1960) discussed the utilization of a semi-structured, thirty-question research interview to measure employee self-actualization. Bonjean and Vance (1968) set forth a short-form, structured instrument as an alternative technique that they felt might better meet the needs of investigators particularly where time, expense, and relative lack of interviewing and analytic skills were factors. In their short form the respondent is given a card listing all the predispositions Argyris found among the employees he studied, for example, "being alone while at work," "having the opportunity to do quality work." The respondent is asked to judge the relative importance of each of these items to him; he is then asked to describe aspects of his present job on the same items. The first judgments are considered his "desired expression" and the second his "actual expression." Self-actualization, which is defined as the relationship between these two, correlated .61 with the initial interview method on thirty-one hospital and retail store employees, and was also related to different forms of "adaptive behavior" experienced by the employee—getting angry with the supervisor, feeling satisfied with his job, thinking about getting another job. This example illustrates a two-stage approach in which Argyris initially attempted to assess variables relevant to theoretical notions about self-actualization by formulating interview questions, and then Bonjean and Vance derived a more structured and less time-consuming technique from this interview. The Bonjean and Vance technique might, of course, be further modified toward a simple objective test that could more easily be used in large-scale studies.

Studies that have dealt with naturalistic observations are far too numerous to review (Barker 1963; Murphy 1962; Weick 1969), and only two particularly relevant examples will be mentioned. Lindemann and Ross (1955), utilizing a predictive test of social adaptation, initially observed and rated fifty children on their adjustment to school based on the child's behavior in a doll play situation, because they felt that this context offered the most promising clues to the emotional integration attained by the child. Nine months later, various ratings on the child's behavior in kindergarten were obtained by a time-sampling observational technique in which each child's location was recorded on a series of classroom maps at five-minute intervals. There were relationships between poor adjustment in the doll play situation and later behavior, for example, behavior in which the child remained in close proximity to others, but failed to interact, and behavior in which two children played together, but excluded others.

Kellam and Schiff (1967) and Kellam (1969) have carried these methods one step further by obtaining ratings from the child's teacher three times during the first grade and once at the end of the third grade. Their methods assess community need by measuring the prevalence of maladaptation in the total population of first-grade children several times each year. Longitudinal measures of prevalence rates provide the base line and outcome measures for a program of prevention and early treatment. Each of the teachers listed ways in which children have difficulty adapting to the first grade. From this pool, five general categories, each of which represented an adaptational task, were formed. The five categories, each rated on four-point scales, were called "social contact," "acceptance of authority," "maturation," "cognitive achievement," and "concentration." There was a sixth global adaptation scale. The authors felt that the teacher's ratings had a face validity derived from the central strategic importance that she occupies with regard to the children in her classroom; that is, the children must adapt to her view of classroom performance. In this approach, large amounts of complex classroom behavioral data are easily reduced to teacher ratings on a few variables. This is efficient, but possibly misleading. For example, the results of an initial intervention program showed an increase in maladaptation by these measures in the intervention as compared to the control schools. The authors suggest that this is because of a change in the standards of the teachers in the intervention schools in the direction of greater expectations. Clearly, in this particular case, additional independent observations of pupil behavior are necessary. On the other hand, the teacher's ratings did have excellent predictive validity, because those children rated as maladapting early in the first grade were nine times more likely to become symptomatic by the end of the first grade, when compared with children rated as adapting.

Changes in relevant variables have also been assessed by Krumboltz (1964) and Thoresen (1967), who categorized statements in group and individual counseling interviews as (1) information seeking, (2) counselor reinforcement of information seeking, (3) non-information seeking, (4) counselor reinforcement of non-information seeking, and (5) counselor cue or questioning responses. Interview categories were correlated with information-seeking behaviors of subjects outside the interview, and results showed that information-seeking responses during the interview, counselor reinforcement of them, and counselor cue responses were positively correlated with information-seeking outside the interview. Counselor reinforcement of information-seeking responses was also highly associated with information seeking during the interview. The importance of these studies resides both in the development of a technique for isolating a single, highly relevant coping variable from the complexity of the interview situation, and in the demonstration that interview reinforcement of this coping style can result in its increased utilization outside the interview situation.

To sum up, the major focus of this section has been on methods that can be used to quantify complex interview and observational data without unnecessarily sacrificing important information. Much more attention must be paid to the relationship between the purpose and the methods utilized in each study. For example, the nagging question in both the Wolff (1964) and Hurwitz (1965) studies is whether information similarly efficient in relating to 17-hydroxycorticosteroid excretion rates and constructive parental coping might not have been obtained from more limited samples of behavior with far less expenditure of effort by both the investigators and the subjects. When relatively global ratings are to be utilized for predictive purposes it may not be necessary to collect such rich, complex data.

Some studies may not need external observers, whereas others must have them. Thus, whereas Kellam's (1967, 1969) studies might have profitably utilized observers to provide external criteria with which to evaluate their intervention program, Lindemann and Ross (1955) could probably have predicted classroom social adaptation by utilizing teachers' ratings as well as by utilizing outside observers in a complex observational study. When an intervention program is to be implemented, external observers may provide essential additional information; when classroom maladaptation is to be predicted, teachers' ratings may be entirely sufficient.

Further research toward a more differentiated understanding of the relationship between free interview and structured questionnaire techniques for assessing the same variables is important. Questionnaires may predict to various external criteria as well as, or better than, interview ratings. For some groups of people or content areas, there may be very high agreement between interview and self-report data, whereas for others the agreement may be low; thus, although a more objective test could be utilized in the former situations, an interview technique would be more appropriate in the latter ones.

The major problems to be solved relate to the cost-benefit trade-offs regarding the use of different methods of reducing complexity in the context of different overriding project goals. The use of a simple cheap method of data collection that amasses largely irrelevant information is obviously wasteful; on the other hand the use of an unnecessarily complicated and time-consuming technique is at best inefficient. The technique and method of data collection and data reduction must be very carefully integrated with the project goals.

FAMILY INTERACTIONAL TECHNIQUES

The systematic use of family interactions in the study of coping patterns is still relatively rare. Goldstein and co-workers (1968) have developed a very important methodology that combines the advantage of relatively free responses to realistic natural situations with standardization of both the interview conditions and the problems presented. Their aim was to determine whether there were consistent coping styles among family members that related to the patterns of psychopathology manifested by an adolescent. They explicitly state that their design is a methodological compromise between sophisticated naturalistic observation with a minimum of standardization and a more rigorously controlled design in which the rich data of spontaneous family interactions cannot be obtained. Initially, there are standardized individual interviews in which each parent and his child are asked to pinpoint a specific problem between parent and child in the areas of achievement, sociability, responsibility, communication with parents, autonomy, and so on. Once the specific problems are identified (and these may be different for each family), each family member is instructed to try to influence other family members. The statements produced are called cue statements, and each subject is asked to predict the response of the person to whom the cue statement is directed. The standardization of problems is achieved through the use of problem ranking of importance, and stimulus comparability is based on the equivalence of rated emotional intensity rather than on the equivalence of objective content. The tape-recorded cue statements to each problem are then played, and each family member individually responds to the others' cue statements. Then the family member hears an expectancy statement, that is, what the other family member thought he would say. The family member is then asked to respond again to the cue statement. Next comes an actual confrontation session where first two, and then all three, of the family members interact. The authors categorize the social influence styles utilized into (1) the use of private, dependent power, (2) information giving, and (3) information seeking. They found relationships between family use of these influence styles and different types of disturbed adolescents.

One of the initial approaches to this area was the "revealed differences technique" utilized by Strodtbeck (1958). Questionnaires are first administered individually to family members. Items on which the individual members express different views are then presented to the family (that is, the differences are revealed), and the family is asked to discuss the item and to see whether they can agree on one of the choices. Item disagreements potentially representing various coalitions are usually used—mother and son agree, father disagrees; father and mother agree, son disagrees; father and son agree, mother disagrees. The major problem is in the scoring of the complex family interactions. Strodtbeck obtained indices of participation, power, and support and related these to other indices of family functioning. Fields (1968) has recently adapted this technique for the assessment of efficacy, which was defined in terms of the child's ability to get his parents to yield to his point of view. Interestingly, she found that the ability of preadolescent and adolescent boys to influence their mothers was related to their overall ego-functioning, where their ability to influence their fathers was not so related. In another adaptation of this type of technique, Kaswan and Love (1969) obtained videotapes of a family's interactions and then had each family member view five or six brief sections of the tape and rate each of the persons interacting in each scene. The family members were then shown profiles of their own ratings and of ratings of the same material made by trained observers. Similarities and contrasts emphasized by the profiles, particularly when seen in conjunction with videotape replays, stimulated evaluation and self-exploration. The authors were most concerned with using this as a technique to stimulate behavior change; however, systematic assessment of coping variables during interaction and confrontation could easily be incorporated.

Ferreira (1963), in other related work, studied decision making by having family members first make choices individually and then meet in a group in order to attempt to come to a family decision. Bauman and colleagues (1967) have utilized marital-couple interaction testing, a technique that includes the testing of individual spouses and the married pair on a set of intelligence test problems. Marital intelligence is defined as the ability of the couple to solve problems and is measured by the I.Q. score achieved by the couple as a unit.

The possibility that some of these techniques may have cross-cultural relevance is indicated by Straus (1968), who obtained data on the ability to solve a laboratory problem for samples of middle-class and working-class families in Bombay, India; Minneapolis, Minnesota; and San Juan, Puerto Rico. In all three samples, working-class family groups were less successful in problem solving than middle-class families. The choice of the task used was in part based on the assumption that working-class persons "do not verbalize well in response to words alone." They tend to think and learn in physical or motoric fashion. It was hoped that a task that involved physical manipulation of objects would allow for such motoric thinking. The task was a game played on a nine-by-twelve-foot court. At the front of the room were three pairs of red and green lights. Each family was given ambiguous instructions and was told that the problem was to figure out how to play the game, a task that seems uniquely generalizable to various extra-experimental settings. There were eight three-minute play periods, and the family's task was to infer the rules of the game with the aid of green lights flashed for correct and red lights for incorrect moves. Despite the great variation in the three cultures, there was considerable concordance in the way middle-class families were differentiated from working-class families.

Argyris (1965a, 1965b) has developed one other technique of interest here, even though it has been utilized primarily in the context of group, rather than family, interactions. He defined a set of categories to measure interpersonal competence—for example, openness, risk taking, owning up to, individuality, trust—that also served as the basis to describe increases or decreases in individual and group competence during T-group and other training. The categories were scored from tape recordings of group sessions. Argyris found that the higher the positive scores on the competence variables, the more the group was perceived by its members and by outsiders as competent on indices such as clarity about goals, generation of alternative ways of thinking about solutions, open expression of feelings, and continual evaluation. The categories were also used as the basis for evaluating the relative effectiveness of lecture versus laboratory education in the subject area of interpersonal relationships and group dynamics. Data indicated that a laboratory approach, with its emphasis on exploration and confrontation, seemed to produce more behavioral change; however, the important point here is the specific conceptualization and development of an assessment technique utilizing interactional data for measuring interpersonal competence, a highly relevant construct. This approach might easily be adapted to the study of family interaction.

There are also a large set of other relevant game techniques that might be utilized to study coping processes in relatively real-life, albeit still experimental, situations. Examples include the prisoner's dilemma game (Rapoport 1960), an inter-nation simulation task (Brody 1963), and several other techniques that have heretofore been used primarily to study interpersonal trust, competition, and cooperation (Deutsch 1958; Deutsch 1962; Shure, Meeher, and Hansford 1965).

TAPE RECORDINGS AND FILMS

The utilization of tape recordings and films, which are ideal media for the relatively quick presentation of complex, real, maximally involving stimuli, is relatively underdeveloped in this area. The major exception is the use of films as stressors with attendant measures of subjects' stress reactions (usually psychophysiological responses), but generally without specific assessment of the actual ways in which the subjects cope with the film stimuli (Lazarus 1966). The type of techniques used by Strupp (1962) in the study of psychotherapists' responses to different patients is most relevant. He showed motion pictures of therapist-patient interactions and stopped the film at various points at which viewing therapists were asked to indicate what the next responses of the therapist should be. This technique is capable of providing a standardized real-life problem situation to which the individual subject must respond. The interest here is in the psychological techniques by which subjects handle and respond to the stimuli of the film, rather than in their psychophysiological reactions. The development of videotapes greatly expands the number and type of stimuli that can be presented to subjects. For example, Geertsma and Reivich (1969) videotaped patients in a brief interview and then showed them one of four types of playback: audio and video, audio alone, video alone, neither audio nor video. Results suggested that self-relevant information mediated via the auditory channel was contextually richer and more effective in eliciting cognitive and affective changes in subjects than information channeled visually. They raise the intriguing possibility that defensive processes may differ with respect to input channel conditions, and that defensive maneuvers may operate less effectively under the video situation.

Rothenberg (1967), in a study that used tape-recorded stimuli in somewhat the same way that Strupp used film stimuli, investigated the development of children's ability to describe and make inferences about the feelings and intentions that occur in adult relationships and studied the relation of this ability to competence in interpersonal relationships and to intrapersonal comfort. The technique consisted of a series of four tape recordings depicting two adults in happy, angry, distressing, and sad situations. The subject was asked to describe each adults' feelings and then to explain why the adult felt the way he did. Responses were scored on a five-point scale, and the level of complexity or sophistication in the understanding of what makes people feel the way they do was determined for each response. Children who were rated as least adequate in interpersonal adjustment in their school classrooms, as well as children attending a child psychiatric clinic, obtained lower scores than their more well adjusted peers when dealing with tapes that depicted possible anxiety-provoking interactions (anger, distress, and sadness). This technique might be modified and made more relevant by presenting problem situations on tape and asking individual subjects how they would handle these situations. This method of presentation is slightly more realistic than having printed problem situations, and subjects would probably feel more involved and might thus give more complete responses.

There have been two very interesting recent uses of films. Pisano (1966) exposed children to a filmed model who was failing in the performance of a task. The model was a "soldier" (called GI Joe and selected from a group of ROTC students partially on his "clean-cut, all-American" appearance) attempting to qualify on a pistol range. During the course of his failure, the soldier consistently enacted the defense of rationalization (for example, "Aw, my finger slipped," "Really, I'm glad I didn't win"). Three response-consequent conditions were provided by the experimenter to the modeled defensive statements as follows: positive or sympathy (for example, "It's too bad that keeps happening"); neutral or no comment; and negative or interpretation (for example, "The worse he does, the more he seems to blame it on the gun"). Following exposure to the model and the subsequent response consequences, the children were placed in a miniature version of the soldier's task in which they attempted to "qualify" on a gun game, electronically controlled to ensure failure. It was hypothesized that the model would serve to elicit increased defensiveness and would, in addition, serve to "shape" the nature of this defensiveness along imitative lines. The results generally supported this prediction. This is a very interesting experimental paradigm for the study of the imitation and modeling of defensive or coping behavior.

The author suggests a number of important lines for further inquiry, including the range of defenses (or coping styles) amenable to imitation, whether established styles can be "reshaped" through appropriate models, and whether styles can be initially acquired through imitation.

In another study, Schwartz (1966) attempted to activate effectance motivation experimentally by utilizing a ten-minute sound motion picture in color, which consisted of random movie scenes (ceramic figures of natives cooking a missionary, a chess game played with cosmetic bottles, a girl swimming, a car motor starting) and the music of *Voodoo Suite* as the sound track, with instructions inferring meaningfulness in the film. Byrne, Nelson, and Reeves (1966) pointed out that the notion of effectance motivation could be extended to include the learned drive to be logical, consistent, and accurate in interpreting one's stimulus world, as well as the desire for certainty and the need to know and to be able to predict. Effectance motivation should be activated in situations in which the meaning of stimuli is unclear, in which there is difficulty in predicting event sequences, and in which reality and fantasy are not clearly differentiated. The control condition in this study used a color film entitled *Highland Lakes Area of Central Texas* showing dam sites, quiet lagoons, parks, lakes, Longhorn caverns' entrances, and the Perdinales River with soft guitar · music as background. Self-report measures indicated, not too surprisingly, that there was greater arousal in the experimental condition than in the control condition. This finding has potentially important implications, because if confusion, disorder, disarray, and blurred reality-fantasy distinctions can really arouse effectance motivation, then the range of relevant naturalistic situations giving rise to greater competence would be almost infinite. More soberly, the link to effectance is rather tenuous; in addition, because not even Texans were aroused by the control film it may be unrepresentatively innocuous.

Glass, Singer, and Friedman (1969) present research implying that the Schwartz movie, rather than arousing effectance, may have had temporary maladaptive consequences. They used a tape recording to deliver 56 and 110 decibels of aversive noise consisting of the following sounds superimposed upon one another: two people speaking Spanish, one person speaking Armenian, a mimeograph machine, a desk calculator, and a typewriter. They found that adaptation to unpredictable, as opposed to predictable, noise resulted in lower tolerance for subsequent frustrations and impaired performance on a proofreading task. These effects seem to be substantially reduced if the subject believes he has control over the noise. People apparently can become accustomed to aversive stimuli, but the work of adaptation may leave the organism less able to cope with subsequent environmental stressors. In any case, the type of motivation aroused by ambiguous situations is much less clear than the probable utility of presenting relevant stimuli by means of films, videotapes, or tape recordings.

ESSAY AND SENTENCE-COMPLETION TECHNIQUES

Although the use of written materials, particularly autobiographies, was suggested by Allport (1961) and Murray (1938), relatively little use has been made of these techniques in the area of assessing coping styles. Again there have been a number of recent studies that point up directions for possible future applications.

Insel (1968) utilized the "Who Am I" (WAI) technique in which subjects' self-descriptions are classified as consensual and external (athlete, girl, married) or subconsensual and internal (happy, bored, interesting). Insel found that subjects presenting themselves via group-relevant or external characteristics used fewer words, were older, were more likely to be married, and tended to be less intuitive and more judgmental in orientation. This general technique was introduced by Bugenthal and Zelen (1950) and has also been successfully used by Kuhn and McPartland (1954) and McPartland, Cumming, and Garretson (1961) among others.

Bush, Hatcher, and Mayman (1969) have assessed externalization-internalization by asking subjects to illustrate through written essays what they felt were the three most difficult crises or personal problems faced by girls during their college years. The essays were rated on the degree to which the experience of conflict was portrayed as internal versus situational and on how attention was distributed within the story between the internal and external referents of the conflict situation. Externalization-internalization correlates with reality attentiveness-inattentiveness and appears to be of importance in determining an individual's capacity to respond to insight therapy.

Winter, Griffith, and Kolb (1968) had students write essays on "How I would ideally like to be in a group" (ideal-self paper) and "How I am actually perceived in groups" (real-self paper). Each student selected a personal-change goal, noted how he planned to measure progress toward this goal and rated his progress after each class session. A content analysis of the self-descriptive essays written by students who were subsequently successful or unsuccessful in attaining self-directed behavior-change goals was conducted. High-change subjects more frequently stated goals with implicit recognition that the goal had not yet been attained. Low-change subjects more frequently described themselves with little recognition of alternative possibilities and showed more tentativeness and uncertainty about themselves.

Hill (1967) has suggested the novel possibility of using a structured autobiography in the construct validation of personality scales. He had 352 male freshmen write structured autobiographies following an outline concerned with relationships with parents and siblings, childhood, adolescence, self-image, and so forth. Content analysis included rating positive or negative affect, categorizing type of punishment used by each parent, and counting the number of favorable or unfavorable adjectives used in different descriptions. The products of high and low scorers were compared on each of six California Psychological Inventory (CPI) scales, and the results provided general evidence for the validity of the manual's description of these scales.

McClain and Andrews (1969) reversed Hill's procedure by using personality scales in the construct validation of an essay technique. They asked subjects to write about "the most wonderful experience or experiences of your life" and had judges classify each experience as a peak or nonpeak experience. Significantly different results on test scores provided evidence that the peak subjects were more self-actualizing than the nonpeak subjects. They suggest that simply letting a person tell of his highest moments might provide information useful in assessing self-actualization.

In another example of an autobiographical technique, Ezekiel (1968) asked Peace Corps trainees to write three essays. The first was about their immediate alternative plans if they were not accepted in the Peace Corps. The second was a brief "mock autobiography" covering the three years after return from the Peace Corps service, and the third was a "mock autobiography" covering the year in which they would be forty years old. The essays were rated on three seven-point scales: differentiation, the extent to which each essay showed complex and detailed mapping of the future; agency, the extent to which the essay showed the future self as the prime agent in determining the course of the person's future life; and demand, the extent to which the subject described a life that was viewed as demanding, long-term, continuing effort. These autobiography dimensions related significantly to four different criteria of overseas performance; ratings by field supervisors, peer nominations, and item and factor analyses of Q-sorts based on extensive field interviews. Relations of autobiography scores to performance were considerably stronger and clearer for males and Protestants than they were for females and Catholics.

Sentence-completion techniques are often preferred to essay techniques because of their greater comparability across subjects and greater efficiency of data handling. Sears and Sherman (1964) have developed a set of relevant sentence completion items, and Loevinger (1966*a*, 1966*b*) has detailed a potentially important model and technique for the systematic assessment of stages in ego development. However, most of the initial uses of the technique involved simply dividing subjects into two presumably opposite groups, such as repressors and sensitizers (Wiener, B. Carpenter, and J. Carpenter 1956) or copers and avoiders. For example, Goldstein (1959) utilized a task of sixty sentence stems such as the following: "If I were stuck. . . ."; "The worst thing a girl can do. . . ."; "I hate. . . ."; "A girl's figure. . . ." Persons who are sensitized to the sexual and aggressive implications of the various stems are identified as copers. Avoiders, on the other hand, characteristically fail to recognize the implications of the stems and are unable to perceive the feelings suggested in the stems as being related to themselves. The distinction parallels that drawn in perceptual situations between persons who show sensitization or vigilance and those who engage in perceptual defense. In Goldstein's study a strong fear appeal received greater acceptance among copers, whereas a minimal fear appeal received greater acceptance among avoiders.

Interestingly, this sentence-completion test was able to differentiate between alcoholics and normals, and between a drunk and sober condition in each group. The fact that the results showed that inebriation significantly decreased the coping behavior of alcoholics, whereas it increased that of normals, amply demonstrates the practical utility of this technique (Pollack 1966).

Andrew (1967) utilized a sentence-completion test in an attempt to predict the rapidity of recovery from surgery. The expectation was that patients could use information if it was compatible with their preferred mode of anxiety reduction. Patients were divided into coper, avoider, and nonspecific defender groups, and an audio tape was prepared to give information about inguinal hernia surgery. The results indicated that the copers recovered well regardless of when they heard the tape; whereas the avoiders recovered more slowly when they heard the tape prior to surgery than the nonspecific defenders did, and also more slowly than did the avoiders who heard the tape after surgery. Importantly, this indicates that information restriction may sometimes be as potentially adaptive as information seeking.

Schroder, Driver, and Streufert (1967) were interested in style rather than content, and they have developed a very intriguing technique for assessing the structural characteristics of verbal responses, which has been applied to essays as well as to incomplete sentence stems. The scoring manual presents a set of general operations for inferring the level of conceptual structure that generated the response. The rater considers the degree of differentiation and the number of degrees of freedom in the rules of integration and the mediating processes underlying the response. Responses are scored along a seven-point scale of integrative complexity. The raters ask the following question: "Regardless of what the person says, what complexity of structure would be required to generate the response?" The authors review studies indicating that people who produce more flexibly integrated responses are also capable of generating more complex integrative behavior in a variety of interpersonal situations.

All these studies, taken together, suggest that essays, autobiographies, and sentence-completion tasks may be particularly useful intermediate-complexity techniques in obtaining information about the individual. They tend to combine the feature of being relatively real and involving for the subject with the feature of only moderately complex data analysis for the investigator. In addition, the data generated may be quite detailed, subtle, and rich. Developments in automated content analyses of written materials will make these techniques even more useful (Stone et al. 1966). In this connection McLaughlin (1966) and Gordon (1969) have already provided systems for the analysis of "Who Am I" information for use with the General Inquirer approach to computer-aided content analysis.

SHORT-STORY AND
PROBLEM-SITUATION TECHNIQUES

There are a surprisingly large number of short-story techniques that have been utilized in this area. One use of the Thematic Apperception Test (TAT) that may serve as a transition from the last section involved a comparison of writing styles across three age (adolescent, late adolescent, and adult) and two academic groups (college and noncollege) (Tooley 1967). Late adolescents were judged to be flamboyant in writing style less often than the other two age groups, and impersonal significantly more often than the other groups. The expressive style of late adolescents was moderate in emotional tone and heavily reliant on intellectualizing defenses.

Coelho, Silber, and Hamburg (1962) attempted to devise an economical and reliable instrument for measuring the coping potential of adolescents during their college freshman year. Subjects wrote stories to accompany ten TAT-type pictures depicting student-oriented scenes. In the first study there were ten students who had shown exceptional competence in college, ten patients hospitalized for emotional difficulties experienced during their freshman year, and ten local state university students who had placed at the eighty-fifth percentile on an advanced placement test. Three variables were scored on fifteen-point scales for each story: (1) solution—that is, whether there was any solution or resolution to the problem situation as defined by the subject; (2) activity—that is, whether the main character was actively striving to bring about the resolution; and (3) favorableness—that is, whether the resolution was favorable to the hero's intended goals.

Results indicated that both normal groups showed higher frequencies of positive ratings on each of the three measures. Two indices of freshman coping behavior were developed: (1) the optimism index was the ratio obtained by comparing the percentage frequency of favorable solutions to the total number of solutions; (2) the effectance index was the ratio obtained by comparing the percentage frequency of favorable solutions to the total number of activity ratings. Effectance refers to satisfying transactions with the environment. The closer the approximation to unity, the higher the level of competence in freshman coping behavior as measured by these two indices, which differentiated between the three groups essentially as expected.

These general results were cross-culturally replicated on a Puerto Rican sample (Field, Maldonado-Sierra, and Coelho 1963). Coelho and co-workers (1969) have also shown that the student-TAT may be highly successful in predicting college dropouts. Precollege student-TAT measures of competence successfully predicted the most vulnerable dropout group, and there was nine times as much chance for a student in the low-competence-rating group to drop out as one in a high-competence-rating group. In still another use of this technique, Newman (1966) gave a hundred freshmen both the student-TAT and a semantic differential on which they rated themselves and their parents. Results indicated a significant relationship between coping behavior on the student-TAT and similarity with parents as rated by the son, and similarity with the son as rated by his father.

Some evidence that a cross-cultural, problem-oriented TAT might be extremely useful is presented by Remmers (1962), who reports findings from samples of 5,000 teenagers in the United States, Puerto Rico, West Germany, and India who responded to a Youth Inventory, a problems checklist adapted to each of the cultures surveyed. Results indicated that teenagers' self-perceived problems could be comparably measured across widely different cultures, that rankings of problem areas across cultures were highly similar, and that health problems were of least concern and post-high-school problems of most concern. This type of study lays excellent groundwork for the decisions about what kinds of TAT-type problem situations might be most relevant for cross-cultural studies.

Whiteley (1966) has independently arrived at a method for assessing adaptive ego-functioning using the TAT that is quite similar to the student-TAT technique. Questions asked of each story include: (1) Was the hero's strategy of action one that included prior consideration of the consequences of his behavior? (2) Did the hero of the story cope with the situation in which the teller of the story placed him? (3) Did the hero's consideration process reflect an awareness of the social realities of the situation? (4) Was the hero's reaction logically related to his long-term interests? (5) Did the hero accept responsibility for his actions? In one study it was found that the heroes in the TAT stories told by superior achievers were more adaptive in their behavior than the heroes in stories told by underachievers. Fields (1968) has simplified Whiteley's scoring criteria for adaptive ego-functioning and has related this to experiences of efficacy within the family, that is, the ability of boys to influence their parents.

Feffer (1966, 1967) attempted to adapt Piaget's concept of decentering to the study of interpersonal behavior by hypothesizing that effective social interaction is a function of each participating individual's ability to consider his behavior from more than one perspective simultaneously. They used a role-taking task (RTT) that required the subject to tell a standard TAT story for an ambiguous picture and then to retell the story from the perspective of each of the TAT figures. Subjects were paired on the basis of similar role-taking performances and were evaluated with regard to effectiveness of social interaction by having one member of the pair attempt to communicate test words via one-word association clues to the other member who did not know the words. One can only hope that the fact that the higher RTT pairs did communicate words more quickly and with fewer clues than the lower RTT pairs might eventually be relevant for the efficacious selection of partners for bridge and other two-person party games. In a further study Lowenherz and Feffer (1969) substantiated their hypothesis that a failure to coordinate perspectives on the RTT occurs when the TAT figures represent defensively isolated aspects of the self-structure.

Korner and Buckwalter (1967), in a rather novel use of the TAT, asked subjects to tell stories that excluded one of the stimuli. Each subject was shown a picture of a boy with his back to the viewer, sitting on a rug and reading a book. The subjects were asked to "make up a story about this picture, but do not use a boy in your story." Responses were classified according to the processes used in eliminating (suppressing) the forbidden stimulus. The authors came up with the somewhat surprising finding that average high-school subjects and highly intelligent graduate students used essentially the same limited number of primitive suppressive methods.

Miller and Swanson (1960) utilized various different TAT and story-completion-type tests to measure the severity of subjects' moral standards, to create conflict, to assess sexual identity, and to study defenses. For example, in order to assess denial, boys were first asked to write imaginative endings to three story beginnings, each of which described a series of events leading to failure. Then the subjects were motivated to do well on a group of tests that were so designed that no one could pass them. The subjects then completed three new stories and denial was defined in terms of the change in the amount of unrealistic fantasy after exposure to failure. In another technique, conflict was created by implying to the boys that their mothers had been interviewed and had indicated various criticisms of them, such as loss of patience with silly humor, boredom with childish interests, embarrassment by clumsy and tactless behavior, and so forth. The authors tabulated discrepancies between the frequencies of defensive endings written for stories presented before and after the arousal of conflict. (The mothers were not these boys' own mothers at all, but were from far, far away, that is, California and not Detroit, the site of the study.)

The authors also aroused sexual conflict by asking each boy to judge the aesthetic values of paintings and photographs of nude females. The subjects, in a relatively benign deception, were told that the ratings would help to find out whether photographers or painters do a better job of portraying the beauty of the human figure. It is questionable whether the pictures utilized (for example, reproductions of Renoir's *Gabriel in an Open Blouse* and Valesquez's *Venus and Cupid*) were in any way representative of either the subjects' or the authors' real-life stimulus environment; however, the adaptation of these pictures for utilization with the Korner excluded-stimulus technique does present some interesting possibilities for studying defensive isolation and suppression. In any case the Miller and Swanson book provides a very rich source of information on the use of standard pictorial and story-completion stimuli in the elicitation and measurement of various motives in experimental setting and will well repay careful reading.

Goldfried and D'Zurilla (1969) discuss a behavioral analytic assessment approach designed to identify, measure, and facilitate effective behavior among college freshmen. Situational analyses were made by male freshmen's self-observations, by observations of freshmen by resident assistants, by interviews with faculty and staff, and by surveys of clinical folders of freshmen who applied for treatment. Subjects were given a list of fourteen areas in which problematic situations were likely to occur and were asked to list those that had occurred to them.

The next goal was to obtain a sample of likely responses to each situation. First, subjects were asked to give a detailed, written account of their likely reactions, and responses were rated by two independent judges on a seven-point scale of effectiveness. Eighty-eight of the most frequently occurring and potentially discriminating problematic situations were chosen. In the next step of response evaluation, the authors selected "significant others" for the purpose of determining explicit and implicit behavioral norms and standards regarding effective behavior in the various problematic situations. The actual measuring-instrument format has sample problem situations of two short paragraphs each and the subject is asked to give his likely responses in each situation. The test is not only to measure general competence, but also to assess separately interpersonal and academic competence. In addition, the authors are attempting to carry out research to study the effects of training in problem solving and decision making on actual test performance. An attempt will be made to train the use of a cognitive problem-solving strategy for dealing with problematic situations of a personal or social nature.

There are at least two aspects of this technique that represent an important advance over other methods. First is the step of response evaluation in which effective behavior is defined by those "significant others" in the environment who make daily decisions about effective behavior. This technique, which has also been recommended by Stern, Stein, and Bloom (1956), is logically similar to that used by Kellam and Schiff (1967). Second is the fact that the procedural assumptions involved in the technique can be systematically studied and, once unwarranted assumptions are identified, the procedure can be modified so as to eliminate the necessity for these assumptions and to maximize predictive power (Kent 1969). As Kent states: "Accurate prediction is thus a matter of successive approximation, rather than a hit-or-miss phenomenon."

Giebink, Stover, and Fahl (1968), who were interested primarily in behavior change, also utilized a logically similar strategy. They devised a problem-story frustration questionnaire consisting of fourteen relatively frequently occurring frustrating situations that were readily observable and had several alternative acceptable responses, but which previous experience had shown were often likely to lead to unacceptable aggressive behavior. They asked their emotionally disturbed boys to give as many alternative responses as they could to each of these situations, and they then instructed the boys in alternative adaptive responses in four experimental situations. They found that the instructed adaptive responses did become part of the boys' verbal and overt behavior response repertoire.

In another approach Sidle and co-workers (1969) developed a two-part coping scale consisting of three stories dealing with problems of college choice, marriage, and examinations. The authors were concerned about the possibility of obtaining relevant information about coping processes from a relatively simple paper-and-pencil measure, and they were also interested in comparing information obtained in an open-ended, or free-response, section with that obtained in a somewhat simpler, but more restrictive, closed-ended section. The strategies included information seeking, talking with others about the problem, attempting to see the humorous aspects of the situation, tension reduction, and so forth. Results indicated that the measure was capable of eliciting information about less socially approved ways of coping, that the ten strategies represented relatively independent ways of coping, and that both free-response and rating sections were important because they tended to elicit somewhat different sources of information about coping strategies.

Gross (1965) also attempted to construct an objective paper-and-pencil measure of characteristic and preferred modes of response to conflictual situations. The situations, presented in short paragraphs, dealt with problem areas common to college students: religion, social and friendship relations, family and authority, occupational and academic success, and heterosexual relationships. Responses to threat were categorized into four groups: (1) acting out; (2) denial and repression; (3) psychological distortion; and (4) appropriate solution seeking. Both the main characters ("Joe College" and "Suzie Coed") and the problem situations utilized (for example, "Joe was invited to a party and somehow neglected to ask what the appropriate dress would be. When he arrived in his best brown suit, he discovered that everyone else was dressed in tuxedos and formal gowns") cast strong doubt that this West Virginia test can safely be generalized for either intercultural, or even intracultural, use.

In a recent paper, Gleser and Ihilevich (1969) describe the development of a defense mechanism inventory (DMI), a paper-and-pencil test that attempts to measure the relative intensity of usage of five major groups of defenses. The inventory consists of ten brief stories (two for each of five conflict areas) followed by four questions regarding the subject's actual behavior, fantasy behavior, and thoughts and feelings in the situations described. Five responses typifying the five defenses (hostility out, projection, principalization, turning against self, and reversal) are provided for each question, and the subject selects the one most representative and the one least representative of his reactions. Various preliminary studies are reported. First, psychologists were able to match stories with conflict areas and responses with defense mechanisms. Second, it was found that the spread and level of defense mechanism scores was strikingly similar under free- and forced-choice instructions. Third, subjects who relied mainly on global defenses (turning against self and reversal) were more field-dependent than subjects who relied excessively on differentiated defenses (turning against object and projection). This first report on the DMI suggests that it may be an extremely useful instrument in further research.

The relatively large number of short-story and problem-situation techniques appears again to be based on the search for methods of intermediate complexity. Most of the research suggests that these are potentially very promising techniques. For example, Coehlo and colleagues (1969) were able to use a TAT technique successfully in one of the first prospective studies of a developmental transition involving stressful experiences in college life, indicating both that short-term longitudinal studies and this type of assessment or coping behavior are feasible and potentially highly valuable. Tooley (1967) also concluded that the TAT could be helpful in studying developmental transitions, and Shanan and Sharon (1965) successfully used it to study the cognitive functioning of Israeli males during the middle years.

The other studies reviewed indicate the wide range of content and experimental and real-life situations to which these types of techniques may be applicable. One of the most exciting developments is the use of the TAT in investigating the extension of Piaget's theory from cognitive to interpersonal behavior. The role-taking task might also help identify specific areas in which interpersonal competence needs to be increased. The introduction of methods by which the judgments of "significant others" about the effectiveness of various adaptive strategies can be systematically integrated into the assessment procedure is also important. Finally, TAT and short-story methods may be potentially useful in cross-cultural comparisons of both problem situations and adaptive strategies.

OBJECTIVE ASSESSMENT TECHNIQUES

The number and range of purportedly relevant new techniques that have been recently developed in this area is bewildering enough to satisfy this author's desire for novelty and stimulus seeking, to arouse his intolerance of ambiguity (hopefully at no permanent adaptational cost), and at the same time to substantially increase his tolerance for unrealistic experiences and his adaptation level for cognitive complexity. For example, Crawford (1967) has developed a Psychological Adjustment Scale, the first group factor of which he labeled "social-economic-environmental competence"; Lazzaro (1968) has presented a seventy-two-item self-report Test of Impulse Control that significantly differentiated between university freshmen and upperclassmen, but unfortunately in the opposite direction from that postulated, indicating, contrary to the current firsthand experience of some campus administrators, that upperclassmen possess greater impulse control than freshmen; Mathis (1967) has published an Environmental Participation Index designed to estimate the relative exposure an individual has had to common American "middle-class" experiences in environmental stimulation; Grinker (1962) has compiled a 700-item questionnaire including categories covering childhood, adolescence, discipline, religious training, stresses and disappointments, evaluation of self, sex, and so on, for use in studying homoclites; Buhler, Brind, and Horner (1968) have utilized a Life Goal Inventory that consists of eighty-six questions referring to twelve general life goals that can be profiled to give various types of healthy, and even a "contented retirement," pattern; Hogan (1969) has developed a sixty-four-item self-report measure of empathy by comparing high- and low-rated empathy groups using the combined MMPI-CPI item pool; Nihira, Foster, and Spencer (1968) and Gunzburg (1968) have developed different instruments to assess the adaptive behavior of mental retardates; and, finally, Wicker (1968) has adapted a semantic differential for rating various situations with dimensions relating to competence or coping (for example, "helped me develop a skill or ability," "helped me have more confidence in myself," "gave me a chance to see how good I am"). This author must admit to further contributing to the complexity by his use of this type of semantic differential to have patients rate their experiences in different psychiatric ward subsettings (Moos, 1968a, 1969).

Moving for a moment to more established techniques, Gough (1966) appraised social maturity by means of the CPI, which is scaled for "folk concepts" theorized to be culturally universal. The optimum constellation of scales to measure social maturity included socialization, responsibility, flexibility, and dominance with positive ratings, and good impression and communality with negative ratings. The initial equation for social maturity was derived by differentiating samples of delinquents and nondelinquents in the United States, and then was cross-culturally validated on a similar Italian sample. Among nondelinquents, the social-maturity equation distinguished between cheaters and noncheaters on course examinations and between high-school students identified as more and less responsible. High scorers on the social-maturity equation are consistently described as dependable, reliable, responsible, mature, and capable; low scorers are consistently seen as distractable, impulsive, defensive, temperamental, and intolerant. Bouchard (1966) has related the CPI sociability scale and the first factor (interpersonal effectiveness) of the CPI to performance under group problem-solving conditions. In other approaches Scarr (1968) has successfully used the Adjective Check List (ACL) in studying grade-school twin girls, and Schaefer (1969) has found the ACL highly valid in identifying the self-concepts of creative high-school boys and girls in different specialty fields. Both the CPI and the ACL are excellent established techniques, and the manuals (Gough 1964, 1965) should be carefully studied as two of the best examples of objective empirical approaches to measurement in this area.

Kipnis (1968) developed an index of social immaturity by adding the scores from two measures of social development: the socialization scale of the CPI and an insolence scale. Results indicated that socially immature students were more visible to their instructors by virtue of their classroom behavior. As freshmen, they were evaluated as more disruptive and as upperclassmen as contributing more to classroom discussion. Socially immature students also had a higher rate of absenteeism and tended to be underachievers in mathematics, but not in introductory psychology. ,This latter finding arouses some curiosity about the factors determining the initial selection of students in psychology and the behavioral sciences, and thus indirectly determining the characteristics of the investigators who later define and study social immaturity.

There are several other relatively established techniques that are relevant to this area. Holland's (1965) Vocational Preference Inventory (VPI) is a personality inventory composed entirely of occupational titles. A person takes the inventory by indicating the occupations that he likes or dislikes. Occupational titles provide subtle stimuli that elicit positive interest and avoid the negative reactions sometimes provoked by obvious personality inventories. In addition, occupational content reduces the subject's need to take, because this content is usually perceived as having no relation to personal adjustment. The rationale of the VPI is that the choice of an occupation is an expressive act that reflects a person's motivation, knowledge, personality, ability, and way of life. The development of adequate adjustive techniques requires accurate discrimination among potential environments. This ability to discriminate potentially dissatisfying and unhealthy environments is imperative for mental health. In this sense the VPI is a miniature performance test of the subject's understanding of his surroundings in relation to himself.

Shostrom (1963) had presented a Personal Orientation Inventory (POI) consisting of 150 two-choice, paired-opposite, comparative value statements. The items are scored for two basic scales of self-actualization: support and time competence. The inventory significantly discriminates between clinically judged self-actualized and non–self-actualized groups (Fisher 1968; Fox, Knapp, and Michael 1968) and is able to show changes that indicate that sensitivity training may result in increased inner directiveness.

Holmes and colleagues (Holmes and Rahe 1967; Komaroff et al. 1968; Masuda and Holmes 1967) have constructed a Social Readjustment Rating Scale (SRRS) consisting of forty-three life events, the occurrence of which usually evokes, or is associated with, some adaptive or coping behavior on the part of the involved individual. Each item contains a life event whose advent is indicative of, or requires, a significant change in an ongoing life pattern.

Roen and Burnes (1967, 1968) have developed a Community Adaptation Schedule (CAS) that consists of 217 questions intended to elicit information about relationships between individuals and their environments. Items were constructed to elicit three modes of response: actual behavior, feeling or affect, and perception or belief. For example, in the question related to savings, one item asks, "How much money do you save?" (behavior); another asks, "How do you feel about your savings program?" (affect); and a third asks, "Do you think you have good money habits or good money sense?" (cognition). Preliminary results indicate that high investment of interest and energy in the community, whether affective, behavioral, or cognitive, is inversely related to the likelihood of social disruption that leads to outpatient care or psychiatric hospitalization.

There are still a number of other newer techniques that deserve special mention. In a very interesting example of developing a technique for a specific situation, King and Schiller (1960) utilized the Driver's Defensive Behavior Inventory (DDBI) to measure the orientations of problem drivers toward their past records of violations and accidents. Twenty-eight statements were classified according to the type of defense mechanism that was represented: "My record may look bad, but I really don't drive that way" (denial); "I think that the police are too strict in enforcing the traffic laws" (projection); and "I believe that since a good driver knows how to handle himself, it doesn't hurt to go over the speed limit once in a while" (rationalization). A measure of the relative use of rationalization was positively related to the level of ego strength in two samples, suggesting the comforting conclusion that rationalizations may be relatively adaptive after all.

Lanyon (1967) has described the construction and validation of an instrument to assess social competence in college males. Items reflect social participation, interpersonal competence, achievement, and environmental mastery. The general emphasis of the items is on extroversion, activity, and decision making at the expense of thinking and reflection. The scale was validated by demonstrating that high and low scorers differed in an antici- pated manner on several MMPI scales, and that socially competent frater- nity members (those with whom their peers preferred to double date) scored higher than socially incompetent members.

Farber (1962) studied the elements of competence in interpersonal rela- tions via a 104-item questionnaire, and Holland and Baird (1968) have de- veloped an Interpersonal Competency Scale (ICS). The scale consists of twenty true-false items—for example, "I have a reputation for being able to cope with difficult people" (no evidence is presented on whether this item has predictive validity for the selection of college administrators or depart- ment chairmen); "I know what I want to do with my life"; "I believe I have good practical judgment"; and "I am good at playing charades." High scorers on the ICS see themselves as sociable, popular, persuasive, energetic people who hope to become influential in community affairs. There were some predictive relationships between ICS freshmen scores and self-ratings, life goals, and achievement in college one year later. However, the evidence thus far indicates that interpersonal competence is a talent unrelated to edu- cation and intellectual abilities in that it has only low relationships to high-school grades. The authors consider the technique to be a rough mea- sure of a general disposition or capacity for interpersonal competence.

There are two further new techniques that have been designed from ex- plicit theoretical notions. Bakan (1966) has postulated two fundamental modalities, agency and communion, which he hypothesizes account for man's psychological growth and adjustment as well as his disintegration and maladjustment. Agency manifests itself in self-protection, self-assertion, self-expansion, isolation, alienation, aloneness, the urge to master, and the repression of thought, feeling, and impulse. Communion manifests itself in the sense of being at one with other organisms, in contact, openness, union, noncontractual cooperation, and in the lack of removal of repression. Bakan has developed a tentative 124-item inventory to measure these constructs— for example, "Friendliness often interferes with one's attempts to reach one's goals" (agency); "I stop thinking about my problems when I am with other people" (communion); "I like working with others" (communion). Brown and Marks (1969) provide some initial evidence for construct validity and point out that the inventory bears little content relationship to standard personality tests such as the CPI or the MMPI.

Alderfer (1967, 1969) was concerned with developing and testing an alter- native to Maslow's need-hierarchy notions and to a simple frustration hy- pothesis for the problem of relating need satisfaction to strength of desires. The alternative theory is based on a threefold conceptualization of human needs: existence, relatedness, and growth (ERG). Alderfer measured both the desire for, and the satisfaction of, these needs in a sample of bank em- ployees, in New York State, and the items are specifically worded for rele- vance to a business organization. For example, satisfaction with existence needs is measured by items like, "Considering the work required, the pay is what it should be"; satisfaction with relatedness needs, by items like, "My boss keeps me informed about what is happening in the company," and "My co-workers are uncooperative unless it's to their advantage," and satisfaction with growth needs, by items like, "My job requires making one or more important decisions every day." Empirical tests were generally supportive of various predictions from the ERG theory, which combines statements relevant to both deficiency and growth motivation. For deficiency motivation, the major cycling of desires is between existence and relatedness needs (which become more desired when not satisfied), whereas for growth motivation the major cycling of desires is between relatedness and growth needs (the latter becoming more desired when they are satisfied). The theory also posits both frustration regression ("The less relatedness needs are satisfied the more existence needs will be desired") and satisfaction progression ("the more relatedness needs are satisfied the more growth needs will be desired"). But according to this theory, that quiescent state of satisfied Nirvana where all has been sufficiently rewarded may never be reached, because "The more growth needs are satisfied the more they will be desired." The paper presents a very intriguing development from Maslow's theory, derives a set of testable predictions, and constructs a measurement technique with which to test these predictions empirically.

Because this author has not been immune to the creative urge, he has been involved in the development of two new techniques for use in psychiatric samples. First, a Ward Initiative Scale (WIS), which attempts to measure the concrete initiatives that patients can take to meet their needs on a psychiatric ward, has been developed (Houts and Moos 1969). The initial form of the WIS measures initiatives in the areas of autonomy, submission, variety, affiliation, and so forth. The subscales closely articulate with the subscales in the Ward Atmosphere Scale, which attempts to measure the social psychological atmospheres of psychiatric wards in terms of the relative emphases on twelve different areas of environmental press (Moos and Houts 1968). The two tests taken together may make it possible to assess some aspects of the person-environment interaction.

In the second approach, patients and therapists in a brief-contact clinic were asked what their goals were in therapy (Houts, MacIntosh, and Moos 1969). They were also asked what means they could use in the psychotherapeutic situation in order to achieve these goals. Therapists were asked similar questions about their goals. This type of means-ends conceptualization may be relevant to other real-life situations.

There are a number of broad personality dispositions that are assessed by relatively standard techniques and that are directly relevant to coping processes. These dispositions are relevant because they purportedly underlie basic ways in which the individual attempts to construe and understand his environment. For example, the Myer-Briggs Type Indicator is thought to measure variables (sensation, intuition, thinking, feeling) that are related to deep-seated individual differences that exercise a wide, but somewhat loose, control over the domains of cognitive functioning, interests, values, and personality development. The other most relevant variables are internal-external control (Rotter 1966), dogmatism (Rokeach 1960), and introversion-extroversion (H. Eysenck and S. Eysenck 1964). Research on these various dispositions has been reviewed relatively recently and thus will not be summarized here (H. Eysenck and S. Eysenck 1969; Lefcourt 1966; Vacchiano, Strauss, and Hockman 1969).

The proliferation of objective techniques almost defies summary. The large number of techniques is undoubtedly related to their simplicity, low cost, and relative efficiency of data handling. Investigators are urged to use stringent criteria to ensure the relevance of the techniques before using them in prospective projects. It should be noted that the general methodology involved in several of the studies mentioned provides important guidelines for the development of new techniques from existing theory (Alderfer 1969; Bakan 1966) or for use in specially relevant specific situations (King and Schiller 1960).

Important issues are raised by Kipnis (1968), who found that socially immature students were more disruptive as freshman and more positively valued as upperclassmen; by Farber (1962), who found both general and specific factors of interpersonal competence; and by Masuda and co-workers (Komaroff, Masuda, and Holmes 1968; Masuda and Holmes 1967), who gave the SRRS to different cultural and subcultural groups and found very high similarities in the perceptions of the extent of social stress caused by different life-change events. Thus some groundwork is being laid for studying the relative costs and benefits of different strategies, the number of different dimensions underlying interpersonal competence, and the potential cross-cultural comparisons of life stresses.

A major issue is the extent of information that can be collected by techniques that admittedly do not adequately mirror the complexities of the real world. Arguments about this tend to be hot and heavy, even though there is as yet very little empirical data actually comparing the relative efficacy of different types of assessment methods in relation to, for example, the different goals discussed in the introduction. Adequate methodological comparison studies of this type are acutely necessary.

BIOGRAPHICAL AND LIFE-HISTORY VARIABLES

Phillips (1968) has made the most comprehensive use of biographical variables in the measurement of social competence. He feels that the key to the prediction of future effectiveness in society lies in asking, "How well has this person met and how well does he now meet the expectations implicitly set by society for individuals of his age and sex group?" Phillips assumes, in a theoretical underpinning of the measure that is explicitly based on Werner (1957), that when development occurs it proceeds from a state of relative diffuseness in organization to a state of increasing differentiation and hierarchical integration. Development progresses along more than a single path, and thus different rates of development may appear in the intellectual, social, and moral spheres. The assumption is that achieved level of psychological development is identical with the person's adaptive potential.

Over the last twenty years, four different scales of social competence have been created: (1) the Phillips premorbid scale; (2) an index based on six biographical items commonly available in routine case records of mental hospitals; (3) the Worcester scale of social attainment; (4) the present scale of social competence. For example, in the present scale, intellectual development is measured by intelligence level, grades of education completed, occupational level, father's occupation, and regularity of employment; social development is assessed by marital status, heterosexual activity, number of organizations, and leadership positions held in organizations; moral development is measured by type of residence, number of people whose work is supervised, voting record, and degree of employment regularity.

Phillips reviews data indicating that: (1) a person's coping potential as indicated by the adequacy of his performance under conditions of experimental stress and his level of psychological development as measured in terms of Rorschach perceptual indices are both related to achieved level of social competence; (2) patients who manifest relatively high levels of premorbid social competence tend to spend shorter periods in hospital, and are less likely to be rehospitalized, than patients of lower premorbid social competence; (3) individuals of higher levels of social competence tend to manifest symptoms reflective of a turning against the self, while symptomatology associated with lower levels of competence indicates either a turning against others or an avoidance of others; (4) thought dominance as opposed to action dominance of symptomatology is associated with higher social competence.

In an interesting recent study reflecting on the issue of "adaptational cost," Ravensborg and Foss (1969) found highly significant differences between completed suicides, natural deaths, and other inpatients on social-competence variables, with suicides tending to be younger, more intelligent, and better educated than the comparison groups.

There has been some recent critical data. Rosen and colleagues (1969) related the three-year posthospital outcomes of eighty-one schizophrenic and eighty-five nonschizophrenic patients to the six-item competence scale and found that among schizophrenic patients social competence was significantly related to incidence and frequency of rehospitalization; whereas among nonschizophrenic patients there was no significant relationship. More critically, in another study, Rosen and co-workers (1968) found that the prognostic value of the six-item scale was based entirely upon its relationship with age of first psychiatric treatment contact.

There is some intriguing data in other areas supporting the usefulness of biographical indices in the measurement of prognosis. For example, Glueck and Glueck (1959) present data suggesting that the social-competence variables of intelligence, education, occupation skill, work habits, and use of leisure time are related to favorable prognosis of delinquents. Holmes and co-workers (1961) utilized the Berle Index, which includes various biographical variables, and found that items such as marital status, educational achievement, and employment regularity discriminated between improved and unimproved patients. Moran and colleagues (1956) have obtained similar data in predicting the outcome of hospital treatment of tuberculosis. The SRRS (1967) mentioned earlier is also a life-event, or essentially biographical, technique; however, it concentrates on life changes specifically requiring various amounts of adaptive or coping behavior. The SRRS also has been shown to be related to both incidence and prognosis of disease.

Schaefer (1969) constructed a 165-item biographical inventory grouped into sections relevant to physical characteristics, family history, educational history, and leisure-time activities. The inventory was able to predict high-school adolescents' creativity scores across sex and specialty fields.

The use of biographical and life-history information dovetails with the new emphasis on unobtrusive measures in the social sciences, because biographical variables are, of course, nonreactive. For example, Barthell and Holmes (1968) studied high-school senior yearbook summaries as a nonreactive archival measure of level of high-school activity. It was found that high-school graduates who were later diagnosed as schizophrenic had participated in significantly fewer activities than did their normal controls, whereas the activity level of later-diagnosed psychoneurotics fell in between that of the schizophrenics and the normals.

When certain global prognostic indices are needed for predictive purposes, various biographical variables may be the simplest, most objective, and most useful data to collect. However, this type of data has less obvious relevance to theories about competence, to the understanding of coping processes, and to possible strategies for changing adaptive behavior.

MULTIMEDIA METHODS

This section briefly comments on two methods that can be utilized with a variety of different types of primary data. The most developed model proposes that the general mechanisms of the ego may take on either defensive or coping functions (Haan 1963, 1969). For example, the classical defense mechanisms concerned with impulse economics are displacement, reaction formation, and repression. Their coping counterparts are sublimation, substitution, and suppression. Defense mechanisms primarily involving cognitive activity with their coping counterparts are: isolation and objectivity, intellectualizing and intellectuality, rationalization and logical analysis. Recently Haan has added a third aspect of ego processes (failure in ego-functioning) in order to describe the processes characteristic of psychotic individuals or the more transient ones of relatively adequate individuals experiencing unmanageable stress. Haan states that "the model is so structured that a coping mechanism, like empathy, a defense mechanism, like projection, and an ego failure, like delusion or ideation, comprise a trio with a quintessential meaning of interpersonal sensitivity, that is, behavior that is attuned to formulating and understanding another's unexpressed or partially expressed thoughts and feelings" (1969, p. 14).

There have been some very interesting findings utilizing this model. For example, coping is generally related to I.Q. acceleration over a twenty-five-year period and defensiveness to I.Q. deceleration (Haan 1963). Upwardly mobile people have a high probability of being seen as coping, with men modulating their impulses and women sublimating them. In another study, Haan (1964) found that responses in the Rorschach situation, at least with normal subjects who are likely to define transactions less rigidly, are better understood in global ego terms than in terms of the specific content or form of Rorschach percepts. Persons who elaborated their Rorschach responses and who affectively or intellectually enjoyed taking the Rorschach had higher coping scores.

In a further study utilizing this model, Weinstock (1967a) correlated ratings on the ten defense mechanism scales with ratings of social class at the subject's birth. Denial was negatively correlated, while intellectualization and projection were positively correlated with social class. These findings lend support to the Miller and Swanson (1960) hypothesis that children of relatively lower-class families tend to employ a more primitive, global, reality-distorting means of defending against conflict, while higher social status is associated with the child's use of more differentiated socially adaptive defenses requiring greater cognitive skill.

Weinstock (1967b) also correlated ratings of parents' personalities and of subjects' childhood family environments with ratings of subjects' use of the ten defense and ten coping mechanisms at thirty years of age. Results indicated that primitive defenses (denial and repression) were related to the father's passivity in the early family environment. More differentiated defenses were related to rejection of the subject in early adolescence. Expressive coping (tolerance of ambiguity, regression in the service of the ego) was correlated with family conflict in adolescence. Weinstock concluded that subjects' imitation of parental behavior played an important role in the development of particular defense and coping mechanisms.

Hunter and Goodstein (1967) investigated the relationship of the Barron Ego Strength Scale to the defense mechanisms of rationalization and denial and the coping mechanism of logical analysis. Forty college subjects took a difficult symbolic reasoning test and were asked to score their own papers and indicate where they stood on faked norms. In a taped standardized interview they were then asked to explain their "poor performance." Subjects with high ego strength used a significantly greater number of coping responses than subjects with low ego strength, and the judges rated the latter as significantly more defensive. Subjects with low ego strength also used more rationalizations.

Alker (1967) studied defensive projection and coping empathy and his overall results supported the assumption that a particular cognitive style was the common basis for both empathy and projection; that is, that the cognitive style of the individual determines which defense and which coping mechanism he chooses in reacting to a situation. The specific finding was that cognitive filtering (narrow category width and high scanning) was associated with both empathy and defensive interpersonal sensitivity. This finding was stronger for males than for females. In a further study, Alker (1968) concluded that minimizing social desirability in a set of items may tend to reduce its effectiveness in discriminating between coping and defensive behavior.

In an important dissertation, Folkins (1967) utilized the model to investigate the effect of anticipation time on reactions to threat of shock. Increases involving seconds (five seconds, thirty seconds, one minute) produced increased disturbance, with maximum disturbance for the one-minute anticipation interval. Three- and five-minute anticipation times produced less disturbance, but twenty-minute anticipation again produced somewhat more disturbance. Coping mechanisms were more in evidence for those anticipation intervals associated with low disturbance, while ego-failure mechanisms were more in evidence for intervals associated with high disturbance. However, coping and ego failure were not directly associated with disturbance in interindividual correlation analyses; only defense mechanisms were associated with low disturbance in these analyses. Folkins concludes that defense, not coping, was the most successful form of ego-functioning in this threat situation. The study is relevant to the question of whether there are typical sequences by which a person attempts to cope with anticipated harm from moment to moment as the confrontation draws nearer. Most interviews revealed a complex pattern that usually included some ratings at each level of ego-functioning.

All these studies indicate that this model can be profitably utilized to analyze data from a variety of different types of situations. There are some rater-reliability problems (Folkins 1967) as well as some disagreements about the assumptions utilized in the model (Lazarus, Averill, and Opton, Chapter 10 of this book), however, the variables are highly relevant, and studies indicate acceptable construct validity. The development of explicit rating criteria for the factor scales of controlled coping, expressive coping, structured defense, and anticognitive defense would make the rating task simpler and might not result in any net loss of relevant information.

Hurvich and Bellak (1968) and Bellak and Hurvich (1969) describe a model whereby materials from clinical interviews, psychological tests, and psychological laboratory procedures are separately rated for adaptive adequacy of ten ego-functions. Thirteen-point scales were developed for use with ratings of two-hour clinical interviews centered on eliciting information relevant to past and present ego-functioning. Rating scales were also developed for assessing the ego-functions from psychological tests—for example, reality testing is assessed from a subject's understanding of intelligence test tasks, from the accuracy of Rorschach form perception, and from distortions of perceptual characteristics of the TAT cards; sense of reality, on the other hand, is gauged from the extent of vagueness, fluidity, and transparency characterizing Rorschach responses and from attributing feelings of strangeness or unreality to TAT characters. One or more laboratory tests were also chosen to measure each ego-function. The method of administration involves some interference with the subject's utilization of the ego-function, and he is evaluated on the adequacy of his performance under the interference conditions. For example, some aspects of autonomous functioning are assessed by the subject's ability to carry out motor coordination when drive-related stimuli are introduced; soundness of judgment is assessed with level of aspiration and time-estimation tasks; sense of reality is evaluated from performance on the rod-and-frame test and response to delayed auditory feedback.

The authors hypothesized and generally found that schizophrenics manifest poorer ego-functioning than neurotics, who in turn show poorer ego-functioning than normals, providing some construct validity for the approach. They are hypothesizing that discriminable ego-function patterns will be found to characterize subgroups within the schizophrenic population and that these patterns will be related to different primary etiologic factors.

The further development of models and empirical methods by which ego-functions may be assessed and directly compared across a wide array of different tasks should prove useful.

SELF-CONCEPTIONS

As Lazarus (1966) has pointed out, certain personality traits such as ego strength and self-esteem may be assumed to reduce vulnerability to threat and to facilitate healthy or adaptive forms of coping. For example, Zimbardo and Formica (1963) have shown that subjects low in self-esteem have a stronger tendency to affiliate under threat than those who are high in self-esteem. Also, Janis (1958) has shown that persons with relatively strong feelings of personal inadequacy are predisposed to be relatively highly influenced by persuasive communications. It is these considerations, together with the theoretical relevance of some of the assessment techniques that have been devised, that give the methods presented in this section prime importance.

Several techniques have been developed that have theoretical relevance particularly in relation to Erikson's theory of ego identity. For example, Rasmussen (1964) examined the relationship of ego identity to psychosocial effectiveness in two groups of Navy recruits. He developed an Ego Identity Scale (EIS) by taking three criteria of health and ill health for each of the first six psychosocial crisis stages mentioned by Erikson. Each derivative was sampled by four items, and the scale thus consists of seventy-two items, half of them cast so as to require a positive response, and half requiring a negative response. A derivative from crisis stage one (basic trust versus mistrust) is that a sense of time perspective occurs; that is, future satisfactions are worth working for and waiting for. A positive statement would be, "If a person wants something worthwhile, he should be willing to wait for it." A negative statement would be, "I lose interest in things if I have to wait too long to get them." The total EIS score significantly differentiated highly adequately from marginally adequately adjusted Navy recruits.

Melges (1969) has operationalized Erikson's eight epigenetic stages by utilizing a semantic-differential technique with three bipolar adjectives defined for each stage, for example, fragmented-integrated, phoney-sincere, and frustrated-satisfied for ego integrity versus despair. A short form of eight basic adjective pairs was found useful in intensive single-case studies of identity crises and depersonalization.

In a somewhat different approach, Marcia (1966, 1967) used semistructured interviews to assess four styles of reacting to the late-adolescent identity crisis: identity achievement, moratorium, foreclosure, and identity diffusion. Marcia also used the ego-identity, incomplete-sentence blank, a twenty-three item semistructured test requiring the subject to complete a sentence "expressing his real feelings" having been given a leading phrase. Two typical stems are: "If one commits oneself . . ." and "When I let myself go, I. . . ." Marcia concluded that the interview based on individual styles was more successful than the incomplete sentences, which treated ego identity as a simple linear quality. One study indicated that identity achievement and moratorium subjects showed superior performance on a stressful concept-attainment task. Foreclosure subjects endorsed authoritarian values, set goals unrealistically high, and had considerable difficulty on the task. In another study, Marcia found that subjects high in identity status were less vulnerable to self-esteem manipulation.

Washburn (1961) constructed items to measure the self-concept as represented in the theories of Erikson, Fromm, Freud, Sarbin, and Maslow. Cluster analyses yielded six patterns ranked from least to most mature: (1) the somatic, primitive self; (2) the submissive, dependent self; (3) the detached, independent self; (4) the outer, controlling self; (5) the inner, controlled self; (6) the integrative, actualizing self. Significant differences in means on tests measuring various self levels were found for contrasting groups of males and females, college preparatory and non-college preparatory high-school students, and college and high-school students.

Coopersmith (1967) has developed a fifty-item Self-Esteem Inventory (SEI) for use with children aged eight to ten. The inventory is concerned with the subject's self-attitude in the areas of peers, parents, school, and personal interests. Coopersmith defined self-esteem from both the perspective of the subject via the SEI and from that of the observer via the rating of the subject's self-esteem behavior. Types of self-esteem were derived from various combinations of the two scores. Generally, there were substantial agreements between self-evaluation and behavioral expression; however, there were groups of subjects demonstrating marked disagreement between self-view and behavior in each of the four possible patterns. In one group, high manifest self-evaluation apparently is a reaction against a low underlying self-evaluation as a result of poor performance and low status. In another group there is low self-evaluation despite excellent performance and high status, and this appears to be due to a striving for unrealistically high goals.

Rosenberg (1965) developed another self-esteem inventory and found an inverse relationship between self-esteem and anxiety in over 5,000 high-school students in New York State. Rosenberg presents an informative discussion of individuals with unstable self-pictures. In general, if an individual has an unclear, uncertain opinion of himself, he is deprived of his most valuable frame of reference and this deprivation is likely to be anxiety provoking.

Other important implications of differences in self-esteem have been indicated in two recent studies by Korman (1966, 1967). He measured self-esteem by utilizing the self-assurance scale of the Ghiselli self-description inventory, a thirty-one item, forced-choice, adjective-pair scale measuring the extent to which the individual perceives himself as being effective in dealing with the problems that confront him. Korman found that individuals with high self-esteem were more likely than those with low self-esteem to choose those occupations that they perceived most likely to fulfill their specific needs and to be in keeping with their self-perceived characteristics. Thus, an individual's self-esteem acts as a "moderator variable" on the extent to which his self-perceived needs are predictive of his occupational choice. In another study, Korman tested and supported the hypothesis that need satisfaction was related to overall satisfaction for individuals with high self-esteem, but not for those with low self-esteem.

In a logically similar approach, Lewis (1966) defined the degree of self-concept implementation as the discrepancy between ideal and actual job ratings and found that as this discrepancy increased both job satisfaction and supervisors' performance ratings decreased.

Ziller, Megas, and DeCencio (1964) have developed a unique nonverbal method in which subjects are required to arrange circles representing the self and other salient social objects on a felt board. For example, in one case the circles were labeled as: psychiatrist, psychologist, social worker, nurse, nurse's aide, other patients, and yourself. Arrangement of the self and social objects along a left-right continuum is equivalent to an evaluation scale of the self and provides an indirect measure of self-esteem. Mossman and Ziller (1968) have proposed that self-esteem is that component of the self system associated with the organism's consistency of social response. They found that the consistency of the level of participation of patients in group therapy sessions was associated with self-esteem. Self-esteem was also positively related to frequency of verbal participation in therapy groups. High self-esteem is regarded as a stabilizing mechanism that enables the organism to suspend judgment concerning self during the information-processing phase of a problem-solving interaction and thereby to persevere, rather than to oscillate, with regard to self-evaluation and self-guiding mechanisms. Ziller and colleagues (1969) have also suggested that persons with low self-esteem should be field-dependent and tend to conform passively to the influence of the prevailing field or context because their behavior is linked to immediate environmental circumstances and is not mediated or integrated by the self-concept.

A number of other measures of self-concept have also been recently described in the literature. For example, Wahler (1968) developed an inventory designed to measure the degree to which subjects differentially emphasized favorable and unfavorable self-descriptive attributes; Tracy (1967), Grant (1967), and Wendland (1968) all worked with the Tennessee Self-Concept Scale, and Wendland found that Negro adolescents do not present a picture of self-devaluation and negative self-esteem in comparison to their white peers, but rather have realistic cynical orientations toward the environment and feelings of isolation from others. Gunderson and Johnson (1965) factor analyzed a self-evaluation inventory given to a population of young, healthy, Navy men and found eight factors, including physical strength, body build, willpower, intelligence, and emotional control; Offer (1966) developed a self-image questionnaire for use with normal adolescents with eleven scales measuring impulse control, emotional tone, body and self-image, external mastery, and superior adjustment; Lentz (1968) developed a self-concept instrument entitled "My Self" for use with primary-grade children; and Rychlak and Legerski (1967) utilized a sorting procedure that required subjects to make forced choices of brief, self-descriptive statements predetermined as representing ascendant dominance or retiring passivity into like-self versus unlike-self categories. Crowne and Stephens (1961) present a summary and critique of earlier studies. The Barron Ego Strength Scale is already a well-known technique and will thus not be reviewed here (Barron 1953; Frank 1967; Stein and Chu 1967).

In an important book, Block (1965) shows that the first two factors of MMPI cannot easily be interpreted in terms of acquiescence and social desirability. He suggests that the first factor be identified as "ego resiliency." The word *resilient* implies the resourcefulness, adaptability, and engagement with his world that characterize an individual placing high on this continuum. Ego resiliency is intended to denote characteristic adaptation capability under the strain of new environmental demands. An individual who is not ego resilient will not be in a state of anxiety if the circumstances in which he functions are for him safe and predictable. The second factor is interpreted in terms of ego control, that is, the individual's characteristic mode of monitoring impulse. The continuum is conceived as representing excessive containment of impulse and delay of gratification at one end (over control), versus insufficient modulation of impulse and an inability to delay gratification at the other (under control). Block further characterizes individuals high and low on each of these factors in his monograph.

Gordon (1969) has presented a comprehensive review of methodologies designed to assess self-conceptions. He discusses four levels of abstraction in the actual content of the self-conception and presents methodological tactics suited to each level. At the most concrete level, specific self-representations are gathered by unstructured, free-response techniques, like the "Who Am I?" or by sentence completion or adjective checklist approaches. At a second level Gordon posits four systemic senses of self (competence, self-determination, unity, and moral worth) and offers a twenty-item self-rating inventory to assess them. He posits a conceptual link between these four senses of self and the four system problems that form the core of the general theory of action (Parsons and Shils 1951), that is, the sense of competence corresponds to the system problem of adaptation, the sense of self-determination to the goal-attainment problem, the sense of unity to the problem of integration, and the sense of moral worth to pattern maintenance. Specific inventory items are derived from the system levels that constitute the situation of action: cultural, social, personality, organism, and surrounding environment. For example, competence is a very general sense of self, but it may be specified by asking for self-ratings on one or more aspects of general performance capacity drawn from each of the five system levels. At the cultural level the individual's being well informed is an important resource, his ability to get along with others is important at the social system level, and his intelligence is one of the chief capacities at the personality level.

The third level is posited as the sense of personal autonomy, and Gordon offers a new thirteen-item personal autonomy scale with five response categories (agree-disagree) for each item. Items include: "I can do what I want without asking someone else's permission"; "I generally make plans on my own"; and "I sometimes have to do things that I think are wrong" (minus item). The fourth level is the level of self-esteem for which Gordon suggests the use of the Rosenberg self-esteem scale. The whole hierarchical structure of self-conceptions posited by Gordon is extremely intriguing, as are his new assessment techniques and their relation to theory. Intercorrelational studies in order to see whether the different levels and senses of self have an empirical reality should probably have high priority.

Several recent studies indicate that there are important environmental effects on self-concept and self-esteem. Carroll (1967) tested the effects of two types of school programs on self-concept and academic achievement over an eight-month interval. Results supported the hypothesis that educable mental retardates in a segregated setting would show less improvement in self-concept than would comparable children in a partially integrated setting. Manasse (1965) explored the effect of the social setting on self-regard of chronic schizophrenics. He hypothesized that self-regard was related to the degree to which a person is able to meet the demands and expectations of his social setting. Two groups of comparable chronic schizophrenics were studied. Group one was hospitalized; group two attended a day-treatment center. Results revealed that the hospitalized group had higher self-regard than the nonhospitalized group. These findings suggest that an environment that demands little enables a person to maintain a relatively positive self-image. On the other hand, an environment that demands a great deal of the same individual may lead to a relatively negative self-image. These basic results have been essentially replicated by Fox (1968) in a study of a job-oriented ward that had a strong push toward patient autonomy and responsibility. Evidence that a Utopian world with high self-esteem for all is still only a fantasy, and that all our actions have both benefits and costs, is indicated by Ziller and co-workers (1969), who found that losing candidates for the Oregon legislature decreased in self-esteem as compared to winning candidates. It is unclear whether this finding is relevant to that of Aronson and Mettee (1968), who discovered that subjects given feedback to decrease their self-esteem temporarily were more likely to cheat rather than lose during a blackjack game under circumstances that made it appear that detection was impossible.

COGNITIVE STYLES

As Inkeles (1966) has pointed out, work on cognitive styles is directly relevant to this area, because these styles are essential components of the individual's equipment for coping with the demands of society. Cognitive styles, like self-conceptions, may exert a loose but decisive control over large areas of experience. They play a role in school performance, channel and limit the choice of occupations, help determine limits of information seeking in stress situations, and have important influences in various other domains such as person perception, interpersonal relationships, types of pathology, and response to different types of psychiatric treatment.

For example, Stern, Stein, and Bloom (1956) have reported on the important role of cognitive styles in the adjustment of freshmen at the University of Chicago. One program stressed and rewarded "abstract analysis and relativity of values and judgment rather than fixed standards," and teachers introduced a good deal of ambiguity and often departed from conventional standards of judgment. Those students whose cognitive styles inclined them to concrete thinking, to insistence on one "correct" answer made up the bulk of the academic casualties at the end of the year.

Only the barest outlines of this vast research area, mainly restricted to newer paper-and-pencil questionnaire techniques, can be given here. Lazarus (1966) has already reviewed a major amount of this work. In addition, Witkin (1962) has covered some of the literature on perceptual measures of cognitive style and has also presented detailed summaries of his own extensive and important research, and thus this will not be reviewed in detail here. Suffice it to say that Witkin argues cogently that research on cognitive styles has important implications for personality theory and for problems of diagnosis and psychotherapy (1965). The general dimension of psychological differentiation is meaningfully related to a variety of other variables, including different forms of pathology, perceptual defense, and certain aspects of patient-therapist interactions (1965). The most impressive aspects of this work relate to the high degree of stability of cognitive styles from childhood to young adulthood (1967) and to the resulting fact that the measures utilized are applicable over a very large age range and thus are suitable for group comparisons in which the subjects of interest vary in age from prepuberty to adulthood. In addition, these measures have already been utilized quite extensively and profitably for both subcultural and cross-cultural comparisons (1967). Recent developments on the techniques by which field-dependence and field-independence may be assessed makes this work of broader potential utility. The field–dependence-independence dimension may be assessed by subtests of the Wechsler Adult Intelligence Scale, by figure drawings, by the embedded-figures test, of which there is a recently adapted paper-and-pencil form, and by the rod-and-frame test, a portable version of which has recently been devised (1968). This body of work should be carefully studied.

Byrne (1961, 1964) developed a Repression-Sensitization Scale (RSS) and found that sensitizers showed greater negative self-description, self-ideal discrepancies, deviant response biases, and poorer CPI-assessed adjustment. A great deal of research has been done utilizing this scale, and the history of work on it illustrates both the benefits and possible costs of introducing a relatively simple, objectively scored, easy-to-use technique. There was initially a great deal of interest in finding correlates of the scale. For example, Lazarus and Alfert (1964) found that repressors had higher levels of skin-conductance reactions to an emotionally arousing film than sensitizers, even though the repressors denied, whereas the sensitizers claimed, subjective distress. Parsons, Fulgenzi, and Edelberg (1969) corroborated this in a group setting and found that repressors had significantly greater amounts of skin conductance than sensitizers and also that they were rated as more aggressive than sensitizers even though they reported themselves as less aggressive. In other studies, MacDonald (1967) showed that attribution of hostility is least in repressors; Feder (1967, 1968) found no relationship between the RSS and the Zigler-Phillips six-item social-competence index, but did find that sensitizers got significantly higher scores on the Cornell Medical Index; Petzel and Gynther (1968) found that sensitizers were better at solving anagrams under ego-oriented instructions and concluded that repressors may be so effective in avoiding or denying stressful stimuli that they cannot cope with unavoidable stress; Weinstein (1966) found that, contrary to his hypothesis, repressors reported more and earlier memories than sensitizers apparently in both a sitting and a lying position; and finally, Schill (1969) found that male repressors demonstrated less ability than male sensitizers to respond to *double-entendre* words with sexual associations. Repressors, then, are generally described as people who use avoidance, repression, denial, and forgetting as primary modes of adaptation, whereas sensitizers approach rather than avoid anxiety and tend to use the defense mechanisms of intellectualization and obsession.

Recent studies have reported various problems with the RSS. For example, Feder (1967) found significant correlations between the scale and both social desirability and acquiescence response set, and Gleser and Ihilevich (1969) report very high correlations between the scale and anxiety.

This raises the basic issue of how the cognitive style of an individual affects the way he will allow himself to respond to paper-and-pencil questionnaires. MacDonald (1967) has pointed out that much of the research evidence pertaining to ego-control patterns has been obtained from questionnaire techniques and that, because repressors by definition deny and sensitizers admit, the resulting data may be indicative of a subject's response style rather than of his adjustment state. Lefcourt (1966), in a very intriguing study, explored the meaning of the RSS dimension by asking subjects their interpretations. Repressors interpreted the scale as an indicator of mental illness, while sensitizers saw it as a measure concerned with honesty with oneself. Subjects were simply asked, "What do you believe this test measures?" and "Describe the sort of person who would fill out the questionnaire in exactly the opposite manner that you did." Repressors viewed the admission of emotionality as a sign of instability, whereas sensitizers viewed it as a reflection of honesty.

One of the most important areas related to cognitive style involves the recent work on cognitive complexity (CC) and differentiation, hierarchical integration, and information processing. The theoretical underpinnings for this work come mainly from Werner (1957) and Kelly (1955). Werner has postulated that the development of cognition involves increased differentiation, articulation, and interdependence of elements by virtue of their integration into a hierarchically organized system. The relative number of constructs in a cognitive system is one index of its degree of cognitive differentiation. Bonarius (1965) lists ten different methods that have been used to assess CC, and Crockett (1965) reviews much of the literature in this area. Zajonc (1960) asks subjects to record and sort all constructs included in his impressions of another person. Two constructs are called similar if they fall in the same group, and the homogeneity of the impression, which is considered a measure of hierarchic integration, is defined by the ratio of the actual to the possible number of similar constructs. Bieri (1961) measures CC by determining the extent to which different interpersonal constructs are actually applied differentially to other persons. Crockett (1965) asks subjects to identify and describe in writing eight different individuals; the number of interpersonal constructs used in the descriptions is taken as the measure of cognitive differentiation.

Research results generally indicate that subjects high in complexity distinguish more clearly between other individuals, assume others are less similar to themselves, develop a greater number of inferences from a particular set of information, are less likely to form stereotypes, are more likely to view others in ambivalent terms, and are better able to assimilate potentially contradictory information about others into unified impressions than are subjects low in complexity. For example, Meltzer, Crockett, and Rosenkrantz (1966) found that under conditions of value congruity, high-complexity subjects utilized potentially incompatible bits of information to form better-organized impressions of another. Miller (1969) found that subjects high in complexity produced more constructs and traits in their descriptions. Adams-Webber (1969) found that persons displaying relatively high cognitive complexity infer the personal constructs of others in social situations more efficiently than do cognitively simple persons.

In other important work in this area, Jones (1965) discusses information deprivation, and Schroder, Driver, and Streufert (1967) cover information processing. The latter authors point out that, given the same amount of information, different people use different conceptual rules in thinking and interrelating elements. They maintain that an adaptive orientation acts first like a set of filters, selecting certain kinds of information, and second, like a program or set of rules that combine these items of information in specific ways. They attempt to show that if the same informational components are described in different ways, different adaptive consequences follow. In changing task environments in which exploration, alternative goals, strategies, and decisions are essential, information-processing variables should be of prime importance. Four points along the dimension of cognitive complexity are described in detail; studies generally supporting the notion that information processing reaches a maximum level of structural complexity at some optimal level of environmental complexity are summarized. Persons capable of using more integratively complex conceptual processes will track more kinds of information, integrate it more complexly, base their actions on more sources of information, generate a greater amount of discrepant information, and develop more, and higher-level, action strategies.

Schroder, Driver, and Streufert (1967) discuss object sorting, the Kelly Reptest, and multidimensional scaling as alternative measures of differentiation, the basic intent of which is to uncover the number, kind, and organization of dimensions employed by subjects in their perceptions of complex stimuli. They also present a manual for assessing the structural characteristics of verbal responses, which has been applied to incomplete sentence stems, and answers to essay questions. This general approach has already been discussed in a previous section.

One of the relevant issues in this area is the extent to which different measures are assessing empirically different constructs and the extent to which there is generality of cognitive complexity across different stimulus domains. Cognitive differentiation and integration are usually seen as depending upon an individual's encounters with empirical phenomena; depending upon the kinds of experiences he has encountered, a person may attain a highly complex set of conceptions with respect to one kind of phenomena and, at the same time, hold undifferentiated conceptions about a different set of objects. For example, a person might use an integratively complex structure for handling interpersonal stimuli, but might have only a simple structure for handling religious stimuli, or vice versa. A person who has attained a high level of differentiation and integration with respect to some sphere may revert to lower-level performance under disorganizing conditions induced by emotional stress. Crockett (1965) has suggested that there are good theoretical reasons to suppose that a complex set of constructs develops with respect to those objects that are of relatively great functional significance to an individual, a supposition that implies only modest generality of complexity across domains. There is some evidence that a person's constructs relative to others with whom he interacts frequently and intimately will be more complex than his constructs relative to categories of people with whom he interacts less intensely.

Cropley (1969) defined the concept of intellectual style as referring to the existence of certain stable idiosyncratic differences among people in the way they go about taking in, processing, and utilizing information obtained from the environment. Two people of equal capacity may differ in the characteristic ways in which they deploy their intellectual resources in coming to grips with information and in the kinds of information they prefer to handle. Four tests of intellectual style were administered: flexibility, originality, category width, and abstractness of intellectual functioning. These variables accounted for significant proportions of the variance in science achievement. The most successful science students were characterized by highly abstract and original thinking and by their characteristic ways of relating apparently discrepant data. In an earlier study (Cropley 1967) it had been found that men graduating with honors came almost exclusively from among those who had been rated highly divergent in their style of thinking on entry into university four years previously. In a generally similar approach, Hoepfner and O'Sullivan (1968) point out that giftedness may be used to describe people with special aptitudes like creative thinking and social intelligence. Thus there is a growing concern with cognitive and intellectual styles, particularly as they may be relevant to the accuracy of prediction of different types of performance over and above the prediction possible from standard intelligence tests.

NOVELTY NEEDS

The concept of man as an active, exploring, stimulus-seeking, and curiosity-seeking organism has given rise to a number of very intriguing new assessment devices that purport to measure various aspects of these tendencies. In early work, which might be considered to be very closely related to cognitive styles, Pervin (1963) found that initially predictable shock was preferable to unpredictable shock even when the predictability did not lead to shock avoidance, but that as exposure to the experimental situations became repetitive, unpredictability became increasingly desirable; Cohen, Stotland, and Wolfe (1955) developed two different measures of need cognition (the desire for more information or understanding) and found that an ambiguous situation produced more frustration than did a structured one, especially for people with high cognition needs; Brim and Hoff (1957) developed a measure of desire for certainty and found that this desire could be increased by situational frustration, such as having to cope with a difficult hidden-figures test; and Budner (1962) developed a scale to measure intolerance of ambiguity, the tendency to perceive ambiguous situations (those characterized by novelty, complexity, or insolubility) as threatening. These and other studies, in conjunction with the theoretical developments in the field, have given rise to new concepts that have in turn elicited new assessment techniques.

For example, Zuckerman and co-workers (1964) have developed a Sensation-Seeking Scale (SSS), which is designed to quantify the construct of "optimal stimulation level." There are fifty-four items pertaining to preferences for extremes of sensation, for new and unfamiliar experiences, for irregularity, and for danger, thrills, or kicks, and so on. The SSS was found to be positively correlated with field independence as measured by the embedded-figures test. In further studies, Zuckerman and Link (1968) found four factors in a version of the SSS given to males: thrill sensation seeking, social sensation seeking, visual sensation seeking, and antisocial sensation seeking. Only the first two factors emerged in the female data. The SSS was positively correlated with autonomy, change, and exhibitionism scores, and negatively correlated with deference, nurturance, orderliness, and affiliation scores on both the Edwards Personal Preference Schedule and the Gough Adjective Checklist. The person characterized by a high degree of sensation seeking tends to be oriented to body sensations, extroverted, thrill seeking, active, impulsive, antisocial, nonconformist, and low on anxiety.

In another study Zuckerman and Schultz (1967) found, in three different universities, that male and female undergraduates who volunteered for hypnosis experiments were significantly higher on the SSS than nonvolunteers. Farley and Farley (1967) predicted and found that extroversion would correlate significantly with the SSS. Kish and Busse (1969) found that SSS scores were negatively related to MMPI depression, repression, and social-introversion scores and positively related to ego strength. Hocking and Robertson (1969) found complex relationships between the SSS and need for stimulation during sensory restriction, and Waters and Kirk (1968) predicted and found positive relationships between SSS scores and risk-taking behavior in a gambling situation.

In case the reader's need for variety is still unsatisfied and he wishes to gamble on a new scale, he can look at the Stimulus Variation-Seeking Scale (SVSS) developed by Penney and Reinehr (1966). The SVSS attempts to measure the amount of exteroceptive stimulus variation seeking customarily sought by an individual. This is defined as approaching and exploring relatively new stimulus situations, incongruous and complex stimuli, and responding so as to vary stimulation. Initial normative data, reliability, and discriminant validity data are presented.

Garlington and Shimota (1964) developed a Change Seeker Index (CSI) that is a measure of the need for variable stimulus input. Examples of CSI items are: "People view me as a quite unpredictable person"; "I tend to act impulsively"; and "It annoys me to have to wait for someone." Reliability, normative data, and initial validity data are presented. McCarroll and colleagues (1967), not to be deterred by complexity, have already analyzed and found high correlations among these three stimulation-seeking scales. They found significantly higher means and correlations among scales obtained for general psychology students than for prefreshman students, suggesting that one year of college experience may lead to more stimulus-seeking behavior. There appears to be some face validity for this conclusion.

Snyder (1968) utilized a more experimental method of obtaining data on stimulation-seeking behavior. He tested two groups of schizophrenic patients for stimulus-seeking behavior before and after undergoing a three-hour period of reduced sensory input, while control groups were tested before and after a three-hour period of routine ward activities. For each of sixty trials, every subject in the positive stimulation groups was required, under threat of shock, to press a button to hear five seconds of music by the Tijuana Brass or to press another button to be left in silence. The total number of avoidance presses, that is presses made prior to the onset of shock was defined as each subject's stimulus-seeking score. The negative stimulation groups were tested under similar conditions, except that they had a choice of pressing a button to hear an automobile horn or a button to be left in silence, but were not permitted to hear music for their button-pressing responses. The results of this experiment did not support any of the initial hypotheses, possibly because individual differences in preference for hearing the Tijuana Brass, automobile horns, or silence were not systematically controlled. It is also possible that allowing an individual to press a button both to escape shock and to have five seconds of silence is such an overwhelmingly positively reinforcing condition that all individual differences are washed out.

In a somewhat different approach, Maddi (1965) has attempted to develop measures of the tendency toward variety. In one study he measured three distinct forms of the need for variety as expressed in thematic apperception: novelty of productions, curiosity, and desire for novelty. Novelty of productions was measured by unusual or infrequent images: for example, unusual role designations of depicted figures, novel interpretations, or unexpected endings. Curiosity was the degree to which the story expressed the process of asking questions or posing problems and attempting to obtain new additional information with which to resolve perplexities. Desire for novelty was defined as description of thoughts, feelings, or actions on the part of the characters that indicated positive concern with new or different experiences. People high in novelty of productions, curiosity, or desire for novelty are assumed to share a strong need for variety, but to differ in the nature of its expression. In a further study, Maddi and Berne (1964) tested and supported the assumption that the desire for novelty and novelty of productions represented, respectively, passive and active forms of the need for variety. Maddi and colleagues (1962) found that subjects exposed to monotonous stimuli scored higher on desire for novelty and lower on novelty of productions than subjects exposed to novel stimuli. They speculate that monotonous experiences may arouse the need for variation, but these experiences temporarily decrease the ability to think in active initiating ways.

Pearson and Maddi (1966) reported the successful development of a structured measure of the active interoceptive form of the tendency toward variety. An instrument was constructed that required the subject to express preference for stimuli varying in degree of novelty. The authors used as items the beginnings of common similes and required the subject to choose between familiar and more novel endings of them.

Acker and McReynolds (1965) have offered an Obscure Figures Test (OFT) as a measure for "cognitive innovation." The test contains forty figures that subjects are asked to interpret in clever and unusual ways. The OFT correlates significantly positively with the SPI, it is able to predict to the criterion of performance in a creative production session, and it is not highly correlated with intelligence (Uribe and McReynolds 1967). Finally, Feirstein (1967) has detailed techniques for assessing the conceptually related construct of tolerance for unrealistic experiences.

Kelly (1966, 1968) believes that the expression of human effectiveness is specific for a particular social environment at a particular point in time, and that it is important to specify the relationships between the functions of different social environments and individual adaptive behavior. He developed a 128-item adaptation scale in an attempt to measure four types of coping behavior: (1) anticipation, that is, the extent to which persons think about future social situations; (2) exploration, that is, preferences for novel social experiences; (3) locus of control; and (4) social effectiveness, that is, a person's perceived power to change the behavior of others. Using definitions of these terms as guides, 600 questionnaire items salient for high-school students were written. They were then honed down to a preliminary instrument of twenty-four items for each of the four major concepts. Most work has been done on the exploration subscale. For example, it was hypothesized that a high-turnover environment would value exploratory behavior so that persons high on exploration would be reputed leaders. Persons low on exploratory behavior would be expected to become casualties of the society and would express unhappiness, alienation, and withdrawal. High- and low-turnover schools were studied, and there was pronounced elevation of the exploratory scores for the deviants at the constant school— that is, students high on exploratory behavior were labeled as deviants in the constant setting.

The exploration subscale was later revised by adding items that would tap an open mind about change, participation, diversive experiences, and current experiences in adopting innovative behavior. The high explorer was seen as a person who valued change, participated in new activities, and who actively worked to bring about change. The additional items relevant to this expanded conceptualization of exploration gave three areas of focus: (1) a cognitive subscale dealing mainly with attitudes toward change; (2) a diversity subscale focusing on participation in a number of activities; and (3) an innovative subscale measuring actual participation in school as a leader and initiator of change. The revised version of the exploration questionnaire consists of sixty items for these three subscales and differentiates between high and low explorers (as chosen by peer nominations) in high schools.

A projective method of assessment of exploratory behavior was also developed. This required the creation of themes that would arouse the student's interests and would sample real events facing high-school students in their day-to-day activities. A set of ten free-response stories was developed. Examples of stories are familiar situations (lunchroom), constructive action (teacher award), student-teacher conflict (school assembly), peer affiliation (school suspension), and so forth. A completely open-ended response format was utilized because it was seen as closer to real life by being unstructured and by encouraging varying responses. Follow-up interviews were included to collect more specific information about the written responses. These techniques for the measurement of exploratory behavior are being developed further; however, one important aspect of this methodology is the development of multiple-assessment techniques for the measurement of different aspects of one construct.

ISSUES AND QUESTIONS

The variety of assessment techniques covered in this review may result in a "blooming, buzzing confusion" unlikely to arouse immediate efficacy experiences. In this section, by way of partial summary, I would like to mention briefly some selected issues that appear to me to have particularly high priority for further research. More general considerations in the selection and evaluation of assessment methodologies are summarized elsewhere (Anastasi 1961; Cronbach 1960).

One important set of issues involves the general questions of which assessment techniques should be used for different specified purposes. Zimbardo (1964) discusses the use of both objective and projective methods; Neugarten's (1961) results suggest that for some subjects the relation between questionnaire and interview data is high, whereas for others it is not; Alderfer (1967) presents data showing that interviews and questionnaires may profitably be used in conjunction with one another; Schroder, Driver, and Streufert (1967) present considerations that objective tests may not be adequate for certain purposes, such as the assessment of integrative complexity; MacDonald (1967) discusses some of the specific problems inherent in the use of paper-and-pencil techniques in the assessment of coping styles; Sidle and co-workers (1969) indicate that both free-response and forced-rating data may be important in assessing coping styles; Folkins (1967) discusses results that indicate that *post hoc* interviews can be utilized to collect valid data about coping processes; and finally, Levine and Spivack (1964), Strodtbeck (1958), and Whiteley and Watts (1969) all discuss some aspect of the more general problem of the relationships between questionnaire responses and behavior. Whiteley and Watts made the disconcerting finding that subjects' stated preferences concerning their styles of decision making correlated significantly with their actual behavior only in the condition in which the decision had no personal consequence. When the subjects were put into a situation where a correct decision presumably had some utility for their future, variables that were activated by the resulting stress began to mediate behavior. The complexity of the relations between attitudes and behavior and some of the considerations relevant to predicting when there will be positive correlations between them and when there will not have been discussed by Warner and DeFleur (1969).

One of the most important recent developments in this area concerns the possibility, with the advent of computer techniques, of empirically comparing different assessment strategies. For example, Butt and Fiske (1968) compared four different approaches of measuring dominance (rational facet, factorial facet, rational trait, factorial trait) at four different levels of evaluation: test statistics (reliability), test intercorrelations, correlations with presumably related variables, and promise of theoretical contribution. Standard and new tests of dominance were given to male undergraduates, female undergraduates, and airmen. It was found that the facet strategy was superior to the trait strategy for basic research purposes, that the rational-facet approach was most promising for theoretical work, and that the factorial-facet approach yielded more relationships with outside variables. There was very great variation in the correlates of dominance, depending upon the particular strategy utilized to measure dominance in the first place (Butt and Fiske 1969). Hase and Goldberg (1967) started with the CPI as their item pool and developed scales by using six different strategies. They found no striking differences in predicting to thirteen criterion measures among scales based on factor-analytic, empirical-group-discriminative, or rational strategies. Studies of this sort can serve as "trial rehearsals" and can help to make explicit the likely costs and benefits of following different specified strategies.

Methodological research is needed at all levels of the assessment process. We need studies that systematically compare different methods of presenting stimuli— printed problem stories, films, audio and videotaped recordings, computer presentation, and so on. Studies should be designed, not merely to predict to a criterion, but rather to compare the efficacy of various alternative methods of prediction (Kelly 1968). For example, under what conditions can semistructured interviews or even simpler objective questionnaires provide as relevant information as longer, free-response interviews? Alternative methodological approaches, possibly adapted from other areas, could be investigated. For example, Loy (1969) assigned swimming coaches to one of four categories on the basis of when they decided to adopt a technological innovation. The categories were based on the year that the coach adopted the innovation, with the earliest adopters being called "innovators" and the latest "laggards." Selected social and psychological characteristics discriminated between the categories: for example, professional status, imaginativeness, educational status, dominance, and sociability. Most importantly, the study provides a methodology by which one can identify known innovators and then compare them with various control groups.

The next issue, which has been of particular interest to me, relates to situational determinants of coping and to the problem of the generality-specificity of trait dimensions. As Lazarus, Averill, and Opton (Chapter 10 of this volume) state, coping and adaptive behavior cannot be studied apart from the environmental context in which it occurs. Mischel (1968) has recently reviewed the literature on specificity, and a variety of other investigators have found that coping processes may depend heavily on the particular environmental context. For example, Argyris (1968) reports that his own interpersonal competence scores varied from 150 to 390, where the lowest score obtained was 10 and the highest 390, depending on the particular group in which he was functioning; he concludes that this competence is an interpersonal or situational ability rather than simply an individual or personal one. In a different example, Visotsky and colleagues (1961) were impressed by the fact that some patients may vary their responses widely as they discern different kinds of behavior in therapeutic personnel. They frequently found that a patient who was described by several staff members as being sullen, uncommunicative, and uncooperative was described by other staff members as being frank, intelligent, and reasonable. The overall problem of the limited generality of "trait" dimensions is relevant to many other areas and is receiving much increased attention. The relevance of the concept of drive, which everyone is assailing on other grounds, has been called into question on the basis of the lack of consistency of supposedly drive-related measures across measurement settings.

Relatively little is actually known about this whole area, which is wide open for further empirical attention. What proportions of behavioral variance can be attributed to persons, settings, modes of response, and their interactions in different experimental and real-life situations? Preliminary results indicate that settings and person-by-setting interactions each contribute significantly to overall behavioral variance in both anxiety and hostility (Endler and Hunt 1968; Endler, Hunt, and Rosenstein 1962). A number of other studies have demonstrated that large differences may occur in the behavior of the same persons in different settings or milieus (Gump, Schoggen, and Redl 1957; Soskin and John 1963; Zinner 1963). Using questionnaire data, we showed that some individuals tended to utilize certain strategies rather than others regardless of the specific problem at hand and that some problem situations tended to elicit the use of certain strategies rather than others regardless of the individual involved (Sidle et al. 1969).

These considerations of course raise many questions. At the minimum they tend to double the complexity of the assessment problem, because they make mandatory the assessment of the environment as well as of the person. The necessity for further work on the environmental side of the person-environment system is particularly acute, because this is as yet a relatively underdeveloped area. Both ecological and perceptual strategies of assessing environments are likely to be of utility. For example, Barker and Gump (1964) have shown that the ecological variables of size and of number of people available in behavior settings may importantly affect developing competences of high-school students. Pace (1963), working with college students, has shown that the information obtained in perceptual measures may be quite different from that obtained with ecological ones. We need to know much more about what environmental dimensions, both perceptual and ecological, might be most meaningfully related to specific types of coping variables. For example, it might be fruitful to attempt to classify environments in terms of the intellectual demands they made upon persons. These considerations are, of course, all relevant to the problem of the person-environment fit, which is discussed in Chapter 11 of this volume.

The whole problem of estimating situational and interaction variance is compounded by the finding that self-esteem may be just that component of the self system that is associated with the organism's consistency of social response. For example, Mossman and Ziller (1968) found that the consistency of the level of participation of patients in group therapy was positively associated with self-esteem. Moos (1968) showed that staff vary their reactions from setting to setting on a psychiatric ward much more than do patients, and Raush and colleagues (1959, 1960) found that normal children show greater differences between settings than do disturbed children.

These considerations are also important because they must sensitize us to the differences between experimental and data-gathering settings and the settings to which we are attempting to extrapolate. Lazarus, Averill, and Opton (Chapter 10 of this book) have pointed out that a person's response may be determined by lower-order dispositions specific to the test situation and only secondarily by the more general dispositions that may be the object of study. This underscores the importance of the analysis of the functional similarities between the test situation and other settings to which prediction is made. All these considerations point up the important need for research on environmental typologies, so that different settings may be more systematically compared.

Another important issue concerns the extent to which idiographic techniques and ipsative research designs will prove fruitful in this area. One problem has to do with specifying the conditions when it is necessary to utilize personally relevant dimensions rather than more general dimensions relevant for all, or at least most, people. There is some data on this point in the comparison between the Kelly Reptest and the Osgood semantic differential technique. The semantic differential generally uses provided dimensions that are the same for everybody, whereas the Reptest uses personal constructs that are uniquely meaningful to the responding individual. Tripodi and Bieri (1963) wanted to determine the comparability of cognitive complexity (CC) scores generated from personal constructs and provided constructs. They had their subjects rate ten persons on five personal constructs using a six-point Likert scale; then each subject rated the same ten persons on five provided constructs. The two methods correlated .50 and the distributions of both types of CC scores were not significantly different. The authors concluded that for research purposes provided constructs were comparable to personal constructs in measuring CC.

Jaspars (1963) reported differences between the results obtained with the semantic differential and the Reptest. The correlations between the results of the two tests were positive for every subject, but they differed largely in size. For example, for the ten most neurotic subjects there was a correlation of only .26 between the structures of the two tests, whereas for the group of the ten least neurotic subjects this correlation was .78. Jaspars concluded that it makes less difference to the normal person than to the neurotic whether or not he has to express himself in provided dimensions. Neurotics may have a more unique cognitive structure than normals, but this cannot be assessed by the semantic differential because, with this instrument, neurotics are "forced into normality."

Cromwell and Caldwell (1962) reported that the ratings on personal constructs were significantly more extreme than on provided constructs. Mitsos (1961) had each subject select nine of twenty-one adjective scales that he felt he could meaningfully use in construing other people. The subjects then applied all twenty-one scales to each of seven concepts. A direct relationship was predicted and found between the personal meaningfulness of the adjective scales and the degree to which the concepts rated by the scales were saturated with meaning. These studies, taken together, indicate that personal constructs may provide more information than provided constructs, possibly especially for neurotic subjects.

The other related problem has to do with the use of ipsative research designs. Various comparisons of normative and ipsative designs appear to show that the ipsative design is capable of providing additional information. For example, Opton and Lazarus (1967) attempted to find discriminating personality items between subjects showing high versus low psychophysiological response to a threatening film and high versus low response to a shock. This normative analysis resulted in no more discriminating items than would be expected by chance. On the other hand, there were many personality differences between subjects who responded relatively more strongly to the film than to the threat of shock, and subjects who responded more strongly to the threat of shock than to the film.

Much more work needs to be done. It is possible that for many purposes regular personality tests can be utilized in ipsative studies; in other situations specific individualized dimensions may be necessary. Chassan (1967) and Shapiro (1970) present further discussions of this area. Chassan's discussion of "intensive design" is important for studying the relationships between changes within an individual over time; it is just such a design that many investigators in this area are using (Melges, Anderson, and Tinklenberg 1969). Chassan has also made the important point that the findings from an intensive study of a single case may well be more generalizable than average group comparison data. It is possible that Q-typing methodology may turn out to have utility for classifying individuals on the basis of similarity of personality patterns (Gordon 1969).

Another general issue is concerned with the number of different dimensions and tests needed to usefully conceptualize and measure different theoretical areas. The most general findings to emerge from empirical correlational studies are that tests that purportedly measure the same constructs usually show low intercorrelations, and that dimensions that appear to be theoretically unitary are empirically far more complex. For example, Lloyd (1966) found no significant correlations between three measures of cognitive style; Vannoy (1965) found that no single unitary dimension could account for intercorrelations among a sample of tests, all of which purportedly measured cognitive complexity-simplicity; Palmer (1968) found the overall consistency so low and the correlations between individual tests so uneven as to cast serious doubt on the hypothesis of a strong unitary process underlying vigilance defense behavior; Stein and Chu (1967) found three factors in Barron's Ego Strength Scale; Smith (1966) found different dimensions of competence in his Peace Corps trainees; and Zuckerman and Link (1968) found four factors in the Sensation-Seeking Scale. There are a host of other examples.

Fiske (1963) has pointed out that it is unlikely that any broad personality variable can adequately be assessed by any single measurement technique; he has formulated an approach in which global personality constructs are analyzed into smaller more homogeneous subconstructs, each of which has its own separate measurement instruments (1966). Pearson (1970) has used this approach in an attempt to demonstrate the lack of comprehensive and representative coverage of the novelty domain by global self-report measures. The tendency toward novelty experiencing was analyzed into four forms in terms of the source of stimulation and the type of subjective experience. The source of experience can either be internal (self-generated) or external to the person, and the subjective quality was classified as either sensation-feeling or cognition. She constructed five specified rational scales, four coordinated with the four separate forms of the tendency toward novelty seeking and one coordinated with desire for novelty. Pearson proposed and found that the resulting four forms of novelty seeking were separable in self-report data, both from one another and from the more global measures of novelty. The results indicated that it is possible to divide the tendency to seek novelty into smaller, more homogeneous subconstructs whose self-report measures do not substantially overlap either with one another or with self-report instruments that measure change or novelty more globally. Thus there are several relatively independent dispositions in the novelty domain that appear not to have been measured by the usual global novelty measures.

This type of conceptual analysis of different content domains with the resulting development of more specific limited-range assessment techniques may help to provide some further clarity in various areas. Gordon's (1969) differentiated analysis of self-conception methodologies is another excellent example.

There are three specific purposes for which further development of assessment techniques would be particularly useful. First, the possibilities of experimentally altering coping and adaptive strategies through modeling and other paradigms are very intriguing. There is a growing body of relevant research relating to the relationship between systematic feedback and behavior change; for example, Kolb, Winter, and Berlew (1968) have assumed that information feedback is crucial for change production and have related this to the feedback model developed by Miller, Galanter, and Pribram (1960). Further studies along the lines of those by Krumboltz and Thoreson (1964), Giebink, Stover, and Fahl (1968), and Pisano (1966) are necessary. More differentiated and specific techniques that are sensitive to change will be needed as interest in these types of studies grows.

Second, we need studies of intermediate or relatively long time span so that the differential balance of costs and benefits of different adaptive strategies may be studied over time. It will thus be necessary to have more integrated assessment methodologies that will permit the simultaneous assessment of multiple possible outcomes. In this connection we need more techniques that systematically assess the individual's prior history of effective coping transactions and that may serve as a base line from which to measure change. Holland and Baird (1968) have pointed out that it should in principle be possible to construct a record of past interpersonal effectiveness that is similar to the nonacademic achievement scales developed in art, music, and literature. Wallace's (1967) attempt to replace traditional dispositional concepts with an abilities conception of personality might help enhance this development. Mechanic's call in Chapter 3 of this volume for behavioral tests that closely approximate real-life tasks is important here, as is Goldfried's (1969) point that we are very much in need of naturalistic studies so that we can learn more about the task requirements of different types of naturally occurring situations.

Third, we need more techniques that have distinct cross-cultural relevance. The general findings of various studies that there are important cross-cultural similarities and that measurement techniques may have general applicability are very encouraging. For example, in one study, Rahe (1969) compared life changes and then scaled results with the SRRS in terms of their ordering between seven different cultural and American subculture groups. The overall correlations between individual groups ranged from .63 to .94, indicating that despite many cross-cultural differences, similarities were far more pronounced. These types of studies are of particular significance for ongoing research that involves comparing "social stress" among inhabitants of various countries. It would be a major step in cross-cultural research if generalizations could be safely made regarding the relative significance of various life changes. The problem of cross-cultural relevance ought to be considered early in the developmental process of each new assessment technique in this area.

On the one hand, the importance of not overburdening an area with new assessment techniques can hardly be overemphasized, because, as has been pointed out, research often follows the availability of techniques rather than the advance of theory (see Chapter 3). Over the long view, however, it is almost uncanny how closely the construction of measurement techniques has followed theory development. In this area alone this has happened with the theories of Werner, Kelly, Erikson, Piaget, Rogers, Maslow, and White, to name only a few. In a sense, assessment methods have been far more responsive to theory than theory has been to the data derived from assessment methods. We often tend to spend time lauding theoretical advances and flaying our assessment methods without fully realizing the extremely close connection between them. The most common case is that research follows the availability of techniques, but the techniques have themselves followed the advance of theory. In addition, it is the assessment methods rather than the theories that derive both the benefits and costs of the informational feedback that tends to follow frequent actual contact with the cold facts of empirical reality.

It is of course true that there are important disadvantages that must be considered in offering new techniques; at the minimum it can be guaranteed that each new technique will claim the research energies of at least one or two investigators and several computers. The availability of an assessment technique in an area, especially a simple one, is an ecological fact that tends to channel research into that area. On the other hand, maximum diversity and variety of new assessment techniques is essential in a newly developing area.

All the considerations set forth here point up the fact that we will still need to experiment systematically with very large numbers of new techniques before we even begin to approach the point where we will have a set of relatively satisfactory measurement tools. I thus, temporarily at least, must take my stand on the side of population growth. On the one hand, I believe that there is an interaction in which different types of assessment methods have unique differential relevance in relation to different purposes and goals; on the other hand, I trust that natural selection will be harsh and that only the fittest shall survive.

REFERENCES

Abram, H. S. Adaptation to open heart surgery: A psychiatric study of response to the threat of death. *American Journal of Psychiatry*, 1965, *122*, 659–667.

Acker, M., and McReynolds, P. The Obscure Figures Test: An instrument for measuring "cognitive innovation." *Perceptual and Motor Skills*, 1965, *21*,815–821.

Adams-Webber, J. Cognitive complexity and sociality. *British Journal of Social and Clinical Psychology*, 1969, *8*, 211–216.

Alderfer, C. Convergent and discriminant validation of satisfaction and desire measures by interviews and questionnaires. *Journal of Applied Psychology*, 1967, *51*, 509–520.

———. An empirical test of a new theory of human needs. *Organizational Behavior and Human Performance*, 1969, *4*, 142–175.

Alker, H. A. Cognitive controls and the Haan-Kroeber model of ego functioning. *Journal of Abnormal Psychology*, 1967, *72*, 434–440.

———. Coping, defense and socially desirable responses. *Psychological Reports*, 1968, *22*, 985–988.

Allport, G. *Pattern and growth in personality.* New York: Holt, Rinehart & Winston, 1961.

Anastasi, A. *Psychological testing.* Rev. ed. New York: Macmillan, 1961.

Andrew, J. M. Coping styles, stress relevant learning and recovery from surgery. Ph.D. dissertation, University of California, Los Angeles, 1967.

Angyal, A. *Foundations for a science of personality.* New York: Commonwealth Fund, 1941.

Argyris, C. *Understanding organizational behavior.* Homewood, Ill.: Dorsey Press, 1960.

――――. Explorations in interpersonal competence, I. *Journal of Applied Behavioral Science,* 1965a, *1,* 58–83.

――――. Explorations in interpersonal competence, II. *Journal of Applied Behavioral Science,* 1965b, *1,* 255–269.

――――. Conditions for competence acquisition and therapy. *Journal of Applied Behavioral Science,* 1968, *4,* 147–177.

Aronson, E., and Mettee, D. Dishonest behavior as a function of differential levels of induced self-esteem. *Journal of Personality and Social Psychology,* 1968, *9,* 121–127.

Bakan, D. *The duality of human existence.* Chicago: Rand McNally, 1966.

Barker, R., ed. *The stream of behavior.* New York: Appleton-Century-Crofts, 1963.

Barker, R., and Gump, P. *Big school, small school.* Stanford, Calif.: Stanford University Press, 1964.

Barron, F. An ego strength scale which predicts response to psychotherapy. *Journal of Consulting Psychology,* 1953, *17,* 327–333.

Barthell, C., and Holmes, D. High school yearbooks: A nonreactive measure of social isolation in graduates who later became schizophrenic. *Journal of Abnormal Psychology,* 1968, *73,* 313–316.

Bauman, G., Roman, R., Borello, J., and Meltzer, B. Interaction testing in the measurement of marital intelligence. *Journal of Abnormal Psychology,* 1967, *72,* 489–495.

Baumrind, D., and Black, A. E. Socialization practices associated with dimensions of competence in preschool boys and girls. *Child Development,* 1967, *38,* 291–327.

Becker, D., and Margolin, F. How surviving parents handled their young children's adaptation to the crisis of loss. *American Journal of Orthopsychiatry,* 1967, *37,* 753–757.

Bellak, L., and Hurvich, M. A systematic study of ego functions. *Journal of Nervous and Mental Disease,* 1969, *148,* 569–585.

Berlyne, D. E. *Conflict, arousal and curiosity.* New York: McGraw-Hill, 1960.

Bieri, J. Complexity-simplicity as a personality variable in cognitive and preferential behavior. In D. Fiske and S. Maddi, eds., *Functions of varied experience.* New York: Dorsey, 1961.

Block, J. *The Q-sort method in personality assessment and psychiatric research.* Springfield, Ill.: Charles C. Thomas, 1961.

――――. *The challenge of response sets: Unconfounding meaning, acquiescence, and social desirability in the MMPI.* New York: Appleton-Century-Crofts, 1965.

Bonarius, J. Research in the personal construct theory of George A. Kelly: Role construct repertory test and basic theory. In B. Maher, ed., *Progress in experimental personality research,* vol. 2. New York: Academic Press, 1965.

Bonjean, C., and Vance, G. A short-form measure of self-actualization. *Journal of Applied Behavioral Science,* 1968, *4,* 299–312.

Bouchard, T. Personality, problem solving procedure, and performance in small groups. Ph.D. dissertation, University of California, Berkeley, 1966.

Brim, O., and Hoff, D. Individual and situational differences in desire for certainty. *Journal of Abnormal and Social Psychology*, 1957, *54*, 225–229.

Brody, R. Some systematic effects of the spread of nuclear weapons technology: A study through simulation of a multi-nuclear future. *Journal of Conflict Resolution*, 1963, 7, 663–753.

Brown, D., and Marks, P. Bakan's biopolar constructs: Agency and communion. *Psychological Record*, 1969, *19*, 465–478.

Budner, S. Intolerance of ambiguity as a personality variable. *Journal of Personality*, 1962, *30*, 29–50.

Bugenthal, J., and Zelen, S. Investigations into the "self-concept": I. The W-A-Y technique. *Journal of Personality*, 1950, *18*, 483–498.

Buhler, C., Brind, A., and Horner, A. Old age as a phase of human life. *Human Development*, 1968, *11*, 53–63.

Burnes, A. J., and Roen, S. R. Social roles and adaptation to the community. *Community Mental Health Journal*, 1967, *3*, 153–158.

Bush, M., Hatcher, R., and Mayman, M. Reality attentiveness-inattentiveness and externalization-internalization in defensive style. *Journal of Consulting and Clinical Psychology*, 1969, *33*, 343–350.

Butt, D., and Fiske, D. Comparison of strategies in developing scales for dominance. *Psychological Bulletin*, 1968, 70, 505–519.

———. Differential correlates of dominance scales. *Journal of Personality*, 1969, *37*, 415–428.

Byrne, D. The repression-sensitization scale: Rationale, reliability and validity. *Journal of Personality*, 1961, *29*, 334–349.

———. Repression-sensitization as a dimension of personality. In B. A. Maher, ed., *Progress in experimental personality research*, vol. 1. New York: Academic Press, 1964.

Byrne, D., Nelson, D., and Reeves, K. Effects of consensual validation and invalidation on attraction as a function of verifiability. *Journal of Experimental and Social Psychology*, 1966, *2*, 98–107.

Carroll, A. W. The effects of segregated and partially integrated school programs on self concept and academic achievement of educable mental retardates. *Exceptional Children*, 1967, *34*, 93–99.

Chassan, J. *Research design in clinical psychology and psychiatry*. New York: Meredith, 1967.

Chodoff, P., Friedman, S., and Hamburg, D. Stress, defenses and coping behavior: Observations in parents of children with malignant disease. *American Journal of Psychiatry*, 1964, *120*, 743–749.

Clifford, R. The Rio Grande flood: A comparative study of border communities in disaster. Disaster Study Number 7. Washington, D.C.: National Academy of Sciences-National Research Council, 1956.

Coelho, G., Hamburg, D., and Murphey, E. Coping strategies in a new learning environment. *Archives of General Psychiatry*, 1963, *9*, 433–443.

Coelho, G., Silber, E., and Hamburg, D. Use of the student-TAT to assess coping behavior in hospitalized normal and exceptionally competent college freshmen. *Perceptual and Motor Skills*, 1962, *14*, 355–365.

Coelho, G., Solomon, F., Wolff, C., Steinberg, A., and Hamburg, D. Predicting coping behavior in college: A prospective use of the student-TAT. *Journal of Nervous and Mental Disease*, 1969, *149*, 386–397.

Cohen, A., Stotland, E., and Wolfe, D. An experimental investigation of need for cognition. *Journal of Abnormal and Social Psychology*, 1955, *51*, 291–297.

Cohen, E. *Human behavior in the concentration camp.* New York: Norton, 1953.

Coopersmith, S. *The antecedents of self-esteem.* San Francisco: Freeman, 1967.

Crawford, P. L. Construction, validation, and factor analysis of a psychological adjustment scale. Ph.D. dissertation, Ohio University, 1967.

Crockett, W. Cognitive complexity and impression formation. In B. A. Maher, ed., *Progress in experimental personality research*, vol. 2. New York: Academic Press, 1965.

Cromwell, R., and Caldwell, D. A comparison of ratings based on personal constructs of self and others. *Journal of Clinical Psychology*, 1962, *18*, 43–46.

Cronbach, L. *Essentials of psychological testing.* 2nd ed. New York: Harper, 1960.

Cropley, A. Divergent thinking and science specialists. *Nature*, 1967, *215*, 671–672.

Cropley, A., and Field, T. Achievement in science and intellectual style. *Journal of Applied Psychology*, 1969, *53*, 132–135.

Crowne, D., and Stephens, M. Self-acceptance and self-evaluative behavior: A critique of methodology. *Psychological Bulletin*, 1961, *58*, 104–121.

Deutsch, M. Trust and suspicion. *Journal of Conflict Resolution*, 1958, *2*, 265–279.

Deutsch, M., and Krauss, R. Studies of interpersonal bargaining. *Journal of Conflict Resolution*, 1962, *6*, 52–76.

Endler, N., and Hunt, J. McV. S-R Inventories of hostility and comparisons of the proportions of variance from persons, responses and situations for hostility and anxiousness. *Journal of Personality and Social Psychology*, 1968, *9*, 309–315.

Endler, N., Hunt, J. McV., and Rosenstein, A. J. An S-R inventory of anxiousness. *Psychological Monographs*, 1962, *76*.

Erikson, E. *Childhood and society.* New York: Norton, 1950.

Eysenck, H., and Eysenck, S. B. G. *Eysenck personality inventory manual.* London: University of London Press, 1964.

————. *Personality structure and measurement.* London: Routledge & Kegan Paul, 1969.

Ezekiel, R. The personal future and Peace Corps competence. *Journal of Personality and Social Psychology*, 1968, *8* (2, pt. 2).

Farber, B. F. Elements of competence in interpersonal relations: A factor analysis. *Sociometry*, 1962, *25*, 30–47.

Farley, F., and Farley, S. V. Extroversion and stimulus seeking motivation. *Journal of Consulting Psychology*, 1967, *31*, 215–216.

Feder, C. Relationship of repression-sensitization to adjustment status, social desirability and acquiescence response set. *Journal of Consulting Psychology*, 1967, *31*, 401–406.

————. Relationship between self-acceptance and adjustment, repression-sensitization and social competence. *Journal of Abnormal Psychology*, 1968, *73*, 317–322.

Feffer, M. Symptom expression as a form of primitive decentering. *Psychological Review*, 1967, *74*, 16–28.

Feffer, M., and Suchotliff, L. Decentering implications of social interaction. *Journal of Personality and Social Psychology*, 1966, *4*, 415–423.

Feirstein, A. Personality correlates of tolerance for unrealistic experiences. *Journal of Consulting Psychology*, 1967, *31*, 387–395.

Ferreira, A. J. Decision making in normal and pathologic families. *Archives of General Psychiatry*, 1963, *8*, 68–73.

Field, P. B., Maldonado-Sierra, E., and Coelho, G. A student-TAT measure of competence: A cross-cultural replication in Puerto Rico. *Perceptual and Motor Skills*, 1963, *16*, 195–198.

Fields, J. Experiences of efficacy within the family, and adaptive ego functioning in the child. Ph.D. dissertation, Boston University, 1968.

Fisher, G. Performance of psychopathic felons on a measure of self-actualization. *Educational Psychology Measurement*, 1968, *28*, 561–563.

Fiske, D. Problems in measuring personality. In J. Wepman and R. Heine, eds., *Concepts of personality*. Chicago: Aldine, 1963.

———. On the coordination of personality concepts and their measurement. *Human Development*, 1966, *9*, 74–83.

Folkins, C. Reactions to threat of pain as a function of anticipation intervals. Ph.D. dissertation, University of California, Berkeley, 1967.

Fowler, H. *Curiosity and exploratory behavior*. New York: Macmillan, 1965.

Fox, J., Knapp, R., and Michael, W. Assessment of self-actualization of psychiatric patients: Validity of the Personal Orientation Inventory. *Educational Psychology Measurement*, 1968, *28*, 565–569.

Fox, P. Cost-effectiveness of mental health: An evaluation of an experimental rehabilitation program. Ph.D. dissertation, Stanford University, 1968.

Frank, G. H. A review of research with measures of ego strength derived from the MMPI and the Rorschach. *Journal of General Psychology*, 1967, 77, 183–206.

Friedman, S., Chodoff, P., Mason, J., and Hamburg, D. Behavioral observations on parents anticipating the death of a child. *Pediatrics*, 1963, *32*, 610–625.

Garlington, W. K., and Shimota, H. E. The change seeker index: A measure of the need for variable stimulus input. *Psychological Reports*, 1964, *14*, 919–924.

Geertsma, R., and Reivich, R. Auditory and visual dimensions of externally medicated self observations. *Journal of Nervous and Mental Disease*, 1969, *148*, 210–223.

Giebink, J., Stover, D., and Fahl, M. Teaching adaptive responses to frustration to emotionally disturbed boys. *Journal of Consulting and Clinical Psychology*, 1968, *32*, 366–368.

Glass, D., Singer, J., and Friedman, L. Psychic cost of adaptation to an environmental stressor. *Journal of Personality and Social Psychology*, 1969, *12*, 200–210.

Gleser, G. C., and Ihilevich, D. An objective instrument for measuring defense mechanisms. *Journal of Consulting and Clinical Psychology*, 1969, *33*, 51–60.

Glueck, S., and Glueck, E. *Predicting delinquency and crime*. Cambridge, Mass.: Harvard University Press, 1959.

Goldfried, M. R., and D'Zurilla, T. J. A behavioral, analytic model for assessing competence. In C. D. Spielberger, ed., *Current topics in clinical and community psychology*, vol. 1. New York: Academic Press, 1969.

Goldstein, M. J. The relationship between coping and avoiding behavior and response to fear-arousing propaganda. *Journal of Abnormal and Social Psychology*, 1959, *58*, 247–252.

Goldstein, M. J., Judd, L., Rodnick, E., Alkire, A., and Gould, E. A method for studying social influence and coping patterns within families of disturbed adolescents. *Journal of Nervous and Mental Disease*, 1968, *147*, 233–251.

Gordon, C. Self-conceptions methodologies. *Journal of Nervous and Mental Disease*, 1969, *148*, 328–364.

Gordon, L. Q typing: An exploration in personality measurement. *Journal of Social Psychology*, 1969, *78*, 121–136.

Gough, H. *The California Psychological Inventory manual*. Rev. ed. Palo Alto, Calif.: Consulting Psychologists Press, 1964.

———. Appraisal of social maturity by means of the CPI. *Journal of Abnormal Psychology*, 1966, *71*, 189–195.

Gough, H., and Heilbrun, A. *The Adjective Check List manual*. Palo Alto, Calif.. Consulting Psychologists Press, 1965.

Grant, C. R. Age differences in self concept from early adulthood through old age. Ph.D. dissertation, University of Nebraska, 1967.

Grinker, R. R., Sr. "Mentally healthy" young males (homoclites). *Archives of General Psychiatry*, 1962, *6*, 405–453.

Gross, R. D. A social situations test as a measure of adjustment mechanisms. Ph.D. dissertation, West Virginia University, 1965.

Gump, P., Schoggen, P., and Redl, F. The camp milieu and its immediate effects. *Journal of Social Issues*, 1957, *13*, 40–46.

Gunderson, E. K., and Johnson, L. C. Past experience, self evaluation and present adjustment. *Journal of Social Psychology*, 1965, *66*, 311–321.

Gunzburg, H. C. *Social competence and mental handicap*. London: Bailliere, Tindall & Cassell, 1968.

Haan, N. Proposed model of ego functioning: Coping and defense mechanisms in relationship to IQ change. *Psychological Monographs*, 1963, 77(8), 1–23.

———. An investigation of the relationships of Rorschach scores, patterns and behavior to coping and defense mechanisms. *Journal of Projective Techniques*, 1964, *28*, 429–441.

———. A tripartite model of ego functioning values and clinical and research applications. *Journal of Nervous and Mental Disease*, 1969, *148*, 14–30.

Hamburg, D., Hamburg, B., and deGoza, S. Adaptive problems and mechanisms in severely burned patients. *Psychiatry*, 1953, *16*, 1–20.

Harlow, H. Mice, monkeys, men and motives. *Psychological Review*, 1953, *60*, 23–32.

Hartmann, H. Comments on the psychoanalytic theory of the ego. *Psychoanalytic Study of the Child*, 1950, *5*, 74–95.

Hartmann, H., Kris, E., and Lowenstein, R. Notes on the theory of aggression. *Psychoanalytic Study of the Child*, 1949, *4*, 9–36.

Hase, H., and Goldberg, L. Comparative validity of different strategies of constructing personality inventory scales. *Psychological Bulletin*, 1967, *67*, 231–248.

Hill, A. H. Use of a structured autobiography in the construct validation of personality scales. *Journal of Consulting Psychology*, 1967, *31*, 551–556.

Hocking, J., and Robertson, M. Sensation Seeking Scale as a predictor of need for stimulation during sensory restriction. *Journal of Consulting and Clinical Psychology*, 1969, *33*, 367–369.

Hoepfner, R., and O'Sullivan, M. Social intelligence and IQ. *Educational Psychology Measurement*, 1968, *28*, 339–344.

Hogan, R. Development of an empathy scale. *Journal of Consulting and Clinical Psychology*, 1969, *33*, 307–316.

Holland, J. L. *Vocational Preference Inventory manual*. 6th rev. Iowa City, Iowa: Educational Research Associates, 1965.

Holland, J. L., and Baird, L. An Interpersonal Competency Scale. *Educational Psychology Measurement*, 1968, *28*, 503–510.

Holmes, T. H., Joffe, J., Ketcham, J., and Sheehy, T. Experimental study of prognosis. *Journal of Psychosomatic Research*, 1961, *5*, 232–252.

Holmes, T. H., and Rahe, R. H. The social readjustment rating scale. *Journal of Psychosomatic Research*, 1967, *11*, 213–218.

Houts, P., MacIntosh, S., and Moss, R. Patient-therapist interdependence: Cognitive and behavioral. *Journal of Consulting and Clinical Psychology*, 1969, *33*, 40–45.

Houts, P., and Moos, R. The development of a Ward Initiative Scale. *Journal of Clinical Psychology*, 1969, *25*, 319–322.

Hunt, J. McV. *Intelligence and experience*. New York: Ronald Press, 1961.

Hunter, C. G., and Goodstein, L. D. Ego strength and types of defensive and coping behavior. *Journal of Consulting Psychology*, 1967, *31*, 432.

Hurvich, M., and Bellak, L. Ego function patterns in schizophrenia. *Psychological Reports*, 1968, *22*, 299–308.

Hurwitz, J. I., Kaplan, D. M., and Kaiser, E. Designing an instrument to assess parental coping mechanisms. In H. J. Parad, ed., *Crisis intervention*. New York: Family Service Association of America, 1965.

Inkeles, A. Social structure and the socialization of competence. *Harvard Educational Review*, 1966, *36*, 265–283.

Insel, S. A. Self presentations in relation to internal and external reference. *Journal of Consulting and Clinical Psychology*, 1968, *32*, 389–395.

Janis, I. *Air war and emotional stress*. New York: McGraw-Hill, 1951.

———. *Psychological stress*. New York: Wiley, 1958.

Jaspars, J. Individual cognitive structures. Paper presented to 17th International Congress of Psychology, Washington, D.C., 1963.

Jones, A. Information deprivation in humans. In B. A. Maher, ed., *Progress in experimental personality research*, vol. 2. New York: Academic Press, 1965.

Kaswan, J., and Love, L. Confrontation as a method of psychological intervention. *Journal of Nervous and Mental Disease*, 1969, *148*, 224–237.

Kellam, S. Adaptation, mental illness and family life in the first-grade classroom of an urban Negro community. Paper presented to the Conference on Coping and Adaptation, Palo Alto, Calif., March 1969.

Kellam, S., and Schiff, S. Adaptation and mental illness in the first-grade classrooms of an urban community. *Psychiatric Research Report*, 1967, *21*, 79–91.

Kelly, G. *The psychology of personal constructs*, vols. 1, 2. New York: Norton, 1955.

Kelly, J. G. Social adaptation to varied environments. Paper presented to American Psychological Association Convention, New York, September 1966.

———. Adaptive behavior in varied high school environments. Unpublished manuscript, Institute for Social Research, University of Michigan, 1968.

Kent, R. Levels of inference in the behavioral-analytic model. Paper presented to Eastern Psychological Association Convention, Philadelphia, April 1969.

King, G. F., and Schiller, M. Ego strength and type of defensive behavior. *Journal of Consulting Psychology*, 1960, *24*, 215–217.

Kipnis, D. Social immaturity, intellectual ability and adjustive behavior in college. *Journal of Applied Psychology*, 1968, *52*, 71–80.

Kish, G., and Busse, W. MMPI correlates of sensation-seeking in male alcoholics: A test of Quay's hypothesis applied to alcoholism. *Journal of Clinical Psychology*, 1969, *25*, 60–62.

Kolb, E., Winter, S., and Berlew, D. Self-directed change: Two studies. *Journal of Applied Behavioral Science*, 1968, *4*, 453–471.

Komaroff, A. L., Masuda, M., and Holmes, T. H. The social readjustment rating scale: A comparative study of Negro, Mexican and white Americans. *Journal of Psychosomatic Research*, 1968, *12*, 121–128.

Korman, A. K. Self esteem variable in vocational choice. *Journal of Applied Psychology*, 1966, *50*, 479–486.

———. Relevance of personal need satisfaction for overall satisfaction as a function of self esteem. *Journal of Applied Psychology*, 1967, *51*, 533–538.

Korner, I. N., and Buckwalter, M. M. Effects of age and intelligence on the operation of suppression. *Journal of Consulting Psychology*, 1967, *31*, 637–639.

Krumboltz, J. D., and Thoresen, C. E. The effect of behavioral counseling in group and individual settings on information seeking behavior. *Journal of Counseling Psychology*, 1964, *11*, 324–333.

Kuhn, M., and McPartland, T. An empirical investigation of self-attitudes. *American Sociological Review*, 1954, *19*, 68–76.

Langford, W. S. The child in the pediatric hospital: Adaptation to illness and hospitalization. *American Journal of Orthopsychiatry*, 1961, *31*, 667–684.

Lanyon, R. I. Measurement of social competence in college males. *Journal of Consulting Psychology*, 1967, *31*, 495–498.

Lazarus, R. *Psychological stress and the coping process.* New York: McGraw-Hill, 1966.

Lazarus, R., and Alfert, E. The short-circuiting of threat. *Journal of Abnormal and Social Psychology*, 1964, *69*, 195–205.

Lazzaro, T. A. The development and validation of the self-report test of impulse control. Ph.D. dissertation, Southern Illinois University, 1968.

Lefcourt, H. Repression-sensitization: A measure of the evaluation of emotional expression. *Journal of Consulting Psychology*, 1966a, *30*, 444–449.

———. Internal versus external control of reinforcement: A review. *Psychological Bulletin*, 1966b, *65*, 206–220.

Lentz, V. B. The development of an instrument for use in understanding the self concepts of children in the primary grades. Ph.D. dissertation, University of North Carolina, 1968.

Levine, M., and Spivack, G. *The Rorschach index of repressive style.* Springfield, Ill.: Charles C. Thomas, 1964.

Lewis, M. V. An analysis of post-high school vocational exploration in terms of self concept theory. Ph.D. dissertation, Pennsylvania State University, 1966.

Lindemann, E., and Ross, N. A follow-up study of a predictive test of social adaptation in pre-school children. In G. Caplan, ed., *Emotional problems of early childhood.* New York: Basic Books, 1955.

Livson, N., and Peskin, H. Prediction of adult psychological health in a longitudinal study. *Journal of Abnormal Psychology*, 1967, *72*, 509–518.

Lloyd, J. The relationship of three measures of cognitive style to variable and constant processes in judging others. Ph.D. dissertation Western Reserve University, 1966.

Loevinger, J. Relation of adjustment to ego development. Unpublished manuscript, Washington University, 1966a.

———. The meaning and measurement of ego development. *American Psychologist*, 1966b, *21*, 195–206.

Lowenherz, L., and Feffer, M. Cognitive level as a function of defensive isolation. *Journal of Abnormal Psychology*, 1969, *74*, 352–357.

Loy, J. Social psychological characteristics of innovators. *American Sociological Review*, 1969, *34*, 73–81.

MacDonald, R. The effects of stress on self-attribution of hostility among ego control patterns. *Journal of Personality*, 1967, *35*, 234–245.

Maddi, S. R., and Berne, N. Novelty of productions and desire for novelty as active and passive forms of the need for variety. *Journal of Personality*, 1964, *32*, 270–277.

Maddi, S. R., Charlens, A., Maddi, D., and Smith, A. Effects of monotony and novelty on imaginative productions. *Journal of Personality*, 1962, *30*, 513–527.

Maddi, S. R., Propost, B., and Feldinger, I. Three expressions of the need for variety. *Journal of Personality*, 1965, *33*, 82–98.

Manasse, G. Self regard as a function of environmental demands in chronic schizophrenics. *Journal of Abnormal Psychology*, 1965, *70*, 210–213.

Marcia, J. E. Development and validation of ego identity status. *Journal of Personality and Social Psychology*, 1966, *3*, 551–558.

———. Ego identity status: Relationship to change in self esteem, "general maladjustment," and authoritarianism. *Journal of Personality*, 1967, *35*, 118–133.

Maslow, A. *Motivation and personality.* New York: Harper, 1954.

Masuda, M., and Holmes, T. H. The social readjustment rating scale: A cross-cultural study of Japanese and Americans. *Journal of Psychosomatic Research*, 1967, *11*, 227–237.

Mathis, H. *Environmental Participation Index manual.* Washington, D.C., Psychometric Studies, October 1967.

McCarroll, J. E., Mitchell, K., Carpenter, R., and Anderson, J. Analysis of three stimulation-seeking scales. *Psychological Reports*, 1967, *21*, 853–856.

McClain, E., and Andrews, H. Some personality correlates of peak experiences: A study in self-actualization. *Journal of Clinical Psychology*, 1969, *25*, 36–38.

McLaughlin, B. The Who Am I dictionary and self-perceived identity in college students. In P. J. Stone et al., eds., *The general inquirer: A computer approach to content analysis.* Cambridge, Mass.: M.I.T. Press, 1966.

McPartland, T., Cumming, J., and Garretson, W. Self-conception and ward behavior in two psychiatric hospitals. *Sociometry*, 1961, *24*, 111–124.

Mechanic, D. *Students under stress.* New York: Free Press, 1962.

Melges, F., Anderson, R., and Tinklenberg, J. Identity and temporal experience. Unpublished manuscript, Stanford University, 1969.

Meltzer, B., Crockett, W., and Rosenkrantz, P. Cognitive complexity value congruity and the integration of potentially incompatible information in impressions of others. *Journal of Personality and Social Psychology*, 1966, *4*, 338–343.

Miller, A. Amount of information and stimulus valence as determinants of cognitive complexity. *Journal of Personality*, 1969, *37*, 141–157.

Miller, D. R., and Swanson, G. E. *Inner conflict and defense.* New York: Holt, 1960.

Miller, G., Galanter, E., and Pribram, K. *Plans and the structure of behavior.* New York: Holt, 1960.

Mischel, W. *Personality and assessment.* New York: Wiley, 1968.

Mitsos, S. Personal constructs and the semantic differential. *Journal of Abnormal and Social Psychology*, 1961, *62*, 433–434.

Moos, R. Differential effects of ward settings on psychiatric patients: A replication and extension. *Journal of Nervous and Mental Disease*, 1968a, *147*, 386–393.

———. A situational analysis of a therapeutic community milieu. *Journal of Abnormal Psychology*, 1968b, *73*, 49–61.

———. Sources of variance in responses to questionnaires and in behavior. *Journal of Abnormal Psychology*, 1969, *74*, 405–412.

Moos, R., and Houts, P. Assessment of the social atmospheres of psychiatric wards. *Journal of Abnormal Psychology*, 1968, *73*, 595–604.

Moran, L., Fairweather, G., and Morton, R. Some determinants of successful and unsuccessful adaptation to hospital treatment of tuberculosis. *Journal of Consulting Psychology*, 1956, *2*, 125–131.

Mossman, B. M., and Ziller, R. C. Self esteem and consistency of social behavior. *Journal of Abnormal Psychology*, 1968, *73*, 363–367.

Murphy, L. *The widening world of childhood.* New York: Basic Books, 1962.

Murray, H. A. *Explorations in personality.* New York: Oxford Press, 1938.

Neugarten, B. L., Havighurst, R. J., and Tobin, S. S. The measurement of life satisfaction. *Journal of Gerontology*, 1961, *16*, 134–143.

Newman, C. A. Some aspects of the relationship between identification with parents in coping behavior. Ph.D. dissertation, University of Maryland, 1966.

Nihira, K., Foster, R., and Spencer, L. Measurement of adaptive behavior: A descriptive system for mental retardates. *American Journal of Orthopsychiatry*, 1968, *38*, 622–634.

Offer, D. Studies of normal adolescents. *Adolescence*, 1966, *1*, 305–320.

Oltman, P. K. A portable rod-and-frame apparatus. *Perceptual and Motor Skills*, 1968, *26*, 503–506.

Opton, E., and Lazarus, R. Personality determinants of psychophysiological response to stress: A theoretical analysis and an experiment. *Journal of Personality and Social Psychology*, 1967, *6*, 291–303.

Pace, R. *College and University Environments Scales, preliminary technical manual.* Princeton, N. J.: Education Testing Service, 1963.

Palmer, R. Patterns of defensive response to threatening stimuli: Antecedents and consistency. *Journal of Abnormal Psychology*, 1968, *73*, 30–36.

Parsons, O., Fulgenzi, L., and Edelberg, R. Aggressiveness and psychophysiological responsivity in groups of repressors and sensitizers. *Journal of Personality and Social Psychology*, 1969, *12*, 235–244.

Parsons, T., and Shils, E. *Toward a general theory of action.* Cambridge, Mass.: Harvard University Press, 1951.

Pearson, P. H. Relationships between global and specified measures of novelty-seeking. *Journal of Consulting and Clinical Psychology*, 1970, *34*, 199–204.

Pearson, P. H., and Maddi, S. R. The Similes Preference Inventory: Development of a structured measure of the tendency toward variety. *Journal of Consulting Psychology*, 1966, *30*, 301–308.

Penney, R. K., and Reinehr, R. C. Development of a stimulus variation seeking scale for adults. *Psychological Reports*, 1966, *18*, 631–638.

Perry, S., Silber, E., and Bloch, D. The child and his family in disaster: A study of the 1953 Vicksburg tornado. Disaster Study Number 5. Washington, D.C.: National Academy of Sciences-National Research Council, 1956.

Pervin, L. The need to predict and control under conditions of threat. *Journal of Personality*, 1963, *31*, 570–587.

Petzel, T., and Gynther, M. Task performance of repressors and sensitizers under ego oriented versus task oriented instructions. *Journal of Consulting and Clinical Psychology*, 1968, *32*, 486–487.

Phillips, L. *Human adaptation and its failures.* New York: Academic Press, 1968.

Pisano, S. F. The modeling of defensive behavior under sympathetic, neutral and interpretive conditions. Ph.D. dissertation, Ohio State University, 1966.

Pollack, D. Coping and avoidance in inebriated alcoholics and normals. *Journal of Abnormal Psychology*, 1966, *71*, 417–419.

Rahe, R. Multi-cultural correlations of life change scaling: America, Japan, Denmark and Sweden. *Journal of Psychosomatic Research*, 1969, *13*, 191–195.

Rapoport, A. *Fights, games and debates.* Ann Arbor: University of Michigan Press, 1960.

Rapoport, R., and Rapoport, R. N. New light on the honeymoon. *Human Relations*, 1964, *17*, 33–56.

Rasmussen, J. E. Relationship of ego identity to psychosocial effectiveness. *Psychological Reports*, 1964, *15*, 815–825.

Raush, H., Dittman, A., and Taylor, T. Person, setting and change in social interaction. I. *Human Relations*, 1959, *12*, 361–378.

Raush, H., Farbman, I., and Llewellyn, L. Person, setting and change in social interaction. II. A normal control study. *Human Relations*, 1960, *13*, 305–332.

Raush, H., Goodrich, W., and Campbell, J. D. Adaptation to the first years of marriage. *Psychiatry*, 1963, *26*, 368–380.

Ravensborg, M., and Foss, A. Suicide and natural death in a state hospital population: A comparison of admission complaints, MMPI profiles and social competence factors. *Journal of Consulting and Clinical Psychology*, 1969, *33*, 466–471.

Remmers, H. H. Cross-cultural studies of teenagers' problems. *Journal of Educational Psychology*, 1962, *53*, 254–261.

Roen, S. R., and Burnes, A. J. *Community adaptation schedule: Preliminary manual.* New York: Behavioral Publications, 1968.

Rogers, C. *On becoming a person.* Boston: Houghton Mifflin, 1961.

Rokeach, M. *The open and closed mind.* New York: Basic Books, 1960.

Rosen, B., Klein, D., Levenstein, S., and Shanian, S. Social competence and post-hospital outcome. *Archives of General Psychiatry*, 1968, *19*, 165–170.

———. Social competence and post-hospital outcome among schizophrenic and non-schizophrenic psychiatric patients. *Journal of Abnormal Psychology*, 1969, *74*, 401–404.

Rosenberg, M. *Society and the adolescent self-image.* Princeton, N.J.: Princeton University Press, 1965.

Rothenberg, B. B. Children's ability to comprehend adults' feelings and motives. Ph.D. dissertation, Cornell University, 1967.

Rotter, J. B. Generalized expectancies for internal versus external control of reinforcement. *Psychological Monographs*, 1966, *80* (whole no. 609).

Rychlak, J. F., and Legerski, A. T. A socio-cultural theory of appropriate sexual role identification and level of personal adjustment. *Journal of Personality*, 1967, *35*, 31–49.

Scarr, S. The adjective check-list as a personality assessment technique with children: Validity of the scales. *Journal of Consulting Psychology*, 1968, *30*, 122–128.

Schaefer, C. The self concept of creative adolescents. *Journal of Psychology*, 1969a, *72*, 233–242.

———. The prediction of creative achievement from a biographical inventory. *Educational Psychology Measurement*, 1969b, *29*, 431–437.

Schill, T. Repressor-sensitizer differences in free associative sex responses to double entendre words. *Journal of Clinical Psychology*, 1969, *25*, 368–369.

Schroder, H., Driver, M., and Streufert, S. *Human information processing.* New York: Holt, Rinehart & Winston, 1967.

Schwartz, M. S. Effectance motivation and interpersonal attraction: Individual differences and personality correlates. Ph.D. dissertation, University of Texas, 1966.

Sears, P., and Sherman, V. *In pursuit of self-esteem.* Belmont, Calif.: Wadsworth, 1964.

Shanan, J., and Sharon, M. Personality and cognitive functioning of Israeli males during the middle years. *Human Development*, 1965, *8*, 2–15.

Shapiro, D., Leiderman, P., and Morningstar, M. Social isolation and social interaction: A behavioral and physiological comparison. In J. Wortis, ed., *Recent advances in biological psychiatry*, vol. 6. New York: Plenum Press, 1964.

Shapiro, M. B. *The reduction of mental distress.* London: Tavistock Publications, 1970.

Shostrom, E. L. *Personal Orientation Inventory: An inventory for the measurement of self-actualization.* Preliminary Manual. San Diego, Calif.: Education and Industrial Testing Service, 1963.

Shure, G., Meeher, R., and Hansford, E. The effectiveness of pacifist strategies in bargaining games. *Journal of Conflict Resolution*, 1965, *9*, 106–117.

Sidle, A., Moos, R., Adams, J., and Cady P. Development of a coping scale: A preliminary study. *Archives of General Psychiatry*, 1969, *20*, 226–232.

Silber, E., Coelho, G., Murphey, E., Hamburg, D., Pearlin, L., and Rosenberg, M. Competent adolescents coping with college decisions. *Archives of General Psychiatry*, 1961*a*, *5*, 517–527.

Sibler, E., Hamburg, D., Coelho, G., Murphey, E., Rosenberg, M., and Pearlin, L. Adaptive behavior in competent adolescents. *Archives of General Psychiatry*, 1961*b*, *5*, 354–365.

Smith, M. B. Explorations in competence: A study of Peace Corps teachers in Ghana. *American Psychologist*, 1966, *21*, 555–566.

Snyder, W. H., Jr. The effects of reduced sensory input on the stimulation seeking behavior of schizophrenics. Ph.D. dissertation, University of South Carolina, 1968.

Soskin, W., and John, V. The study of spontaneous talk. In R. Barker, ed., *The stream of behavior.* New York: Appleton-Century-Crofts, 1963.

Stein, K. B., and Chu, C. Dimensionality of Barron's Ego Strength Scale. *Journal of Consulting Psychology*, 1967, *31*, 153–161.

Stern, G., Stein, M., and Bloom, B. *Methods in personality assessment.* Glencoe, Ill.: Free Press, 1956.

Stone, P., Dunphy, D., Smith, M., and Ogilvie, D., eds. *The general inquirer: A computer approach to content analysis.* Cambridge, Mass.: M.I.T. Press, 1966.

Strassman, H., Thaler, M., and Schein, E. A prisoner of war syndrome: Apathy as a reaction to severe stress. *American Journal of Psychiatry*, 1956, *112*, 998–1003.

Straus, M. A. Communication, creativity and the problem solving ability of middle and working class families in three societies. *American Journal of Sociology*, 1968, *73*, 417–430.

Strodtbeck, F. Family interaction, values and achievement. In D. McClelland, A. Baldwin, U. Bronfenbrenner, and F. Strodtbeck, eds., *Talent and society.* Princeton, N.J.: Van Nostrand, 1958.

Strupp, H. Patient-doctor relationships: Psychotherapist in the therapeutic process. In A. J. Bachrach, ed., *Experimental foundations of clinical psychology.* New York: Basic Books, 1962.

Thoresen, C. E., and Krumboltz, J. D. Relationship of counselor reinforcement of selected responses to external behavior. *Journal of Counseling Psychology*, 1967, *14*, 140–144.

Tooley, K. Expressive style as a developmental index in late adolescence. *Journal of Projective Techniques and Personality Assessment*, 1967, *31*, 51–59.

Tracy, G. T. A methodological study of the desirability response set on the Tennessee Department of Mental Health Self-Concept Scale. Ph.D. dissertation, University of Miami, 1967.

Tripodi, T., and Bieri, J. Cognitive complexity as a function of own and provided constructs. *Psychological Reports*, 1963, *13*, 26.

Uribe, B., and McReynolds, P. Comparison of two measures of innovative performance. *Perceptual and Motor Skills*, 1967, *25*, 777–780.

Vacchiano, R. B., Strauss, P. S., and Hockman, L. The open and closed mind: A review of dogmatism. *Psychological Bulletin*, 1969, *71*, 261–273.

Vannoy, J. Generality of cognitive complexity-simplicity as a personality construct. *Journal of Personality and Social Psychology*, 1965, *2*, 385–396.

Visotsky, H., Hamburg, D., Goss, M., and Lebovits, B. Coping behavior under extreme stress: Observations of patients with severe poliomyelitis. *Archives of General Psychiatry*, 1961, *5*, 423–448.

Wahler, H. J. The self description inventory: Measuring levels of self evaluation behavior in terms of favorable and unfavorable personality attributes. *Journal of Clinical Psychology*, 1968, *24*, 40–45.

Wallace, J. What units shall we employ? Allport's question revisited. *Journal of Consulting Psychology*, 1967, *31*, 56–64.

Warner, L., and DeFleur, M. Attitude as an interactional concept: Social constraint and social distance as intervening variables between attitudes and action. *American Sociological Review*, 1969, *34*, 153–169.

Washburn, W. C. Patterns of self conceptualization in high school and college students. *Journal of Educational Psychology*, 1961, *52*, 123–131.

Waters, L., and Kirk, W. Stimulus-seeking motivation and risk-taking behavior in a gambling situation. *Educational Psychology Measurement*, 1968, *28*, 549–550.

Weick, K. Systematic observational methods. In G. Lindzey and E. Aronson, eds., *Handbook of social psychology*, vol. 2. 2nd ed. London: Addison-Wesley, 1969.

Weinstein, I. P. The recall of memories as a function of repressing and sensitizing defenses and body position. Ph.D. dissertation, Michigan State University, 1966.

Weinstock, A. R. Longitudinal study of social class and defense preferences. *Journal of Consulting Psychology*, 1967a, 31, 539–541.

———. Family environment and the development of defense and coping mechanisms. *Journal of Personality and Social Psychology*, 1967b, *5*, 67–75.

Wendland, M. M. Self-concept in southern Negro and white adolescents as related to rural-urban residence. Ph.D. dissertation, University of North Carolina, 1968.

Werner, H. *Comparative psychology of mental development*. New York: International Universities Press, 1957.

White, R. Motivation reconsidered: The concept of competence. *Psychological Review*, 1959, *66*, 297–333.

Whiteley, J. M. A method for assessing adaptive ego functioning using the Thematic Apperception Test. *Journal of Experimental Education*, 1966, 34, 1–21.

Whiteley, R., and Watts, W. Information cost, decision consequence and selected personality variables as factors in pre-decision information seeking. *Journal of Personality*, 1969, *37*, 325–341.

Wicker, A. Undermanning performances and students' subjective experiences in behavior settings of large and small high schools. *Journal of Personality and Social Psychology*, 1968, *10*, 255–261.

Wiener, M., Carpenter, B., and Carpenter, J. Determination of defense mechanisms for conflict areas from verbal material. *Journal of Consulting Psychology*, 1956, *20*, 215–219.

Winter, S. K., Griffith, J. C., and Kolb, D. A. Capacity for self direction. *Journal of Consulting and Clinical Psychology*, 1968, *32*, 35–41.

Witkin, H. A. *Psychological differentiation*. New York: Wiley, 1962.

———. Psychological differentiation and forms of pathology. *Journal of Abnormal Psychology*, 1965, *70*, 317–336.

———. A cognitive-style approach to cross-cultural research. *International Journal of Psychology*, 1967, *2*, 233–250.

Witkin, H. A., Goodenough, D., and Karp, S. Stability of cognitive style from childhood to young adulthood. *Journal of Personality and Social Psychology*, 1967, *7*, 291–300.

Wolff, C., Friedman, S., Hofer, M., and Mason, J. Relationship between psychological defenses and mean urinary 17-hydroxycorticosteroid excretion rates. I. A predictive study of parents of fatally ill children. *Psychosomatic Medicine*, 1964*a*, *26*, 576–591.

Wolff, C., Hofer, M., and Mason, J. Relationship between psychological defenses and mean urinary 17-hydroxycorticosteroid excretion rates. II. Methodologic and theoretical considerations. *Psychosomatic Medicine*, 1964*b*, *26*, 592–608.

Zajonc, R. The process of cognitive tuning in communication. *Journal of Abnormal and Social Psychology*, 1960, *61*, 159–167.

Ziller, R., Hagey, J., Smith, M., and Long, B. Self esteem: A self social construct. *Journal of Consulting and Clinical Psychology*, 1969, *33*, 84–95.

Ziller, R., Megas, J., and DeCencio, D. Self social constructs of normal and acute psychiatric patients. *Journal of Consulting Psychology*, 1964, *28*, 59–63.

Zimbardo, P. Relationship between projective and direct measures of fear arousal. *Journal of Abnormal and Social Psychology*, 1964, *68*, 196–199.

Zimbardo, P., and Formica, R. Emotional comparison and self-esteem as determinants of affiliation. *Journal of Personality*, 1963, *31*, 79–96.

Zinner, L. The consistency of human behavior in various situations: A methodological application of functional ecological psychology. Ph.D. dissertation, University of Houston, 1963.

Zuckerman, M., Kolin, E., Price, L., and Zoob, I. Development of a sensation seeking scale. *Journal of Consulting Psychology*, 1964, *28*, 477–482.

Zuckerman, M., and Link, K. Construct validity for the sensation seeking scale. *Journal of Consulting and Clinical Psychology*, 1968, *32*, 420–426.

Zuckerman, M., Persky, H., Link, K., and Basu, G. Experimental and subject factors determining responses to sensory deprivation, social isolation and confinement. *Journal of Abnormal Psychology*, 1968, *73*, 183–194.

Zuckerman, M., and Schultz, D. Sensation-seeking and volunteering for sensory deprivation and hypnosis experiments. *Journal of Consulting Psychology*, 1967, *31*, 358–363.

V

COPING
AND ADAPTATION

V

GOETHE
AND ADAPTATION

13

Coping and Adaptation: Steps toward a Synthesis of Biological and Social Perspectives

DAVID A. HAMBURG, GEORGE V. COELHO, AND JOHN E. ADAMS

BIOLOGICAL CONCEPTS OF ADAPTATION AND THE ROLE OF BEHAVIOR IN HUMAN EVOLUTION

From a biological perspective, adaptation means reproductive success of a *population*. In the modern synthesis of evolutionary theory, biological adaptation is centrally concerned with the genetic development of populations of organisms in response to demands placed upon them by their environments. Such biological adaptation is most often a compromise between the long-range and the immediate requirements of survival. As stated by Simpson, "Adaptation in general may be regarded as a complex of processes (and results of processes) bringing about and maintaining an organism-environment relationship useful to individual organisms and populations" (1958, p. 521). Adaptation is thus a dynamic, evolving, unending process. As environments change, so must organisms change if they are to survive. Although the emphasis in evolutionary theory is usually placed on populations of organisms, it is important to note that reproductive success of a population involves all phases of the life cycle of the *individual* organism and that such success is most commonly favored by individual adaptation to his particular environment. Although biological adaptation is the result of natural selection, it centrally involves behavior as a vital element in the shaping of evolutionary change. As complex organisms have evolved, behavior has become an exceedingly important factor in meeting adaptive tasks which contribute to species survival. Such fundamental tasks would include finding food and water, avoiding predators, achieving fertile copulation, caring for the young, and preparing the young to cope effectively with the specific requirements of a given environment. Finally, adaptive behavior functions through a social system. The role of behavior in adaptation is not only a function of individuals, but of groups as well. The present volume in general and this chapter in particular attempt to highlight certain aspects of these species, individual, and group adaptational processes, with particular emphasis on behavior as an instrumental factor.

In recent years, there has been an intensification of research on human evolution and the evolution of human behavior. Sources of information include the enlarging fossil record, prehistoric archaeology, chemical dating methods, study of the few remaining hunting-and-gathering societies, and especially the study of nonhuman primates. Sherwood Washburn, with his students and colleagues, has led the way in this new wave of research on human evolution. Their overriding concern is a deeper understanding of social behavior and organization in contemporary human development and the problems of adaptation to constant environmental change. As Chapter 1 suggests, direct observation of primate behavior in natural habitats over many years can be helpful in understanding the ways in which structure and behavior are adapted to environmental conditions. Some generalizations can be made about long-term primate adaptive patterns based on the pooled observations of a great variety of field studies in natural habitats.

All species of monkeys and apes studied so far live in *social groups* that include both sexes and all ages. Although there is much variation in the size and structure of the groups—the most common groups vary between about ten and fifty, but among gibbons the group consists of a pair of adults and their offspring, whereas it may be as large as a few hundred among some baboons and macaques—with differing patterns of group cohesion, interanimal dominance, and sex behavior, all monkeys and apes spend the greater part of their lives in close association with other members of the same species. In general, among both tree-living and ground-living primates, the infant nonhuman primate is given much special attention and care that ensures its survival. In all species of monkeys and apes for which data are available, it is apparent that the *mother-infant relationship* is an important part of the groupwide matrix of social relations. Infant survival depends on the adaptation of the whole group. Thus, the mother with a newborn is the focus of attention, being very attractive to other group members, and the mother-infant relationship is the most intense (in terms of time, energy, and emotion) in the primate group, outlasting any other social bond. Within the chimpanzee community, for example, the only highly stable social unit over a long time interval is the mother and her offspring. These units form a set of stable subgroups within a community, and offspring keep returning to the mother from time to time, even when they are fully adult. Recently, similar observations of enduring mother-offspring relations have been made in a long-term study of rhesus macaque groups.

In addition to the importance of the mother-infant social structure, developmental time for the individual is also vital. Many of the Old World monkeys require several years before they become fully adult, whereas the time required by the great apes is longer. For the chimpanzee, fourteen to sixteen years may be required before full maturity is attained in the wild. This maturation period is, of course, longest in humans, and there is thus a broad trend toward prolongation of immaturity as one moves along the phylogenetic scale. It is important to note that this characteristic carries with it certain short-term adaptive disadvantages. For example, the mother cannot move as freely as she otherwise would, and other members of the group must similarly restrict their activities and make adjustments to take account of the infant's movement limitations. There are, in addition, reproductive limitations, because typically the adult female primate does not become sexually receptive again until most or all of the lactation period has passed. What kind of broader adaptive gain could possibly overcome disadvantages of this kind? The principal gain probably is that this very long protected time can be utilized for learning. It is long enough so that simple elements of learning can be combined in very complex sequences that can then be adapted to the specific conditions of a given environment, whatever those conditions may be. Adapting to a very diverse array of environments thus becomes feasible through the shaping of behavior in the long protected interval of immaturity.

If a system of this sort is to work effectively, the mother should be motivated to protect the young, and the young should be motivated to seek her protection. Moreover, the young should be motivated to explore the environment and to learn how to take its salient features into account. Over a very long time period, natural selection favors these behavior patterns because in the long term they enhance the capacity for dealing with highly varied environments. In this framework, it is useful to view mother-infant relations as a sort of implicit preparation of the young for adult life. Field studies of nonhuman primates have revealed a number of such instances of behavioral rehearsal. A striking example is the juvenile female primate's interest in, and experience with, younger siblings and other infants in the group. This interest begins very early and goes all the way through the life span in the higher primate species for which relevant data are so far available. The specific adaptive importance of such behavior is suggested by the significant sex difference in the attractiveness of the young to males and females. Although there is also evidence of male interest in the young, this appears more variable, both from species to species, and from one time to another in the individual male's life span. By contrast, female interest in the young is very strong and persistent, and by the time the adult female in the natural habitat has offspring of her own she is typically an experienced infant handler and has developed considerable competence in a broad range of maternal behavior.

A second important primate adaptive pattern demonstrated in field studies is *exploratory behavior*. This is manifested in visual searching of the environment and in examination of objects. Over an extended period, such exploration leads to familiarity with the home range, and information accumulates regarding food sources, water sources, probable location and behavior of predators, and trees that offer safety. The deeply ingrained nature of exploratory behavior has been documented in experimental studies, where maintenance of other behaviors has been repeatedly achieved through the use of opportunity for exploration as a reward. The basic finding is that primates will work persistently and will solve problems in order to see, hear, or manipulate. It has been further shown that different classes of objects have different reward value within each sensory sphere. For example, in regard to visual preferences, bright is chosen over dull, clear over fuzzy, moving over still, and color over black and white. Of particular interest is the fact that the most effective of all rewards in maintaining responsiveness at a high level is the sight and sound of other monkeys. This last is true even for monkeys raised from birth in total isolation. In aggregate, these visual preferences seem to have considerable relevance for the natural environment, for the monkey seems to prefer the kinds of stimuli that have had adaptive significance for its species in the long course of its evolution. In experiments of this sort, evidence has also accumulated indicating that novelty increases exploratory behavior, especially when the mother is near the young primate. Fear on the other hand decreases exploration. Altogether, from both field and experimental work, there is growing evidence of selective motivation for exploratory behavior, especially in the young primate.

The exploratory tendencies described above may be usefully linked to the concept of *observational learning*. In these settings one monkey learns from watching another. For example, in experimental food-choice situations the observing animal has been shown to learn from the incorrect as well as the correct responses of the operator. Newer field studies suggest the adaptive significance of *observational learning in a social context*, for the following is a recurrent sequence: (1) close observation of one animal by another; (2) imitation by the observing animal of the behavior of some observed animal; and (3) the later practice of the observed behavior. The practice component occurs particularly in the group play behavior of young animals. Such social learning seems to be crucial in the development of adaptive behavior in nature, because young nonhuman primates have the opportunity for consistent, close-range observation of behavior utilized by adults in meeting the adaptive problems of their habitat. This generalization clearly applies in such diverse behavioral spheres as food getting, defense, predation, attachment, sex, shelter seeking, threat, attack, deference, and cooperation. In all likelihood, this full access to observation of effective adults in all spheres of adaptive behavior also characterized most human societies in earlier evolutionary eras.

To this point we have emphasized the positive aspects of behavioral consistency and change as a force in the development of the human species. It is also important to note that the time scale of evolution highlights a dilemma in the contemporary human situation. There have been mammals on earth for well over fifty million years. Primates appeared early among the mammals and have been present for at least fifty million years. We have recently learned that a distinctly manlike form has existed for several million years, and our own species has been in existence for about forty thousand years. Agriculture has been a significant environmental factor for man for less than ten thousand years, and the industrial revolution began only about two hundred years ago and has become widespread even more recently.

Problems that concern us so urgently today—the enormous population growth, urbanization with its difficult consequences, a physically sedentary way of life, environmental damage, and resource depletion—are largely very recent problems for man. We see, then, that some of the chief features of the contemporary environment are products of the most recent phase of development, much of which has taken place even within our lifetime. The biological equipment of the human organism is mostly very old. In addition to obvious physical characteristics, some of our emotional response tendencies and learning orientations are probably a part of that biological equipment, built into the organism because they worked well in adaptation over many thousands and even millions of years. There has been precious little time for change in that equipment since the industrial revolution began two centuries ago, and yet the circumstances of our present life are largely a product of that revolution. We do not know how well we are suited to the world in which we now live, but we must try to understand the forces that molded our species.

We have mentioned above the important contribution of studies of non-human primates to the understanding of man's biological and behavioral past. Evidence from several lines of biological research indicates that the chimpanzee has a closer relationship to man than any other living animal. Important new discoveries have revealed close similarity between man and chimpanzee in chromosomes, blood proteins, immune responses, and DNA. Moreover, continuing neuro-anatomical research has shown increasingly that the circuitry of man's brain resembles more closely that of the chimpanzee than it does that of any other species, including other apes and monkeys. Thus an understanding of the behavior of the chimpanzee may contribute to a fuller understanding of the origins of human behavior and adaptive response in the face of new and potentially threatening situations. The most relevant program of research on chimpanzee behavior in their natural habitat is that being conducted by Dr. Jane Van Lawick-Goodall at the Gombe National Park in Tanzania. This research clearly demonstrates that wild chimpanzees are highly intelligent and very social primates who are capable of close and enduring attachments. They show an extensive repertoire of gestural and postural communication patterns, some of which bear remarkable similarities to our own, for example, in greeting, threat, attack, submission, and reassurance. The chimpanzee not only uses tools effectively for many purposes, but also makes simple tools. He hunts other mammals for food, cooperates with other chimpanzees to do so, and shares the prey with them afterward. Family ties extend throughout the life span. Chimpanzee adolescence is characterized by striking changes in various behavior patterns, including sex, aggression, attachment, and deference. These adolescent behavioral changes show clear sex differences.

To illustrate the way in which knowledge about primate behavior may be relevant to man, let us review briefly what is known about the primate equivalent of what is clearly a major current social problem for man, namely, destructive aggression. When are primates likely to threaten and fight with one another, or to threaten and fight with members of other species? The following is a summary of situations likely to elicit such behavior in chimpanzees:

1. When there is competition over food, especially if highly desirable foods are spatially concentrated or in short supply.
2. When an infant is being defended by its mother.
3. If a contest occurs over the dominance prerogatives of two individuals of similar social rank.
4. As a redirection of aggression: for example, when a low-ranking male has been attacked by a high-ranking male, it often turns to attack an individual subordinate to itself.
5. With failure of one animal to comply with a signal given by the aggressor.
6. When a familiar animal appears strange or different: for example, due to paralytic disease.
7. When changes in dominance status occur, over time, especially among the adolescent and young adult males.
8. When a female in estrus does not respond to an adult male's courtship.
9. When relative strangers meet.
10. In the hunting and killing of small animals.
11. When a chimpanzee is suffering from a presumably painful injury.

If one surveys the contexts listed above in which aggressive behavior is most likely to occur in the natural habitat, much of the information can be condensed into two general categories: (1) defense and (2) access to valued resources. Within each of these categories, a variety of animals or objects or activities may be involved. So behaving aggressively in contexts of defense and of access to valued resources may well have given selective advantage in the zoological sense to higher primates. In effect, such behavior, if adequately regulated, can be an enforcer of many adaptive requirements, such as those involving food, water, and protection from predation.

These observations raise questions for future research regarding similarities in the contexts of aggressive behavior between chimpanzee and man. Of special interest in this connection are the following: (1) Is the heavy reliance upon dominance relations in chimpanzees (and other higher primate species) in some way a precursor of the ubiquitous status differentiations in human societies? (2) Is the redirection of aggression downward in the dominance hierarchy in some way related to the widespread human tendency toward the scapegoating of lower-status individuals or groups? (3) Is the turbulence in adolescent behavior, especially the male "aggression spurt," related to similar phenomena in human adolescence and at least partially dependent on developmental changes in sex hormones? Even with the answers to these questions, however, we would still face the even more crucial issue that the adaptability of aggressive behavior in past environments gives no assurance whatever that similar behavior will function adaptively in the very different environment of contemporary man.

In summary, evolutionary adaptation is formulated as reproductive success of a population. Reproductive success of a population is positively correlated with reproductive success of individual members of that population, which is, in turn, positively correlated with the absence of intense and prolonged suffering, and with effective social behavior. When the environment is stable in its main features over long periods of time, guidelines for behavior emerge that are, on the average, useful for the population. Such guidelines for behavior tend to be taught early in life, are shaped by powerful rewards and punishments, are strongly charged emotionally, and are supported by norms important for group cooperation in meeting developmental needs. Such early learning of guidelines for adaptive behavior tends to induce lifelong commitments. On the average, over long time spans, they prepare the young to meet the adaptive requirements of the environment by fulfilling the roles of adult life.

Evolutionary research has taught us that variability in structure and function is crucial in meeting new conditions for a population. In other words, when there is a drastic change in environmental conditions, some genes that had formerly been of little adaptive utility may now become exceedingly important. The same principle applies to behavior; that is, there is much long-run adaptive utility in preserving in populations a wide range of behavior patterns. But the questions remain: What are these alternative behavior patterns, and can they be mobilized to assist man in dealing with a very rapidly changing world?

FROM ADAPTATION IN EVOLUTION TO COPING IN CONTEMPORARY SOCIAL CHANGE

Although biological adaptation means reproductive success of a population, the important variable can never be numbers alone. Reproductive success means progeny able to utilize environmental opportunities and avoid catastrophes. For example, the size of the population must be related to the carrying capacity of the land, and this in turn varies with technology. Against the background of subsistence uncertainties, marginality, and threats of natural disaster that have characterized so much of human experience, new technological leverage has historically been quite attractive. Given this fundamental incentive, technology is often pursued vigorously, and it, in turn, transforms society. One such transformation occurred rather promptly in the wake of the industrial revolution, another between

1870 and 1900 when an acceleration in the impact of science and technology occurred, and a third acceleration has been evident since World War II. On the time scale of evolution, these are exceedingly recent changes, and their rate is extraordinarily rapid. As we have previously discussed in terms of biological factors, so in times of such rapid technological and social change old guidelines for *behavior* become uncertain or discredited. Previously learned guidelines may be poorly suited to new conditions, but these established guidelines, if they have worked well for long periods, are difficult to change. They are difficult to change for the person in his lifetime, and they are also difficult to change for the population. The problems in changing such behavior patterns are substantially related to the fact that self-esteem and close interpersonal relationships are dependent upon them. Yet the need for change in behavior is actually greatest when drastic environmental changes are occurring. At the extreme, failure to change behavior in such circumstances may result in considerable risk of extinction—for the person, for the society, and even for the species.

Goldschmidt, in Chapter 2, has incisively summarized these processes of cultural transformations and the crucial role of institutional supports in the maintenance of self-esteem in the crisis of change. He emphasizes that the growth of technology involves change in the life circumstances of the population, with alterations in the concentration of population, the accumulation of goods, the degree to which people may lead a settled life, their opportunities for leisure, and an increase in the area over which there is communication. These changed circumstances require and make possible divergent ways of meeting the needs of all social systems. Though no society is a perfectly functioning mechanism, its institutions are instrumentalities through which group life can be maintained and through which the individual can be supplied with minimally necessary satisfactions of both his physical needs and his culturally conditioned wants. Whatever the nature of the society, the social imperatives continue, but the pattern in which they operate will vary. This variation is dependent, in large measure, on the character of that technology and the size and circumstances of the population that it supports. These various forces require that the institutions of society, like the populations they serve, undergo evolutionary change.

For millions of years, primate (including human) societies have been meeting the adaptive requirements of their populations. They have done this in many ways, depending in substantial part on the environmental conditions they had to meet. Individuals have been prepared throughout a lengthy childhood development for their roles in the particular social system. Each social system thus supports, channels, and facilitates adaptive behavior throughout the life cycle. It is as though the culture gives instructions: "This is the way we meet this problem"; "These are the acceptable limits of behavior in coping with this adaptive requirement." While technological changes offer hope of meeting adaptive requirements more effectively, social systems must also change to utilize these technological opportunities. This in turn elicits changes in socialization practices as individuals are prepared for effective roles in their modified social systems. To repeat once more an earlier theme, a very rapid rate of change poses distinctive problems for the culture, because these socialization practices must change rapidly enough to meet emerging conditions.

The experiences of childhood and adolescence may be viewed as preparation for adult behavior. In contemporary society, when survival requirements seem easier to meet (at least in the short run), there is considerable uncertainty about the values that should guide the shaping of behavior during the years of growth and development. What do we want our children to be when they grow up? The mere fact that this question is so frequently asked implies a choice rather than a simple acceptance of traditional values, but the choices themselves are often difficult and require individual decision making.

Just as studies of animal structure and function have shown that a variety of biological solutions are possible for a given environmental problem, so too a variety of social solutions may be utilized in meeting common human predicaments. Underlying this diversity, however, are fundamental human social needs. As Goldschmidt puts it, ". . . in human societies there are recurrent problems requiring institutionalized solutions. These problems are the result of a combination of two generic circumstances: (1) the vicissitudes of the environment within which the society must maintain life; and (2) the preprogrammed, self-seeking characteristics of the human animal that must be curbed or channelized" (p. 19). In addition, though different cultures arrange these matters in remarkably different ways, individuals in all cultures seem to require a dependable basis for self-esteem and a sense of belonging in a valued group. Goldschmidt further points out that institutional systems, through a variety of subsystems, provide for the human cooperation that has been essential in species survival. These institutions provide the mechanisms for collaborative social action and supply ways in which the individual's requirements can be effectively meshed with those of his community. Although we have so far stressed diversity in social organization, it is also important to point out that some behavior patterns are so effective in meeting fundamental human problems that they have tended to appear over and over again in different cultures and in different parts of the world. As an example, the pattern of extensive food-sharing in hunting-and-gathering societies has such powerful advantages that it seems to be a universal part of that way of life.

Goldschmidt's chapter provides an important bridge between the biological study of behavior as adaptation through the long course of human evolution and the coping behavior of groups in contemporary social change. He emphasizes human consistency in the face of cultural diversity and hypothesizes that differentially patterned behavior in different cultures relates fundamentally (though certainly not exclusively) to the ecological circumstances under which the cultures operate. Underlying the diverse expression of social organization of the human animal is the need for a positive self-image.

Mechanic, in Chapter 3, provides an important interdisciplinary bridge between Goldschmidt's concern with institutional supports for self-esteem and positive self-image and White's emphasis (in Chapter 4) on defense, not as an end in itself, but as a set of mechanisms that facilitate continuing striving for competence and mastery. He argues that the early studies on coping behavior paid insufficient attention to the social environment, especially with regard to the capacity of the individual through group attachments to reconstruct a harsh social reality and to preserve the self-esteem of its members in adversity. At the individual level, Mechanic describes personal adaptation as having three fundamental components: (1) coping capabilities, (2) motivation to meet environmental demands, and (3) maintenance of psychological equilibrium.

Mechanic, like Goldschmidt, White, and George, puts strong emphasis on the necessity to maintain self-esteem in stressful circumstances. "We all maintain our sense of self-respect and energy for action through perceptions that enhance our self-importance and self-esteem, and we maintain our sanity by suppressing the tremendous vulnerability we all experience in relation to the risks of the real world" (pp. 37–38). He further reiterates Goldschmidt's inclusion of culture as a powerful force. "Man's abilities to cope with the environment depend on the efficacy of the solutions that his culture provides, and the skills he develops are dependent on the adequacy of the preparatory institutions to which he has been exposed" (p. 33). In more general terms, adequacy in meeting adaptive tasks is seen to depend substantially on support, guidance, and facilitation of significant other people and the society at large.

There is, however, more to adaptation than protecting the self. Adaptation is anticipatory as well as reactive. People tend to approach their environment with plans, to calculate and recalculate their risks and opportunities, to take on tasks they feel they can handle, to seek actively for information and feedback, to prepare for probable difficulties, to provide multiple buffers against defeat, to keep some options open, to distribute commitments, to set the stage for new efforts by practice and rehearsal, and to try a variety of hypotheses in resolving any important problem.

It is also important to note again that the tasks change over time, so preparation to meet them must change as well. This includes the development of new social institutions (or at least the substantial modification of existing ones) to assist the individual in acquiring strategies that have a reasonable probability of effectiveness in meeting vital tasks. Methodologically, this viewpoint argues strongly for studies that provide close observation of individual subjects in their social networks over an extended period of time, coping with real problems of major personal significance. Behavior that is apparently defensive in one phase may serve coping functions viewed over time in reference to the overall organism's survival strategy.

Tragically, the past few decades have offered abundant opportunity to observe ways in which people cope with man's inhumanity to man. They have provided examples of extreme hardship probably comparable to any in human history. In an attempt to make some of these concepts more vivid, we should now like to summarize a particularly poignant example of coping under extreme stress. This involves observations that have emerged from the Nazi concentration camps. Coping variables in this setting have been most clearly illustrated by the work of Eitinger (in press). We mention here some of his main findings, based on direct observations in the camps followed by semistructured interviews and medical examinations over many years. Eitinger asks how it was that some people were able to survive this prolonged ordeal physically and psychologically. A certain physical minimum of survival possibilities had to be present in order for coping behavior to have had any chance of effectiveness, for many otherwise effective copers were simply overwhelmed by crushing events. Given this physical minimum of survival possibilities, Eitinger has been especially interested in patterns of coping behavior that tended not only to foster physical survival, but to maintain mental health both during the stay in the camp and in the years afterward. A significant finding was that "identification with the aggressor" was not commonly used by inmates and, when it was used, tended to have damaging effects on self-esteem and interpersonal relationships in the long run. Inmates were found to be substantially helped if they felt they had *something to live for*. The notion of a "contract with fate," in which it was believed by the prisoner that every misfortune and trauma he suffered would spare his beloved in another camp, did not occur frequently. The prisoners who fared best in the long run were those who for one reason or another could retain their personality system largely intact—where previous interests, values, and skills could to come extent be carried on during the period of incarceration. Very fortunate in this respect were some members of service professions, such as physicians, nurses, clergymen, and social workers.

Another route of coping that proved effective in the long run involved *linkages with valued groups*. For example, prisoners who were able to stay together with some member of their family or to remain in contact with some of their prewar peers benefited from such relationships. Strong identification with ethnic or national groups proved quite supportive. When Norwegian prisoners were asked many years later what helped them most to survive, their answers very often conveyed a strong thrust: "being together with other Norwegians." In essence, the maintenance of self-esteem, a sense of human dignity, a sense of group belonging, and a feeling of being useful to others all seemed to contribute significantly to survival in both physical and psychological terms. On the other hand, conditions of high physical and psychological vulnerability are summarized by Eitinger as follows: "Prisoners who were completely isolated from their family, bereft of all contact with groups to whom they were related before the war, people who very quickly abandoned themselves and their innermost values, people who were completely overwhelmed by the notion that they had nobody and nothing to struggle or to live for, all felt completely passive and had lost their ability to retain some sort of self-activity. They were those who most usually succumbed." The above, and other work on survival under extreme conditions, suggests the importance both of group supports and of individual strategies in adaptation.

DEVELOPMENT OF COMPETENCE IN THE LIFE CYCLE IN CONTEMPORARY SOCIETIES

Developmental Tasks and Coping Strategies: Basic Considerations

Clearly implicit in many of the chapters in this volume, and also in the seminal writings of Erik Erikson (1959), are the concepts of tasks and strategies. That is, requirements for effective adaptation (tasks) and the variety of ways in which these requirements may be met (strategies). We shall now expand somewhat on these concepts, drawing particularly on studies of the young human's coping with the inevitable crises of the maturational process.

The development of competence for meeting the tasks of modern, industrial societies within the individual life span is a very complex process covering many years. What are the tasks for which long-term preparation must be undertaken? Alex Inkeles has provided an insightful description.

Effective participation in a modern industrial and urban society requires certain levels of skill in the manipulation of language and other symbol systems, such as arithmetic and time; the ability to comprehend and complete forms; information as to when and where to go for what; skills in interpersonal relations which permit negotiation, insure protection of one's interests, and provide maintenance of stable and satisfying relations with intimates, peers, and authorities; motives to achieve, to master, to persevere; defenses to control and channel acceptably the impulses to aggression, to sexual expression, to extreme dependency; a cognitive style which permits thinking in concrete terms while still permitting reasonable handling of abstractions and general concepts; a mind which does not insist on excessively premature closure, is tolerant of diversity, and has some components of flexibility; a conative style which facilitates reasonably regular, steady, and persistent effort, relieved by rest and relaxation but not requiring long periods of total withdrawal or depressive psychic slump; and a style of expressing affect which encourages stable and enduring relationships without excessive narcissistic dependence or explosive aggression in the face of petty frustration (1966, pp. 265–283).

Contemporary man in a technological society faces challenges to his adaptive development that are truly unprecedented. He has to cope with environmental changes that he has generated through his own powers, but that have consequences for his behavior and social relations that are stressful in ways he has not experienced before. As we have described earlier, nonhuman primates and early man were organized around one small society for a whole lifetime. Until very recently, much after the onset of the industrial revolution, men lived and worked in a relatively rural, stable environment that was physically and socially bounded by familiar events. For most of the time that man has existed, it was also an open society in the sense that, for the most part, social behavior and social communication was mediated by face-to-face interaction. Adaptive tasks were perceived in terms of their immediacy for survival, and the range of potential strategies was relatively circumscribed. Natural selection has favored those populations whose members were, on the whole, organized effectively to meet these tasks. In the very large, complex, and rapidly changing societies of recent times the contributions of individuals to such effectiveness have often been obscured, and preparation for effectiveness is more complicated than ever before.

The long, tortuous route toward competence in the complex tasks of adult life depends in part on behavioral tendencies that evolution has built into the human infant. Concomitantly, in every society, the child must be assisted in the development of competence in vital adaptive tasks. White has contributed much in recent years to our understanding of the early steps toward competence:

This behavior includes visual exploration, grasping, investigatory behavior of young animals and children. Effectance motivation must be conceived to involve satisfaction—a feeling of efficacy—in transactions in which behavior has an exploratory, varying, experimental character and produces changes in the stimulus field. Having this character, the behavior leads the organism to find out how the environment can be changed and what consequences flow from these changes.

In higher animals and especially in man, where so little is innately provided and so much has to be learned about dealing with the environment, effectance motivation independent of primary drives can be seen as an arrangement having high adaptive value. Considering the slow rate of learning in infancy and the vast amount that has to be learned before there can be an effective level of interaction with surroundings, young animals and children would simply not learn enough unless they worked pretty steadily at the task between episodes of homeostatic crisis. . . . Crawling and walking, attention and perception, language and thinking, exploring novel objects and places, manipulating the surroundings, and producing effective changes in the environment . . . all of these behaviors have a common biological significance: They all form part of the process whereby the animal or child learns to interact effectively with his environment (1959, pp. 297–333).

For any species, some patterns of behavior are easy to learn, some fairly difficult, and some exceedingly difficult. In general, patterns that have been valuable in species survival are easy to learn. It seems likely that hormonal influences on brain development may have important mediating roles. One way in which this can occur is through the development of attention, for attention is crucial to the learning processes. Hormonal influences during a sensitive period of brain development may render a certain class of stimuli more interesting to the organism at a later stage. Although largely hypothetical at this point, this line of inquiry is amenable to experimental analysis in nonhuman primates and to direct observation in human infants. Such work is a crucial frontier in research on infancy.

Lois B. Murphy is an authentic pioneer in the study of coping behavior, especially in respect to its development (1962). Indeed, some years ago, she persuaded us to adopt the term *coping* for our studies of behavioral adaptation in life-threatening situations, and she has had similar influences on other workers in the field. Among her many contributions, her description of three-year-olds, brought for the first time from their homes to her study center, provided an insightful window into simple coping strategies of early life, strategies that contain some of the basic building blocks out of which complex strategies in later life are created. Her careful, direct observation of behavior in a new situation has shown much about the ways in which children overcome their fears, increase relevant information, and acquire some competence in respect to the novel tasks. Significantly, these studies were extended in time beyond this revealing initial encounter, with observations made in many sessions over several years. These longitudinal observations permitted insight into some ways in which early temperament may predispose toward different styles of coping, and the gradual building, testing, and sharpening of coping strategies over extended periods of time. It is particularly interesting to see the various ways in which children of different temperamental orientations tend to scan their environment for areas of likely competence. Whether familiarity with the environment grows slowly or rapidly, and by whatever route, ways are found of testing the environment and one's own capacities in relation to it, discovering in due course features of the situation that are promising for oneself.

The observations of Lois Murphy remind us that coping begins from birth. The baby has to cope initially with the problems of the feeding process. His coping involves managing inner resources while meeting outer exigencies in a feedback relationship with the mothering one. The realities of inner, as well as outer, environmental demands have to be managed.

Coping, for Murphy as for White, involves imaginative and innovative behavior. The infant and child are frequently confronted with new experiences, obstacles, frustrations, dangers as well as opportunities, for which they have no ready-made devices or management strategies. Much of the child's coping is original, to him at least, and even creative in the sense of trial and error. Success in these intrinsic coping challenges may bring expressions of gratifying mastery. In this context, part of the mother's task is not to teach, but to respond to what the baby initiates. Murphy documents the individual differences that must be recognized in children's coping resources and resilience, as well as in differences in support from the environment. She underlines the consequences of these developmental differences for the infant's ability to weather such stresses sufficiently to permit continued growth and increased capacity to reach workable relationships with the environment.

Unfortunately the study of coping has not been a conspicuous feature of the major longitudinal studies so far conducted. There are, however, intriguing leads from some of them, particularly the University of California's guidance study directed by Jean MacFarlane (1964). Developmental studies in this field deserve much greater attention in the future.

Developmental Tasks and Coping Strategies:
Illustrations from Two Transitions of the
Life Cycle—Puberty and Menopause

The major transitions present challenges and opportunities for new learning and personal development. At the same time, they have stressful aspects that, from a clinical viewpoint, are often seen as precipitating factors in psychiatric and medical casualties. The major transitions of the life cycle, such as puberty or the menopause, not only reflect a drastic change in the internal environment, but often occur concomitantly with major changes in the social environment. Turning now to these later stages in the life cycle, we shall pursue more deeply, through two specific examples, the definition of tasks and strategies for given developmental crisis periods.

In Chapter 6, Beatrix Hamburg calls attention to early adolescence as an important and neglected phase of human development that lends itself admirably to analysis in terms of developmental tasks and coping strategies. This discussion has the merit of explicitly linking biological, psychological, and sociocultural processes. It is thus related to other work on developmental crises, including Erik Erikson (1959) on late adolescence, Greta Bibring (1961) on pregnancy, and Theresa Benedek (1959) on parenthood.

Beatrix Hamburg points out that the coming of age in modern technological societies is an increasingly long and complex process. Over at least the past two centuries, there has been a significant trend toward the earlier onset of physiological maturation, while the achievement of full social maturity has tended to be increasingly delayed. The former presumably rests upon nutritional and hygienic changes, while the latter has to do with the increasingly complex educational requirements for a high technology society. There is thus now nearly a decade in which, by most criteria, the adolescent in our society is neither child nor adult. This prolongation of adolescence is very pertinent to the by now classic formulation of the "identity crisis" by Erikson. It reflects major social changes and suggests formidable problems of improvising new coping strategies to meet rapidly changing socioenvironmental conditions. Although there is increased recent interest in the study of the adolescent period, Hamburg points out that most attention has been given to the last few years of it, with a focus on boys. She clarifies the need for additional data on the earlier phase of adolescence for both sexes and the need for additional data on females at all levels. Because there are strong indications of significant differences among the various subsets of adolescents, she also points to the need for clarification of tasks and strategies, not only by sex and by age level, but also by social class and ethnic group.

The dominant theme of early adolescence is hormonal change and, as a result of this change, a growth spurt and the development of secondary sex characteristics. Hamburg emphasizes the need for further studies, utilizing newer methods of measuring sex hormones and their metabolites, or the relationship between hormonal changes and the frequently observed behavioral changes, especially in the sphere of sexuality, aggressiveness, and emotional vulnerability. Conversely, she also points out the differential social and psychological consequences of early versus late physical maturation. This effect is perhaps most strikingly seen in the advantage conferred upon the early maturing boy. The early onset of exceptional size and strength has tended traditionally to be highly valued in males, and it is thus conducive to the growth of self-esteem and the development of lasting competences.

The interaction of biological and social factors is further demonstrated by the fact that, with the earlier onset of puberty, it tends to coincide in American society with the transition from elementary school to junior high school. There are marked differences between the junior high school and the elementary school as social environments. Thus, a drastic change in environmental conditions occurs both internally and externally at about the same time. This is a heavy load upon the organism and represents a sharp discontinuity with past experience. A great many adolescents are inadequately prepared to cope with this conjunction of stressful events. Despite these and other stresses, systematic and large-scale survey research indicates considerable coping effectiveness on the part of a large proportion of the young adolescent population. All too little is known of the mechanisms through which such coping effectiveness is accomplished. There is evidence that for a significant number of adolescents such adaptation is still based on the assimilation of traditional values and skills, but as increasing numbers of families offer a wider range of opportunities, they also provide fewer guidelines for adolescent behavior. Although coping studies of college freshmen conducted at the National Institute of Mental Health (NIMH) have shown that the peer group can provide much support, guidance, and facilitation for the somewhat older adolescent, the substitution of peer pressure for parental guidance in the younger age group can produce considerable emotional turbulence. Research is clearly needed into the sources and consequences of different coping strategies in early adolescence; and systematic studies on the transition from elementary school to junior high school, in an approach similar to the work already done on the transition from high school to college, would be most helpful.

We have just considered the stressful conjunction of puberty with the transition from elementary school to junior high school and emphasized the frequent coincidence between biological and social transformations. The same issues arise with the menopause, for in the years during which far-reaching endocrine changes are occurring, leading to the end of a woman's reproductive period, other events frequently occur in her life that have threatening implications. We shall first review some of the tasks that often have threatening implications for the woman in the menopausal period, at least in American society, and then consider coping strategies through which women often meet the task requirements.

Not all the tasks to be considered here pertain to any given woman, but it is not unusual for several tasks to make a direct impact upon her at the same time of life. The following are tasks or issues of the menopausal period that deserve consideration, partly because they are often clinically significant in problems of the developmental phase. (1) The likelihood of serious illness is greater at this time of life than it had been before. Indeed, such risks are higher for the woman than at any time since her own infancy. This risk applies as well to significant others such as husbands, siblings, and friends. The serious illness or death of a close friend during this time may heighten the individual's sense of vulnerability. (2) This is an era when there is a rather high probability of having chronically ill parents. Such situations may be quite burdensome, especially because social arrangements for the elderly in highly mobile, rapidly changing societies are often inadequate. (3) Concerns about the loss of youthfulness may be personally threatening, especially in cultures that place great value on youth and manifest strong ambivalence toward the elderly. Preoccupations about loss of attractiveness, diminishing sexuality, and fading vigor may enter into these concerns. (4) This is a time when children are likely to be "lost" in the sense that they have more or less disappeared from the home and intimate contact has diminished. Their need for their parents is much less than it was at an earlier time and they may show striking deviation from parental values. This situation, which has sometimes been referred to as the "empty nest syndrome," is particularly salient for a woman whose self-esteem has been based to a large extent upon her value as a mother. (5) When faced with the empty nest, the woman must decide what to do with the time made available by the departure of her children. This presents opportunities, but it is also often associated with a sense of loss, and the opportunities themselves may pose difficult choices. (6) The woman's husband may well be undergoing concurrent transitions in his own life, making him less available in time and emotional commitment than he had been in some earlier phases of their marriage. He may, for example, be experiencing serious disappointment in regard to long-term career aspirations. He may also be having concerns similar to hers, such as those having to do with the loss of youthful vigor. If sufficiently absorbed in a major personal transition of his own, the husband may be less available to his wife when she needs him most.

The menopausal era, and we speak not only of the menopause itself, but also of commonly associated events, may thus pose extremely difficult and distressing tasks for the individual living through it. These task requirements sometimes cannot be satisfactorily met, and hence the prominence of clinical disorders in this period. In the general population, however, these tasks may elicit a variety of strategies that often do, in fact, reach substantial effectiveness in meeting task requirements. These strategies tend to evolve over rather long periods of time and are better measured on a scale of months and years than of days and weeks. Although there has so far been little systematic research on this subject, some observations from clinical and community settings suggest some of the strategies often employed.

First, there are avoidance tendencies, involving psychological processes through which people minimize awareness of threatening implications of their life circumstances. One example is avoidance with respect to onset, that is, a tendency to deny that menopause itself has set in, or that one of the associated changes is in fact occurring. There may be fleeting thoughts about the changes that are occurring, but these thoughts are quickly rejected. With the external evidence of distress, the husband or a friend may suggest consulting a gynecologist or other physician, but this possibility may be only briefly considered and then rejected. The woman may feel she is too young, or that the symptoms are not significant, or that they are different in kind from those of the menopause. There are thus many bases for avoiding (at least for a while and either automatically or deliberately) potentially disturbing implications.

Another kind of avoidance involves patterns of behavior that have the functional effect of reassuring oneself about the persistence of youthfulness. There are various ways of providing such reassurance, for example, by increasing expenditures on clothing, often in youthful styles. This approach may also involve styles of behavior that are perceived by the individual as being youthful—in politics, or athletics, or in the activities of an organization that has been associated prominently with young people. It is as if the person were saying: "I can still do things that young people do. I'm identified with them. I'm like they are. I'm a young person myself, because chronological age is not what is important, it is spirit, activity, and appearance that are important." Another example of this functional reassurance about youthfulness is in changes in sexual behavior, for example extramarital affairs, where again an important part of the personal significance often is the reassurance about youth. These then are ways of struggling against the implication that there is some kind of decline signaled by the menopause itself or by some change associated in time with the menopause. It is important to note that avoidance tendencies shade quite naturally into other behavior on a time scale of months or even years. What was avoidance at one period may become something else later.

Let us next consider the *seeking of information* as a coping strategy in the menopausal era. For illustrative purposes, we shall restrict ourselves to information about the menopause itself. Women commonly talk with their peers about menopause, and much "incidental learning" is thus acquired. A friend may have mentioned, a year or two before, that she herself had been having some menopausal difficulty, had been apprehensive about it, or had found a doctor who was helpful. Such information may be filed away, and the friend who made the remark may now be approached with further questions.

The seeking of information in medical areas is exceedingly important at this time. Many physicians have found that questions on this subject are often emotionally charged and they find it helpful to listen carefully for latent concerns implied in a woman's questions. What do these changes mean to her? For example, some women think that menopause means much greater risk of cancer, and when such latent concerns are explored, realistic assurance can often follow.

Peers and physicians are not the only resource people who provide pertinent information. The extended family is still important, though less so than in earlier historical times. A woman's mother, or an older female relative, may be important in this regard. If the relative is respected and has learned from her own menopausal experience, she can offer advice or information on a relatively nonthreatening basis. For many women, this is an especially trustworthy and credible source of guidance. The historical importance of this resource points up one of the dilemmas of recent changes in society. In earlier times, if a woman survived to menopausal age, she usually had around her older female members of the extended family who could tell her what to expect and how she might cope. With the increased development of a mobile nuclear family, the menopausal woman is more likely than ever before to undergo this transitional experience in a setting where she has no such relatives available. The woman may, of course, have created something like an extended family through a network of friends, suggesting one of the ways in which we must improvise to make readily available the sources of information and emotional support that the extended family traditionally provided.

This brings us to another strategy that is commonly employed, namely the *making of new friendships* or the deepening of existing ones at this time of life. This may occur in a variety of ways, and one of the incentives is often the "loss" of children. It may also be motivated by some drifting apart of husband and wife without physical separation or divorce. Whatever the motivation, the observable fact is that many women (and men) reach out to others at this phase. Such reaching out very often involves peers, because one can learn from them about the menopause and associated problems. There is a feeling that "we are all in the same boat," not only with respect to menopause, but in "losing" our children and experiencing other similar dilemmas. Age peers may reasonably be expected, on the average, to be more sympathetic and more understanding because one's own experience is quite salient to them. Despite the above, friendships with other age levels may also be quite significant. These relationships may occur with much older people, equivalent to parental age. Reaching out to such persons may operate in the context of seeking information, but other psychological processes may also be involved. It may be useful to a woman in the menopausal era to treat an older woman in the way she would like to be treated herself. This is particularly so if she is concerned about the loyalty of her children as they become less dependent on her. Even unconsciously, she may be motivated to provide her children with a model of responsibility to parents. If she is concerned, perhaps for the first time in her life, about the aging process, she thinks of her own ultimate need for help and thus provides for younger significant others a model of consideration, sensitivity, and reliability. She may hope, albeit vaguely, that sooner or later these qualities may be applied to her.

Just as friendships may be initiated or deepened in this era, so too may activities. This may occur in both the recreational and occupational spheres. An important feature of recreational activity is that it can provide a focus for social activity and peer contact, a focus that need not be intensely personal, but nevertheless friendly and encouraging. Recreation is also likely to provide a sense of involvement, distraction from concerns, absorption in activity, and relief of tensions. It may also have additional connotations of youthfulness and in that sense may provide a reaffirmation of vitality. Intensification or renewal of activity in the occupational sphere is often clearest in the case of a woman who already has a firm professional base. She may have been working part time in her profession over the years and now expands into full-time work; or if she has been out of her profession for a while, she may now undertake some "retooling" in order to reenter an active professional life. Both men and women sometimes make drastic shifts in occupational activity in this phase of life. Such shifts may be a response to boredom, may reflect a striving for social contribution, and may have the potential for invigorating the individual's life. There are, however, risks connected to such a shift, for one may not be very good at the new enterprise or may find it more difficult than anticipated. Although it may not be easy to reach the level of competence attained in a prior occupational activity, for those who can tolerate the uncertainties and persist in their efforts, the rewards may be profound. Such a "new career" strategy can be viewed broadly enough so that it need not be occupational in the sense of working for a living or a full-time job. What we mean by "career" in this context is that it is a serious and fully engaging commitment. From her own activities, the person develops a sense that she is clearly competent in the direction of her new commitment whether it is a hobby, special interest, or a job; this is confirmed by feedback from others.

A strategy providing elements of both activity and relationship is seen in the search for "substitute children," both within and beyond the family. A woman who sees her own children in some sense moving out of her life may well try to preserve the parent-child mode of interaction, but with different individuals. If she has felt quite competent in the mothering role, and it has been an important basis for her self-esteem, she may find that while she can no longer be useful in that way to her own children, perhaps she can be useful to others. Children of neighbors, of friends of the family, or of other family members may serve in this capacity.

When specifically focused on occupational activities, such coping strategies may be difficult for women to implement because social arrangements are still fairly rudimentary for the acquiring of advanced competence. This is an area where rapid social change may be anticipated. Until recently, most women, even those with a college education, had not planned to enter complex occupational activity. Much of their self-esteem rested of their roles as wives and mothers, and on other family relationships. Circumstances are changing, however, and today a woman in her forties may often feel a need to find new ways of being useful and capable. It is plausible for her to seek training for specialized skills, but the social arrangements are not yet well established, especially for the woman who wants to undertake such activities gradually while continuing to devote a substantial part of her time to home and family. Social innovations are being sought to facilitate such transitions, and it is a recurring theme of this book that rapid social change calls for new social arrangements. These must be capable of providing assistance, guidance, facilitation, or support for individual coping strategies.

For many women, means must be devised during this life period for establishing new kinds of relationships with her children. Some parents in this era intensify demands on their children, while others become hyperindependent. Most parental behavior actually falls between these two ends of the spectrum, and, with many variations, there is a basic process of reaching a new equilibrium between parents and children. An equilibrium is established that facilitates mutual interests, mutual respect, and mutual support in time of stress. Over months or years, the relation between parent and mature offspring evolves in a way that conveys the message that, while there is a different basis for the relationship, there has not been an abandoning of each other. There is instead a recognition of changing interests and changing personal commitments, with enduring ties and mutual loyalty.

Some women become grandparents during the menopausal era. With tongue in cheek, it is said that grandparents get on singularly well with their grandchildren because they have a "common enemy." Whether on that basis or some other, there is often a striking mutual benefit situation between grandparents and grandchildren. From the child's point of view, the most obvious impression is that these are loving, doting, generous people who require very little from the child. They are perhaps the closest one comes to unconditional love. From the grandparents' point of view, it is gratifying to have the kind of unabashed fondness and appreciation that grandchildren can give. It may also bestow a renewed sense of usefulness in helping to care for the child and in advising the young mother. In the nuclear, mobile family, with the grandparents often living far away, their visits may become highly meaningful to the children. It is also frequently the case that grandchildren serve as a vehicle to improve the relationship between grandparents and their own children. The young parents may well come to be more understanding about the difficulties of the parental generation and compassionate about the complexities of caring for young children.

Religious commitment may be for some an important strategy for coping with problems of this era, and an intensification of religious interests often occurs. The potential for intervention of supernatural protective forces is always welcome for many people, and especially so when health may be in jeopardy. Religious involvement may also provide a sense of belonging, particularly because religious organizations so often are vehicles for friendship, social centers, and sources of intellectual stimulation. Such religious affiliations may provide relatively uncritical acceptance and the clarity of rules is helpful in that it allows the individual to readily determine what one is supposed to do in order to be a worthwhile human being.

We turn finally to one of the most important strategies of this life era that may have wide applicability at other times of stress. This is the strategy of *self-appraisal*. It involves a careful stock-taking and may well lead to new ways of thinking of oneself such that long-held self-perceptions may be significantly modified, and new emphasis may be given to characteristics, qualities, or skills that were relatively ignored at an earlier time. Although it may involve making a virtue of necessity, in this instance the woman tends to think of herself as having certain assets that she may not have really appreciated before. These might include maturity, experience, judgment, knowledge, wisdom, or psychological stamina. She may thus come to see herself as useful to other people by virtue of the knowledge and judgment she has accumulated. These qualities also offer the opportunity for mutual appreciation among peers. They can share experiences of stress and coping, recall personally significant occasions of mastery, and appreciate each other's valued attributes.

The above relatively detailed account of tasks and strategies in the menopausal era may serve to suggest ways in which many nodal points and major transitions of the life cycle might be analyzed in future research. A similar delineation of tasks and strategies might usefully include the following phases of the individual life cycle: (1) the attainment of coordination between mother and infant; (2) the initial transition to an out-of-home facility (school, day-care center); (3) puberty; (4) major educational transitions; (5) the first serious occupational commitment; (6) marriage; (7) the first pregnancy; (8) geographic moves; (9) childrens' milestones; (10) economic setbacks; and (11) retirement. Each of these situations presents stressful challenges of practical importance and can precipitate casualty reactions in some individuals.

Other questions must also be asked, including why the tasks of a given situation are more threatening for some persons than for others. To what extent are reactions in each era influenced by biologically based individual differences, social factors, such as major early experiences, complex technology, geographic and social mobility, economic stability in the heterogeneity and scale of society? Further, are coping strategies suggested by biologically based individual differences, for example those that influence activity level in early life, family and other early attachments, models in the culture, or educational and occupational settings?

Many illuminating glimpses into these matters are available in the present volume. But much of this territory remains to be explored, and we hope some readers will be stimulated to take up the task.

INDIVIDUAL COPING STRATEGIES:
PROBLEM SOLVING AND DECISION MAKING
IN STRESSFUL CIRCUMSTANCES

In the absence of definitive cultural guidelines and institutionally defined pathways for social adaptation, individuals must improvise and make personal decisions at every stage of the life cycle and in a great variety of stressful situations. This complex process is well exemplified in several chapters in this volume. With the earlier sections of this chapter as background, we shall now consider in some detail a number of the concepts and formulations presented by the various contributors. In this effort we will make an explicit attempt to underline those areas in which there is apparent theoretical agreement and conceptual concordance, as well as those in which there is disagreement or lack of clarity.

Robert W. White (Chapter 4) has made many fundamental contributions in the area of coping and adaptation (1959, 1972). For him, *adaptation* is the central concept and *strategy of adaptation* is the superordinate category under which are subsumed the terms *defense, mastery*, and *coping*. Defense is concerned with danger and safety, mastery with defeat and victory, and coping with difficult and unusual conditions. Defense is used in a psychoanalytic sense, referring centrally to protection against anxiety. Mastery emphasizes successful performance, the end result, in meeting task requirements. Coping essentially refers to the ongoing adaptive processes of meeting task requirements under exceptionally difficult circumstances. For White, coping involves creative, not routine, action, reflective, not reflexive, behavior.

White calls attention to the complexity of the behavioral processes involved and the many tasks that have to be managed all at once if an individual is to come to terms with environmental demands. He uses a military metaphor, saying, "adaptation often calls for delay, strategic retreat, regrouping of forces, abandoning of untenable positions, seeking fresh intelligence and deploying new weapons" (p. 50). This approach allows for temporizing tactics in the strategy of adaptation—a theme dealt with by other contributors as well. Sometimes adaptation to a severely frustrating reality is possible only if full recognition of the bitter truth is for a considerable time postponed. White emphasizes "that adaptation does not mean either a total triumph over the environment or a total surrender to it, but rather a striving toward an acceptable compromise" (p. 52). This formulation raises the issue of acceptable to whom and by what criteria. We are thus led back to the biological considerations of species survival considered earlier, and to the social definition of acceptability considered by Goldschmidt and Mechanic.

If the human animal is to conduct effective transactions with the environment, three broad conditions must be met, and met in a coordinated way: (1) adequate information must be secured, but neither ignorance nor overload will be useful; (2) satisfactory internal conditions must be maintained, including both effective regulation of physiological functions and the control of emotional distress, so as to foster the processing of information and action based upon it; (3) autonomy or freedom of movement must be maintained and care must be taken to avoid the risks of "only one right way" and the disaster of "no way out." In respect to transitions, large and small, White makes a point of considerable generality. "There is, of course, always a little risk in newness, so what is required is a cautious approach allowing time to assess both the risk and the possibility of benefits" (p. 59).

With respect to internal organization, White, like other contributors (Goldschmidt, Mechanic, Murphy, Janis, Adams, Lindemann, and George), emphasizes the great importance of maintaining self-esteem. "No adaptive strategy that is careless of the level of self-esteem is likely to be any good" (p. 61). Though self-esteem may have to be maintained in the short run by defensive avoidance and self-deception, long-term avoidance of real problems tends to be maladaptive, at least if the stakes are high. Where important problems can be foreseen, or where early warning signals exist, then psychological preparation becomes exceedingly useful. "The use of strategies of adaptation in advance, in anticipation of problems that still lie ahead, would appear to be a peculiarly human attribute" (p. 63).

The NIMH studies of competent adolescents coping with the transition from high school to college have shown an extensive repertoire of adaptive strategies serving to increase information about college, to keep anxiety and depression within tolerable limits, to sustain a self-image of adequacy, and to provide encouragement that the new environment will offer pathways to satisfaction. In commenting on these studies in Chapter 4, White concludes:

Whatever distortions and defensive operations may have crept into their college-oriented behavior, these were greatly overbalanced by substantial increases in realistic information, in realistic expectations, and in actual competence through role rehearsal. . . . One of the great advantages of research on coping is that it brings back into the psychological and psychiatric literature the persistence, the will to live, the courage, and indeed the heroism that are as much a part of human nature as the evasions, and petty impulse gratifications that bulk so large in our thinking about psychopathology (p. 64).

This orientation can clearly be useful in psychotherapy and related helping situations. Many people can benefit from specific information regarding tasks and strategies relevant to their current circumstances. When a new pattern of action is undertaken that holds reasonable promise of effectiveness, emotional responses tend to change concomitantly, and the more effective the action, the less the distress. We can recall in our own experiences the gain in confidence and the reduction in anxiety that ended to follow effective performance of an act that had previously been subject to considerable misgiving. Clinicians must learn which strategies are useful in which situations, and which of these are closest to the patient's available repertoire. Behavioral scientists could help many individuals cope with their predicaments if their investigations could build a substantial inventory of (1) common problem situations, (2) feasible strategies, (3) probability of preparation for each strategy in various human populations (for example, cultures and subcultures).

Closely related to White's use of the term *strategy* is the concept of *crisis intervention* developed by Erich Lindemann in his pioneering studies of the responses to stress in clinical and community settings. Adams and Lindemann in Chapter 7 use *crisis* to refer to "a situation in which one or several individuals are confronted with adaptive tasks that demand the mobilization of new resources in psychological competence, and social skills" (p. 127). Two general types of crises are delineated: (1) the "developmental crisis," which has been studied by Erikson, Bibring, and Benedek; and (2) the "situational crisis," which has been particularly studied by Caplan and Lindemann. These various crises are viewed both from the standpoint of (1) their situational requirements, and (2) phases over time in which personal and social resources are mobilized. We are here again dealing with tasks and strategies. "The critical issue arises over the choice of patterns of adaptation. These may be regressive and defensive, functioning primarily for the protection of the self from disintegration, or may represent efforts to master the environment, restructure the task ahead, and solve the problems of dealing with a novel situation" (p. 128).

Adams and Lindemann focus on the coping strategies of individuals suffering from long-term illness or disability in which major and permanent changes in behavior are often obligatory, especially in the design of new interpersonal roles. New forms of behavior and new social encounters must be anticipated and rehearsed. This involves facing some anxiety and depression in respect to the riskier possibilities of the new situation. As in other contributions in this volume, emphasis is placed on the need for support, guidance, and facilitation by significant others, be they in professional or nonprofessional roles. There is a focus on the adaptive tasks embedded in the situation of long-term disability, especially from the point of view of the patient's need to reshape certain social roles in relation to those of significant others. One of the principal tasks is accommodating to the necessity of being permanently different in some important respect.

A significant point is reached after the initial period of denial, when experiences and behavior analogous to mourning are observed. The accustomed life style and its range of functions and rewards are not abandoned without pain, and the attending depression must be accepted before new functions and roles can be learned. There must be detailed review of the major tasks faced by the individual and his environment. These include defense against recurring negative emotions, the maintenance of a sense of value in the face of impaired functioning, the search for models for the successful creation of a new life style, and the development of access to reference groups whose values and goals support a new set of roles. Specific coping strategies must be collaboratively developed to approach each of these major challenges.

The patient needs to test his modified self and reaffirm his worth as a person, and thus the maintenance of self-esteem is again seen as a primary task in a variety of crisis situations. It is important to note that this need not rest upon the patient's characteristic behavior patterns at a given moment, but may draw heavily upon his sense of movement toward an image of himself in the future. He is important not only for what he is today, but also for what he can become. Because serious physical impairments usually require some change of a person's goals, successful adaptation implies a *range* of potentially satisfying goals, and some flexibility in choosing among them. If such an orientation has been part of the pre-illness socialization experience of the individual, the probability of effective coping in his new condition is enhanced. In these processes, much can be gained from the opportunity to observe, and identify with, others who can serve as models for new patterns of role behavior, for example, persons who have been effective in coping with similar disability. Here, as elsewhere, the importance of early and continuous involvement of significant others in supporting the patient's self-esteem is emphasized. This applies not only to family and friends, but often to key figures in schools and industrial settings as well. Thus, as Goldschmidt and Mechanic point out, the individual's coping processes may be powerfully facilitated not only by his primary group, but also by institutional arrangements that are culturally valued.

Although Adams and Lindemann concentrate specifically on effective adaptation to physical disability, the principles outlined have applicability in other areas as well. The study of coping behavior in a wide range of settings may thus provide important clues to the understanding and facilitation of individual and social change.

In general, work on coping and adaptation arising in the disciplines of psychology and psychiatry has dealt in detail with the person, but very little with the environment. John French and his collaborators make an explicit effort to bridge this gap and do so in a way that leads toward quantitative measures. They conceive of the person-environment fit in terms of discrepancies between demands and supplies and conceptualize the demand and the corresponding supply on commensurate dimensions. By thus measuring them on the same scale, they move toward a more intimate integration of the person and environment than has been customary.

Adjustment requires change and for French this implies improvement of a poor fit between person and environment. In appraising deprivation, the person tends to evaluate the magnitude, importance, immediacy, and duration of his deprivation against those suffered by his reference group. In attempting to correct such experiences of deprivation, one may do so either by changing the environment or changing oneself. This last includes the possibility of simply changing one's view of oneself or one's view of the environment.

Linking with Adams and Lindemann, French points out that environmental demands may be reduced to meet limited abilities, as in the case of serious injury. Linking with psychoanalytic formulation, they indicate that the accuracy of self-assessment may be decreased to allow protection from overwhelming fear. As in other chapters in this volume, considerable significance is again attached to self-esteem.

By his careful research on the strategies of decision making in wartime combat, naturally occurring disasters, surgical stress, and other difficult choice points, Irving Janis has had strong impact not only in psychology, but in other disciplines as well. An example of his interdisciplinary influence is evident in this volume in Alexander George's use of Janis's decision-making model in a political context (Chapter 9). In his contribution to the present volume, Janis is concerned mainly with the characteristics of individuals that influence their responses to fear-arousing communications. A number of clinical and experimental observations indicate that in general the effectiveness of warnings in eliciting coping behavior depends upon: (1) who sends the message, that is, trust in the competence and integrity of the communication source; (2) what the message says, that is, information about ways to cope with the threat; and (3) the predispositions of the person to whom it is said, that is, distinctive characteristics of the individual. Although Janis and his colleagues have contributed substantially in the first two areas, it is the third that is the focus of attention here.

Janis draws attention to two general classes of predispositional factors: (1) ego-involvement; and (2) chronic level of anxiety. Ego-involvement refers to the degree to which the individual perceives the threat as relevant to his personal goals, decisions, and social commitments, while chronic level of anxiety refers to an individual's sensitivity to a wide range of potentially stressful events.

To first consider ego-involvement in the threat, studies of smokers and drinkers indicate that highly ego-involved persons, when presented with a warning message about the consequences of smoking or drinking, tend to become more vigilant and more interested than others in obtaining information about the threat. They also, however, tend to be more reluctant than others to conclude that the danger is sufficiently great to require protective action. When commitment to a long-term pattern of behavior is firmly established, change is resisted unless: (1) the risks are high in the foreseeable future, especially in regard to survival, self-esteem, or relations with significant others; or (2) alternate courses of action are reasonably attractive (for example, substitute gratifications).

In an effort to clarify predispositional differences in ego-involvement, Janis builds a model of the decision-making process in stressful circumstances of this kind. The model describes a series of steps, starting with challenging information, that lead the individual toward reconsidering his present views and actions. These steps are: (1) appraisal of *challenge;* (2) appraisal of *recommended alternatives* for meeting the challenge; (3) making a *tentative decision* about the best available policy; (4) *committing oneself* to the new policy; (5) *adherence* to the new policy despite challenges. In the cases studied, the policy involves issues such as giving up cigarette smoking or giving up alcoholic beverages. However, the policy might well be a course of action toward higher education in the high school–college transition studies described by White or an administrative decision as described by George.

Janis considers various ways in which motivation for change can be enhanced and skills for implementing such motivation may be acquired. For example, the near-miss experience of combat described by Grinker and Spiegel (1945) challenges one's feelings of personal vulnerability. An experience of narrow escape in a situation of high stakes, as commonly occurs for instance in automobile accidents, may strongly enhance a person's motivation to change high-risk behavior, for example, heavy alcohol intake. In a similar way, but on a scale of lower intensity, emotional role playing may serve as a device for challenging complacency. It may also offer a vehicle for acquiring specific skills useful in relation to the task at hand. Here as elsewhere, the opportunity to observe persons of demonstrated effectiveness as they cope with the problem can be of great value. The availability of such models does not, however, ensure that they will be utilized, for some individuals seem to need explicit training in an interpersonal orientation so that they may work toward a meshing of self-and-other perceptions, mutual accommodation, and a sharing of benefits.

It is interesting to read Alexander George's contribution in the light of those made by Goldschmidt, Mechanic, and Janis. George looks at problems of stress and coping in individual, group, and organizational contexts. Although he focuses on high-level political decision making, it is likely that his analysis has considerable generality in other situations. In studying presidential decisions, George uses an extreme case to highlight vividly a set of processes that are important over a much wider range of situations. In reading his paper it may be useful to substitute for "president" terms like "executive," "administrator," "leader," or "person whose decisions affect the lives of many others." In this particular historical arena of great contemporary interest, his analysis again illuminates Goldschmidt's and Mechanic's emphasis upon *social* support, guidance, and facilitation for individual coping efforts.

George attempts to understand not only processes that tend to maintain the decision maker's psychological equilibrium, but also the quality of his decisions. The arena in which he examines these issues is certainly a stressful one, affecting as it does the lives of a great many people. The decision-making model developed by Janis and utilized by George is one that links the individual to his small-group and organizational settings. When multiple, conflicting stakes are aroused in a difficult situation, the individual decision maker undertakes a sort of "balance-sheet" assessment, comparing his current policy with proposed new ones. In doing so, he examines the anticipated utility of these alternative policies, both for himself and for other people who are particularly significant to him. He similarly examines the various policies in relation to anticipated approval and disapproval, again both in the way he views himself and the way he will be viewed by others. George points out that the political decision maker (and the individual decision maker in many difficult situations) often has to operate under the following limitations: (1) incomplete information about the situation; (2)

inadequate knowledge of the relation between ends and means, so that he cannot predict with high confidence the consequences of choosing a given course of action; and (3) difficulty in formulating a single criterion for use in choosing the best available option. In such a setting, strategies for dealing with cognitive complexity become essential. George describes a set of such strategies that have been illustrated in research on political decision making. They have much overlap with strategies employed in other situations of cognitive complexity.

These difficult situations typically pose multiple stakes for the decision maker that cannot readily be reconciled. He must, therefore, have ways of dealing with such decisional conflicts. George describes three broad strategies: (1) avoiding the conflict; (2) resolving the conflict; and (3) accepting the conflict. For each of these strategies, he delineates several tactics through which they can be implemented. In respect to the small-group context, George points out that "coping takes place not only via intrapsychic ego-functions of the individual, but also by means of the interpersonal processes within the small group to which he belongs" (p. 190). His observations on the nature of such facilitating relationships in face-to-face groups have a good deal in common with the recent research literature on group psychotherapy.

The administrative decision maker typically copes with the difficult problems he faces within the framework of a large-scale organization. All large-scale organizations have structural characteristics of hierarchy, specialization, and centralization that have inherent risks and constraints. But George emphasizes that organizations may also provide reinforcement for the individual's constructive, adaptive ego-functions. For example, organizations can assist a political leader in a stressful situation in facing up to the need for seeking and utilizing relevant information and advice; and they can provide him with specialized assistance relevant for problem solving. Formal organization structures can also compensate for or overcome some of the disruptive influences of small groups.

A major theme running through George's analysis both of small groups and of the organizational context has to do with the strong advantages of explicitly considering a wide range of alternatives, including unpleasant ones, before making a major decision. This issue appears to be of great importance over a wide range of coping issues and is by no means limited to stressful political decisions. George considers a variety of factors in the small group and the large organization that tend either to inhibit or to facilitate a consideration of multiple alternatives. For instance, he says, "because conflict over policy and advocacy is inevitable within a complex organization, one solution lies in the direction of ensuring that multiple advocates within the system will cover the range of interesting policy options on any given issue" (pp. 206–207). He points out the advantages of planning procedures that encourage critical, broad-gauged consideration of many overlapping and competing factors that are embedded in a particular problem. In so doing, alternative courses of action can be formulated with increasing clarity, and the advantages and limitations of each can then be assessed in a way that draws upon the best available evidence, involving not only protection of the decision maker's self, but also giving serious consideration to the welfare of others.

George makes some suggestions for organizational interventions to improve the quality of decision-making processes. These suggestions have some interesting analogies with psychotherapeutic interventions on the level of the individual or the small group. Among other suggestions, he points out the desirability of organizational early warning systems. Because it is so difficult under most stressful circumstances to make anything like an optimal decision, there is an urgent need for monitoring the course of the transaction with the environment in such a way as to detect early warning signals, when untoward consequences are beginning to appear, but before irreversible damage has occurred. This has great relevance both for individuals making personally important decisions in stressful situations (for example, at the level of the family), and for social problems in a rapidly changing society (for example, technology assessment).

In the final section of his paper, George identifies from recent historical cases some factors that increase the risk of malfunction in the decision-making processes. These malfunctions tend to occur under the following conditions: (1) when the decision maker and his advisors agree too readily on the nature of the problem and on a single response to it; (2) when advisors take up alternatives with the decision maker, but cover only a narrow range of options; (3) when there is no advocate for an unpopular option; (4) when advisors work out their own disagreements over alternative possibilities without the decision maker's knowledge and then present him with a single recommendation; (5) when advisors agree privately among themselves that the decision maker should face up to a distressing situation, but no one is willing to alert him to it; (6) when the decision maker is largely dependent upon a single channel of information; (7) when the underlying assumptions of a plan have been evaluated only by the advocates of that option; (8) when the decision maker does not arrange for a well-qualified group to examine carefully the negative judgment offered by one or more advisors on a preferred course of action; (9) when the decision maker is impressed by a consensus among his advisors, but does not thoroughly examine the adequacy of its basis. Making explicit these sources of interference with effective problem solving enhances future opportunities for coping with stressful decision-making situations.

Richard Lazarus, another major contributor to our understanding of coping and adaptation, views coping in a way that is similar to White's. In Chapter 10, Lazarus, Averill, and Opton define coping as "problem solving efforts made by an individual when the demands he faces are highly relevant to his welfare (that is, a situation of considerable jeopardy or promise), and when these demands tax his adaptive resources" (pp. 250–251). Their contribution is particularly significant because it relates currents in psychological research that have been largely separate in the past. One of these currents is research on problem solving, where studies usually involve relatively low stakes to the individual and the focus is on deliberate, flexible, reality-oriented efforts at mastery. On the other hand, when the personal stakes are high, the focus of inquiry usually shifts to more rigid, primitive, and less realistic efforts at mastery. As Lazarus and his co-workers point out, "There is no reason why the student of problem solving should not also concern himself with the context of high drive, emotion, and psychopathology" (p. 250). Although strongly committed to experimental research, they draw upon several sources of information and ideas: (1) psychoanalytic and clinical observations; (2) biological research; and (3) studies of problem solving. Like others in this volume, they emphasize that coping is a transaction between an individual and his environment, and that "coping can never be assessed or evaluated without regard to the environmental demands that create the need for it in the first place. It is essential that we discover how each type of situation initiates, shapes, and constrains the form of coping" (p. 258).

One of Lazarus's central concepts is *appraisal*, which is a perception distinguishing the potentially harmful from the potentially beneficial or irrelevant. Appraisal involves not only a response to the perception of some threatening condition, but also potential avenues of solution or mastery. Lazarus and his colleagues extend the process of appraisal in time, referring to *secondary appraisal* in which a range of coping alternatives is delineated, and *reappraisal* in which the original perception may be changed from threatening to benign, or vice versa. They emphasize that emotional responses and coping strategies flow from these mediating appraisals, and their experimental studies have contributed significantly to clarification of the factors influencing appraisal, as well as of the relation of appraisal to emotional response, coping strategy, and physiological concomitants. A point is made of the need for a description and classification system for coping processes, antecedents, and consequences. In our view, an evolutionary, adaptive orientation is helpful in this regard.

In their chapter, Lazarus and his colleagues undertake to clarify two classes of determinants of coping behavior: situational determinants and personality determinants. In regard to situational factors, they point out that the informational significance of environmental stimulation may arise through three broad classes of input: (1) the selection pressures of human evolution; (2) socialization processes that are characteristic of a culture; and (3) personal experiences that are relatively idiosyncratic. Evolution may have built into the human organism a sensitivity to certain stimuli, particularly in childhood, that tend to generate similar emotional responses and coping inclinations in most members of the species. Moreover, all cultures must deal with certain recurrent aspects of the human predicament, even though the content may vary greatly from one culture to another. As an example, what is considered insulting varies a good deal across cultures, but all cultures have some commonly understood transactions that are insulting in personal significance. The developing individual is exposed not only to these general cultural patterns, but also to variations and deviations from these themes as transmitted by his unique combination of family and personal experiences.

Lazarus and his co-workers also consider the effect of intensity and duration of situational factors on coping responses. They point out that under severe stress, with relatively intense emotional responses, developmentally earlier and simpler forms of coping are more likely to appear than are novel and complex ones. Elsewhere, the literature indicates that it is very difficult for individuals to improvise under high-stress conditions, and it is much more likely that long-established, overlearned patterns of response will be applied rather than new ones specifically tailored to the situation. If highly adaptive patterns have been well ingrained, good function may appear even under very high stress, and indeed this principle has been effectively utilized in preparing astronauts to cope with the hazards and contingencies of space flight. With respect to the duration of stress, they point out that when threats appear suddenly and are expected by the individual to continue over some period of time, there is likely to be a greater intensity of emotional disturbance. Under such circumstances more disorganization of coping can be anticipated than when threats are perceived as emerging gradually.

Lazarus and his co-workers are further interested in situational factors that tend to "pull" for intrapsychic or for interpersonal modes of coping. If the situation is appraised as one that cannot be changed externally—if the personal environment is essentially intractable—then an effort is made to manipulate it internally. If, on the other hand, promising ways of changing the environment for the better are envisioned, however dimly, then the possibilities for direct action are explored. Such direct action largely, though not entirely, involves relationships with other people.

In respect to personality determinants of coping responses, Lazarus and his colleagues believe that some personality dispositions may contribute to specific coping behaviors because they provide orientations toward particular stimulus objects. These orientations shape or constrain the range of coping processes that are available to an individual in a given situation. A simple but meaningful example might be that a person who is consistently hostile to the police will find difficulty in asking for police protection when he is threatened. In other words, personality dispositions tend to define a range of permissible responses for the individual in a particular situation, whereas the boundaries of this range appear to be set largely by the basis on which the individual's self-esteem is formulated and by his appraisal of how significant others would view him in the situation. This brings us back to the authors' heavy emphasis on the mediating role of appraisal, in which the choice of coping strategy depends on how the situation is assessed by the individual. For any given situation, there is much consistent individual difference in the way the situation tends to be defined. These long-term dispositions to define certain situations in certain ways are crucial to the study of personality. It is unfortunate that personality research has for so long neglected such coping dimensions. Just as situational factors may pull for intrapsychic as against interpersonal coping responses, so too personality factors strongly influence this choice. Individuals who feel competent to deal with a threatening situation are more likely to undertake interpersonal, direct-action responses, as compared with those who have a low sense of competence or power. In pursuing questions of this kind, these authors emphasize the interaction of situational and personality variables, and thus point to the need for a new integrative unit of analysis. For this purpose, they use the concept *appraised significance of the situation*. This concept is quite similar to concepts used elsewhere in the stress literature, such as *personal meaning* and *definition of the situation*.

Indeed, the contribution of Lazarus and his colleagues links closely with other contributions in the area and suggests certain recurrent themes that are probably of basic importance. Because appraisal processes presumably occur in terms of motivational relevance for the individual, they therefore center on issues of personal survival, self-esteem, close relations with significant others, and belonging in valued groups. The dispositional variables of Lazarus are quite similar to the person variables of French. The situation variables of Lazarus are quite similar to the environment variables of French. Lazarus's view of coping as a transaction between individual and environment, strongly shared by Grinker and others, is closely related to French's concept of adjustment in terms of person-environment fit. Lazarus's concept of appraised *significance of the situation* draws together several major facets of stress and coping. In appraising the significance of the situation, the person is asking, "What does it mean to me? How will it affect my future? What implications does it have for survival, self-esteem, interpersonal relations, group belonging, and meeting task requirements?" These questions are fundamental in the analysis of human coping behavior in the greatest variety of stressful circumstances.

Lazarus's emphasis on reappraisal processes relates to White's and Murphy's concern with the development of coping strategies over extended periods of time. The ability to reevaluate decisions and policies from time to time seems fundamental to coping with complex and changing environments. In the rapid movement of modern societies, the individual finds much utility in making temporal and interpersonal differentiation—in effect, to say, "That was then, and this is now." In other words, as environmental conditions change drastically within the individual's life span he makes reappraisals and new policy decisions, sorting out different eras in his life, relating to current individuals and situations primarily in terms of their own characteristics rather than in terms of assumptions derived from contact with other (and often quite different) individuals and situations. But appraisal and reappraisal are not enough, and action must follow by way of implementing a new appraisal.

Lazarus also touches on criteria for estimating the adequacy of coping responses. They include flexibility, rationality, and effectiveness. We think these criteria can be spelled out as follows: (1) flexibility—behavior varies with environmental conditions (including both internal and external environments); (2) rationality—the individual utilizes problem-solving capacities of the human brain (including the accumulated experience of relevant human groups embedded in culture as a way of life); and (3) effectiveness— the behavior meets task requirements or changes the task in a way that meets the criteria of the individual and his significant others.

Recurrent coping themes in the various chapters of this volume are thus apparent. They briefly include: (1) appraisal; (2) motivation (including hope); (3) information seeking and utilization; (4) contingency planning; (5) rehearsal, trial actions; (6) feedback; and (7) social influences: channeling priorities, preparation, prescription. Explicit attention to these variables in future research on man's adaptation to his complex and changing environment will not only increase our basic understanding of human development, but will also offer useful clues for assisting those in distress.

METHODOLOGICAL CONSIDERATIONS: TOWARD THE STRENGTHENING OF RESEARCH ON COPING AND ADAPTATION

The ground-breaking studies of human coping behavior have mainly relied on interview and direct observation, often in very difficult circumstances. Such studies have had great value and will continue to have such value in the future. At the same time, there is a need to develop assessment techniques to delineate coping variables that are as specific and reliable as it is possible to make them, given the complexity of the subject matter.

Moos's contribution to this volume (Chapter 12) is the most thorough, informative review so far undertaken in an attempt to analyze techniques relevant to the study of coping behavior. He considers methods and procedures for the assessment of such variables as self-esteem, self-actualization, identity, exploratory behavior, stimulus-seeking motivation, and feelings of efficacy and competence. He reviews a broad range of measures pertinent both to everyday stresses and to major transitions or crises. He is concerned not only with measurement in basic research, but also with the potential utility of assessment for intervention programs in education, mental health, and organizational development. Variables related to the environment as well as to the person are documented, emphasizing the theoretical orientations of French and Lazarus, among others. He makes a serious effort to preserve the complexity of the subject's response, while reducing the complexity of data analysis. Each technique is examined on three dimensions: the stimulus situation, the responses, and the analysis of data. He covers techniques in the areas of interview and observation, family interaction, tape recordings and films, essay and sentence-completion techniques, short-story and problem-situation techniques, objective-assessment techniques, biographical and life-history variables, multimedia methods, self-conception techniques, cognitive styles, and novelty-need assessments.

This comprehensive review provides a reasonable basis for deciding on assessment techniques for a specified purpose. Developments in computer technology hold much promise for an empirical comparison of different assessment techniques and the integration of data from various techniques brought to bear on a given problem.

Moos indentifies three particular purposes for which further development of assessment techniques would be especially useful: (1) the possibility of altering coping strategies experimentally through interventions such as modeling and information feedback; (2) the possibility of balancing costs and benefits of different coping strategies through intermediate and long time spans (months or years); and (3) the possibility of understanding major cultural differences in coping behavior by developing techniques that have cross-cultural comparability.

The work of Lazarus and his colleagues, more than any other represented in this volume, is a serious effort to deal with coping responses in a laboratory setting. Typically, their work involves four response dimensions: verbal reports, physiological changes, expressive reactions, and behavioral actions. They emphasize the desirability of using a combination of measures to provide a reasonably adequate view of these complex responses. Their work touches on the sometimes unappreciated difficulty with a dichotomous classification between intrapsychic response and direct action response (mainly interpersonal). Bridging categories are needed, because responses to threat in fact typically involve an interplay between intrapsychic mechanisms and direct actions upon the environment. At least two such bridging concepts appear to be useful in much stress research: (1) the processes of appraisal and reappraisal described by Lazarus; and (2) the processes of seeking and utilizing information described by Hamburg and Adams (1967).

An important suggestion implicit in the chapter by Lazarus and his colleagues, and explicit in the work of Lois Murphy and Beatrix Hamburg, is the desirability of studying coping responses developmentally. The Lazarus experiments are cross-sectional, but similar experiments can be conducted at different age levels, in different eras of development, and even in various field situations. In particular, the combination of experimental and field methods deserves further attention.

Lazarus and his co-workers employ four basic experimental strategies in studying emotional and coping responses to threatening stimulation: (1) direct experimental manipulation of the appraisal-reappraisal process; (2) indirect experimental manipulation of appraisal-reappraisal; (3) observation and inference from self-reports; and (4) selection of experimental subject on the basis of relevant personality dispositions. They use a sources-of-variance model in which they examine three main types of variables pertinent to stress and coping: responses, situations, and persons. We have already indicated that they obtain four different types of response data and point to the problem of integrating these different responses. They deliberately vary situations in order to determine whether a particular kind of situation tends to "pull" for a particular kind of coping response. They systematically vary the kinds of persons who are exposed to a given threat in order to clarify the ways in which established personality characteristics tend to shape coping responses.

Janis's valuable clinical observations and experimental hypotheses have already had a highly stimulating impact on behavioral science. To test these hypotheses more fully, we need more precise and reliable measures of emotional responses. These should focus on both transient fluctuations and on long-term dispositions. The papers of Moos and Lazarus are helpful in this regard, and the long-range perspective given by Mechanic has important methodological implications for such research. As White has noted, effective coping often requires tackling more than one task at a time. In this vein, important decisions sometimes have to be made more or less simultaneously, and important decisions are often linked in sequence. For example, in Janis's study of men who resist the draft, this decision in itself is a prelude to other decisions. The next branch could be whether to take a legal or illegal course of draft resistance. If a legal course is chosen, there are other branches: for example, whether to apply for conscientious objector status, to emigrate, to undertake legal challenge, and so on. Thus, carefully designed studies of decision-making processes in real-life situations may have great potential for future understanding, particularly if they have at least a modestly longitudinal character. Also, it will be important to examine decisions of rather different character. Decisions made regarding such grossly noxious stimuli as surgery, tornadoes, possibility of malignant disease, and risk of going to jail are certainly difficult and distressing, often dramatically so. But other decisions that do not involve grossly noxious stimuli may also, in their way, be difficult and challenging. Such decisions include choice of college, career, marital partner, and size of family. They too deserve serious investigation.

An important recurrent theme throughout this volume is the role of the perceptual organization and cognitive processes in shaping adaptive behavior. This theme has many variations. It is presented in terms of information seeking in the service of monitoring self-esteem (White; Adams and Lindemann); vigilance (Janis); appraisal and reappraisal processes (Lazarus, Averill, and Opton); perceptual organization of the interpersonal and symbolic environment (Murphy; Mechanic). Methods are suggested by these authors that include obtaining *prospective* data of a short-term longitudinal character, through combinations of field and experimental techniques.

To develop an adequate methodology in the area of coping, future researchers will need to pay attention to, and make adjustments for, multiple sets of validating evidences that bear simultaneously on the following basic considerations discussed earlier: (1) short-term and long-term behavioral aspects of adaptation to a critical episode; (2) welfare of the individual and of the group to which he belongs; and (3) what the actor does to the environment, and how the environmental challenge is perceived by the actor.

CONCLUDING COMMENT

Research on coping behavior emphasizes processes of human problem solving in the direction of adaptive change. It brings into focus transactions of individuals or groups that are effective in meeting the requirements or utilizing the opportunities of specific environments. It highlights possibilities for enhancing the competence of individuals through developmental attainments, including ways of learning from exceptionally difficult circumstances. It is also beginning to suggest ways in which such stressful circumstances may be modified to diminish human suffering.

The study of adaptation links biological sciences, social sciences, and the clinical professions. The findings and implications of these studies are beginning to be useful in psychotherapy, counseling, rehabilitation, preventive intervention, and in the practice of physicians, nurses, social workers, and teachers. Much, however, remains to be done in providing dependable information within the framework that has been constructed by workers in this field.

New information about coping patterns under specified conditions could benefit both individuals and institutions challenged by crises of social change. Such information, respecting the nature of human biology and the nature of social systems, could both help individuals acquire coping skills and assist institutions in anticipating typical or recurring coping exigencies.

We have touched on a variety of stressful circumstances, especially major transitions of the life cycle, that occur in a fairly predictable way. Unfortunately, only a few of these have so far been the subject of multiple studies that provide reasonably dependable information in some depth. For most stressful situations, we must do the best we can, as a practical matter, with fragments of information about the tasks embedded in the situation and the ways in which these tasks can be met effectively. We hope this volume provides a useful framework for analysis of stressful situations and that it will stimulate a new wave of coping studies. In due course, it should be possible to construct a coping "table-of-the-elements": (1) a roster of stressful situations; (2) the tasks embedded in each of these situations; (3) the range of strategies employed in the general population in meeting these tasks; (4) the distribution of these strategies by pertinent biological and social criteria—for example, age, sex, ethnic group; and (5) the risks, costs, opportunities, and benefits associated with each strategy in each situation, taking into account relevant factors such as cultural and subcultural settings. It is not difficult to imagine the utility of such knowledge for physicians, educators, and psychotherapists. We hope that this volume carries the inquiry in a direction whose promise can be at least dimly seen.

REFERENCES

Benedek, T. Parenthood as a developmental phase. *Journal of American Psycho-analytical Association*, 1959, *1*, 389.

Bibring, G. L. A study of the psychological processes in pregnancy and the earliest mother-child relationship. *The Psychoanalytic Study of the Child*, 1961, *16*, 9–73.

Eitinger, L. *Coping with aggression.* In press.

Erikson, E. Identity and the life cycle. *Psychological Issues*, 1959, *1* (1).

Grinker, R. R., and Spiegel, J. P. *Men under stress.* Philadelphia: Blakiston, 1945.

Hamburg, D. A., and Adams, J. E. A perspective on coping: Seeking and utilizing information in major transitions. *Archives of General Psychiatry*, 1967, *17*, 277–284.

Inkeles, A. Social structure and the socialization of competence. *Harvard Educational Review*, 1966, *36*, 265–283.

MacFarlane, J. W. Perspectives on personal consistency and change: The guidance study. *Vita Humana*, 1964, *7*, 115–126.

Murphy, L. B. *The widening world of childhood: Paths toward mastery.* New York: Basic Books, 1962.

Simpson, G. G. Behavior and evolution. In A. R. Roe and G. G. Simpson, eds., *Behavior and evolution.* New Haven, Conn.: Yale University Press, 1958.

White, R. W. Motivation reconsidered: The concept of competence. *Psychological Review*, 1959, *66*, 297–333.

———. *The enterprise of living.* New York: Holt, Rinehart & Winston, 1972.

Index